NINTH

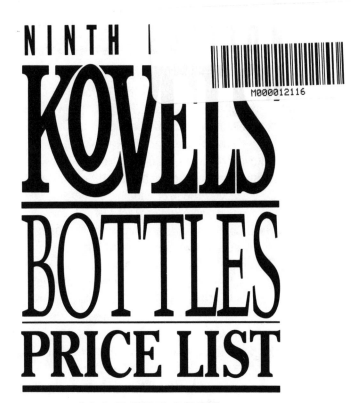

KOVELS
BOTTLES
PRICE LIST

ILLUSTRATED

RALPH AND TERRY KOVEL

CROWN PUBLISHERS, INC.
NEW YORK

To Zoe, who learned to love bottles at an early age, and to Lee, Kim, and Al.

BOOKS BY RALPH AND TERRY KOVEL

American Country Furniture 1780–1875
Dictionary of Marks—Pottery & Porcelain
A Directory of American Silver, Pewter and Silver Plate
Kovels' Advertising Collectibles Price List
Kovels' American Silver Marks
Kovels' Antiques & Collectibles Price List
Kovels' Antiques & Collectibles Fix-It Source Book
Kovels' Book of Antique Labels
Kovels' Bottles Price List
Kovels' Collector's Guide to American Art Pottery
Kovels' Collector's Source Book
Kovels' Depression Glass & American Dinnerware Price List
Kovels' Guide to Selling Your Antiques & Collectibles
Kovels' Illustrated Price Guide to Royal Doulton
Kovels' Know Your Antiques
Kovels' Know Your Collectibles
Kovels' New Dictionary of Marks—Pottery & Porcelain
Kovels' Organizer for Collectors
Kovels' Price Guide for Collector Plates, Figurines, Paperweights,
and Other Limited Editions

Copyright © 1992 by Ralph Kovel and Terry Kovel
Special photographs by Benjamin Margalit
All rights reserved. No part of this book may be reproduced or
transmitted in any form or by any means, electronic or mechanical,
including photocopying, recording, or by any information storage and
retrieval system, without permission in writing from the publisher.
Published by Crown Publishers, Inc., 201 East 50th Street,
New York, New York 10022. Member of the Crown Publishing Group.
CROWN is a trademark of Crown Publishers, Inc.
Manufactured in the United States of America
Library of Congress Cataloging-in-Publication Data
Kovel, Ralph M.
Kovels' bottles price list / by Ralph and Terry Kovel. — 9th ed.
p.   cm.
Includes bibliographical references and index.
1. Bottles—United States—Catalogs.   I. Kovel, Terry H.
II. Title.
NK5440.B6K6   1992
748.8'2' 0973075—dc20   92-5192
CIP

ISBN: 0-517-58944-3
10   9   8   7   6   5   4   3   2   1
First Edition

Contents

Keep Up on Bottle Prices All Year Long

Have you kept up with prices? They change! Last year a collector-dealer discovered several boxes of never-used, mint bottles. It was a treasure trove of rare bottles, each worth $75 to collectors. When the news came out that there were now many mint examples available, the price fell to $20. Prices change with discoveries, auction records, even historic events. Every entry and every picture in this book is new and current thanks to modern computer technology, making this book a handy overall price guide. But you also need current news about bottles.

Books on your shelf get older each month, and prices do change. Important sales produce new record prices. Rarities are discovered. Fakes appear. You will want to keep up with developments from month to month rather than from year to year. *Kovels on Antiques and Collectibles,* a nationally distributed, illustrated newsletter, includes up-to-date information on bottles and other collectibles. This monthly newsletter reports current prices, collecting trends, landmark auction results for all types of antiques and collectibles, including bottles, and tax, estate, security, and other pertinent news for collectors.

Additional information and a free sample newsletter are available from the authors at P.O. Box 420420, Palm Coast, Florida 32142.

Clues to the Contents of This Book

Some product slogans brag, "We did it right the first time." We know that anything can be improved; and, once again with a new book, we have put in a few extra features. This is the all-new, better-than-ever, ninth edition of *Kovels' Bottles Price List*. We wrote the first bottle price guide 21 years ago. This year, the book's format has been updated to reflect the changing interests of the 1990s. Paragraphs have been expanded. The histories of companies and their products have been researched and we have tried to note any important changes in ownership of modern brands. A new color picture section tells the history of the past 20 years of bottle collecting in America. All of the prices listed are new. They are compiled from sales and offerings of the past year. You will find that many modern bottles are no longer listed by brand, because collector interest has lagged. We still have complete listings of the more popular modern bottles such as Jim Beam and Ezra Brooks. The pictures of old bottles are all new and were taken with special equipment so they are clearer and more informative.

"Go-withs," the bottle-related items that are bought and sold at all the bottle shows, are listed in their own section at the end of the book. Jar openers, advertisements, corkscrews, bottle caps, and other items that picture or are used with bottles have been classified as bottle go-withs. There is also a complete bibliography and a listing of publications included in this book to aid you in further research. This list was completely checked and is accurate as of February 1992. The national and state club lists are accurate as of February 1992. Unfortunately, addresses do change; and if you cannot find one of the listed clubs, write us, P.O. Box 22200-B, Beachwood, Ohio 44122.

Note: Bottles holding alcoholic beverages must be sold empty to conform with the law in most states. To sell a filled liquor bottle, you must have a liquor license from the state where you live or where you sell the bottle. It is illegal to ship full bottles across state lines. The value is the same for full or empty liquor bottles.

DEFINITIONS

Novice collectors may need a few definitions to explain the terms used in this book. The *pontil mark* is a scar on the bottom of a bottle. It was made by the punty rod that held the glass for the glass blower. If the scar is rough, it is called a *pontil*. If it is smoothed out, it is called a *ground pontil*. *Free blown* means that the glass was blown by the glassmaker using a blow pipe. It was not poured into a mold. A *kick-up* is the deep indentation on the bottom of a bottle. It is very often found on wine bottles. *Whittle marks* are the irregular marks that look like the rough surface of a piece of whittled wood. They are found on bottles that were made before 1900 and were caused by hot glass being blown into a cold mold. *Embossed* lettering is raised lettering. *Etched* lettering was cut into the bottle with acid or a sharp instrument. *Bubbles, teardrops,* or *seeds* describe types of bubbles that form in glass. A *seam* is the line left on the bottle by the mold. It goes up the neck of the bottle. If it goes over the lip, the bottle was machine-made. An *applied lip* is handmade and applied to the bottle after the glassmaker has formed the bottle. A *sheared lip* is found on bottles made before 1840. The top of the bottle was cut from the blowpipe with shears and the result is the sheared lip. The *2-piece,* or *BIMAL,* mold was used from about 1860 to 1900. The *3-piece mold* was used from 1820 to 1880. The automatic bottle machine was invented in 1903 and *machine-made* bottles were made after that date. If glass that was made from 1880 to 1914 is left in strong sunlight, it often turns colors. This is because of the chemical content of the old glass. Bottles can turn purple, pale lavender, or shades of green or brown. These bottles are called *sun-colored*. *Black glass* is not really black. It is very dark olive green or olive amber and appears black unless seen in a bright light. *Milk glass* is an opaque glass made by using tin or zinc in the mixture. Although most milk glass is white, it is correct to call colored glass of this type "blue" or "green" milk glass. There are a few other terms that relate to only one type of bottle and these terms have been identified in the proper paragraphs.

Bottle clubs and bottle shows have set the rules for this edition of *Kovels' Bottles Price List*. We have used the terms preferred by the collectors and have tried to organize the thousands of listings in easy-to-use form. Many abbreviations have been included that are part of the bottle collectors' language. The abbreviations used by John Tibbits in his book *How to Collect Antique Bottles* are listed below and appear throughout the book.

ABM means automatic bottle machine.

BIMAL means blown in mold, applied lip, open pontil.

DUG means literally dug from the ground.

FB means free blown.

IP mens iron pontil.

ISP means inserted slug plate. Special names could be embossed on a bottle, especially a milk bottle, with a special plate inserted in the mold.

OP means open pontil.

SC means sun-colored.

SCA means sun-colored amethyst.

To make the descriptions of the bottles as complete as possible, an identification number has been added to the description in some categories. The serious collector knows the important books about a specialty, and these books have numbered lists of styles of bottles. Included in this book are identification numbers for flasks from McKearin, bitters from Ring, and fruit jars from Creswick. The full titles of the books used are included in the Bibliography and listed in the introductory paragraph for each category.

Medicine bottles include all medicine bottles, except those under the more specific headings such as "Bitters" or "Sarsaparilla." Other related bottles may be found listed under "Drugs." Modern bottles of major interest are listed under the brand name. Unfortunately, we could not offer a complete list of all modern bottles in a pocket-sized book.

If you are not a regular at bottle shows, it may take a few tries to become accustomed to the method of listing. If you cannot find a bottle, try several related headings. For instance, hair products are found under "Cosmetic."

Many named bottles are found under "Medicine," "Food," "Fruit Jar," etc. If your fruit jar has several names, such as "Ball Mason," look under "Fruit Jar, Ball" or "Fruit Jar, Mason." If no color is listed, the bottle is clear.

The prices shown for bottles are the *actual* prices asked for or bid for bottles during the past year. We know collectors try to get discounts, so some of these bottles may have sold for a little less. Prices vary in different parts of the country and, if more than one price for a bottle has been recorded, a range is given. Because of the idiosyncrasies of the computer, it was impossible to place a range on prices of bottles that are illustrated. The price listed is an average.

Spelling is meant to help the collector. If the original bottle spelled "Catsup" as "Ketchup," the latter is the spelling that appears. The abbreviation "Dr." for doctor may appear on bottles as "Dr" (no period) or "Dr." (period). We have included a period each time to keep the computer alphabetizing more consistent except for bottles of Dr Pepper. The period was omitted by the company in 1950 and we use whatever appeared on the bottle. If a word is written "Kennedy's," "Kennedys'," or "Kennedys," we have placed the apostrophe or omitted it as it appeared on the bottle. A few bottles are included that had errors in the original spelling in the bottle mold. The error is explained. Medicine, bitters, and other bottle types sometimes use the term "Dr." and sometimes use just the last name of the doctor. We have used the wording as it appears on the bottle. "Whiskey" is used even if the bottle held Scotch or Canadian or was spelled "Whisky." The rules of computer alphabetizing are followed.

Every bottle or go-with illustrated in black and white is indicated by the abbreviation "Illus" in the text. Color pictures are priced in the center section where they appear.

We welcome any information about clubs, prices, or content for future books but cannot give appraisals by mail. We have tried to be accurate but cannot be responsible for any errors in pricing or information that may appear.

Ralph M. Kovel, Life Member, Federation of Historical Bottle Clubs; Senior Member, American Society of Appraisers
Terry H. Kovel, Life Member, Federation of Historical Bottle Clubs; Senior Member, American Society of Appraisers

Acknowledgments

We want to thank the following companies and collectors who knowingly or unknowingly helped us to find pictures and prices for this book. Many were participating in bottle shows and they graciously let us disturb them while we photographed their stock. Many stopped by to watch and make encouraging remarks. Special thanks go to the Southern Region & Memphis

Bottle Collectors Club who helped us set up a booth, set up lights, find electric outlets, and do the dozens of other things needed to photograph bottles at the National Bottle and Advertising show in Memphis, Tennessee. All of the color pictures in this book were taken at the show. Many of the bottles are rarities proudly brought to us by their owners. Part of the fun of writing our books is meeting the collectors. Our special thanks to Norma and Bill Smith, Ed Provine, and Bob Simmons, who were so helpful at the Memphis show; and to Cecil Munsey, Gene Bradberry and the others who helped us locate the rarities at the show. More special thank you's to The Heart of Ohio Bottle Club, who arranged for us to attend one of their shows. Dan Arman and the others were gracious and helpful.

The catalogs are an important source of price information. The auction houses have been more than generous with both information and pictures. Thanks to the bottle auctions, especially Skinner, Inc., Western Glass Auctions, Glass-Works Auctions, Norman C. Heckler, Harmer Rooke, and Collectors Auction Services. Other auction galleries that helped were BBR Auctions, DuMouchelle's Art Galleries, Inc., Early Auction Company, Garth's Auctions, Inc., Oliver's Auction Gallery, Richard Opfer Auctioneering, Inc., and Richard W. Withington, Inc. The information about clubs and publications was the result of many calls and letters. We thank all who answered, but especially Barbara Harms of the Federation of Historical Bottle Clubs. Last but not least, thank you to Adam Koch, who not only keeps us informed about bottle news but also has a large car and took our oversized purchases home from the Memphis show.

And to these others who knowingly or unknowingly contributed prices to this book, we say "Thank you": Curtis & Rena Abbott; Carl & Sherry Abell; Edmund Acela; Clarence & Betty Acker; Bob & Jackie Adams; Bill Agee; Sandy & Sylvia Andromeda; Bill Annable; *Antique Bottle & Glass Collector;* The Antique Bottles & Stoneware Shop; Antique to Ancient— Rock & Gift Shop; Archaeology Hobbyist (Gene Blasi); Daniel & Karen Arman; David & Linda Arman; Elwin & Ethel Armstrong; Carolyn Arnold; Attic to Basement Collectiques; Jerry Atwell; Anthony Augustyn; *Avon Collectors Newsletter; Avon Times;* Richard & Berny Baldwin; Ken Barnes; Norman Barnett; Vern & Linda Ann Bauckman; Sheldon Baugh; Jim Beam Brands Co. (Toni Clark); Dr. Benson; Blue & Grey Farm Antiques (Henry Heflin); *Bottles & Extras; British Bottle Review;* Chris Brown; Chuck Bukin; Don Leonard & Jackie Burns-Leonard; *The Candy Gram;* Tom & Deena Caniff; Phyllis Christ; George & Barbara Comp; Ken Cornell; Earl W. Cron; Roy Dudiak; Roger Durflinger; Tom & Jeanette Eccles; Bill Egleston Inc.; Mike & Monica Elling; Patty Elwood; Marvin Engel; *Federation Glass Works;* Neal & Mary Jane Ferguson; Ralph D. Finch; Tim & Lois Ford; 4 in 1 Bottle & Decanter Club; *Fruit Jar Newsletter;* Mike Garrett; Leigh Giarde; Glenmore Distilleries (Chris Morris); Good Ol' Boy Antiques; Wayne & Nancy Gray; Jim Hagenbuch; George Hansen; Bob & Barbara A. Harms; Billy Harrelson; John Hathaway; Michael Henrich; James E. Herring; Parker Higby; Tim Hinkle; Hoffman Originals (Ed

Wertheimer); Keith L. Holt; Homestead Collectibles; The Howells; Tom & Vic Hug; International Association of Jim Beam Bottles & Specialties Club (Shirley Sumbles); Mart W. James; Johnny Reb's Outpost (Ray Davenport); Bob Kay; Mike King; Sonia Kirchner; Adam Koch; Bill Koster; Kruse International; Brian LaBrake; Herman & Arlene Lorcher; Stanley Lower; Sonny & Melody Mallory; Jerry McCann; Mary Ann McGirr; Pat McKelvey; Marshall McMasters; C.B. Meares; Middle Tennessee Bottle & Collectors' Club; Leo J. Miller; *Miniature Bottle Collector;* Monsen & Baer; H.F. Montague Enterprises (Mildred Maguire); Mr. B's Antiques and Collectibles; Old Trenton Country Store (Bob & Bev Parks); Carl & Gail Onufer; Gary L. Piper; Glen Poch; Don & Sarah Ramsey; Bob Rice; Marvin L. Ridgeway; Carlton G. & Mary H. Riggin; Tom "Big Knife" Rightmer; Carlyn Ring; Mike Ritter; Rick Ronczka; Jan Rutland; Jim Scharnagel; Larry & Linda Shope; Ski Country, Ltd. (Steve Braton); James P. Slowiak; John Slowiak; Thom Smith; *Soda Mart;* Burton Spiller; James R. Stebbins; Jack Stecher; Mark Steinmetz; Darrel & Norma Story; Joy & Carl Sturm; Vic Svendsen; Edwin R. Tardy; Sam & Eloise Taylor; Art & Jewel Umburger; Paul Van Vactor; Jim & Linda Wallace; Richard Watson; Drew West; Wild Turkey (Olivia Witt); John Wilson; Ben S. Wood; Mike Wood; Peter P. Zimbelman.

A book like this requires much painstaking research and proofreading. Thank you to Edie Smrekar, Harriet Goldner, Marcia Goldberg, Gay Hunter, Gloria Pearlman, Nancy Saada, and the others who helped with the book. Sharon Squibb and Ken Sansone at Crown Publishing made it all look right. Benjamin Margalit took most of the black and white and many of the color pictures, showing all of us that good pictures of glass bottles are possible.

Publications of Interest
to Bottle Collectors
SEE THE CLUB LIST FOR OTHER PUBLICATIONS

NEWSPAPERS

These are general newspapers with some articles and ads for bottles.

Antique Trader Weekly
P.O. Box 1050
Dubuque, Iowa 52004-1050

Collector's News
P.O. Box 156
Grundy Center, Iowa 50638

NEWSLETTERS

Bitters Report
P.O. Box 1253
Bunnell, Florida 32110

Creamers
P.O. Box 11
Lake Villa, Illinois 60046

Fruit Jar Newsletter
364 Gregory Avenue
West Orange, New Jersey
07052-3743

Just For Openers
6126 McPherson
St. Louis, Missouri 63112

Kovels on Antiques and
Collectibles

P.O. Box 22200-B
Beachwood, Ohio 44122

The Milk Route
4 Ox Bow Road
Westport, Connecticut 06880-2602

MAGAZINES

Antique Bottle & Glass
Collector
Box 187
East Greenville, Pennsylvania
18041

Bottles and Extras
P.O. Box 154
Happy Camp, California 96039

British Bottle Review
2 Strafford Avenue
Elsecar, Barnsley
S. Yorkshire, S74 8AA, England

The Miniature Bottle
Collector
P.O. Box 2161
Palos Verdes Peninsula,
California 90274

Bottle Clubs

There are hundreds of bottle clubs that welcome new members. This list is arranged by state and city so you can find the club nearest your home. If no club is listed nearby, we suggest you contact the national organizations (see below). Any active bottle club that is not listed and wishes to be included in future editions of *Kovels' Bottles Price List* should send the necessary information to the authors, P.O. Box 22200-B, Beachwood, Ohio 44122. Information in this list has been compiled with the help of the National Federation of Bottle Clubs and The Miniature Bottle Collector.

NATIONAL CLUBS

Many of these clubs have local chapters & shows. Write them for more information.

AMERICAN
  BREWERIANA
  ASSOCIATION, INC.
P.O. Box 11157
Pueblo, Colorado 81001

AMERICAN
  COLLECTORS OF
  INFANT FEEDERS
5161 West 59th Street
Indianapolis, Indiana 46254

AVON TIMES
P.O. Box 9868
Kansas City, Missouri 64134

COCA-COLA
  COLLECTORS CLUB
  INTERNATIONAL
P.O. Box 49166
Atlanta, Georgia 30359-1166

CROWN COLLECTORS
  SOCIETY
  INTERNATIONAL
4300 San Juan Drive
Fairfax, Virginia 22030

DR PEPPER
  COLLECTORS CLUB
1529 John Smith
Irving, Texas 75061

FEDERATION OF
  HISTORICAL BOTTLE
  CLUBS
14521 Atlantic
Riverdale, Illinois 60627

FIGURAL BOTTLE
  OPENER
  COLLECTORS
117 Basin Hill Road
Duncannon, Pennsylvania
  17020

HOFFMAN NATIONAL
  COLLECTORS CLUB
P.O. Box 37341
Cincinnati, Ohio 45222

INTERNATIONAL
  ASSOCIATION OF JIM
  BEAM BOTTLE AND
  SPECIALTIES CLUB
5013 Chase Avenue
Downers Grove, Illinois
  60515-4399

INTERNATIONAL
  CHINESE SNUFF
  BOTTLE SOCIETY
2601 North Charles Street
Baltimore, Maryland 21218

INTERNATIONAL
  SWIZZLE STICK
  COLLECTORS
  ASSOCIATION
P.O. Box 1117
Bellingham, Washington
  98227-1117

JELLY JAMMERS
  (jelly jars)
R.R. 1, Box 23
Boggstown, Indiana 46110

LILLIPUTIAN BOTTLE
  CLUB
5626 Corning Avenue
Los Angeles, California
  90056

NATIONAL
  ASSOCIATION OF
  AVON COLLECTORS
  CLUB
P.O. Box 7006
Kansas City, Missouri 64113

NATIONAL
ASSOCIATION OF
BREWERIANA
ADVERTISING
2343 Met-To-Wee Lane
Wauwatosa, Wisconsin
53226

NATIONAL PRIVY
DIGGERS
ASSOCIATION
5208 Jules Verne Court
Tampa, Florida 33611

NATIONAL SKI
COUNTRY BOTTLE
CLUB
1224 Washington Avenue
Golden, Colorado 80401

PAINTED SODA
BOTTLE
COLLECTOR'S
ASSOCIATION
9418 Hilmer Drive
LaMesa, California 91942

PEPSI-COLA
COLLECTORS CLUB
P.O. Box 1275
Covina, California 91722

PERFUME & SCENT
BOTTLE NEWS
P.O. Box 6965
Rockford, Illinois
61125-6965

SARATOGA-TYPE
BOTTLE
COLLECTORS
SOCIETY
238 South Street
Mechanicville, New York
12118

SOCIETY OF INKWELL
COLLECTORS
5136 Thomas Avenue South
Minneapolis, Minnesota
55410

TIN CONTAINER
COLLECTORS
ASSOCIATION
P.O. Box 440101
Aurora, Colorado 80044

TOPS & BOTTOMS
CLUB (for Renee
Lalique bottles only)
P.O. Box 15555
Plantation, Florida 33317

WESTERN WORLD
AVON CLUB
P.O. Box 23785
Pleasant Hill, California
94523

STATE CLUBS

Alabama

Mobile Bottle Collectors
Club
8844 Lee Circle
IRVINGTON, ALABAMA
36544

Montgomery Bottle &
Insulators Club
2021 Merrily Drive
MONTGOMERY,
ALABAMA 36111

Arizona

Indian Country Antique
Bottle & Relic Society
3818 Hilltop Drive
JONESBORO, ARIZONA
72401

Phoenix Antique Bottle &
Collectors Club
1939 West Waltann Lane
PHOENIX, ARIZONA
85023

Arkansas

Little Rock Antique
Bottle Collectors Club
#7 Rockwood
CABOT, ARKANSAS
72023

California

California Miniature Bottle
Club
1911 Willow Street
ALAMEDA, CALIFORNIA
94501

Miniature Bottle Club of
Southern California
836 Carob
BREA, CALIFORNIA
92621

Lilliputian Miniature
Bottle Club
5626 Corning Avenue
LOS ANGELES,
CALIFORNIA 90056

Los Angeles Historical
Bottle Club
P.O. Box 60762 Terminal
Annex
LOS ANGELES,
CALIFORNIA 90060

'49er Historical Bottle
Association
P.O. Box 561
PENRYN, CALIFORNIA
95663

San Luis Obispo Bottle
Society
124-21st Street
PASO ROBLES,
CALIFORNIA 93446

Golden Gate Historical
Bottle Society
6019 Arlington Boulevard
RICHMOND,
CALIFORNIA 94805

San Bernardino County
Historical Bottle &
Collectibles Club
P.O. Box 6759
SAN BERNARDINO,
CALIFORNIA 92412

San Diego Antique Bottle
Club
P.O. Box 5137
SAN DIEGO,
CALIFORNIA 92165

San Jose Historical Bottle
Collectors Association
P.O. Box 5432
SAN JOSE, CALIFORNIA
95150

Northwestern Bottle
Collectors Association
P.O. Box 1121
SANTA ROSA,
CALIFORNIA 95402

Sequoia Antique Bottle &
Collectable Society
P.O. Box 3695
VISALIA, CALIFORNIA
93278

Colorado

Southern Colorado Antique
Bottle Collectors
843 Ussie Avenue
CANON CITY,
COLORADO 81212

Pikes Peak Antique Bottle &
Collectors Club
P.O. Box 2012
COLORADO SPRINGS,
COLORADO 80901

Antique Bottles &
Collectables of Colorado
P.O. Box 245
LITTLETON, COLORADO
80160

Western Slope Bottle Club
P.O. Box 354
PALISADE, COLORADO
81526

Connecticut

Southern Connecticut
Antique Bottle Collectors
Association
34 Dartmouth Drive
HUNTINGTON,
CONNECTICUT 06484

Delaware

Tri-State Bottle Collectors &
Diggers Club
730 Paper Mill Road
NEWARK, DELAWARE
19711

Florida

M-T Bottle Collectors
Association Inc.
P.O. Box 1581
DELAND, FLORIDA 32720

SunCoast Antique Bottle
Collectors Association
5305 8th Avenue South
GULFPORT, FLORIDA
33707

Antique Bottle Collectors of
North Florida
P.O. Box 14796
JACKSONVILLE,
FLORIDA 32238

Central Florida Insulator
Collectors Club
707 N.E. 113th Street
MIAMI, FLORIDA 33161

Mid-State Antique Bottle
Collectors, Inc.
3400 East Grant Avenue
ORLANDO, FLORIDA
32806

Georgia

Southeastern Antique
Bottle Club
1546 Summerford Court
DUNWOODY, GEORGIA
30338

Hawaii

Hawaii Historical Bottle
Collectors Club
P.O. Box 90456
HONOLULU, HAWAII
96835

Illinois

Metro-East Bottle & Jar
Association
309 Bellevue Drive
BELLEVILLE, ILLINOIS
62223

Midwest Miniature Bottle
Club
836 Tam O'Shanter
BOLINGBROOK,
ILLINOIS 60439

First Chicago Bottle Club
P.O. Box A3382
CHICAGO, ILLINOIS
60690

Antique Bottle Collectors
of Northern Illinois
215 Coventry
MT. PROSPECT, ILLINOIS
60056

Indiana

Midwest Antique Fruit Jar
& Bottle Club
P.O. Box 38
FLAT ROCK, INDIANA
47234

Fort Wayne Historical
Bottle Club
6793 C.R. 55
SPENCERVILLE,
INDIANA 46788

Iowa

Iowa Antique Bottlers
Route 1, Box 145
MILTON, IOWA 52570

Kansas

Southeast Kansas Bottle
& Relic Club
P.O. Box 471
CHANUTE, KANSAS
66720

North Central Kansas
Antique Bottle &
Collectors Club
336 East Wisconsin
RUSSELL, KANSAS 67665

Kentucky

Kentuckiana Antique
Bottle & Outhouse
Society
5801 River Knolls Drive
LOUISVILLE, KENTUCKY
40222

Maine

New England Antique Bottle
Club
P.O. Box 897
ROCKPORT, MAINE
04856

Massachusetts

Berkshire Antique Bottle
Association
R.D. 1 Hill Road
WEST STOCKBRIDGE,
MASSACHUSETTS 01266

Michigan

Great Lakes Miniature
Bottle Club
P.O. Box 230460
FAIR HAVEN, MICHIGAN
48023

Flint Antique Bottle &
Collectable Club
3201 Lapeer Street
FLINT, MICHIGAN 48503

Kalamazoo Antique Bottle
Club
204 Monroe
KALAMAZOO,
MICHIGAN 49007

Huron Valley Bottle &
Insulators Club
6349 West Silver Lake Road
LINDEN, MICHIGAN 48451

Metropolitan Detroit
Antique Bottle Club
465 Moran Road
GROSSE POINT FARMS,
MICHIGAN 48236

Minnesota

Minnesota First Antique
Bottle Club
5001 Queen Avenue North
MINNEAPOLIS,
MINNESOTA 55430

North Star Historical
Bottle Association
3308-32nd Avenue South
MINNEAPOLIS,
MINNESOTA 55406

Missouri

St. Louis Antique Bottle
Collectors Association
10118 Schuessler
ST. LOUIS, MISSOURI
63128

Nebraska

Nebraska Antique Bottle
& Collectors Club
14835 Drexel Street
OMAHA, NEBRASKA
68137

Nevada

Las Vegas Bottle Club
2632 East Harman
LAS VEGAS, NEVADA
89121

Antique Bottle Collectors
of Reno & Sparks
P.O. Box 1061
VERDI, NEVADA 89439

New Hampshire

Yankee Antique Bottle
Club
P.O. Box 702
KEENE,
NEW HAMPSHIRE
03431

Merrimack Valley Antique
Bottle Collectors
776 Harvey Road
MANCHESTER,
NEW HAMPSHIRE
03103

New Jersey

South Jersey Heritage
Bottle & Glass Club
P.O. Box 122
GLASSBORO,
NEW JERSEY
08028

North Jersey Antique Bottle
Collectors Association
251 Vista View Drive
MAHWAH, NEW JERSEY
07430

Jersey Shore Bottle Club
P.O. Box 995
TOMS RIVER,
NEW JERSEY
08754

New York

Long Island Antique
Bottle Association
P.O. Box 147
BAYPORT, NEW YORK
11705

Empire State Bottle
Collectors Association
P.O. Box 3421
SYRACUSE, NEW YORK
13220

Western New York
Miniature Liquor Club
P.O. Box 182
CHEEKTOWAGA,
NEW YORK 14225

Finger Lakes Bottle
Collectors Association
399 Dubois Road
ITHACA, NEW YORK
14850

Genesee Valley Bottle
Collectors Association
Box 7528
ROCHESTER, NEW YORK
14615

Hudson Valley Bottle Club
144 County Route 1
WARWICK, NEW YORK
10990

Ohio

Ohio Bottle Club, Inc.
P.O. Box 585
BARBERTON, OHIO 44203

Southwestern Ohio
Antique Bottle & Jar Club
273 Hilltop Drive
DAYTON, OHIO 45415

Findlay Antique Bottle Club
407 Cimarron Ct.
FINDLAY, OHIO 45840

Bottle Hunter Club
22000 Shaker Blvd.
SHAKER HEIGHTS, OHIO
44122

Oklahoma

Oklahoma Territory Bottle &
Relic Club
1300 South Blue Haven
Drive
MUSTANG, OKLAHOMA
73064

Tulsa Antique Bottle and
Relic Club
P.O. Box 4278
TULSA, OKLAHOMA
74519

Oregon

Northwest Mini Club of
Portland
P.O. Box 6551
PORTLAND, OREGON
97228

Oregon Miniature Bottle
Club
P.O. Box 70201
EUGENE, OREGON 97401

Pennsylvania

Washington County Antique
Bottle & Insulator Club
RD 2, Box 342
CARMICHAELS,
PENNSYLVANIA 15320

Laurel Valley Bottle Club
P.O. Box 131
LIGONIER,
PENNSYLVANIA 15658

Ligonier Historical Bottle
Collectors
P.O. Box 188
LIGONIER,
PENNSYLVANIA 15658

Forks of the Delaware Bottle
Collectors Association
2996 Georgetown Road
NAZARETH,
PENNSYLVANIA 18064

Bedford County Bottle Club
P.O. Box 116
LOYSBURG,
PENNSYLVANIA 16659

Kiski Mini Beam &
Specialties Club
816 Cranberry Drive
MONROEVILLE,
PENNSYLVANNIA 15146

Pittsburgh Antique Bottle
Club
209 Palomino Drive
OAKDALE,
PENNSYLVANIA 15071

Del-Val Miniature Bottle
Club
653 Parlin Street
PHILADELPHIA,
PENNSYLVLANIA 19116

Pennsylvania Bottle
Collectors Association
251 Eastland Avenue
YORK, PENNSYLVANIA
17402

Tennessee

Memphis Bottle
Collectors Club
4098 Faxon Avenue
MEMPHIS, TENNESSEE
38122

Middle Tennessee Bottle
Collectors Club
2405 Pennington Bend Road
NASHVILLE, TENNESSEE
37214

Texas

Austin Bottle & Insulator
Collectors
1614 Ashberry Drive
AUSTIN, TEXAS 78723

Gulf Coast Bottle & Jar
Club
P.O. Box 1754
PASADENA, TEXAS 77501

Utah

Utah Antique Bottle & Relic
Club
517 South Hayes
MIDVALE, UTAH 84047

Virginia

Potomac Bottle Collectors
8411 Porter Lane
ALEXANDRIA, VIRGINIA
22308

Historical Bottle Diggers
of Virginia
145 Third Street
BROADWAY, VIRGINIA
22815

Richmond Area Bottle
Collectors Association Inc.
524 Bayliss Drive
RICHMOND, VIRGINIA
23235

Apple Valley Bottle
Collectors Club
P.O. Box 2201
WINCHESTER, VIRGINIA
22601

Washington

Washington Bottle
Collectors Association
5492 Hannegan Road
BELLINGHAM,
WASHINGTON 98226

Wisconsin

Milwaukee Antique
Bottle Club
2343 Met-To-Wee Lane
WAUWATOSA,
WISCONSIN 53226

OTHER SOURCES

Museum of Beverage
Containers & Advertising
1055 Ridgecrest Drive
Goodlettsville, Tennessee
37072

National Bottle Museum
Society
P.O. Box 621
Ballston Spa, New York
12020

Rakow Library
Corning Museum of Glass
One Museum Way
Corning, New York
14830-2253

AUCTION GALLERIES

Sales held at these galleries during the past year are reported in the price
list.

BBR Auctions
2 Strafford Avenue
Elsecar, Barnsley
S. Yorkshire, S74 8AA,
England

Collectors Auction Services
327 Seneca Street
Oil City, Pennsylvania
16301

DuMouchelle's Art
Galleries, Inc.
409 E. Jefferson Avenue
Detroit, Michigan 48226

Early Auction Co.
123 Main Street
Milford, Ohio 45150

Garth's Auctions, Inc.
P.O. Box 369
Delaware, Ohio 43015

Glass-Works Auctions
P.O. Box 187
East Greenville,
Pennsylvania 18041

Harmer Rooke
3 East 57th Street
New York, New York 10022

Norman C. Heckler
Bradford Corner Road
Woodstock Valley,
Connecticut 06282

Richard Opfer
Auctioneering, Inc.
1919 Greenspring Drive
Timonium, Maryland 21093

Western Glass Auctions
1288 West 11th Street,
Suite 230
Trady, California 95376

Oliver's Auction Gallery
P.O. Box 337
Kennebunk, Maine 04043

Skinner, Inc.
357 Main Street
Bolton, Massachusetts 01740

Richard W. Withington, Inc.
Hillsboro, New Hampshire
03244

Bibliography

GENERAL

Antique Bottles Collectors Encyclopedia with Price Guide. S. Yorkshire, England: B.B.R. Publishing, 1986.

Fred's Price Guide to Modern Bottles. Issued quarterly (P.O. Box 1423, Cheyenne, Wyoming 82003). (Price lists for modern bottles.)

Freeman, Larry. *Grand Old American Bottles*. Watkins Glen, New York: Century House, 1964.

Ketchum, William C., Jr. *A Treasury of American Bottles*. Indianapolis: Bobbs-Merrill Company, 1975.

Kovel, Ralph and Terry. *Kovels' Antiques & Collectibles Price List 1992*. 24th edition. New York: Crown Publishers, 1991.

————. *Kovels' Know Your Antiques*. New York: Crown Publishers, 1981.

McKearin, George L. and Helen. *Two Hundred Years of American Blown Glass*. New York: Crown Publishers, 1950.

Montague, H.F. *Montague's Modern Bottle Identification & Price Guide*. 3rd edition. Privately printed, 1984 (P.O. Box 4059, Overland Park, Kansas 66204).

Munsey, Cecil. *The Illustrated Guide to Collecting Bottles*. New York: Hawthorn Books, Inc., 1970.

Stockton, John. *Victorian Bottles: A Collector's Guide to Yesterday's Empties*. North Pomfret, Vermont: David & Charles, 1981.

Toulouse, Julian Harrison. *Bottle Makers and Their Marks*. Nashville, Tennessee: Thomas Nelson & Sons, 1971.

AVON

Avon 8. Pleasant Hill, California: Western World Publishing, 1985.

Avon 8: Supplement 1. Pleasant Hill, California: Western World Publishing, 1987.

Hastin, Bud. *Bud Hastin's Avon Bottle Collector's Encyclopedia*. 11th edition. Privately printed, 1988 (P.O. Box 43690, Las Vegas, Nevada 89116).

————. *Avon Collectibles Price Guide*. 1st edition. Privately printed, 1991 (P.O. Box 9868, Kansas City, Missouri 64134).

BEAM

Cembura, Al, and Constance Avery. *A Guide to Jim Beam Bottles*. 12th edition. Privately printed, 1984 (139 Arlington Ave., Berkeley, California 94707).

Honeyman, Betty, ed. *Jim Beam Bottles: A Pictorial Guide.* Downers Grove, Illinois: International Association of Jim Beam Bottle and Specialties Clubs, 1982. Price guide updated 1990.

BARBER

Holiner, Richard. *Collecting Barber Bottles,* Paducah, Kentucky: Collector Books, 1987.

Namiat, Robert. *Barber Bottles with Prices.* Radnor, Pennsylvania: Wallace-Homestead Book Co., 1977.

BEER

Bull, Donald, et al. *American Breweries.* Privately printed, 1984 (P.O. Box 106, Trumbull, Connecticut 06611).

Friedrich, Manfred, and Donald Bull. *The Register of United States Breweries 1876–1976.* 2 volumes. Privately printed, 1976 (P.O. Box 106, Trumbull, Connecticut 06611).

BITTERS

Ring, Carlyn. *For Bitters Only.* Privately printed, 1980 (P.O. Box 357, Sun Valley, Idaho 83383).

Ring, Carlyn, and Sheldon Ray. *For Bitters Only: Update & Price Guide.* Privately printed, 1984 (P.O. Box 357, Sun Valley, Idaho 83383).

Watson, Richard. *Bitters Bottles,* Nashville, Tennessee: Thomas Nelson & Sons, 1965.

_____. *Supplement to Bitters Bottles.* Nashville, Tennessee: Thomas Nelson & Sons, 1968.

BLACK GLASS

Morgan, Roy, and Gordon Litherland. *Sealed Bottles: Their History and Evolution (1630–1930).* Burton-on-Trent, England: Midland Antique Bottle Publishing, 1976.

_____. *A Bottle Collector's Guide: European Seals, Case Gins and Bitters.* London: Latimer New Dimensions Ltd., 1976.

CANDY CONTAINERS

Eikelberner, George, Serge Agadjanian, and Adele L. Bowden. *The Compleat American Glass Candy Containers Handbook.* Privately printed, 1986 (6252 Cedarwood Rd., Mentor, Ohio 44060).

Eikelberner, George, and Serge Agadjanian. *American Glass Containers.* Privately printed, 1967 (River Rd., Belle Mead, New Jersey 08502).

_____. *More American Glass Candy Containers.* Privately printed, 1970 (River Rd., Belle Mead, New Jersey 08502).

Long, Jennie D. *An Album of Candy Containers.* 2 volumes. Privately printed, 1978, 1983 (P.O. Box 552, Kingsburg, California 93631).

COCA-COLA

Bates, Paul and Karen. Numerous computer-generated lists. Privately printed (Ridgecrest Dr., Goodlettsville, Tennessee 37072).

Coca-Cola Company. *The Coca-Cola Company . . . An Illustrated Profile.* Atlanta, Georgia: The Coca-Cola Company, 1974.

Goldstein, Shelley and Helen. *Coca-Cola Collectibles with Current Prices and Photographs in Full Color.* 4 volumes and Index. Privately printed, 1971–1980 (P.O. Box 301, Woodland Hills, California 91364).

Hill, Deborah Goldstein. *Price Guide to Coca-Cola Collectibles.* Radnor, Pennsylvania: Wallace-Homestead Book Co., 1991.

Hoy, Anne. *Coca-Cola: The First Hundred Years.* Atlanta, Georgia: The Coca-Cola Company, 1986.

Mix, Richard. *The Mix Guide to Commemorative Coca-Cola Bottles.* Privately printed, 1990 (P.O. Box 558, Marietta, Georgia 30061-0558).

Munsey, Cecil. *The Illustrated Guide to the Collectibles of Coca-Cola.* New York: Hawthorn Books, Inc., 1972.

Petretti, Allan. *Petretti's Coca-Cola Collectibles Price Guide.* Radnor, Pennsylvania: Wallace-Homestead Book Co., 1991.

Schmidt, Bill and Jan. *The Schmidt Museum Collection of Coca-Cola Memorabilia.* Privately printed, 1986 (P.O. Box 647, Elizabethtown, Kentucky 42701).

Shartar, Martin, and Norman Shavin. *The Wonderful World of Coca-Cola.* Privately printed, 1978 (2181 Sylvan Road S.W., Atlanta, Georgia 30344).

Wilson, Al. *Collectors Guide to Coca-Cola Items.* Gas City, Indiana: L-W Book Sales, 1985.

COLOGNE, SEE PERFUME

CURES, SEE MEDICINE; SARSAPARILLA

DECANTER

Davis, Derek Co. *English Bottles & Decanters 1650–1900.* New York: World Publishing Co., 1972.

DRUG, SEE MEDICINE

FIGURAL, SEE ALSO BITTERS

Revi, Albert Christian. *American Pressed Glass and Figure Bottles.* New York: Thomas Nelson & Sons, 1964.

Umberger, Jewel and Arthur L. *Collectible Character Bottles.* Privately printed, 1969 (Corker Book Company, 819 W. Wilson, Tyler, Texas 75701).

Wearin, Otha D. *Statues that Pour: The Story of Character Bottles.* Privately printed, 1965 (Sage Books, 2679 South York St., Denver, Colorado).

FLASKS

McKearin, Helen, and Kenneth M. Wilson. *American Bottles & Flasks and Their Ancestry.* New York: Crown Publishers, 1978.

Roberts, Mike. *Price Guide to All the Flasks*. Privately printed, 1980 (840 Elm Court, Newark, Ohio 43055).

Thomas, John L. *Picnics, Coffins, Shoo-Flies*. Privately printed, 1974 (P.O. Box 446, Weaverville, California 96093).

Van Rensselaer, Stephen. *Early American Bottles & Flasks*. Revised edition. Privately printed, 1969 (J. Edmund Edwards, 61 Winton Place, Stratford, Connecticut 06497).

FOOD, SEE ALSO FRUIT JARS; VINEGAR

Alberts, Robert C. *The Good Provider: H.J. Heinz and His 57 Varieties*. Boston: Houghton Mifflin Company, 1973.

Reddock, Richard D. and Barbara. *Planters Peanuts*. Radnor, Pennsylvania: Wallace-Homestead Book Co., 1978.

FRUIT JARS

Bowditch, Barbara. *American Jelly Glasses: A Collector's Notebook*. Privately printed, 1986 (400 Dorchester Rd., Rochester, New York 14610).

Brantley, William F. *A Collector's Guide to Ball Jars*. Muncie, Indiana: Ball Corporation, 1975.

Creswick, Alice. *The Fruit Jar Works*. 2 volumes. Privately printed, 1987 (0-8525 Kenowa S.W., Grand Rapids, Michigan 49504).

———. *Red Book: The Collector's Guide to Old Fruit Jars*. No. 6. Privately printed, 1990 (0-8525 Kenowa S.W., Grand Rapids, Michigan 49504).

Roller, Dick. *The Standard Fruit Jar Reference*. Privately printed, 1983 (607 Driskell, Paris, Illinois 61944).

Toulouse, Julian Harrison. *Fruit Jars: A Collector's Manual*. Jointly published by Nashville, Tennessee: Thomas Nelson & Sons, and Hanover, Pennsylvania: Everybody's Press, 1969.

INK

Covill, William E., Jr. *Ink Bottles and Inkwells*. Taunton, Massachusetts: William S. Sullwold Publishing, 1971.

Rivera, Betty and Ted. *Inkstands and Inkwells*. New York: Crown Publishers, 1973.

JAR, SEE FRUIT JAR

MEDICINE

Baldwin, Joseph K. *A Collector's Guide to Patent and Proprietary Medicine Bottles of the Nineteenth Century*. Nashville, Tennessee: Thomas Nelson & Sons, 1973.

Blasi, Betty. *A Bit About Balsams: A Chapter in the History of Nineteenth Century Medicine*. Privately printed, 1974 (5801 River Knolls Dr., Louisville, Kentucky 40222).

Burton, Jean. *Lydia Pinkham Is Her Name*. New York: Farrar, Straus and Company, 1949.

Wilson, Bill and Betty. *19th Century Medicine in Glass*. Privately printed, 1971 (Box 245, Amador City, California 95601).

MILK GLASS

Belknap, E.M. *Milk Glass*. New York: Crown Publishers, 1959.

Ferson, Regis F. and Mary F. *Yesterday's Milk Glass Today*. Privately printed, 1981 (122 Arden Rd., Pittsburgh, Pennsylvania 15216).

MILK

Giarde, Jeffrey L. *Glass Milk Bottles: Their Makers and Marks*. Bryn Mawr, California: The Time Travelers Press, 1980.

MINERAL WATER, SEE SODA

MINIATURES

Cembura, Al, and Constance Avery. *A Guide to Miniature Bottles*. Privately printed, 1973 (139 Arlington Ave., Berkeley, California 94708).

Kay, Robert E. *Miniature Beer Bottles & Go-Withs*. Privately printed, 1980 (216 No. Batavia Ave., Batavia, Illinois 60510).

Keegan, Alan. *Scotch in Miniature: A Collector's Guide*. Privately printed, 1982 (Chiisai Bin, P.O. Box 1900, Garden Grove, California 92642).

Maund, David L. and Mike Barbakoff. *Two Hundred and One Rare Scotch Whisky Miniatures*. Privately printed, 1991 (Briscoe Publications, P.O. Box 2161, Palos Verdes, CA 90274).

Triffon, James A. *The Whiskey Miniature Bottle Collection*. 2 volumes. Privately printed, 1979, 1981 (available from Chiisai Bin Imports, P.O. Box 90245, Los Angeles, California 90009).

NURSING

Ostrander, Diane Rouse. *A Guide to American Nursing Bottles*. Privately printed, 1984 (Will-O-Graf, P.O. Box 24, Willoughby, Ohio 44094).

PEPPER SAUCE, SEE PICKLE

PEPSI-COLA

Rawlingson, Fred. *Brad's Drink: A Primer for Pepsi-Cola Collectors*. Privately printed, 1976 (FAR Publications, Box 5456, Newport News, Virginia 23605).

Stoddard, Bob. *Introduction to Pepsi Collecting*. Privately printed, 1991 (P.O. Box 1548, Pomona, California 91769).

Vehling, Bill, and Michael Hunt. *Pepsi-Cola Collectibles (with prices)*. 2 volumes. Gas City, Indiana: L-W Book Sales, 1988, 1990.

PERFUME, COLOGNE, AND SCENT

Baccarat: The Perfume Bottles. Privately printed, 1986 (Addor Associates, Inc., P.O. Box 2128, Westport, Connecticut 06880).

Forsythe, Ruth A. *Made in Czechoslovakia*. Privately printed, 1982 (Box 327, Galena, Ohio 43021).

Gaborit, Jean-Yves. *Perfumes: The Essences and Their Bottles*. New York: Rizzoli International Publications, Inc., 1985.

Martin, Hazel. *A Collection of Figural Perfume & Scent Bottles*. Privately printed, 1982 (P.O. Box 110, Lancaster, California 93535).

North, Jacquelyn Y. Jones. *Commercial Perfume Bottles*. West Chester, Pennsylvania: Schiffer Publishing, Ltd., 1986.

_____. *Perfume, Cologne and Scent Bottles*. West Chester, Pennsylvania: Schiffer Publishing, Ltd., 1986.

Sloan, Jean. *Perfume and Scent Bottle Collecting with Prices*. Radnor, Pennsylvania: Wallace-Homestead Book Co., 1986.

Utt, Mary Lou, and Glen and Patricia Bayer. *Lalique Perfume Bottles*. New York: Crown Publishers, 1985.

PICKLE

Zumwalt, Betty. *Ketchup Pickles Sauces*. Privately printed, 1980 (P.O. Box 413, Fulton, California 95439).

POISON

Durflinger, Roger L. *Poison Bottles Collectors Guide*. Privately printed, 1972 (132 W. Oak St., Washington Court House, Ohio 43160).

Kuhn, Rudy. *Poison Bottle Workbook*. Privately printed, 1988 (3954 Perie Lane, San Jose, California 95132).

Stier, Wallis W. *Poison Bottles: A Collectors' Guide*. Privately printed, 1969 (P.O. Box 243, Rockland, Idaho 83271).

ROYAL DOULTON

Dale, Jean. *The Charlton Standard Catalog of Royal Doulton Jugs*. Privately printed, 1991 (Charlton Press, 2010 Yonge St., Toronto, Ontario M4S 1Z9, Canada).

SARSAPARILLA

DeGrafft, Joan. *American Sarsaparilla Bottles*. Privately printed, 1980 (47 Ash St., North Attleboro, Massachusetts 92760).

Shimko, Phyllis. *Sarsaparilla Bottle Encyclopedia*. Privately printed, 1969 (Box 117, Aurora, Oregon 97002).

SKI COUNTRY

Ski Country Collector's Guide and Catalog of Decanters. Privately printed, 1983 (1224 Washington Ave., Golden, Colorado 80401).

SCENT, SEE PERFUME

SODA, SEE ALSO COCA-COLA; PEPSI-COLA

Bates, Paul and Karen. Numerous computer-generated lists by subject. Privately printed (Ridgecrest Dr., Goodlettsville, Tennessee 37072).

Bowers, Q. David. *The Moxie Encyclopedia*. Vestal, New York: The Vestal Press Ltd., 1984.

Dietz, Lawrence. *Soda Pop*. New York: Simon & Schuster, 1973.

Ellis, Harry E. *Dr Pepper, King of Beverages*. Dallas, Texas: Dr Pepper Company, 1979.

Fowler, Ron. *Ice-Cold Soda Pop 5 Cents*. Privately printed, 1981 (4110 48th N.E., Seattle, Washington 98105).

Herbetta, Victoria. *America Goes POP*. Privately printed, 1982 (P.O. Box 8154, Houston, Texas 77004).

Morrison, Tom. *Root Beer Advertising: A Collector's Guide*. Privately printed, 1990 (2930 Squaw Valley Dr., Colorado Springs, Colorado 80918).

TONIC, SEE MEDICINE

VINEGAR

Smith, Levin J. *White House Vinegar Book*. Privately printed, 1971 (P.O. Box 102, Independence, Virginia 24348).

WHISKEY

Barnett, R.E. *Western Whiskey Bottles*. Privately printed, 1992 (Box 109, Lakeview, Oregon 97640).

Spaid, David, and Henry Ford. *The One Hundred and One Rare Whiskeys*. Privately printed, 1989 (P.O. Box 2161, Palos Verdes, California 90274).

Westcott, David. *Westcott Price Guide to Advertising Water Jugs*. Privately printed, 1991 (P.O. Box 245, Deniliquin, NSW, 2710 Australia).

WINE

Dumbrell, Roger. *Understanding Antique Wine Bottles*. Suffolk, England: Antique Collectors' Club, 1983.

GO-WITHS

Byrne, Thomas. *The U.S. Beer Coaster Guide*. Privately printed, 1980 (P.O. Box 173, East Hanover, New Jersey 07936).

Congdon-Martin, Douglas. *America For Sale*. West Chester, Pennsylvania: Schiffer Publishing Ltd., 1991.

Edmonson, Barbara. *Historic Shot Glasses*. Bend, Oregon: Maverick Publications, 1985.

_____. *Old Advertising: Sprits Glasses*. Bend, Oregon: Maverick Publications, 1988.

Hake, Ted, and Russ King. *Price Guide to Collectible Pin-Back Buttons 1896–1986*. Privately printed, 1986 (Hake's Americana & Collectible Press, P.O. Box 1444, York, Pennsylvania 17405).

Klug, Ray. *Antique Advertising Encyclopedia*. 2 volumes. Gas City, Indiana: L-W Book Sales, 1978, 1985.

Robinson, Joleen A., and Kay F. Sellers. *Advertising Dolls*. Paducah, Kentucky: Collector Books, 1980.

---------------------------- **AESTHETIC SPECIALTIES** ----------------------------

In 1979 the first bottle was released by ASI, or Aesthetic Specialties, Inc., of San Mateo, California. It was a ceramic vodka bottle that was made to honor the 1979 Crosby 38th National Pro–Am Golf Tournament. According to the company president, Charles Wittwer, 400 cases of the bottle were made. The company continued making bottles: the 1979 Kentucky Derby bottle (600 cases); 1909 Stanley Steamer (5,000 cases in three different colors made in 1979); 1903 Cadillac (2 colors made in 1979, gold version, with and without trim, made in 1980); World's Greatest Golfer (400 cases in 1979); World's Greatest Hunter (1979); 38th and 39th Crosby Golf Tournaments (1979 and 1980); 1981 Crosby 40th Golf Tournament (reworked version of World's Greatest Golfer, 100 cases); Crosby Golf Tournaments (1982, 1983, and 1984); Telephone Service Truck (1980); Ice Cream Truck (1980); 1910 Oldsmobile (1980, made in three colors); Packard (1980); 1911 Stanley Steamer (1981, 1,200 cases); 1937 Packard (1981, produced with McCormick); 1914 Chevrolet (1981); and Fire engine (1981).

AESTHETIC SPECIALTIES, Bing Crosby, 38th, 1979 .... 12.00
  Bing Crosby, 41st, Otter, 1982 .... 40.00
  Bing Crosby, 42nd, Seal, 1983 .... 40.00
  Cadillac, 1903 Model, White, 1979 .... 45.00
  Golfer, World's Greatest, 1979 .... 32.00
  Hunter, World's Greatest, 1979 .... 26.00
  Kentucky Derby, 1979 .... 25.00
  Model T Ice Cream Truck, 1980 .... 55.00
  Model T Telephone Truck, 1980 .... 50.00
  Oldsmobile, 1910 Model, 1980 .... 70.00
  Stanley Steamer, 1909 Model, Black, 1978 .... 45.00
    ALPHA, see Lewis & Clark
    AUSTIN NICHOLS, see Wild Turkey

---------------------------- **AVON** ----------------------------

David H. McConnell started a door–to–door selling company in 1886. He recruited women as independent sales representatives to sell his perfume. The company was named the California Perfume Company even though it was located in New York City. The first product was a set of five perfumes called Little Dot. In 1928 it was decided that CPC was too limiting a name so a new line called Avon was introduced. By 1936, the Avon name was on all of the company's products, including perfumes, toothbrushes, and baking items. Avon became a public company in 1946. Collectors want the bottles, jewelry, and sales awards, but there is also interest in the early advertising and pamphlets. For information on national and local clubs, books, and other publications, contact the National Association of Avon Collector Clubs, P.O. Box 7006, Kansas City, MO 64113.

AVON, Abraham Lincoln, 1971 .... 2.00
  Aladdin's Lamp, 1971 .... 6.00
  Alpine Flask, 1966 .... 15.00 To 35.00
  American Beauty Fragrance Jar, No Tassel, 1934–1943 .... 22.00
  American Schooner, 1972 .... 2.00
    AVON, ANGEL, see also Heavenly Angel
  Angler, 1970 .... 4.00
  Apothecary, Decanter, 1972 .... 160.00
  Army Jeep, 1974 .... 3.50 To 8.00
  Atlantic 4–4–2, 1973 .... 5.00
  Attention Fragrance, 1943, Box 35.00
    AVON, AUTO HORN, see Avon, It's A Blast
  Auto Lantern, 1973 .... 9.50
  Avon Calling 9.50
  Avon Calling, 1969 .... 5.50
  Avon Calling, 1973, 1905 Phone 3.25
  Avonshire Candleholder, 1973 .... 6.00
  Avonshire, Decanter, 1973 .... 5.00
    AVON, BARBER BOTTLE, see Avon, Close Harmony
  Barber Pole, 1974 .... 2.00
    AVON, BASEBALL MITT, see Avon, Fielder's Choice
  Bath Urn, Opalescent, 1963 .... 12.00 To 14.00

Bay Rum, Jug, 1962 .... 8.00
Bay Rum, Keg, 1965 ....9.50 To 12.50
Be My Valentine Cologne, Miniature 1.50
Beautiful Awakening, 1973 .... 3.00
Bell, Birthday, Crystal, 1986 .... 15.00
Bell, Bunny, 1984 ....6.00 To 17.50
Bell, Cape Cod, Hostess, 1979 .... 12.00 To 20.00
Bell, Cape Cod, Hostess, 1980 .... 12.00
Bell, Centennial, Box, 1986 .... 12.00
Bell, Christmas, 1973, Hobnail 5.00
Bell, Christmas, 1973, Mikasa 20.00
Bell, Christmas, 1978, Emerald 5.00
Bell, Christmas, 1978, Joyous ....2.00 To 3.00
Bell, Christmas, 1980, Snowflake, Crystal ....5.00 To 8.00
Bell, Christmas, 1981, Moonlight Glow ....6.00 To 9.00
Bell, Christmas, 1987 .... 14.00
Bell, Country, 1985 ....4.00 To 5.00
Bell, Crystal Song, 1975 ....3.00 To 7.50
Bell, Hospital, 1976 .... 7.00
Bell, Hospitality, 1976 ....3.00 To 7.50
Bell, Hostess, Cherub, 1978 .... 12.00
Bell, Hudson Manor, 1978 .... 15.00 To 20.00
Bell, Hummingbird, 1985 .... 13.00
Bell, Independence, 1976 .... 22.00
Bell, Liberty, 1971 ....4.00 To 5.00
Bell, Mid–America Club Convention, Souvenir, 1984 .... 25.00
Bell, Rosepoint, 1977 ....5.00 To 10.00
Bell, Tapestry, 1981 .... 25.00
Belle, Fragrance, 1965 .... 7.50
Betsy Ross, 1976 .... 12.00
Big Bolt, 1976 .... 2.00
Big Game Rhino, 1972 .... 4.00
Big Rig, 1975 ....3.00 To 6.00
Biplane, Clear 75.00
Bird of Paradise, Decanter, 1970 ....4.00 To 6.00
Bird's Egg, Autumn, 1984 .... 7.00
Bird's Egg, Spring, 1984 .... 7.00
Black Lady, Club, 1984 .... 15.00 To 17.50
Black Telephone, Man's, Contents, Box 25.00
Blunderbuss Pistol, 1780, 1976 ....5.00 To 8.00
   AVON, BOOT, see also Avon, Western Boot
Boot, Leather Spray Cologne, 1966 .... 2.50
Boots 'n Saddle, 1980 .... 7.00
Bowling Pins Set, 1960 .... 6.00
Bright Chipmunk, Candle, 1978 .... 4.00
Bucking Bronco, 1971 .... 3.00
Buffalo Nickel, 1971 .... 10.00
Cable Car, 1974 .... 6.00
Cadillac, 1968 .... 8.00
California Perfume Co., Anniversary Keepsake, 1976 .... 2.00
California Perfume Co., Daphne Talcum Powder, 1920 .... 55.00
California Perfume Co., Demonstrator Set, 4 Bottles, Box, 1923 .... 300.00
California Perfume Co., Gold Coast, 1977 .... 32.50
California Perfume Co., Talc For Men, 1929 .... 55.00
California Perfume Co., Trailing Arbutus Talc, 1923 .... 3.00
California Perfume Co., Venetian Carnation, Glass Stopper 150.00
California Perfume Co., Vernafleur Adherent Powder, 1925 .... 45.00
Candle, Flaming Tulip, 1973 .... 5.00
Candle, Floral Medley, 1971 ....4.00 To 5.00
Candle, Sunshine Rose Fragrance 5.00
Candle, Winter Lights, 1978 .... 4.50
Candleholder, Planter, Bunny, 1977–1978 .... 10.00
Candleholder, Regency Cologne, 1973–1974 .... 8.00

Candleholder, Teddy Bear, 1980 .... 18.00
Candlestick, Cape Cod, 1975 .... 8.00
Candlestick, Charisma, 1974 .... 8.00
Candlestick, Danish Modern, 1970 .... 4.50
Candlestick, Flaming Tulip, 1973 .... 10.00
Candlestick, Goblet, Cape Cod, 1977 .... 11.00
Candlestick, Goblet, Cape Cod, Bayberry Candle, 1976 .... 8.00
Candlestick, Heart & Diamond, 1979 .... 6.00
Candlestick, Hurricane, Cape Cod, Glass Chimney, 1985, 13 In. 25.00
Candlestick, Milk Glass, Frosted, 1st Christmas, 1967 .... 3.50
Candlestick, Regency, 1973 .... 8.00
Candy Dish, Lead Crystal, Frosted, 1978 .... 12.50
   AVON, CANNON, see also Avon, Defender Cannon; Avon, Revolutionary Cannon
Cannonball Express 4–6, 1976 .... 5.00
Capital, Decanter, 1970 .... 10.00
Captain's Choice, 1964 .... 4.00 To 9.00
Captain's Pride, In Stand, 1970 .... 8.00
Car, Auburn, Bobtail Speedster, 1983 .... 20.00
Car, Bugatti, 1927 Model, 1974 .... 10.00
Car, Cadillac, Solid Gold, 1969–1973 .... 8.00 To 10.00
Car, Checker Cab, 1926 Model, 1977 .... 5.00
Car, Chrysler, Town & Country, 1948 Model, 1976 .... 8.00 To 10.00
Car, Cord, 1937 Model, 1974–1976 .... 8.00 To 20.00
Car, Duesenberg, 1970–1972 .... 8.00
Car, Duesenberg, Silver, 1970–1972 .... 22.00
Car, Dune Buggy, 1971–1973 .... 8.00
Car, Electric Charger, 1970 .... 3.00
Car, Electric Charger, 1970–1972 .... 8.00
Car, Ford, 1936 Model, Orange, 1976–1977 .... 33.00
Car, Futura, 1969 .... 15.00
Car, Jaguar, 1973–1976 .... 8.00
Car, Packard Roadster, 1970 .... 5.00 To 6.00
Car, Pierce Arrow, 1933 Model, 1975 .... 10.00
Car, Rolls Royce, 1937 Model, 1972–1975 .... 8.00
Car, Stanley Steamer, Silver, 1971 .... 10.00
Car, Stanley Steamer, Silver, 1978 .... 4.00 To 10.00
Car, Sterling Six, Amber, 1968–1970 .... 6.00
Car, Straight Eight, Green, 1969–1971 .... 8.00 To 22.00
Car, Thunderbird, 1955 Model, 1974–1975 .... 12.00
Car, Touring T, Silver, 1978 .... 6.00
Car, Volkswagen Bus, 1975–1976 .... 10.00
Car, Volkswagen, Black, 1970–1972 .... 5.00 To 10.00
Car, Volkswagen, Blue, 1973–1974 .... 5.00 To 7.00
Car, Volkswagen, Decanter, Rabbit, 1980–1982 .... 4.00
Car, Volkswagen, Red, 1972 .... 5.00 To 7.00
Casey's Lantern, Amber, 1966 .... 15.00 To 25.00
Casey's Lantern, Amber, Box, 1966 .... 45.00
Casey's Lantern, Green, 1966 .... 20.00
Casey's Lantern, Red, 1966 .... 20.00
   AVON, CAT, see Avon, Ming Cat
Catch–A–Fish, 1976–1978 .... 5.00
Cement Mixer, 1979 .... 3.00
Chess Set, 1972–1978, 5 Piece .... 50.00 To 150.00
Chimney Lamp, 1973 .... 6.00
China Teapot, 1973 .... 20.00
Christmas Tree, 1974 .... 2.50
Church Mouse Groom, 1979 .... 1.20
Classic Lion, 1973 .... 3.00
Classic Vase, 1985 .... 35.00
Classics, 1969 .... 5.00

Avon, Dollars 'n' Scents

Avon, Occur! Cologne, 3/4 X 2 1/4 In.

AVON, CLOCK, see Avon, Beautiful Awakening; Avon, Daylight Shaving Time; Avon, Enchanted Hours; Avon, Fragrance Hours; Avon, Leisure Hours; Avon, No Cause For Alarm

Close Harmony, With Tip, 1963	12.00
Club, Black Lady, 1984	20.00
AVON, COFFEE MILL, see Avon, Country Store Coffee Mill	
Collectors Corner	25.00
Cologne Gems, 1966–1967	4.00 To 6.00
Colonial Boy, Decanter, 1975	2.25
Colonial Girl, Decanter, 1975	3.50
Colonial Mist, 1967	1.00
Come Rain Or Shine, 1983	15.00
Conair 1200, Blow Dryer, 1978	3.00
Cookie Jar, Patchwork, 1972	12.00
Cookie Jar, Teddy Bear, 1979	28.00
Corncob Pipe, 1974–1975	1.00
Cotillion Perfume, 1953	20.00
Cotillion Powder Sachet, 1964	6.00
Cotillion Precious Pair, 1971	3.00
Country Kitchen Hand Lotion, 1973	12.00
Country Kitchen Hand Lotion, 1974	4.00
Country Lantern, 1979	5.00
Country Store Coffee Mill, 1972	8.00
Country Store, Coffee Mill, 1970	3.50
Country Talc Shaker, 1977	3.00
Country Vendor, 1973	5.00
Courting Carriage, 1973	2.00
Courting Lamp, 1970	5.00 To 12.00
Courting Lamp, Ruby, Test Bottle	100.00
Courting Rose, Yellow, 1977	5.00
Covered Wagon, 1970	2.00
Cream Lotion, 1942	14.00
Creamer, Cape Cod, 1981	7.00
Cup & Saucer, Cape Cod, 1990	12.00
Decanter Set, Cape Cod, 1977–1980, 9 Piece	45.00
Decanter, Cape Cod, 1977	11.00 To 18.00
Decanter, Classic, 1969	2.00
Decanter, E. T., 1983	2.00
Decanter, Homestead, 1973	2.00
Decanter, Statue of Liberty, 1986	7.00

Decanter, Unicorn, 1974 .... 3.50
Defender Cannon, 1966 ....8.00 To 14.00
Delft Blue Pomander, Skin Softener, 1972 .... 4.00
Delicate Dove, 1974–1976 .... 4.00
Devotee Treasure Box, Award, 1966 .... 20.00
  AVON, DOG, see Avon, Lady Spaniel; Avon, Old Faithful
Dollars 'n' Scents ....*Illus* 30.00
Dolphin Miniature, 1973 .... 3.00
Dolphin, 1968 .... 3.00 To 4.00
Dovecote, 1974 .... 3.00
Dr. Hoot, 1975–1976 .... 6.00
  AVON, DUCK, see Avon, Mallard Duck; Avon, Mallard–In–Flight; Avon,
  Wild Mallard Ceramic Organizer
Duck Decoy Pomander, 1974–1975 .... 3.00 To 4.00
Dueling Pistol 1760, 1973–1974 .... 3.00 To 5.00
Dutch Girl, 1970 .... 2.20
Dutch Girl, 1973 .... 4.00
Dutch Maid, 1977 .... 4.00
Eagle, Porcelain, 1982–1983 .... 18.00
Egg Set, 4 Seasons, 1987 .... 36.00 To 40.00
Egg, 4 Seasons, Autumn, 1987 .... 8.00 To 10.00
Egg, 4 Seasons, Summer, 1977 .... 8.00 To 15.00
Egg, 4 Seasons, Winter, 1977 .... 8.00
Eiffel Tower, 1970 .... 5.00
  AVON, ELECTRIC CHARGER, see Avon, Car, Electric Charger
Elegante Cologne, 1956 .... 9.50
Elegante, 1971 .... 5.00
Emerald Accent, Decanter, 1982 .... 10.00
Empire Green Bud Vase, 1974 .... 3.00
Enchanted Hours, 1972 .... 1.40
Fan Rocker, Box, 1962–1963 .... 4.00
Fantasque Elegant Evening Set, 1985 .... 3.50
Fielder's Choice, 1971 .... 2.50
Fire Fighter, 1910 .... 10.00
  AVON, FISH, see Avon, Dolphin; Avon, Sea Spirit
Fishing Reel 6.00
Flamingo, 1971 .... 4.00
Flirtatious Frog Pomander, 1980 .... 5.00
Flower Bell Cologne Mist 4.00
Fly–A–Balloon, 1975–1977 .... 5.00
  AVON, FOOTBALL HELMET, see Avon, Opening Play
Ford, 1936 .... 10.00
Fragrance Bell, 1965 .... 4.50
Fragrance Belle, 1965 .... 9.00
Fragrance Fling Trio, 1968 .... 4.00
Fragrance Hours, 1971 .... 4.00
French Telephone, 1971 .... 20.00 To 30.00
Futura, 1969 .... 7.00 To 18.00
Fuzzy Bear, 1977 .... 3.00
Gallery Ginger Jar, Porcelain, 1983 .... 65.00
Garden Girl, Contents, Box, 1978 .... 10.00
Garden Girl, Yellow, 1978–1979 .... 5.00
Gavel, 1967–1968 .... 8.00 To 10.00
Gentle Moments, 1975 .... 20.00
Gentlemen's Collection, 1968 .... 10.00
Goblet, '94 Anniversary, 1980 .... 3.00
Goblet, George & Martha Washington, 1975–1977, Pair 15.00
Goblet, George Washington, 1975–1977 .... 10.00
Goblet, Water, Cape Cod, 1977 .... 19.00
Goblet, Water, Cape Cod, 1979 .... 9.00
Goblet, Wine, Cape Cod, 1976 .... 10.00
  AVON, GOLD CADILLAC, see Avon, Car, Cadillac
Golden Promise, Box, 1947 .... 17.00

Golden Thimble, 1972 .... 2.50
    AVON, GOLF, see Avon, Perfect Drive
Golf Cart 8.00
Gone Fishing, 1973–1975 .... 5.00
Good Luck Elephant, 1975 .... 4.00
Grecian Pitcher, 1972–1976 .... 5.00
Hawaiian Delights, 1962 .... 3.00 To 4.00
Haynes Apperson 1902, 1973–1974 .... 10.00
    AVON, HEAD, see Avon, Warrior
Hearth Lamp, 1973 ....8.00 To 17.00
Hearthside Cream Sachet, 1976 .... 3.00
Hearts & Diamonds Candle, 1973 .... 8.00
    AVON, HELMET, see Avon, Opening Play
Her Prettiness, 1969–1972 .... 5.00
Here's My Heart, 1948–1949 .... 9.00
Highway King, 1977 .... 3.00
Hurricane Lamp, 1973 .... 19.00
Icicle, Box, 1967–1968 .... 3.00
Imperial Garden Ceramic Vase, 1973–1975 .... 12.50
It All Adds Up, 1978 .... 2.00
It's A Blast, 1970–1971 .... 8.75
Jolly Santa, 1978 .... 1.00
Just A Twist, 1977–1978 .... 10.00
Just For Kicks, 1974 .... 2.50
Just Two Set, 1965 .... 10.00 To 50.00
Kangaroo Two, 1978 .... 4.00 To 8.75
Keepsake Cream Sachet, Box, 1973 .... 1.50
Keepsake, 1967 .... 8.75
Keynote, 1967 .... 10.00
Kitten's Hideaway, 1974–1976 .... 2.50
Koffee Klatch, 1971–1974 .... 2.50
La Belle Telephone, 1974–1976 .... 2.25 To 5.00
Lady Spaniel, 1974 .... 10.00
    AVON, LAMP, see Avon, Courting Lamp; Avon, Hurricane Lamp; Avon,
      Ming Blue Lamp; Avon, Parlor Lamp; Avon, Tiffany Lamp
    AVON, LANTERN, see also Avon, Casey's Lantern
Lantern, Auto, 1973 .... 7.00 To 8.75
Lantern, Whale Oil, 1974–1975 .... 10.00
Lavender & Lace, 1970–1972 .... 3.00
Lavender Powder Sachet, 1944–1945 .... 5.00
Leisure Hours, 1970 .... 3.00
Lennox Bowl, 1980 .... 15.00
Liberty Dollar, 1970–1972 .... 10.00
Lincoln, 1971–1972 .... 4.00
Linus, 1968–1974 .... 4.00
Little Dream Girl, 1980 .... 2.50
Little Jack Horner, 1979 .... 4.00
Little Red Riding Hood, 1985 .... 15.00
Log Cabin 10.00
Lollipop Double Dip, 1968 .... 1.00
Looking Glass, 1970 .... 4.00
Looney Lather Bubble Bath, 1971 .... 4.00
Lucy Bubble Bath, 1970–1972 .... 4.00
Mallard Duck, 1967 .... 6.00 To 7.00
Mallard In Flight, 1974 .... 5.00
Marine Binoculars, 1973 .... 4.00 To 8.75
Mary Non–Tear Shampoo, 1968 .... 4.00
Master Organizer Set, 1970 .... 30.00
McConnells Store Set, 1982 .... 25.00
Meadow Bird, 1975–1976 .... 4.00
Ming Blue Lamp, 1974 .... 4.00 To 6.00
Ming Cat, White Glass, 1971 .... 5.00
Moonwind Mist–Bath Oil, 1972 .... 4.00

Motorbike, Black, 1977, Europe 6.00
Mrs. Albee, 1987 .... 85.00
Mug, Lewis & Clark, 1985 .... 10.00
Mug, We're Hot, With Candy 7.50
Mug, Wright Brothers, 1985 .... 10.00
My First Call 15.00
My First Call, Box 20.00
NAAC, 1st Annual Club, 1972 .... 120.00 To 140.00
NAAC, 2nd Annual Club, 1973 .... 60.00
NAAC, 3rd Annual Club, 1974 .... 25.00
NAAC, 4th Annual Club, 1975 .... 40.00
NAAC, 5th Annual Club, 1976 .... 30.00 To 45.00
NAAC, 6th Annual Club, 1906 Avon Lady, 1977 .... 40.00
NAAC, 7th Annual Club, 1978 .... 15.00 To 55.00
NAAC, 8th Annual Club, 1979 .... 25.00
NAAC, 9th Annual Club, 1980 .... 15.00 To 20.00
NAAC, 10th Annual Club, 1981 .... 16.00
NAAC, 11th Annual Club, 1982 .... 17.00
NAAC, 12th Annual Club, 1983 .... 16.00
NAAC, 13th Annual Club, 1984, Black 20.00
NAAC, 15th Annual Club, 1986 .... 19.00
NAAC, 1st Convention, 1980 .... 25.00 To 30.00
NAAC, 2nd Convention, 1981 .... 20.00
NAAC, 3rd Convention, 1982 .... 20.00
NAAC, 4th Convention, 1983 .... 40.00
NAAC, 5th Convention, 1984 .... 45.00
NAAC, 6th Convention, 1985 .... 40.00
NAAC, 7th Convention, 1986 .... 35.00
NAAC, 8th Convention, 1987 .... 18.00
Nearness, 1955–1959 .... 3.00
No Cause For Alarm, Decanter, 1979–1980 .... 3.00
Occur! Cologne, 3/4 x 2 1/4 In. ....*Illus* 2.00
Old Faithful, 1970 .... 1.60
On The Avenue, 1978–1979 .... 3.00
Opening Play, 1968–1969 .... 12.00 To 20.00
Oriental Egg, Delicate Blossoms, 1975–1976 .... 5.00
　　　AVON, OWL, see Avon, Dr. Hoot; Avon, Precious Owl
Pampered Persians, Decanter, 1974–1976 .... 3.00
Parlour Lamp, 1971 .... 10.00
Pass Play, 1973–1975 .... 4.00
Pearl Lumiere Roses Cologne, 1974 .... 3.00
Pepperbox Pistol 1850, 1982–1983 .... 5.00
Perfect Drive, 1975–1976 .... 5.00 To 8.75
Persian Pitcher, 1974 .... 3.00
Piano, Decanter, 1972 .... 3.00
Pine Bath Oil, Box, 1940 .... 35.00
　　　AVON, PIPE, see also Avon, Uncle Sam Pipe
Pipe, American Eagle, 1974 .... 3.00
Pipe, Bloodhound, 1976 .... 15.00 To 20.00
Pipe, Bulldog, 1972 .... 4.00 To 15.00
Pipe, Calabash, 1974 .... 5.00 To 15.00
Pipe, Collector's, 1973 .... 15.00
Pipe, Dutch, 1973 .... 5.00
Pipe, Uncle Sam, 1975 .... 15.00 To 20.00
Pipe, Wild Mustang, Decanter, 1976–1977 .... 20.00
　　　AVON, PISTOL, see also Avon, Pepperbox Pistol
Pistol, Blunderbuss, 1976 .... 10.00
Pistol, Colt Revolver, 1975 .... 10.00
Pistol, Derringer, 1977 .... 5.00 To 7.00
Pistol, Dueling, I, 1973 .... 11.00
Pistol, Dueling, II, 1974 .... 10.00
Pistol, Philadelphia Derringer, 1980 .... 9.00
Pistol, Thomas Jefferson Hand Gun, 1978 .... 9.00

Avon, Snail, Box, 1968–1969, 2 In.

Pistol, Volcanic Repeating, 1979	11.00
Pitcher, Car, Straight 8, 8 Matching Tumblers	45.00
Pitcher, Mt. Vernon Sauce, 1977	7.00
Pitcher, Water, Cape Cod, 1984	11.00 To 15.00
Pony Express, 1971	3.50
Pony Post, 1972	3.00 To 10.00
Pot Belly Stove, 1970–1971	10.00
Powder Sachet, 1972	4.00 To 10.00
Precious Owl Cream Sachet, 1972	4.00
President Lincoln Bust, Gold, 1979	85.00
President Lincoln, Gold, 1973	8.75
President Washington Bust, White, 1974–1976	4.00 To 80.00
AVON, PUMP, see Avon, Town Pump	
Pyramid of Fragrance, 1969	9.00
Quill Pen	7.00
Rain Or Shine, Greeting Candle, 1973	20.00
Rapture, Foaming Bath Oil, 1965	3.00
Ready For An Avon Day, Box	15.00
Recruiting Mrs. Albee, 1989–1990	100.00
Remember When Radio, Decanter, 1972	5.00
Renaissance Trio, 1966–1967	10.00
Revolutionary Cannon, 1975	2.50
Ring Around Rosie, 1966–1967	7.00
AVON, ROOSTER, see Avon, Country Kitchen	
Rose Fragrance Jar, White Flower Lid, 1946	45.00
Royal Apple, 1972	2.50
Royal Coach, White, 1972–1973	3.00
Royal Elephant, 1977–1979	3.00
Royal Orb, 1965–1966	10.00
Royal Swan, Aqua, 1971	3.00
Salt & Pepper, Buttercup, 1974	3.50
Salt & Pepper, Cape Cod, 1978	8.00 To 8.50
Salt & Pepper, Wooden Soldier	10.00
Saltshaker, Buttercup, 1974	2.00
Saltshaker, Cape Cod, 1978	4.00
Scentiments Cologne, 1978–1979	3.00
Scimitar, 1968–1969	8.00 To 20.00
Sea Horse Miniature, 1973	4.00
Sea Horse, 1970	3.00 To 4.00
Sea Spirit, Topaz, 1973–1976	3.00

Secretaire Lilac Bath Oil, 1972–1975 .... 4.50
Sentimental Doll, 1970 .... 2.00
Side Wheeler, 1971–1972 .... 15.00
Sign of Spring, 1974 .... 4.00
Six Shooter, 1962–1963 .... 22.00
Skin Freshener, 1936 .... 10.00
Snail, Box, 1968–1969, 2 In. ....*Illus* 16.00
Snail, Clear, Screw Cap, 1973 .... 39.00
Snowman, Petite, 1973 .... 5.00
Somewhere Bath Oil, 1962 .... 15.00
Song of Spring, Blue Bird, 1977 .... 7.00
Spanish Senorita, 1975–1976 .... 5.00
Spashu & Poolu, Box, 1970 .... 3.00
Spice O' Life Set, 1966 .... 11.00
Spicy Treasures Set, 1968 .... 8.00
Splash 'n' Spray, 1968 .... 16.00
Spring Creation Set, 1953 .... 18.00
Star Signs, 1975 .... 4.00
　　AVON, STEER HORNS, see Avon, Western Choice
Stein, Age of The Iron Horse, 1982 .... 45.00
Stein, American Armed Forces, 1990 .... 30.00 To 45.00
Stein, Blacksmith, 1985 .... 50.00
Stein, Car Classic, 1979 .... 20.00
Stein, Car Classic, 1979, Miniature .... 10.00 To 37.50
Stein, Collector's, 1976 .... 18.00 To 30.00
Stein, Ducks of American Wilderness, 1988 .... 22.00 To 50.00
Stein, Fire Fighter, 1989 .... 22.00 To 55.00
Stein, Fishing, 1990 .... 22.00 To 28.00
Stein, Flying Classics, 1981 .... 45.00
Stein, Gold Rush, 1987 .... 22.00 To 50.00
Stein, Great American Football, 1982 .... 18.00
Stein, Great American Football, 1983 .... 45.00
Stein, Hunter's, 1972 .... 5.00 To 9.50
Stein, Indians of The American Frontier, 1988 .... 25.00 To 50.00
Stein, Racing Car, 1989 .... 22.50 To 55.00
Stein, Shipbuilder, 1986 .... 50.00
Stein, Sporting, 1978 .... 20.00
Stein, Sporting, 1978, Miniature 30.00
Stein, Tall Ships, 1977 .... 20.00 To 40.00
Stein, Tall Ships, 1977, Miniature 30.00
Stein, Western Roundup, 1980 .... 20.00
Stein, Western Roundup, 1980, Miniature .... 10.00 To 45.00
Sterling Six, 1968–1970 .... 8.75
Stop 'n Go, 1974 .... 10.00
Sugar & Creamer, Currier & Ives, 1982 .... 8.00
Super Charge, 1976 .... 10.00
Super Shift, 1978 .... 10.00
Super Sleuth Magnifier, 1979 .... 6.00
Sure Catch, Milk Glass, 1977 .... 4.00
Swan Lake, 1972 .... 3.00
Sweet Tooth Terrier, 1979–1980 .... 2.00
　　AVON, SWORD, see Avon, Scimitar
　　AVON, TELEPHONE, see Avon, Avon Calling; Avon, French Telephone;
　　Avon, La Belle Telephone
Thomas Flyer, 1974–1975 .... 8.00
Tic Toc Tiger, 1967–1969 .... 4.00
Tiffany Lamp, 1973 .... 5.00
Tiffany Lamp, Blue, Brazil 20.00
To A Wild Rose Cream Sachet, Box 2.00
To A Wild Rose Perfume, 1950 .... 80.00
Toofie On Guard, 1968–1969 .... 3.00
Town Pump, Decanter, 1968 .... 2.00
Treasure Chest, Box, 1973 .... 30.00

Tribute, Silver Warrior, 1967 .... 9.00
Tub Talk, Blue & Yellow, 1969 .... 5.00
Ultra Mist Atomizer, 1980–1981 .... 5.00
Unicorn, 1974–1975 .... 4.00
Vase, Bud, Emerald, 1971 .... 2.00
Vase, Bud, Ruby Red, 1970 .... 5.00
Vase, Spring Bouquet, Green, 1981 .... 8.00
Vase, Spring Bouquet, Red, 1981 .... 5.00
Vase, Spring Dynasty, 1982–1983 .... 3.50
Viking Discoverer, 1977–1979 .... 15.00
Viking Horn, 1966 ....8.00 To 10.00
       AVON, WARRIOR, see also Avon, Tribute
Warrior, 1967, Silver ....8.00 To 12.00
Warrior, 1968, Frosted 5.00
Warrior, 1971, Clear 5.00
Washington Bottle, 1970–1972 .... 8.75
Western Boot, 1973–1978 .... 2.00
Western Choice Steer Horns, 1967 .... 10.00 To 12.00
Western Saddle, 1971 .... 3.50
Whale Organizer Set, 1973 .... 20.00
Whistle Tots, Brazil, 1966–1967 .... 5.00
Wild Mallard Ceramic Organizer, 1978 .... 12.50 To 20.00
Wild West, Bullet, 1977–1978 .... 8.00
Winnebago Motor Home, 1978–1979 .... 8.00

BALLANTINE

Ballantine's Scotch was sold in figural bottles in 1969. The five bottles were shaped like a golf bag, knight, mallard, zebra, or fisherman. Ballantine also made some flasks and jugs with special designs.

BALLANTINE, Charioteer, Flask, 1969 .... 5.00
   Discus Thrower, Flask, 1969 .... 10.00
   Fisherman, 1969 ....*Illus* 10.00
   Gladiator, Flask, 1969 .... 5.00
   Golf Bag, 1969 ....*Illus* 8.00
   Knight, 1969 .... 12.00
   Mallard, 1969 .... 15.00
   Zebra, 1969 ....18.00 To 20.00

Ballantine, Fisherman, 1969

Ballantine, Golf Bag, 1969

BARBER

The nineteenth–century barber either made his own hair tonic or purchased it in large containers. Barber bottles were used at the barbershop or in the home. The barber filled the bottles each day with hair oil, bay rum, tonic, shampoo, witch hazel, rosewater, or some other cosmetic. He knew what was inside each bottle because of its distinctive shape and color. Most of the important types of glass were used for barber bottles. Spatter glass, milk glass, cranberry, cobalt, cut, hobnail, vaseline, and opalescent glass were used alone or in attractive combinations. Some were made with enamel–painted decorations. Most of the bottles were blown. A pontil mark can be found on the bottom of many bottles. These special fancy bottles were popular during the last half of the nineteenth–century. In 1906 the Pure Food and Drug Act made it illegal to use refillable, nonlabeled bottles in a barbershop and the bottles were no longer used.

BARBER, 8 Fern–Like Patterns, 4–Piece Mold, Globular, 4 1/4 In.	55.00
Amethyst, Bulbous, Sheared Mouth, Pontil, Ribbed, 6 3/4 In.	99.00
Amethyst, Enameled Design, Ribbed, Pontil, Rolled Lip, 7 1/2 In.	132.00
Amethyst, Multicolored Enameled Design, Bulbous, Pontil, 7 5/8 In.	66.00
Amethyst, Multicolored Enameled Design, Bulbous, Ribbed, 7 7/8 In.	99.00
Amethyst, Red & White Enameled, Ribbed, Pontil, 6 1/2 In.	60.00
Amethyst, Red, White & Gold Enameled, Ribbed, 7 1/2 In.	55.00
Amethyst, Tooled Collar, 1870–1920, 4 1/2 In.	84.00
Amethyst, White Enameled, Mary Gregory Type, Ribbed, 1890, 8 In.	265.00
Amethyst, White, Yellow & Red Enameled, Ribbed, OP, 7 3/4 In.	121.00
Applied Floral, Sky Blue, OP, 1880, 8 In.	220.00
Applied Flower, Yellow Green, Ribbed, OP, 1880, 7 3/4 In.	110.00
Applied Flowers, Amethyst, Porcelain Stopper, OP, 1880, 7 3/4 In.	88.00
Applied Flowers, Light Blue, Frosted, 1880, 7 7/8 In.	143.00
Art Nouveau, Clear, Imperial Red Interior, OP, 1870–1920, 8 1/4 In.	341.00
Bay Rum, Amethyst, Enameled Gristmill, White, OP, 7 1/2 In.	413.00
Bay Rum, Clear, ABM, Cylinder, 8 3/4 In.	30.00
Bay Rum, Milk Glass, Hand Painted Floral, OP, 8 In.	231.00
Bay Rum, Opalescent, Hand Painted Birds & Bay Rum, OP	139.00
Bay Rum, Owl Drug Co., Clear, Tooled Top, 1900–1910, 6 1/2 In.	22.00
Blue & White Striped, 9 In. ....*Illus*	350.00
Bright Green, Multicolored Enameled Design, Bulbous, 8 1/4 In.	66.00
Bright Light Blue, Modified Bell, Pontil, 7 7/8 In.	110.00
Bulldog Picture, Ess–Tee–Dee, Clear, 1890, 8 In.	33.00
Clear, Village Horse Scene, Fluted Neck, Rolled Neck, 7 1/8 In.	121.00
Cobalt Blue, Turn Mold, 1890, 8 7/8 In.	33.00
Coin Spot, Citron, White, Yellow & Orange Enameled, OP, 8 In.	110.00
Coin Spot, Light Green, Polished Pontil, 1870–1920, 6 7/8 In.	68.00
Coin Spot, Robin's–Egg Blue, Segmented Body, Long Neck, 6 3/4 In.	66.00
Cranberry Glass, Broken Swirl, Ribbed, Pontil	89.00
Cranberry Glass, Inverted Coin Spot, Bulbous, Long Neck, 6 3/4 In.	83.00
Cranberry Glass, White Opalized Stripes, Segmented, Bulbous, 7 In.	77.00
Cranberry, 26 White Stripes To Left, 8 1/4 In.	220.00
Daisy & Fern, Lemon Yellow Opalized	120.00
Diamond, Cranberry, 9 Panels, Mold Blown, Fancy, 6 1/2 In.	77.00
Emerald Green, White, Yellow, Orange Enameled Design, OP, 7 7/8 In.	187.00
Enameled Daisy & Dot Design, Ribbed, Sapphire, OP, 7 1/4 In.	115.00
Enameled Daisy & Floral, Ribbed, 1890–1920, 3 3/4 In.	84.00
Enameled Daisy Design, Medium Blue, OP, 1870–1920, 7 In.	53.00
Enameled Daisy, Gold Flowers Design, Amethyst, Ribbed, OP, 7 In.	136.00
Enameled Design, Deep Yellow Green, Ribbed, OP, 7 5/8 In.	104.00
Enameled Design, Lavender, Ribbed, OP, 1880–1920, 7 In.	110.00
Enameled Design, Ribbed, Deep Amethyst, OP, 1870–1920, 8 In.	95.00
Enameled Floral, Amethyst, Ribbed, OP, 1880–1900, 7 1/2 In.	149.00
Enameled Flower, Bright Yellow Green, Ribbed, Squatty, 6 7/8 In.	44.00
Enameled Flower, Electric Blue, Ribbed, Bulbous, Pontil, 6 3/4 In.	110.00
Enameled Flower, Light Blue, Corset Waist, Pontil, 8 In.	66.00
Enameled Flower, Looped Arch Design, Emerald Green, OP, 6 1/2 In.	121.00
Enameled Flowers, 12 Ribs, Citron, Sheared Lip, Pontil, 7 1/4 In.	94.00
Green Speckles, Tapering Ribbed, Wrap Around, Bulbous Base, 12 In.	137.00

Barber, Blue & White Striped, 9 In.

Barber, Hobnail, Blue, 7 In.

Barber, Milk Glass, Stopper, 11 1/2 In.

Barber, Witch–Hazel, Label, 8 In.

Green, Wapler Barber Supply House, 7 1/2 In. 65.00
Hair Tonic, Clear, Stopper, Label, Rectangular, 5 1/2 In. 35.00
Hand Painted Floral, Jos. C. Kuhn, Ground Lip, 8 5/8 In. ....*Illus* 303.00
Hobnail, Blue, 7 In. ....*Illus* 57.00
Hobnail, Golden Yellow 63.00
Hobnail, Yellow Amber 45.00
Milk Glass, Blue, Enameled Flowers, Ground Stopper, 9 5/8 In. 154.00
Milk Glass, C. Everett Ackron, Lavender, Cottage, 8 3/4 In. 385.00

Milk Glass, Floral, Thomas Hilt Toilet Water, 8 1/2 In. 231.00
Milk Glass, Hand Painted Owl, L. Hood, Ground Lip, 10 1/8 In. 468.00
Milk Glass, Hand Painted, Multicolored Floral, Tapered, 8 1/2 In. 185.00
Milk Glass, J. H. Morton, Bay Rum, Painted Floral, 8 3/4 In. 413.00
Milk Glass, Opalescent, Enameled Cherub Scene, Conical, 7 1/2 In. 220.00
Milk Glass, Opalescent, Melon Sides, Coin Spot, 6 7/8 In. 73.00
Milk Glass, Painted Flowers, Hegener Barber Supplies, 8 3/4 In. 165.00
Milk Glass, Pretty Woman Picture, W. L. Doremus, Bay Rum, 10 1/2 In. 798.00
Milk Glass, Stopper, 11 1/2 In. ....*Illus* 30.00
Opalescent Hobnail, Blue, Pontil 39.00
Opalescent Swirled, Cranberry, Rolled Lip, 1890–1910, 7 1/4 In. 231.00
Opalized Clear, Fern, Segmented Body, Long Neck, 7 In. 66.00
Opalized Clear, White Hobnail Pattern, Polished Pontil, 7 In. 104.00
Opalized Cranberry & White, Stars & Stripes Pattern, 7 In. 303.00
Opalized Cranberry, Daisy & Fern Pattern, Melon Sides, 7 In., Pair 149.00
Opalized Cranberry, Daisy & Fern, Satin Finish, Segmented, 7 In. 88.00
Opalized Cranberry, White Hobnail Pattern, Polished Pontil, 7 In. 110.00
Opalized Robin's–Egg Blue, Herringbone, 7 3/8 In. 523.00
Opalized Turquoise, Swirl Ribbed, Polished Pontil, 7 In. 275.00
Opalized White, Spanish Lace, Polished Pontil, 7 In. 121.00
Opalized Yellow Green, Melon Sides, Rolled Lip, 7 1/4 In. 77.00
Over The Top Hair Tonic, U.S. Troops Charging, 1890–1920, 8 5/8 In. 385.00
Painted Cherubs & Border Design, Fiery Opalescent, Conical 300.00
Quilted Pattern, Cornflower Blue, Pontil, 1890–1910, 7 1/2 In. 303.00
S. L. Potteiger Tonic, Woman's Bust, Conical, Sprinkler, 8 1/2 In. 467.00
Sea Foam, Opalescent, Hand Painted Birds & Sea Foam, OP 139.00
Set, Clambroth, 12–Sided, 7 5/8–In. Shaving–Paper Vase, JHK, 4 Pc. 298.00
Set, Clambroth, Fluted, 7–In. Shaving–Paper Vase, MH Co., 5 Piece 275.00
Swirled Right White Stripes, Clear, 6 1/4 In. 90.00
Thumbprint, Art Nouveau Portrait Design, Yellow Green, 8 In. 315.00
Thumbprint, Dot & Daisy Enameled, Yellow Amber, 7 3/4 In. 100.00
Vegederma, Mary Gregory Type Design, Yellow Green, OP, 7 5/8 In. 633.00
Vegederma, Queen of Hair Tonics, Woman's Head Profile, 6 7/8 In. 418.00
White Applied Designs, Amethyst, Bulbous Neck, OP, 1880, 7 3/4 In. 110.00
White Enameled Design, Gilt, Emerald Green, Brown Horizontal Band 90.00
White Enameled Flowers, Amethyst, 1900 .... 88.00
White Stars & Stripes, Cranberry, Polished Pontil, 7 In. 357.00
White Stripes Swirled Right, Clear, 6 1/4 In. 90.00
Witch–Hazel, Label, 8 In. ....*Illus* 75.00
Yellow Green, Ribbed, Green, Orange, White & Pink Enameled, OP, 9 In. 330.00
Yellow Green, White, Orange & Yellow Enameled Design, OP, 8 In. 55.00
  BATTERY JAR, see Oil

--------------------------------- BEAM ---------------------------------

The history of the Jim Beam company is confusing because the progeny of the founder,
Jacob Beam, favored the names David and James. Jacob Beam had been a whiskey
distiller in Virginia and Maryland before moving to Kentucky in 1788. He was selling
Kentucky Straight Bourbon in bottles labeled *Beam* by 1795. His son David continued to
market Beam bourbon. His grandson, David M. Beam, was the next to inherit the
business. One of David M.'s brands was Old Tub, started in 1882 at Beam's Clear Springs
Distillery No. 230. The company was called David M. Beam. The next Beam family
member in the business was Col. James B. Beam, son of David M., who started working
at the distillery in 1880 at the age of 16. By 1914 he owned the Early Times Distillery
No. 7 in Louisville, Kentucky. J. B. Beam and B. H. Hurt were partners in the distillery
from 1892 to 1899. In 1915, when the colonel died, the distillery was acquired by S.L.
Guthrie and some partners. Then T. Jeremiah Beam, son of James B. Beam, inherited the
James Beam Company, and with his cousin, Carl Beam, continued to make the famous
bourbon. Booker Noe, Baker Beam, and David Beam, sixth–generation descendants of
Jacob Beam, continued in the business. Today, Jim Beam Brands is a wholly–owned
subsidiary of American Brands, Inc.

Beam, Armanetti, Award Winner, 1969

Beam, Benjamin Franklin,
Saturday Evening Post Cover, 1975

Beam bottles favored by today's collectors are made as containers for Kentucky Straight Bourbon. In 1953, the company began selling some Christmas season whiskey in special decanters shaped like cocktail shakers instead of the usual whiskey bottles. The decanters were so popular that by 1955 the company was making Regal China bottles in special shapes. Executive series bottles started in 1955 and political figures in 1956. Customer specialties were first made in 1956, decanters (called *trophy series* by collectors) in 1957, and the state series in 1958. Other bottles are classed by collectors as Regal China or Glass Specialty bottles. The rarest Beam bottle is the First National Bank of Chicago bottle; 117 were issued in 1964. The Salute to Spiro Agnew bottle made in 1970 was limited to 196. Six men making counterfeits of the very rare Beam bottles were arrested in 1970.

The company has also made many other advertising items or *go–withs* such as ashtrays and openers. The International Association of Jim Beam Bottle & Specialties Clubs (5013 Chase Ave., Downers Grove, IL 60515–4399) has regional and sectional meetings. They sell a book *Jim Beam Bottles: A Pictorial Guide* and a price list is also available.

Bottles are listed here alphabetically by name or as Convention, Executive, or Political. This is because beginning collectors find it difficult to locate bottles by type. Miniature bottles are listed here also. Go–withs are in the special section at the end of the book.

BEAM, A–C Spark Plug, 1977 .... 22.00 To 29.00
  ABC Florida, 1973 .... 10.00
  AHEPA, 1972 .... 6.00
  Aida, Opera, 1978 .... 125.00
  Alaska Purchase, 1966 .... 5.00
  Alaska, 1958, State .... 48.00 To 52.00
  Amaretto, Crystal, 1975 .... 2.00 To 3.00
  Amber, Crystal, 1973 .... 5.00
  Ambulance, Emergency, White, 1985 .... 30.00 To 45.00
  American Brands, 1989 .... 275.00
  American Cowboy, 1981 .... 15.00
  AMVETS, 25th Anniversary of American Wars, 11 3/4 In. .... 5.00 To 6.00
  Angelo's Delivery Truck, 1984 .... 190.00
  Antioch, 1967 .... 5.00 To 8.00
  Antique Trader, 1968 .... 5.00
  Appaloosa, 1974 .... 10.00 To 12.00
  Arizona, 1968, State 5.00
  Armadillo, 1981 .... 12.00 To 15.00
  Armanetti, Award Winner, 1969 ....*Illus* 7.00

Armanetti, Fun Shopper, 1971 .... 8.00 To 9.00
Armanetti, Vase, 1968 .... 5.00 To 6.00
Armenetti, Bacchus, 1970 .... 10.00
Army Jeep, Regal China, 1987 .... 25.00 To 35.00
Azur–Glo, Crystal, 1975 .... 2.00 To 4.00
Barney's Slot Machine, 1978 .... 20.00 To 25.00
Barry Berish, Presidential, 1984 .... 90.00
Barry Berish, Presidential, 1985 .... 90.00
Barry Berish, Presidential, 1986 .... 90.00
Bartender's Guild, Crystal, 1973 .... 9.00
Baseball, 1969 .... 23.00 To 25.00
Bass Boat, 1988 .... 18.00 To 35.00
Beam Pot, 1980 .... 12.00
Beatty Burro, Glass, 1970 .... 18.00
Beaver Valley Club, 1977 .... 10.00 To 13.00
Bell Ringer, A Fore Ye Go, 1970 .... 8.00 To 10.00
Bell Ringer, Plaid Apron, 1970 .... 7.00 To 8.00
Bell Scotch, 1969 .... 10.00 To 23.00
Bell Scotch, Miniature, 1969 .... 15.00 To 17.00
Benjamin Franklin, Saturday Evening Post Cover, 1975 ....*Illus* 5.00
Big Apple, 1979 .... 12.00
Bing Crosby, 29th National Pro–AM, 1970, 12 In. .... 5.00 To 6.00
Bing Crosby, 30th, 1971 .... 5.00 To 8.00
Bing Crosby, 31st, 1972 .... 20.00 To 22.00
Bing Crosby, 32nd, 1973 .... 20.00 To 25.00
Bing Crosby, 33rd, 1974 .... 25.00
Bing Crosby, 34th, 1975 .... 57.00
Bing Crosby, 35th, 1976 .... 22.00 To 25.00
Bing Crosby, 36th, 1977 .... 18.00 To 22.00
Bing Crosby, 37th, 1978 .... 18.00
Binnions' Horseshoe, 1970 .... 8.00 To 10.00
Black Katz, 1968 .... 14.00
Blue Crystal, 1971 .... 5.00
Blue Daisy, 1967 .... 5.00
Blue Fox, 1967 .... 92.00
Blue Goose, 1971 .... 5.00
Blue Goose, 1979 .... 12.00
Blue Hen, 1982 .... 18.00 To 20.00
Blue Jay, 1969, Trophy .... 8.00 To 10.00
Blue Slot Machine, 1967 .... 10.00
Bluegill, 1974, 9 3/4 In. .... 15.00 To 18.00
Bob Hope Desert Classic, 14th, 1973 .... 10.00
Bob Hope Desert Classic, 15th, 1974 .... 10.00 To 14.00
Bohemian Girl, 1974 ....*Illus* 15.00
Bonded Gold, 1975 .... 5.00
Bonded Mystic, 1979 .... 5.00 To 8.00
Bonded Silver, Regal, 1975 .... 5.00
Boothill, 1972 .... 8.00
Boris Godunov, Opera, 1982 .... 350.00
Bowling Proprietors, 1974 .... 6.00
Box Car, 1983 .... 45.00
Boy With Cherries, Collector's Editon, Vol. IV, 1969 .... 5.00
Boy's Town, 1973 .... 9.00 To 11.00
BPAA, Bowling Proprietors, 1974 .... 5.00
BPO Does, 1971 .... 5.00 To 6.00
Broadmoor Hotel, 1968 .... 5.00 To 7.00
Buccaneer, Multicolor, 1982 .... 52.00
Buccaneer, Solid Gold, 1982 .... 52.00
Buffalo Bill, 1971 .... 6.00
Bulldog, 1979 .... 25.00
Cable Car, 1968 .... 5.00 To 6.00
Cable Car, 1983 .... 37.00 To 39.00
Cal Neva, 1969 .... 7.00

California Derby, With Glasses, 1971	35.00
California Mission, 1970	15.00
Camellia City Club, 1979	20.00
Cameo, Blue, 1965	4.00 To 5.00
Cannon With Chain, 1970	2.00 To 3.00
Canteen, 1979	15.00
Captain & Mate, 1980	10.00
Cardinal, Female, 1973, Trophy	10.00
Cardinal, Male, 1968, Trophy	29.00 To 32.00
Carmen, Opera, 1978	20.00
Carolers, Holiday, 1988	50.00
Carolers, Presidential, 1988	80.00
Cat, Siamese, 1967	9.00 To 10.00
Catfish, 1981, Trophy	20.00
Cathedral Radio, 1979	10.00 To 15.00
Cedars of Lebanon, 1971	5.00 To 6.00
Charisma, Decanter, 1970, 12 1/2 In.	11.00
Charlie McCarthy, 1976	*Illus* 25.00
Chateau Classic Cherry, 1976	2.00
Chateaux, 1953	28.00
Cherry Hills Country Club, 1973	6.00
Chevrolet, Bel Air, 1957 Model, Black, 1988	75.00 To 90.00
Chevrolet, Bel Air, 1957 Model, Gold, 1988	135.00 To 150.00
Chevrolet, Bel Air, 1957 Model, Red, 1987	94.00
Chevrolet, Bel Air, 1957 Model, Red, 1988	80.00
Chevrolet, Camaro, Blue, 1969 Model	49.00 To 66.00
Chevrolet, Camaro, Green, 1969 Model	85.00 To 117.00
Chevrolet, Camaro, Pace Car, 1969 Model	69.00
Chevrolet, Camaro, Silver, 1969 Model	95.00
Chevrolet, Convertible, Black, 1957 Model	75.00 To 89.00
Chevrolet, Convertible, Cream, 1957 Model	110.00
Chevrolet, Convertible, Red, 1957 Model	79.00
Chevrolet, Corvette Stingray, 1963 Model, Black, 1987	120.00
Chevrolet, Corvette, Black, 1955 Model	125.00
Chevrolet, Corvette, Black, 1957 Model	75.00
Chevrolet, Corvette, Black, 1978 Model, 1984	69.00 To 140.00
Chevrolet, Corvette, Blue, 1954 Model	85.00
Chevrolet, Corvette, Blue, 1963 Model	150.00
Chevrolet, Corvette, Bronze, 1984 Model	95.00
Chevrolet, Corvette, Bronze, 1986 Model	89.00

Beam, Bohemian Girl, 1974   *Beam, Charlie McCarthy, 1976*   *Beam, International Chili Society, 1976*

Chevrolet, Corvette, Copper, 1955 Model 79.00
Chevrolet, Corvette, Copper, 1957 Model 125.00
Chevrolet, Corvette, Gold, 1984 Model 95.00
Chevrolet, Corvette, Pace Car, 1978 Model 175.00
Chevrolet, Corvette, Pace Car, Yellow, 1986 .... 79.00
Chevrolet, Corvette, Red, 1955 Model 125.00
Chevrolet, Corvette, Red, 1963 Model, 1988 .... 49.00 To 65.00
Chevrolet, Corvette, Red, 1978 Model, 1988 .... 55.00
Chevrolet, Corvette, Red, 1984 Model, 1988 .... 49.00
Chevrolet, Corvette, Red, 1986 Model 89.00
Chevrolet, Corvette, Silver, 1963 Model, 1988 .... 49.00 To 65.00
Chevrolet, Corvette, White, 1953 Model .... 110.00 To 125.00
Chevrolet, Corvette, White, 1957 Model 125.00
Chevrolet, Corvette, White, 1978 Model, 1985 .... 45.00 To 55.00
Chevrolet, Corvette, Yellow, 1963 .... 45.00
Chevrolet, Corvette, Yellow, 1978 Model, 1985 .... 45.00
Chevrolet, Dark Blue, 1957 .... 75.00
Chevrolet, Turquoise, 1957 .... 65.00
Chevrolet, Yellow Hot Rod, 1957 Model, 1988 .... 69.00 To 79.00
Cheyenne, 1967 .... 5.00
Chicago Art Museum, 1972 .... 12.00
Chicago Club Loving Cup, 1978 .... 15.00
Chicago Cub, 1985 .... 28.00 To 35.00
Chicago Fire, 1971 .... 15.00
Chocolomi, 1976 .... 2.00
Christmas Tree, 1986 .... 100.00
Christmas Tree, Paperweight, 1986 .... 35.00
Christmas, 1973 .... 15.00
Churchill Downs, Kentucky Derby, 95th, Pink Roses, 1969 .... 6.00
Churchill Downs, Kentucky Derby, 96th, Double Roses, 1970 .... 24.00
Churchill Downs, Kentucky Derby, 97th, Horse & Rider, 1971 .... 7.00
Churchill Downs, Kentucky Derby, 98th, Horse & Rider In Wreath, 1972 .... 6.00
Churchill Downs, Kentucky Derby, 100th, 1974 .... 10.00
Circus Wagon, 1979 .... 25.00
Civil War, North, 1961 .... 10.00 To 25.00
Civil War, South, 1961 .... 25.00 To 42.00
Cleopatra, Rust, 1962 .... 5.00
Cleopatra, Yellow, 1962 .... 15.00
Clint Eastwood, 1973 .... 12.00 To 14.00
Clock, Antique, 1985 .... 35.00 To 39.00
Coach Devaney, Nebraska, 1972 .... 10.00
Cocktail Shaker, 1953 .... 4.00 To 6.00
Coffee Grinder, Antique, 1979 .... 10.00 To 12.00
Coffee Warmer, Pyrex, Gold Metal Band, 1956 .... 5.00
Coffee Warmer, Pyrex, Gold, 1954 .... 10.00
Coho Salmon, 1976 .... 15.00
Colin Meads, 1984 .... 185.00
Collectors Edition, Vol. 1, Aristide Braunt, 1966 .... 2.00
Collectors Edition, Vol. 1, Laughing Cavalier, 1966 .... 2.00
Collectors Edition, Vol. 1, Mardi Gras, 1966 .... 2.00 To 3.00
Collectors Edition, Vol. 1, On The Terrace, 1966 .... 7.00
Collectors Edition, Vol. 2, George Gisze, 1967 .... 2.00
Collectors Edition, Vol. 2, Night Watch, 1967 .... 2.00
Collectors Edition, Vol. 2, The Jester, 1967 .... 3.00
Collectors Edition, Vol. 3, American Gothic, 1968 .... 2.00 To 4.00
Collectors Edition, Vol. 3, Buffalo Hunt, 1968 .... 4.00
Collectors Edition, Vol. 3, Hauling In The Gill Net, 1968 .... 5.00
Collectors Edition, Vol. 3, Indian Maiden, 1968 .... 2.00 To 5.00
Collectors Edition, Vol. 3, The Scout, 1968 .... 4.00
Collectors Edition, Vol. 3, Whistler's Mother, 1968 .... 2.00
Collectors Edition, Vol. 4, Balcony, 1969 .... 2.00
Collectors Edition, Vol. 4, Emile Zola, 1969 .... 5.00
Collectors Edition, Vol. 4, Judge, 1969 .... 5.00

Collectors Edition, Vol. 4, Sunflowers, 1969 .... 2.00 To 5.00
Collectors Edition, Vol. 5, Au Cafe, 1970 .... 2.00
Collectors Edition, Vol. 5, Galah Bird, 1979 .... 14.00
Collectors Edition, Vol. 5, Old Peasant, 1970 .... 2.00
Collectors Edition, Vol. 5, Titus At Writing Desk, 1970 .... 5.00
Collectors Edition, Vol. 6, Charles I, 1971 .... 2.00 To 4.00
Collectors Edition, Vol. 7, Maidservant, 1972 .... 4.00
Collectors Edition, Vol. 7, Prince Baltasor, 1972 .... 2.00
Collectors Edition, Vol. 8, Frederic F. Chopin, 1973 .... 2.00
Collectors Edition, Vol. 9, Cardinal, 1974 .... 2.00 To 4.00
Collectors Edition, Vol. 10, Fruit Basket, 1969 .... 5.00
Collectors Edition, Vol. 10, Largemouth Bass, 1975 .... 3.00
Collectors Edition, Vol. 10, Sailfish, 1975 .... 3.00
Collectors Edition, Vol. 11, Bighorn Sheep, 1976 .... 3.00 To 5.00
Collectors Edition, Vol. 11, Chipmunk, 1976 .... 5.00
Collectors Edition, Vol. 12, Labrador Retriever, 1977 .... 3.00
Collectors Edition, Vol. 12, Pointer, 1977 .... 5.00
Collectors Edition, Vol. 12, Springer Spaniel, 1977 .... 3.00
Collectors Edition, Vol. 14, Cottontail Rabbit, 1978 .... 3.00
Collectors Edition, Vol. 14, Mule Deer, 1978 .... 3.00
Collectors Edition, Vol. 15, Cowboy, 1979 .... 3.00
Collectors Edition, Vol. 15, Indian Trapper 1908, 1979 .... 2.00
Collectors Edition, Vol. 15, Lt. S. C. Robertson 1890, 1979 .... 2.00 To 5.00
Collectors Edition, Vol. 16, Mallard, 1980 .... 3.00
Collectors Edition, Vol. 17, Great Elk, 1981 .... 3.00
Collectors Edition, Vol. 17, Pintail Duck, 1981 .... 3.00
Collectors Edition, Vol. 18, Cardinal, 1982 .... 4.00
Collectors Edition, Vol. 18, Whitetail Deer, 1982 .... 4.00
Collectors Edition, Vol. 19, Scarlet Tanager, 1983 .... 4.00
Colorado Centennial, 1976 .... 15.00
Colorado Springs, 1972 .... 5.00 To 10.00
Colorado, State, 1959 .... 25.00 To 27.00
Convention, No. 1, Denver, 1971 .... 5.00 To 10.00
Convention, No. 2, Anaheim, June 19–25, 1972 .... 25.00 To 37.00
Convention, No. 3, Detroit, 1973 .... 10.00 To 19.00
Convention, No. 4, Lancaster, 1974 .... 7.00
Convention, No. 5, Sacramento, 1975 .... 5.00 To 11.00
Convention, No. 6, Hartford, 1976 .... 5.00
Convention, No. 7, Louisville, 1977 .... 5.00
Convention, No. 8 Chicago, 1978 .... 10.00
Convention, No. 9, Houston, 1979, Cowboy .... 25.00 To 59.00
Convention, No. 9, Houston, 1979, Tiffany On Rocket 49.00
Convention, No. 10, Norfolk, 1980 .... 20.00 To 25.00
Convention, No. 11, Las Vegas, 1981 .... 20.00
Convention, No. 12, New Orleans, 1982 .... 29.00
Convention, No. 13, St. Louis, 1983, Budweiser 151.00
Convention, No. 14, Hollywood, Florida, 1984 .... 20.00
Convention, No. 15, Las Vegas, 1985 .... 40.00
Convention, No. 16, Boston, Mass., 1986 .... 55.00
Convention, No. 17, Louisville, 1988 .... 65.00
Convention, No. 18, Portland, 1989 .... 29.00
Convention, No. 19, Kansas City, 1990 .... 45.00
Cowboy 1902, 1979 .... 12.00
Cowboy, American, 1981 .... 12.00
Cowboy, Houston, Convention Gift, Color, 1979 .... 250.00
Cowboy, Houston, Convention Gift, Tan, 1979 .... 250.00
CPO, 1974 .... 12.00
Crappie, 1979, Trophy 15.00
Crispus Attucks, Glass, 1976 .... 4.00 To 5.00
CRLDA, 1973 .... 6.00 To 7.00
Dancing Scot, Short, 1963 .... 75.00
Dancing Scot, Tall, 1964 .... 25.00
Dancing Scot, Tall, Couple, 1964 .... 195.00

Dark Eyes Vodka Jugs, 1978 .... 6.00
Delaware, 1972, State 6.00
Delco Battery, 1978 .... 25.00
Delft Blue, 1963 .... 5.00
Delft Rose, 1963 .... 6.00
Denver Rush To Rockies, 1970 .... 10.00
Dining Car, 1982 .... 80.00
Distillery, Red Fox, 1973 ....800.00 To 1200.00
District Executive Urn, 1986 .... 36.00
Dodge City, 1972 .... 6.00
Doe, 1963 .... 23.00 To 25.00
Don Giovanni, Opera, 1980 .... 165.00
Duck Decoy, 1988, 375 Ml. .... 25.00 To 30.00
Duck, 1957, Trophy 25.00
Ducks Unlimited, No. 1, Mallard, 1974 .... 35.00 To 50.00
Ducks Unlimited, No. 2, Wood Duck, 1975 .... 47.00 To 48.00
Ducks Unlimited, No. 3, 40th Anniversary, 1977 .... 45.00 To 50.00
Ducks Unlimited, No. 4, Mallard, 1978 .... 39.00
Ducks Unlimited, No. 5, Canvasback Drake, 1979 .... 35.00 To 40.00
Ducks Unlimited, No. 6, Blue–Winged Teal, 1980 ....*Illus* 50.00
Ducks Unlimited, No. 7, Green–Winged Teal, 1981 .... 40.00 To 45.00
Ducks Unlimited, No. 8, Woody & His Brood, 1982 .... 40.00 To 45.00
Ducks Unlimited, No. 9, American Widgeons, 1983 .... 40.00 To 45.00
Ducks Unlimited, No. 10, Mallard, 1984 .... 60.00 To 65.00
Ducks Unlimited, No. 11, Pintail, Pair, 1985 .... 35.00
Ducks Unlimited, No. 12, Redhead, 1986 .... 19.00
Ducks Unlimited, No. 13, Bluebill, 1987 .... 25.00 To 50.00
Ducks Unlimited, No. 14, Gadwall Family, 1988 .... 20.00 To 39.00
Ducks Unlimited, No. 15, Black Duck, 1989 .... 32.00 To 50.00
Ducks Unlimited, No. 16, Canada Goose, 1989 .... 75.00
Ducks Unlimited, No. 17, Tundra Swan, 1991 .... 54.00
Duesenberg, 1934 Model J, Dark Blue, 1981 .... 150.00
Duesenberg, 1934 Model J, Light Blue, 1981 .... 100.00
Duesenberg, 1935 Convertible, Coupe, Gray, 1983 .... 245.00
Eagle, 1966, Trophy 12.00
Elks Club, 1968 .... 5.00 To 6.00
Elks National Foundation, 1978 .... 12.00 To 13.00
Emmett Kelly, 1973 .... 24.00 To 53.00
Ernie's Flower Cart, 1976 .... 25.00
Evergreen State Club, 1974 .... 12.00
Executive, 1955, Royal Porcelain 390.00
Executive, 1956, Royal Gold Round 80.00
Executive, 1957, Royal Di Monte 45.00
Executive, 1958, Gray Cherub 250.00
Executive, 1959, Tavern Scene 49.00
Executive, 1960, Blue Cherub 80.00
Executive, 1961, Golden Chalice 40.00
Executive, 1962, Flower Basket .... 25.00 To 36.00
Executive, 1963, Royal Rose 30.00
Executive, 1964, Royal Gold Diamond 30.00
Executive, 1965, Marbled Fantasy 40.00
Executive, 1966, Majestic 22.00
Executive, 1967, Prestige .... 7.00 To 10.00
Executive, 1968, Presidential 7.00
Executive, 1969, Sovereign .... 5.00 To 10.00
Executive, 1970, Charisma 10.00
Executive, 1971, Fantasia 10.00
Executive, 1972, Regency 12.00
Executive, 1973, Phoenician 10.00
Executive, 1974, Twin Cherubs 12.00
Executive, 1975, Reflections In Gold ....*Illus* 12.00
Executive, 1976, Floro De Oro 12.00
Executive, 1977, Golden Jubilee 12.00

Executive, 1978, Yellow Rose of Texas .... 12.00 To 16.00
Executive, 1979, Mother of Pearl Vase .... 14.00 To 16.00
Executive, 1980, Titian ....*Illus*   14.00
Executive, 1981, Royal Filigree, Cobalt Deluxe 25.00
Executive, 1982, Americana Pitcher 26.00
Executive, 1983, Musical Bell 35.00
Executive, 1984, Musical Bell, Noel .... 20.00 To 25.00
Executive, 1985, Italian Marble Vase .... 20.00 To 32.00
Executive, 1986, Bowl, Italian Marble .... 25.00 To 32.00
Executive, 1987, Indigo & Pearl Gray Swirls 30.00
Executive, 1988, 2 Young Doves 19.00
Expo 74, 1974 .... 9.00
Falstaff, Opera, 1979 .... 150.00
Father's Day, 1988 .... 19.00
Fiesta Bowl, 1973 .... 10.00
Figaro, Opera, 1977 .... 174.00
Fighting Bull, 1981, Trophy 15.00
Fiji Islands, 1971 .... 5.00
Fire Chief's Car, 1981 .... 125.00
Fire Engine 1867, Steam Powered, 1978 .... 125.00 To 300.00
Fire Pumper Truck, 1867 Model, Mississippi, 1978 .... 125.00
Fire Pumper Truck, 1917 Model, 1982 .... 90.00 To 125.00
Fire Pumper Truck, 1930s, 1988 .... 45.00 To 54.00
First National Bank of Chicago, 1964 .... 2400.00
Five Seasons Club, 1980 .... 7.00 To 10.00
Fleet Reserve, 1974 .... 7.00
Florida Shell, 1968 .... 5.00
Football Hall of Fame, 1972 .... 14.00
Football, 1989 .... 57.00
Ford, Fire Chief, 1928 Model, 1988 .... 110.00
Ford, Fire Chief, 1934 Model, 1988 .... 49.00
Ford, Fire Pumper Truck, 1935 Model, 1988 .... 49.00
Ford, International Delivery Wagon, Black, 1984 .... 85.00 To 95.00
Ford, International Delivery Wagon, Green, 1984 .... 95.00
Ford, Model A, 1903 Model, Black 40.00
Ford, Model A, 1903 Model, Red, 1978 .... 35.00
Ford, Model A, 1928 Model, 1980 .... 70.00
Ford, Model A, 1938 Model, Parkwood Supply, 1984 .... 150.00
Ford, Model A, Angeles Liquor 195.00
Ford, Model A, Fire Truck, 1930 Model, 1983 ....*Illus*   175.00

Beam, Executive, 1975, Reflections In Gold   *Beam, Executive, 1980, Titian*

Ford, Model T, 1913 Model, Black, 1974 .... 35.00 To 45.00
Ford, Mustang, 1964 Model, Black 110.00
Ford, Mustang, 1964 Model, Red 49.00
Ford, Mustang, 1964 Model, White 39.00
Ford, Paddy Wagon, 1930 Model, 1984 ....57.00 To 125.00
Ford, Phaeton, 1929 Model, 1982 .... 49.00 To 52.00
Ford, Pickup Truck, 1930s, 1988 .... 59.00
Ford, Pickup Truck, Angelo's, 1990 .... 80.00
Ford, Police Car, 1929 Model, Blue, 1982 .... 79.00
Ford, Police Car, 1929 Model, Yellow, 1983 .... 395.00
Ford, Police Car, 1934 Model, Black & White 65.00
Ford, Police Car, 1934 Model, Yellow 95.00
Ford, Police Tow Truck, 1935 Model, 1988 .... 24.00
Ford, Roadster, 1934 Model, Cream, 1990 .... 65.00 To 80.00
Ford, Salesmen's Award, Black, 1980 .... 838.00
Ford, Salesmen's Award, Yellow, 1980 .... 389.00
Ford, Thunderbird, 1956 Model, Black, 1986 ....75.00 To 225.00
Ford, Thunderbird, 1956 Model, Blue, 1986 .... 85.00
Ford, Thunderbird, 1956 Model, Gray, 1986 .... 65.00
Ford, Thunderbird, 1956 Model, Green, 1986 .... 65.00
Ford, Thunderbird, 1956 Model, Yellow, 1986 .... 55.00
Ford, V8, Tow Truck, 1988 .... 35.00
Ford, Woody Wagon, 1929 Model, 1984 ....*Illus*	55.00
Foremost, Black & Gold, 1956 ....240.00 To 250.00
Foremost, Gray & Gold, 1956 .... 250.00
Foremost, Speckled Beauty, 1956 .... 350.00
Fox, Blue, 1967 .... 80.00
Fox, Distillery Red, 1973 .... 1400.00
Fox, Gold, 1969 .... 45.00
Fox, Green, 1965 .... 20.00
Fox, On Dolphin, 1980 .... 15.00
Fox, Rennie The Runner, 1974 .... 14.00
Fox, Rennie The Surfer, 1975 .... 16.00
Fox, Uncle Sam, 1971 .... 10.00
Fox, White, 1969 .... 45.00

Beam, Ford, Model A, Fire Truck, 1930 Model, 1983

Beam, Ford, Woody Wagon, 1929 Model, 1984

Beam, Train, Tank Car, 1983

Franklin Mint, 1970 .... 6.00
Gare St. Lazare, 1970 .... 5.00
Gem City Club, 1983 .... 44.00
George Washington, 1976 .... 14.00
Germany, Hansel & Gretel, 1971 .... 6.00
Germany, Pied Piper, 1974 .... 6.00
Germany, Wiesbaden, 1973 .... 7.00
Gibson Girl, 1983 .... 90.00
Gladiolas Festival, 1974 .... 7.00
Glen Campbell, 1976 .... 11.00
Globe, Antique, 1980 ....6.00 To 10.00
Golden Gate Casino, 1969 .... 79.00
Golden Nugget Casino, 1969 .... 50.00
Golf Cart, Regal China, 1986 ....25.00 To 30.00
Goose, Blue, 1979 .... 14.00
Grand Canyon, 1969 .... 5.00
Gray Poodle, 1970, Trophy 12.00
Great Dane, 1976, Trophy 12.00
Great Expectations, Dickens, Holiday, 1988, 750 Ml. 54.00
Green China Jug, Pussy Willow, 1965 .... 6.00
Guitarist 5.00
Hannah Dustin, 1973 .... 15.00
Harley–Davidson, 1988 .... 175.00
Harolds Club Or Bust 10.00
Harolds Club, Covered Wagon, 1969 ....7.00 To 15.00
Harolds Club, Man In Barrel, No. 1, 1957 .... 395.00
Harolds Club, Man In Barrel, No. 2, 1958 .... 150.00
Harolds Club, Nevada, Gray, 1963 .... 100.00
Harolds Club, Nevada, Silver, 1964 .... 100.00
Harolds Club, Pinwheel, 1965 .... 40.00
Harolds Club, Reno 15.00
Harolds Club, Silver Opal, 1957 .... 20.00
Harolds Club, Slot Machine, Blue, 1967 .... 12.00
Harolds Club, Slot Machine, Gray, 1968 .... 5.00
Harolds Club, VIP, 1967 .... 55.00
Harolds Club, VIP, 1968 .... 60.00
Harolds Club, VIP, 1969 .... 275.00
Harolds Club, VIP, 1970 .... 50.00
Harolds Club, VIP, 1971 .... 50.00
Harolds Club, VIP, 1972 .... 22.00
Harolds Club, VIP, 1973 .... 20.00
Harolds Club, VIP, 1974 .... 15.00
Harolds Club, VIP, 1975 .... 15.00
Harolds Club, VIP, 1976 .... 20.00
Harolds Club, VIP, 1977 .... 25.00
Harolds Club, VIP, 1978 .... 25.00
Harolds Club, VIP, 1979 .... 30.00
Harolds Club, VIP, 1980 .... 30.00
Harolds Club, VIP, 1981 .... 95.00
Harolds Club, VIP, 1982 .... 95.00
Harp Seal, Sierra Club, 1987 .... 24.00
Harrah's Club, Nevada, Gray, 1963 .... 680.00
Harrah's Club, Nevada, Silver, 1963 .... 495.00
Hatfield, 1973 .... 20.00
Hawaii Aloha, 1971, 11 In. 6.00
Hawaii Paradise, 1978 .... 15.00
Hawaii, 1959, State 32.00
Hawaii, 1967, State 35.00
Hawaiian Open, 7th, Pineapple, 1972 .... 7.00
Hawaiian Open, 8th, Golfball, 1973 .... 8.00
Hawaiian Open, 9th, Tiki God, 1974 .... 7.00
Hawaiian Open, 10th, Menehune, 1975 .... 14.00
Hawaiian Open, 11th, Outrigger, 1975 ....*Illus* 13.00

Hawaiian Open, 11th, US Emblem, 1975 .... 8.00
Helmet & Boots, Short Timer, 1984 .... 18.00 To 29.00
Hemisfair, San Antonio, 1968 .... 10.00
Hoffman, 1969 .... 6.00
Home Builders, 1978 .... 24.00
Hone Heke, 1981 .... 195.00
Hongi Hika, 1980 .... 195.00
Horse, Black, Trophy, 1962 .... 17.00 To 24.00
Horse, Brown, 1962 .... 17.00
Horseshoe Club, Reno, 1969 .... 8.00
Hyatt House, Chicago, 1971 .... 10.00
Hyatt Regency, New Orleans, 1976 .... 12.00
Idaho, 1963, State 50.00
Illinois, 1968, State 6.00
Indian Chief, 1979 .... 12.00
Indianapolis Sesquicentennial, 1971 .... 8.00
Indianapolis Speed Race, 1970 .... 6.00
International Chili Society, 1976 ....*Illus* 10.00
International Petroleum, 1971 .... 5.00
Jackelope, 1971 .... 10.00
Jaguar, 1981, Trophy 20.00
Jewel Tea Wagon, 1974 .... 75.00
Jim Beam Jug, Black, 1982 .... 35.00
Jim Beam Jug, Dark Blue, 1982 .... 35.00
Jim Beam Jug, Dark Green, 1982 .... 35.00
Jim Beam Jug, Light Blue, 1982 .... 35.00
John Henry, 1972 .... 18.00
Kaiser International, 1971 .... 5.00
Kangaroo, 1977 .... 16.00
Kansas, 1960, State 50.00
Kentucky Colonels, 1970, 12 In. 5.00
Kentucky, Black Horsehead Stopper, 1967 .... 12.00
Kentucky, White Horsehead Stopper, 1967 .... 30.00
Key West, Florida, 1972 .... 6.00
King Kamehameha, 1972 .... 9.00
King Kong, 1976 .... 8.00
Kiwi Bird, 1974, Trophy 10.00
Koala Bear, 1973 .... 16.00
Labrador Retriever, 1987 .... 20.00
Laramie Centennial Jubilee 1868–1968, 1968 .... 6.00
Largemouth Bass, 1973, Trophy 15.00
Las Vegas, 1969 .... 6.00
Legion Music, Joliet Legion Band, 1978 .... 15.00

Beam, Hawaiian Open, 11th, Outrigger, 1975   *Beam, Richard's, New Mexico, 1967*

Light Bulb, 1979	14.00
Lombard, Lilac, 1969	5.00
London Bridge With Medallion, 1969	185.00
London Bridge, 1971	8.00
Louisville Downs, 1st Pro–AM, 1977	12.00
Madame Butterfly, Opera, 1977	225.00
Magpies, 1977	18.00
Maine, 1970, State	6.00
Mare & Foal, 1982	12.00
Marina City, 1962	20.00
Marine Corps, 1975	30.00
Martha Washington, 1975	10.00
McCoy, 1973	15.00
Mephistopheles, Opera, 1979	165.00
Mercedes Benz 450SL, Red, 1987	45.00
Mercedes Benz, Blue, 1974	35.00
Mercedes Benz, Gold, 1974	75.00
Mercedes Benz, Green, 1974	45.00
Mercedes Benz, Mocha, 1974	39.00
Mercedes Benz, Red, 1974	39.00
Mercedes Benz, Sand Beige, Pa., 1974	35.00
Mercedes Benz, Silver–Australia, 1974	150.00
Mercedes Benz, White, 1974	45.00
Mermaid, 1984	65.00
Michigan, 1972, State	6.00
Milwaukee Stein, 1972	45.00
Mint 400, 3rd, China Stopper, 1970	90.00
Mint 400, 4th, Metal Stopper, 1971	8.00
Mint 400, 5th, 1972	8.00
Mint 400, 6th, 1973	9.00
Mint 400, 7th, 1975	9.00
Mint 400, 8th, 1976	10.00
Montana, 1963, State	65.00
Monterey Bay Club, 1977	10.00
Mortimer Snerd, 1976	25.00
Mr. Goodwrench, 1978	29.00
Mt. St. Helens, 1980	25.00
Multi–Glo, 1975	6.00
Musicians On Wine Cask, 1964	5.00
Muskie, 1971, Trophy	15.00
National Licensed Beverage Assoc., 1975	5.00
Nevada, 1963, State	35.00
New Hampshire Eagle, 1971	20.00
New Hampshire, 1967, State	6.00
New Jersey, Blue Gray, 1963, State	52.00
New Jersey, Yellow, 1963, State	52.00
New Mexico Bicentennial, 1976	10.00
New Mexico, 1972, State	5.00
New York Big Apple, 1979	10.00 To 12.00
New York World's Fair, 1964	9.00
Noel, Executive Bell, 29th, 1983	30.00
Noel, Executive Bell, 30th, 1984	25.00
North Dakota, 1964, State	60.00
Northern Pike, 1978, Trophy	15.00
Nutcracker, 1978	18.00
Nutcracker, Holiday, 1989	125.00
Nutcracker, Holiday, 1990	49.00
Nutcracker, Presidential, 1989	75.00
Oatmeal Jug, 1966	45.00
Oh Kentucky, 1981	75.00
Ohio State Fair, 1973	6.00
Ohio, 1966, State	5.00
Oldsmobile, 1904 Model, 1972	45.00

Beam, Ducks Unlimited, No. 6,   Beam, Panda Bears, 1980,   Beam, Political, Elephant,
    Blue–Winged Teal, 1980   Trophy   1976, Drum

Olsorita Eagle Race Car, No. 48, 1975	59.00
Oregon Liquor Control, 1984	32.00
Oregon, 1959, State	22.00
Osco Drug, 1987	40.00
Owl, L. V. N. H., 1982	45.00
Paddy Wagon, 1984	120.00
Panda Bears, 1980, Trophy .....*Illus*	20.00
Passenger Car, 1981	50.00
Paul Bunyan, 1970	9.00
Pearl Harbor Survivors, 1976	10.00
Pearl Harbor, 1972	18.00
Pennsylvania Dutch Club, 1974	12.00
Pennsylvania, 1967, State	6.00
Perch Pretty, 1980, Trophy	15.00
Permian Basin Oil Show, 1972	5.00
PGA, 1971, 10 1/2 In.	6.00
Pheasant, 1960, Trophy	12.00
Phi Sigma Kappa, 1973	5.00
Police Patrol Car, 1930s, Black & White, 1989	72.00
Police Patrol Car, 1930s, Yellow, 1989	125.00
Political, Democratic, Convention, 1988 .....10.00 To 35.00	
Political, Donkey & Elephant, 1960, Campaigners, Pair	30.00
Political, Donkey & Elephant, 1964, Boxers, Pair	16.00
Political, Donkey & Elephant, 1968, Clowns, Pair	10.00
Political, Donkey & Elephant, 1976, Drums, Pair	16.00
Political, Donkey & Elephant, 1980, Superman, Pair	24.00
Political, Donkey & Elephant, 1984, Computers, Pair	30.00
Political, Donkey, 1968, Clown .....5.00 To 22.00	
Political, Donkey, 1972, Football	7.00
Political, Donkey, 1980, Superman	12.00
Political, Donkey, 1984, Computer	15.00
Political, Elephant, 1964, Boxer	22.00
Political, Elephant, 1970, Spiro Agnew	1200.00
Political, Elephant, 1972, Miami Beach	550.00
Political, Elephant, 1972, San Diego	20.00
Political, Elephant, 1972, Washington, D. C., Feb. 10 Dinner	550.00
Political, Elephant, 1976, Drum .....*Illus*	8.00
Political, Elephant, 1980, Superman	10.00
Political, Republican, Convention, 1988	35.00
Ponderosa, 1969	6.00

Ponderosa, One Millionth Visitor, 1972	10.00
Pony Express, 1968	8.00
Portland Bottle & Rose, Convention, Red, 1988	35.00
Portland Bottle & Rose, Convention, Yellow, 1988	35.00
Portland Rose Festival, 1972	8.00
Poulan Chain Saw, 1979	28.00
Preakness, Pimlico, 1975	6.00
Prima Donna, 1969	8.00
Proprietor's Own, Crystal, 1968	10.00
Queensland, 1978	22.00
Rabbit, Texas, 1971	8.00
Rainbow Trout, 1975, Trophy	15.00
Ralph's Market, 1973	14.00
Ramada Inn, 1976	8.00
Red Mile, 1975	12.00
Redwood Empire, 1967, 12 3/4 In.	6.00
Reidsville, 1973	5.00
Reno, 1964	5.00
Republic of Texas Club, 1980	16.00
Richard's, New Mexico, 1967	*Illus* 7.00
Robin, 1969, Trophy	8.00
Rocky Marciano, 1973	20.00
Rubber Capitol Club, 1973	15.00
Ruby, Crystal, 1967	9.00
Ruidoso Downs, 1968	6.00
Sahara Invitational, 1971	7.00
Sailfish, 1957	25.00
Samoa, 1973	7.00
San Diego, 1968	5.00
San Francisco Cable Car, 1983	35.00
Santa Claus, 1983	150.00
Santa Fe, 1960	125.00
Screech Owl, 1979	22.00
Seafair, 1972	29.00
Seattle World's Fair, 1962	18.00
Seoul, Korea, 1988	60.00
Setter, 1958	30.00
Sheraton Hotel, 1975	8.00
Showgirl, Blond, Las Vegas Convention Gift, 1981	50.00
Showgirl, Brunette, Las Vegas Convention Gift, 1981	50.00
Shriner, El Kahir Pyramid, 1975	18.00
Shriner, Indiana, 1970	6.00
Shriner, Moila, Camel, 1975	12.00
Shriner, Moila, Sword, 1972	25.00
Shriner, Rajah, 1977	25.00
Shriner, Western Association, 1980	20.00
Siamese Cat, 1967, Trophy	12.00
Sigma Nu Kentucky, 1977	10.00
Smith's North Shore Club, 1972	18.00
Smoke Glo, 1975	4.00
Smoked Geni, 1964	9.00
Snow Goose, 1979	15.00 To 40.00
South Carolina, 1970, State	6.00
South Dakota, Mt. Rushmore, 1969	6.00
Space Shuttle, 1987	30.00
Spenger's Fish Grotto, 1977	20.00
Sports Car Club of America, 1976	15.00
St. Bernard, 1979, Trophy	30.00
St. Louis Arch, 1964	15.00
St. Louis Club, 1972	10.00
Stanley Steamer, 1909	75.00
Statue of Liberty, 1975	10.00
Stone Mountain, 1974	8.00

Beam, Telephone, 1919 Dial, 1980

Beam, Zimmerman Liquors, Eldorado,
Gray Blue, 1978

Sturgeon, 1980, Trophy 15.00
Stutz Bearcat, 1914, Gray, 1977 .... 49.00 To 55.00
Stutz Bearcat, 1914, Yellow, 1977 .... 55.00
Submarine Redfin, 1970 .... 6.00
Superdome, 1975 .... 5.00
Swagman, 1979 .... 15.00
Sydney Opera House, 1977 .... 18.00
Te Rauparaha, 1982 .... 200.00
Telephone, 100 Digit, 1983 .... 50.00
Telephone, 1897 Model, 1978 .... 47.00
Telephone, 1919 Dial, 1980 ....*Illus* 47.00
Telephone, Battery, 1982 .... 25.00
Telephone, French Cradle, 1979 .... 20.00 To 25.00
Telephone, Wall Set, 1975 .... 20.00 To 55.00
Texas Rabbit, 1971 .... 5.00
Thailand, 1969 .... 5.00
Thomas Flyer, Blue, 1976 .... 65.00
Thomas Flyer, White, 1976 .... 75.00
Tiffany Poodle, 1973 .... 20.00
Tigers, 1977 .... 15.00
Tobacco Festival, 1973 .... 11.00 To 15.00
Tombstone, 1970 .... 6.00
Train, Baggaage Car 39.00
Train, Box Car, Brown 35.00
Train, Box Car, Yellow 55.00
Train, Bumper 6.00
Train, Caboose, General Stark, Gray, 1972 .... 8.00
Train, Caboose, Gray, 1988 .... 40.00 To 55.00
Train, Caboose, Yellow, 1987 .... 40.00 To 65.00
Train, Casey Jones Accessory Set 60.00
Train, Casey Jones Box Car 49.00
Train, Casey Jones Bumpers 12.00
Train, Casey Jones Caboose, 1989 .... 34.00 To 52.00
Train, Casey Jones Tank Car 54.00
Train, Casey Jones Track 12.00
Train, Casey Jones With Tender, 1989 .... 39.00
Train, Coal Tender 35.00
Train, Combination Car, 1988 .... 59.00
Train, Dining Car 85.00
Train, Flat Car, 1988 .... 30.00 To 37.00

Train, General Locomotive, 1988	69.00
Train, Grant Locomotive	69.00
Train, Log Car, 1988	65.00
Train, Lumber Car, 1987	20.00
Train, Observation Car, 1987	20.00
Train, Passenger Car	39.00
Train, Tank Car, 1983 *Illus*	25.00
Train, Track	10.00
Train, Turner Locomotive, 1982	125.00
Train, Water Tower, 1987	25.00
Train, Wood Tender	49.00
TraveLodge, 1972	8.00
Treasure Chest, 1979	10.00
Trout Unlimited, 1977	15.00
Truth Or Consequences, 1974	8.00
Turquoise China Jug, 1966	6.00
Turtle, 1975	23.00
Twin Bridges Club, 1971	40.00
U.S. Open, 1972	10.00
Veterans of Foreign Wars, 1971	10.00
Viking, 1973	12.00
Volkswagen, Blue, 1973	45.00 To 49.00
Volkswagen, Red, 1973	49.00
Von's 75th Anniversary, 1981	35.00
Walleyed Pike, 1977, Trophy	15.00
Washington Bicentennial, 1976	12.00
Washington State, 1975, State	5.00
Water Tower, 1987	20.00 To 30.00
Waterman, Norfolk Convention Gift, 1980, Pair	60.00
West Virginia, 1963, State	150.00
WGA, 1971	5.00
Wolverine Club, 1975	10.00
Woodpecker, 1969, Trophy	8.00
Wyoming, 1965, State	52.00
Yellow Katz, 1967	20.00
Yellowstone, 1972	5.00
Yosemite, Decal Map, 1967, 11 In.	5.00
Yuma Rifle Club, 1968	25.00
Zimmerman Liquors, 2–Handled Jug, 1965	65.00
Zimmerman Liquors, 50th Anniversary, 1983	40.00
Zimmerman Liquors, Art Institute	10.00
Zimmerman Liquors, Bell, Dark Blue, 1976	6.00
Zimmerman Liquors, Bell, Light Blue, 1976	6.00
Zimmerman Liquors, Blue Beauty, 1969, 10 In.	10.00
Zimmerman Liquors, Cherubs, Lavender, 1968	5.00
Zimmerman Liquors, Cherubs, Salmon, 1968	7.00
Zimmerman Liquors, Eldorado, Gray Blue, 1978 *Illus*	5.00
Zimmerman Liquors, Peddler, 1971	5.00
Zimmerman Liquors, Vase, Green, 1972	7.00
Zimmerman Liquors, Z, 1970	10.00

BEER

History says that beer was first made in America in the Roanoke Colony of Virginia in 1587. It is also claimed that the Pilgrims brought some over on the already crowded Mayflower. William Penn started a brewery in 1683. By the time of the Civil War, beer was made and bottled in all parts of the United States. In the early years the beer was poured from kegs or sold in ordinary unmarked black glass bottles. English stoneware bottles were in common use in this country from about 1860 to 1890. Excavations in many inner cities still unearth these sturdy containers. A more or less standard bottle was used by about 1870. It held a quart of liquid and measured about 10 inches high. The early ones were plain and had a cork stopper. Later bottles had embossed lettering on the sides. The lightning stopper was invented in 1875 and many bottles had various types of wire and lever–type seals that were replacements for the corks. In the 1900s Crown corks were used. It wasn't long before plain bottles with paper labels appeared, but cans were soon the containers preferred by many. The standard thick–topped glass beer bottle shape of the 1870s, as well as modern beer bottles, are included in this category. The bottles can be found in clear, brown, aqua, or amber glass. A few cobalt blue, milk glass, or red examples are known. Some bottles have turned slightly amethyst in color from the sun. Collectors are often interested in local breweries and books listing the names and addresses of companies have been written. (See Bibliography.) Beer bottle collectors often search for advertising trays, signs, and other *go–withs* collected as *breweriana*. These are listed under Go–Withs at the end of this book.

BEER, A. J. Gleason, Stoneware, Gray, 1855 .... 45.00
  A. Pearsall, Flint, Mich., Bright Lime Green, Tooled Mouth, 11 1/4 In. 193.00
  Adam Scheidt Brewing Co., Baltimore, Amber, Blob Top 12.00
  Atlanta Brewing & Ice Co., Lager, Atlanta, Stoneware, 9 In. ....*Illus* 125.00
  Bartholomay Brewery, Rochester, N. Y., Deep Amber, Wheel Picture, Blob 19.00
  Bass & Co., Pale Ale, White, Cork, Carlton China, 3 3/4 In. 31.00
  Bernard Fischer, Philadelphia, Pa., Aqua 18.00
  Blown, Dark Olive, 9 In. 30.00
  Blown, Deep Root Beer Amber, Applied Mouth, 7 7/8 In. 71.00
  Blown, Deep Root Beer Amber, Pontil, 8 1/2 In. 350.00
  Bohemian Brewing Co., Kansas City, Ring Top 5.00
  Buffalo Brewing Co., Monogram, San Francisco Agency, Amber, 1/2 Pt. 25.00
  Buffalo Brewing Co., Sacramento, Calif., Amber, Vertical Slug, 1/2 Pt. 25.00
  Buffum, Amber 50.00
  Bunker Hill Lager Beer, Amber, Wire Bail, Stopper 25.00
  C. Conrad & Co., Original Budweiser, U.S. Pat. No. 6376, Aqua, Small 25.00
  C. D. Postel, Amber, Blob Top, Sheafs of Wheat 65.00
  Chas. Jolly, Philadelphia, Dark Lime, 1890, 10 1/2 In. 55.00
  Chas. Jolly, Philadelphia, Pa., Yellow Green 50.00
  Chicago Lager Beer, San Francisco, Blob Top 150.00
  Cobalt Blue, Pt. 15.00
  Columbia Brewing Co., Logansport, Ind., Amber, Blob Top, 11 1/2 In. 9.00
  Columbia Brewing Co., Logansport, Ind., Aqua, Blob Top, Pony, 6 1/2 In. 9.00
  D. Lagrange, Moravia, N. Y., Golden Amber, Slug Plate, Snap Wire Top 22.00
  D. P. Rockefeller & Bro., Sunbury, Pa., Snap Wire Top 15.00
  Dr. Cronk's Beer, Bright Yellow Green, 12–Sided, IP, 9 1/2 In. 963.00
  E. Bigelow, Springfield, Mass., Medium Green, IP, 6 1/4 In. 105.00
  Empire Bottling, 47 Great Jones St., N. Y., Amber, Tenpin Shape, 8 In. 45.00
  Enis Bros., Utica, N. Y., Aqua, Blob, BIM, Slug Plate, Qt. 18.00
  Enterprise Brewing, San Francisco, Calif., Amber, Qt. 5.00
  Excelsior Bottling Works, Schenectady, N. Y., Citron, Blob, BIM, Pt. 16.00
  Foss–Schneider Brewing Co., Cincinnati, Oh., Aqua, Blob Top, 12 In. 9.00
  Fred Koch Brewery, Dunkirk, N. Y., Amber, Crown Top, BIM, Pt. 18.00
  Fredricksburg Bottle Co., San Francisco, Monogram, Amber, 1/2 Pt. 20.00
  G. A. P., Ale, Blob, Yellow Olive, Slug Plate, 1881, 10 1/2 In., Qt. 50.00
  G. B. Seely's Son, New York, Embossed Bartender, Blob, Qt. 19.00
  Geo. A. Ticoulet, Sacramento, Amber, Split 18.00
  Golden Age Beer, Spokane, Wash., Partial Label, 1/2 Gal. 15.00
  Golden Gate Bottling Works, Bear Picture, San Fran., Amber, 1/2 Pt. 75.00
  Hartmann & Fehrenbach Brewing Co., Amber, Blob Top, Flying Horse 19.00
  Hinckel Brewing Co., Boston, Mass., Clear, Blob Top, 9 3/4 In. 17.50
  Hoster, Columbus, Ohio, Amber, Blob Top, Seed Bubbles 10.00
  I. Sutton & Co., Covington, Ky., Cobalt Blue, 12–Sided, IP, 8 1/2 In. 1100.00
  Indianapolis Brewing Co., Aqua, Angel On Globe, Blob Top, 11 1/2 In. 9.00
  Joseph Herb Brewing Co., Milan, Oh., Amber, Crown Top, BIM, Pt. 18.00
  Kornahrens–Fitschen, Philadelphia, XXX Porter Ale, Green, Squat 100.00
  L. Jung, Milwaukee, Amber, Blob 6.00
  Louis Heineman, Philadelphia, Pa., Aqua, Slug Plate 18.00
  McAvoy Brewing Co., Malt Marrow, Amber, Blob Top, 8 In. 6.00
  Miller 1000 Beer, 12 Oz. 2.00
  Milwaukee Lager Beer, J. Gahm, Boston, Light Amber, Blob Top 20.00
    BEER, MINIATURE, see Miniature, Beer

Moerlein Grest Brewing Co., Old Jug Lager, Nashville, Stoneware 65.00
National Bottling Works, Light Amber, Blob Top, Eagle, Qt. 75.00
National Brewing, San Francisco, Amber, Blob Top 10.00
National Lager Beer, H. Rohrbacher, Stockton, Amber, Split 25.00
P. O. C., Bar, 31 1/2 In. 100.00
Pacific Bottling, San Francisco, Amber, J Monogram, Split 125.00
Patrick Henry 35.00
Peter Mugler Brewer, Sisson, Calif., Light Amber, 1/2 Pt. 75.00
S. W. Utter, Nassau, N. Y., Amber, Blob Top, Pt. 8.00
Santa Clara Bottling Works, Amber, Split 40.00
Santa Clara Bottling Works, San Jose, Amber, Qt. 40.00
Schlitz Royal Ruby, Labels, 7 Oz. 40.00
Schlitz, Royal Ruby, Anchor Glassworks, 1950s, ABM Lip, Qt. .... 50.00 To 60.00
Sedges & Butler, Dark Brown, Fat, Chunky Neck, Flared Lip, 8 1/2 In. 157.00
Sonora Brewing Co., Sonora, Calif., Monogram, Amber, Qt. 30.00
Weiss Beer, McKinney & Co., Philadelphia, Aqua, Octagonal, 7 1/2 In. 88.00
   BENNINGTON, see Pottery

----------------------------------- BININGER -----------------------------------

Bininger and Company of New York City was a family–owned grocery and dry goods
store. It was founded by the 1820s and remained in business into the 1880s. The store
sold whiskey, wine, and other liquors. After a while they began bottling their products in
their own specially designed bottles. The first bottles were ordered from England but it
wasn't long before the local glass factories made the Bininger's special figural containers.
Barrels, clocks, cannons, jugs, and flasks were made. Colors were usually shades of amber,
green, or puce.

BININGER, A. M. & Co., Gin 1595.00
A. M. & Co., Old Kentucky, N. Y., Barrel, Orange Amber 160.00
A. M. & Co., Bourbon, Barrel, Amber, OP, 8 In. 198.00
A. M. & Co., Bourbon, Barrel, Amber, OP, 9 3/8 In. 165.00
A. M. & Co., Bright Green, Tapered, IP, 9 1/4 In. 2310.00
A. M. & Co., Cannon Shape, Great Gun Gin, Red Golden Amber, 12 In. 1045.00
A. M. & Co., Cannon Shape, Medium Amber, 12 3/8 In. 300.00
A. M. & Co., Cannon Shape, Medium Golden Amber, 12 1/4 In. 467.00

Beer, Atlanta Brewing & Ice
Co., Lager, Atlanta,
Stoneware, 9 In.

Bininger, Kentucky Bourbon,
Amber, Label

Bininger, Knickerbocker,
Amber, Handle, Pt.

A. M. & Co., Jug, Amber, Applied Handle & Spout, 8 In. 385.00
A. M. & Co., Jug, Olive, Applied Handle & Spout, 7 3/4 In. 1155.00
A. M. & Co., Old Dominion Wheat Tonic, Olive Green, 9 3/4 In. 80.00
A. M. & Co., Old Kentucky Bourbon, Olive, Applied Mouth, 10 In. 88.00
A. M. & Co., Old Kentucky Bourbon, Yellow Amber, Square, 9 7/8 In. 132.00
A. M. & Co., Old London Dock Gin, Amber, Square, Qt. 20.00
A. M. & Co., Old London Dock Gin, Green, Open Bubble On Lip 60.00
A. M. & Co., Old London Dock Gin, Olive Green, Civil War .... 55.00 To 95.00
A. M. & Co., Pinkish Puce, Square, 9 7/8 In. 413.00
A. M. & Co., Urn Shape, Chocolate Amber, 10 In. 143.00
A. M. & Co., Urn Shape, Medium Amber, Handle, 8 3/4 In. 2200.00
Alarm Clock, Regulator, Deep Golden Amber, Pontil, Pt. 357.00
Bourbon, Barrel, Dark Amber, Double Collar, 1861–1864, 8 In. 170.00
Clock, Regulator, Golden Amber, 5 3/4 In. 143.00
Clock, Regulator, Liquor, OP 275.00
Clock, Regulator, Yellow Amber, 5 3/4 In. 220.00
Flask, Traveler's Guide, Teardrop, Golden Amber, Pocket, 6 3/4 In. 198.00
Kentucky Bourbon, Amber, Label ....*Illus*   60.00
Knickerbocker, Amber, Handle, Pt. ....*Illus*   800.00
Night Cap, Golden Amber, Oval, 1860–1870, Pt. 230.00
Night Cap, Orange Amber, OP, 7 3/4 In. 198.00
Whiskey, Green, Handle 830.00

──────────────── **BISCHOFF** ────────────────

Bischoff Company has made fancy decanters since it was founded in 1777 in Trieste, Italy.
The modern collectible Bischoff bottles have been imported into the United States since
about 1950. Glass, porcelain, and stoneware decanters and figurals are made.

BISCHOFF, African Head, 1962 .... 13.00
Alpine Pitcher, 1969 .... 25.00
Amber Flower, Leaf, 1952 .... 30.00
Antique Candlestick, 1958 .... 22.00
Ashtray, Girl With Harp, 1958, Miniature 12.00
Bacchus Pitcher 12.00
Bell Tower, 1959 .... 20.00
Bell Tower, 1960 .... 36.00
Black Cat, 1969 .... 20.00
Cameo Pitcher, 1962 .... 20.00
Canteen, Floral, 1969 .... 20.00
Chariot Urn, 1966 .... 23.00
Chinese Boy, 1962 .... 35.00
Chinese Girl, 1962 .... 35.00
Christmas Tree, 1957 .... 45.00
Clown Candlestick, 1963 .... 8.00
Coronet Crystal, 1952 .... 32.00
Dancers, 1961 .... 13.00
Deer, 1969 .... 12.00
Dog, Alabaster, 1969 .... 40.00
Dog, Dachshund, 1966 .... 45.00
Duck, 1964 .... 45.00
Egyptian Ashtray, 1961 .... 15.00
Egyptian Dancers, 1961 .... 12.00
Egyptian Musical Trio, 1959 .... 20.00
Egyptian Musicians, 1963 .... 15.00
Emerald Rose, 1952 .... 48.00
Festival, 1957 .... 47.00
Fish Ashtray, 1961 .... 20.00
Fish, Ruby, 1969 .... 31.00
Fruit Bowl, 1966 .... 30.00
Grecian Vase, 1969 .... 15.00
Green Rose, 1954 .... 35.00
Jungle Scene, Ruby 25.00
Mask, Columbian, 1963 .... 30.00

Mask, Nigerian, 1970	15.00
Modern Vase, 1959	30.00
Opaline, 1957	45.00
Pagentry Vase, 1962	24.00
Pink Rose, 1954	32.00
Pirate, 1970	20.00
Porcelain Cameo, 1953	15.00
Red Bell, Rose, 1957	45.00
Red Bell, Striped, 1957	31.00
Rooster Ashtray, 1962	20.00
Ruby Etched, 1952	35.00
Ruby Flowers, 1953	35.00
Silver Aqua Green, 1954	30.00
Spanish Boy, 1961	30.00
Spanish Girl, 1961	32.00
Topaz Basket, 1958	30.00
Tower of Fruit, 1964	15.00
Venetian Blue Green, 1953	30.00
Watch Tower, 1960	10.00
White Pitcher, 1960	15.00
Wild Geese Pitcher, 1969	25.00
Yellow Vase, 1959	23.00

BITTERS

Bitters seems to have been an idea that started in Germany during the seventeenth century. A tax was levied against gin in the mid–1700s and the clever salesmen simply added some herbs to the gin and sold the mixture as medicine. Later, the medicine was made in Italy and England. Bitters is the name of this mixture. By the nineteenth century, bitters became a popular local product in America. One brand had over 59% alcohol (about 118 proof). It was usually of such a high alcoholic content that the claim that one using the product felt healthier with each sip was almost true. Although alcoholism had become a problem and social drinking was frowned upon by most proper Victorians, the soothing bitters medicine found wide acceptance. At that time there was no tax on the medicine and no laws concerning ingredients or advertising claims.

The word *bitters* must be embossed on the glass or a paper label must be affixed to the bottle for the collector to call the bottle a bitters bottle. Most date from 1862, the year of the Revenue Act tax on liquor, until 1906, the year the Food and Drug Act placed restrictions on the sale of bitters as a medicinal cure. Over 1,000 types are known. Bitters were sometimes packaged in figural bottles shaped like cabins, human figures, fish, pigs, barrels, ears of corn, drums, clocks, horses, or cannons. The bottles came in a variety of colors. They ranged from clear to milk glass, pale to deep amethyst, light aqua to cobalt blue, pale yellow to amber, and pale to dark green. A bottle found in an unusual color commands a much higher price than a clear bottle of the same shape. The numbers used in the entries in the form R–00 refer to the book *For Bitters Only* by Carlyn Ring. Each bottle is pictured and described in detail in the book. There is a newsletter for collectors: *The Bitters Report,* P.O. Box 1253, Bunnell, FL 32110.

BITTERS, African Stomach, Spruance, Stanley & Co., Amber, 9 5/8 In., R–A16	130.00
Alpine, Decanter, Yellow Green, Spout, Handle, 6 1/2 In., R–A9	77.00
American Deobstruent, Label, R–A47	30.00
American Life, Omaha, Amber, R–A48	3900.00
Angostura Bark, Amber, 7 In., R–A68	65.00
Angostura Bark, Eagle Liqueur Dist., Amber, Globe, 7 7/8 In., R–A68	70.00
Angostura, Emerald, Whiskey Shape, Embossed Shoulder, R–A64	20.00
Arabian, Lawrence & Weichselbaum, Amber, 9 3/4 In., R–A80	500.00
Aromatic German, Seiferth & Co., Pittsburgh, Square, 9 1/8 In.	1210.00
Aromatic Orange Stomach, Nashville, Amber, 10 1/8 In., R–A90	412.00
Atwood's Jaundice, Georgetown, Mass., Aqua, 12–Sided, R–A122	75.00
Atwood's Jaundice, M. Carter & Son, Georgetown, 12–Sided, R–A123	35.00
Atwood's Jaundice, Mass., Aqua, 11–Sided, 6 In., R–A121	15.00
Atwood's, Free Sample	7.00
Augauer, Chicago, Bright Green, Label, R–A134	75.00

Bitters, Brown's Celebrated
Indian Herb, Brilliant Amber,
R-B223

Bitters, Fish, W.H. Ware,
Medium Amber, R-F44

Bitters, Pineapple, W. & Co.,
N.Y., Deep Amber, OP,
8 1/4 In., R-P100

Augauer, Olive Green, R–A134 .... 130.00
Baker's Orange Grove, Amber, Square, 9 1/2 In., R–B9 .... 176.00 To 225.00
Baker's Orange Grove, Apricot, Rope Corners, 9 1/2 In., R–B9 .... 400.00
Baker's Orange Grove, Yellow, 9 1/2 In., R–B9 .... 425.00 To 725.00
Barrel, Deep Sapphire Blue, Square Mouth, 9 3/4 In., R–B171 .... 1210.00
Barto's Great Gun, Cannon, Amber, 1865–1870, 11 In., R–B32 .... 3150.00
Bavarian, Hoffheimer Brothers, Deep Olive Green, 9 1/4 In., R–B34 .... 550.00
Begg's Dandelion, Sioux City, Iowa, Amber, R–B53 .... 325.00
Bell's Cocktail, Jas. M. Bell, Amber, 10 In., R–B58 .... 425.00 To 495.00
Bennet's Wild Cherry Stomach, San Francisco, Amber, 9 In., R–B74 .... 270.00
Berkshire, Amann & Co., Pig, Cincinnati, Amber, 9 In., R–B81 .... 660.00
Berkshire, Amann & Co., Pig, Cincinnati, Amber, 9 1/2 In., R–B81. 2 .... 1045.00
Berkshire, Amann & Co., Pig, Cincinnati, Amber, 9 5/8 In., R–B81 .... 990.00
Berkshire, Amann & Co., Pig, Cincinnati, Amber, 10 1/2 In., R–B81. 4 .... 1430.00
Best Bitters In America, Amber, 9 1/4 In., R–B92 .... 2150.00
Big Bill Best, Amber, Tapering Square, 12 1/8 In., R–B95 .... 110.00
Blue Mountain, Aqua, R–B128 .... 95.00
Boerhaves Holland, B. Page Jr. & Co., Aqua, 7 5/8 In., R–B134 .... 550.00
Boker's Stomach, Lady's Leg, Amber, Label, 12 3/8 In., D–B138 .... 55.00
Boneset, Essex Chemical Works, Aqua, Cylinder, 9 1/2 In., R–B146 .... 45.00
Bourbon Whiskey, Barrel, Cherry Puce, 1870, 9 3/4 In., R–B171 .... 495.00
Bourbon Whiskey, Barrel, Deep Claret, R–B171 .... 275.00
Bourbon Whiskey, Barrel, Medium Topaz, 9 1/4 In. 1155.00
Bourbon Whiskey, Puce, Applied Mouth, 9 1/4 In., R–B171 .... 165.00 To 415.00
Boyer's Stomach, Cincinnati, Clear, Tooled Lip, R–B184 .... 65.00
Brady's Family, Amber, R–B193 .... 295.00
Brophy's, Nokomis, Illinois, Aqua, R–B217 .... 70.00
Brown's Celebrated Indian Herb, Amber, 12 In., R–B223 .... 325.00 To 875.00
Brown's Celebrated Indian Herb, Amber, 12 In., R–B226 .... 253.00 To 550.00
Brown's Celebrated Indian Herb, Brilliant Amber, R–B223 ....*Illus* 425.00
Brown's Celebrated Indian Herb, Golden Amber, R–B226 .... 250.00
Brown's Celebrated Indian Herb, Green, 12 In., R–B225 .... 2950.00
Brown's Celebrated Indian Herb, Honey Amber, 12 In. R–B225 .... 275.00
Brown's Celebrated Indian Herb, Painted, R–B223 .... 400.00
Brown's Celebrated Indian Herb, Yellow Amber, 12 1/4 In., R–B226 .... 385.00
Brown's Celebrated Indian Herb, Yellow Green, R–B225 .... 2950.00
Brown's Iron, Embossed, Front & Back Labels, Contents, R–B231 .... 40.00
Brown's Iron, Medium Amber Base, Light Amber Top, R–B231 .... 45.00
Brown's Jamaica Ginger 15.00
Buhrer's Gentian, Deep Aqua, 8 1/4 In., R–B251 .... 115.00

Burdock Blood, Foster Milburn Co., Aqua, 8 1/4 In., R–B262 .... 36.00
Burgundy Bitters, R. P. Burwell, Amber, 8 1/4 In., R–B266 .... 303.00
C. Brinckerhoff's Health Restorative, New York, $1. 00, Light Olive 425.00
C. Gautiers Native Wine Bitters, Olive Yellow, 9 5/8 In., R–G8 .... 963.00
C. H. Atwood's, Emerald Green, Fluted Shoulder, Label, R–A129 .... 65.00
    BITTERS, C. W. ROBACK'S, see Bitters, Dr. C. W. Roback's
    BITTERS, CABIN, see Bitters, Drake's Plantation; Bitters, Golden; Bitters,
    Kelly's Old Cabin; Bitters, Old Homestead Wild Cherry
Caldwell's Herb, Great Tonic, IP, Amber, R–C8 .... 150.00
California Fig, San Francisco, Amber, R–C18 .... 67.00
Canteen, John Hart & Co., Blue Green, 9 3/4 In., R–C34 .... 900.00 To 990.00
Canton, Star, Lady's Leg, Medium Amber, R–C35 .... 350.00
Carmeliter Stomach, Square, Amber, 10 1/4 In., R–C52 .... 75.00
Carmeliter, Variant, Amber 95.00
Caroni, Green, 5 In., R–C60 .... 60.00
Catawba Wine, Grapes, Deep Olive Amber, 9 3/8 In., R–C85 .... 880.00
Catawba Wine, Olive Green, R–C85 .... 1700.00
Catawba Wine, Yellow Emerald Green, Grapes, 9 1/2 In., R–C85 .... 1870.00
Celebrated Crown, F. Chevalier & Co., Amber, Square, 8 7/8 In. 325.00
Cha's Schlitz German Wine, Amber, Triangular, 10 1/8 In., R–G32 .... 688.00
Clark & White, Saratoga Type, Pt. 45.00
Clark & White, Saratoga Type, Qt. 32.00
Clarke's Compound Mandrake, Aqua 48.00
Clarke's Sherry Wine, Aqua, Rectangular, 7 7/8 In., R–C165 .... 55.00
Clarke's Sherry Wine, Aqua, Variant, 7 1/2 In., R–C165 .... 70.00
Clarke's Sherry Wine, Rockland, Me., Aqua, 8 In., R–C164 .... 71.50
Clarke's Sherry Wine, Rockland, Me., Aqua, 9 3/4 In., R–C162 .... 65.00
Clarke's Vegetable Sherry Wine, Aqua, 14 In., R–C155 .... 193.00
Clarke's Vegetable Sherry Wine, Sharon, Mass., Aqua, 14 In. 550.00
Cognac Bitters, S. Steinfeld's, Green, Cylinder, 11 1/8 In., R–C187 .... 440.00
Congress & Empire, Embossed Back, Green, Qt. 58.00
Constitution, Seward & Bentley, Dark Amethyst, 9 3/8 In., R–C222 .... 1650.00
Cooley's Anti–Dispeptic Or Jaundice, Aqua, 6 1/4 In., R–C228 .... 650.00
Corn Juice, Coffin Flask Shape, Aqua, 8 In. 605.00
Covert's Modoc Stomach Bitters, Amber, R–C241 .... 175.00
Curtis Cordial Calisaya, Amber, 11 3/4 In., R–C261 .... 688.00
Curtis Cordial Calisaya, Olive Yellow, 11 1/2 In., R–C261 .... 3550.00
Damiana Bitters, Baja, Calif., Lewis Hess, Teal, 11 1/2 In., R–D5 .... 25.00
Damiana, Aqua, Small Burst Bubble, Cylinder, Clear, R–D4. 5 .... 28.00
David Andrews Vegetable Jaundice, Tomb Shape, Aqua, 8 In., R–A57 .... 675.00

Bitters, Dr. A.W. Coleman's
Anti Dyspeptic & Tonic, 9 In.,
R-C194

Bitters, Dr. Anthony's
Angostura, Philadelphia

Bitters, Lash's, Paper Label,
Amber, 9 In., R-L32

Davis Vegetable Pain Killer, OP, 8 1/4 In., R–D30 .... 23.00
De Witts Stomach, Chicago, Amber, Tooled Lip, 9 3/8 In., R–D64 .... 121.00
DeKuyper Orange, Green, Label, Tooled Lip, 7 3/4 In., R–D40 .... 26.00
DeKuyper Orange, Green, Spout, Pewter, 2 Labels, R–D40 .... 26.00 To 45.00
Devil–Cert Stomach, Clear, ABM Lip, Pt., 8 In., R–D59 .... 30.00 To 55.00
Diamond's Blood Bitters, Buffalo, N. Y., Amber, 7 1/2 In., R–D70 .... 209.00
Digestine, P. J. Bowlin Liquor Co., Amber, 8 1/8 In., R–D73 .... 300.00
Dingens Napoleon Cocktail, Yellow Amber, IP, 10 In., R–N3 .... 2860.00
Doyle's Hop Bitters, 1872, Amber, 10 In., R–D94 .... 49.00
Doyle's Hop Bitters, 1872, Label, Contents, Amber, R–D93 .... 35.00
Doyle's Hop Bitters, Berries & Leaf, Amber 9 1/2 In. R–D93 .... 25.00 To 55.00
Doyle's Hop Bitters, Doyle's Upside Down, Amber, 9 1/2 In., R–D95 .... 330.00
Dr. A. S. Hopkin's Union Stomach, Label, Amber, R–H181 .... 40.00
Dr. A. S. Hopkin's Union Stomach, Yellow, Square, 9 5/8 In., R–H180 .... 121.00
Dr. A. W. Coleman's Anti Dyspeptic & Tonic, 9 In., R–C194 ....*Illus* 2500.00
Dr. A. W. Coleman's Anti Dyspeptic, Deep Olive Green, R–C194 .... 775.00
Dr. Anthony's Angostura, Philadelphia ....*Illus* 425.00
Dr. Ashbaugh's Plant & Root, J. C. Tilton, Yellow, 9 In., R–A101 .... 467.00
Dr. Ball's Vegetable Stomachic, Northboro, Mass., OP, R–B14f 165.00
Dr. Baxter's Mandrake, Label, 6 1/2 In., R–B36 .... 30.00
Dr. Bell's Blood Purifying, English Remedy, Amber, 9 5/8 In., R–B56 .... 77.00
Dr. Bell's Blood Purifying, R–B56 .... 80.00
Dr. Blake's Aromatic, N. Y., Aqua, OP, R–B120 .... 95.00
Dr. C. W. Roback's Stomach, Cincinnati, O., Olive, 9 5/8 In., R–R73 .... 2870.00
Dr. C. W. Roback's Stomach, Cincinnati, O., Orange Amber, R–R74 .... 195.00
Dr. C. W. Roback's Stomach, Cincinnati, O., Yellow, 10 In., R–R73 .... 605.00
Dr. Caldwell's Herb, Amber, Triangular, 12 1/2 In., R–C9 .... 137.00
Dr. Campbell's Scotch, Amber, Strap Flask, 6 1/4 In., R–C31 .... 253.00
Dr. Campbell's Scotch, Medium Amber, R–C31 .... 150.00
Dr. Copp's White Mountain, Aqua, Oval, Tolled Lip, 8 1/4 In. R–C232 .... 125.00
Dr. Dunlap's Anchor, Grand Rapids, Mich., Amber, 10 3/8 In., R–D122 .... 578.00
Dr. Dunlap's Anchor, Orange Amber, 10 1/8 In., R–D122 .... 330.00
Dr. F. F. W. Hogguers, Detroit, Mich., Amber, 9 1/4 In., R–H141 .... 358.00
Dr. Fenner's, Capitol, Aqua, 9 In., R–C39 .... 42.00 To 45.00
Dr. Fisch's, Fish Shape, Amber, 11 3/4 In., R–F44 .... 135.00
Dr. Flint's Quaker, Providence, R. I., Globby Lip, Flat Panel, R–F59 .... 33.00
Dr. Geo. Pierce's Indian Restorative, Aqua, OP, R–P96 .... 120.00 To 135.00
Dr. Geo. Pierce's Indian Restorative, Aqua, R–P95 .... 45.00 To 75.00
Dr. Geo. Pierce's Indian Restorative, Green Aqua, OP, R–P96 .... 130.00
Dr. Geo. Pierce's Indian Restorative, Lowell, Ma., Aqua, 8 In., R–P96 .... 148.00
Dr. Gruessie–Altherr's, Krauter, Amber, Cylinder, Label, R–G122 .... 25.00
Dr. H. F. Weis Medicine Co., Rhine Stomach, Dayton, O., Amber, Square 100.00
Dr. Harter's Wild Cherry, Amber, Rectangular, 7 1/2 In., R–H51 .... 85.00
Dr. Harter's Wild Cherry, Dayton, O., Amber, 4 3/8 In., R–H48 .... 25.00
Dr. Harter's Wild Cherry, Dayton, O., Amber, 7 3/4 In., R–H46 .... 30.00
Dr. Harter's Wild Cherry, St. Louis, Light Amber, 2 3/4 In., R–H54 .... 35.00
Dr. Henley's Wild Grape Root IXL, Blue Green, Round, 12 In., R–H84 .... 70.00
Dr. Henley's Wild Grape Root IXL, Green, 1868, 12 In., R–H84 .... 2100.00
Dr. Henley's Wild Grape Root, Aqua, R–H85 .... 55.00 To 70.00
Dr. Hoofland's German, Bubbles, Aqua, 9 1/2 In., R–H168 .... 45.00
BITTERS, DR. HOSTETTER'S, see Bitters, Dr. J. Hostetter's
Dr. J. Hostetter's Stomach, Amber, 8 3/4 In., R–H197 .... 10.00
Dr. J. Hostetter's Stomach, Dark Amber, 1860, 9 3/4 In., R–H194 .... 176.00
Dr. J. Hostetter's Stomach, Deep Olive Amber, R–H194 .... 130.00
Dr. J. Hostetter's Stomach, Dense Olive Green, 10 In., R–H195 .... 116.00
Dr. J. Hostetter's Stomach, Yellow, Square, 9 In., R–H194 .... 358.00
Dr. J. Hostetter's, W. McG & Co., Olive Green, R–H195 .... 50.00
Dr. Jacob's, Aqua, Rectangular, Label, Pontil, 8 3/8 In., R–J11 .... 328.00
Dr. Jaynes' Alkaseptic, Label, Embossed, Box 18.00
Dr. John Bull's Cedron, Louisville, Ky., Amber, 10 In., R–B254 .... 688.00
Dr. Langley's Root & Herb, 76 Union, Green Aqua, 6 1/8 In., R–L26 .... 47.50
Dr. Langley's Root & Herb, Aqua, 6 1/8 In., R–L26 .... 110.00
Dr. Langley's Root & Herb, Aqua, 7 1/8 In., R–L22 .... 66.00

Dr. Langley's Root & Herb, Boston, Apple Green, 8 3/4 In., R–L22 .... 55.00
Dr. Langley's Root & Herb, Boston, Aqua, Cloudy, 8 1/4 In., R–L21 .... 55.00
Dr. Langley's Root & Herb, Boston, Aqua, Round, 7 1/4 In., R–L22 .... 30.00
Dr. Langley's Root & Herb, Boston, Light Green, 6 1/2 In., R–L22 .... 75.00
Dr. Langley's Root & Herb, Deep Blue Green, Label, R–L20 .... 200.00
Dr. Langley's Root & Herb, Light To Apple Green, 8 3/4 In., R–L21 .... 82.50
Dr. Langley's Root & Herb, Teal, Applied Mouth, 8 1/2 In., R–L25 .... 93.50
Dr. Loew's Celebrated Stomach, Yellow Green, 3 7/8 In., R–L112 .... 100.00
Dr. Loew's Stomach, Christy Co., Yellow Green, 9 1/4 In., R–L116 .... 522.00
Dr. Lovegood's XX Family, Cabin, Amber, 10 5/16 In., R–L124 .... 1850.00
Dr. M. C. Ayer Restorative, Smoky Gray, 8 7/8 In., R–A144 .... 170.00
Dr. Manly Hardy's Genuine Jaundice, Bangor, Aqua, R–H34 .... 135.00 To 150.00
Dr. Patrick's, Terre Haute, Ind., Semi–Cabin, Amber, 10 1/4 In. 743.00
Dr. Petzold's Genuine German, Pat. 1884, Amber, 10 1/4 In., R–P75 .... 143.00
Dr. Petzold's Genuine German, Pat. 1884, Amber, 8 In., R–P76 .... 88.00
Dr. Renz's Herb, Olive, Amber Tones, 1862–1874, 9 7/8 In., R–R37 .... 176.00
Dr. S. W. Roback's Stomach, Olive, 9 5/8 In., R–R73 .... 2700.00
Dr. Sawen's Life Invigorating, Utica, Medium Amber, Square, R–S41 .... 55.00
Dr. Sawen's Life Invigorating, Utica, N. Y., Golden Amber, R–S41 .... 65.00
Dr. Shepard's Compound, Wahoo Bitters, Aqua, 7 1/2 In., R–S99 .... 198.00
Dr. Sims' Anti–Constipation, Nashville, Tenn., 7 In., R–S188 .... 245.00
Dr. Skinner's Sherry Wine Bitters, Aqua, OP, 8 5/8 In., R–S116 .... 171.00
Dr. Soule's Hop, 1872, Red Amber, Striations, 9 7/8 In., R–S145 .... 132.00
Dr. Soule's Hop, 1872, Yellow, Orange Cast, 9 7/8 In., R–S145 .... 121.00
Dr. Soule's Hop, Amber, 8 In., R–S147 .... 280.00
Dr. Stephen Jewett's Health Restoring, Aqua, R–J37 ....85.00 To 145.00
Dr. Stoever's, Amber, Square, Beveled Edges, 9 3/4 In., R–S199 .... 170.00
Dr. Stoughten's National, Amber, Square, 10 In., R–S208 .... 1700.00 To 1870.00
Dr. Thatcher's Liver & Blood Syrup, ABM, 8 In. 25.00
Dr. Thos Hall's California Pepsin Wine Bitters, Amber, R–H11 .... 145.00
Dr. Tompkins' Vegetable, Green, 8 5/8 In., R–T36 .... 825.00
Dr. Von Hopf's, Chamberlain, Des Moines, Amber, R–V28 ....65.00 To 250.00
Dr. Walker's, Vinegar, Label, Aqua, R–W11 .... 30.00
Dr. Walkinshaw's Curative, Batavia, N. Y., Amber, Label, R–W14 .... 450.00
Dr. Washington's American Life, Amber, 9 1/4 In., W–53 .... 193.00
Dr. Wheeler's Tonic Sherry Wine, Aqua, 9 3/8 In., R–W87 .... 2100.00 To 2420.00
Dr. Wonser's U.S. A. Indian Root, Dark Amber, 11 In., R–W146 .... 2200.00
Dr. Wood's Sarsaparilla & Wild Cherry, Aqua, 9 In., W–151 .... 165.00
Drake's Plantation, 4 Log, Golden Amber, 10 1/4 In., R–D110 .... 72.00
Drake's Plantation, 4 Log, Yellow Amber, 10 1/4 In., R–D110 .... 88.00
Drake's Plantation, 5 Log, Pat. 1862, Amber, 9 3/4 In., R–D109 .... 253.00
Drake's Plantation, 6 Log, Amber, 10 1/8 In., R–D104 .... 99.00
Drake's Plantation, 6 Log, Amber, 10 In., R–D108 .... 48.00
Drake's Plantation, 6 Log, Amber, R–D103 .... 120.00
Drake's Plantation, 6 Log, Amber, R–D105 .... 57.50
Drake's Plantation, 6 Log, Arabesque, Deep Medium Amber, Crude Lip 250.00
Drake's Plantation, 6 Log, Blue Green, 9 7/8 In., R–D105 .... 3450.00
Drake's Plantation, 6 Log, Bright Green, 10 In., R–D102 .... 2310.00
Drake's Plantation, 6 Log, Citron, R–D104 .... 275.00 To 500.00
Drake's Plantation, 6 Log, Dark Amber, 9 3/4 In., R–D105 .... 110.00
Drake's Plantation, 6 Log, Deep Puce, R–D105 .... 210.00
Drake's Plantation, 6 Log, Light Amber, Flat Corners, R–D104 .... 200.00
Drake's Plantation, 6 Log, Light Amber, R–D105 .... 65.00
Drake's Plantation, 6 Log, Light Apricot, R–D104 .... 225.00
Drake's Plantation, 6 Log, Olive Yellow, R–D108 .... 600.00
Drake's Plantation, 6 Log, Yellow Olive, 9 7/8 In., R–D105 .... 231.00
Drake's Plantation, 6 Log, Yellow, R–D104 .... 275.00
Drake's Plantation, Cabin, Black Amethyst, 10 In., R–D105 .... 220.00
E. J. Rose Magador, Amber, 8 3/4 In., R–R47 .... 65.00
E. R. Clarke's Sarsaparilla, Sharon, Mass., Aqua, OP, R–C154 .... 154.00
E. Wideman & J. Chappaz, Copper Puce, Lady's Leg, 11 1/2 In. 578.00
Eagle Angostura Bark, Amber, 7 In., R–E2 .... 75.00
   BITTERS, EAR OF CORN, see Bitters, National, Ear of Corn

Electric Brand, Amber, Tooled Lip, Labels, R–E32 .... 35.00
Electric Brand, Square, Amber, 8 1/2 In., R–E30 .... 10.00
Electric, Amber, 2 Labels, Tooled Lip, 8 1/2 In., R–E33 .... 32.00
Electric, H. E. Bucklen & Co., Chicago, Amber, 10 In., R–E31 .... 35.00 To 50.00
Emerson Botanic, Augusta, Maine, Label, R–E41 .... 35.00
Excelsior, Saratoga Type, Green, Pt. 48.00
F. Brown Boston, Sarsaparilla & Tomato, Sparkling, Aqua, OP, R–S36 .... 165.00
Ferro Quina Stomach Blood Maker, Amber, Lady's Leg Neck, R–F39 .... 75.00
Fish, W. H. Ware, Amber, Pat. 1866, 11 3/4 In., R–F46 .... 165.00 To 187.00
Fish, W. H. Ware, Chocolate Amber, Pat. 1866, 11 5/8 In., R–F46 .... 475.00
Fish, W. H. Ware, Medium Amber, R–F44 ....*Illus* 450.00
Fish, W. H. Ware, Yellow Green, Pat. 1866, 11 5/8 In., R–F46 .... 1430.00
Fowler's Stomach Bitters, Yellow Amber, Square, 9 7/8 In., R–F76 .... 468.00
Fritz Reuter Gin, Milk Glass, Case, 10 1/8 In., R–R40 .... 413.00
Genuine Bull Wild Cherry, Clear, Rectangular, 8 1/2 In., R–G15 .... 125.00
Geo. Benz & Sons Appetine, Black Amethyst, Square, Dug, 8 In., R–A78 .... 575.00
German Balsam, Milk Glass, R–G18 .... 400.00
Gilbert's Sarsaparilla, Enosburgh Falls, Amber, 8 5/8 In., R–G42 .... 303.00
Globe Tonic, Light Golden Amber, Embossed 2 Sides, Square, R–G49 .... 75.00
Globe, Byrne Bros. & Co., Cannon, Yellow Amber, 10 3/4 In., R–G47 .... 575.00
Globe, Byrne Bros. & Co., N. Y., Amber, Bell Shape, 11 In., R–G47 .... 220.00
Goff's Herb, Camden, N. J., Aqua, Embossed, Label, 3 3/4 In., R–G59 .... 25.00
Golden, Geo. C. Hubbel & Co., Aqua, Cabin, 10 1/4 In., R–G63 .... 210.00 To 380.00
Granger, Baltimore, Honey Amber, 8 1/2 In., R–G90 .... 295.00
Graves & Son Tonic Bitters, Semi–Cabin, Aqua, 10 In., R–G96 .... 330.00
Greeley's Bourbon Whiskey, Barrel, Burgundy, 9 1/4 In., R–G102 .... 231.00
Greeley's Bourbon Whiskey, Barrel, Puce, 9 1/8 In., R–G102 .... 110.00
Greeley's Bourbon Whiskey, Barrel, Strawberry, 9 In., R–G102 .... 605.00
Greeley's Bourbon Whiskey, Gasoline Puce, Barrel, 9 In., R–G102 .... 385.00
Greeley's Bourbon, Barrel, Deep Copper, 9 3/8 In., R–G101 .... 319.00
Greeley's Bourbon, Barrel, Gray Brown, 9 3/8 In., R–G101 .... 187.00
Greeley's Bourbon, Barrel, Medium Olive Green, R–G101 .... 1250.00
Greeley's Bourbon, Barrel, Medium Puce, 9 1/4 In., R–G101 .... 185.00
Greeley's Bourbon, Barrel, Medium Red Puce, R–G101 .... 275.00
Greeley's Bourbon, Barrel, Olive To Smoky Olive, 9 1/4 In., R–G101 .... 523.00
Greeley's Bourbon, Barrel, Peach Puce, 9 1/8 In., R–G101 .... 330.00
Greeley's Bourbon, Barrel, Puce Amber, 9 In., R–G101 .... 176.00
Greeley's Bourbon, Barrel, Smoky Apricot, R–G101 .... 300.00
Greeley's Bourbon, Barrel, Smoky Olive Green, 9 1/8 In., R–G101 .... 605.00
Greeley's Bourbon, Barrel, Yellow Olive, 9 1/2 In., R–G101 .... 295.00
Greer's Eclipse, Amber, Square, 8 3/4 In., R–G112 .... 80.00
Gwilym Evans Quinine, Aqua, Rectangular, 7 1/8 In., R–E58 .... 45.00
Gwilym Evans Quinine, Blue Aqua, BIMAL, 7 In., R–E57 .... 50.00
H. H. Warner & Co., Tippecanoe, Gold Amber, 9 In., R–Pg. 456 .... 66.00
H. H. Warner & Co., Tippecanoe, Light Honey Amber, R–Pg. 456 .... 75.00
H. P. Herb Wild Cherry, Cabin, Green, Rope Corners, 8 3/4 In., R–H94 .... 3800.00
H. P. Herb Wild Cherry, Cabin, Reading, Pa., Amber, 10 In., R–H93 .... 264.00
H. P. Herb Wild Cherry, Cabin, Reading, Yellow Olive, 10 In., R–H93 .... 1705.00
Hagan's, Amber, Triangular, Applied Mouth, 9 3/4 In., R–H5 .... 330.00 To 440.00
Hall's, Barrel, Light Amber, R–H10 .... 130.00
Hall's, Barrel, Medium Amber, Applied Mouth, 9 1/2 In., R–H9 .... 2350.00
Hall's, Barrel, New Haven, Est. 1842, Yellow, 9 1/8 In., R–H10 .... 440.00
Hall's, Barrel, New Haven, Yellowish Amber, 9 In., R–H10 .... 143.00
Hall's, Barrel, Orange Amber, R–H10 .... 120.00
Hall's, Barrel, Yellow, Square Collar Lip, 1860–1880, 9 In., R–H10 .... 264.00
Hanlan's Tuna, Purple, Cylinder, Embossed Base, 9 1/4 In., R–H24 .... 50.00
Hartwig Kantorowicz, Berlin, Green, Cylinder 195.00
Hartwig Kantorowicz, Brilliant Emerald Green, R–L106 .... 1450.00
Hartwig Kantorowicz, Paris, Milk Glass, Gin Shape, 8 7/8 In., R–106 .... 60.00
Hartwig Kantorowicz, Posen, Hamburg, Milk Glass, Gin Shape, R–L106 .... 35.00
Hathaway's Celebrated Stomach, Amber, Square, 10 In. 165.00
Hathorn, Amber, Saratoga Type 18.00
Herkules Bitters, Ball, AC Monogram, Yellow Green, 7 3/8 In., R–H98 .... 1925.00

Holland Import Co., Buffalo, Lady's Leg, Yellow Amber, 12 1/2 In. 357.00
Holtzermann's Patent Stomach, Cabin, Amber, 9 1/2 In., R–H155 .... 1100.00
Holtzermann's Patent Stomach, Cabin, Amber, 9 3/4 In., R–H154 .... 143.00
Holtzermann's Patent Stomach, Cabin, Medium Amber, R–H154 .... 235.00
Holtzermann's Patent Stomach, Red Amber, 9 7/8 In., R–H154 .... 168.00
Holtzermann's Stomach, Clear, Bar, White Enameled, 11 In., R–Pg. 246 .... 264.00
Holtzermann's Stomach, Medium Amber, Applied Mouth, R–H155 .... 625.00
Hops & Malt, Amber, Square, 10 In., R–H186 .... 44.00
Hops & Malt, Semi–Cabin, Amber, Labels, 9 1/4 In., R–H186 .... 750.00
Hops & Malt, Sheaf of Grain, Amber, 9 3/8 In., R–H187 .... 743.00
Host Stomach, I. G. Co. 5.00
    BITTERS, HOSTETTER'S, see Bitters, Dr. J. Hostetter's
    BITTERS, HUBBELL CO., see Bitters, Golden
Hunkidori Stomach, H. B. Matthews, Medium Amber, 9 In., R–H211 .... 115.00
Hutching's Dyspepsia, Amber, R–L217 .... 220.00
    BITTERS, INDIAN QUEEN, see Bitters, Brown's Celebrated Indian Herb
J. F. L. Capitol, Pineapple, Yellow, Amber, 9 1/8 In., R–C40 .... 250.00 To 275.00
J. T. Wiggins Gentian Bitters, Amber, Square, 9 3/4 In. 550.00
John Moffat, New York, Phoenix, Aqua, $1. 00, 5 1/2 In., R–M112 .... 72.00
John Moffat, New York, Phoenix, Aqua, $1. 00, 5 3/8 In., R–M113 .... 65.00
John Roots, Buffalo, N. Y., Emerald Green, 10 1/4 In., R–R90. 4 .... 770.00
Johnson's Calisaya, Burlington, Vt., Bright Amber, 10 In., R–J45 .... 85.00
Johnson's Indian Dyspeptic, Aqua, Rectangular, 6 1/4 In., R–J46 .... 165.00
Jones's Indian Specific Herb, Indian, Amber, 9 1/8 In., R–J51 .... 1072.00
Jones's Universal Stomach, Amber, 9 1/4 In., R–J53 ....77.00 To 121.00
Kaiser Wilhelm, Clear, 10 1/8 In., R–K5 .... 30.00
Kelly's Old Cabin, Pat. 1863, Deep Olive, 9 1/8 In., R–K21 ....*Illus* 4350.00
Kelly's Old Cabin, Pat. 1863, Yellow Amber, 9 1/8 In., R–K21 .... 975.00
Kelly's Old Cabin, Pat. March 1870, Amber, 9 3/8 In., R–K22 .... 797.00
Keystone Tonic, McLain Bros., Ill., Honey Amber, Square 975.00
Kimball's Jaundice, Backward S, Light Olive, IP, 7 In., R–K42 .... 375.00
Kimball's Jaundice, Olive Amber, Rectangular, IP, 7 In., R–K42 .... 330.00
Lacour's, Sarsapariphere, Yellow Amber, 9 3/8 In., R–L3 .... 797.00
Lancaster N. Y., Barrel, Amber, Square Collar, 9 1/4 In. 105.00
Landsberg's Century, Adler Co., 1776–1886, Amber, 11 1/4 In., R–L13 .... 2035.00
Langley's Root & Herb, Blue Green, R–L23 .... 75.00
Lash's Bitters Natural Tonic Laxative, Amber, ABM, Square, R–L33 .... 10.00
Lash's Kidney & Liver, Amber, 9 In., R–L35 .... 10.00
Lash's, Amber, Backbar, R–L41 .... 65.00
Lash's, Paper Label, Amber, 9 In., R–L32 ....*Illus* 37.00
Leak's Kidney & Liver, Amber, 9 3/4 In., R–L53 .... 50.00
Lerpaiger's Burgundy Wine, Green, Cylinder 295.00
Lippman's Great German, Amber, 10 In., R–L98 .... 165.00
    BITTERS, LITTHAUER STOMACH, see also Bitters, Hartwig Kantorowicz
Litthauer's Stomach, Berlin, Milk Glass, Gin Shape, 9 1/2 In., R–L10 .... 100.00
Litthauer's Stomach, Milk Glass, R–L101 .... 85.00
Lohengrin Gin, Von Buton, Germany, Milk Glass, 9 1/8 In., R–L117 .... 198.00
Loveridge's Wahoo, Salt Glazed, Stoneware Jug, Handle, R–Pg. 310 .... 825.00
Lyons, New Haven, Conn., Amber, Square, 1860–1890, 9 In., R–L141 .... 220.00
Malt Bitters Co., Boston, Embossed, Green, Blob Top, 9 In., R–M20 .... 30.00
    BITTERS, MANDRAKE, see Bitters, Dr. Baxter's
Marshall's Square, Amber, 8 5/8 In., R–M40 .... 35.00
McKeever's Army, Cannonballs, Drum, Amber, 11 In., R–M58 .... 1595.00 To 1870.00
Mexican, Henry C. Weaver, Gold Amber, Rectangular, 9 3/8 In., R–M78 .... 1945.00
Mishler's Herb, Amber, 9 In., R–M101 .... 30.00
Morning Star, Inceptum, Amber, 1860–1870, 12 7/8 In., R–M135 .... 198.00
Morning Star, Inceptum, Yellow Amber, Triangular, 5 In., R–M136 .... 1265.00
Moulton's Olorosa Bitters, Pineapple, Aqua, 11 3/8 In., R–M145 .... 253.00
Mrs. Leonard's Dock & Dandelion, Clear, Labels, 8 In., R–L74 .... 220.00
National Tonic, Burgundy, 12 3/8 In., R–N13 .... 1210.00
National, Ear of Corn, Amber, 12 1/4 In., R–N8 .... 220.00
National, Ear of Corn, Amber, 12 5/8 In., R–N8 .... 400.00
National, Ear of Corn, Amber, Sloping Collar, 12 3/8 In., R–N8 .... 176.00

Bitters, Kelly's Old Cabin,
Pat. 1863, Deep Olive,
9 1/8 In., R-K21

Bitters, Old Sachem &
Wigwam Tonic, Barrel,
Orange Amber, R-O46

Bitters, Zingari, F. Rahter,
Lady's Leg, Puce, 11 5/8 In.,
R-Z4

National, Ear of Corn, Aqua, 12 1/2 In., R–N8 .... 2640.00
National, Ear of Corn, Burgundy, 12 1/2 In., R–N8 .... 1150.00
National, Ear of Corn, Deep Golden Amber, 12 1/2 In., R–N8 .... 253.00
National, Ear of Corn, Deep Puce, 12 1/2 In., R–N8 .... 1150.00
National, Ear of Corn, Deep Reddish Puce, 12 3/8 In., R–N8 .... 550.00
National, Ear of Corn, Golden Yellow, R–N8 .... 160.00
National, Ear of Corn, Medium Amber, 12 1/2 In., R–N8 .... 247.00
National, Ear of Corn, Medium Pink Puce, 12 1/4 In., R–N8 .... 1100.00
National, Ear of Corn, Puce Amber, 12 5/8 In., R–N8 .... 330.00
National, Ear of Corn, Yellow Amber, 12 1/4 In., R–N8 .... 286.00
National, Ear of Corn, Yellow, Amber Tint, 12 1/2 In., R–N8 .... 240.00
New York Hop, Aqua, 9 1/2 In., R–N28 .... 180.00
O K Plantation, Amber, Triangular, 11 1/4 In., R–O13 .... 750.00
O'Leary's 20th Century, Amber, 8 5/8 In., R–O55 .... 83.00
O'Leary's 20th Century, Medium Amber, 8 1/2 In., R–O55 .... 85.00
O. P. Bissell's, Peoria, Ill., Amber, Embossed, 7 1/2 In., R–B110 .... 195.00
Old Dr. ASM, Solomon's Great Indian, Directions On Back, R–O137 .... 75.00
Old Dr. Aurent's, IXL Stomach, R–O137 .... 375.00
Old Homestead Wild Cherry, Cabin, Amber, 9 3/4 In., R–O37 .... 231.00
Old Homestead Wild Cherry, Cabin, Apricot, R–O37 .... 2550.00
Old Homestead Wild Cherry, Cabin, Chocolate Amber, 10 In., R–O37 .... 286.00
Old Homestead Wild Cherry, Cabin, Deep Amber, 9 1/2 In., R–O37 .... 170.00
Old Homestead Wild Cherry, Cabin, Golden Amber, 9 3/4 In., R–O37 .... 440.00
Old Homestead Wild Cherry, Cabin, Yellow Amber, R–O37 .... 350.00
Old Sachem & Wigwam Tonic, Barrel, Green, 9 1/2 In., R–O46 .... 2585.00
Old Sachem & Wigwam Tonic, Barrel, Lemon Yellow, 9 3/8 In., R–O46 .... 3150.00
Old Sachem & Wigwam Tonic, Barrel, Moss Green, 9 3/8 In., R–O46 .... 2350.00
Old Sachem & Wigwam Tonic, Barrel, Orange Amber, R–O46 ....*Illus* 190.00
Old Sachem & Wigwam Tonic, Barrel, Reddish Puce, 9 1/4 In., R–O46 .... 468.00
Old Sachem & Wigwam Tonic, Bright Yellow Green, R–O46 .... 3150.00
Old Sachem & Wigwam Tonic, Golden Amber, 9 1/4 In., R–O46 .... 242.00
Old Sachem & Wigwam Tonic, Grayish Moss Green, R–O46 .... 2350.00
Old Sachem & Wigwam Tonic, Medium Apricot Puce, 9 1/4 In., R–O46 .... 350.00
Oswego, Two Stars, 25 Cents, Golden Amber, Small, R–O93 .... 125.00
Pagliano Girolamo, Yellow Green, OP, 4 1/8 In. 70.00

Pepsin, R. W. Davis Drug Co., Yellow Green, 8 1/8 In., R–P44 .... 176.00
Peruvian, Monogram In Shield, Light Amber, Square, R–P65 .... 65.00
    BITTERS, PIG, see Bitters, Berkshire; Bitters, Suffolk
Pineapple, A. L. Lacraix, Aqua, Pat. 1870, 9 1/8 In., R–P101 .... 1045.00
Pineapple, A. L. Lacraix, Pat. Oct. 1st, 1870, Aqua, R–P101 .... 950.00
Pineapple, W. & Co., N. Y., Blue Green, OP, 8 3/8 In., R–P100 .... 2750.00
Pineapple, W. & Co., N. Y., Deep Amber, OP, 8 1/4 In., R–P100 ....*Illus* 198.00
Pineapple, W. & Co., N. Y., Golden Amber, 8 1/2 In., R–P100 .... 187.00 To 325.00
Pineapple, W. & Co., N. Y., Medium Green, 1855–1865, 8 1/2 In., R–P100 .... 1210.00
Pineapple, W. & Co., N. Y., Olive Green, IP, 8 3/8 In., R–P100 .... 1100.00
Pineapple, W. & Co., N. Y., Orange Amber, Double Collar, 9 In., R–P100 .... 193.00
Prickly Ash, Amber, 9 1/4 In., R–P141 .... 25.00
Prickly Ash, Yellow Amber, 9 1/4 In., R–P141 .... 30.00
Professor B. E. Mann's Oriental Stomach, Amber, 10 In., R–M29 .... 467.00
Prune Stomach & Liver, Amber, 9 1/2 In., R–P151 .... 65.00
Prussian, Medium Amber, 8 1/2 In., R–P152 .... 350.00
Punch Stomach & Liver, Amber 55.00
Quaker, Lenox, Mass., Aqua, Label, 9 In., R–Q1 .... 40.00
Reed's, Lady's Leg, Amber, Bubbly, 12 1/2 In., R–R28 .... 192.00
Reed's, Lady's Leg, Light Amber, Partial Amber, 12 1/2 In., R–R28 .... 325.00
Renault, Amber, Man With Hat, Label, Stopper, 3 3/4 In., R–R35 .... 6.50
Renes's Magic Oil, Label, Embossed 8.00
Rex's Kidney & Liver, Yellow Amber, 9 1/2 In., R–R43 .... 30.00
Rising Sun, Yellow Amber, 9 1/4 In., R–R66 .... 140.00
Roderic's Cough Balsam, Label, Embossed 15.00
Royal Pepsin Stomach, Amber, 8 7/8 In., R–R113 .... 75.00
Royal Pepsin Stomach, Red Amber, 6 3/8 In., R–R115 .... 40.00
Royce's Sherry Wine, Aqua, 8 In., R–R119 .... 62.00
Rush's, Amber, 8 7/8 In., R–R124 .... 45.00
Russ, San Domingo, Rectangular, 9 7/8 In., R–R126 .... 500.00
Russ, St. Domingo, Amber, 9 7/8 In., R–R125 .... 75.00
Russ, St. Domingo, Bright Yellowish Green, 9 7/8 In., R–R125 .... 450.00
Russ, St. Domingo, N. Y., Yellow Olive, Square, 10 In., R–R125 .... 495.00
Russian Imperial Tonic, Aqua, 9 In., R–R133 .... 725.00 To 800.00
S. B. Rothenberg, Milk Glass, Sole Agent U.S., R–B82 .... 180.00
S. O. Richardson's, South Reading, Mass., Aqua, OP, R–R57 .... 55.00 To 75.00
    BITTERS, S.T. DRAKE'S, see Bitters, Drake's Plantation
Sarracenia Life, Tucker, Mobile, Medium Amber, 9 1/4 In., R–S34 .... 175.00
Saxlehner's Hunyadi Janos Bitterquell, Green, 9 1/4 In., R–Pg. 420 .... 15.00
Sazerac Aromatic, Milk Glass, 10 1/4 In., R–S48 .... 798.00
Sazerac Aromatic, Milk Glass, Lady's Leg, 12 In., R–S47 .... 300.00
Schroeder's, Louisville, Ky., Lady's Leg, Amber, 11 7/8 In., R–S64 .... 358.00
Secrestat, Black Glass, 3–Piece Mold, Applied Seal, 12 In. 98.00
Simon's Centennial, Golden Amber, Applied Lip, 1860–1880, R–S110 .... 1210.00
Smiths Druid, Barrel, Medium Orange Amber, 9 1/2 In., R–S124 .... 880.00
Smyrna Stomach, Dayton, Oh., Lady's Leg, Amber, Square, R–S134 .... 200.00
Sol Frank's Panacea, Lighthouse, Amber, 10 1/4 In., R–F79 .... 495.00
Sol Frank's Panacea, Lighthouse, Dark Amber, 10 1/4 In., R–F79 .... 1430.00
Solomons' Invigorating, Brilliant Cobalt Blue, R–S140 .... 450.00
Star Kidney & Liver, Amber, R–S173 .... 25.00
Steketee's Blood Purifying, Amber, 9 5/8 In., R–S188 .... 110.00
Stoddard, Phelp's Arcanum, Worcester, Mass., Light Olive, Pontil 875.00
Strang Murray & Co., New York, Lady's Leg, Amber, 11 3/4 In. 72.00
Suffolk, Philbrook & Tucker, Pig, Amber, 10 In., R–S217 .... 425.00
Suffolk, Philbrook & Tucker, Pig, Golden Amber, 10 In., R–S217 .... 495.00
Swan, McFarland Bros., Meadville, Pa., Amber, 9 1/2 In., R–S229 .... 300.00
Swiss Stomach, Arnold Koch, Amber, 9 3/8 In., R–S242 .... 259.00 To 345.00
Thomas Hurley's Stomach, Yellow Amber, 10 1/2 In., R–H214 .... 650.00
Von Hopfs Curacoa, Chamberlain & Co., Amber, 7 1/2 In., R–V28 .... 50.00
Von Koster Stomach, Amber, Square, 8 7/8 In., R–V32 .... 132.00
W. L. Richardson's, So. Reading, Hinged Mold, Aqua, 7 1/2 In., R–R58 .... 85.0
Wait's Kidney & Liver, California, Amber, R–W6 .... 40.00
Walker's Cocktail, Lady's Leg, Amber, 11 In., R–W12 .... 578.00 To 625.00

Walker's Tonic, Lady's Leg, Deep Amber, 10 7/8 In., R–W13 .... 775.00
Warner's German Hop, Reading, Mich., Yellow Amber, 1880, 10 In., R–G2 .... 303.00
Warner's Safe Tonic, Rochester, N. Y., Amber, 9 1/2 In., R–W346 .... 33.00
Webb's Improved Stomach, Jackson, Mich., Amber, 9 In., R–W60 .... 132.00
West India Stomach, Red Amber, 8 1/2 In., R–W78 .... 45.00 To 65.00
Wheeler's Genuine, Aqua, Embossed, Oval, 9 1/4 In., R–W85 .... 95.00
White's Stomach, Medium Amber, 9 5/8 In., R–W101 .... 787.00
William Allen's Congress, Aqua, 10 In., R–A29 .... 110.00
William Allen's Congress, Cherry Puce, 10 In., R–A29 .... 1090.00
William Allen's Congress, Deep Aqua, Applied Mouth, 10 In., R–A29 .... 143.00
William Allen's Congress, Emerald, 10 In., R–A29 .... 525.00
William Allen's Congress, Pink Puce, 10 In., R–A29 .... 4550.00
Wm. Frank & Sons, Globular, IP, Similar To R–M121 .... 850.00
Wood's Tonic Wine, Cincinnati, Oh., Aqua, 9 1/2 In., R–W153 .... 165.00
Wryghte's Bitters, London, Deep Olive–Green, 6 In., R–W165 .... 385.00
Yerba Buena, Amber, 9 1/2 In., R–Y3 .... 55.00
Yochim Stomach, Amber, Label, 8 3/4 In., R–Y5 .... 100.00
Zingari, F. Rahter, Lady's Leg, Amber, 12 In., R–Z4 .... 110.00
Zingari, F. Rahter, Lady's Leg, Puce, 11 5/8 In., R–Z4 ....*Illus* 6710.00
Zu Zu, Amber, Applied Mouth, 8 7/8 In., R–Z9 .... 187.00
Zu Zu, Whiskey Neck, Amber 225.00

BLACK GLASS

Black glass is not really black. It is dark green or brown. In the seventeenth century, blown black glass demijohns were used to carry liquor overseas from Europe. They were usually heavy glass bottles that were made to withstand shipping. The kick–up bottom also helped deter breakage. Many types of bottles were made of very dark glass that appeared black. This was one of the most common colors for glass wine bottles of the eighteenth and early–nineteenth centuries.

BLACK GLASS, Bladder, Dark Olive Green, Free–Blown, 1720–1730, 9 3/4 In. 561.00
Bubbly, Reddish Amber, Crude, 6 In. 125.00
Case, Free–Blown, Rectangular, Seed Bubbles, 9 In. 172.00
Case, Olive Amber, Free–Blown, Pontil, Swirls & Seeds, 9 In. 156.00
Cylinder, Octagonal, Swirl of Bubbles Around Body, 10 1/8 In. 741.00
Dutch Kidney, Olive Green, String Lip, Pontil, 5 5/8 In. 625.00
Dutch Onion, Bright Green, Bubbles, 1730, 7 3/4 In. 66.00
Dutch Onion, Horse's Hoof Shape, Applied String Rim, 8 In. 98.00
Dutch Onion, Olive Amber, Applied String Rim, OP, 8 7/8 In. 130.00
Dutch Onion, Olive Amber, Wide Mouth, OP, 8 1/8 In. 750.00
Dutch Onion, Pontil Top of Kick–Up, 1700–1730, 7 1/2 In. 72.00
Dutch Onion, Pontil, 1720–1730, 7 3/8 In. 88.00
Dutch Onion, String Rim, Flared Lip, 1720–1730, 7 7/8 In. 100.00
Dutch Onion, Tooled Lip, String Rim, 1720–1730, 7 In. 73.00
English Mallet, Amber, Applied String Lip, Pontil, 8 3/4 In. 100.00
English Mallet, Deep Olive Amber, Double Pontil, 7 5/8 In. 230.00
English Mallet, Deep Olive Amber, Pontil, 7 7/8 In. 120.00
English Mallet, Olive Amber, Pontil, 6 3/4 In. 275.00
English Onion, Dark Olive Amber, Pontil, 5 1/2 In. 275.00
Flattened Octagonal, Bubbles, 1770, 9 1/8 In. 234.00
H. Ricketts & Co., Bristol, Cylinder, 3–Piece Mold, 11 In. 58.00
Lady's Leg, Porter, OP, 1770, 8 In. 98.00
Mallet, Neck Striations, Misshapen Form, 1740, 5 3/4 In. 309.00
Octagonal, Lady's Leg Neck, Pontil, 8 In. 127.00
Onion, Olive Amber, OP, String Lip, 6 3/8 In. 149.00
Porter, Olive Green, OP, Large Bubbles, 1770, 8 In. 95.00
Rose & Co. Ltd., Roses, Champagne Shape, 13 1/4 In. 73.00
Shaft & Globe, Free–Blown, Short Neck, 1680 .... 1148.00
Truffle, Free–Blown, Pontil End of Kick–Up, 11 1/2 In. 344.00
Truffle, Free–Blown, Pontil Top Deep Kick–Up, 8 1/2 In. 246.00
Truffle, Free–Blown, Pontil Top Deep Kick–Up, 11 1/2 In. 2542.00
Utility, Cylinder OP, Qt. 29.00
Whiskey, Pontil, Qt. 19.00

Blown, Gothic Design, Mold Blown, 13 In.   *Blown, Light Green, Tall Neck, Mold Blown, 12 In.*

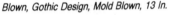

Whitney & Son, Shrewsbury, Flattened, 1860–1870, 7 1/2 In. 39.00
Wine, Cylinder, Pontil, Dip Mold 1800, Qt. 39.00
    BLACKING, see Household, Blacking

─────────────────────────────── **BLOWN** ───────────────────────────────

The American glass industry did not flourish until after the Revolution. Glass for windows and blown-glass bottles were the most rewarding products. The bottles were blown in large or small sizes to hold liquor. Many glassworks made blown and pattern-molded bottles. Midwestern factories favored twisted swirl designs. The colors ranged from green and aquamarine to dark olive green or amber. Sometimes blue or dark maroon bottles were blown. Some were made of such dark glass they are known as *black glass* bottles.

BLOWN, 16 Ribs, Swirled Right, Deep Amethyst, Flaring Lip, Pontil, 5 3/4 In. 1760.00
3-Piece Mold, Medium Green, 6 3/4 In. 2125.00
Amber, Flared Lip, 5 In. 35.00
Apothecary, Green, Olive Tone, Sheared Lip, OP, 11 1/16 In. 275.00
Aqua, OP, 1830, 9 In. 75.00
Bulbous, Olive Green, Short Neck, Pontil, 1820–1850, 4 1/2 In. 1045.00
Champagne, Deep Olive Green, OP, 10 1/2 In. 425.00
Chestnut, Aqua, Rolled Lip, 3 3/8 In. 77.00
Chestnut, Deep Burgundy, 3-Piece Mold, Handle, 1860–1890, 7 3/4 In. 28.00
Chestnut, Seedy Olive Green, Long Neck, 1780–1820, 6 5/8 In. 137.00
Club, 16 Ribs, Swirled, Aqua, 8 3/8 In. 190.00
Club, 16 Ribs, Swirled, Aqua, Midwestern, 8 1/4 In. 35.00
Club, Aqua, Midwestern, 9 In. 95.00
Club, Light Green, Midwestern, 8 In. 275.00
Cruet, Entwined Circle Pattern 10.00
Decanter, 3-Piece Mold, Clear, 3 Neck Rings, New England 165.00
Decanter, 3-Piece Mold, Olive Green, Keene 800.00
Decanter, 3-Piece Mold, Sunburst Stopper, 1825–1840 .... 110.00
Decanter, Bar, Pale Yellow Green, Stopper, Kent, Ohio 5000.00
Decanter, Bright Canary, 6 Concave Panels & Neck, 9 7/8 In. 743.00
Decanter, Stopper, 1850, 1/2 Pt. 55.00
Decanter, Stopper, 7 1/2 In. 75.00
Flattened Bladder Shape, Root Beer Amber, OP, Rolled Lip, 8 1/8 In. 187.00
Flytrap, Clear, Bulbous, Wide Neck Band, 1860–1880, 7 1/2 In. 82.00
Globular, Aqua, 9 1/2 In. 40.00
Globular, Olive Amber, Pontil, 12 1/2 In. 190.00
Globular, Olive Amber, Sloping Collared Mouth, Pontil, 9 3/8 In. 165.00

Gothic Design, Mold Blown, 13 In. ....*Illus*   65.00
Jar, 3–Piece Mold, Yellow Green, Stopper, Globular, Pontil, 7 3/8 In. 5500.00
Jar, Amethyst, Square Sides, Flared Rim, 8 In. 325.00
Jar, Blue Green, Straight Sides, Cylinder, Pontil, 7 In. 176.00
Jar, Food, Deep Olive Amber, Pontil, Tooled & Flared Lip, 12 7/8 In. 231.00
Jar, Food, Medium Olive Amber, Pontil, Tooled & Flared Lip, 10 In. 121.00
Jar, Green Aqua, Cylindrical, 1830–1850, 8 In. 187.00
Jar, Light Blue Green, Bubbly, Pontil, 1840–1850, 8 7/8 In. 286.00
Jar, Truffle, Deep Olive Amber, Pontil, 12 1/8 In. 160.00
Jar, Utility, Olive Amber, Rolled Lip, Pontil, 7 1/4 In. 450.00
Jar, Wide Mouth, Deep Aqua, Green Tint, Pontil, 6 5/8 In. 375.00
Jar, Wide Mouth, Deep Olive Yellow, Flared Lip, OP, 4 3/4 In. 235.00
Jar, Wide Mouth, Olive Green, Pontil, 8 1/8 In. 450.00
Jug, Aqua, Cylindrical, Long Conical Shoulder, Handle, 8 1/8 In. 120.00
Jug, Whiskey, Puce, Bulbous, Handle, OP, 8 In. 65.00
Light Green, Tall Neck, Mold Blown, 12 In. ....*Illus*   55.00
Ludlow, Brilliant Green, Yellow Tones, OP, 8 1/4 In. 140.00
Ludlow, Medium Olive Amber, Rolled Lip, OP, 10 1/2 In. 100.00
Ludlow, Olive Amber, 8 7/8 In. 35.00
Ludlow, Olive Amber, 9 1/2 In. 100.00
Ludlow, Olive, Applied Lip, 5 1/4 In. 100.00
Medium Olive Amber, Applied String Lip, OP, 4 In. 253.00
Olive Amber, Rolled Collared Mouth, Pontil, 11 3/4 In. 285.00
Pale Yellow Green, Flared Lip, 5 3/4 In. 55.00
Pear Shape, Smoky Aqua, Thin Flared Lip, Pontil, 3 7/8 In. 78.00
Pocket, Flattened Teardrop, Golden Amber, Pontil, 4 3/4 In. 110.00
Ribbed, Amethyst, Bulbous, Applied Handle, Late 1800s, 7 7/8 In. 45.00
Rolling Pin, Green Aqua, Applied & Tooled Knobs, 1840–1860, 14 In. 55.00
Swirled, 24 Ribs, Amber, 8 3/4 In. 200.00
Toilet Water, 3–Piece Mold, Boston, Cobalt, Stopper, 6 1/2 In. 577.00
Utility, Citron, Pontil, 5 7/8 In. 176.00
Utility, Flared Lip, 3 In. 9.00
Utility, Larson Type, Swirl, Deep Amethyst, Turned Lip, 5 3/4 In. 55.00
Utility, No Neck, Laid–On Ring Lip, 7 1/2 In. 350.00
Utility, Pale Green, Flared Lip, OP, 1800–1820, 3 In. 231.00
Utility, Squaw Vine, Label, Thin Flared Lip, 4 In. 25.00
Whimsy, Animal Shape, Cobalt Blue, 16 Ribs, 1840–1870, 7 x 9 1/4 In. 473.00
Whiskey, Dark Red Amber, Inverted Cone, Pontil, 10 1/4 In. 203.00
Wine Taster, Aqua, Rolled Lip, Pontil, 5 1/4 In. 50.00
Wine, Medium Olive Green, String Lip, OP, 8 5/8 In. 55.00
    BROOKS, see Ezra Brooks
    C.P.C., CALIFORNIA PERFUME COMPANY, see Avon
    CABIN STILL, see Old Fitzgerald
    CALABASH, see Flask

──────────────── **CANDY CONTAINER** ────────────────

The first figural glass candy containers date from the nineteenth century. They were made to hold candy and to be used later as toys for children. These containers were very popular after World War I. Small glass or papier–mache figural bottles held dime–store candy. Cars, trains, airplanes, animals, comic figures, telephones, and many other imaginative containers were made. The fad faded in the Depression years but returned in the 1940s. Today many of the same shapes hold modern candy in plastic bottles. The paper labels on the containers help a little with the dating. In the 1940s the words *Contents* or *Ingredients* were included on the labels. Earlier, this information was not necessary. Screw tops and corks were used. Some of the most popular early shapes have been reproduced in Taiwan and Hong Kong in recent years. A club with a newsletter is Candy Container Collectors of America, P.O. Box 8708, Canton, OH 44711–8708.

CANDY CONTAINER, Angel, Felt, Creazeoni, Florence, Italy, Box 125.00
Auto, Tin Roof & Wheels 825.00
Auto, With Tassels 175.00
Baby Sweeper, Metal Handle, Tin Wheels, Closure, Contents 605.00
Barney Google, Paint Touches, Closure 165.00

Battleship, Miniature	18.00
Billiken, Painted	120.00
Billikin	30.00
Boat, Titled Colorado, Red Tin Cover, Rigging	275.00
Boat, Victory Glass, Jeannette, Pa., Candy	35.00
Boot, Clear	10.00
Boot, Etched Rick I Love You Penny, Clear, 3 In.	20.00
Boy, On Drum, Original Paint	66.00
Brown Derby, Looks Like Suede, Oval Hat Box, 7 1/4 In.	125.00
Bulldog, Base Screw Closure, 4 1/4 In.	60.00
Bureau, Original Paint Traces On Closure	110.00
Bus, Greyhound	135.00
Bus, Jitney, Tin Wheels, Painted	330.00
Carpet Sweeper, Baby's, Repro Closure & Wheels	160.00
Charlie Chaplin, Closure, Contents	77.00
Chick, Dress, Shoes, Removable Head, Papier–Mache, Germany	168.00
Chick, In Shell Car, No Closure	183.00
Chicken, Crowing, Painted, Contents, Closure	242.00
Chicken, On Nest, J. H. Millstein Co.	25.00
Chicken, On Oblong Nest, 3 1/8 In.	20.00
Chicken, On Sagging Basket, 3 1/4 In.	25.00
Clock, Mantel, Scroll Work, Paper Face	120.00 To 145.00
Clock, Opaque White, Gold Painted Face, Closure	145.00
Colorado Boat, Replaced Top	150.00
Crystal Palace	175.00
Dirigible, Closure	143.00
Dog By Barrel, L. E. Smith	165.00
Dog, By Barrel	100.00 To 180.00
Dog, Hound Pup, Large Glass Hat, 3 1/2 In.	12.50
Dog, Hound Pup, Screw Top	13.00
Duck, Large Bill, Original Paint, Closure	137.00
Egg, Metal	10.00
Electric Coupe, Vail Brothers, 1913	35.00
Electric Iron, Play Toy Co.	22.50
Elephant, Swallow–Tail Suit	300.00
Fire Engine, Large Boiler, Bell Shaped Radiator	60.00
Football	40.00
Girl, Wearing Hat, Bisque Head & Limbs, Germany, 10 In.	750.00
Goblin Head	325.00
Gun, Amber	10.00
Gun, Clear Turning To Amethyst, Screw Cap, 7 3/4 In.	15.00
Gun, West Spec. Co., 5 3/4 In.	15.00
Horse With Cart, Glass	35.00
Hot Doggie, Blue, Closure	1045.00
House, All Glass, Tall Chimney	150.00
House, Painted, Closure	137.00
House, Red, Bisque Santa In Courtyard, Snowman, Blue Fence	129.00
Independence Hall, Tin Closure	66.00
Jack–O'–Lantern	185.00
Jack–O'–Lantern, Painted, No Top, Metal Bail	110.00
Kewpie, Standing, By Barrel, Painted, Coin Slot, Closure	160.00
Kiddie Kar	150.00
Lamp, Kerosene, Tin, Glass Globe, Tin Shade	100.00
Lantern, Barn, Large	32.50
Lantern, Pat. Dec. 20, '04, 3 3/4 In.	30.00
Lantern, Tin Top & Bottom, No Handle	18.00
Lantern, Twins On Anchor, 5 1/2 In.	15.00
Learned Fox, 5 1/4 In.	100.00
Liberty Bell, With Hanger	35.00
Liberty Motors Airplane, Painted, Complete	3850.00
Little Red Riding Hood, Tin, Lovel & Covel Co.	195.00
Locomotive No. 1028, Stough No. 5	5.00
Log Cabin, Village, Glass Liner, Bracket	550.00

Mailbox, All Glass	125.00
Man, On Motorcycle, Original Paint, Closure	577.00
Mounted Policeman, Original Closure, Some Paint Loss	3500.00
Naked Child, Sucking Thumb, Germany	48.00
Nurser, Doll's	15.00
Opera Glass, Opaque White, Tin Screw	165.00
Owl, Original Paint & Closure, 4 3/8 In.	100.00
Pencil, Baby Jumbo, Candy, 5 1/2 In.	15.00
Piano, Tin Closure	165.00
Pipe, Clear Glass, Wicker Bowl, Amber Mouthpiece	40.00
Powder Horn, Cap, Patent Applied On Base	50.00
Pretty Maid Washing Machine, Glass Tub, Metal Base	170.00
Pumpkin Head, Policeman, Repainted	400.00
Pumpkin Head, Witch, Repro Closure & Repaint	315.00
Pumpkin, Papier-Mache	25.00
Puss In Boots, High Top Shoe, Milk Glass, Gold Paint	25.00
Rabbit Family	604.00
Rabbit, Double, Dressed As Uncle Sam, 23 In.	3520.00
Rabbit, Laid Back Ears, Rectangular Base, 4 1/2 In.	60.00
Rabbit, Nibbling Carrot, 4 1/2 In.	35.00
Rabbit, Original Closure	700.00
Rabbit, Pushing Cart, Plastic, 1950s	24.00
Rabbit, Pushing Chick, In Shell Cart, Painted, Closure	465.00
Rabbit, Pushing Wheelbarrow, Original Closure, 4 1/8 In.	135.00
Rabbit, Running, On Log	300.00 To 603.00
Rabbit, Running, On Log, Gold, Painted, 4 x 3 1/8 In.	150.00
Rabbit, Running, On Log, No Closure	66.00
Rabbit, With Basket, Screw Top	75.00
Rabbit, With Collar, Screw Closure, 5 1/2 In.	60.00
Radio, No Closure	66.00
Radio, Original Paint, Closure	125.00
Radio, Touches of Paint, Closure	120.00
Rapid Fire Cannon, Glass Walls, Tin, Painted	275.00
Reindeer, Pewter Horse & Glass Eyes	395.00
Reindeer, Santa On Sled, Sitting On Flat Box	1475.00
Rocking Horse, With Clown, Blue Tinted, No Closure	100.00
Rocking Horse, With Clown, Clear, No Closure	93.00
Rooster, Crowing, Screw Closure, 5 1/8 In.	175.00
Rooster, On Box	59.00
Safe, Milk Glass, Penny Trust Co., Metal Slide Closure	125.00
Santa Claus, By Square Chimney	672.00
Santa Claus, In Banded Coat	669.00
Santa Claus, Red, White & Black Candy, Closure	176.00
Santa Claus, With Double Cuff, 4 1/2 In.	65.00
Silk Drawstring Top, Children Lithograph, Square, 1870	150.00
Skookum, By Tree Stump	681.00
Space Gun	25.00
Spark Plug, Clear ....*Illus*	100.00
Spirit of Goodwill, Complete	95.00
Spirit of St. Louis, Clear, Grapeville, Pa.	660.00
Suitcase, Clear	45.00
Suitcase, Milk Glass, 2 Piece	150.00
Suitcase, Opaque White, Dutch Girl Side, Metal Handle	198.00
Suitcase, Red, Holly Sprig	35.00
Tank, World War I	110.00
Telephone, Candlestick, Round Center	12.00
Telephone, Cardboard Shield, Cork, H. B. Waters, 5 1/8 In.	383.00
Telephone, Crosetti's Desk Type, Label, Contents	20.00
Telephone, Painted, Closure, Receiver, Contents	160.00
Telephone, Redlichs No. 1, Wooden Receiver, 9 3/8 In.	405.00
Telephone, Redlichs No. 4, Pewter Top, Label, 4 3/8 In.	25.00
Telephone, Victory Glass, Jeannette, Pa.	47.50
Telephone, West Co.	25.00

Telephone, Wooden Receiver 35.00
Toonerville, Depot Line, No Closure 385.00
Touring Car, Streamlined 18.00
Train, New York Central, Locomotive, Coal Car, 2 Cars 495.00
Uncle Sam's Hat, Original Paint, No Closure 33.00
Windmill, Candy Guaranteed, 5 3/4 In. 320.00
    CANNING JAR, see Fruit Jar
    CASE, see Gin

COCA–COLA

Coca–Cola was first served in 1886 in Atlanta, Georgia. John S. Pemberton, a pharmacist, originated the syrup and sold it to others. He was trying to make a patent medicine to aid those who suffered from nervousness, headaches, or stomach problems. At first the syrup was mixed with water; but in 1887, Willis E. Venable mixed it with carbonated water, and Coca–Cola was made. Pemberton sold his interest in the company to Venable and a local businessman, George S. Lowndes, in 1888. Later that year, Asa Griggs Candler, an owner of a pharmaceutical company, and some business friends became partners in Coca–Cola. A short time later they purchased the rest of the company. After some other transactions, Asa Candler became the sole owner of Coca–Cola for a grand total of $2,300. The first ad for Coca–Cola appeared in the *Atlanta Journal* on May 29, 1886. Since that time the drink has been sold in all parts of the world and in a variety of bottles. The *waisted* bottle was first used in 1916. Over 1,000 commemorative Coca–Cola bottles have been issued. The company advertised heavily, and bottles, trays, calendars, signs, toys, and lamps, as well as thousands of other items, can be found. See listings under Go–Withs at the back of the book.

Coca–Cola written in script was trademarked in 1893. *Coke* was registered in 1945. There is a national club with a newsletter, The Cola Clan, P.O. Box 49166, Atlanta, GA 30359–1166. You can learn from the national about local meetings. Price guides and books about the history of Coca–Cola are listed in the Bibliography. The Schmidt Coca–Cola Museum in Elizabethtown, Kentucky, is associated with Coca–Cola bottlers. The Coca–Cola Company Archives (One Coca–Cola Plaza, Atlanta, GA 30313) can answer questions about Coca–Cola memorabila. The World of Coca–Cola Museum on Martin Luther King Dr. in Atlanta has exhibits of interest to collectors.

COCA–COLA, Abbeville, S. C., 1915 .... 30.00
    Abbeville, S. C., 1923 .... 50.00
    Albermarle, N. C., Block Letters, Round Slug .... 15.00 To 20.00
    Aqua, Straight–Sided Crown Cap, Property of PCGW, 6 1/2 Oz. 40.00
    Baseball Winter Meetings, Hollywood, Fla., 1981 .... 110.00

Candy Container, Spark Plug, Clear

Berlin, N. H., Green, Straight Sides, Contents, 7 Oz.	75.00
Birmingham, Al., Green, Script On Lower Reverse & Obverse	20.00
Birmingham, Al., Script On Shoulders	20.00
Biscoe, N. C., Straight Sides	12.00
Bristol, Tenn., Aqua, Straight Sides, Dug	35.00
Bristol, Va., Orange Amber, Small Slug Plate	125.00
Canada, Aqua	16.00
Canada, Dark Green, Misprint	80.00
Canada, Light Green	32.00
Canton, Oh., Amber	35.00
CC Soda, Biscoe, N. C. Misspelled, Property of Alabama Misprint	30.00
Chase City, Va., Block Letters Base, Aqua, Straight Sides	9.00
Chattanooga, Tenn., Hutchinson	55.00
Chester, S. C., Script At Shoulder, Straight Sides	20.00
Christmas, Cameron, Wisconsin	30.00
Christmas, Des Moines, Iowa	20.00
Christmas, Green, 1923	18.50
Christmas, Texarkana, Tex.	15.00
Christmas, Westminster, Md., 6 Oz.	8.00
Clemson, National Champions, 1981	3.00
Cleveland, Oh., Amber	40.00
Clifton Forge, Ice & Bottling Works, Va., Straight Sides	25.00
Columbus, Oh., Bottling Co., Amber	25.00
Concord, N. C., Script At Shoulder, Light Green, Straight Sides	20.00
Crimson Tide, Paul "Bear" Bryant, 9 1/2 In. ....*Illus*	3.00
Cumberland, Md., Straight Sides	8.00
Durham, N. C., Deep Aqua, Coke In Script, Slug Plate	25.00
Durham, N. C., Script At Shoulder & Base, Aqua .... 15.00 To 20.00	
Eddie Robinson, Winningest Coach, Basketball, 1984 ....*Illus*	8.00
Fayetteville, N. C., Hutchinson	75.00
Fresno, Calif., Aqua, 1915	15.00
Frisco City, Ala., Dark Green, Straight Sides	14.00
Fulmer's Beverages, 18 Panels, Alliance, Oh., ABM, 7 3/4 In.	15.00
Gilley's, Pasadena, Texas, Feb. 1984, 10 Oz. ....*Illus*	15.00
Greek, Painted Label	1.50
Greensboro, N. C., Script In Middle, Green, Straight Sides	20.00
Hartsville, S. C.	350.00
High Point, N. C., Script At Shoulder & Base, Straight Sides	25.00
High Point, N. C., Smoky, Straight Sides	12.00
Honolulu, Trademark, U.S. Patent Office	25.00

Coca–Cola, Johnny Lee,
Steak Fry & Street Dance, 1986
Coca–Cola, Ty Cobb, The Georgia Peach,
1983
Coca–Cola, Eddie Robinson,
Winningest Coach, Basketball, 1984

Coca–Cola, Unforgettable Forties, 1984,
10 Oz.
Coca–Cola, Jimmy Carter,
39th President of U.S., 10 Oz.
Coca–Cola, Gilley's, Pasadena, Texas,
Feb.1984, 10 Oz.

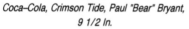

Coca–Cola, Crimson Tide, Paul "Bear" Bryant, 9 1/2 In.

Coca–Cola, Seltzer, Big Chief, Stockton, Calif., 12 In.

Huntington, W. Va., Script In Middle, Oval, Straight Sides 20.00
Huntsville, Ala., Amber, Script Lower Obverse 100.00
Hygeia Bottling Works, Pensacola, Fla., Straight Sides 25.00
Jackson, Tenn., Amber, Circle Arrow, BIMAL 100.00
Jimmy Carter, 39th President of U.S., 10 Oz. ....*Illus* 85.00
Johnny Lee, Steak Fry & Street Dance, 1986 ....*Illus* 35.00
Kenford, N. C., Straight Sides 25.00
Knoxville, Tenn., Amber, Script Lower Obverse 30.00
Lexington, Ky., Amber .... 35.00 To 40.00
Macon, Ga., Deep Aqua, Coke In Script, Slug Plate 25.00
Macon, Ga., Reversed N & Script Front 20.00
Macon, Ga., Script In Middle & Base, Straight Sides 22.00
Majestic Bottling Co., Missoula, Ribbed, Clear, ABM, 8 3/4 In. 8.00
Memphis, Tenn., Arrows, Straight Sides, Amber 22.00
Newark, Oh., Bottling Co., Aqua 15.00
No Returns, Clear 2.00
Olympics, Los Angeles, Sam The Eagle, 1984 .... 4.00
Pennsboro, W. Va., Honeycomb Design, Green, Straight Sides 12.00
Philadelphia, Pa., Hutchinson 65.00
Pittsburgh, Pa., Amber, Contents, 6 1/2 Oz. 30.00
Pittsburgh, Pa., Hutchinson 55.00
Portland, Me., Bottling Co., Oval Slug Plate Front, ABM 10.00
Prince of Wales, Lady Diana, Wedding, July 29, 1981, England 35.00
Richmond, Va., Hutchinson 40.00
Roanoke, Va., Hutchinson 50.00
Rocky Mount, N. C., Straight Sides 8.00
Rome, Ga., Script Lower Obverse 20.00
Royal Palm Soda, Bulged Shoulder, Pale Green, ABM, Cylinder 12.00
Seltzer, Big Chief, Stockton, Calif., 12 In. ....*Illus* 35.00
Seltzer, Mt. Lassen Siphon Water, Susanville, Calif. .... 120.00 To 129.00
Seltzer, Susanville, Calif. 129.00
Siler City, N. C., Soda Water, Light Green, Emblem, Stars 20.00
Soda Water, Jamestown, N. Y., 6 Stars Shoulder, Square, 7 3/4 In. 10.00
Springfield, Oh., Hutchinson 45.00
Syrup Jug, 1 Gal. 15.00
Tallahassee, Fla., Bottling Co., Cylinder, ABM, 7 3/4 In. 10.00
Tupelo, Miss., Amber, 1915–1916 .... 250.00 To 395.00
Ty Cobb, The Georgia Peach, 1983 ....*Illus* 250.00
Unforgettable Forties, 1984, 10 Oz. ....*Illus* 35.00
University of N. C. Tarheels, Nat. Basketball Champions, 1982 .... 4.00

Wal–Mart 25th Anniversary, 1962–1987, Montgomery, Ala. 15.00
Warren, Oh., CCB Co., Inc., 4 Stars Shoulder, ABM, 6 1/2 Oz. 12.00
Washington, N. C., Hutchinson 55.00
Wilmington, N. C., Hutchinson 75.00
Winston, N. C., Script At Shoulder, Green, Straight Sides 70.00
York, Pa., Bottling Works, Aqua, ABM, 7 5/8 In. 12.00

———————————— COLLECTORS ART ————————————

Collectors Art bottles are made of hand–painted porcelain. The bird series was made in the 1970s. The first issued was the bluebird, then the meadowlark, canary, hummingbird, parakeet, and cardinal. Only 12 birds were issued each year and each was limited to 1,200 pieces. The later editions included bulls (1975), dogs, other animals, and a 1971 Corvette Stingray.

COLLECTORS ART, Afghan Hound, 1975, Miniature 20.00
Basset Hound, 1977, Miniature 22.00
Black Angus, 1975, Miniature 14.00
Blue Bird, 1971, Miniature ....*Illus* 25.00
Blue Jay, 1972, Miniature .... 20.00 To 26.00
Brahma Bull, 1973 .... 32.00 To 35.00
Brahma Bull, 1975, Miniature 20.00
Bunting, 1973, Miniature .... 17.00 To 20.00
Canary, 1971, Miniature ....*Illus* 27.00
Cardinal, 1971, Miniature .... 24.00 To 30.00
Charolais Bull, 1974 .... 23.00
Charolais Bull, 1975, Miniature 20.00
Chipmunks, 1972, Miniature 17.00
Collie, 1976, Miniature .... 20.00 To 21.00
Corvette Stingray, 1971 .... 19.00
Corvette, Red, Plain Tires, 1971 .... 20.00
Dachshund, 1977, Miniature 22.00
Dalmatian, 1976, Miniature 27.00
Doberman, Black, 1976, Miniature 23.00
Goldfinch, 1972, Miniature .... 20.00 To 21.00
Hereford, 1972 .... 38.00
Hereford, 1975, Miniature .... 22.00 To 24.00
Hummingbird, 1971, Miniature .... 20.00 To 24.00
Irish Setter, 1976, Miniature 20.00
Koala, 1972, Miniature .... 26.00 To 33.00
Meadowlark, 1971, Miniature ....*Illus* 26.00
Mexican Fighting Bull, 1975, Miniature .... 20.00 To 24.00
Oriole, 1972, Miniature .... 20.00 To 22.00
Parakeet, 1971, Miniature .... 21.00 To 24.00

Collectors Art, Blue Bird,   *Collectors Art, Meadowlark,*   *Collectors Art, Canary,*
1971, Miniature   *1971, Miniature*   *1971, Miniature*

Pointer, 1976, Miniature	18.00
Poodle, Black, 1976, Miniature	19.00
Poodle, White, 1976, Miniature	19.00
Rabbits, 1972, Miniature	26.00 To 45.00
Raccoons, 1973, Miniature	25.00 To 26.00
Robin, 1972, Miniature	19.00 To 20.00
Schnauzer, 1976, Miniature	20.00
Shepherd, Black, 1976, Miniature	28.00
Shepherd, Brown, 1976, Miniature	15.00
Skunks, 1972, Miniature	20.00 To 26.00
St. Bernard, 1977, Miniature	20.00
Texas Longhorn, 1974	33.00
Texas Longhorn, 1975, Miniature	21.00 To 23.00

COLOGNE

Our ancestors did not bathe very often and probably did not smell very good. It is no wonder that the perfume and cologne business thrived in earlier centuries. Perfume is a liquid mixture with alcohol. Cologne is a similar mixture but with more alcohol, so the odor is not as strong or as lasting. Scent was also popular. It was a perfume with some ammonia in the mixture so it could be used to revive someone who felt faint. The mixture dictated the type and size of bottle. Scent bottles usually had screw tops to keep the ammonia smell from escaping. Because its odor did not last as long as that of perfume, cologne was used more often and was sold in larger bottles. Cologne became popular in the United States about 1830; the Boston and Sandwich Glass Company of Sandwich, Massachusetts, was making cologne bottles at that time. Since cologne bottles were usually put on display, they were made with fancy shapes, brightly colored glass, or elaborate labels. Blown figural and scroll bottles were favored. The best-known cologne bottle is the 1880 Charlie Ross bottle. It has the embossed face of Charlie, a famous kidnap victim—a strange shape to choose for a cologne bottle! Today the name *perfume* is sometimes used incorrectly as a generic term meaning both cologne and perfume. Old and new bottles for cologne, perfume, and scents are collected.

COLOGNE, see also Perfume; Scent

COLOGNE, Amethyst, Swirled Left, Dark & Light, 16 Ribs, 5 3/4 In.	715.00
Aqua, 12–Sided, OP, Rolled Lip, 8 7/8 In.	66.00
Aqua, Fancy, OP, 5 5/8 In.	50.00
Ball Shape, Hand Painted Morning Glories, Porcelain, Footed	286.00
Barrel, Clear, OP, Miniature	100.00
Basket Shape, Aqua, Label	12.00
Bell Shape, Cobalt Blue, Gold Leaf Design, Stopper, 7 1/2 In.	110.00
Blown, Medium Apple Green, Cut Stopper, Hexagonal, 5 1/2 In.	660.00
Brilliant Cobalt Blue, 3–Piece Mold, Pontil, 6 In.	187.00
Bust of Kossuth, Aqua, OP, 5 3/4 In.	231.00
Canteen, Figural, Army Green & Navy Blue, Encased In Plaster, Pair	44.00
Clear, 3–Piece Mold, Blown Stopper, OP, 5 1/4 In.	33.00
Clear, 3–Piece Mold, OP, Type 4, 5 7/8 In.	38.50
Clear, Label Under Glass, 1880–1910, 10 In.	495.00
Cobalt Blue, 3–Piece Mold, Stopper, Type 4, 5 3/8 In.	182.00
Cobalt Blue, Flared Lip, 12–Sided, 6 1/8 In.	72.00
Cobalt Blue, Sheared & Flared Lip, 6 In.	171.00
Corset Waist, Clear, Octagonal, 5 5/8 In.	121.00
Corset Waist, Lavender Blue, Octagonal, 5 7/8 In.	688.00
Cut Glass, Fluted Base & Neck, Etched Word Cologne, 8 5/8 In.	83.00
Cut Glass, Recliner, Starburst, Smelling Salts, Screw Cap, 7 In.	40.00
Dancing Indian Maidens, Double, Aqua, Triangular, OP	165.00
Dancing Indians, Aqua, OP, Rolled Lip, 4 7/8 In.	132.00
Deep Cobalt Blue, 3–Piece Mold, Blown, 5 1/2 In.	132.00
Deep Purple, 3–Piece Mold, Blown, Boston & Sandwich, 1825–1840	210.00
Deep Sapphire Blue, 3–Piece Mold, 1825–1840, 6 In.	165.00
Diamond Pattern, Amethyst, Stopper, Square, 1880–1900, 4 In.	100.00
Diamond Points, Deep Amethyst, Square, 1860–1880, 6 3/8 In.	600.00
Dorothy Perkins, Lilac, 5 1/4 In.	15.00
Flared & Rolled Lip, 12–Sided, Medium Sapphire Blue, 7 3/8 In.	154.00

Flared & Tooled Lip, 12–Sided, Teal, 5 1/2 In.	148.00
Flared Lip, Amethyst, Center Rib, Square, 5 1/2 In.	231.00
Flared Lip, Clear, Fancy, OP, 5 1/2 In.	60.00
Flared Lip, Clear, Fancy, Pontil, 1830–1850, 4 1/4 In.	88.00
Flared Lip, Clear, Fancy, Pontil, 9 3/8 In.	88.00
Flared Lip, Deep Cobalt Blue, OP, 4 In.	798.00
Floral Design, America, c.1870	825.00
Fountain Shape, Clear, Flared Mouth, Pontil, 4 1/2 In.	121.00
Geometric, Clear, Concave Sides	15.00
Grumpy, From Snow White & 7 Dwarfs, Figural, Russia, Contents	40.00
Houbigant, Quelques Fleurs, Clear, Gold French Courtesans, Stopper	187.00
Hourglass, Sapphire, Pontil, 1860–1870, Hexagonal, 4 5/8 In.	990.00
Imperial, Hobnail, Pair	20.00
Jug, Old Holland Cologne, Stoneware, Brown Shoulders, Miniature	25.00
Limoges, Porcelain, Hand Painted Bluebirds, Roses, Stopper	154.00
Lucien Lelong, Solid, 4 1/2 In.	15.00
Medium Cobalt Blue, OP, Rolled Lip, 5 1/2 In.	660.00
Milk Glass, Beaded Ribbing, Round, 8 In.	60.00
Milk Glass, Blue, Flared Lip, Pontil, 5 In.	22.00
Milk Glass, Blue, Tooled Lip, Pontil, 10 7/8 In.	94.00
Milk Glass, Blue, Waisted, Enameled Design, OP, 6 3/4 In.	55.00
Milk Glass, Cobalt Blue Overlay, Flared Lip, 7 3/4 In.	220.00
Milk Glass, Leaves & Lion's Heads, No Stopper, 6 1/2 In.	32.00
Milk Glass, Vertical Ribbing, Swirling Stars Band, 7 1/2 In.	88.00
Molded, Tam O'Shanter Stopper, Pontil, New England, 1825–1840, 6 In.	105.00
Monument, D. Mitchell, Amethyst, Flared Lip, 6 1/2 In.	1008.00
Monument, Deep Cobalt Blue, Flared Lip, 6 3/8 In.	1265.00
Monument, Emerald, Turquoise Tint, New England, 1860–1880, 12 In.	1650.00
Monument, Opalescent Gray Blue, Pontil, 4 1/2 In.	467.00
Monument, Opalescent, Blown Stopper, Pontil, 4 1/2 In.	523.00
Muted Diamond, 12–Piece Mold Amethyst, Stiegel–Type, 4 3/4 In.	176.00
Opalescent, Gold Paint, Flared Lip, Pontil, 5 1/2 In.	38.50
Paneled, 12–Sided, Deep Amethyst, New England, 1860–1880, 7 3/8 In.	275.00
Paneled, 12–Sided, Deep Emerald, New England, 1860–1880, 4 3/4 In.	440.00
Paneled, 12–Sided, Light Peacock Opaque Blue, 7 3/8 In.	620.00
Paneled, 12–Sided, Medium Amethyst, Wavy, Wide Mouth, 7 1/4 In.	197.00
Pitkin Type, Ribs Swirled To Right, Amethyst, Pontil, 6 In.	165.00
Ricksecker Sweet Clover, Milk Glass, Gold Words, 8 1/2 In.	176.00
Rolled Lip, 12–Sided, Light Teal, 5 In.	77.00
Rolled Lip, 12–Sided, Teal, 6 3/8 In.	94.00
Rue De La Cloche, Small	3.50
Sandwich, Medium Amethyst, Thumbprint Pattern, Square, 5 3/4 In.	550.00
Sandwich, Rib Beaded, Fiery Opalescent, 5 1/2 In.	121.00
Sloping Shoulders, 12–Sided, Amethyst, Tooled Lip, 4 7/8 In.	99.00
Sloping Shoulders, 12–Sided, Cobalt Blue, 6 1/4 In.	770.00
Sloping Shoulders, 12–Sided, Teal, Flared & Rolled Lip, 4 3/4 In.	198.00
Tappan, Germany, Small	3.50
Tooled Lip, 12–Sided, Deep Cobalt Blue, 4 3/4 In.	121.00
Tooled Lip, 12–Sided, Medium Teal, Smooth Base, 1860–1880, 5 1/2 In.	165.00
Tosca, Clear, Molded Scalloped Stopper	22.00
Vantine, Buddha, 6 3/4 In.	70.00
Vigny, Heure Intime, Clear, Quilted Design, Stopper	28.00
Yardley, 5 1/2 In.	10.00

CORDIAL

Cordials are liqueurs that are usually made to be drunk at the end of the meal. They consist of pure alcohol or cognac, plus flavors from fruits, herbs, flowers, or roots. A cordial may also be a medicinal drink. Curacao is a cordial containing orange peel, Creme de Menthe contains mint, Triple Sec has orange and cognac, and Kummel has coriander and caraway seeds.

CORDIAL, Allover Roses, Black Olive, Flattened Form, Squatty, 9 3/8 In.	66.00
Caley, Vivid Green, Cone, Embossed Large Crown, 10 1/2 In.	44.00

Clark's California Cherry Cordial, Amber, Rectangular, 8 In.	25.00
Cloud's, Medium Amber, Rectangular, Tapered Body, 10 1/8 In.	66.00
Crown Cordial & Extract Co., New York, Clear, 1/2 Gal.	10.00
Danciger's Cherry Flavor, Men Harvesting Label, 1915, Qt.	19.00
Dr. Ira Warren's Pulmonic Cherry Cordial, Aqua, Rectangular, 7 In.	450.00
Dr. RX, Cascara Cordial, Amber, Bimal, Label, 9 In.	10.00
Enameled Bird & Floral Scene, Rectangular, Bohemia, 6 1/2 In.	360.00
Enameled Floral, Multicolored, Opaque White, Bohemia, 4 3/4 In.	220.00
Enameled Floral, Pewter Collar, Pontil, Bohemia, Dated 1772, 5 In.	275.00
Enameled Floral, Pewter Collar, Rectangular, Bohemia, 5 1/2 In.	148.00
Enameled Floral, Pewter Threads, Mid–Late 18th Century, 5 5/8 In.	200.00
Enameled Floral, Pontil, Mid–18th Century, 5 1/4 In.	195.00
Ginger Cordial D. M., Reading, Pa., Label, BIMAL, 1880–1890, Qt.	69.00
L. Rose & Co., Black Green, Thin Neck, Vine Embossed, 12 In.	61.00
Mrs. E. Kidder's Dysentery Cordial, Aqua, OP, 7 1/2 In.	150.00
Mrs. E. Kidder's Dysentery Cordial, Boston, Aqua, OP, 6 1/2 In.	66.00
Rowat & Co., Aqua, Long Tapering Neck, Stopper, 14 In.	13.00
T. J. Dunbar Schiedam Cordial Schnapps, Olive, Label	125.00
T. J. Dunbar Schiedam Cordial Schnapps, Teal Blue, Label	125.00
Wishart's Pine Tree, Green, 8 In.	79.00
Wishart's Trade, Pine Tree, Tar Cordial, Amber, Square	35.00 To 59.00

——————————————— COSMETIC ———————————————

Cosmetics of all kinds have been packaged in bottles. Hair restorer, hair dye, creams, rosewater, and many other product bottles can be found. The early bottles often had paper labels, which add to their value.

COSMETIC, Agonsair For Children's Hair, Aqua, 6 1/2 In.	12.00
Barker's Chevoux Tonique For The Hair	40.00
Barry Trico Hair	16.00
Batchelor's Liquid No. 2 Hair Dye, Aqua, OP	15.00
Big 4 Dressing Pomade, Straightener, Label, 1930s, 2 1/2 In.	7.00
Bogle's Electric No. 2 Hair Dye, Variant, Overall Stain, Aqua, OP	30.00
Buckingham Whisker Dye, BIMAL, 4 7/8 In.	8.00
Burger's Hair Restorative, N. Y., Clambroth, 6 3/4 In.	1155.00
Burger's Hair Restorative, N. Y., Red Opalescent, 7 In.	1100.00 To 1500.00
Catalan Hair Renewer, Cobalt Blue, Tooled Lip, Hexagonal, 6 In.	100.00
Chew's No. 1 Hair Dye, Aqua, OP	35.00
Circassian Hair Oil, A. L. Scovill, Rectangular, 5 3/4 In.	35.00
Clock's Excelsior Hair Restorer, Aqua, Rectangular, 7 1/4 In.	15.00
D. Damschinsky's Liquid Hair Dye, Small	3.50
Danderine For The Hair, ABM, 4 1/2 In.	4.00
Davis's Hyperion For The Hair, Haze	45.00
DeWitt's Fragrant Hair Dressing, Label, 25 Cents, 6 1/2 In.	10.00
Dr. D. Jayne's Hair Tonic, Philadelphia, Aqua, Oval, Pontil	45.00
Dr. Fahrney's Health Restorer, Hagerstown, Md., Amber, 7 1/4 In.	17.00
Ebony Black Hair Dye, Golden Peacock, Paris, Tn., 1940s, 3 In.	4.00
Eureka, Hair Restorative, P. J. Reilly, San Francisco, Aqua, 7 In.	750.00
Eureka, Infallible Hair Restorative, Clear, 1860, Oval, 6 In.	30.00
George's No. 1 Hair Dye, Clear, OP, Large	45.00
Gilman's No. 1 Hair Dye, Clear, OP	35.00
Gilman's No. 2 Hair Dye, Aqua, OP	30.00
Glover's Royal Scalp & Mange Remedy, Amber	15.00
Hagon's Cleanser For Children's Hair, Aqua, 6 1/2 In.	14.00
Hall's Hair Renewer, Peacock Blue, Tooled Top, Box, 7 1/4 In.	143.00
Hall's Hair Renewer, Peacock, No Stopper, Rectangular, 6 3/8 In.	25.00
Harrison's Columbian Hair Dye, Clear	25.00
Harrison's Hair Color Restorer, Reading, Amber, 6 1/2 In.	18.00
Hays's Hair Health, Amber, BIMAL, 6 1/2 In.	6.00
Houbigant–Chardin, Paris Et Londres, Amethyst, 1870, 5 3/4 In.	44.00
I. Terry's Hair Dye, Cohoes, N. Y., No. 2, Aqua, OP, 3 In.	18.00
J. M. Curtis, Cure For Baldness, Aqua, Whittled, 7 3/4 In.	303.00
Jar, Golden Peacock Cream Tonic, Hair, Milk Glass, 2 3/8 In.	8.00

Cosmetic, LeVarn's Golden Wash Shampoo,
Mettowee Toilet, 8 In.

Cosmetic, Penslar's Hair Tonic, Green,
Paper Label, Woman's Picture

Jar, Golden Peacock Vanishing Cream, Milk Glass, 1930s, 2 3/8 In. 6.00
Jerome's Hair Color Restorer, Amethyst, Flared Lip, 6 1/4 In. 1320.00
Jerome's Hair Color Restorer, Cobalt Blue, Flared Lip, 6 3/8 In. 413.00
John H. Woodbury Dermatological Institute, Man's Face, 7 In. 36.00
Joslyn's Kalothricos, Hair, Aqua, OP 55.00
L. S. Bliss, Unrivaled Hair Tonic, Aqua, OP, 6 7/8 In. 110.00
LaRoque's Oxygenated Cream of Lilies, For Hair, Aqua, Blown, Label 28.00
LeVarn's Golden Wash Shampoo, Mettowee Toilet, 8 In. ....*Illus* 120.00
LeVarn's Hair Tonic & Dandruff Cure, Granville, N. Y., 7 1/2 In. 66.00
Lilac After Shave, Parfum Int., Chicago, Ill., 6 1/2 In. 10.00
Louden & Co., Hair Tonic, Clear, Rolled Lip 40.00
Lyon's Kathairon, OP 15.00
Lyon's Powder, B & P, Light Amber, Embossed 35.00
Mrs. Allen's World Hair Balsam, Aqua, OP, 6 3/4 In. 77.00
Mrs. Allen's World Hair Restorer, Dark Amethyst, 7 1/8 In. 253.00
Mrs. Allen's World Hair Restorer, Golden Amber, 7 In. 20.00
Mrs. Allen's World Hair Restorer, Honey Amber .... 22.00 To 25.00
Nadinola Cream Complexion Beautifier, Nat'l. Toilet, Milk Glass 25.00
Newbro's Herpicide, Kills The Dandruff Germ, Lady's Leg, 7 In. 18.00
Odell Hair Trainer, Boy's Head Label, 1 Pt., 9 1/4 In. 15.00
Oldrige's Balm of Columbia Restoring Hair, Crude, 5 1/2 In. 150.00
Owl Drug Co., Quinine Hair Tonic, 2 Wing, Clear, Stopper, 6 In. 61.00
Parker's Hair Balsam, Amber, 7 1/2 In. 4.00
Penslar's Hair Tonic, Green, Paper Label, Woman's Picture .... *Illus* 65.00
Pepsodent Antiseptic, Lever Bros., Box, 1 3/4 x 3 3/4 In. 5.00
Pepunek's Hair-O-Dress, Victory Label, Muncie, Ind., 6 In. 12.00
Perry's Hungarian Balm For Hair, Aqua, OP, 5 3/4 In. 105.00
Phalon's Magic Hair Dye, No. 1, Aqua, OP, Large 35.00
Pierce's Rosetta Hair Tonic, Boston, Mass., Aqua, OP 145.00
Pond's Extract, Aqua, OP, 4 In. 35.00
Pond's Extract, Rectangular, 4 1/2 In. 30.00
Pothe Hair Dye, Boston, Fancy, Aqua, OP 35.00
Professor Wood's Hair Restorative, Rectangular, 7 1/4 In. 45.00
Roehl's Reliable Hair Restorer, Amber, 7 7/8 In. 22.00
Rowland's Macassar Oil, For Hair, Hatton, London, Clear, OP 63.00

Rubifoam For The Teeth, Clear, BIMAL, 4 In. 3.00
St. Clair's Hair Lotion, Deep Cobalt Blue, Glob Top, 7 1/4 In. 125.00
Stephan's Y-5 Hair Groom, Sold Only By Barbers, 9 1/2 In. 15.00
Storr's Chemical Hair Invigorator, Aqua, OP, 5 3/4 In. .... 85.00 To 98.00
Teel Liquid Dentifrice, Proctor & Gamble, 1945, Box, 2 x 4 In. 15.00
Unrivaled Hair Tonic, L. S. Bliss, Mass., Aqua, OP, 6 7/8 In. 125.00
Velno's Magic Hair Oil, Aqua, Flared Lip 25.00
W. C. Montgomery's Hair Restorer, Black Amethyst, 7 1/2 In. 200.00
Wilson's Hair Colorer, Deep Aqua 50.00

CURE

Collectors have their own interests and a large group of bottle collectors seek medicine bottles with the word *cure* embossed on the glass or printed on the label. A cure bottle is not a *remedy bottle*. The word *cure* was originally used for a medicine that treated many diseases. A *specific* was made for only one disease. The Pure Food and Drug Act of 1906 made label changes mandatory and the use of the word *cure* was no longer permitted.

CURE, see also Medicine; Bitters
CURE, Alexander's Sure Cure, Contents, Label 42.00
   Arctic Frost Bite Cure, Aqua, Label, BIMAL, 2 1/2 In. 12.00
   B. Catarrh Cure, Smith Bros., Fresno, Calif., Cylindrical, Embossed 35.00
   B. W. Hair & Son Asthma Cure, London, Amber, 6 1/2 In. 26.00
   Baker's Vegetable Blood & Liver Cure, Greenville, Tenn., Amber, 9 In. 385.00
   Bauer's Cough Cure, Aqua, BIMAL, Sample 7.00
   Bauer's Imperial Mange Cure, Amber, Rectangular, 7 In. 8.50
   Bennett's Magic Cure, Deep Cobalt Blue, 5 1/4 In. 400.00
   Brown's Blood Cure, Philadelphia, Bright Yellow Green, 6 1/4 In. 231.00
   Calberts Derby Cure, Aqua, Embossed 13.00
   Chaul-Moo-Gra, East Indian Cure 25.00
   Craig's Kidney & Liver Cure Company, Amber, Applied Mouth, 9 1/2 In. 55.00
   Cramer's Cough Cure, Aqua, BIM, 6 In. 6.00
   Cramer's Cure, Melvin & Badger Co., Boston, Mass., Spout, Miniature 5.00
   Cramer's Kidney Cure, Albany, N. Y., Sample, Aqua, 4 1/4 In. 9.00
   Cramer's Kidney Cure, Aqua, Free Sample, 4 1/4 In. 16.00
   Da Costa Radical Cure, Dr. Morris' Syrup of Tar, 3 Indented Panels 35.00

Cure, Foley's Kidney Cure, Chicago, Ill.,
Paper Label, 9 1/4 In.

Dixon's Dystemper Cure, Elkhart, Ind., Contents, Clear, 5 In.	27.00
Dr. Craig's Cough & Consumption Cure, Orange Amber, 8 In.	625.00
Dr. D. M. Bye's Combination Oil Cure, Indianapolis, Cork, 4 1/4 In.	22.00
Dr. Dewitt's Liver Blood & Kidney Cure, Baltimore, Amber, 8 3/4 In.	225.00
Dr. Kaufmann's Angelic Rheumatism Cure	25.00
Dr. Kilmer's Swamp Root Kidney Cure, Sample, 3 In.	7.00
Dr. L. E. Keeley's Double Chloride of Gold Cure, Drunkenness, Spout	75.00
Dr. L. E. Keeley's Gold Cure For Drunkenness, 1880–1890, 5 1/2 In.	197.00
Dr. M. M. Fenner's Kidney & Backache Cure, Amber	20.00
Dr. Parker's Cough Cure	10.00
F. F. Ganter's Magic Chicken Cholera Cure, Glasgo, Ken., Amber, 6 Oz.	35.00
Faith Whitcomb's Balsam Cures Coughs, Colds, Consumption, Aqua, 9 In.	150.00
Farzier's Dystemper Cure, Nappanee, Ind.	8.00
Fenner's Kidney & Backache Cure, Label	45.00
Foley's Kidney & Bladder Cure, Amber	25.00
Foley's Kidney Cure, Chicago, Ill., Paper Label, 9 1/4 In. ....*Illus*	45.00
Great Dr. Kilmer's Swamp Root Kidney, Liver, Bladder Cure Specific	8.00
H. H. Warner & Co., Tippecanoe, Medium Amber	75.00
Hall's Catarrh Cure, Aqua, Round, 4 3/4 In.	8.00
Hart's Swedish Asthma Cure, Buffalo, Amber	15.00
Hicking's Syrup of Tamarinds, Cures Coughs & Colds, Aqua, 5 1/2 In.	45.00
Himalaya Kola Compound Cure For Asthma, Amber, Smooth Base	15.00
Hires Cough Cure, Aqua, Ring Top	15.00
J. Stanford Gregory, Instant Cure of Pain, N. Y., Aqua, OP, 4 5/8 In.	88.00
Jackson's Antizyme Fever Cure, Aqua, Small	9.00
Jackson's Fever Cure, Aqua, 4 1/2 In.	14.00
Kendall's Spavin Cure, Amber, 12 Panels, BIMAL, 5 1/2 In.	7.50
Langenbach's Dysentery Cure, Amber, Embossed, Label, BIMAL	35.00
Langenbach's Dysentery Cure, Embossed	20.00
Langenbach's Dysentery Cure, Embossed, Contents	30.00
Langenbach's Dysentery Cure, Label	25.00
Melbourne, Golden Amber, Label	40.00
Melbourne, Red Amber	30.00
Munyon's Inhaler Cures Colds, Emerald Green, Cylinder, 4 1/4 In.	20.00
One Minute Cough Cure, E. C. DeWitt & Co., Aqua, Rectangular, 4 1/8 In.	7.00
Original Dr. Craig's Kidney Cure, Rochester, Amber, 9 1/2 In.	105.00
Original Kidney & Liver Cure, Rochester, Medium Amber, 9 3/4 In.	500.00
Park's Liver & Kidney Cure, Amber, Rectangular, 1870–1880, 9 3/4 In.	77.00
Park's Liver & Kidney Cure, H. Wells, Leroy, N. Y., Aqua, 9 3/4 In.	55.00
Piso's Cure For Consumption, Hazeltine & Co., Aqua, BIM, 5 1/2 In.	18.00
Polar Star Cough Cure, Cornflower Blue	45.00
Rhodes Fever & Ague Cure, Aqua, OP, 1850, 7 1/2 In.	198.00
Rhodes Fever & Ague Cure, Label, Box	30.00
Rock's Cough & Cure, Sozodont, 2 In.	8.00
Russian Rheumatic Cure, Box	55.00
S. B. Catarrh Cure, Aqua, Round, 7 1/2 In.	22.00
Sanford's Radical Cure, Sapphire, Label, Dark, 1880s, Rectangular	165.00
Shiloh's Consumption Cure	20.00
Shiloh's Consumption Cure, Aqua, Label, 4 1/4 In.	17.00
Shiloh's Consumption Cure, Aqua, Taper Top, 6 In.	15.00
Sloan's Sure Colic Cure	8.00
Spark's Kidney & Liver Cure, Camden, N. J., Amber, Oval, 9 3/8 In.	357.00
Spohn's Distemper Cure, Aqua	15.00
Upham's Fresh Meat	20.00
Veno's Lightning Cough Cure, Aqua, 5 1/2 In.	10.00
Warner's Safe Cure, 4 Cities, Black	150.00
Warner's Safe Cure, Concentrated, Amber, 5 5/8 In.	20.00
Warner's Safe Cure, London, Bright Green, 4 5/8 In.	364.00
Warner's Safe Cure, London, Green, 1/2 Pt.	85.00
Warner's Safe Cure, London, Nervine, Straw, Pt.	60.00
Warner's Safe Cure, London, Yellow Amber, Applied Top, 9 1/8 In.	55.00
Warner's Safe Cure, Melbourne, Red Amber, Tooled Collar, 9 5/8 In.	32.00
Warner's Safe Cure, Rochester, Yellow, 7 1/4 In.	66.00

Cyrus Noble, Carousel, Horse, White Charger, 1979
Cyrus Noble, Carousel, Tiger, 1979
Cyrus Noble, Carousel, Horse, Black Flyer, 1979
Cyrus Noble, Carousel, Lion, 1979

Warner's Safe Cure, Yellow, Reproduction 35.00
Warner's Safe Diabetes Cure, London, Deep Red Amber, Pt., 9 3/8 In. 82.00
Warner's Safe Diabetes Cure, Melbourne, Amber, 9 1/2 In. 104.00
Warner's Safe Kidney & Liver, Amber, Blob Top 15.00
Warner's Safe Kidney & Liver, Rochester, Amber, 9 1/2 In. .... 15.00 To 55.00
Warner's Safe Kidney & Liver, Slug Plate Variant, Amber 39.00
Warner's Safe Nervine, London, Light Olive Yellow, 9 3/8 In. 95.00
Warner's Safe Nervine, Rochester, Medium Amber, 9 1/2 In. 165.00
Warner's Safe Rheumatic Cure, Rochester, N. Y., Amber, Blob Top, 9 In. 105.00
Wm. Radam's Microbe Killer, Golden Amber, 10 3/8 In. 213.00
Woods Peppermint Cure, Purple, BIMAL 50.00

CYRUS NOBLE

This complicated story requires a cast of characters: Cyrus Noble, a master distiller; Ernest R. Lilienthal, owner of Bernheim Distillery; Crown Distillers, trade name of Lilienthal & Company; Haas Brothers, successor to Lilienthal & Co.; and another Ernest R. Lilienthal, president of Haas Brothers Distributing and grandson of the original Ernest Lilienthal. Cyrus Noble was in charge of the quality of the whiskey made at the Bernheim Distillery in Kentucky. He was said to be a large man, over 300 pounds, and liked to taste his own product. According to the stories, he tasted to excess one day, fell into a whiskey vat, and drowned. The company, as a tribute, named the brand for him in 1871 and so Cyrus Noble Bourbon came into being.

Ernest R. Lilienthal, the original owner of Bernheim Distillery, moved to San Francisco and opened Lilienthal & Company with the trade name of Crown Distillers. Their best-selling brand was Cyrus Noble. It was made in three grades and sold by the barrel. The company later became Haas Brothers Distributing Company.

In 1901 John Coleman, a miner in Searchlight, Nevada, was so discouraged with the results of his digging that he offered to trade his mine to Tobe Weaver, a bartender, for a quart of Cyrus Noble whiskey. The mine was named Cyrus Noble and eventually produced over $250,000 worth of gold.

One of the early bottles used for Cyrus Noble whiskey was amber with an inside screw top; it was made from the 1860s to 1921. Haas Brothers of San Francisco marketed special Cyrus Noble bottles from 1971 to 1980. The first, made to commemorate the company's 100th anniversary, pictured the miner, the unfortunate John Coleman. Six thousand bottles were made and sold, filled, for $16.95 each. Tobe Weaver, the fortunate bartender, was pictured in the next bottle. A mine series was made from 1971 to 1978, the full size about 14 inches high and the miniatures about 6 inches; a wild animal series from 1977 to 1978; and a carousel series in 1979 and 1980. Other series are birds of the forest, olympic bottles, horned animals, and sea animals. W. A. Lacey, a brand of 86 proof blended whiskey distributed by Haas Brothers, was also packed in a variety of figural bottles. They are listed separately under Lacey.

CYRUS NOBLE, Assayer, 1972	175.00
Assayer, 1974, Miniature	10.00 To 15.00
Bartender, 1971	170.00 To 240.00
Bartender, 1974, Miniature	15.00 To 17.00
Bear & Cubs, 1978, 1st Edition	72.00 To 85.00
Bear & Cubs, 1980, Miniature	17.00
Beaver & Kit, 1978, Miniature	17.00
Blacksmith, 1974	50.00
Blacksmith, 1976, Miniature	18.00
Buffalo Cow & Calf, 1977, 1st Edition	115.00
Buffalo Cow & Calf, 1977, 2nd Edition	70.00
Buffalo Cow & Calf, 1977, Nevada Edition	90.00
Buffalo Cow & Calf, 1979, Miniature	17.00
Burro, 1973	70.00
Burro, 1975, Miniature	10.00 To 13.00
Carousel, Horse, Black Flyer, 1979	*Illus* 35.00
Carousel, Horse, White Charger, 1979	*Illus* 35.00
Carousel, Lion, 1979	*Illus* 35.00
Carousel, Pipe Organ, 1980	20.00
Carousel, Tiger, 1979	35.00
Carousel, Tiger, 1979	*Illus* 39.00
Deer & Mule, 1980	48.00
Deer, White Tail Buck, 1979	48.00 To 70.00
Delta Suicide Table, 1971, 4 Piece	265.00
Dolphin, 1979	45.00
Elk, Bull, 1980	45.00
Gambler's Lady, 1976	50.00
Gambler's Lady, 1977, Miniature	80.00
Gambler, 1974	50.00
Gambler, 1975, Miniature	12.00 To 13.00
Gold Miner, 1970	325.00
Gold Miner, 1974, Miniature	10.00 To 20.00
Harp Seal, 1979	50.00
Landlady, 1977	24.00
Landlady, 1978, Miniature	23.00
Middle of Piano, Trumpeter, 1979	42.00
Middle of Piano, Trumpeter, 1979, Miniature	16.00
Mine Shaft, 1978	40.00
Mine Shaft, 1979, Miniature	20.00
Miner's Daughter, 1975	40.00 To 45.00
Miner's Daughter, 1976, Miniature	15.00 To 20.00
Moose & Calf, 1977, 2nd Edition	70.00
Moose & Calf, 1977, Nevada Edition	70.00
Moose & Calf, 1979, Miniature	15.00
Mountain Lion & Cubs, 1977, 1st Edition	*Illus* 75.00
Mountain Lion & Cubs, 1979, Miniature	15.00
Mountain Sheep, 1st Edition, 1978	110.00
Mountain Sheep, 2nd Edition, 1979	60.00
Music Man, 1977	30.00
Music Man, 1978, Miniature	30.00
Oklahoma Dancers, 1978	25.00 To 28.00
Olympic Skater, 1980	25.00
Owl In Tree, 1980	35.00
Penguins, 1978	50.00
Penguins, 1980, Miniature	18.00
Sea Turtle, 1979	40.00
Seal Family, 1978	41.00

Seal, Harp, 1979 .... 50.00
Snowshoe Thompson, 1972 .... 175.00
Snowshoe Thompson, 1976, Miniature 22.00
South of The Border, Dancer, 1978 .... 25.00
Tonopah, Octagonal, Milk Glass, 1972 ....*Illus* 165.00
USC Trojan, 1980 .... 35.00
Violinist, 1976 .... 36.00
Violinist, 1978, Miniature 30.00
Walrus Family, 1978 .... 45.00
Walrus Family, 1980, Miniature .... 13.00 To 20.00
Whiskey Drummer, 1975 .... 45.00
Whiskey Drummer, 1977, Miniature 21.00

*Cyrus Noble, Mountain Lion & Cubs,
1977, 1st Edition*

*Cyrus Noble, Tonopah,
Octagonal, Milk Glass, 1972*

*Dant, Field Bird Series,
No. 3, Prairie Chicken, 1969*

Dant, Ft.Sill, 1969

Dant, Indy 500, 1969

--------------------------------- DANT ---------------------------------

Dant figural bottles were first released in 1968 to hold J. W. Dant alcoholic products. The figurals were discontinued after a few years. The company made an Americana series, field birds, special bottlings, and ceramic bottles. Several bottles were made with *errors*. Collectors seem to have discounted this in determining value.

DANT, Alamo, 1969	5.00
American Legion, 1969	5.00 To 6.00
Atlantic City, 1969	6.00
Boeing 747, 1970	7.00
Boston Tea Party, 1968	5.00
Boston Tea Party, Eagle Right, 1968	10.00
Burr–Hamilton Duel, 1969	8.00
Constitution & Guerriere, 1969	6.00
Field Bird Series, No. 1, Ringnecked Pheasant, 1969	8.00
Field Bird Series, No. 2, Chukar Partridge, 1969	8.00
Field Bird Series, No. 3, Prairie Chicken, 1969 ....*Illus*	8.00
Field Bird Series, No. 4, Mountain Quail, 1969	8.00
Field Bird Series, No. 5, Ruffled Grouse, 1969	8.00
Field Bird Series, No. 6, California Quail, 1969	8.00
Field Bird Series, No. 7, Bob White, 1969	8.00
Field Bird Series, No. 8, Woodcock, 1969	8.00
Ft. Sill, 1969 ....*Illus*	10.00
Indy 500, 1969 ....*Illus*	8.00
Mt. Rushmore, 1969	7.00 To 8.00
Patrick Henry, 1969	6.00
Paul Bunyan, 1969	7.00
Pot Bellied Stove, 1966	10.00
San Diego Harbor, 1969	5.00
Washington At Delaware, 1969	6.00

------------------------- DAVIESS COUNTY -------------------------

Daviess County ceramic bottles were made from 1978 to 1981. The best–known were the American Legion Convention bottles. About 14 figural bottles were made, including a series of large tractor trailers and Greensboro Golf Tournament souvenirs.

DAVIESS COUNTY, American Legion, Boston, 1980	15.00 To 18.00
American Legion, Hawaii, 1981	18.00 To 25.00
American Legion, Houston, 1979	15.00
American Legion, New Orleans, 1978	20.00
Greensboro Open, Golf Ball & Tee, 1981	25.00
Iowa Hog, 1978	30.00
Jeep CJ-7, Yellow, 1979	25.00
Kentucky Long Rifle, 1978	35.00
Mallard Decoy, 1989	35.00
Oil Tanker, Gulf, 1979	30.00
Pontiac Trans Am, 1980	25.00

----------------------------- DECANTER -----------------------------

Decanters were first used to hold the alcoholic beverages that had been stored in kegs. The undesirable sediment that formed at the bottom of old wine kegs was removed by carefully pouring off the top liquid, or decanting it. At first a necessity, the decanter later became merely an attractive serving vessel. A decanter usually has a bulbous bottom, a long neck, and a small mouth for easy pouring. Most have a cork or glass stopper. They were popular in England from the beginning of the eighteenth century. By about 1775 the decanter was elaborate, with cut, applied, or enameled decorations. Various early American glassworks made decanters. Mold–blown decanters were the most popular style and many were made in the East and the Midwest from 1820 to the 1860s. Pressed glass was a less expensive process introduced in about 1850, and many decanters were made by this method. Colored Bohemian glass consisting of two or three cased layers became popular in the late–nineteenth century. Many decanters are now made for home or restaurant use or with special logos to promote products. Bar bottles, decanter–like bottles

Decanter, Vanilla, Backbar, 11 In.

Drug, P.H.Schneider Drug Co., Trinidad, Colo., 7 1/2 Oz.

with brand names in the glass, were used from about 1890 to 1920 in saloons. The law no longer permits the use of bar bottles because no bottle may be refilled from another container.

DECANTER, see also Beam; Bischoff, etc.

DECANTER, Art Glass, Cobalt Blue, Threaded, Corset Waist, Stopper, 10 In.	150.00
Ball, Juice, Paneled, Clear, Qt.	8.00
Blown, 2 Applied Rings, Bulbous Lip, Wheel Stopper, 9 1/4 In.	45.00
Blown, 2 Applied Rings, Mushroom Stopper, 7 7/8 In.	25.00
Blown, 3–Piece Mold, 3 Applied Rigaree Rings, Stopper, 8 In.	175.00
Blown, 3–Piece Mold, Clear, Flared, Stopper, Pontil, 1/2 Pt.	358.00
Blown, 3–Piece Mold, Cobalt Blue, Stopper, 5 3/16 In.	467.00
Blown, 3–Piece Mold, Flared Mouth, Stopper, Pontil, 1/2 Pt.	495.00
Blown, 3–Piece Mold, Hollow Ribbed Stopper, 9 In.	235.00
Blown, 3–Piece Mold, Olive Green, Pontil, Qt.	880.00
Blown, 3–Piece Mold, Pale Violet Tint, Cone, Stopper, Qt.	275.00
Blown, 3–Piece Mold, Stopper	175.00
Blown, 3–Piece Mold, Vaseline Tint, Flared, Pontil, Pt.	165.00
Blown, 3–Piece Mold, Wine, Stopper, Label, 9 In.	350.00
Blown, 3–Piece Mold, Yellow Green, Pontil, Pt.	550.00
Blown, Golden Amber, Large Mushroom Lip, Pontil, 10 1/2 In.	660.00
Blown, Medium Olive Yellow, Applied Mouth, OP, 10 3/8 In.	450.00
Clear, Painted Floral Design, Hollow Stopper, Pontil	15.00
Columbian Exposition, Clear, Whiskey, Gold Lettering	50.00
Cut Glass, Catto's Old Highland Whiskey, Square Base, 10 In.	182.00
Cylinder, Long John In Border, Cut Glass Stopper, 11 In.	91.00
Dark Green, Applied Rings, Small	660.00
Decorative, Clear, Stopper	100.00
HMS New Zealand, Sir John Jellicoe, Black Glaze, Sepia, 12 In.	500.00
Keene, 3–Piece Mold, Olive Green	880.00
Keene, Geometric, 3–Piece Mold	425.00
Keene, Green	425.00
Laid On Neck Ring, OP, 1820–1840, Qt.	39.00
Olive Green, Long Neck, IP, 1845–1860, 7 1/4 In.	120.00
St. Jacob's Bitters, Engraved, Leaf Border, Bell Base, 8 7/8 In.	150.00
Vanilla, Backbar, 11 In. *Illus*	125.00

Watson's Whiskey, HM King George V, Blue, White, Hexagonal, 12 In.	837.00
Whiskey, Amber, Bell Shape, Indented Label Panel, Stopper, 5th	95.00
Zanesville Swirl, Amber	450.00

─────────────────── **DEMIJOHN** ───────────────────

A demijohn is a very large bottle that is usually blown. Many held alcoholic beverages, molasses, or other liquids. It was usually bulbous with a long neck and a high kick-up. Early examples have open pontils. Many were covered with wicker to avoid breakage when the bottles were shipped. A demijohn could hold from one to ten gallons. Most early demijohns were made of dark green amber or black glass. By the 1850s the glass colors were often aqua, light green, or clear.

DEMIJOHN, 3-Piece Mold, Olive Green, Tapered, 3 Gal.	75.00
3-Piece Mold, Yellow Green, OP, 1 1/2 Gal.	42.00
Blown, 2-Piece Mold, Kidney, Yellow Green, Pontil, 1840, 19 In.	242.00
Blown, Flattened Sides, Olive Amber, OP, 12 3/4 In.	400.00
Blown, Sloping Collar, New England, 1840-1860, 11 1/4 In.	25.00
Blown, Yellow Amber, Applied Mouth, Pontil, 11 1/2 In.	65.00
Blue Green, Tapered, OP, Gal.	45.00
Bright Green, Large Applied Lip, Rough Pontil, 12 In.	66.00
Citron, Flat Bottom, Gal.	35.00
Congress, Green, OP, 15 In.	30.00
Cylinder, Blue Green, IP, 1/2 Gal.	39.00
Cylinder, Blue Green, IP, Gal.	49.00
Dark Aqua, Flat Bottom, Gal.	25.00
Dip Mold, Golden Amber, OP, Gal.	79.00
Dip Mold, Olive Amber, OP, 3 Qt.	45.00
Heart Shape, Citron Green, OP, 1/2 Gal.	98.00
Kidney Shape, Amber, OP, Qt.	29.00
Kidney Shape, Aqua, IP, Qt.	19.00
Light Kelly Green, Flat Bottom, Gal.	25.00
Light Olive Amber, 2 Piece, 12 1/4 In.	66.00
Micro-Mini, Embossed To Look Wicker Covered, OP, 3 In.	37.00
Moss Green, Flat Bottom, Gal.	25.00
Olive Amber, 14 1/2 In.	150.00
Olive Citron, Dip Mold, OP, 2 Gal.	69.00
Olive Green, Flattened Sides, Sloping Collar, Pontil, 19 1/2 In.	100.00
Olive Green, OP, 1850, 14 1/2 In.	25.00

─────────────────── **DICKEL** ───────────────────

George Dickel Tennessee sour mash whiskey was sold in figural bottles in about 1967. The golf club, powder horn, and ceramic jug were widely advertised then but are of limited interest to today's collectors.

DICKEL, Golf Club, 1967	7.00
Golf Club, 1979, Miniature	7.00
Jug, Ceramic	8.00
Powder Horn, 1/2 Gal.	70.00
Powder Horn, Gal.	200.00
Powder Horn, Miniature	8.00
Powder Horn, Qt.	12.00

─────────────────── **DOUBLE SPRINGS** ───────────────────

Double Springs of Louisville, Kentucky, made ceramic figural bottles from 1968 to 1978. They had a classic car series made by the Century Porcelain Company, a Bicentennial series, and other figural bottles.

DOUBLE SPRINGS, Bentley, 1927 Model, 1972	30.00
Bicentennial, Colorado, 1976	14.00
Bicentennial, South Dakota, 1976	14.00
Cadillac, 1913 Model, 1971	26.00
Cord, 1937 Model, 1978	18.00
Coyote, Gold, 1971	10.00

Ford, Model T, 1910 Model, 1970	24.00
Georgia Bulldog, 1971	10.00
Kentucky Derby, With Glass, 1964	10.00
Matador, 1969	12.00
Mercedes Benz, 1975	12.00
Milwaukee Buck, 1971	12.00
Owl, Brown, 1968	12.00
Owl, Red	12.00
Owl, Red, 1968	12.00
Peasant Boy, 1968	5.00
Peasant Girl, 1968	5.00
Rolls Royce, 1912 Model, 1971	36.00
Stanley Steamer, 1909 Model, 1971	27.00
Stutz Bearcat, 1919 Model, 1970	35.00

DRUG

Druggists and apothecaries had many types of bottles. A few large, decorative bottles were kept in the window or on the shelves as ads. A series of matching labeled bottles often held special drugs and herbs. Small bottles were used to dispense medicines to customers. A drugstore often had special bottles made with the name and location of the store embossed on the glass. Drug bottles come in many sizes, shapes, and colors. If the original printed label can be found, it adds to the value.

DRUG, A. N. Clarke, Beverly, Mass., Embossed, OP, Large	25.00
Alfred B. Taylor Druggist, Philadelphia, Aqua, Cylinder, 1/2 Pt.	25.00
Alfred Helgeson, Vermillion, S. D., Monogram	10.00
Apothecary, Benjamin Green, Portsmouth, N. H., Cobalt Blue, 7 1/2 In.	55.00
Apothecary, Blown, Yellow Olive Amber, Smooth Base, 12 1/2 In.	325.00
Apothecary, Clear, Ground Glass Stopper, 8 1/2 In.	15.00
Apothecary, Cobalt Blue, Label, Ext. Wild Indigo, Stopper	99.00
Apothecary, Cobalt Blue, Stopper, 15 In., Gal.	195.00
Apothecary, Cobalt Blue, Stopper, OP, 5 In.	59.00
Apothecary, Cobalt Blue, Stopper, OP, 7 In.	79.00
Apothecary, Cobalt Blue, Stopper, Square, 5 1/2 In.	45.00
Apothecary, Cobalt Blue, Stopper, Square, 6 3/4 In.	49.00
Apothecary, Deep Peacock Blue, Polished Pontil, 1850, 9 1/4 In.	88.00
Apothecary, Salem, Mass, 12–Sided, OP	25.00
Apothecary, Tr. Digital, Cobalt Blue, Gold Label Under Glass, 5 In.	69.00
Apothecary, Tr. Digital, Cobalt Blue, Gold Label Under Glass, 8 In.	89.00
Apothecary, Warren Glass Works, Cobalt Blue, Glass Label, 1/2 Gal.	125.00
B & P, Lyons Powder, Medium Olive Green, OP, 4 1/4 In.	215.00
B. W. Fetters Druggist, Philadelphia, Light Blue Green	25.00
Billings Geyser, Blob	55.00
C. Heimstreet & Co., Troy, N. Y., Sapphire Blue, Octagonal, OP, 7 1/4 In.	158.00
C. W. Snow & Co., Druggists, Syracuse, N. Y., Cobalt Blue, 8 1/4 In.	121.00
Calomel, Gilbert Bros. & Co., Inc. Baltimore, 8 Labeled Vials, Box	20.00
Columbus Wholesale Drug Co., Hydrogen Peroxide, Brown, 5 In.	4.00
De Witts Creosant Expectorant, Chicago, Ill., Box, 6 1/2 In.	4.00
Display, Engraved Cross Hatched Design, Stopper, 1850–1870, 35 In.	413.00
Display, Engraved Leaf & Grape Cluster, Stopper, 1850–1870, 37 In.	385.00
Dr. H. W. Jackson, Druggist, Olive Amber, OP, 4 1/4 In.	668.00
Dr. J. D. Knott, Monticello, Ill., Amber, 3 1/2 In.	10.00
Dr. M. M. Fenner's Peoples Remedies, Fredonia, 1872–1891, Aqua, 7 1/2 In	8.50
E. S. Reed's Son Apothecary, Milk Glass, Heart Stopper, 4 5/8 In.	121.00
Eddy & Co., Central Drug Store, Sonora, Calif, 7 3/8 In.	22.00
Embossed, 4 Quarts–True Measure, Pedestal, No Cover	88.00
Fish Bowl Jar, Rexall Store	35.00
Frank E. Morgan & Sons, Philadelphia, Cobalt Blue, Burst Bubble	89.00
G. W. Merchant, Chemist, Emerald, OP, Applied Mouth, 5 1/2 In.	176.00
G. W. Merchant, Chemist, Lockport, N. Y., Blue Green, OP, 7 In.	798.00
G. W. Merchant, Chemist, Lockport, N. Y., Yellow Green, 5 1/2 In.	440.00
G. W. Merchant, Lockport, N. Y., Medium Blue Green, OP, 5 1/2 In.	264.00
Geo. C. Frye, Portland, Me., Apothecary, Mortar & Pestle Picture, 4 In.	15.00

Globe Tobacco Co., Detroit, Amber, Lid, Handle, Oct. 10, 1882, 7 1/4 In. 58.00
Grand Opera House Drug Store, W. N. Janvier, Springfield, O., BIM, 3 In. 12.00
GWL Drug Co., Light Amethyst, 1 Wing, Owl Misspelled, 9 7/8 In. 165.00
Heil's Drug Store, The Prescription Store, Prescott, Ariz., 5 7/8 In. 15.00
Henshaw Ward & Co., Druggist, Boston, Yellow Green, OP, 9 In. 446.00
Hollis Genuine Essence of Rose, Thomas Hollis, Druggist, OP, Label 55.00
Hood's Tooth Powder, Small 3.50
J. Levinson Leasing Pharmacist, Napa, Calif., 4 3/8 In. 9.50
Jar, Boro–Phen Douche Powder, Waterbury Chemical, St. Louis, 4 3/4 In. 10.00
Jar, Dr. King's New Life Pills Always Satisfy, Square, 14 x 5 In. 400.00
Jar, Hy–Geen Astringent Powder, Vaginal Douche, S. Pheiffer, 5 1/2 In. 8.00
Jar, Hy–Gen–Ol Douche Powder, Allen & Co., St. Louis, Mo., 5 1/2 In. 12.00
Jas. Tarrant Druggist, N. Y., Oval 30.00
Jn. Wyeth & Bro. Apothecaries, Philadelphia, Aqua, Cylinder, Pt. 25.00
John J. Smith, Louisville, Ky., Deep Aqua, Applied Mouth, 6 In. 39.00
Julias Deetkan, Deadwood, S. D. 10.00
Katz & Besthoff Pharmacists, New Orleans, Cobalt Blue, 7 3/4 In. 45.00
Keystone Drug Co., Deer Lodge, Mont., BIMAL, 2 7/8 In. 8.00
Laughlin & Bushfield Druggists, Va., Deep Aqua, Cylinder, 7 3/4 In. 121.00
Laughlin & Bushfield Druggists, Wheeling, Va., Aqua, 8 7/8 In. 143.00
Licorice Lozenges, Ribbed Rings Above & Below Label, Adam's M, Amber 65.00
Lowe & Reeds Compound Chlorine Tooth Wash 125.00
Melvin & Badger, Apothecaries, Cobalt Blue, Irregular Hexagon, 5 In. 88.00
Melvin & Badger, Apothecaries, Poison, Boston, Cobalt Blue, 5 In. 58.00
Merchants Chemists, Lockport, Teal, IP 150.00
Meyer Bros. Aspirin Tablets, 100 In Box, 2 1/8 x 3 7/8 x 1 1/2 In. 5.00
Moses Atwood's, None Genuine Without My Name, Complete Label 50.00
Mullen Drug Co., Warren, Pa., Bright Yellow Green, 7 1/8 In. 83.00
Owl Drug Co., 2 Wings, Amber, Tooled Top, 1895–1908, 8 In. 105.00
Owl Drug Co., 7 In. ....*Illus* 42.00
Owl Drug Co., Citrate of Magnesia, Pry Off Lid 25.00
Owl Drug Co., Embossed Owl, Clear 15.00
Owl Drug Co., Huile D'Olive, Clear, Tooled Top, 1895–1905, 9 In. 110.00
Owl Drug Co., Lewiston, Idaho, Tooled Top, 1900–1908, 4 3/4 In. 66.00
Owl Drug Co., Light Amethyst, Slug Plate, Pat. Jan. 5, 1892, 3 3/4 In. 33.00
Owl Drug Co., Milk Glass, Label, 1 Wing, 1895–1905, 3 3/8 In. 275.00
Owl Drug Co., San Francisco, Amber, Rounded Back, 1895–1900, 8 3/8 In. 99.00
Owl Drug Co., San Francisco, Calif., Rectangular, 7 1/2 In. 25.00
Owl, Cobalt Blue, Tooled Top, 1892–1895, 9 1/2 In. 440.00
P. H. Schneider Drug Co., Trinidad, Colo., 7 1/2 Oz. ....*Illus* 4.00
Perks Drugstore, Houlton, Me., Amber, 4 1/4 In. 28.00
Pharmacy, Puce, Glass Topper, 10 In. 20.00
Pill, Medium Green, TM On Side, Square, 2 In. 125.00
Purity Drug Co., Fowler's Solution, Muskogee, 4 3/4 In. ....*Illus* 85.00
Quillaim Terry's Prescription, Druggist, Terry, S. D. 7.00
R. J. Bennet's Pharmacist, Nevada City, Calif. 20.00
Robert's Drug Store, Goldfield, Nev. 220.00
Rumford Chemical, Teal, Large 12.50
Rushton Clark & Co., Chemist, Aqua, Applied Top, OP, 9 1/2 In. 105.00
Sam'l Felt, Jr., Druggist, Fluid Extract Cascara Sagrada, Teal, 8 In. 20.00
Scott's Emulsion Cod Liver Oil, Aqua, Crown Top, Man, Fish, 7 1/2 In. 3.00
Selburt Co., Cleveland, 6th City, 4 1/2 In. ....*Illus* 3.00
Show Jar, Pressed Glass, Cylindrical, 26 In. 407.00
Show Jar, Pressed Glass, Hexagonal, 23 In. 239.00
Southern Pacific Co., Hospital Dept., 5 1/2 In. 15.00
Sozodont For Teeth & Breath, Clear, Square, BIM, 2 1/2 In. 6.00
Steinhauser & Eaton, Green, Mortar & Pestle Design, 8 3/4 In. 121.00
Sun Drug Co., Los Angeles, Winged Mortar & Pestle, Amber, 5 3/4 In. 187.00
Sun Drug Co., Los Angeles, Winged Mortar & Pestle, Amber, 8 3/4 In. 413.00
Sutcliffe, McAllister & Co., Louisville, Yellow Green, OP, 5 1/2 In. 743.00
Swank's Pharmacy, Germantown, Cobalt Blue, 5 1/4 In. 53.00
T. E. Jenkins & Co. Chemists, Louisville, Deep Aqua, OP, 6 5/8 In. 93.00
Thomas Prescription Druggist, San Jose, Calif. 27.50

Ezra Brooks, American Legion, Chicago, 1972

Ezra Brooks, West Virginia Mountain Lady, 1972

Thos. A. Spivey, Pharmacist, Rio Vista, Calif., 5 7/8 In.	22.50
Towne Secombet Allison, Prescription Druggists, San Bernadino, 6 In.	12.50
Twenty Grand Aspirin, 100 Tablets, Box, 3 7/8 x 2 x 1 1/4 In.	4.00
U.S. A. Hospital Dept., Yellow Amber, Applied Mouth, 9 In.	264.00
U.S. A. Med's Dept., Drippy Applied Top, Green Striation, Aqua, 9 In.	125.00
W. J. M. Gordon Pharmacist, Cincinnati, Oh., Round, IP, 7 In.	30.00
W. W. Quillan Druggist, Sioux Falls, S. D.	10.00
Wing & Sisson Druggists, Coxsackie, N. Y., Aqua, Label, 1850, 7 3/8 In.	165.00
Wm. A. Leader Druggist, Columbia, Pa., OP, 1850, 5 7/8 In.	28.00
Wm. Radams Microbe Killer, Amber, Pat. Dec. 13, 1881, 1887–1906, 10 In.	132.00
Wm. S. Kimball & Co., Rochester, N. Y., Tobacco Jar, Amber, 7 In.	69.00

Drug, Owl Drug Co., 7 In.

Drug, Purity Drug Co., Fowler's Solution, Muskogee, 4 3/4 In.

Drug, Selburt Co., Cleveland, 6th City, 4 1/2 In.

————————————— **EZRA BROOKS** —————————————

Ezra Brooks fancy bottles were first made in 1964. The Ezra Brooks brand was purchased by Glenmore Distilleries Company of Louisville, Kentucky, in 1988, three years after Ezra Brooks had discontinued making decanters. About 300 different ceramic figurals were made between 1964 and 1985. The Ezra Brooks distillery in Owensboro, Kentucky, continues to produce 90–proof bourbon for Glenmore Distilleries.

EZRA BROOKS, American Legion, Chicago, 1972 ....*Illus*   70.00
  American Legion, Denver, 1972 ....   15.00
  American Legion, Hawaii, 1973 ....   10.00
  American Legion, Houston, 1971 ....   40.00
  American Legion, Miami Beach, 1974 ....   10.00
  AMVET, Dolphin, 1974 ....   10.00
  AMVET, Polish Legion, 1978 ....   8.00
  Arizona, 1969 ....   5.00
  Auburn, Boat Tail, 1932 Model, 1978 ....   20.00
  Auburn, War Eagle, 1982 ....   22.00
  Badger, Boxer, 1973 ....   15.00
  Badger, Football, 1974 ....   15.00
  Badger, Hockey, 1974 ....   11.00
  Bareknuckle Fighter, 1971 ....   12.00
  Basketball Player, 1974 ....   15.00
  Bear, 1968 ....   7.00
  Bear, California Golden, 1968 ....   6.00
  Beaver, 1972 ....*Illus*   9.00
  Bengal Tiger, 1979 ....   27.00
  Big Daddy Lounge, 1969 ....   7.00
  Big Red, No. 1, Football, 1970 ....   20.00
  Big Red, No. 2, With Hat, 1971 ....   18.00
  Bird, Canadian Honker, 1975 ....   13.00
  Bird, Eagle, Gold, 1971 ....   16.00
  Bird, Snow Egret, 1980 ....   23.00
  Bordertown, 1970 ....   9.00
  Bowler, 1973 ....5.00 To 6.00
  Bucket of Blood, 1970 ....   6.00
  Bucking Bronco, 1973 ....   12.00
  C. B. Convoy, 1976 ....   7.00
  Cable Car, Brown, 1968 ....   12.00
  Cannon, Antique, 1969 ....   6.00
  Card, Jack of Diamonds, 1969 ....   7.00
  Card, King of Clubs, 1969 ....7.00 To 9.00
  Card, Queen of Hearts, 1969 ....   7.00
  Casey At Bat, 1973 ....   25.00

Ezra Brooks, Beaver, 1972   *Ezra Brooks, Fox, Redtail, 1979*   *Ezra Brooks, Razorback Hog, 1969*

Ezra Brooks, Clown, No. 4, Keystone Cop, 1980
Ezra Brooks, Clown, No.5, Cuddles, 1980
Ezra Brooks, Clown, No.6, Tramp, 1980

Cheyenne Shootout, 1970	8.00
Chicago Fire Team, 1974	25.00
Christmas Tree, 1979	15.00
Cigar Store Indian, 1968	9.00
Clown, No. 1, Smiley, 1970	25.00
Clown, No. 2, Cowboy Hat, 1979	25.00
Clown, No. 3, Pagliacci, 1979	20.00
Clown, No. 4, Keystone Cop, 1980 ....*Illus*	36.00
Clown, No. 5, Cuddles, 1980 ....*Illus*	25.00
Clown, No. 6, Tramp, 1980 ....*Illus*	25.00
Clown, With Accordion, 1971	25.00
Clown, With Balloons, 1973	22.00
Club, No. 1, Distillery, 1970	7.00
Club, No. 2, Birthday Cake, 1971	16.00
Club, No. 3, Map, 1972	14.00
Clydesdale, 1974	13.00
Colonial Drummer, 1974	10.00

Ezra Brooks, Equestrian, 1974

Ezra Brooks, Keystone Cops, 1971

Corvette, 1957 Model, 1977	98.00
Corvette, 1962 Model, Mako Shark, 1979	15.00
Corvette, Indy Pace Car, 1978	41.00
Court Jester, 1971	9.00
Dakota Cowboy, 1975	30.00
Dakota Cowgirl, 1976	20.00
Dakota Farmers Elevator, 1978	21.00
Deadwagon, 1970	9.00
Deer, Whitetail, 1974	19.00
Delta Belle, Riverboat, 1969	8.00
Dollar, Silver Bottle, 1969	7.00
Drum & Bugle, Conquistador, 1971	8.00
Dueling Pistol, Flintlock, 1968	9.00 To 10.00
Dueling Pistol, Japanese, 1968	35.00
Duesenberg, 1971	25.00 To 29.00
Eagle, Gold, 1971	18.00
Elephant, Asian, 1973	15.00
Elephant, Big Bertha, 1970	11.00
Elk, 1972	28.00
English Setter, Bird Dog, 1971	11.00 To 12.00
Equestrian, 1974 ....*Illus*	9.00
Ez Jug, No. 1, 1977	16.00
Ez Jug, No. 2, 1980	20.00
F. O. E. Eagle, 1978	17.00
F. O. E. Eagle, 1980	36.00
F. O. E. Eagle, 1981	34.00
Fire Engine, 1971	19.00
Fisherman, 1974	11.00
Football Player, 1974	10.00
Ford Mustang, Indy Pace Car, 1979	25.00
Ford Thunderbird, 1956 Model, Blue, 1976	75.00 To 80.00
Ford Thunderbird, 1956 Model, Yellow, 1976	67.00 To 75.00
Foremost Astronaut, 1970	7.00
Foremost Dancing Man, 1969	10.00
Fox, Redtail, 1979 ....*Illus*	40.00
Fresno Grape, 1970	9.00
Gamecock, 1970	12.00
Gator, No. 1, Passing, 1972	11.00
Gator, No. 2, Running, 1973	12.00
Gator, No. 3, Blocker, 1975	21.00
Gavel & Block, VIP, 1982, 200 Ml.	12.00
Gavel, President, 1982, 750 Ml.	28.00
Georgia Bulldog, 1972	20.00
Goldpanner, 1969	6.00
Gopher, Minnesota Hockey Player, 1975	17.00
Grandfather Clock, 1970	8.00
Greensboro Open, Golfer, 1973	19.00 To 25.00
Greensboro, Open, Club & Ball, 1977	20.00
Groucho Marx, 1977 ....*Illus*	41.00
Hambletonian, 1970	11.00
Hardy, Oliver, 1976 ....*Illus*	16.00
Harold's Club Dice, 1968	7.00
Hereford, 1971	14.00
Horseshoe Club, Horseshoe, 1970	9.00
Idaho Skier, 1972	10.00
Indian, Ceremonial, 1970	16.00
Indy Pace Car, Pontiac, 1980	20.00
Indy Race Car No. 21, 1970	20.00 To 40.00
Indy Race Car No. 3, Norton Spirit, 1982	65.00
Indy Race Car, No. 1, Gould Charger, 1982	65.00
Indy Race Car, No. 2, 1982	65.00
Indy STP No. 20, G. Johncock, 1983	75.00
Iowa Farmer's Elevator, 1978	31.00

Ezra Brooks, Groucho Marx, 1977

Ezra Brooks, Hardy, Oliver, 1976
Ezra Brooks, Laurel, Stan, 1976

Iowa Farmer, 1977	60.00
Jayhawk, Kansas, 1969	9.00
Kachina, No. 1, Morning Singer, 1971	75.00
Kachina, No. 2, Hummingbird, 1973	45.00
Kachina, No. 3, Antelope, 1974	60.00
Kachina, No. 4, Maiden, 1975	23.00 To 25.00
Kachina, No. 5, Longhair, 1976	35.00
Kachina, No. 6, Buffalo Dancer, 1977	33.00
Kachina, No. 7, Mudhead, 1978	40.00
Kachina, No. 8, Drummer, 1979	54.00
Kachina, No. 9, Watermelon, 1980	10.00
Katz Cat, Gray, 1969	9.00
Katz Cats, Philharmonic, 1970, Pair	84.00
Keystone Cops, 1971 *Illus*	32.00
Laurel, Stan, 1976 *Illus*	14.00
Liberty Bell, 1969	7.00
Lincoln Continental, 1941 Model, 1979	23.00
Lion On Rock, 1971	8.00
Liquor Square, 1972	7.00
Lobster, 1970	17.00
Longhorn Steer, 1971	24.00
Macaw, Blue & Gold, 1980	36.00
Maine Potato, 1973	9.00
Man of War, 1969	15.00
Max The Hat Zimmerman, 1976	25.00
Minuteman, 1975	12.00
Moose, 1972	26.00
Motorcycle, 1971	10.00
Mr. Merchant, 1970	10.00
Mule, Missouri, 1971	10.00
New Hampshire, Man On Mountain, 1970	9.00
New Hampshire, Statehouse, 1970	9.00
Nugget Classic, 1970	10.00
Nugget Classic, Gold, 1970	12.00
Nugget Rooster, 1969	25.00
Oil Gusher, 1969	6.00
Old Ez Owl, No. 1, Miniature	15.00
Old Ez Owl, No. 3, Snowy, 1980	29.00
Old Ez Owl, No. 4, Scops, 1981	25.00
Ontario Racer No. 10, 1970	20.00
Panda, 1972	15.00 To 16.00
Phoenix Bird, 1971	22.00
Phonograph, 1970	15.00

Pirate, 1971 .... 6.00
Political, Donkey, New York, 1976 .... 12.00
Political, Elephant, Kansas City, 1976 .... 14.00
Potbelly Stove, 1968 .... 9.00
Quail, 1970 .... 8.00
Raccoon, 1978 .... 38.00
Ram, 1972 .... 18.00
Razorback Hog, 1969 ....*Illus* 15.00
Reno Arch, 1968 .... 6.00
Rooster Fighting Gamecock 14.00
Saddle, Silver, 1972 .... 27.00
Sailfish, 1971 .... 8.00
Salmon, Washington, 1971 .... 22.00
Sea Captain, 1971 .... 10.00
Seal, Gold, 1972 .... 12.00
Senator, 1972 .... 14.00
Setter, With Bird, 1970 .... 12.00
Shark, White, 1977 .... 10.00
Shriner, Clown, 1978 .... 14.00
Shriner, King Tut Guard, 1979 .... 18.00
Shriner, Sphinx, 1980 .... 9.00
Silver Spur Boot, 1971 .... 9.00
Ski Boot, 1972 .... 9.00
Slot Machine, 1971 .... 20.00
Snowmobile, 1972 .... 12.00
Snowy Owl, 1979 .... 25.00
South Dakota Air National Guard, 1976 .... 19.00 To 24.00
Spirit of '76, 1974 .... 8.00
Spirit of St. Louis, 1977 .... 9.00
Stagecoach, Overland Express, 1969 .... 8.00
Stonewall Jackson, 1974 .... 25.00
Strongman, 1974 .... 10.00
Sturgeon, 1975 .... 24.00
Tank, 1972 .... 16.00
Tecumseh, 1969 .... 7.00
Telephone, 1971 .... 10.00 To 15.00
Tennis Player, 1973 .... 10.00
Ticker Tape, 1970 .... 8.00
Tonopah, 1972 .... 12.00
Totem Pole, No. 1, 1972 .... 9.00
Totem Pole, No. 2, 1973 .... 11.00
Tractor, Fordson, 1971 .... 17.00
Trail Bike, 1972 .... 11.00
Train, Casey Jones, 1980 .... 15.00
Train, Iron Horse, 1969 .... 15.00
Trojan Horse, 1974 .... 15.00
Trojan USC, 1973 .... 12.00
Trout & Fly, 1970 .... 8.00 To 9.00
Truckin' An' Vannin', 1976 .... 24.00
Turkey, White, 1971 .... 20.00
Vermont Skier, 1972 .... 13.00
VFW, Blue, 1973 .... 8.00
Water Tower, Chicago, 1969 .... 7.00
Weirton Steel, 1974 .... 15.00
West Virginia Mountain Lady, 1972 ....*Illus* 21.00
West Virginia Mountain Man, 1970 .... 65.00
Whale, Washington, 1972 .... 20.00
Wheat Shocker, Kansas, 1971 .... 6.00
Whooping Crane, 1982 .... 19.00
Wichita Centennial, 1970 .... 7.00
William Penn, 1981 .... 60.00
Winston Churchill, 1969 .... 6.00
Zimmerman Top Hat, 1968 .... 7.00

--- **FAMOUS FIRSTS** ---

Famous Firsts Ltd. of Port Chester, New York, was owned by Richard E. Magid. The first figural bottles, issued in 1968, were a series of race cars. The last figurals were made in 1985.

FAMOUS FIRSTS, Animals, Mother & Baby, 1981, Miniature, 6 Piece	210.00
Balloon, 1971	19.00 To 35.00
Bear, Pitcher, 1975	18.00
Bell, Alpine, Black, 1970, 200 Ml.	35.00
Bell, Alpine, Bronze, 1970, 200 Ml.	15.00
Bell, St. Pol, 1970	20.00
Bennie Bowwow, 1973 *Illus*	12.00
Bersaglieri, 1969	30.00
Bugatti Royale, 1973, 750 Ml.	395.00
Butterfly, 1971	24.00
Butterfly, 1971, Miniature	15.00
Cable Car, 1973, 500 Ml.	46.00
Cable Car, 1973, Miniature	20.00
Centurion, 1969	37.00
China Clipper, 1979	125.00
Circus Lion, 1979	25.00
Circus Tiger, 1979	25.00
Coffee Mill, Blue, 1971	20.00 To 35.00
Coffee Mill, Orange, 1971	35.00
Corvette Stingray, 1963 Model, Red, 1975, 500 Ml.	95.00
Corvette Stingray, 1963 Model, White, 1970, Miniature	18.00
Corvette Stingray, 1963 Model, White, 1979, 200 Ml.	95.00
DeWitt Clinton Engine, 1969, Miniature	10.00 To 15.00
Dino Ferrari, Red, 1983, 200 Ml.	60.00
Dino Ferrari, White, 1975	30.00
Don Sympatico, Brown, 1973	18.00
Don Sympatico, Orange, 1973	18.00
Duesenberg, 1980	110.00
Duesenberg, 50th Anniversary, Red, 1982	215.00
Egg House, 1975	10.00
Fireman, 1980	50.00
Fireman, 1981, Miniature	10.00
Garibaldi, 1969	35.00
Geisha Doll, 1978, Miniature, 3 Piece	40.00
Golfer, He, 1973	33.00

Famous Firsts, Bennie Bowwow, 1973
Famous Firsts, Minnie Meow, 1973

Famous Firsts, Swiss Chalet, 1974

Golfer, She, 1973	33.00
Her, Filomena, 1973	20.00
Hippo, Baby, 1980	59.00
Honda Motorcycle, 1975	60.00
Hurdy Gurdy, 1971	15.00
Indy Racer, No. 11, 1971	30.00
Indy Racer, No. 11, 1973, Miniature	20.00
Leopard, Pitcher, 1975	18.00
Liberty Bell, 1976, Miniature	10.00
Lockheed Transport, Jungle, 1982, 200 Ml.	65.00
Lockheed Transport, Marine Gray, 1982, 200 Ml.	65.00
Lockheed Transport, USAF Gray, 1982, 200 Ml.	65.00
Lockheed, 1979, 200 Ml.	58.00
Lotus Racer, No. 2, 1971	25.00
Marmon Wasp Golden, No. 32, 1971, 1/2 Pt. ..	25.00
Marmon Wasp No. 32, No. 1, 1968, 500 Ml. ...	65.00
Marmon Wasp No. 32, No. 2, 1968, Miniature .... 15.00 To	19.00
Minnie Meow, 1973 ....*Illus*	18.00
Monkey, Pitcher, 1975	18.00
Mustang, 1974	125.00
Napoleon, 1969	20.00
National Racer, No. 8, 1972, 500 Ml.	58.00
National Racer, No. 8, 1972, Miniature	35.00
Owl, Pitcher, 1975	18.00
Panda, Baby, 1980	85.00
Panda, Baby, 1981, Miniature	25.00
Panther, Pitcher, 1975	18.00
Pepper Mill, 1978 .... 10.00 To	18.00
Phonograph, 1969, Miniature	20.00
Porsche Targa, 1979, 500 Ml.	40.00
Renault Racer, No. 3, 1969	65.00
Riverboat, Natchez Mail Packet, 1975, 500 Ml.	47.00
Riverboat, Robert E. Lee, 1971 .... 72.00 To	75.00
Rooster, Richardo, 1973	16.00
Roulette Wheel, 1972 .... 15.00 To	20.00
Scale, Lombardy, 1970	28.00
Sewing Machine, 1979, Miniature	20.00
Ship, China Clipper, 1979	130.00
Ship, Sea Witch, 1976	75.00
Ship, Sea Witch, 1980, 200 Ml.	23.00
Ship, Yankee Clipper, Pitcher, 1975	16.00
Skier, He, 1973	17.00
Skier, Jack, 1975	24.00
Skier, Jill, 1975	24.00
Skier, She, 1973	17.00
Spirit of St. Louis, 1969, Pt.	125.00
Spirit of St. Louis, 1972, Miniature	58.00
Swiss Chalet, 1974 ....*Illus*	33.00
Telephone, Floral, 1973	20.00
Telephone, French, Blue, 1969	30.00
Telephone, French, White, 1973, Miniature .... 13.00 To	18.00
Telephone, French, Yellow, 1969	30.00
Telephone, Johnny Reb, 1973	25.00
Telephone, Yankee Doodle, 1973	30.00
Tennis, He, 1973	24.00
Tennis, She, 1973	29.00
Tiger, Pitcher, 1975	18.00
Winnie Mae, Airplane, 1972, 1/2 Pt.	63.00
Winnie Mae, Airplane, 1972, Miniature	35.00
Winnie Mae, Airplane, 1972, Pt.	95.00
Yacht America, 1970, 13 In. .... 32.00 To	35.00
Yacht America, 1978, Miniature	26.00
Zebra, Pitcher, 1975	18.00

Figural, Book, Coming Thro'
The Rye, Blue, Pottery, 5 In.

Figural, Dog, Amber, 10 In.

Figural, Monkey, Our Boy
Fine Cologne, 4 3/4 In.

FIGURAL

Figural bottles are specially named by the collectors of bottles. Any bottle that is of a recognizable shape, such as a human head, a pretzel, or a clock, is considered to be a figural. There are no restrictions as to date or material. Figurals are also listed by brand name or type in other sections of this book.

FIGURAL, see also Bitters; Cologne; Perfume; Pottery; Royal Doulton

FIGURAL, Baby, Crying	75.00
Baltimore Monument, Sesquicentennial, Baker Bros., Amber, 9 In.	2310.00
Banjo, Lavender, 9 In.	20.00
Barrel, Colman's, Mustard	45.00
Barrel, Cuervo, Wooden	10.00
Barrel, Flattened, Signed Green, Lambeth, 6 1/2 In.	200.00
Barrel, Gingerette, Bar, Clear, Spigot Base, Lid, 11 1/2 In.	36.00
Barrel, Globe Tobacco Co., Detroit, Oct. 10th, 1882, Amber, 1/2 Gal.	14.00
Barrel, Nottingham–Type Salt Glaze, Impressed 1 Gal., 10 1/2 In.	100.00
Barrel, Pottery, Spigot Hole Front, Coat of Arms, 15 1/2 In.	126.00
Barrel, Schweppes, Deep Blue Top, Blue Base, Bourne Denby, 11 In.	253.00
Barrel, Unembossed, Brilliant Pea Green, 1870, 9 7/8 In.	308.00
Bear, Deep Amethyst ....50.00 To 65.00
Bear, Opaque White, 11 In.	77.50
Bear, Pomade, Deep Amethyst, New England, 1870–1890, 3 3/4 In.	143.00
Bear, Sitting, Dense Amethyst, Tooled Mouth, 11 1/8 In.	33.00
Beer Mug, Clear, 2 1/4 In.	9.00
Book, Coming Thro' The Rye, Blue, Pottery, 5 In. ....*Illus*	250.00
Book, Departed Spirits, Bennington–Type Pottery, Brown, 5 5/8 In.	275.00
Book, Departed Spirits, Pottery, Cream, Brown & Green, 5 1/2 In.	345.00
Boot, Saratoga Dressing, Aqua, Tooled Lip, 4 Ft. 2 In.	22.00
Boot, Woman's, Impressed Diamonds, Orange, Salt Glaze, 4 In.	273.00
Boot, Woman's, Jones Pub, Newington, Salt Glaze, 4 1/4 In.	400.00
Boy & Girl, Climbing Tree, 12 In. ....*Illus*	110.00
Boy, Milk Glass, Yellow, Clear Frosted Head, Late 1800s, 6 3/4 In.	550.00
Candlestick, Ryenbende, Miniature	13.00
Cannon, B & Co., Amber, Round Collar, Ring Lip, 1865–1880, 11 In.	990.00
Chinese Man, Standing, Aqua, Embossed DK, c.1850, 10 1/2 In.	4125.00
Cigar, Amber	25.00
Coachman, Amber, Van Dunck, Netherlands, 8 1/2 In.	88.00
Coachman, Pottery, Rockingham Glaze, 1850–1880, 10 3/8 In.	110.00
Column, Metal Columbus Atop, Milk Glass, 1895–1900, 18 In.	330.00
Crying Baby, T. P. S. & Co., Clear, 6 1/8 In.	55.00
Cucumber, Stoneware, Green & Cream Mottled Glaze, 11 3/4 In.	88.00
Daniel O'Connell, Flask, Irish Reform Cordial, 7 3/4 In.	746.00
Dice, Clear, 1890–1910, 1 1/16 In., Pair	99.00

Bottles have been made since ancient times and have been collected since the Roman Empire. But skip to the twentieth century. In the 1900s the wealthy collected paintings, antiquities, coins, stamps, and glass. Early American historic flasks and blown bottles soon attracted some early collectors. A few bottle history books were available after 1871, but the first book for collectors was written in 1921. That was the start of serious bottle collecting.

In 1947 James Thompson classified bitters bottles in his book. In 1959 the Antique Bottle Collectors Association of California met for the first time. The club had a newsletter, the main source of information about bottles until 1965. That year, *Western Collector* magazine started a section called "Bottle World." Our 1967 book, *Know Your Antiques,* told how to date a bottle from the lip, neck, type of closure, and bottom of the bottle. We said, "Bottle collecting is among the top three hobbies in the nation."

Lists of bottle clubs and publications are an indication of interest each year. Our first bottle price book listing old and new bottles was published in 1971. It also listed 2 national clubs, 226 local clubs, 4 bottle publications, and a bibliography of 135 books. Bottles changed hands at swap meets, bottle shows, and antiques shops. Bottle digging became a family pastime. Experts wrote about how to probe a privy, excavate a dump, or search tree roots near a swamp. Collectors wanted perfect bottles. If a paper label remained, it was removed so the clear glass could glow in the window. Today, the label, even if damaged, adds to the value because many advertising collectors want a complete package. The box, instructions, and go-withs are saved. Labels should be pristine for the bottle to be worth top dollar.

Modern bottles were made to sell consumers. Avon cosmetics seemed to be selling the packaging more than the contents. Liquor companies discovered the advantages of putting beverages in attractive containers, especially those made in an on-going series.

Bottle collecting has changed. Modern bottles peaked in 1982, and now although still collected, they are no longer considered "good investments." Antique bottles are still an important collectible. Historic flasks, bitters, and blown perfume bottles are sold at Americana auctions and shows. Supply is limited, prices are high. The top-priced flask in our 1971 book was $850. The current record price for a flask is $40,700, bid for *two* different bottles in 1988. Condition, rarity, and color still determine value. It also helps if two well-to-do collectors are bidding on the same bottle.

Bitters, cures, inks, medicines, candy containers, figurals, fruit jars, sodas, and other types of bottles have been studied, numbered, and classified in easily obtainable books. While bottle digs, shows, and clubs attract thousands, numbers are down from the 1980s and back to 1970s levels. Popularity of collectibles seems to go in twenty-five year cycles. The first ten years, starting about 1965, pioneer collectors studied and bought bottles. Books were written, clubs formed, and information became available. Others joined the search, prices rose, and by 1975 at the Charles Gardner collection auction, top interest and dollars were seen. Since then, the number of collectors has fallen, but the cycle is starting again. New collectors are seeking perfumes, milk bottles, fruit jars, and "painted" soda bottles. And record prices were seen at 1988–1990 auctions: Harrison's Columbian ink sold for $26,400, Wynkoop's sarsaparilla for $13,000, Macallan Scotch whiskey for $7,000.

LITTLE FOLKS GIFT BOX

AVON

Avon started calling loudly to bottle collectors in 1965. They offered a men's after-shave in a stein-shaped decanter or an amber glass boot. Collectors liked these modern figural bottles, and soon thousands of collectors realized that fancy bottles sold. Buy a bottle of cologne, use the contents, sell the empty bottle for more than you paid for it full. Even figural plastic containers, perfume bottles, and other Avons were instant collectibles. Two early price books about Avons appeared, the 1969 book *Bud Hastin's Avon Collector's Guide* and the 1969 book *Western Collector's Handbook and Price Guide to Avon Bottles*. New editions appeared over the years. Our 1971 bottle price book listed thirteen pages of Avons with prices such as $9 to $15 for the Viking Horn and $2.75 for the Boot spray cologne. These same bottles are in this book at $8 to $10 for the Viking Horn and $2.50 for the boot. Not a good investment, especially if you consider the 337% inflation since 1971. The early and rare Avon bottles, like these from 1927 marked California Perfume Company, bring good prices; so do attractive figurals in perfect condition, mint in the box. Children's sets like this one pictured in the 1927 catalog are very rare. Over 14,000 items are listed in the Avon price books and new ones appear each year, so there are plenty of Avons waiting to be collected.

BARBER
Early twentieth-century barber bottles with under-glass labels, unusual shapes, or colorful mixtures of glass bring the best prices today. This is a crossover collectible of interest to those who want bottles and those interested in medical and barber antiques. The blue and white 9-inch bottle is $350, the more common hobnail only $57. The unusual witch hazel bottle is $75.

BEAM

Modern liquor bottles were the collectible of the 1970s. The first true listing and price guide for Jim Beam bottle collectors appeared in 1968 and was updated yearly until 1985. Collector interest diminished by 1985, and today there is a small but enthusiastic group of collectors of modern figural liquor bottles. This Beam 1982 J.B. Turner locomotive bottle is worth $125, but many Beams sell for under $10. Other modern liquor bottles have been popular with collectors and are still bought and sold. The Ski Country bottles like these 1974 redwing blackbirds were made as part of a set. Value: $29–$50.

BEER

Beer bottle collectors want two different types. Some search for the bottles made before the automatic bottle machines were used. Many of these are found at bottle digs, so condition is often poor. Some want more recent bottles with known brand names or attractive labels. This rare, old, 18-inch amber glass bottle marked "E. Anheuser Co., St. Louis" is valued by the owner at $5,000.

BITTERS

Bitters are among the top-priced bottles collected. Especially popular and expensive are the figural bottles that held bitters. The record price of $16,500 was set in 1975 for a sapphire blue Old Homestead Wild Cherry Bitters. An aqua Indian Queen broke the record in 1991 for $16,700. Prices for these bottles, *counterclockwise from bottom right:* golden amber Suffolk pig, $495; Lash's bitters with paper label, $37; Jackson's Stoverall honey amber bottle, $2,500; amber G. L. Herrick Keystone Tonic bitters, $3,000; Dr. S. Mansfield Highland bitters, root beer color, $2,500.

DRUG

Any bottle used in a drugstore is part of this group of bottles. Prized are those with the embossed word "drug" or nineteenth-century examples with pontilled bottoms. This yellow-green bottle held Swain's Panacea from Philadelphia. Value: $300.

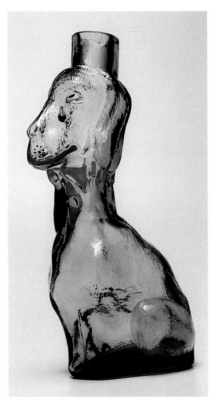

FIGURAL

Figural bottles have charmed collectors since ancient times. Price is determined by age, rarity, and appeal. The 12-inch enamel-decorated bottle shaped like a Spanish woman is worth $45. There is a companion male bottle. A more whimsical figural bottle like the 10-inch dog of amber glass is $32.

FIRE GRENADE
Fire grenades or fire extinguishers are rare because once used they are destroyed. These amber "hand grenades" are *top:* Barnum's, June 26, 1869, $975; Healy's "upside down," $875; *bottom:* Flagg's, Aug. 4, 1868, $650; and Hayward's, Aug 8, 1871, $345.

FLASKS

Historic flasks are identified by number and design in the McKearin books. Collectors can tell exactly what they have and record it for other collectors. Perhaps this is one reason flasks sell well—prices can be compared. Of course, the problem of how to describe a color remains because a "honey amber" may be worth more than an "amber" or a "reddish amber." The brown anchor flask made at the Ravenna Glass Works is worth $600. The historic flask could be called the king of the bottle world, but some prefer the non-royal buxom woman pictured on the glass label of this 6½-inch flask. Value, $450.

FRUIT JAR

Age, rarity, and color determine the value of fruit jars. This amber Globe jar marked "Pat. May 25, 1866" is not rare, so it is valued at $63. A cobalt blue fruit jar would be more expensive.

MILK

Colored glass milk bottles are rare. A few were made in amber or green glass. It was thought the color kept the milk fresher. This green bottle marked "Weckerle" is priced at $100.

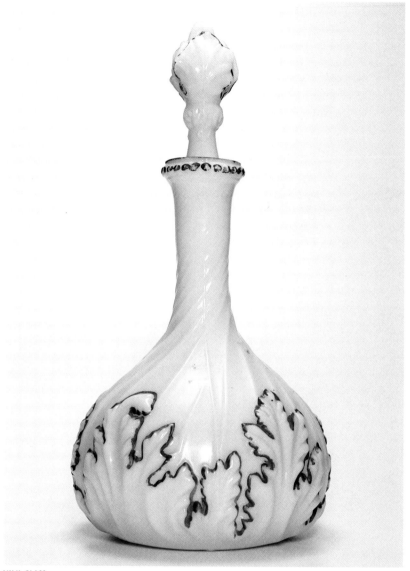

MILK GLASS
Milk glass was used to make many types of dinnerwares, dresser sets, vases, and other decorative objects in the nineteenth century. Bottles were also made. This milk glass decanter, or backbar bottle, decorated with gold paint is worth $125. Notice the elaborate molded decoration, typical of the Victorian style.

MINIATURE

There is something fascinating for most collectors about tiny replicas of bigger objects. Collectors of bottles also like miniatures. In the 1940s, bar owners often gave customers humorous miniature pottery bottles like this 3¾-inch-high dog. It is worth $24. Other miniature pottery giveaways like this pictured golfers, babies, attractive women, drunks, and other appropriate subjects. Prices can go over $100 for a good miniature. Most were made in Germany or Japan. But don't ignore the more traditional bottle-shaped miniatures that held samples of food or medicine or single servings of alcoholic beverages.

OPPOSITE PAGE: Miniature jugs were used as samples or giveaway promotions from the early 1900s. This cabinet holds pottery jugs less than 3 inches high.

A group of miniature jugs offered for sale at a 1991 bottle show.

Shelf 1, left to right: Elk's Pride Whiskey, Jno. S. Law, Carlisle, Pa., $150; Drink Old "New Hope" Sour Mash, $150; Compliments of Wheeler & Beagle, Detroit, Mich., $85; Compliments of C. E. Reed, Pure Wines & Liquors, $175; *Shelf 2:* Old Continental Whiskey, $50; Benton, Myers & Co., Cleveland, Ohio, $75; R.H. Parker Rye, Compliments Jos. Jellison, Montpelier, Ind., $125; Metropolitan Club, Freiberg & Kahn, Cincinnati, Ohio, $50; *Shelf 3:* Helmet Rye, Max Fruhauf & Co., Cincinnati, Ohio, $95; A Jug of Joy-Germa-Viki Cure, Syracuse, N.Y., $300; Cracking Club Whiskey, Schwabacher & Co., 1911, $75; C.H. Goodwin, Iron Mountain Saloon, Monroe, La. (a favorite of the dealer, so not for sale); *Shelf 4:* Try Karolina Korne, Gulf Distilling Co., Pensacola, Fla., $4; Original Hoffman House Rye Whiskey, H.F. Corbin & Co., Cincinnati, Ohio, $95; Compliments of J.C. Moore Jug House Co., Delta, La. (another favorite); Compliments of J. Freis, 150 Quincy St., Cleveland, Ohio, $85.

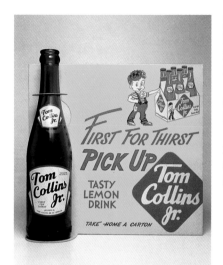

SODA

Naturally carbonated water was sold in the United States by 1818. Artificial carbonation began in 1830. Embossed blob-top bottles held the drink. In the 1980s, collectors started buying pyro-decorated modern soda bottles. Earlier collectors sought Coke or Pepsi memorabilia. This bottle of Tom Collins Jr., a 1940s nonalcoholic drink, and display sign is priced $30. The record 1991 price for a soda is $15,180 for a 6-sided deep amethyst bottle embossed "Blagrove's Superior Aerated Mineral Water, Brooklyn."

STIEGEL-TYPE

Bottles actually made by the Stiegel glassworks in the eighteenth century are probably all in museum collections. Bottles similar in appearance, made in the nineteenth and twentieth centuries, usually in Europe, are offered for sale as Stiegel-type. The peasant-like decorations and colors make them popular. This pair of 7-inch-high bottles was for sale at $400.

STONEWARE

Many stoneware bottles were made in England and Canada, and the tradition of the dark and light tan bottle was carried on in the United States. The "old fashioned" nineteenth-century style packaging of this beverage included the two-tone glaze and the Victorian type design for the black printed words. "Old Jug Lager" came in several similar bottles.

PERFUME, SCENT & COLOGNE

Perfume, scent, and cologne bottles are often confused with one another. Perfume was used to create a pleasant odor and scent to revive those who were fainting. Scent is smelling salts—perfume with ammonia salts added for a sharp vapor. The bottles are different. Scent bottles were usually free-blown or blown in a mold. The opening was large. Hinged lids were used. Scent bottles were rarely made after the nineteenth century. Cologne is similar to perfume but has more alcohol in the mixture. Cologne bottles often have atomizer tops. Perfume bottles have a small opening and a dauber as a stopper. The 1980s saw a surge of interest in twentieth-century commercial bottles, especially those by Lalique. This pink perfume bottle with floral decoration sold for $225. There is a club for collectors, the Perfume & Scent Bottle Collectors, P.O. Box 6965, Rockford, Ill. 61125-6965.

POISON

"You collect *poison* bottles?" might be the reaction of friends, but a shelf of unusual cobalt blue poisons is really a collection to envy. The problem of how to safely store poison was probably first solved in Denmark in the early nineteenth century when special apothecary jars were marked + + + to indicate poison. A law was passed in New York in 1829 that required the word "Poison" appear on appropriate containers. The skull and crossbones was officially used as a symbol on poisons in America beginning in 1853. By the 1870s, poisonous liquids were put in special bottles made with raised bumps or lines on the outside so they would feel different from ordinary bottles. Many were made of cobalt blue or other colored glass. By the 1930s, it was decided that the fancy colors and marking attracted children, so the philosophy changed and poison was put in simple containers with safety closures. Today collectors want any container that held poison, even labeled bottles

for rat and roach killers. The most desirable poison bottles are still the older colored examples. The 3-inch amber Jacobs bottle and the cobalt blue bottle are examples of collectible poisons.

NAILSEA-TYPE

Glass was made in Bristol, England, from 1788 to 1873. The distinctive glass had loopings of white or colored glass as the decoration. The name of one glass house, Nailsea, has become the collector's name for this glass, but a more accurate name is Nailsea-type. Often the bottles were made with rounded bottoms and could not be kept upright on the shelf. Gemel bottles, used to serve oil and vinegar, and flasks were made this way. This 7 ½-inch Nailsea-type flask is worth $480. The added stand solves the problem of the rounded bottom.

WHISKEY

Many collectors limit their bottle collections by displaying bottles used by only one industry. Beer, milk, soda water, or whiskey are popular choices. This cobalt whiskey bottle has a paper label that identifies it as "Caspers, Roanoke, Virginia." The Grand Army Encampment bottle labeled "Sept. 1895, Louisville, Kentucky," was a souvenir of a reunion of the Union troops.

Figural, Santa In Chimney, Whiskey, 5 1/2 In.   *Figural, Viking, Creme De Menthe, 12 1/2 In.*

Dice, Milk Glass	250.00
Dog, Amber, 10 In. ....*Illus*	32.00
Dog, Lime Green, Cambridge, 8 In.	8.00
Dog, Sitting, Pottery, Tan & White, Germany, 9 In.	20.00
Donkey, Italian Wine, Leather Cover ....9.00 To 12.00	
Dutch Girl, G. G. Delft, Holland, Cracked Hat Closure	82.00
Ear of Corn, Figural, Fitzpatrick & Co., 9 1/4 In.	1320.00
Eiffel Tower, Clear, Pontil, 14 3/4 In.	55.00
Elephant, Italian Wine, Leather Cover ....9.00 To 12.00	
Elephant, Uplifted Trunk, Frosted, 1900–1920, Pontil, 10 3/4 In.	154.00
Elk's Tooth, Milk Glass, Clock Face Above Elk's Head, 3 7/8 In.	66.00
Fat Man, Pochman & Harrison Mustard, Chicago, Screw Cap, 1/2 Pt.	5.00
Fish, Amber, 6 In.	30.00
Fish, Amber, 10 In.	8.00
Fish, Clear To Light Aqua, 3–In. Neck, 14 In.	10.00
Fish, Italian Wine, Green Glass	4.00
Friar John, Crushing Grapes, Italian Wine	14.00
George Washington, Clear, Umberger Garibaldi, Italy	25.00
Girl, Cazanove Bordeaux, France Bresse, Painted Porcelain	65.00
Globe, Clear, Smooth Lip, Pt.	5.00
Globe, Korbeline, Mosaic Type, Embossed, Clear, 7 In.	7.50
Grant's Tomb, Milk Glass, Metal Bust of Grant, 11 1/8 In.	303.00
Hat, 3–Piece Mold, Deep Sapphire, New England, 2 1/4 In.	413.00
Hessian Soldier, Clear, 7 Ft. 4 In.	44.00
Horsehead, Roman, Italian Wine	12.00
Horseshoe, Las Vegas	12.00
Hound, Seltzer, Orange Amber, Large	118.00
FIGURAL, INDIAN QUEEN, see Bitters, Brown's Celebrated	
Klondike Or Gold Nugget, Milk Glass, Original Closure	65.00
Kummel Bear, Black Amethyst, 11 In.	55.00
Kummel Bear, Deep Olive Green, 11 In.	30.00
Lady With Bird, Salt Glaze, Denby & Codnor Park, Derbyshire, 8 In.	410.00
Liberty Bell, Blended Whiskey, 200th Birthday, 11K Gold, 7 In.	12.00
Log, Uncle Tom's, Clear, Tooled Top, 3 1/2 In.	24.00
Man On Barrel, Dark To Medium Brown, Toby Jug Type, 6 3/4 In.	182.00
Man On Barrel, Success To Reform, Reform Flask, Denby, 7 3/4 In.	200.00
Mercedes, Italian Wine	22.00
Monkey, Our Boy Fine Cologne, 4 3/4 In. ....*Illus*	85.00
Monkey, Sitting, Milk Glass, Lip Crazed, 4 1/2 In.	143.00
Moses, Poland Springs Water, Honey Amber, 11 In.	83.00

Old Crow, Chess Set, Playing Rug, Complete 550.00
Old Tom, On Barrel, Oldfield & Co., 10 1/2 In. 191.00
Old Tom, On Barrel, Reform Flask, Oldfield & Co., 6 In. 318.00
Oyster, Clear, Ground Lip, Screw Cap 50.00
Pig, Bourbon In A Hog, Clear 65.00
Pig, Clear, Mouth Seal, 3 1/2 x 7 1/2 In. 66.00
Pig, Drink While It Last From The Hog's —, Amethyst, 6 3/4 In. 175.00
Pig, Pottery, Tan Glaze, Blue Eyes, 1850–1880, 6 1/2 In. 220.00
Pig, Rosenbaum Bros. Old Kentucky, Unglazed Pottery, 6 7/8 In. 303.00
Pig, Something Good In A Hog's – He Won't Squeal, Clear 79.00
Pig, Stoneware, Brown Glaze, 2 1/4 x 5 In. 187.00
Pig, We Trust G. A. R., Pottery, Salt Glazed, Blue Slip, 7 In. 242.00
Pig, Whiskey 1875, Pottery, Put Your Mouth To My, 9 In. 1760.00
Pipe, Alpine, Italian Wine 12.00
Pistol, 6 Shooter, USA Avor, Clear, Silver Inside, BIM, 5 In. 32.00
Pistol, Chianti Wine, Emerald Green, ABM, 17 In. 26.00
Pistol, Embossed Pat. Applied For, 5 1/4 In. 65.00
Policeman, Black, Screw Cap Head, 9 In. 75.00
Powder Horn, Diamond Pattern, Clear 35.00
Pretzel, Brown Pottery 30.00
Purse, Crisscross, Clasp, Slip Glaze Deep Red To Orange, 5 7/8 In. 209.00
Purse, F. Dark Wine & Spirit Merchant, Varied Salt Glaze, 6 In. 255.00
Purse, Woven, Clasp, Duke of Wellington, Chelsea, Salt Glaze, 5 In. 164.00
Rooster, Italian Wine, Leather Cover 15.00
Sailor, Standing, Smoking Pipe, Allover Orange, 8 1/3 In. 164.00
Santa Claus, Clear, Square Collared Mouth, N. J., 12 1/4 In. 120.00
Santa Claus, Milk Glass, 1880–1900, 12 1/2 In. 33.00
Santa In Chimney, Whiskey, 5 1/2 In. ....*Illus* 185.00
Shoe, Old Fashioned, Aqua, Heel Pontil, Seed Bubbles, 5 1/4 In. 50.00
Skeleton, Word Poison, Brown & White Glaze, Pottery, Stopper, 8 In. 88.00
Skull, Clear, 3–Piece Mold, 1890–1910, 4 In. 633.00
Sweet Potato, Ceramic, Late 19th Century, 7 In. 65.00
Teddy Roosevelt, Medium Amethyst, 6 3/8 In. 132.00
Three Cherubs, Holding Globe, Depose, Clear, Period Stopper, 12 In. 44.00
Tiger, Reclining, Italian Wine 14.00
Tipstaff, Crown Top, S. Green, Lambeth, Dark Brown, Red Orange, 9 In. 273.00
Titulus, Italian Wine 7.00
Turkey, Italian Wine, Leather Cover 18.00
Uncle Sam, Clear, Tooled Lip, Screw Cap Missing, 9 1/2 In. 121.00
Viking, Creme De Menthe, 12 1/2 In. ....*Illus* 350.00
Violin, Lavender, Music On Back, 10 In. 15.00
Violin, Light Green, 6 In. 10.00
Violin, Light Green, Seed Bubbles, 10 In. 12.00

Figural, Boy & Girl, Climbing Tree, 12 In.

Figural, Woman, Upside Down, 14 In.

Fire Grenade, Barnum's Hand, June 26, 1869, Amber, 6 In.

Fire Grenade, Flagg's Hand, Aug.4, 1868, Amber, 6 1/2 In.

William IV, Deep Brown Top, Cream, Glaze, 6 3/4 In.	91.00
William IV, Reform Cordial, Light Brown Matte, 8 In.	137.00
Wolf, Seated, With Book, Ceramic, Germany, 4 7/8 In.	44.00
Woman's Bust, Mi Lola Cigar Co., Milwaukee, Knob Lid, 6 1/2 In.	60.00
Woman, Pottery, Rockingham Type Glaze, 8 3/4 In.	149.00
Woman, Upside Down, 14 In. ....*Illus*	110.00
Zorro, Sandeman, Black Cup, Left Shoulder, Label, Wedgwood, 10 In.	9.00
Zorro, Sandeman, Black Cup, Right Shoulder, Label, Wedgwood, 10 In.	9.00
Zorro, Sandeman, White Cup, Left Shoulder, Wedgwood, 10 In.	12.00

FIRE GRENADE

Fire grenades were popular from about 1870 to 1910. They were glass containers filled with a fire extinguisher such as carbon tetrachloride. The bottle of liquid was thrown at the base of a fire to shatter and extinguish the flames. A particularly ingenious *automatic* type was hung in a wire rack; theoretically, the heat of the fire would melt the solder of the rack and the glass grenade would drop into the fire. Because they were designed to be destroyed, not too many have survived for the collector. Some are found today that still have the original contents sealed by cork and wax closures. Handle these with care. Fumes from the contents are dangerous to your health.

FIRE GRENADE, American Fire Extinguisher, Quilted, Footed, Square, 6 In.	231.00
Barnum's Hand Fire Ext. Diamond, Aqua, Square, 6 In.	220.00
Barnum's Hand, Diamond, Aqua, June 25th, 1869, 6 1/8 In.	358.00
Barnum's Hand, June 26, 1869, Amber, 6 In. ....*Illus*	975.00
C. & N. W. Ry., Clear, Ground Lip, 17 3/4 In.	130.00
Chicago Northwestern Railroad, Tube, Broken Neck, Clear	45.00
Dri–Gas, Chattanooga, Tenn., Clear, ABM, 11 In.	187.00
Flagg's Hand, Aug. 4, 1868, Amber, 6 1/2 In. ....*Illus*	650.00
Harden's Hand, Flat, English Star, Cobalt Blue, Contents, Pt.	60.00
Harden's Hand, Footed, Cobalt Blue, 1/2 Pt.	165.00
Harden's Hand, Improved, 2 Piece, Iron Clamp, Colorless, 5 In.	275.00
Harden's Hand, Pale Green, 6 1/2 In.	350.00
Harden's Hand, Quilted, Footed, Blue, Contents, 1/2 Pt.	165.00
Harden's Hand, Quilted, Footed, Blue, Contents, Pt.	80.00
Harden's Hand, Quilted, Footed, Cobalt Blue, 1/2 Pt.	165.00
Harden's Hand, Quilted, Turquoise, 1870–1900, 6 In.	50.00
Harden's Hand, Star In Circle, Clear, May 27, '84, 8 In.	468.00
Harden's Hand, Star In Circle, Yellow Green, 7 7/8 In.	357.00
Harden's Hand, Star, Blue, Pt.	80.00
Harden's Hand, Star, Cobalt Blue, Contents, 6 1/2 In.	121.00

Harden's Hand, Star, Deep Cobalt Blue, 6 3/4 In. ....148.00 To 198.00
Harden's Hand, Star, Large, Turquoise, Contents, 6 1/2 In. 100.00
Harden's Hand, Star, Pat. '84, Turquoise, 6 1/2 In. 165.00
Harden's Hand, Star, Turquoise, 6 1/2 In. 83.00
Harden's Hand, Turquoise, 5 1/8 In. 75.00
Harden's Hand, Turquoise, Pat. No. 1 Aug. 8, 1871 & 1883, 6 In. 121.00
Harden's Hand, Yellow Green, 7 3/4 In. 300.00
Harden's Sprinkler, Deep Cobalt Blue, 17 In. 670.00
Harkness Fire Destroyer, Cobalt Blue, Pt. 475.00
Harkness Fire Destroyer, Cobalt Blue, Unembossed, 6 1/4 In. 231.00
Hayward's Hand, Amber, 6 1/8 In. 110.00
Hayward's Hand, Apple Green, Pat. Aug. 8, 1871, 6 1/4 In. 253.00
Hayward's Hand, Aqua, 7 1/2 In. 170.00
Hayward's Hand, Cobalt Blue, 6 In. 275.00
Hayward's Hand, Diamond Panel, Clear, Pt. 225.00
Hayward's Hand, Golden Amber, Spherical, 4 Panels, 6 1/4 In. 91.00
Hayward's Hand, Medium Amber, 6 In. 140.00
Hayward's Hand, Pale Aqua, Contents, 5 7/8 In. 165.00
Hayward's Hand, Pleated, Aqua, Contents, Lead Seal, Pt. 225.00
Hayward's Hand, Pleated, Aqua, Contents, Pt. 225.00
Hayward's Hand, Turquoise, Aug. 8, 1871, Contents, 6 In. 523.00
Hayward's Hand, Yellow Amber, Pat. Aug. 8, 1871, 6 1/8 In. 83.00
Hayward's Hand, Yellow Green, Aug. 8, 1871, 6 1/2 In. ....*Illus* 345.00
Hayward's Hand, Yellow Green, Aug. 8, 1871, 6 1/4 In. 242.00
Healy's Hand, U Upside Down, Amber, 11 In. ....*Illus* 875.00
Imperial, Bright Yellow Green, 6 1/2 In. 350.00
Kalamazoo Rockford, Medium Deep Cobalt 100.00
Kalamazoo, Cobalt Blue 525.00
L. B., Medium Sapphire Blue, Pt., 5 1/4 In. 1000.00
Nutting, NHS Monogram, Yellow, Orange Cast, 7 1/8 In. 137.00
Pat. Nov. 28, 1884, Golden Amber, Contents, 6 1/4 In. 798.00
Pinoxic, Green 175.00
Pyro–Ball, Staten Island, Rack & 4 Light Bulb–Shaped Balls 137.00
Rockford Hand, Kalamazoo, Bright Cobalt Blue, 10 3/4 In. 330.00
Rockford Hand, Kalamazoo, Cobalt Blue, 10 3/4 In. 275.00
Shu–Stop, Automatic Fireman On Wall, Holder, Pear Shape 55.00
Sinclair, Unembossed, Cobalt Blue, 7 1/8 In. 120.00
Systeme Labbe, Grenade Extincteur, Paris, Amber, 5 1/2 In. 350.00
FITZGERALD, see Old Fitzgerald

Fire Grenade, Hayward's Hand,
Yellow Green, Aug.8, 1871, 6 1/2 In.

Fire Grenade, Healy's Hand, U Upside Down,
Amber, 11 In.

Flask, 10 Diamond Pattern, Brown, 5 1/2 In.   Flask, Anchor, Brown, Ravenna Glass Co.,
                                                                    8 In.

FLASK

Flasks have been made in America since the eighteenth century. Hundreds of styles and variations were made. Free–blown, mold–blown, and decorated flasks are all popular with collectors. Prices are determined by rarity, condition, and color. In general, bright colors bring higher prices. The numbers used in the entries in the form McK G I–000 refer to the book *American Bottles and Flasks* by Helen McKearin and Kenneth M. Wilson. Each flask listed in that book is sketched and described and it is important to compare your flask with the book picture to determine value, since many similar flasks were made.

Many reproductions of flasks have been made, most in the last 20 years, but some as early as the nineteenth century. The reproduction flasks that seem to cause the most confusion for the beginner are the Lestoil flasks made in the 1960s. These bottles, sold in grocery stores, were filled with Lestoil, a liquid cleaner, and sold for about 65 cents. Three designs were made: a Washington Eagle, a Columbia Eagle, and a ship Franklin Eagle. Four colors were used—purple, dark blue, dark green, and amber—and mixes were also produced. Over one million of the flasks were made and they now are seen at the collectible shows. The only mark on the bottles was the name Lestoil on the stopper. Other reproductions will be found marked *Nuline* or *Taiwan*.

FLASK, 10 Diamond Pattern, Brown, 5 1/2 In. ....*Illus*   1600.00
15–Piece Mold, Diamond, Deep Green Aqua, Pontil, 1/2 Pt. 495.00
16 Ribs, Swirled Left, Midwest, Yellow Green, Pontil, 6 1/2 In. 477.00
20 Ribs, Midwest, Citron, Sheared Mouth, Pontil, Pt. 660.00
24 Ribs, Swirled Right, Bright Yellowish Amber, Globular, 7 7/8 In. 358.00
33rd National Encampment, 1899, Philadelphia, Pa., Pocket, 5 1/8 In. 330.00
A. Hamfeldt Wines & Liquors, Ottawa, Ill., Oval 50.00
Admiral Dewey, Eagle, Flags, Canteen Form, 1890–1910, 1/2 Pt. 110.00
Anchor, Brown, Ravenna Glass Co., 8 In. ....*Illus*   600.00
Barley Bree, William Gillies & Co., Pottery, 3 Men Drinking, 5 In. 237.00
Black & White Looping, Red Ground, Stand, 7 1/2 In. ....*Illus*   480.00
Blown, Aqua, OP, 1830, Oval, 6 1/4 In. 77.00
Blown, Midwestern, Amber, 11 In. 325.00
Blown, OP, Rolled Out Lip, Cork, 1840, 6 In. 33.00
Blown, Sunburst Shape, Ribbed, Cobalt Blue, 1/2 Pt. 1100.00
Bonnie Bros., Louisville, Ky., Whiskey, Purple, Pt. 25.00

Chapin & Gore, Chicago, Sour Mash, 1867, Amber, Side Strap 75.00
Chestnut, 12 Diamond, Clear, Flared Mouth, Pontil, 5 5/8 In. 175.00
Chestnut, 12 Ribs, Dark Amethyst, Terminal Ring, 5 3/8 In. 650.00
Chestnut, 16 Ribs, Midwest, Green Aqua, OP, 1820–1840, 6 1/8 In. 105.00
Chestnut, 18 Diamond, Citron Shading To Amber At Neck, 6 3/8 In. 1600.00
Chestnut, 18 Ribs, Swirled To Right 175.00
Chestnut, 18 Ribs, Swirled, Midwest, Aqua, 6 1/4 In. 135.00
Chestnut, 18 Ribs, Swirled, Midwest, Light Green 175.00
Chestnut, 22 Ribs, Midwest, Aqua, Pontil, 1/2 Pt. 165.00
Chestnut, 24 Ribs, Orange Amber, OP, Zanesville, 1/2 Pt. 195.00
Chestnut, 32 Ribs, Amethyst, Terminal Ring, Mantua, 5 In. 1525.00
Chestnut, Amber, Applied Handle, 9 In. 50.00
Chestnut, Blown, New England, Deep Olive, c.1820, 1/2 Pt. 100.00
Chestnut, Expanded Diamond Popcorn, Clear, 5 1/4 In. 95.00
Chestnut, Flat, Clear, Rows of Controlled Bubbles, OP, 4 1/2 In. 40.00
Chestnut, Free–Blown, Medium Olive Yellow, OP, 4 1/2 In. 100.00
Chestnut, Free–Blown, Medium Olive, OP, Rolled Lip, 6 1/2 In. 88.00
Chestnut, Free–Blown, Olive Amber, Rolled Lip, OP, 5 1/8 In. 70.00
Chestnut, Free–Blown, Olive Green, 1790–1830, 5 1/2 In. 176.00
Chestnut, Free–Blown, Thin, No Pontil Mark, 1800–1830, 6 1/4 In. 330.00
Chestnut, Free–Blown, Yellow Amber, Rolled Lip, OP, 4 1/2 In. 275.00
Chestnut, Green, Handle, Flat, OP, Large 135.00
Chestnut, Light Olive Green, Pontil, 1790–1830, 5 1/4 In. 143.00
Chestnut, Medium Olive Yellow, OP, Rolled Lip, 6 In. 121.00
Chestnut, Medium Yellow Amber, OP, Rolled Lip, 6 3/4 In. 154.00
Chestnut, Midwest, Citron, 4 7/8 In. 155.00
Chestnut, Midwest, Golden Amber, OP, Zanesville 180.00
Chestnut, Yellow Amber, Sheared Mouth, Pontil, 6 1/4 In. 132.00
Clasped Hands & Eagle, Medium Moss Green, Variant, 1870s, Qt. 550.00
Coffin, Clear, Says Full Quart 6.00
Crown & Lion, Aqua, Sheared Lip, France, Mid–19th Century 50.00
Daniel Shea, Haymarket Square, Boston, Amber, Strap Side, 1/2 Pt. 65.00
Enameled, Floral, 3 Crossed Swords 1 Side, America Other, 5 In. 210.00
Fleur–De–Lis Side, Diamond Pattern, Teardrop, Green, 8 1/2 In. 55.00
For Auld Lang Syne, Flattened Pottery, Kilted Highlander, 6 In. 91.00
Gen. U.S. Grant, Picture, Metal Cap, Flattened Rectangular, 1/2 Pt. 330.00
Granite Glass Co., Stoddard, N. H., Olive Amber, Pontil, Pt. 143.00
Green Strap Side, Pt. 35.00
Half Barrel Shape, Merry Christmas & Happy New Year, Clear, 1/2 Pt. 94.00
Horse's Head, Stirrup, Amethyst Tint, BIMAL 55.00
Hound & Horseman, Amber 385.00
James Buchanan & Co. Ltd., Olive Green, Lion & Unicorn, 1900, Qt. 29.00
Jas. Eadie, Grangetown Hotel, Aqua, Rectangular, 1/2 Pt. 35.00
Leon Greenberg, Calif. Wine Agency, Hartford, Conn., Coffin 35.00
Light Green, New London, 1/2 Pt. 440.00
Lions & Shield, Acorns & Leaves, Cobalt Blue, Pontil, 1840–1860, Pt. ... 352.00
McK G I–001, Washington & Eagle, Light Blue Green, Pontil, Pt. 396.00
McK G I–002, Washington & Eagle, Aqua, Pt. 200.00
McK G I–006, Washington & Eagle, Clear, Amethyst Tint, OP, Pt. 1045.00
McK G I–011, Washington & Eagle, Aqua, OP, Pt. 468.00
McK G I–014, Washington & Eagle, Aqua, Pontil, Pt. 121.00
McK G I–014, Washington & Eagle, T. W. D., Aqua, Pt. .... 140.00 To 170.00
McK G I–016, Washington & Eagle, Aqua, Pontil, Pt. 350.00
McK G I–017, Washington & Taylor, Aqua, Pt. 150.00
McK G I–020, Washington & Monument, Aqua, Pt. 90.00
McK G I–021, Washington & Monument, Aqua, OP 150.00
McK G I–024, Washington & Taylor, Aqua, Sheared Mouth, Pt. 132.00
McK G I–030, Washington, Citron, OP, Albany, 1/2 Pt. 330.00
McK G I–031, Washington & Jackson, Dark Olive Green 150.00
McK G I–033, Washington & Jackson, Olive Amber, Pt. 165.00
McK G I–034, Washington & Jackson, Olive Amber, Pt. 143.00
McK G I–037, Washington & Taylor, Aqua, Qt. 65.00
McK G I–037, Washington & Taylor, Clear Green, Pontil, Qt. 176.00

McK G I–037, Washington & Taylor, Hinge Base, Aqua, OP, Qt. 95.00
McK G I–037, Washington & Taylor, Light Yellow Green 200.00
McK G I–038, Washington & Taylor, Aqua, Double Collar Lip, Pt. 65.00
McK G I–038, Washington & Taylor, Emerald Green, OP, Pt. 440.00
McK G I–038, Washington & Taylor, Medium Green, 1850, Pt. 330.00
McK G I–038, Washington & Taylor, Olive Green, Pontil, Pt. 550.00
McK G I–039, Washington & Taylor, Pink Amethyst, Thin, Sheared Lip 2970.00
McK G I–040a, Washington & Taylor, Aqua, Pt. 65.00
McK G I–041, Washington & Taylor, Olive Green, 1/2 Pt. 25.00
McK G I–042, Washington & Taylor, Aqua, Pontil, Dyottville, Qt. 180.00
McK G I–042, Washington & Taylor, Light Blue Green, Pontil, Qt. 110.00
McK G I–043, Washington & Taylor, Aqua, Sheared Mouth, Pontil, Qt. 55.00
McK G I–043, Washington & Taylor, Deep Amber, OP, Qt. 577.00
McK G I–045, Washington & Taylor, Aqua, Double Collared, Qt. 44.00
McK G I–046, Washington & Taylor, Aqua, Qt. 55.00
McK G I–047, Washington, Light To Medium Blue Green, Qt. 215.00
McK G I–048, Washington, Father of His Country, Aqua, Applied Mouth 60.00
McK G I–048, Washington, Father of His Country, Blue Green, Pt. 110.00
McK G I–050, Washington & Taylor, Aqua, 1840–1850 .... 66.00
McK G I–051, Washington & Taylor, Dark Sapphire, Qt. 895.00
McK G I–051, Washington & Taylor, Deep Chocolate, OP, Qt. 1595.00
McK G I–051, Washington & Taylor, Medium Blue Green, Dyottville 231.00
McK G I–051, Washington & Taylor, Sapphire Blue, Pontil, Qt. 358.00
McK G I–052, Washington & Taylor, Medium Blue Green, Pontil, Pt. 171.00
McK G I–052, Washington & Taylor, Yellow Amber, OP, Pt. 715.00
McK G I–053, Washington & Taylor, Aqua, Pt. 70.00
McK G I–054, Washington & Taylor, Olive Yellow, Qt. 193.00
McK G I–055a, Washington & Taylor, Pale Yellow Green, Pontil, Pt. 110.00
McK G I–059, Washington & Sheaf, Aqua, 1/2 Pt. .... 60.00 To 90.00
McK G I–061, Washington & Washington, Aqua, Sheared Mouth, Qt. 77.00
McK G I–071, Taylor & Ringgold, Aqua, OP, Pt. .... 127.00 To 190.00
McK G I–076, Taylor & Eagle, Aqua, OP, Pt. 3345.00
McK G I–077, Taylor & Eagle, Deep Aqua, Pt. 385.00
McK G I–080, Lafayette & Clinton, Coventry, Olive Amber, Pt. 500.00
McK G I–080, Lafayette & Clinton, Medium Olive Green, Pt. 121.00
McK G I–082, Lafayette & Clinton, Yellow Olive, Pontil, 1/2 Pt. 3520.00
McK G I–085, Lafayette & Liberty, Medium Olive Green, Coventry 275.00
McK G I–086, Lafayette & Liberty, Yellow Amber, 1/2 Pt. 325.00
McK G I–090, Lafayette & Eagle, Aqua, Sheared Mouth, Pontil, Pt. 220.00
McK G I–090, Lafayette & Eagle, Pale Aqua, Pt. 154.00
McK G I–093, Lafayette & Eagle, Blue Green, Pt. 1400.00
McK G I–094, Franklin & Dyott, Aqua, Sheared Mouth, Pontil, Pt. 88.00
McK G I–094, Franklin & Dyott, Deep Amber, Pontil, 1826–1830, Pt. 2090.00
McK G I–096, Franklin & Dyott, Aqua, OP, Qt. 250.00
McK G I–097, Franklin & Franklin, Aqua, OP, Qt. .... 121.00 To 175.00
McK G I–099, Jenny Lind, Calabash, Aqua, IP 88.00
McK G I–099, Jenny Lind, Calabash, Deep Emerald Green 688.00
McK G I–099, Jenny Lind, Calabash, Olive Yellow, OP 1045.00
McK G I–103, Jenny Lind & Glasshouse, Calabash, Aqua, OP, Qt. 84.00
McK G I–104, Jenny Lind, Calabash, Cornflower Blue, Qt. 750.00
McK G I–104, Jenny Lind, Calabash, Medium Yellow Green, IP 1430.00
McK G I–107, Jenny Lind, Calabash, Aqua, Pontil, Qt. 55.00
McK G I–108, Jenny Lind & Lyre, Aqua, OP, Pt. .... 575.00 To 850.00
McK G I–109, Jenny Lind & Lyre, Aqua, Sheared Lip, Pontil, Qt. 800.00
McK G I–110, Jenny Lind & Lyre, Aqua, Sheared Lip, Pontil, Qt. 950.00
McK G I–112, Kossuth & Frigate, Calabash, Aqua, OP 242.00
McK G I–113, Kossuth & Tree, Calabash, Bright Yellow Green 225.00
McK G I–113, Kossuth & Tree, Calabash, Deep Emerald Green 805.00
McK G I–113, Kossuth & Tree, Calabash, Olive Yellow, Pontil, Qt. 231.00
McK G I–113, Kossuth & Tree, Calabash, Pale Green, IP, Qt. 77.00
McK G I–114, Byron & Scott, Olive Amber 300.00
McK G I–114, Byron & Scott, Yellow Amber, Pontil, 1/2 Pt. .... 126.00 To 231.00
McK G I–117, Columbia & Eagle, Kensington, Aqua, OP, Pt. 605.00

McK G I–118, Columbia & Eagle, Kensington, Aqua, OP, 1/2 Pt. 230.00
McK G I–121, Columbia & Eagle, Aqua, OP, Pt. .... 215.00 To 500.00
McK G I–121, Columbia & Eagle, Aqua, Pontil, Pt. 358.00
McK G I–122, Columbia & Eagle, Clear, Stringy Striations, Thick, Pt. 4180.00
McK G I–123a, Cleveland & Stevenson, Rooster, Amber, Pt. .... 357.00 To 375.00
McK G I–124, Cleveland & Stevenson, Rooster, Amber, 1/2 Pt. 412.00
McK G II–003, Double Eagle, 3–Piece Mold, Olive, Pontil, 1/2 Pt. 9900.00
McK G II–003, Double Eagle, Aqua, Pontil, Pt. 154.00
McK G II–006, Eagle & Cornucopia, Pale Aqua, OP, Pt. .... 154.00 To 200.00
McK G II–007, Eagle & Sunburst, Medium Aqua, Pontil, 1820–1830, Pt. 525.00
McK G II–007, Eagle & Sunburst, Yellow Green, OP, Pt. 2475.00
McK G II–009, Eagle & Snake, Pale Vaseline, OP, Pt. 3575.00
McK G II–012, Eagle & Inverted Cornucopia, Light Blue Green 375.00
McK G II–016, Eagle & Cornucopia, Deep Aqua, OP, 1/2 Pt. 154.00
McK G II–019, Eagle & Morning Glory, Aqua, OP, Pt. .... 330.00 To 358.00
McK G II–022, Eagle & Lyre, 3–Piece Mold, Clear, Stopper, 8 1/4 In. 121.00
McK G II–023, Eagle & Flower, Deep Aqua, OP, Pt. 165.00
McK G II–024, Double Eagle, Aqua, OP, Pt. 165.00
McK G II–024, Double Eagle, Light Green, Pt. 350.00
McK G II–024, Double Eagle, Medium Yellow Green, OP, Pt. 253.00
McK G II–024, Double Eagle, Sapphire Blue, Pontil, Kentucky, Pt. 2750.00
McK G II–025, Double Eagle, Aqua, Pt. 135.00
McK G II–025, Double Eagle, Deep Chocolate Amber, OP, Pt. 770.00
McK G II–026, Double Eagle, Ice Blue, IP, Qt. 330.00
McK G II–026, Double Eagle, Light Blue Green 275.00
McK G II–026, Double Eagle, Medium Green, Pontil, Kentucky, Qt. 225.00
McK G II–029, Eagle, Aqua, Laid On Ring, 1/2 Pt. 75.00
McK G II–030, Double Eagle, Aqua, 1/2 Pt. 300.00
McK G II–032a, Double Eagle, Aqua, OP, Pt. 265.00
McK G II–032a, Double Eagle, Pale Green Aqua, OP, Pt. 190.00
McK G II–033, Eagle & Louisville, Aqua, 1/2 Pt. 154.00
McK G II–037, Eagle & Ravenna, Deep Golden Amber, IP, Pt. 467.00
McK G II–038, Eagle & Dyottville, Brilliant Amethyst, Pt. 688.00
McK G II–039, Eagle & Plain, Reverse, Aqua, Smooth Base, Pt. 77.00
McK G II–040, Double Eagle, Bright Medium Blue Green, Pontil, Pt. 715.00
McK G II–040, Double Eagle, Emerald Green, Kensington, Pontil, Pt. 1100.00
McK G II–041, Eagle & Tree, Aqua, Pt. 130.00
McK G II–042, Eagle & Frigate, Aqua, Pontil, Pt. 77.00
McK G II–043, Eagle & Cornucopia, Aqua, Pontil, 1/2 Pt. 182.00
McK G II–045, Eagle & Cornucopia, Aqua, 1/2 Pt. 140.00
McK G II–048, Eagle & Flag, Coffin & Hay, Aqua, OP, Qt. 175.00
McK G II–048, Eagle & Flag, Coffin & Hay, Emerald Green, OP, Qt. 1595.00
McK G II–050, Eagle & Stag, Aqua, OP, 1/2 Pt. .... 155.00 To 250.00
McK G II–052, Eagle & Flag, Aqua, Pt. 100.00
McK G II–053, Eagle & Flag, Aqua, Pt. ....90.00 To 150.00
McK G II–054, Eagle & Flag, Aqua, OP, Pt. 139.00
McK G II–054, Eagle & Flag, Aqua, Pontil, Pt. 99.00
McK G II–055, Eagle & Grapes, Gray Aqua, OP, Qt. 75.00
McK G II–055, Eagle & Grapes, Medium Blue Green, OP, Qt. 745.00
McK G II–060, Eagle & Oak Tree, Amber, OP, 1/2 Pt. 965.00
McK G II–060, Eagle & Oak Tree, Pale Yellow Green, Pontil, 1/2 Pt. 550.00
McK G II–061, Eagle & Willington, Deep Green, 1860s, Qt. 275.00
McK G II–061, Eagle & Willington, Olive Green, Sloping Collar, Qt. 155.00
McK G II–062, Eagle & Willington, Emerald Green, Applied Top, Pt. 385.00
McK G II–063, Eagle & Willington, Olive Green, 1/2 Pt. 150.00
McK G II–066, Eagle & New London, Yellow, Qt. 1430.00
McK G II–071, Double Eagle, Dark Amber, Pontil, 1/2 Pt. 110.00
McK G II–072, Eagle & Cornucopia, Olive Amber, OP, Pt. 175.00
McK G II–073, Eagle & Cornucopia, Golden Amber, OP, Pt. 109.00
McK G II–073, Eagle & Cornucopia, Green, Pt. 125.00
McK G II–073, Eagle & Cornucopia, Medium Olive Green, OP, Pt. 98.00
McK G II–073, Eagle & Cornucopia, Olive Amber, Pt. 70.00
McK G II–076, Eagle & Concentric Ring, Bright Yellow Green, Qt. 633.00

McK G II–076a, Eagle & Concentric Ring, Light Green, Pt. 4400.00
McK G II–080, Double Eagle, Granite Glass, Yellow Olive, Pontil, Qt. 560.00
McK G II–082, Double Eagle, Olive Amber, Pt. 83.00
McK G II–084, Double Eagle, Olive Amber, Pt. 60.00
McK G II–085, Double Eagle, Olive Amber, 1/2 Pt. 65.00
McK G II–086, Double Eagle, Deep Olive Amber, Pontil, 1/2 Pt. 87.00
McK G II–088, Double Eagle, Yellow Amber, OP/1/2 Pt. 105.00
McK G II–092, Double Eagle, Amber, Pt. 125.00
McK G II–092, Double Eagle, Aqua, IP, Pt. .... 49.00 To 72.00
McK G II–101, Double Eagle, Olive Green, Applied Mouth, Qt. 275.00
McK G II–105, Double Eagle, Dark Emerald Green 265.00
McK G II–106, Double Eagle, Deep Olive Green, OP, Pt. 149.00
McK G II–109, Double Eagle, Sapphire Blue, Pittsburgh, 1/2 Pt. 770.00
McK G II–130, Double Eagle, Aqua, Pt. .... 44.00 To 55.00
McK G II–142, Eagle & Indian, Aqua, Qt. .... 99.00 To 115.00
McK G II–142, Eagle & Indian, Cornflower Blue, Qt. 150.00
McK G II–142, Eagle & Indian, Light Aqua, Qt. 150.00
McK G II–142, Eagle & Indian, Shooting Arrow, Aqua, Qt. 150.00
McK G III–004, Cornucopia & Urn, Deep Olive Green, OP, Pt. 88.00
McK G III–004, Cornucopia & Urn, Green, Pt. 125.00
McK G III–004, Cornucopia & Urn, Olive Amber, OP, Pt. 65.00
McK G III–004, Cornucopia & Urn, Olive Green, Pt. 55.00
McK G III–004, Cornucopia & Urn, Teal, Coventry, Pt. 225.00
McK G III–005, Cornucopia & Urn, Olive Green, OP, 6 3/4 In. 66.00
McK G III–007, Cornucopia & Urn, Olive Amber, 1/2 Pt. 65.00
McK G III–007, Cornucopia & Urn, Olive Green, 1/2 Pt. 55.00
McK G III–007, Cornucopia & Urn, Olive Yellow, OP, 1/2 Pt. 121.00
McK G III–011, Cornucopia & Urn, Olive Green, Sheared, OP, 1/2 Pt. 84.00
McK G III–012, Cornucopia & Urn, Olive Amber, Pontil, 1/2 Pt. 165.00
McK G III–014, Cornucopia & Urn, Emerald Green, OP, 1/2 Pt. 385.00
McK G III–014, Cornucopia & Urn, Green, OP, 1/2 Pt. 495.00
McK G III–015, Cornucopia & Urn, Bright Yellow Green, 1/2 Pt. 400.00
McK G III–016, Cornucopia & Urn, Aqua, OP, Pt. 225.00
McK G III–016, Cornucopia & Urn, Cobalt Blue, Lancaster, IP, Pt. 743.00
McK G III–016, Cornucopia & Urn, Lancaster, Sapphire Blue, Pt. 1150.00
McK G III–017, Cornucopia & Urn, Blue Green, OP, Pt. .... 226.00 To 245.00
McK G III–017, Cornucopia & Urn, Medium Blue 495.00
McK G IV–001, Masonic & Eagle, Light Blue Green, Pontil, Pt. 187.00
McK G IV–001, Masonic & Eagle, Light Green, Pontil, Pt. 187.00
McK G IV–001, Masonic & Eagle, Medium Blue Green, Pontil, Pt. 154.00
McK G IV–001a, Masonic & Eagle, Light To Bluish Green, OP, Pt. 143.00
McK G IV–003, Masonic & Eagle, Medium Blue Green, Pontil, Pt. 220.00
McK G IV–007, Masonic & Eagle, Deep Aqua, Pontil, Pt. .... 295.00 To 325.00
McK G IV–007, Masonic & Eagle, Medium Yellow Green, OP, Qt. 605.00
McK G IV–007a, Masonic & Eagle, Light Green Aqua, Pontil, Pt. 330.00
McK G IV–014, Masonic & Eagle, Yellow Green, Pontil, 1/2 Pt. 357.00
McK G IV–016, Cornucopia & Urn, Ice Blue, OP, Pt. 200.00
McK G IV–016, Masonic & Eagle, Olive Green, Pontil, Pt. 1705.00
McK G IV–017, Masonic & Eagle, Light Yellow Amber, Pt. 175.00
McK G IV–017, Masonic & Eagle, Olive Amber, Pontil, Keene, Pt. 143.00
McK G IV–018, Masonic & Eagle, Olive Amber, Pontil, Keene, Pt. 176.00
McK G IV–018, Masonic & Eagle, Yellow Amber, OP, Pt. 85.00
McK G IV–019, Masonic & Eagle, Golden Amber, Pontil, Keene, Pt. 132.00
McK G IV–019, Masonic & Eagle, Yellow Amber, Pontil, Pt. 180.00
McK G IV–020, Masonic & Eagle, Deep Amber, OP, Pt. 195.00
McK G IV–021, Masonic & Eagle, Olive Green, Pt. .... 135.00 To 220.00
McK G IV–026, Masonic & Eagle, NEG, Olive Amber, OP, 1/2 Pt. 990.00
McK G IV–028, Masonic, Blue Green, Pt. 265.00
McK G IV–032, Masonic & Eagle, Aqua, Pt. 250.00
McK G IV–032, Masonic & Eagle, Citron, Pontil, Pt. 1100.00
McK G IV–032, Masonic & Eagle, Red Amber, OP, Zanesville, Pt. 425.00
McK G IV–032, Masonic Farmer's Arms & Eagle, Amber, 1820s 247.00
McK G IV–032, Masonic Farmer's Arms & Eagle, Golden Amber, Pt. 495.00

McK G IV–032, Masonic Farmer's Arms & Eagle, Medium Green, OP, Pt.		330.00
McK G IV–032, Masonic Farmer's Arms & Eagle, Reddish Amber, Pt.		242.00
McK G IV–032, Masonic Farmer's Arms & Eagle, Yellow Olive, OP, Pt.		2035.00
McK G IV–032, Masonic Farmer's Arms & Eagle, Zanesville, Aqua		273.00
McK G IV–034, Masonic Farmer's Arms & Frigate, Aqua, Pontil, Pt.		242.00
McK G IV–036, Masonic & Frigate, Light Yellow Green		170.00
McK G IV–036, Masonic Farmer's Arms & Frigate, Yellow Green		155.00
McK G IV–037, Masonic & Eagle, Pale Aqua, Pontil, Pt.		110.00
McK G IV–037, Masonic & Eagle, T. W. D., Aqua, OP, Pt.		138.00
McK G IV–042, Clasped Hands Shield & Eagle, Calabash, Citron, OP		305.00
McK G IV–043, Masonic & Star, Olive Green, Sheared Lip, OP, Pt.		210.00
McK G V–001b, Success To The Railroad, Yellow Amber, OP, Pt.		2530.00
McK G V–002, Success To The Railroad, Aqua, Pt.		400.00
McK G V–003, Success To The Railroad, Forest Green, Keene, Pt.		242.00
McK G V–003, Success To The Railroad, Golden Olive Amber, OP, Pt.		84.00
McK G V–003, Success To The Railroad, Yellow Olive, Pt.	132.00 To	400.00
McK G V–004, Success To The Railroad, Bright Yellow Amber		500.00
McK G V–004, Success To The Railroad, Green		275.00
McK G V–005, Success To The Railroad, Forest Green, Mt. Vernon, 1820s		193.00
McK G V–005, Success To The Railroad, Golden Amber, Mt. Vernon, Pt.		170.00
McK G V–005, Success To The Railroad, Horse, Deep Yellow Amber, Pt.		88.00
McK G V–005, Success To The Railroad, Olive Green, Pontil, Pt.		150.00
McK G V–006, Success To The Railroad, Olive Amber, Pt.		137.00
McK G V–006, Success To The Railroad, Olive Green, Pt.		176.00
McK G V–008, Success To The Railroad, Olive Amber, Pontil, Pt.		132.00
McK G V–009, Railroad & Eagle, Medium Olive Amber, Pontil, Pt.		185.00
McK G V–010, Railroad & Eagle, Yellow Olive, Pontil, 1/2 Pt.		363.00
McK G VI–001, Monument, A Little More Grape, Copper, Puce, 1/2 Pt.		2420.00
McK G VI–004, Corn For The World, Bright Yellow, Olive Tone, Qt.		578.00
McK G VI–004, Corn For The World, Gold Amber, Qt.		413.00
McK G VI–005, Corn For The World, Baltimore Monument, Aqua, Qt.		88.00
McK G VIII–001, Sunburst, Clear, OP, Pt.		440.00
McK G VIII–001, Sunburst, Yellow Green, OP, Pt.		800.00
McK G VIII–002, Sunburst, Bright Medium Green, Pontil, Pt.		550.00
McK G VIII–002, Sunburst, Clear Yellow Green		380.00
McK G VIII–003, Sunburst, Bright Olive Green, OP, Pt.		330.00
McK G VIII–003, Sunburst, Medium Yellow Olive, OP, Pt.		395.00
McK G VIII–003a, Sunburst, Yellow Amber, OP, Pt.		358.00
McK G VIII–005, Sunburst, Olive Amber		1000.00
McK G VIII–005a, Sunburst, Light Olive Amber, Pontil, Pt.		1100.00
McK G VIII–007, Sunburst, Yellow Olive, OP, Pt.		330.00
McK G VIII–008, Sunburst, Olive Amber, Pt.		231.00
McK G VIII–009, Sunburst, P. & W., Medium Olive Amber, Pontil, 1/2 Pt.		350.00
McK G VIII–009, Sunburst, P. & W., Olive Amber, Pontil, 1/2 Pt.		325.00
McK G VIII–009, Sunburst, P. & W., Yellow Olive, Pontil, 1/2 Pt.		143.00
McK G VIII–010, Sunburst & Keen, P. & W., Green		390.00
McK G VIII–010, Sunburst & Keen, P. & W., Medium Amber, OP, 1/2 Pt.		275.00
McK G VIII–014, Sunburst, Brilliant Yellow Green, Pontil, 1/2 Pt.		1485.00
McK G VIII–018, Sunburst, Yellow Amber, OP, 1/2 Pt.		550.00
McK G VIII–020, Sunburst, Aqua Green, OP		250.00
McK G VIII–020, Sunburst, Aqua, Sheared Lip, Pontil, Pt.		110.00
McK G VIII–020, Sunburst, Yellow Amber, OP, Pt.		1925.00
McK G VIII–022, Sunburst, Medium To Deep Claret, OP, Pt.		8855.00
McK G VIII–024, Sunburst, Aqua, 1/2 Pt.		200.00
McK G VIII–025, Sunburst, Medium To Deep Pink Puce, OP, 1/2 Pt.		6325.00
McK G VIII–027, Sunburst, Deep Aqua, 1/2 Pt.		187.00
McK G VIII–027, Sunburst, Light Aqua, Pontil, 1/2 Pt.		195.00
McK G VIII–027, Sunburst, Pale Green, Pontil, 1/2 Pt.		55.00
McK G VIII–029, Elongated Sunburst, Aqua, Sheared Lip, Pontil, Pt.		165.00
McK G VIII–029, Elongated Sunburst, Light Blue Green, OP, Pt.		175.00
McK G IX–001, Scroll, Aqua, IP, Qt.		61.00
McK G IX–001, Scroll, Variant, Cobalt Blue, IP, Qt.		2100.00
McK G IX–001, Scroll, Variant, Medium Citron, IP, Qt.		425.00

McK G IX–002, Scroll, Aqua, OP, Qt. 100.00
McK G IX–002, Scroll, Black Olive, IP, Qt. 600.00
McK G IX–002, Scroll, Bright Medium Green, OP, Qt. 633.00
McK G IX–002, Scroll, Bright Sapphire Blue, IP, Qt. .... 400.00 To 495.00
McK G IX–002, Scroll, Clambroth, Pontil, Qt. 478.00
McK G IX–002, Scroll, Light Emerald Green, Tubular Pontil, Qt. 200.00
McK G IX–002, Scroll, Moonstone, Amethyst Tint, Pontil, Qt. 200.00
McK G IX–002, Scroll, Olive Yellow, Tubular Pontil, Qt. 800.00
McK G IX–002, Scroll, Pink Moonstone, Qt. 550.00
McK G IX–003, Scroll, Olive Yellow, White Flecks, Flared Mouth, Qt. 825.00
McK G IX–004, Scroll, Aqua, IP, Qt. 106.00
McK G IX–006, Scroll & Louisville, Aqua, IP, Qt. 72.00
McK G IX–008, Scroll & Louisville, Aqua, Pt. 185.00
McK G IX–009, Scroll & Louisville, Brilliant Yellow, IP, Pt. 2805.00
McK G IX–010, Scroll, Amber, Sheared Lip, Pontil, Pt. 300.00
McK G IX–010, Scroll, Aqua, IP, Pt. .... 61.00 To 83.00
McK G IX–010, Scroll, Jade Green, OP, Pt. 523.00
McK G IX–010, Scroll, Moonstone, Sheared Lip, Pontil, Pt. 425.00
McK G IX–010, Scroll, Yellow Amber, OP, Lancaster, Pt. 231.00
McK G IX–010, Scroll, Yellow, IP, Pt. 625.00
McK G IX–010a, Scroll, Aqua, Pt. 75.00
McK G IX–010a, Scroll, Sapphire Blue, Tooled Round Collar, Pt. 1200.00
McK G IX–010a, Scroll, Sapphire, Pt. 1485.00
McK G IX–010b, Scroll, Deep Olive Yellow, IP, Pt. 385.00
McK G IX–010b, Scroll, Medium Emerald Green, IP, Pt. 300.00
McK G IX–011, Scroll, 6 Circular Mold Indents Around Neck, Aqua 85.00
McK G IX–011, Scroll, Aqua, OP, Pt. 72.00
McK G IX–011a, Scroll, Deep Olive Yellow, OP, Pt. 688.00
McK G IX–012, Scroll, Dark Olive, Sheared Lip, Pontil, Pt. 450.00
McK G IX–014, Scroll, Aqua, Sheared Lip, Pontil, Pt. 250.00
McK G IX–014, Scroll, Yellow Olive, Pt. 880.00
McK G IX–016, Scroll, Dark Olive Amber, Long Neck, Pontil, Pt. 425.00
McK G IX–023, Scroll, Aqua, Pt. 100.00
McK G IX–024, Scroll, A On 1 Side, Yellow Green, Pontil, Pt. 2400.00
McK G IX–025, C Scroll, Aqua, OP, Pt. 60.00
McK G IX–027, Scroll, S. McKee & Co., Smoky Amber, Aqua Streaked, Pt. 6000.00
McK G IX–028, Scroll, Rough & Ready, Aqua, Tubular Pontil, Pt. 600.00
McK G IX–029, Scroll, Aqua, OP, 2 Qt. 413.00
McK G IX–029, Scroll, Aqua, Pontil, 1840–1860, 1/2 Gal. Plus 220.00
McK G IX–030a, Scroll, Aqua, Ground Pontil, Gal. 450.00
McK G IX–034, Scroll, Brilliant Emerald Green, 1/2 Pt. 1980.00
McK G IX–034, Scroll, Olive Yellow, Flared Mouth, Pontil, 1/2 Pt. 1125.00
McK G IX–036, Scroll, Medium Emerald Green, Sheared Lip, 1/2 Pt. 600.00
McK G IX–036, Scroll, Sapphire Blue, Tooled Mouth, Pontil, 1/2 Pt. 4180.00
McK G IX–037, Scroll, Aqua, 1/2 Pt. 60.00
McK G IX–037, Scroll, Sapphire Blue, Pontil, 1/2 Pt. 2300.00
McK G IX–038, Scroll, Aqua, OP, 1/2 Pt. 231.00
McK G IX–038a, Scroll, Apple Olive Green, Pontil 1/2 Pt. 1425.00
McK G IX–039, Scroll, BP & B, Light Green, Amber Streaks, 1/2 Pt. 950.00
McK G IX–040, Scroll, Clear, Sheared & Fire Polished Lip, Miniature 600.00
McK G IX–041, Scroll, Anchor, Fleur–De–Lis, Deep Aqua, OP, 1/2 Pt. 3795.00
McK G IX–041, Scroll, Anchor, Fleur–De–Lis, Emerald Green, 1/2 Pt. 600.00
McK G IX–042, Scroll, Anchor, Fleur–De–Lis, Amethyst, 1/2 Pt. 1500.00
McK G IX–043, Scroll, Corset Waist, J. R. & Son, Aqua, OP, Pt. 550.00
McK G IX–043, Scroll, J. R. & Son, Amethyst, Streaks, Pt. 4750.00
McK G IX–045, Scroll, Pt. 390.00
McK G IX–047, Scroll, R. Knowles & Co., Aqua, Pontil, Pt. 1200.00
McK G IX–047, Scroll, R. Knowles & Co., Green Aqua, OP, Pt. 1320.00
McK G IX–048, Scroll, McCarthy & Torreyson, Aqua, Pt. 835.00
McK G IX–049, Scroll, McCarthy & Torreyson, Aqua, Pontil, Qt. 1100.00
McK G IX–051, Scroll, Hearts & Flowers, Aqua, OP, Qt. .... 1300.00 To 2310.00
McK G X–001, Stag & Willow Tree, Good Game, Aqua, OP, Pt. 99.00
McK G X–002, Stag & Willow Tree, Good Game, Aqua, 1/2 Pt. 253.00

McK G X–003, Sheaf of Wheat & Grapes, Aqua, 1/2 Pt. 120.00
McK G X–006, Gen. Taylor Never Surrenders, Pale Green, 1/2 Pt. 242.00
McK G X–008, Sailboat & Star, Aqua, Sheared Mouth, Pontil, 1/2 Pt. 148.00
McK G X–008, Sloop & Star, Light Yellow Green, OP, 1/2 Pt. 187.00
McK G X–008a, Sloop & Star, Light Green, 1/2 Pt. 225.00
McK G X–009, Sloop & Star, Aqua, Pontil, 1/2 Pt. 100.00
McK G X–009, Sloop & Star, Medium Green Aqua, 1/2 Pt. 245.00
McK G X–015, Summer & Winter, Aqua, Pt. .... 45.00 To 82.50
McK G X–015, Summer & Winter, Bright Yellow Green, Pt. 165.00
McK G X–015, Summer & Winter, Medium Yellow Green, Pt. 935.00
McK G X–016, Summer & Winter, Aqua, Round Collar, 1/2 Pt. 55.00
McK G X–018, Summer & Winter, Emerald, Qt. 250.00
McK G X–022, Cabin & Flag, Hard Cider, Pt. 2500.00
McK G X–024, Jared Spencer, Medallions & Diamond, Yellow Amber, Pt. 11000.00
McK G X–030, Great Western Deer Hunter, Aqua, Pt. 358.00
McK G X–032, Ship & Columbian Jubilee, Amber, Coffin, Pt. 660.00
McK G XI–008, For Pike's Peak, Prospector, Deep Aqua, Qt. 72.00
McK G XI–017, Prospector & Eagle, Aqua, Pt. 85.00
McK G XI–022, For Pike's Peak, Prospector, Eagle, Aqua, Pt. 65.00
McK G XI–024, For Pike's Peak, Prospector, Eagle, Medium Amber, Qt. 633.00
McK G XI–027, For Pike's Peak, Prospector, Eagle, Aqua, Pt. 55.00
McK G XI–028, For Pike's Peak, Prospector, Eagle, Golden Amber, Pt. 775.00
McK G XI–030, For Pike's Peak, Prospector, Eagle, Aqua, Qt. 55.00
McK G XI–034, For Pike's Peak, Prospector, Eagle, Yellow Olive, Qt. 880.00
McK G XI–035, For Pike's Peak, Prospector, Eagle, Blue Green, Pt. 176.00
McK G XI–035, For Pike's Peak, Prospector, Eagle, Yellow Green, Pt. 550.00
McK G XI–046, For Pike's Peak, Prospector, Hunter, Yellow Green, Pt. 743.00
McK G XI–050, For Pike's Peak, Prospector, Hunter, Blue Green, Pt. 330.00
McK G XI–050, For Pike's Peak, Prospector, Hunter, Medium Amber, Pt. 633.00
McK G XI–052, For Pike's Peak, Prospector, Hunter, Blue Aqua, 1/2 Pt. 105.00
McK G XII–002, Waterford, Clasped Hands & Eagle, Aqua, Qt. 248.00
McK G XII–003, Union. Clasped Hands & Eagle, Yellow Olive, Qt. 715.00
McK G XII–005, Union, Clasped Hands & Eagle, Cobalt Blue, Qt. 660.00
McK G XII–007a, Union, Clasped Hands & Eagle, Aqua, Qt. 61.00
McK G XII–029, Union, Clasped Hands & Eagle, Golden Amber, 1/2 Pt. 110.00
McK G XII–033, Union, Clasped Hands & Eagle, Orange Amber, 1/2 Pt. 149.00
McK G XII–039a, Union, Clasped Hands & Cannon, Aqua, Pt. 88.00
McK G XII–040, Union, Clasped Hands & Cannon, Amber, Pt. 198.00
McK G XII–040, Union, Clasped Hands & Cannon, Aqua, Smooth Base, Pt. 150.00
McK G XII–040, Union, Clasped Hands & Cannon, Light Amber, Pt. 220.00
McK G XII–040, Union, Clasped Hands & Cannon, Yellow, Pt. 468.00
McK G XII–041, Union, Clasped Hands & Cannon, Orange Amber, Pt. 175.00
McK G XII–043, Union, Clasped Hands & Eagle, Calabash, Amber, IP, Qt. 209.00
McK G XIII–004, Hunter & Fisherman, Calabash, Amber 137.00
McK G XIII–004, Hunter & Fisherman, Calabash, Aqua, IP, Qt. 85.00
McK G XIII–005, Hunter & Fisherman, Calabash, Aqua, Qt. 38.00
McK G XIII–012, Soldier & Ballet Dancer, Golden Amber, Pt. 357.00
McK G XIII–013, Soldier & Dancer, Olive Green, Pt. 850.00
McK G XIII–015, Soldier & Daisy, Calabash, Aqua, IP, Qt. .... 129.00 To 143.00
McK G XIII–016, Army Dragoon & Hound, Aqua, Double Collared, Qt. 55.00
McK G XIII–016, Army Dragoon & Hound, Yellow Olive, OP, Qt. 440.00
McK G XIII–017, Horse & Hound, Aqua, Smooth Base, Whittled, Pt. 150.00
McK G XIII–019, Flora Temple, Reddish Amber, Qt. 242.00
McK G XIII–021, Flora Temple, Amber, Handle, Pt. .... 253.00 To 275.00
McK G XIII–021, Flora Temple, Puce Amber, Handle, Pt. 197.00
McK G XIII–021, Flora Temple, Puce, Missing Handle, Pt. 150.00
McK G XIII–021, Flora Temple, Reddish Puce, Pt. .... 253.00 To 300.00
McK G XIII–023, Flora Temple, Light Blue Green, Pt. 358.00
McK G XIII–023, Flora Temple, Olive Green, Pt. 935.00
McK G XIII–035, Sheaf of Wheat, Westford Glass, Red Amber, Pt. 132.00
McK G XIII–036, Sheaf of Wheat, Westford Glass, Red Amber, Pt. 165.00
McK G XIII–037, Sheaf of Wheat, Westford Glass, Olive Green, 1/2 Pt. 125.00
McK G XIII–038, Sheaf of Grain & Star, Brilliant Olive Yellow, Qt. 468.00

Flask, Black & White Looping, Red Ground,
Stand, 7 1/2 In.

Flask, Merry Christmas & Happy New Year,
Cap, 6 In.

McK G XIII–039, Sheaf of Grain & Star, Bright Green, OP, Pt.	475.00
McK G XIII–040, Sheaf of Grain, Star, Medium Teal, OP, 1/2 Pt.	440.00
McK G XIII–045, Sheaf of Grain, Star, Calabash, Amber, IP	330.00
McK G XIII–048, Anchor & Sheaf of Wheat, Baltimore Glass, Aqua, Qt.	84.00
McK G XIII–052, Anchor & Sheaf of Wheat, Calabash, Aqua, OP	187.00
McK G XIII–052, Anchor & Sheaf of Wheat, Calabash, Cobalt Blue	2695.00
McK G XIII–053, Anchor & Eagle, Resurgam, Aqua, Pt.	60.00
McK G XIII–053, Anchor & Eagle, Resurgam, Yellow, Olive Tone, Pt.	468.00
McK G XIII–054, Anchor & Eagle, Resurgam, Round Collar, Aqua	175.00
McK G XIII–059, Anchor, Baltimore & Cabin, Aqua, OP, Pt.	175.00
McK G XIII–075, Key, Coffin Shape, Aqua, Pt.	25.00
McK G XIV–001, Traveler's & Companion, Gold Amber, Striations	137.00
McK G XIV–004, Traveler's Companion & Star, Light Green, Pt.	358.00
McK G XIV–007, Traveler's Companion & Star, Bright Yellow, 1/2 Pt.	825.00
McK G XIV–007, Traveler's Companion & Star, Olive Tone, 1/2 Pt.	413.00
McK G XV–002, Clyde Glass Works, Pale Green Aqua, Pt.	50.00
McK G XV–005, Cunningham & Ihmsen, Aqua, Strap Side, Pt.	60.00
McK G XV–007, Granite Glass Co., Stoddard, N. H., Red Amber, Pt.	132.00
McK G XV–015, Newburgh Glass Co., Pat. Feb. 27, 1866, Olive Green, Pt.	550.00
Merry Christmas & Happy New Year, Cap, 6 In. ....*Illus*	450.00
Merry Christmas & Happy New Year, Pumpkin Seed, Clear	15.00
Merry Christmas, Santa Claus, Label, Ovoid, Metal Cap, Pocket, 1/2 Pt.	990.00
Midwest, 16 Ribs, Sapphire Blue, Spout, OP, 1820–1850, 9 1/2 In.	1840.00
Midwest, 24 Ribs, Swirled Left, Golden Amber, Globular, 8 1/2 In.	357.00
Midwest, 24 Ribs, Swirled Left, Light Citron, 7 1/2 In.	770.00
Midwest, 24 Ribs, Swirled Left, Light Honey Amber, 7 3/8 In.	880.00
Midwest, 24 Vertical Ribs, Golden Amber, Pocket	175.00
Midwest, 26 Ribs, Swirled Right, Medium Golden Amber, 8 1/4 In.	385.00
Midwest, Aqua, Club, OP, Qt.	45.00
Midwest, Aqua, Flattened, Vertical Ribs, Flared Lip, 5 In.	105.00
Midwest, Chestnut, Swirl	1750.00
Midwest, No Pattern, Aqua, Globular, OP, 8 1/4 In.	140.00
Miss Prettyman, Mr. & Mrs. Caudle Other Side, Lambeth, 5 1/2 In.	309.00
Miss Prettyman, Mr. & Mrs. Caudle Other Side, Lambeth, 8 In.	331.00
Munich, Riemerschmid	10.00

Nottingham, Stoneware, Lineker 195.00
Nottingham, Stoneware, Perry 175.00
Old Joe Gideon Whiskey, St. Louis, 1904, Amber Stained, 1/2 Pt. 25.00
Oregon Import Co., Portland, Ore, Amber, 1/2 Pt. 15.00
P. W. Cavanaugh, Merry Christmas & Happy New Year, Pocket, 6 In. 1073.00
Picnic, Light Honey Amber, Embossed Try It 45.00
Pitkin Type, 18 Ribs, Sapphire Blue, Pontil, 1/2 Pt. 1430.00
Pitkin Type, 18 Ribs, Swirled Right, Yellow Olive, 5 In. 495.00
Pitkin Type, 20 Ribs, Swirled Right, Yellow Green, 4 3/8 In. 605.00
Pitkin Type, 24 Broken Ribs, Swirled Left, Bright Yellow, 7 1/8 In. 413.00
Pitkin Type, 24 Ribs, Swirled Left, Yellow Green, 1800–1880, Pt. 303.00
Pitkin Type, 24 Ribs, Swirled Right, Clear To Yellow, 3 1/4 In. 187.00
Pitkin Type, 31 Broken Ribs, Swirled Right, Olive Green, 6 In. 303.00
Pitkin Type, 31 Ribs, Swirled Left, Olive Green, 6 5/8 In. 176.00
Pitkin Type, 31 Ribs, Swirled Left, Yellow Olive, Pontil, 6 3/4 In. 385.00
Pitkin Type, 32 Broken Ribs, Swirled Left, Green Aqua, 1810–1840 .... 275.00
Pitkin Type, 32 Broken Ribs, Swirled Right, Olive, Pontil, 5 7/8 In. 358.00
Pitkin Type, 32 Broken Ribs, Swirled, Light Green, Midwest, 1820–1840 .... 198.00
Pitkin Type, 32 Ribs, Swirled Left, Green Aqua, Lip Pontil, 6 3/4 In. 250.00
Pitkin Type, 32 Ribs, Swirled Left, Olive, Pontil, 6 1/4 In. 110.00
Pitkin Type, 36 Broken Ribs, Swirled Left, Olive Yellow, OP, 1/2 Pt. 275.00
Pitkin Type, 36 Broken Ribs, Swirled Left, Olive, OP, 5 3/8 In. 458.00
Pitkin Type, 36 Broken Ribs, Swirled Right, Olive Amber, 5 3/8 In. 1980.00
Pitkin Type, 36 Broken Ribs, Swirled, Light Olive, New England, 5 In. 220.00
Pitkin Type, 36 Ribs, Swirled Left, Bright Green, Pontil, 6 3/4 In. 220.00
Pitkin Type, 36 Ribs, Swirled Left, Golden Amber, 6 1/8 In. 687.00
Pitkin Type, 36 Ribs, Swirled Left, Medium Yellow Amber, OP, 5 In. 385.00
Pitkin Type, 36 Ribs, Swirled Left, Olive Amber, New England, 5 In. 210.00
Pitkin Type, 36 Ribs, Swirled Left, Olive Green, Pontil, 5 1/8 In. 352.00
Pitkin Type, 36 Ribs, Swirled Left, Olive, 1790–1830, 5 1/4 In. 220.00
Pitkin Type, 36 Ribs, Swirled Left, Yellow Olive, 5 1/8 In. 330.00
Pitkin Type, 36 Ribs, Swirled Left, Yellow Olive, 6 1/4 In. 413.00
Pitkin Type, 36 Ribs, Swirled Right, Light Olive, 7 1/8 In. 798.00
Pitkin Type, 36 Ribs, Swirled Right, Yellow, Olive Tone, OP, 5 1/4 In. 303.00
Pitkin Type, 38 Ribs, Swirled Right, Olive Amber, Pontil, 7 In. 630.00
Pitkin Type, Swirled Left, Deep Purple, Shear Top, OP, 1/2 Pt. 85.00
Pocket, We Drank From Same Canteen, Pottery, 1861–1865, 4 7/8 In. 231.00
Pocket, Woman, Arabian Dress, Clear, Metal Neck Band & Cap, 5 1/4 In. 963.00
Pocket, Woman, Early Swimsuit Label, Clear, Cap, 5 3/4 In. 385.00
Poison, Quilted, Pale Amethyst, Pontil, 1830–1840, 5 1/4 In. 240.00
Porter, Stoneware, Bailey & Dabell, 1810 .... 350.00
Porter, Stoneware, Dabell 98.00
Porter, Stoneware, Eaglesfield 78.00
Porter, Stoneware, Killingley 78.00
Porter, Stoneware, Perry 165.00
Porter, Stoneware, Turner, Seal 156.00
Pottery, Green Woven Top, Plaited Handle, Stopper, 5 1/2 In. 36.00
Pumpkinseed, Clear, Embossed Clock & Regulator, Pt. 39.00
Pumpkinseed, J. H. Duke & Bro., Clear, Tooled Lip, 1880–1900 .... 44.00
Pumpkinseed, Light Amber, Crooked Neck, Double Collar, 4 3/4 In. 50.00
Pumpkinseed, Mendels O. P. S. Whiskey, San Francisco, Aqua, 1/2 Pt. 75.00
Pumpkinseed, Picnic, Medium Amber, 5 1/4 In. 66.00
Pumpkinseed, Picnic, Yellow Green, Tooled Lip, 1880–1900 .... 242.00
Pumpkinseed, Union Pacific Tea Co., N. Y., Elephant, Est. 1873 .... 110.00
Pumpkinseed, Whiskey, Embossed Try It, Yellow Amber, 1/4 Pt. 53.00
Redware, 2 Black Splotches Under Glaze, Stopper, Pt. 63.00
Redware, Brown Albany Glaze, 7 1/2 In. 130.00
Redware, Glazed, Flat Sides, Ovoid, 7 3/4 In. 125.00
Remember The Maine, Picture, Feb. 15th, 1898, Cap, Pocket, 1/2 Pt. 297.00
Ribbed, Swirled Right, Amethyst, Sheared Mouth, Pontil, 1930, 6 In. 330.00
Saddle, Emerald, Rigaree 40.00
Scroll, Aqua, IP, Qt. 15.00
Scroll, Aqua, Sheared Neck, Graphic Pontil, 6 1/2 In. 45.00

Flask, Stampede, Whiskey, 6 In.   Flask, Victorian Lady, 6 1/2 In.

Scroll, Clevenger, Cobalt Blue, OP, 1900s, Pt.	69.00
Somers Conn. Bottle Club, Commemorative, Milk Glass	8.00
Spirits, Blown, Cobalt Blue, White Petal Design, Rectangular, 7 In.	743.00
Stampede, Whiskey, 6 In. ....*Illus*	15.00
Stoddard Type, Amber, 1/2 Pt.	16.00
Sunburst, Deep Forest Green, Coventry, 1820s, 1/2 Pt.	440.00
Take A Drink, Golden Amber, Wicker Cover, No Cap, 1/2 Pt.	137.00
U.S. Warship Maine, Sunk Havana, 1898, Ship, Ovoid, Pocket, 1/2 Pt.	357.00
Victorian Lady, 6 1/2 In. ....*Illus*	450.00
Violin, Cobalt Blue, ABM, Fancy	25.00
W. B. Bond & Co., Newark, N. J., Amber, Strap, Qt.	12.00
Walther's Peptonized Post, Pittsburgh, Pa., Amber, Fifth	35.00
Ward's Hotel, Gloucester, N. J., Light Amethyst, Slug Plate, BIM, 8 In.	38.00
Wharton's Whiskey, Teardrop Shape, Amber, Pocket	139.00
Whitney's Glass Works, Amber, 1/2 Pt.	19.00
Wm. Jackson & Co., Dockhead London, Black Glass, Flattened Hip, 6 In.	449.00
Wormser Bros., San Francisco, Dark Amber, Colored Top	165.00

———————————————— **FOOD** ————————————————

Food bottles include all of the many grocery store containers, such as those for catsup, horseradish, jelly, and other foodstuffs. Vinegar bottles and a few other special bottles are listed under their own headings.

FOOD, A & P Extract, Small	3.50
A–1 Sauce, Midget	12.00
A. J. C. Tomato Sauce, Pale Purple, Australia	9.00
Acker's Select Tea, Yellow Green, Crown Lid, Square, 11 1/8 In.	303.00
American Condensed Milk Co., San Francisco, Screw Top, Amethyst, Pt.	25.00
American Oyster Co., Trade AOCO Mark, Providence, R. I., Pt.	15.00
Anchovy Paste, Burgess's, London, Barrel, Pottery, 3 1/2 In.	18.00
As You Like It Horseradish, Crock, Stenciled, Small	25.00
Baker's Flavoring Extracts, Aqua, Square Ring Lip, BIM, 4 3/4 In.	14.00
Balsam Honey, Aqua, Rolled Lip, OP, Cylinder, 3 3/4 In.	25.00
Becker's Pure Horseradish, Buffalo, Aqua, Round, 4 1/4 In. .... 12.00 To 17.00	
Benton Myers & Co., Fruit Juices, Cleveland, Cream Pottery, 3 5/8 In.	38.00

Berry, Aqua, OP, 13 1/2 In. 66.00
Billet, Zatek Chocolate, Penna. Chocolate Co., Pittsburgh, Knobbed Lid 495.00
Blossom Brand Prepared Mustard, Glass Lid, Wire Bail, Label, Pt. 18.00
Blue Ribbon Coffee, Clear, Aqua Lid & Band, Qt. 7.00
Blueberry, Olive Amber, Double Collared Mouth, 1860–1872, 11 1/4 In. 425.00
Borden's Malted Milk, Jar, Porcelain Label, Tin Lid, 8 3/4 In. 319.00
Borden's Milk, Has No Equal, Embossed, Light Amethyst, 7 In. 30.00
Bristol Farm Plum Preserves, Clear, Label, Pt. 5.00
Brooke Bond Improved Blend Tea, White On Green, England, Pt. 13.00
Brown's Jamaica Ginger 6.00
Bunker Hill Horseradish, Aqua, Label, Small 12.00
Bunte Mustard, Chicago, ABM, Lid, 4 3/4 In. 14.00
California Fig Syrup Co., Wheeling, W. Va., Clear 12.00
California Orange Cider, Green, Turn Mold, Blob Top, Qt. 15.00
   FOOD, CALIFORNIA PERFUME CO., see Avon, California Perfume Co.
Chico's Peanuts, Jar, Tin Litho Lid, Yellow Ground, Black, Red, 11 In. 231.00
Cleveland Fruit Juice Co., Safety Valve, Clear, 1/2 Gal. 6.00
Condiment, Emerald Green, Fluted, BIMAL, 6 1/4 In. 4.00
Cracker, For Bar Use, Square, Cover 330.00
Crosse & Blackwell Mustard, Coat of Arms, Pottery, 4 3/8 In. 53.00
Crown Celery Salt, Horton Cato & Co., Yellow Amber, 8 In. 182.00
Crown Cordial & Extract Co., N. Y., Aqua, 1/2 Gal. 10.00
Cuyuga County Tomato Catsup, Levanna, N. Y., Aqua, Swirls, 10 In. 60.50
CW Mustard, Atlas E–Z Seal, Label, Clear, Pt. 6.00
D & G, Embossed, Multi–Ring, 11 In. 20.00
Derby Peter Pan Peanut Butter, Label, No Lid, 12 Oz. 6.00
Dr. G. S. Waits Flavorings, Will Not Bake Out, Freeze Out, Clear 12.00
E. C. Hazard & Co. Queen Olives, N. Y., Yellow Green, 6 7/8 In. 66.00
Elwood Cooper Pure Olive Oil, Santa Barbara, Cal., Seal, Aqua, 11 In. 40.00
Empress Marmalade, Gold Ground, Ship In Oval, 5 In. 45.00
Forget–Me–Not Pure Horseradish White Vinegar & Brine, Aqua, 6 Oz. 15.00
French's Medford Brand Prepared Mustard, Clear, Pt. 3.00
G. L. W. B. Fleur–De–Lis Brand Sugar Syrup, C. M. Tice, Boston, 1/2 Gal. 8.00
G. L. W. B. Verampshire Brand Pure Honey, C. Tice & Co., Boston, Pt. 8.00
Geneseo Kitchen Jam, Glass Lid, Clear 33.00
Geo. Barret, Pure Macerated Spices, N. Y., Aqua, OP, 5 In. 88.00
Giessen's Union Mustard, N. Y., Eagle, Clear, OP, 4 5/8 In. 88.00
Golden Crown Table Syrup, Pt. 6.00
Grapefruitola, F. M. Williams, Bar, Pewter Top, 1913, 12 In. 79.00
Hartshorn's Pure Extract Ginger, Label, Embossed, ABM, 5 In. 5.00
Heinz Tomato Ketchup, Pittsburgh, U.S. A., Fancy, Odd Shape 15.00
Honey Tolu, Beehive Picture, Aqua, Rectangular, 6 In. 20.00
Horlick's Malted Milk, Jar, Raised Letter On Reverse, 9 1/2 In. 220.00
Horlick's Malted Milk, Racine, Wisc., London, Eng., Clear, 1/2 Pt. 8.00
Huckleberry, Aqua, 10 Upper Panels, Round Collared Lip, 11 1/2 In. 88.00
J. F. G. Peanut Butter, Figural, Globe, 8 Oz. 10.00
J. Fau Prunes Dente Bordeaux, Clear, Aqua Tint, 8 1/2 In. 99.00
Jar, Waneta Cocoa, Boston, Qt. 25.00
Jumbo Brand Apple Butter, Elephant Head, Clear, 1 Lb. 30.00
Jumbo Brand Peanut Butter, Elephant Head, Clear, 1 Lb. 4.00
Jumbo Brand Peanut Butter, Elephant Head, Clear, Fishbowl, Bail, 2 Lb. 30.00
Jumbo Brand Peanut Butter, Elephant Head, Clear, Lantern, Bail, 2 Lb. 22.00
Jumbo The Bottled Health Food, No Lid, 1 Lb. 5.00
Kaukauna Klub, Pottery, Blue Letters, Lid, Weir Clamp, 1/2 Pt. 12.00
L A Nut Brand, Screw Cap, Clear, Nut House On Nut, With Man, Pt. 4.00
Lake Horseradish, Denver 10.00
LC Extract, Label, Almanac, Corkscrew, Box 180.00
Lime Juice, Arrow Design, Dark Olive Amber, Applied Top, 10 1/4 In. 125.00
Lime Juice, Deep Olive Amber, Arrow Design, 10 1/4 In. 88.00
M. D. Espy, IP 68.00
Maine Condensed Milk Co., Clear, Hexagonal, Pt. 18.00
Manzanilla Olives, Franklin MacVeach & Co., Label, 7 In. 10.00
Mayday Peanut Butter, Kenton, Oh., Metal Screw Cap, Round, 1/2 Pt. 4.00

Food, Mustard, W.Diedz & Co., 4 3/4 In.   *Fruit Jar, Banner, July 14, 1908, Wide Mouth, Lid, Blue, 7 1/4 In.*

Mellin's Food, Free Sample, Aqua, BIMAL, 3 1/2 In. 6.00
Moland's Quaker City Dried Beef, P. G. Co., No. 3, Phila., Round, 1/2 Pt. 4.00
Mrs. Chapin's Mayonnaise, Boston, Mass., Clear, Pt. 3.00
Mrs. Chapin's Mayonnaise, Drey Bosses, Pt. 6.00
Mrs. Chapin's Salad Dressing, Boston, Mass., Clear, Pt. 4.00
Mustard Pot, Sarreguemines Dijon France, Porcelain, Tin Crown Top 40.00
Mustard, Giessens Union Mustard, Clear, Green Tin 125.00
Mustard, Jar, Dark Olive Amber, Rolled Lip, 3 7/8 In. 77.00
Mustard, McK GII–44, 3-Piece Mold, Blown, Lid, 4 3/4 In. 176.00
Mustard, W. Diedz & Co., 4 3/4 In. ....*Illus* 85.00
Mustard, W. Diedz & Co., Aqua, Round, OP, Rolled Lip, 5 In. 60.00
N. W. Opermann Mustard Factory, Aqua, OP, 4 3/4 In. 209.00
Ocean Spray Cranberry Juice Cocktail, Fruit Jar, 1930–1980, Qt. 22.00
Old Style Mustard, Clear, Label, Pt. 5.00
Olive Oil, Norwich, Conn., Label 10.00
    FOOD, PEPPER SAUCE, see Pepper Sauce
Phelps' Mayonnaise, Batavia, N. Y., Round, 1/2 Pt. 6.00
    FOOD, PICKLE, see Pickle
Pioneer Catsup, Amber, Hexagonal, 9 1/4 In. 176.00
Planter's Peanuts, Jar, Lettering, Peanut Corners & Handle, 14 In. 220.00
Planter's Peanuts, Jar, Lettering, Peanut Handle, 9 In. 60.00
Planter's Peanuts, Jar, Peanut Handle, Gold, Label, 13 In. 110.00
Planter's Peanuts, Jar, Peanut Handle, Letters On Sides, 8 1/2 In. 242.00
Planter's Peanuts, Jar, Peanut Handle, Yellow, Label, 12 1/2 In. 132.00
Pot, Pure Honey, Winfield, Cream Pottery, 4 7/8 In. 31.00
Pot, Russian Caviar Co., Haymarket S. W., Transfer, Pottery, 3 1/3 In. 18.00
Pure Horseradish, H. D. Geer, Three River, Mass., Aqua, 7 In. 8.25
R. J. C. Mustard, Aqua, Hexagonal, OP, 6 1/4 In. 33.00
Red Dragon Extract, Embossed Dragon 10.00
Robert Gibson & Sons Lozenge Makers, Aqua, England, 1870, 13 In. 33.00
Rock Maple Vermont Maple Syrup, Paper Label, Round, 1/4 Pt. 12.00
Royal Mint Sauce, Green, Globular, BIM 35.00
Sandwich Mustard, Diamond Pattern 75.00
Sanitas Grape Food, Los Gatos, Calif., Amber, Hand Holds Grapes, 6 In. 30.00
Shaker Syrup, No. 1, Canterbury, N. H. 135.00
Shriver's Oyster Ketchup, Baltimore, Olive Green, IP, 7 In. 1155.00
Smucker's Jelly, Clear, Round, 1 3/4 In. 5.00
Sun Jar, Q. T. W. Closure, Aqua 50.00
T. A. Bryan & Co's. Perfection Tomato Sauce, Amber, 8 1/2 In. 413.00
T. H. McGruder & Co., Extra Superfine Olive Oil, Olive Green, 11 In. 20.00

Valentine's Meat Juice, Amber, Teardrop Shape, BIM, 3 1/2 In.	14.00
Vermont Maple Co–Op, Essex Junction, Vt., Crown Top, 1/2 Pt.	15.00
Victoria's Yogurt, Jar, Orange Writing, 1/2 Pt. .... 10.00 To	12.00
W. T. Estcott Chocolates & Bonbons, Philadelphia, Screw Cap, 1912, Pt.	15.00
Wampole's Milk Food, Jar, Ground Lip, Zinc Lid, 1/2 Gal.	18.00
Wan–Eta Cocoa, Boston, Amber, No Screw Cap, Pt.	10.00
Wan–Eta Cocoa, Boston, Amber, Zinc Cover, Qt.	8.00
Wan–Eta Cocoa, Boston, Clear, 1/2 Pt.	4.00
Welch's Grape Juice, Howdy Doody, Kagran, Dated 1946, 1 1/2 Pt.	100.00
Wendell & Espy Mince Meat, Philadelphia, Aqua, Square, 8 In.	495.00
Yacht Club Salad Dressing, Chicago, Clear, BIM, 5 In.	9.00
Yami Yogurt Trade Mark Reg. Bulgarian Cultured Milk, Jar, 8 Oz.	7.50

───────────────────────── **FRUIT JAR** ─────────────────────────

Fruit jars made of glass have been used in the United States since the 1850s. More than 1,000 different jars have been found with varieties of closures, embossing, and colors. The date 1858 on many jars refers to a patent and not the age of the bottle. Be sure to look in this listing under any name or initial that appears on your jar. If not otherwise indicated, the jar listed is of clear glass and quart size. The numbers used in the entries in the form C–0 refer to the book *Red Book of Fruit Jars Number 6* by Alice Creswick. A publication for collectors is Fruit Jar Newsletter, 364 Gregory Avenue, West Orange, NJ 07052-3743.

FRUIT JAR, A Stone & Co., Phila. Lugs In Mouth, 2 Qt., C–2750–3	650.00
A. B. G. M. Co., Wax Sealer, Aqua, Qt., C–7	35.00
A. D. & H. Chambers Union, Pittsburgh, Wax Sealer, Blue, Qt., C–580	148.00
A. G. Smalley & Co., Amber, Round, Lid & Band, Qt., C–2646	60.00
A. G. Smalley & Co., Boston & New York, Glass Lid, 1/2 Pt., C–2645	8.00
A. G. Smalley & Co., Pat. April 7, 1896, Square, 1/2 Pt., C–2646	12.00
A. Kline, Patent Oct. 27, '63, Blown Stopper, Aqua, Qt., C–1422	123.00
A. Kline, Aqua, No Stopper, 1/2 Gal., C–1427	50.00
A. Stone & Co., Philadelphia, Deep Aqua, IP, Wax Ring, Qt., C–2753	935.00
Acme L. G. Co., Star, Pat. Nov. 30th, 1858, Aqua, 1/2 Gal., C–15	165.00
Acme, L. G. Co., Star, 1893, Aqua, Pt., C–14	148.00
Adams & Co., Pittsburgh, Pa., Aqua, Qt., C–17	578.00
Air–Tight, Aqua, Applied Wax Sealer, IP, Qt., C–81	143.00
All Right, Aqua, Repro Closure, Pat. Jan. 28, 1868, Qt., C–61	138.00
All Right, Pat. Jan. 28th, 1868, Aqua, 1/2 Gal., C–61	99.00
Amazon Swift Seal, In Circle, Blue, 1/2 Gal., C–70	12.00
Amazon Swift Seal, In Circle, Blue, Qt., C–69	10.00
American, Eagle & Flag, Light Green, Qt., C–73 .... 100.00 To	138.00
American, NAG Co., Aqua, Porcelain Lined, 1/2 Gal. C–75	30.00
American, NAG Co., Porcelain Lined, Aqua, Midget, C–75	148.00
Anchor Hocking Mason, H In Anchor, Clear, Pt., C–81	1.00
Anchor, Block Letters, Clear, Lid & Band, Qt., C–77	35.00
Arthur Burnham & Gilroy, Philadelphia, Yellowware, Pt., C–98	250.00
Atherholt, Fisher, Aqua, Qt., C–103	300.00
Atlas E–Z Seal, Amber, Qt., C–111	33.00
Atlas E–Z Seal, Apple Green, Qt., C–17	10.00
Atlas E–Z Seal, Aqua, Qt., C–107	36.00
Atlas E–Z Seal, Clear, 1/2 Pt., C–112 .... 4.00 To	6.00
Atlas E–Z Seal, Cornflower Blue, Clear Lid, Pt., C–109	10.00
Atlas E–Z Seal, Deep Olive, 2 Qt., C–109	35.00
Atlas E–Z Seal, Light Olive, Clear Lid, Qt., C–109	9.00
Atlas E–Z Seal, Olive Green, 1/2 Gal., C–109	23.00
Atlas E–Z Seal, Olive Green, Bell Shape, Matching Lid, Pt., C–109	40.00
Atlas E–Z Seal, Olive, Stubby, Pt., C–116	35.00
Atlas Improved Mason, Aqua, Qt., C–138	15.00
Atlas Junior Mason, Clear, 2/3 Pt., C–139	9.00
Atlas Junior Mason, Clear, Lid, 1/2 Pt., C–139	9.00
Atlas Mason Improved Pat., Aqua, Pt., C–145	12.00
Atlas Mason Improved Pat., Light Blue, Pt., C–146	7.00
Atlas Mason's Patent, Amethyst, 1/2 Gal., C–150	15.00
Atlas Mason's Patent, Aqua, Qt., C–150	3.00

Atlas Mason's Patent, Light To Yellow Green, ABM, Qt., C–150	50.00
Atlas Strong Shoulder Mason, Aqua, Pt., C–163	3.00
Atlas Strong Shoulder Mason, Bank, Zinc Lid, 1/2 Pt., C–162	9.00
Atlas Strong Shoulder Mason, Green, Qt., C–161	7.00
Atlas Wholefruit, Clear, Pt., C–170	4.00
Atlas Wholefruit, Clear, Qt., C–170	2.00
Atlas, Good Luck, Clover, Lightning Closure, Pt., C–128	5.00
Atlas, Good Luck, Clover, Lightning Closure, Qt., C–128	4.00
Atmospheric, Whitall's Patent June 18th, 1861, Aqua, Lid, 8 In.	85.00
Automatic Sealer, Aqua, Qt., C–177	98.00
Avon, Lightning Cover, Deep Blue Aqua, Modern, Pt.	8.00
B. B Wilcox, Pat. Mar. 26th, 1867, Blue Aqua, Qt., C–3008	44.00
B. B. Wilcox 3, Pat. March 26th, 1867, Aqua, Qt., C–3004	73.00
Ball Home Canning, William G. Hannah, Bust, 1981, Teal, Qt.	60.00
Ball Ideal, 1976 Office Building, Blue, Pt., C–244	23.00
Ball Ideal, Bicentennial, Eagle, Blue, 1/2 Pt., C–243–1	8.00
Ball Ideal, Bicentennial, Edmund F. Ball, Blue, Qt., C–241	75.00
Ball Ideal, Pat. July 14, 1908, Blue, Qt., C–222	2.00
Ball Mason, Aqua, Shoulder Seal, Hahne & Co., Qt., C–297	100.00
Ball Mason, Yellow Green, Amber Striations, Qt., C–280	83.00
Ball Masons Patent 1858, Aqua, Qt., C–330	8.00
Ball Pat. Applied For, Aqua, Tin Lid & Wire, Qt., C–327	330.00
Ball Pepfect (Error), Blue, Pt., C–353	10.00
Ball Perfect Mason, Amber, Ribbed, 1/2 Gal., C–333	18.00
Ball Perfect Mason, Blue, Fluted Lip, Bead Bubble, Pt., C–332	18.00
Ball Perfect Mason, Deep Emerald Green, Qt., C–339	60.00
Ball Perfect Mason, Deep Olive Amber, 1/2 Gal., C–339	60.00
Ball Perfect Mason, Deep Olive Amber, Pt., C–339	80.00
Ball Perfect Mason, Green, Block Letters, Pt., C–332	14.00
Ball Perfection, Blue, Zinc Band, Pt., C–399	75.00
Ball Refrigerator & Freezer Jar, Clear, Pt., C–364	2.00
Ball Sanitary Sure Seal, Blue, Date, Lighting Closure, Qt., C–367	11.00
Ball Square Mason, Clear, Pt., C–381	15.00
Ball Square Mason, Pt., C–382	14.00
Ball Standard, Aqua, Wax Seal, Qt., C–384	4.00
Ball Sure Seal, Clear, Narrow Mouth, Lightning Seal, Pt., C–391–5	20.00
Ball Sure Seal, Clear, Old–Style Lightning Seal, Pt., C–393	20.00
Ball Sure Seal, Ghost Sanitary, Lightning Cover, Pt., C–390	20.00
Baltimore Glass Works, Aqua, Qt., C–399	273.00
Banner, Circle, Pat. Feb. . 9th, 1864, Aqua, Qt., C–403	98.00
Banner, July 14, 1908, Wide Mouth, Lid, Blue, 7 1/4 In. ....*Illus*	13.00
Beaver, Aqua, 2 Qt., C–426–1	65.00
Beaver, Aqua, Imperial Qt., C–424	30.00
Beaver, Clear, Lid, Midget Pt., C–423	73.00
Beaver, Golden Amber, Canada, 1860–1880, Qt.	275.00
Beechnut, T. M. Amethyst, No Cap, Pt., C–432	6.00
Bloeser, Aqua, Clamp, Qt., C–468	248.00
Bloeser, Aqua, Qt., C–468	180.00
Bowker's Pyrox, Label, Clear, Dunkley Clamp, 1/2 Pt., C–490	8.00
Brockway Clear–Vu Mason, Round, Ground Lip Lid, Band, Pt., C–514	7.00
Brockway Clear–Vu Mason, Square, Ground Lip Lid, Band, Pt., C–514	11.00
Buckeye No. 2, Deep Aqua, 1/2 Gal., C–528	150.00
Buckeye No. 3, Aqua, Qt., C–528	198.00
FRUIT JAR, C F J CO., see Fruit Jar, Mason's C F J Co.	
C. Burnham & Co., Mfg., Aqua, Pt., C–544	600.00
Calcutt's, Clear, Lid, 1/2 Gal., C–549	30.00
Canton Domestic, Amethyst, Smooth Lip, Pt., C–566	75.00
Canton Domestic, Sun Colored Amethyst, Pt., C–566	98.00
Canton, Clear, 1/2 Gal., C–565	90.00
Canton, Slug Plate, Clear, Qt., C–563–1	98.00
Champion Syrup Refining Co., Indianapolis, Aqua, Qt., C–584	30.00
Champion, Pat. Aug. 31, 1869, Aqua, Qt., C–583	190.00
Chas. M. Higgins & Co., Brooklyn, N. Y., Clear, 1/2 Pt.	10.00

Fruit Jar, E.C.Flaccus & Co., Stag's Head, No Lid, 6 In., C–1016

Fruit Jar, Easy Trade VJC Co., Wire Bail, Lid, 9 In., C–878

Chef Trademark, Berdan Co., Ball–Made, Chef In Circle, Pt., C–590 .... 10.00
Chef Trademark, Clear, Lightning Closure, Pt., C–591–1 .... 7.00
Cincinnati, Oh. On Tin Lid, June 9, 1863, Aqua, 1/2 Gal., C–544 .... 210.00
Clark's Peerless, Aqua, Pt., C–606 ....8.00 To 10.00
Clarke Fruit Jar Co., Cleveland, Oh., Aqua, Qt., C–603 .... 48.00 To 80.00
Clarke, Cleveland, Oh., Original Clamp, Aqua, 1/2 Gal., C–603 .... 73.00
Cohansey Glass Mfg. Co., Aqua, Ground Lip, 1 1/2 Pt., C–626–1 .... 15.00
Cohansey Glass Mfg. Co., Pat. '77, Aqua, Barrel, 1/2 Gal., C–633 .... 83.00
Cohansey Mfg. Co., Pat. March 20, '77, Aqua, Qt., C–633 .... 128.00
Cohansey, Arched, Aqua, 1/2 Gal., C–628 .... 43.00
Columbia, Aqua, Pt., C–638 .... 30.00
Conserve, Clear, Ground Lip, Glass Lid, Wire Bail, Pt., C–652 .... 15.00
Cromwell Preserving Jar, Clear, Alloy Lid, 6 3/4 In., C–670 .... 25.00
Crown Emblem, Aqua, Qt., C–679 .... 4.00
Crown Mason, Embossed Lid, Band, Pt., C–703 .... 9.00
Crown, Canada, 1/2 Imperial Pt., C–689 .... 10.00
Crown, T. Eaton Co., Ltd., 190 Yonge St., Toronto, Clear, Pt., C–701 .... 75.00
Crystal Jar Co., Clear, Qt., C–706 .... 23.00
Cs & Co., Light Green, Stopper, Qt., C–715 .... 15.00
Cunningham & Co., Pittsburgh, Pa., Aqua, Qt., C–724 .... 33.00
Cunningham & Co., Pittsburgh, Pa., Cork, Blue, c.1860, Qt., C–722 .... 3960.00
Cunningham & Ihmsen, Aqua, Wax Seal, Qt., C–745 .... 22.50
Daisy, F. E. Ward & Co., Aqua, Qt., C–743 .... 9.00
Dandy Dark, Trademark, Amber, 1/2 Gal., C–751 .... 148.00
Darling Imperial, Below ADM Monogram, Aqua, Midget Pt., C–754 .... 215.00
Darling Imperial, Monogram, Aqua, Qt., C–754 .... 38.00
Dexter, Fruits & Vegetables Circle Name, Aqua, 1/2 Gal., C–774 .... 68.00
Dictator, D. I. Holcomb, Dec. 14, 1869, Aqua, Qt., C–783 .... 88.00
Dodge Sweeney California Butter, Aqua, 1 1/2 Qt., C–796 .... 325.00
Doolittle, Block Letters, Clear, Qt., C–809–1 .... 38.00
Double Safety, Clear, 1/2 Gal., C–818 .... 8.00
Double Safety, Clear, 1/2 Pt., C–816 .... 10.00 To 16.00
Double Safety, Clear, 1/2 Pt., C–818 .... 10.00
Double Safety, Clear, Qt., C–817 .... 4.00
Double Safety, Dark Green, 3/4 Pt., C–818 .... 10.00
Double Safety, Kivlan Onthank Co., Lightning Closure, Pt., C–821 .... 6.00
Drey Improved Ever Seal, Aqua, Lightning Closure, Pt., C–835 .... 7.00
Drey Improved Ever Seal, Clear, Qt., C–835 .... 1.00
Drey Perfect Mason, 1/2 Pt., C–846 .... 12.00
Drey Square Mason, Carpenter's Square, Clear, Qt., C–847 .... 6.00

E. C. Flaccus & Co., Stag's Head, Green, Label, Pt., C–1016 .... 825.00
E. C. Flaccus & Co., Stag's Head, Milk Glass, Pt., C–1016 .... 400.00
E. C. Flaccus & Co., Stag's Head, No Lid, 6 In., C–1016 ....*Illus* 35.00
Eagle, Aqua, 1/2 Gal., C–872 .... 125.00
Eagle, Aqua, Qt., C–873 .... 100.00
Easy Trade VJC Co., Wire Bail, Lid, 9 In., C–878 ....*Illus* 30.00
Eclipse, Aqua, 1/2 Gal., C–884 .... 525.00
Eclipse, Aqua, Qt., C–885 .... 448.00
Economy Sealer, Pat. Sept. 15th, 1885, Aqua, Qt., C–906 .... 18.00
Electric Trade Mark, Aqua, Pt., C–919 .... 9.00
Electric, Globe, Aqua, 1/2 Gal., C–921 .... 85.00
Electric, Globe, Aqua, Pt., C–921 .... 134.00
Electrolux, Clear, Screw Threads, Round, Sprayer Top, Pt. 4.00
Empire, Clear, Pt., C–925 .... 8.00
Erie Lightning, Aqua, Qt., C–942 .... 48.00
Eureka 1, Aqua, No Lid, Qt., C–948 .... 58.00
Eureka, Green Tint, Dunbar, W. Va., 1/2 Pt., C–945 .... 20.00
Eureka, Pat. Dec. 27th, 1864, Aqua, Qt., C–948 .... 68.00
Everlasting, Jar In Flag, Aqua, 1/2 Gal., C–952 .... 28.00
Everlasting, Jar In Flag, Green, Double Wire Clamp, Qt., C–952 .... 18.50
Excelsior, 1860, Screw Lid, 7 1/2 In. ....*Illus* 675.00
Excelsior, Basket of Fruit, Aqua, Zinc Band, Qt., C–957 .... 633.00
F. B. Co., Aqua, Wax Sealer, Qt., C–987 .... 18.00
F. C. G. Co., Wax Sealer, Amber, 1/2 Gal., C–988 .... 130.00
Farm Family, Ground Lip Lid, Pt., C–980 .... 10.00
Favorite Trademark, Aqua, Pt., C–985 .... 28.00
Federal, Draped Flag, Light Green, Qt., C–996 .... 148.00
Flaccus Bros., Steers Head, Bright Green, Pt., C–1013 .... 853.00
Flaccus Bros., Steers Head, Clear, Pt., C–1010 .... 190.00
Flaccus Bros., Steers Head, Milk Glass, Lid, Pt., C–1014 .... 330.00
Flaccus Bros., Steers Head, Milk Glass, Pt., C–1013 .... 155.00
Forster, Clear, Qt., C–1024 .... 15.00
    FRUIT JAR, FOSTER, see Fruit Jar, Sealfast
Franklin Dexter, Aqua, 1/2 Gal., C–1034 .... 33.00
Franklin Fruit Jar, Aqua, Zinc Lid, Midget, C–1033 .... 231.00
Franklin No. 1, Aqua, Qt., C–1033-1 .... 55.00
Franklin, Aqua, Midget, C–1033 .... 220.00
Fridley & Cornman's, Pat. Oct. 25, 1857, Aqua, Qt., C–1038 .... 598.00
Fruit Keeper, GCCO, Aqua, 1/2 Gal., C–1042 .... 44.00
Fruit Keeper, GCCO, Aqua, Pt., C–1042 .... 34.00
Fruit Keeper, GCCO, Aqua, Qt., C–1042 .... 38.00
Fruit Keeper, GCCO, Green, Pt., C–1042 .... 60.00
Galloway's Everlasting, Feb. 8th, 1870, Wax Sealer, Pt., C–1045 .... 38.00
Gem, CFJ, Aqua, Midget Pt., C–1078 .... 133.00
Gem, H. F. J. Co. In Iron Cross, May 10, 1870, Aqua, Midget, C–1059 .... 33.00
Genuine Boyds Mason, Green, 1/2 Gal., C–497 .... 5.00
Genuine Boyds Mason, Shepherds Crook, Aqua, Qt., C–495 .... 18.00
Geo. D. Brown, Reproduction Clamp, Pt., C–525 .... 35.00
Gilberds Improved Jar, Aqua, Qt., C–1108 .... 185.00
Glass Bros., London, Ontario, Stoneware, Lid, Pt., C–1119 .... 450.00
Glassboro Trade 1 Mark Improved, Aqua, 1/2 Gal., C–1116 .... 18.00
Globe Tobacco Co., Lid, Amber, 1/2 Gal. 32.00
Globe, Amber, Pt., C–1123 .... 85.00
Globe, May 25, 1866, Amber, Wire Bail, Lid, Qt., C–1123 ....*Illus* 63.00
Globe, Yellow Amber, Lid & Metal Closure, Qt., C–1124 .... 105.00
Green Mountain, C. A. Co., In Circle, Aqua, Pt., C–1151 .... 10.00 To 12.00
Green Mountain, C. A. Co., Light Aqua, Pt., C–1152 .... 12.00
Green Mountain, C. A. Co. In Frame, Clear, 1/2 Gal., C–1152 .... 18.00
Green Mountain, C. A. Co. In Frame, Pt., C–1152 .... 10.00
Gregory's Pat. Aug. 17, 1869, Aqua, Qt., C–648 .... 498.00
Griffen's Patent, Aqua, Glass Lid, 1/2 Gal., C–1154 .... 75.00
Griffin's Pat. Oct. 7, 1862, Aqua, Lid, Original Clamp, Qt., C–1155 .... 148.00
Griswold's Pat. 1862, Clambroth, Amethyst Tint, Qt., C–1156 .... 1540.00

Fruit Jar, Excelsior, 1860, Screw Lid,
7 1/2 In.

Fruit Jar, Globe, May 25, 1866, Amber,
Wire Bail, Lid, Qt., C–1123

H & C, Aqua, Haze, Qt., C–1159	8.00
H & S, Philadelphia, Screw Lid, 5 1/2 In. ....*Illus*	2500.00
H. A. Johnson, Home Made Preserves, Boston, Mass, Qt.	48.00
H. W. Pettit, Amethyst, Pt., C–2362	12.00
Hahne & Co., Star, Newark, Mason's Pat. 1858, Blue, Pt., C–1165	27.00
Haine's 3 Patent March 1st, 1870, Aqua, Qt., C–1170 ....80.00 To	88.00
Haine's Combination, Aqua, Qt., C–1168	188.00
Hamilton Glass Works, Aqua, Qt., C–1190	198.00
Hannum & Hawk, Cleveland, O., Cork–Seat Type Finish, 1/2 Pt.	5.00
Hansee's Palace Home Jar, Clear, Qt., C–1206	45.00
Hazel Atlas E–Z Seal, Aqua, Pt., C–1127	36.00
Hazel Atlas E–Z Seal, Cornflower Blue, Pt., C–1127	23.00
Hazel Atlas E–Z Seal, Ghost Lightning, Aqua, Qt., C–1231	16.00
Hazel Atlas E–Z Seal, Ghost Lightning, Green, Qt., C–1128	22.00
Hazel Atlas Preserve Jar, Clear, Pt., C–1231	8.00
Helme's Railroad Mills, Amber, Zinc Band, Pt., C–1235	77.00
FRUIT JAR, HERO CROSS, see Fruit Jar, Mason's Cross	
Hero Improved, Aqua, Tin Lid, Qt., C–1241	53.00
Hero Improved, Aqua, Whittled, Qt., C–1241	26.50
Heroine, Aqua, 1/2 Gal., C–1249	50.00
High Grade, Aqua, Zinc Lid, 1880–1890, Qt., C–1253	165.00
Hollieanna Mason, Clear, Pt., C–1258	16.00
Hom–Pak Mason, Clear, Qt., C–1262 ....2.00 To	7.00
Honest Mason Jar Pat. 1858, Amethyst, Qt., C–1264	15.00
Howe Jar, Scranton, Pa., Aqua, Qt., C–1274 ....48.00 To	60.00
Ideal Imperial, Aqua, Qt., C–1282	23.00
Imperial Trademark, Hand, Holding Mace, Aqua, Qt., C–1291	395.00
Independent Jar, Clear, Midget, C–1308	100.00
Independent Jar, Zinc Lid, 1/2 Gal., C–1308	33.00
J & B, Pat. July 14, 1889, Aqua, 1/2 Gal., C–1321	75.00
J & B, Pat. June 14, 1898, Aqua, Repro Cap, Pt., C–1321	50.00
J. C. Lefferts, Pat. Feb'y 15th, 1859, Qt.	598.00
J. Ellwood Lee Co., Label, Lid, Amber, Qt., C–1469	120.00
J. P. Smith Son & Co., Pittsburgh, Wax Sealer, Aqua, Qt., C–2670	28.00
J. T. Kinney, Aqua, Qt., C–1420	145.00
J. W. Beardsley's Sons, Vacuum Cap, Jelly–Type, 3 1/2 Oz.	9.00
Jeannette Mason Home Packer, J In Square, Clear, Qt., C–1324	1.00
Jewel, Canada, Clear, Qt., C–1331	2.00
John M. Moore's Mfg., Aqua, 1/2 Gal., C–2205	185.00
John M. Moore's Mfg., Aqua, Qt., C–2205	245.00

Johnson & Johnson, N. Y., Cobalt Blue, Screw Band, Qt., C–1341–1	358.00
Johnson & Johnson, New Brunswick, Amber, Qt., C–1340	16.00
Jumbo Good Enuf For Me, Clear, Pt., C–1347	4.00
Jumbo Peanut Butter, Elephant's Head, Tapered, 4 Oz., C–1347	19.00
Jumbo The Bottled Health Food, No Lid, Clear, 1 Lb., C–1347	5.00
Kerr Self Sealing Mason, 65th Anniv. 1903–1968, Gold, Qt., C–1387	33.00
Kerr Self Sealing, Mason, Clear, 1/2 Pt., C–1370	2.00
Kerr Self Sealing, Mason, Clear, Midget Pt., C–1376–1	2.00
Kerr Self Sealing, Mason, Light Green, Pt., C–1376	12.00
Kilner Jar Improved, Reg., Clear, Qt., C–1409	10.00
Kilner, Green Aqua, Smooth Lip, Pt., C–1406	18.00
King, On Banner, Below King's Head, Clear, Pt., C–1417	15.00
Knowlton Vacuum, Aqua, 1/2 Gal., C–1432 .... 22.00 To	45.00
Knowlton Vacuum, Aqua, Qt., C–1432	46.00
Knowlton Vacuum, Star, Aqua, Qt., C–1432	23.00
Knox Genuine Mason, Clear, Band, Pt., C–1434	25.00
Knox Mason, Marked Metal Lid, Band, Clear, 1/2 Pt., C–1434	16.00
L & W, Aqua, Kline Stopper, Qt.	48.00
L. Cohansey, Pat. McH 20, 77, Wax Sealer, Glass Lid, Aqua, Qt., C–633	138.00
Lafayette, Below Profile of Lafayette, Aqua, Qt., C–1450	785.00
Lafayette, Script, Aqua, 1/2 Gal., C–1450–1	123.00
Lafayette, Script, Aqua, Qt., C–1452	120.00
Lamb Mason, Round, Lamb Ground Lip Lid, Band, Pt., C–1455	6.00
Leader, Amber, Qt., C–1465	148.00
Legrand Ideal, Aqua, No Lid, Qt., C–1472	80.00
Legrand Ideal, LIJ, Monogram, Pat. July, 5, '98, Aqua, Qt., C–1472	168.00
Leotric, In Circle, Aqua, Pt., C–1476	4.00
Lightning, Golden Amber, Qt., C–1505	50.00
Lightning, Medium Olive Yellow, Pt., C–1499	350.00
Lightning, Medium Yellow Amber, Qt., C–1499	80.00
Lightning, Trademark, Cornflower Blue, Qt., C–1501	63.00
Lightning, Trademark, Deep Cornflower Blue, 2 Qt., C–1501	150.00
Lightning, Trademark, Putnam, Aqua, 1 1/2 Pt., C–1499	38.00
Lightning, Yellow Olive, 1/2 Gal., C–1499	275.00
Lightning, Yellow, Olive Tones, Qt., C–1499	185.00
Lockport Mason, Ghost Reversed Lockport, Aqua, Pt., C–1513	15.00
Longlife, Amber, Sprouter, Label, 1978, Qt., C–1517–1	12.00
Lustre, R. E. Tongue, Frame, Aqua, Qt., C–1557	8.00
M. G. Co., Citron, Wax Sealer, Tin Lid, Qt., C–2170–3	75.00
Made In Canada Perfect Seal, Wm. ADJ, Shield, Clear, Qt., C–2345	2.00
Magic Fruit Jar, Star, Green Aqua, Pt., C–1606	300.00
Magic Fruit Jar, Star, Pale Green, Qt., C–1606	176.00
Magic Star, Aqua, Qt., C–1606	75.00
Magic, Star, Amber, 1/2 Gal., C–1606	648.00
Magic, Star, Amber, Qt., C–1606	648.00
Marion Jar, Mason's Pat. Nov. 30th, 1858, Aqua, Pt., C–1625	18.00
Mascot Disk Immerser, Milk Glass, Zinc Lid, Qt., C–1628	225.00
Mascot Trademark, Pat. Improved, Clear, Immerser Lid, Qt., C–1628	165.00
Mascot Trademark, Pat. Improved, Clear, Qt., C–1630	168.00
Mason Patent, N. C. L. Co., Light Blue Aqua, Midget, C–1862	180.00
Mason WG Co., Qt., C–1659	150.00
Mason's 1 Patent Nov. 30th, 1858, Aqua, 1/2 Gal., C–2027–1	15.00
Mason's 2 Patent, H C & T, Aqua, Ground Lip, 1/2 Gal., C–1883–2	22.00
Mason's 7 Patent Nov. 30th, 1858, Aqua, Qt., C–1779	325.00
Mason's 7 Patent Nov. 30th, 1858, Aqua, Zinc Lid, Midget, C–2058	143.00
Mason's 8 Patent, Aqua, Midget, C–2061	175.00
Mason's 25 Patent, Aqua, Ground Lip, Qt., C–2089	12.00
Mason's 404 Patent Nov. 30th, 1858, Aqua, Midget, C–2126	176.00
Mason's BC Co. Improved, Aqua, 1/2 Gal.	58.00
Mason's BC Co. Improved, Aqua, Qt.	58.00
Mason's CFJ Co., Patent Nov. 30, 1858, Yellow Olive, Qt., C–1754	118.00
Mason's CFJ Co., Patent Nov. 30th, 1858, Aqua, Midget Pt., C–1754	12.00
Mason's CJF Co., Light Yellow Green, Midget, C–1920	110.00

Mason's Cross, Aqua, Qt., C–1240–1 .... 48.00
Mason's Cross, Medium Orange Amber, Qt., C–1939 .... 85.00
Mason's Crystal, Clear, Qt., C–1846 .... 28.00
Mason's Improved, Clyde, N. Y., Aqua, Midget, C–1713 .... 39.00
Mason's Improved, Hourglass, Aqua, Midget Pt., C–1869 .... 75.00
Mason's Improved, Yellow, 1/2 Pt., C–1695 .... 120.00
Mason's Keystone, Nov. 30, 1858, Green, 1/2 Gal., C–2020 .... 530.00
Mason's LGCO, Pat. Nov. 30th, 1858, Cornflower Blue, Midget, C–1970 .... 358.00
Mason's Patent Nov. 30th, 1858, Amber, Qt., C–1787 .... 149.00
Mason's Patent Nov. 30th, 1858, Amber, Zinc Lid, Qt., C–1787 .... 176.00
Mason's Patent Nov. 30th, 1858, Aqua, Insert, Midget Pt., C–1871 ...... 65.00
Mason's Patent Nov. 30th, 1858, Aqua, Midget Pt., C–1869 .... 85.00
Mason's Patent Nov. 30th, 1858, Aqua, Zinc Lid, Midget, C–1787 .... 39.00
Mason's Patent Nov. 30th, 1858, Christmas, Aqua, Pt., C–1782 .... 73.00
Mason's Patent Nov. 30th, 1858, Clear, 1/2 Gal., C–1766 .... 14.00
Mason's Patent Nov. 30th, 1858, Clear, Star Base, Midget, C–1907 ..... 39.00
Mason's Patent Nov. 30th, 1858, Clyde, N. Y., Aqua, Midget, C–1921 ...... 61.00
Mason's Patent Nov. 30th, 1858, Cornflower, Lid, Midget, C–1861 .... 253.00
Mason's Patent Nov. 30th, 1858, Red Amber, 1/2 Gal., C–1780 .... 110.00
Mason's Patent Nov. 30th, 1858, Vaseline, 1/2 Gal., C–1838 .... 39.00
Mason's Patent Nov. 30th, 1858, Yellow To Aqua, Midget, C–1784 .... 176.00
Mason's Patent Nov. 30th, 1858, Yellow, Snowflake, Midget, C–1875 .... 1265.00
Mason's Patent, Aqua, Olive Striations, 1/2 Gal., C–1787 .... 110.00
Mason's Patent, Moore Bros., Aqua, Pt., C–1889 .... 8.00
Mason's Patent, Orange Amber, 1/2 Gal., C–1787 .... 100.00
Mason's SG Co., Pat. Nov. 30th, 1858, Aqua, Qt. 6.00
Mason's Union, Shield, Aqua, Qt., C–2133 .... 105.00 To 125.00
Mason, Arched, Citron, Qt., C–1644 .... 30.00
Mason, Arched, Pt., C–1644 .... 4.00
Mason, Medium Amber, Pt., C–1665 .... 150.00
Mason, of 1872, Aqua, Pt., C–1750–1 .... 158.00
Masons, Tudor Rose, Clear, Embossed, Zinc Lid, 1/2 Gal., C–1875 .... 42.50
McDonald New Perfect Seal, Blue, Pt., C–2148 .... 9.00
McMechen's Always The Best, Old Virginia, Clear, Pt., C–2161 .... 123.00
McMechen's, Wheeling, W. Va., Square, No Cover, 1/2 Pt., C–2161 ...... 40.00
Medford Preserved Fruit, Buffalo, Aqua, 1/2 Gal., C–2163 .... 154.00
Medford Preserved Fruit, Buffalo, Cornflower, 2 Qt., C–2163 .... 240.00
Metro E–Z Pak Mason, Clear, Zinc Lid, Pt., C–2165 .... 2.00
Millville Atmospheric, Amber, 1/2 Gal., C–2181 .... 3950.00
Millville Atmospheric, Aqua, 1/2 Gal., C–2183 .... 130.00
Millville Atmospheric, Aqua, Qt., C–2181 .... 28.00
Millville WT Co. Improved G. Iz. B., Aqua, 1/2 Gal., C–2187 .... 65.00
Millville WT Co. Improved, Aqua, Qt., C–2187 .... 68.00
Millville–Whitall's Patent, Aqua, Iron Yoke, 1/2 Pt., C–2185 .... 154.00
Mission Trademark Mason, Calif., Aqua, 1/2 Pt., C–2190 .... 58.00
Mission Trademark Mason, Calif., Pt., C–2190 .... 5.00
Model Jar, Patent Aug. 27, 1867, Rochester, N. Y., Aqua, Qt., C–2195 .... 283.00
Model Mason, Pale Amethyst, Qt., C–2196 .... 14.00
Mrs. C. E. Kellner Preserving Co., Aqua, Safety Valve, Pt. 68.00
Mrs. Chapin's Mayonnaise, Boston, Mass., Clear, Pt., C–585 .... 3.00
Mrs. G. E. Haller, Aqua, Glass Stopper, Pt., C–1178 .... 275.00
Mrs. G. E. Haller, Patent Feb. 25 '73, Blown Stopper, Qt., C–1178 ..... 135.00
My Choice, Aqua, 1/2 Gal., C–2217 .... 198.00
Myers Test Jar, Aqua, Qt., C–2218 .... 130.00
NE Plus Ultra Airtight, Aqua, No Glass Lid, 1/2 Gal., C–477 .... 633.00
New Paragon, No Closure, Qt., C–2289 .... 65.00
NW Electroglass Mason, Clear, Qt., C–2253 .... 8.00
Ohio Quality Mason, Clear, Pt., C–2263 .... 13.00
Owl, Milk Glass, Pt. 83.00
Pansy, Paneled, Clear, Qt., C–2286 .... 198.00
Pearl, Aqua, Qt., C–2318 .... 38.00 To 43.00
Peerless, Aqua, Repro Clamp, Qt., C–2322 .... 100.00
Perfect Seal, Vines, Pt., C–2348 .... 8.00

Perfect Seal, Vines, SCA, Pt., C–2349 .... 8.00
Perfection, Clear, Qt., C–2330 .... 100.00
Phoenix Surgical Dressing Co., Amber, Lid & Closure, Qt., C–2364 .... 303.00
Potter & Bodine, Philadelphia, Aqua, 1/2 Gal., C–2381 .... 150.00
Potter & Bodine, Philadelphia, Aqua, Qt., C–2381 .... 123.00
Presto Supreme Mason, Ill. Glass, Aluminum Cap, 1/2 Pt., C–2415 .... 8.00
Presto Supreme Mason, Owens, Illinois Glass, 1/2 Gal., C–2406 .... 3.00
Presto Supreme Mason, Owens, Illinois Glass, 1/2 Pt., C–2406 .... 5.00
Protector, Aqua, Lid, 7 1/2 In., C–2420 ....*Illus* 55.00
Protector, Recessed Panels, Aqua, Qt., C–2421–1 .... 48.00
Puritan, Aqua, 1/2 Gal., C–2425 .... 163.00
Putnam Glass Works, Zanesville, Oh., Qt., C–2428 .... 33.00
Queen, Aqua, Patent Nov. 2, 1869, Qt., C–2433 .... 24.00
Queen, CFJ Co., Aqua, Monogram Back, Screw Band, Qt., C–2434 .... 20.00
Queen, Circled By Patent Dates, Aqua, Whittled, Qt., C–2432 .... 43.00
Queen, Clear, Pt., C–2439 .... 4.00
Queen, SKO, Clear, 1/2 Pt., C–2437 .... 18.00
Queensland, Pineapple, Green, Qt., C–2450 .... 123.00
Quick Seal, In Circle, Blue, Lightning Closure, Pt., C–2452 .... 6.00
Quick Seal, In Circle, Blue, Lightning Closure, Qt., C–2451 .... 5.00
Quick Seal, Patent July 14, 1908, Clear, Qt., C–2454 .... 2.00
R. E. Tongue & Bros. Co., Inc., Philadelphia, Aqua, Pt. 14.00
    FRUIT JAR, RAILROAD, see Fruit Jar, Helme's
Red Over Key Mason, Aqua, Pt., C–2476 .... 15.00
Reed's Patties, Reed Candy Co., Chicago, 1/2 Gal., C–2483 .... 40.00
Retentive, Aqua, 2 Qt., C–2498 .... 250.00
Richelieu Preserved Fruit, Safety Valve Type, Clear, Pt. 14.00
Root Mason, Aqua, Pt., C–2510 .... 7.00 To 7.50
Royal of 1876, Green Aqua, Qt., C–2515 .... 135.00
Royal, Black, Qt., C–2513 .... 3250.00
Royal, Clear, Amethyst Tint, Qt., C–2514 .... 180.00
Royal, Clear, Qt., C–2515–1 .... 4.00
S. B. Dewey Jr., Rochester, N. Y., Stopper, Aqua, C–771 .... 330.00
Safety Valve, Aqua, Greek Key, 1/2 Gal., C–2539 .... 22.00 To 38.00
Safety Valve, Green, Clear Lid, Pt., C–2538 .... 80.00
Safety, Amber, Original Clamp, Pt., C–2538 .... 130.00
Safety, Aqua, Glass Lid, Wire Clamp, 1/2 Gal., C–2538 .... 40.00
Samco Super Mason, Aqua, Milk Glass Lid, Band, Pt., C–2548 .... 8.00
Samco Super Mason, Clear, Zinc Lid, 1/2 Gal., C–2548 .... 4.00
Schaffer, Rochester, N. Y., Aqua, 1/2 Gal., C–2561 .... 198.00

Fruit Jar, H & S, Philadelphia, Screw Lid, 5 1/2 In.

Fruit Jar, Protector, Aqua, Lid, 7 1/2 In., C-2420

Fruit Jar, Strittmatters Pure Honey, Blue, Screw Lid, 5 1/2 In.

Fruit Jar, Sun, Trademark, Wire Bail, Lid, 7 3/4 In., C–2761

Schaffer, Rochester, N. Y., Aqua, Glass Domed Lid, Qt., C–2561 .... 177.00
Sealfast, Clear, Qt., C–2577 .... 3.00
Security Seal FCG Co., Clear, Small Mouth, Pt., C–2608 .... 6.00
Security Seal, In Triangles, Clear, Pt., C–2608 .... 5.00
Sierra Mason, Calif., Clear, Pt., C–2627 .... 65.00
Silicon, In Circle, Aqua, Qt., C–2629 .... 12.00
SKO Queen Trademark, Adjust. Wide Mouth, Clear, 1/2 Pt., C–2448 .... 15.00
SKO Queen, Clear, Unembossed Lid, Pt., C–2446 .... 10.00
Smalley Full Measure, Amber, Zinc Lid, Qt., C–2648 .... 48.00
Smalley's Nu–Seal, In Diamonds, Clear, 1/2 Pt. 48.00
Southern Double Seal Mason, Clear, 1/2 Gal., C–2680 .... 38.00
Spratt's Patent, July 18, 1854, Lead Lid, C–2687 .... 350.00
Standard From Foote, Baer & Co., Cleveland, Aqua, Qt., C–2707 .... 28.00
Standard, Shepherd's Crook, Aqua, Wax Sealer, Qt., C–2711 .... 25.00
Standard, W. McC & Co., Aqua, Qt., C–2701 .... 18.00
Standard, W. McC & Co., Wax Sealer, Sky Blue, Qt., C–2706 .... 148.00
Star Glass Co., New Albany, Ind., Aqua, 1/2 Gal., C–2729 .... 40.00
Star Glass Co., New Albany, Ind., Aqua, Qt., C–2729 .... 38.00
Star, Below Stippled Star, Clear, 1/2 Gal., C–2719 .... 48.00
    FRUIT JAR, STEER'S HEAD, see Fruit Jar, Flaccus Bros.
Stevens Tin Top, Pat. July 27, 1875, Aqua, Wax Sealer, Qt., C–2739 .... 73.00
Strittmatters Pure Honey, Blue, Screw Lid, 5 1/2 In. ....*Illus* 65.00
Sun, Aqua, 1/2 Gal., C–2761 .... 130.00
Sun, In Circle, Radiating Rays, Aqua, Qt., C–2761 .... 68.00
Sun, Trademark, Wire Bail, Lid, 7 3/4 In., C–2761 ....*Illus* 75.00
Superior A. G. Co., In Circle, Aqua, Pt., C–2770 .... 14.00
Sure Seal, Blue, Bulge Neck, Pt., C–2773 .... 12.00
Swasey Double Safety, In Frame, Clear, Pt., C–2776 .... 9.00
Swayzee's Improved Mason, Aqua, 1/2 Gal., C–2780 .... 10.00
Swayzee's Improved Mason, Aqua, Qt., C–2780 .... 5.00
T. M. Sinclair & Co. Ltd., Dunkley Lid, Clamp, Qt., C–2637 .... 20.00
Telephone, Trademark Reg. Whitney Glass Works, Aqua, Pt., C–2791 .... 8.00
Texas Mason, Map of Texas, Clear, Zinc Cover, Pt., C–2796 .... 15.00
Trademark Dandy, Dark Amber, 1/2 Gal., C–751 .... 185.00
Trademark Keystone Registered, Clear, Pt., C–1391 .... 7.00
Trademark Lightning Putman, Aqua, 26 Oz., C–1491–2 .... 20.00
Trademark Lightning Putnam, Amber, Pt., C–1499 .... 44.00
Trademark Lightning Reg. U.S. Patent Office, Aqua, Qt., C–1493 .... 2.00
Trademark Lightning, Aqua, Pt., C–1501 .... 4.00
Trademark Lightning, Citron, Qt., C–1501 .... 135.00

Union 3, Wax Sealer, Burst Bubble, C–2850 .... 10.00
Union, Beaver Falls Glass Co., Aqua, 1/2 Gal., C–2844 .... 33.00
Vacuum Seal, Detroit, Mi., Patent Nov. 1st, 1904, Clear, Qt., C–2870 .... 128.00
Van Vliet Improved, Pat. May3–81, Aqua, Cylinder, Qt., C–2879 .... 523.00
Van Vliet, Aqua, Qt., C–2878 .... 425.00
Veteran, Bust, Pt., C–2884 .... 28.00
Victory 1, Circled By Patent Dates, Aqua, Qt., C–2890–1 .... 48.00
Victory, In Shield, Clear, 2 Side Clamps, Pt., C–2897 .... 4.00
Victory, Kivlan & Onthank, Boston, Toggle Clamp, 1/2 Pt., C–2897 .... 12.00
W. M. Telephone Jar, Aqua, Pt., C–2790 .... 8.00
Wears Jar, In Stippled Frame, Clear, Pt., C–2918 .... 8.00
Wears, Clear, 1/2 Pt., C–2919 .... 40.00
Wears, In Circle, Clear, Pt., C–2917 .... 11.00
Weideman, Boy, Clear, Pt., C–2931 .... 10.00
Western Pride, Patent June 22, 1875, Aqua, Whittled, Qt., C–2945 .... 148.00
Whitney Mason 2, Patent 1858, Aqua, Qt., C–2973 .... 8.00
Whitney Mason, 3 Above 5 Dots, Patent 1858, Aqua, Qt., C–2991–1 .... 6.00
Whitney Mason, 5 Dots Below, Pat. 1858, Light Olive, Pt., C–2990 .... 14.00
Whitney Mason, Dot Below Mason, Patent 1858, Aqua, Pt., C–2986–1 .... 8.00
Wide Mouth, Olive Amber, Rolled Lip, 8 1/2 In. 85.00
Winslow Improved Valve, Aqua, Qt., C–3021 .... 296.00
Winslow, Aqua, Glass Lid, Wire, 1/2 Gal., C–3022 .... 63.00
Wm. Frank & Sons, Pittsburgh, Aqua, Wax Sealer, Qt., C–1031 .... 28.00
Woodbury Improved, W. G. W., Pt., Qt., 1/2 Gal., 3 Piece, C–3030 .... 120.00
Worcester, Aqua, Qt., C–3034 .... 160.00

GARNIER

The house of Garnier Liqueurs was founded in 1859 in Enghien, France. Figurals have been made through the nineteenth and twentieth centuries, except for the years of Prohibition and World War II. Julius Wile and Brothers, a New York City firm established in 1877, became the exclusive U.S. agents for Garnier in 1885. Many of the bottles were not sold in the United States but were purchased in France or the Caribbean and brought back home. Only miniature bottles were sold in the United States from 1970 to 1973. From 1974 to 1978, Garnier was distributed in the United States by Fleischmann Distilling Company. In 1978 the Garnier trademark was acquired by Standard Brands, Inc., the parent company of Julius Wile Sons and Company and Fleischmann Distilling Co., and few of the full-sized bottles were again sold in the United States. Standard Brands has since merged with Nabisco Brands, Inc.

GARNIER, Acorn, 1910 .... 40.00
Aladdin's Lamp, 1963 .... 40.00
Alfa Romeo, 1913 Model, 1969 .... 25.00
Alfa Romeo, 1924 Model, 1969 .... 24.00 To 25.00
Alfa Romeo, 1929 Model, 1969 .... 24.00 To 25.00
Apollo, 1969 .... 20.00
Aztec, 1965 .... 16.00
Baby Foot, 1963 .... 15.00
Bacchus, 1967 .... 23.00
Baseball Player, 1970 .... 18.00
Bellows, 1969 .... 16.00
Blue Bird, 1970 .... 15.00
Bouquet, 1966 .... 20.00
Bulldog 20.00
Bullfighter, 1963 .... 18.00 To 20.00
Burmese Man, 1965 .... 20.00
Butterfly, 1970, Miniature 10.00
Candlestick, 1955 .... 40.00
Candlestick, Bedroom, 1967 .... 22.00
Candlestick, Glass, 1965 .... 20.00
Cannon, 1964 .... 50.00
Cardinal, 1969 .... 14.00
Cards, Miniature, 1970 .... 11.00
Carrossee Coach, 1970 .... 27.00

Cat, Black, 1962	22.00
Chalet, 1955	45.00
Chimney, 1956	56.00
Chinese Man, 1970	18.00 To 20.00
Chinese Woman, 1970	18.00 To 20.00
Christmas Tree, 1956	60.00
Citroen, 1922 Model, 1970	26.00
Clock, 1958	25.00
Clown's Head, 1931	75.00
Clown, No. 20, 1910	42.00
Clown, With Tuba, 1955	18.00
Cocker Spaniel, 1970	20.00
Coffee Mill, 1966	25.00
Coffeepot, 1962	32.00
Collie, 1970	20.00
Country Jug, 1937	30.00
Deer	12.00
Diamond Bottle, 1969	13.00
Drunkard, Milord, 1956	22.00
Duck, No. 21, 1910	15.00
Duckling, 1956	38.00
Duo Firefly, 1959	15.00
Egg House, 1956	75.00
Eiffel Tower, 1950	20.00
Elephant, No. 66, 1932	7.00
Elephant, No. 183, 1961	20.00
Empire Vase, 1962	15.00
Fiat, 1913 Model, Nuevo, 1969	25.00
Fiat, 1924 Model, 1969	25.00
Football Player, 1970	16.00
Ford, 1913 Model, 1969	25.00
Fountain, 1964	28.00
German Shepherd, 1970	18.00
Giraffe, 1961	34.00
Goddess, 1963	42.00
Goldfinch, No. 11, 1970	15.00
Goose, 1955	18.00
Greyhound, 1930	75.00
Guitar & Mandolin	16.00
Harlequin, No. 166, 1958	35.00
Hockey Player, 1970	18.00
Hula Hoop, 1959	27.00
Humoristiques, 1934, Miniature	25.00
Hunting Vase, 1964	28.00
Inca, 1969	15.00
Indian Princess	12.00
Indian, 1958	16.00
Indy 500, No. 1, 1970	20.00
Jockey, 1961	25.00 To 26.00
LaDona, 1963	35.00
Lafayette	20.00
Laurel Crown, 1963	20.00
Locomotive, 1969	20.00
Log, Quarter, 1958	28.00
Log, Round, 1958	24.00
Loon, 1970	15.00
Maharajah, 1958	75.00
Marquis, 1931	75.00
Marseilles, 1970	20.00
Meadowlark, 1969	15.00
MG, 1913 Model, 1970	24.00
Mocking Bird, 1970	12.00
Montmartre, 1960	15.00

Napoleon, 1969	25.00
Oasis, 1959	20.00
Oriole, 1970	12.00
Packard, 1930 Model, 1970	25.00
Painting, 1961	28.00
Paris Monuments, 1966	20.00
Parrot, 1910	33.00
Partridge, No. 177, 1961	30.00
Pegasus, 1958	55.00
Pelican, 4 1/2 In.	50.00
Penguin, 1930	75.00
Pentanque, Balls	35.00
Pheasant, 1969	28.00
Policeman, Bahamas, 1970	20.00
Policeman, New York, 1970	20.00
Policeman, Paris, 1970	20.00
Pony, 1961	30.00
Poodle, Black, 1954	15.00
Poodle, White, 1954	15.00
Quail Valley, 1969	10.00
Rainbow, No. 142, 1955	28.00
Renault, 1911 Model, 1969	25.00
Roadrunner, 1969	14.00
Robin, 1970	12.00
Rolls Royce, 1908 Model, 1970	25.00
Rooster, Black, 1952	15.00
Rooster, Maroon, 1952	20.00
Rouen Vase, 1962	25.00
Scarecrow, 1960	30.00
Sheriff, Cowboy, 1958	22.00
Snail, 1959	62.00
Soccer Shoe, 1962	35.00
Soldier, 1949, Miniature	34.00
Soldier, Faceless, 1949	60.00
SS France, 1962	105.00
SS Queen Mary, 1970	25.00
St. Tropez, 1961	25.00
Stanley Steamer, 1907 Model, 1970	24.00 To 25.00
Tam Tam, 1961	50.00
Taxi, Paris, 1960	50.00
Teapot, No. 180, 1961	18.00
Tierce, Musical, 1965	40.00
Trout, 1967	20.00
Violin, 1966	30.00
Watch, Blue, 1966	25.00
Water Pitcher, 1965	15.00
Watering Can, 1958	15.00
Woman, With Jug, 1930	45.00
Young Deer, 1964	30.00

─────────────────── **GEMEL** ───────────────────

Gemel bottles are made in pairs. Two bottles are blown separately then joined together, usually with the two necks pointing in different directions. Gemels are popular for serving oil and vinegar or two different types of liqueurs.

GEMEL, Double Blown, Applied Foot & Rigaree, 7 1/4 In.	50.00
Double Blown, Clear, Cranberry & White Looping, 9 1/2 In.	55.00
Double Blown, Clear, White Looping, Amethyst Lip, Wafer Foot, 8 In.	25.00
Double Blown, Clear, White Looping, Applied Clear Rigaree, 8 1/2 In.	25.00
Double Blown, Clear, White Looping, Cobalt Blue Lip, 8 1/2 In.	35.00
Double Blown, Light Blue, White Looping, S. J., 7 3/4 In.	50.00
Double Blown, Stiegel–Type, Diamond–Quilted, Flowers, 6 3/8 In.	10.00
Double Blown, Stiegel–Type, Diamond–Quilted, Rigaree, 6 3/4 In.	20.00

Double Blown, Stiegel–Type, Diamond–Quilted, Rigaree, 8 In. 25.00

GIN

The word *gin* comes from the French word *genieve,* meaning juniper. It is said that Count de Morret, a brother of King Henry IV, made a drink of distilled spirits, juniper berries, and other substances. One of the earliest types of gin was what today is called *Geneva* or *Holland's* gin. It is made from a barley malt grain mash and juniper berries. The alcohol content is low and it is usually not used for cocktails. In some countries it is considered medicine. In England and America, the preferred drink is dry gin, which is made with juniper berries, coriander seeds, angelica root, and other flavors. The best dry gin is distilled, not mixed by the process used during Prohibition to make *bathtub* gin. Another drink is Tom gin, much like dry gin but with sugar added. Gin bottles have been made since the 1600s. Most of them have straight sides. Gin has always been an inexpensive drink, which is why so many of these bottles were made. Many were of a type called *case bottles* today. The case bottle was made with straight sides so that 4 to 12 bottles would fit tightly into a wooden packing case.

GIN, Avan Hoboken & Co., Olive Green, Case, Shoulder Seal AH, Qt. 58.50
     Avan Hoboken, Rotterdam, Case, Seal On Shoulder, Large 65.00
     Backbar, 10 Ribs, Gold Yellow, Silver Painted Letters, 1860–1890, 11 In. 110.00
     GIN, BININGER, see Bininger
     Blown, 3–Piece Mold, Gin Embossed, Clear, Stopper, 1825–1840, Qt. 303.00
     Blown, Olive Amber, Square Tapered, Mushroom Mouth, Pontil, 9 1/4 In. 77.00
     Blown, Yellow Green, Straight Sides, Square, Pontil, 10 7/8 In. 198.00
     Case, Engraved Floral, Rectangular, Late 18th Century, Bohemia, 1/2 Pt. 88.00
     Case, Flared Lip, Large Ring Pontil, 1800–1840, 10 1/4 In. 565.00
     Case, Green, Yellow Tint, Dip Mold, OP, Flared Lip, 9 7/8 In. 121.00
     Case, Medium Olive Amber, Dip Mold, OP, Flared & Rolled Lip, 9 3/4 In. 94.00
     Case, Medium Olive Amber, Dip Mold, OP, Flared, 11 1/4 In. 165.00
     Case, Olive Amber, Dip Mold, Flared & Rolled Lip, Pontil, 19 5/8 In. 1760.00
     Charles London Cordial, Light Olive Amber, Square, Qt. 50.00
     Coats & Co., Original Plymouth Gin, Plymouth, England, Bar, 8 1/2 In. 678.00
     Decraauwe Hengst, Schiedam, Black Glass, Case, Blob Lip, 11 3/8 In. 182.00
     DeKuyper, Olive, Seal D. K., Geneva, Paper Heart–Shaped Label, 11 In. 48.00
     Dip Mold, Medium Olive Yellow, Case, OP, 10 1/8 In. 100.00

Gin, J.J. Peters, Trademark,   *Gin, Melcher's Finest,*   *Ginger Beer, Hudor Co.,*
10 In.   *Geneva, Montreal, 10 1/2 In.*   *Buffalo, N.Y., Pottery, Cap,*
                                          7 1/2 In.

Dip Mold, Olive Amber, Case, Flared & Rolled Lip, OP, 15 1/2 In. 578.00
Dip Mold, Olive Amber, Case, OP, Seed Bubbles, 10 7/8 In. 121.00
Dip Mold, Wide Mouth, Medium Olive Amber, OP, 8 7/8 In. 750.00
Dip Mold, Wide Mouth, Medium Olive Amber, OP, 9 In. 643.00
Gilby, Barrel 15.00
Gordon's Dry, Aqua, Rectangular, 8 1/2 In. 20.00
Hartwig Kantorowicz, Josef Loewenthal, Milk Glass, Case, 9 3/8 In. 77.00
Hartwig Kantorowicz, Posen, Hamburg, Paris, Milk Glass, Case 50.00
Herman Jansen Schiedam, Olive Green 34.00
J. H. Henkes, Delfshaven, Holland, Case, Olive, Label 30.00
J. J. W. Peters, Trademark, 10 In. .... *Illus* 45.00
J. T. Daly Club House, Dark Emerald Green, Applied Top, 8 3/4 In. 94.00
J. W. Peters, Embossed Dog, Grass Green, Case 37.00
L. Lyons Pure Ohio Catawba Brandy Gin, Dense Amber, 13 1/2 In. 209.00
Melcher's Finest, Geneva, Montreal, 10 1/2 In. ....*Illus* 18.00
Olive Green, Tapered, Bubbles, 10 In. 15.00
Olive Tree, Embossed, 9 In. 340.00
Olive Tree, Embossed, Sloping Collar, 9 1/2 In. 176.00
Royal I. A. I. N. Bataui, Amethyst, Tooled Top, 12 In. 94.00
V. Hoytema & Co., Olive Green, Embossed, 11 In. 26.00
Van Dulken Weiland & Co., Pig Snout, Black Glass, Bubbles, 9 3/8 In. 156.00
Vandenbergh & Co., Light Olive, Bell, Ribbon, Flat Lip, Case, 10 1/2 In. 45.00
W. Hasekamp & Co., Schnapps, Lynx Picture, Black Glass, 8 7/8 In. 91.00
Wister's Club House, Dark Blue Green, Case, IP, 9 1/2 In. 121.00

──────────────── **GINGER BEER** ────────────────

Ginger beer was originally made from fermented ginger root, cream of tartar, sugar, yeast, and water. It was a popular drink from the 1850s to the 1920s. Beer made from grains became more popular and very little alcoholic ginger beer was made. Today it is an alcohol–free carbonated drink like soda. Pottery bottles have been made since the 1650s. A few products are still bottled in stoneware containers today. Ginger beer, vinegar, and cider were usually put in stoneware holders until the 1930s. The ginger beer bottle usually held 10 ounces. Blob tops, tapered collars, and crown tops were used. Some used a cork, others a Lightning stopper or inside screw stopper. The bottles were of shades of brown and white. Some were salt glazed for a slightly rough, glassy finish. Bottles were stamped or printed with names and usually the words *ginger beer.*

GINGER BEER, A. G. Barr, Blob Top 22.00
A. G. Scott, Blue Shoulder Transfer, Spanish, 10 1/4 In. 73.00
Anchor Picture, Stoneware 16.00
Andrew A. Watt & Co. Ltd., Londonderry, Crown Cap, Castle, 7 In. 45.00
Arliss Robinson & Co., Sutton, Surrey, Blue Top, 6 3/4 In. 105.00
Arthur Craig & Co., Design In Shield, Gray, 8 3/4 In. 34.00
Axe & Mason, Town, 2 Roses Transfer 55.00
C. W. Southern, Belper, 3 Story House In Oval, 8 1/2 In. 85.00
C. Wooley & Son, Dalkeith, Heart–Shaped Transfer, 8 3/4 In. 33.00
Charles Bailey, Henley, Oxon., Round Black Print, White 36.00
Charles Moore, Glasgow, Dark Green Top, Stoneware, 8 In. 273.00
Cross & Co., Vancouver, British Columbia 45.00
Double Eagle Bottling Co., Cleveland, Oh. 22.00
Forbes, Maxwell & Co., Aberdeen, Black Initials, 8 1/2 In. 33.00
G. & C. Moore, Edinburgh & Glasgow, Pink, Brown Bird Transfer 182.00
Golden Key Brand, E. L. Drewry, Winnipeg, Manitoba, Qt. 85.00
Green Top Valance, Top Half Green, Swing Stopper, 8 3/4 In. 86.00
H. McCauley, Apothecaries, Eagle, Blob Top, Pottery, 8 3/4 In. 362.00
Hendry's, Edinburgh, Scotsman & Banner Transfer, 8 1/2 In. 49.00
Hop Bitters, Sam'l Vincent, All White, Blob Top, 8 In. 39.00
Hudor Co., Buffalo, N. Y., Pottery, Cap, 7 1/2 In. ....*Illus* 55.00
J. F. Giering & Brother, Youngstown, Oh., Crock 65.00
J. Horne & Co., Glasgow 36.00
J. Robertson & Co., Edinburgh, No Swing Stopper, 8 3/4 In. 98.00
J. W. Green Limited, Green Top, Stoneware, 6 7/8 In. 36.00
James B. Flawith, Durham, Port Dundas Train Picture, 8 In. 164.00

James Wilson, Pulteneytown, Turret Building, 8 7/8 In.	91.00
Lawrence's & Sons, Yarmouth, Shield & Medals, Pottery, 7 In.	128.00
Lee & Green Co., Buffalo, N. Y.	22.00
Lighton Bros., Sheffield, Lion, Holding Hamilton	36.00
MacLachan, Glasgow & Belfast, 3–Turretted Castle	40.00
Manchester Champagne, 1870s	6.00
Mappins Masbro' Old Brewery, Rotherham, Horse & Rider, 8 In.	63.00
Middlemas, Kelso, Black Transfer, 8 1/4 In.	34.00
Nottingham, Ford, Parr, Chocolate Top	109.00
Nottingham, Harrison, Smith	109.00
Nottingham, Hart, Glass	63.00
Nottingham, Holmes	109.00
Nottingham, Thraves, Andrew	90.00
Oldensburg Works, Century Brand, H. N. Daniels	22.00
Pain & Bayles, Ipswich, Classic Scroll & Castle, 6 1/2 In.	98.00
Queens Ale & Stout, Aulton, Aberdeen, Blob Top, Transfer, 8 In.	39.00
Randall & Sons, Chesterfield, Cork, Church Spire, 8 In.	78.00
Robert Haldane, Glasgow, Beast's Head Trademark	36.00
Robert Henderson, Stoneware, Negro Drinking, 7 7/8 In.	237.00
Rose & Co., Doctor's Stout, Man Picture, Pottery, 7 3/4 In.	57.00
Sang & Co., Elgin, Blue Transfer, Swing Stopper, Pottery, 9 In.	362.00
T. A. Minnitt Home Bakery, Nottingham, Oval Transfer, 8 1/4 In.	328.00
T. Armstrong & Son, Invalid Dublin Stout, Pottery, 8 1/4 In.	38.00
T. W. Swift, Derby, Deep Blue Top, Cream Base, 7 In.	39.00
Thompson Ltd., Aberdeen, Red Brown Top, Black Glaze, Transfer	33.00
W. A. Scott, Montrose, Central Hotel Picture, 8 3/4 In.	205.00
W. H. Roome, Sailing Ship, Pottery, Red Brown Top, 8 In.	195.00
W. H. Wood, Durham & Sunderland, Durham Cathedral, 8 In.	68.00
Ye Old Country Stone, Felix Dist., Vancouver, BC	20.00

GLUE

Glue and paste have been packaged in bottles since the nineteenth century. Most of these bottles have identifying paper labels. A few have the name embossed in the glass.

GLUE, Carter's Photolibrary Paste, Screw Cap, Amethyst, Qt.	17.00
Commercial Paste Co., Columbus, Oh., Screw Threads, Clear, Qt.	10.00
Major's Rubber Cement, Small	3.50
Silicious Cement, Aqua, OP, Triangular	20.00
Spalding's, Haze, OP	8.00

GRENADIER

The Grenadier Spirits Company of San Francisco, California, started making figural porcelain bottles in 1970. Twelve soldier–shaped fifths were in Series No. 1. These were followed by Series 2 late in 1970. Only 400 cases were made of each soldier. The company continued to make bottles in series, including the 1976 American Revolutionary Army regiments in fifths and tenths, and many groups of minibottles. They also had series of club bottles, missions, foreign generals, horses, and more. The brothel series was started in 1978 for a special customer, Mr. Dug Picking of Carson City, Nevada. These are usually sold as *Dug's Nevada Brothel* and are listed in this book under *Miniature*. The Grenadier Spirits Company sold out to Fleishmann Distilling Company and stopped making bottles about 1980. Jon–Sol purchased the remaining inventory of bottles.

GRENADIER, Alabama Roughs, 1975, Miniature	10.00
Eugene, 1970	25.00
Father's Gift, 1979 .... 21.00 To	23.00
Father's Gift, 1979, Miniature	10.00
Fire Chief, 1973	95.00
Fireman Statue, 1974	450.00
Ford T–Bird, No. 15, Bud Moore, 1979	30.00
Fray Junipero Serro, 1974	20.00
Fray Junipero Serro, 1979, Miniature	12.00
Frosty The Snowman, 1978	25.00
Frosty The Snowman, 1980, Miniature .... 12.00 To 14.00	

Horse, American Saddle Bred, 1978 .... 25.00 To 30.00
Horse, American Thoroughbred, 1978 .... 20.00 To 22.00
Horse, Appaloosa, 1978 .... 20.00
Horse, Arabian, 1978 .... 16.00
Horse, Tennessee Walking, 1978 .... 20.00
Jester, 1977 .... 45.00
Joan of Arc, 1972 .... 60.00
Mission San Carlos, 1977 .... 20.00
Mission San Francisco, 1978 .... 25.00
Mission San Gabriel Archangel, 1978 .... 15.00
Mission Santa Clara De Asis, 1978 .... 15.00
Moose Lodge, 1970 .... 15.00
Mr. Spock, Bust, 1979 .... 22.00 To 25.00
Mr. Spock, Standing, Gold, 1979 .... 100.00
Pontiac Trans Am, 1979 .... 30.00
San Fernando Electric Mfg. Co., 1976 .... 65.00
Santa Claus, Green Sack, 1978 .... 28.00
Santa Claus, Green Sack, 1980, Miniature 14.00
Soldier, 1st Officers Guard, 1970 .... 15.00 To 20.00
Soldier, 1st Officers Guard, 1971, Miniature 12.00
Soldier, 1st Pennsylvania, 1970 .... 20.00 To 26.00
Soldier, 1st Regiment Virginia Volunteers, 1974, Miniature 10.00
Soldier, 2nd Maryland, 1969 .... 29.00 To 30.00
Soldier, 2nd Regiment, US Sharpshooters, 1975, Miniature 18.00
Soldier, 3rd New York, 1970 .... 17.00 To 20.00
Soldier, 4th Virginia Cavalry, 1975, Miniature 15.00
Soldier, 6th Wisconsin Regiment, 1975, Miniature 12.00
Soldier, 14th Virginia Cavalry, 1975, Miniature 17.00
Soldier, Baron Johann DeKalb, 1978 .... 30.00
Soldier, Baron Von Steuben, 1978 .... 20.00
Soldier, Baylor's 3rd Continental, 1969 .... 20.00 To 23.00
Soldier, Billy Mitchell, 1975 .... 30.00
Soldier, Captain, Confederate, 1970 .... 25.00
Soldier, Captain, Union Army, 1970 .... 30.00
Soldier, Captain, Union Army, 1975, Miniature 15.00
Soldier, Comte De Rochambeau, 1978 .... 25.00
Soldier, Connecticut Governor's Foot Guard, 1972 .... 23.00
Soldier, Continental Marines, 1969 .... 26.00
Soldier, Corporal, French, 1970 .... 25.00
Soldier, Corporal, French, 1973, Miniature 15.00
Soldier, Count Pulaski, 1978 .... 50.00
Soldier, Dragoon 17th, 1970 .... 25.00
Soldier, General Custer, 1970 .... 27.00
Soldier, General MacArthur, 1975 .... 30.00
Soldier, General Robert E. Lee, 1974 .... 22.00
Soldier, General Ulysses S. Grant, 1975 .... 20.00
Soldier, George Washington, On Horse, 1974 .... 27.00
Soldier, Indiana Zouve, 1975, Miniature 15.00
Soldier, Jeb Stuart, 1970 .... 20.00
Soldier, Jeb Stuart, 1970, Miniature 15.00
Soldier, John Paul Jones, 1976 .... 22.00 To 23.00
Soldier, Kings African Rifle Corps, 1970 .... 16.00 To 22.00
Soldier, Kings African Rifle Corps, 1970, Miniature 15.00
Soldier, Kings African Rifle Corps, 1970, Qt. 28.00
Soldier, Lannes, 1970 .... 16.00 To 20.00
Soldier, Lassal, 1969 .... 28.00 To 35.00
Soldier, Marquis De Lafayette, 1978 .... 20.00
Soldier, Marquis De Lafayette, 1979, Miniature 10.00
Soldier, Mosby's Ranger, 1975, Miniature 20.00
Soldier, Murat, 1970 .... 16.00
Soldier, Napoleon, 1969 .... 16.00 To 25.00
Soldier, New York Highlander, 1975, Miniature 12.00
Soldier, Ney, 1969 .... 17.00 To 20.00

Soldier, Officer 3rd Guard Regiment, 1971	23.00
Soldier, Officer 3rd Guard Regiment, 1971, Miniature	14.00
Soldier, Officer, British, 1970	27.00
Soldier, Scots Fusileer, 1971	18.00
Soldier, Scots Fusileer, 1975, Miniature	12.00
Soldier, Sergeant Major, Coldstream Guard, 1971	27.00
Soldier, Teddy Roosevelt, 1976	23.00
Soldier, Teddy Roosevelt, 1977, Miniature	8.00
Soldier, Texas Ranger, 1977	30.00
Soldier, Texas Ranger, 1979, Miniature	10.00
Soldier, Thaddeus Kosciuszko, 1978	16.00
Soldier, Von Steuben, 1978	20.00
Soldier, Washington Blue Rifles, 1974, Miniature	13.00

HAIR PRODUCTS, see Cosmetic; Medicine
HAND LOTION, see Cosmetic; Medicine

HOFFMAN

J. Wertheimer had a distillery in Kentucky before the Civil War. Edward Wertheimer and his brother Lee joined the business as young men. When Edward Sr. died at age 92, his son Ed Wertheimer Jr., became president. Edward Jr.'s sons, Ed Wertheimer III and Thomas Wertheimer, also worked in the family company. L. & E. Wertheimer Inc. made the products of the Hoffman Distilling Company and the Old Spring Distilling Company, including Old Spring Bourbon, until 1983 when the company was sold to Commonwealth Distillery. Hoffman Originals, later called the Hoffman Club, was founded by the Wertheimers in 1971 to make a series of figural bottles. The first was the Mr. Lucky series, started in 1973. These were leprechaun–shaped decanters. Five series of leprechauns were made. Other series include wildlife, decoy ducks (1977–1978), Aesop's fables, C. M. Russell (1978), rodeo (1978), pool–playing dogs (1978), belt buckles (1979), horses (1979), Jack Richardson animals, Bill Ohrmann animals (1980–1981), cheerleaders (1980), framed pistols (1978), political (1980), and college football (1981–1982). The miniature Hoffman bottles include series such as leprechauns (1981), birds (1978), dogs and cats (1978–1981), decoys (1978–1979), pistols on stands (1975), Street Swingers (musicians, 1978–1979), pistols (1975), wildlife (1978), and horses (1978).

HOFFMAN, A. J. Foyte, No. 2, 1972	104.00
Aesop's Fables, Androcles & The Lion, 1978	16.00
Aesop's Fables, Fox & Grapes, 1978	16.00
Aesop's Fables, Goose With The Golden Egg, 1978	16.00
Aesop's Fables, Hare & The Tortoise, 1978	16.00
Alaska Pipeline, 1975	24.00
Animal, Bear & Cub, Fishing, 1981	60.00
Animal, Bear & Cub, In Tree, 1978	35.00
Animal, Big Trouble On The Trail, 1979	325.00

Hoffman, Animal, Mountain Goat & Puma, 1981

Animal, Big Trouble On The Trail, 1979, Miniature 350.00
Animal, Big Trouble On The Trail, White, Gold, 1979 .... 225.00
Animal, Bobcat & Pheasant, 1978 .... 43.00
Animal, Bobcat & Pheasant, 1978, Miniature 10.00
Animal, Doe & Fawn, 1975 .... 29.00
Animal, Falcon & Rabbit, 1978 .... 25.00
Animal, Falcon & Rabbit, 1978, Miniature 10.00
Animal, Fox & Eagle, 1978 .... 45.00
Animal, Fox & Rabbit, 1981 .... 40.00
Animal, Jaguar & Armadillo 25.00
Animal, Kangaroo and Koala Bear, 1978 .... 36.00
Animal, Lion & Crane, 1979 .... 25.00
Animal, Lion & Sheep, 1977, 3 Piece 160.00
Animal, Lynx & Rabbit, 1981 .... 49.00
Animal, Mountain Goat & Puma, 1981 ....*Illus* 65.00
Animal, Musk Ox, 1979, Pair 49.00
Animal, Owl & Chipmunk, 1978 .... 32.00
Animal, Panda, 1976 .... 55.00
Animal, Panda, 1976, Miniature 12.00
Animal, Penguins, 1979 .... 48.00
Animal, Pup Seals, 1979, Miniature 20.00
Animal, Rams, Fighting, 1977, 4 Piece 215.00
Animal, Stranger This Is My Land, 1978 .... 295.00
Animal, Wolf & Raccoon, 1978 .... 46.00
Animal, Wolf & Raccoon, 1978, Miniature 14.00
Betsy Ross, 1974 ....32.00 To 39.00
Big Red Machine, 1973 .... 34.00
Bird, Blue Bill, 1978, Miniature 12.00
Bird, Blue Jay, 1979, Pair 37.00
Bird, Dove, Closed Wing, 1979 .... 18.00
Bird, Dove, Open Wing, 1979 .... 18.00
Bird, Eagle, Bicentennial, 1976 .... 30.00
Bird, Eagle, Open Wing, 1979 .... 20.00
Bird, Egret, Baby, 1979, 200 Ml. 14.00
Bird, Love Birds, 1979 .... 15.00
Bird, Swan, Closed Wing, 1980, 100 Ml. 16.00
Bird, Swan, Open Wing, 1980, 200 Ml. 16.00
Bird, Titmouse, 1979 .... 25.00
Bird, Turkeys, 1980, 200 Ml. 35.00
Bird, Wood Ducks, 1980 .... 29.00
Cat, Miniature, Set of 6 .... 65.00
Cat, Perry Persian, 1981, 50 Ml. 10.00
Cat, Sammy Siamese, 1981, Miniature 12.00
Cat, Suzie Siamese, 1981, Miniature 12.00
Cat, Tom Cat, 1981, Miniature, 50 Ml. 12.00
Cheerleader, Dallas, 1979 .... 25.00
Cheerleader, Dallas, Topless 95.00
Children of The World, France, 1978 .... 24.00
Children of The World, Jamaica, 1979 .... 24.00
Children of The World, Mexico, 1979 .... 24.00
Children of The World, Panama, 1979 .... 24.00
Children of The World, Spain, 1979 .... 24.00
Children of The World, Yugoslavia, 1979 .... 24.00
College, Auburn Tigers, Helmet, 1981 .... 25.00
College, Clemson Tigers, 1981 .... 30.00
College, Georgia Bulldogs, Helmet, 1981 .... 40.00
College, Kansas State Wildcats, Helmet, 1981 .... 22.00
College, Kentucky Wildcat, Basketball, 1979 .... 35.00
College, Kentucky Wildcat, Helmet, 1981 .... 24.00
College, LSU Tiger, No. 1, 1978 .... 34.00
College, LSU Tiger, No. 2, 1981 .... 38.00
College, Mississippi Southern Golden Eagle, 1982 .... 46.00
College, Mississippi State Bulldog, 1977 .... 44.00

College, Mississippi University Rebel, 1977	45.00
College, Missouri Tiger, 1981	22.00
College, Nebraska Cornhusker, 1981	39.00
College, Nevada Wolfpack, 1979	39.00
College, Ohio State, Fan, 1982	40.00
College, Oklahoma Sooners, Helmet, 1981	39.00
Convention, Leprechaun In Barrel, 1982	40.00
Cowboy & Puma, 1978	295.00
Dog, Alfy Afghan, 1981	27.00
Dog, Beagle, 1978	27.00
Dog, Boston Terrier, 1978, Miniature	27.00
Dog, Boxer, 1978, Miniature	27.00
Dog, Cocker Spaniel, 1978, Miniature	27.00
Dog, Coon Dog, 1979	49.00
Dog, Dachshund, 1978, Miniature	27.00
Dog, Dalmatian, Miniature	27.00
Dog, Dog & Squirrel, 1981	45.00
Dog, Percy Poodle, 1981, Miniature	20.00
Dog, Pointer, 1979	41.00
Dog, Pool Hustler, 1979	110.00
Dog, Scotch Terrier, 1978, Miniature	27.00
Dog, Scotty Terrier, 1981, Miniature	19.00
Dog, Setter, 1979	37.00
Dog, Springer Spaniel, 1979	51.00
Dog, Terry Terrier, 1981, Miniature	12.00
Donahue Commemorative, 1972	25.00
Donahue Sunoco, No. 66, 1972	85.00
Duck, Blue Wing Teal, 1978	20.00
Duck, Decoy, Canada Goose, 1977	19.00
Duck, Decoy, Canvasback, 1978, Miniature, Pair	15.00
Duck, Decoy, Golden Eye, 1978, Miniature, Pair	12.00
Duck, Decoy, Green Winged Teal, 1977, Miniature, Pair	17.00
Duck, Decoy, Loon, 1978	33.00
Duck, Decoy, Mallard, 1977, Miniature, Pair	13.00
Duck, Decoy, Merganser, 1978	20.00
Duck, Decoy, Merganser, 1978, Miniature	12.00
Duck, Decoy, Pintail, 1977, Miniature, Pair	14.00
Duck, Decoy, Redhead, 1977, Miniature, Pair	11.00
Duck, Decoy, Ruddy Duck, 1978, Miniature, Pair	11.00
Duck, Decoy, Widgeon, 1978	28.00
Duck, Decoy, Wood Duck, 1977, Miniature, Pair	14.00
Duck, Decoy, Wood Duck, 1978	38.00
Duck, Mallard, Closed Wing, 1982	18.00
Duck, Mallard, Open Wing, 1982	18.00
Generation Gap, 1976, Miniature, Pair	5.00 To 12.00
Horse, Appaloosa Yearling, 1979, Miniature	15.00
Horse, Arabian Stallion, 1979, Miniature	15.00
Horse, Mare & Colt, 1979	35.00
Horse, Proud Arabian, 1979, Miniature	15.00
Horse, Quarter Horse, 1979, Miniature	15.00
Horse, Shetland Pony, 1979, Miniature	15.00 To 25.00
Horse, Thoroughbred, 1979, Miniature	15.00
Horses, 1979, Miniature, 6 Piece	88.00
Johncock Commemorative, 1973	15.00
Johncock No. 20, 1974	80.00
Lady Godiva, 1974	24.00 To 29.00
Locomotive, 1981	75.00
Locomotive, 1981, 200 Ml.	75.00
Mr. Baker, 1978	35.00
Mr. Baker, 1978, Miniature	10.00 To 12.00
Mr. Barber, 1980	25.00
Mr. Barber, 1980, Miniature	12.00
Mr. Bartender, 1975 ....*Illus*	30.00

Hoffman, Mr.Bartender, 1975

Hoffman, Mr.Doctor, 1974

Mr. Blacksmith, 1976	35.00
Mr. Blacksmith, 1976, Miniature	10.00 To 12.00
Mr. Butcher, 1979, Miniature	12.00
Mr. Carpenter, 1979	30.00
Mr. Charmer, 1974	20.00
Mr. Charmer, 1974, Miniature	10.00 To 11.00
Mr. Cobbler, 1973	20.00
Mr. Cobbler, Miniature	10.00
Mr. Dancer, 1974	20.00
Mr. Dancer, 1974, Miniature	15.00
Mr. Dentist, 1980	24.00
Mr. Dentist, 1980, Miniature	12.00
Mr. Doctor, 1974 ....*Illus*	25.00
Mr. Doctor, 1974, Miniature	15.00
Mr. Electrician, 1978	34.00
Mr. Electrician, 1978, Miniature	13.00
Mr. Farmer, 1980	25.00
Mr. Farmer, 1980, Miniature	10.00
Mr. Fiddler, 1974	22.00
Mr. Fiddler, 1974, Miniature	20.00
Mr. Fireman, 1976	65.00
Mr. Fireman, 1976, Miniature	21.00 To 25.00
Mr. Fireman, Retired, 1983, Miniature	15.00
Mr. Guitarist, 1975, Miniature	10.00
Mr. Harpist, 1974	17.00 To 20.00
Mr. Harpist, 1974, Miniature	5.00 To 10.00
Mr. Lucky & Rockwell, 1980, Miniature	47.00
Mr. Lucky, 1974, Miniature	9.00 To 10.00
Mr. Lucky, Caroliers, 1979	25.00
Mr. Lucky, Caroliers, 1979, Miniature	15.00
Mr. Lucky, Organ Player, 1979	25.00
Mr. Lucky, Organ Player, 1979, Miniature	15.00
Mr. Lucky, Retired, 1978, Miniature	20.00
Mr. Lucky, Retired, With Wooden Chair, 1981	42.00
Mr. Lucky, Retired, With Wooden Chair, 1981, Miniature	35.00
Mr. Lucky, White & Gold, 1981	185.00
Mr. Lucky, White & Gold, 1981	95.00
Mr. Mailman, 1976	35.00
Mr. Mailman, 1976, Miniature	16.00
Mr. Mechanic, 1979	30.00
Mr. Mechanic, 1979, Miniature	12.00
Mr. Organ Player, 1979	28.00
Mr. Photographer, 1980	28.00

Mr. Photographer, 1980, Miniature 15.00
Mr. Plumber, 1978 .... 27.00
Mr. Plumber, 1978, Miniature .... 10.00 To 12.00
Mr. Policeman Retired, 1986, Miniature ....*Illus* 30.00
Mr. Policeman, 1975 .... 30.00
Mr. Policeman, 1975, Miniature 15.00
Mr. Railroad Engineer, 1980 .... 29.00
Mr. Railroad Engineer, 1980, Miniature 15.00
Mr. Salesman, Miniature 15.00
Mr. Sandman, 1974 .... 20.00
Mr. Sandman, 1974, Miniature 5.00
Mr. Saxophonist, 1975 .... 25.00
Mr. Saxophonist, 1975, Miniature ....8.00 To 12.00
Mr. Stockbroker, 1976 ....*Illus* 42.00
Mr. Tailor, 1979, Miniature .... 10.00 To 12.00
Mr. Teacher, 1976 .... 22.00
Mr. Teacher, 1976, Miniature 14.00
Mr. Tourist, 1980 .... 24.00
Mr. Tourist, 1980, Miniature 15.00
Mrs. Lucky, 1974 .... 20.00
Mrs. Lucky, 1974, Miniature ....5.00 To 10.00
Mrs. Lucky, Retired, Miniature 10.00
Pistol, Civil War Colt, Framed, 1978 .... 28.00
Pistol, Civil War Colt, With Stand, 1975, Miniature 15.00
Pistol, Colt 45 Automatic, Framed, 1978 .... 26.00
Pistol, Colt 45 Automatic, With Stand, 1975, Miniature 18.00
Pistol, Derringer, Gold, Framed, 1979 .... 24.00
Pistol, Derringer, Silver, Framed, 1979 .... 24.00
Pistol, Dodge City Frontier, Framed, 1978 ....25.00 To 27.00
Pistol, Dodge City Frontier, With Stand, 1975, Miniature 17.00
Pistol, German Luger, Framed, 1978 ....5.00 To 15.00
Pistol, German Luger, With Stand, 1975, Miniature 11.00
Pistol, Kentucky Flintlock, With Stand, 1975 ....15.00 To 25.00
Pistol, Lawman, With Stand, 1978, Miniature 25.00
Pistol, Tower Flintlock, 1975 .... 26.00
Political Donkey, 1980 .... 15.00
Political Elephant, 1980 .... 15.00
Rodeo Championship Saddle 30.00
Rodeo, Bareback Rider, 1978 .... 27.00
Rodeo, Belt Buckle, Bareback Riding, 1979 ....15.00 To 25.00
Rodeo, Belt Buckle, Calf Roping, 1979 .... 25.00
Rodeo, Belt Buckle, Nile, 1978 ....15.00 To 17.00
Rodeo, Belt Buckle, Saddle Bronc Riding, 1979 .... 24.00

Hoffman, Mr.Policeman Retired, 1986, Miniature

Hoffman, Mr.Stockbroker, 1976

Rodeo, Belt Buckle, Steer Wrestling, 1978 .... 22.00
Rodeo, Belt Buckle, Team Roping, 1979 .... 15.00
Rodeo, Brahma Bull Riding, 1978 .... 40.00
Rodeo, Bull Riding, 1979 .... 21.00
Rodeo, Calf Roping, 1978 .... 35.00
Rodeo, Clown, 1971 .... 39.00
Rodeo, Roping, 1978 .... 36.00
Rodeo, Saddle Bronc Riding, 1978 .... 10.00
Rodeo, Steer Wrestling, 1978 .... 40.00
Russel, Buffalo Hunter, 1978 .... 30.00
Russel, Buffalo Man, 1976 .... 25.00
Russel, Buffalo Man, 1976, Miniature 10.00
Russel, Cowboy, 1978 .... 30.00
Russel, Flathead Squaw, 1976 .... 15.00 To 18.00
Russel, Flathead Squaw, 1976, Miniature 10.00
Russel, Half Breed Trader, 1978 .... 34.00
Russel, Last of 5000, 1975 .... 15.00
Russel, Miscellaneous, Bust, 1978 .... 19.00 To 24.00
Russel, Miscellaneous, I Rode Him, 1978, 2 Piece 35.00
Russel, Northern Cree, 1976 .... 36.00
Russel, Prospector, 1976 .... 21.00
Russel, Prospector, 1976, Miniature 10.00
Russel, Red River Breed, 1976 .... 25.00
Russel, Red River Breed, 1976, Miniature 10.00
Russel, Scout, 1978 .... 35.00
Russel, Stage Robber, 1978 .... 30.00
Russel, Stagecoach Driver, 1976 .... 19.00
Russel, Stagecoach Driver, 1976, Miniature 10.00
Russel, Trapper, 1976 .... 19.00 To 25.00
Russel, Trapper, 1976, Miniature 10.00
Rutherford, No. 3, 1974 .... 70.00
Soldier, Concord Soldier, 1973 .... 20.00
Soldier, Queen's Rangers, 1978, Miniature, 4 Piece 50.00
Soldier, Tennessee Volunteers, Helmet, 1981 .... 25.00
Street Swingers, Accordian Player, 1978, Miniature 15.00
Street Swingers, Bass Player, 1979, Miniature 15.00
Street Swingers, Clarinet Player, 1978, Miniature 15.00
Street Swingers, Cymbal Player, 1978, Miniature 15.00
Street Swingers, Drummer, 1979, Miniature 15.00
Street Swingers, Fiddler, 1978, Miniature 15.00
Street Swingers, Mandolin Player, 1979, Miniature 15.00
Street Swingers, Saxaphone Player, 1978, Miniature 15.00
Street Swingers, Tuba Player, 1978, Miniature 15.00
Street Swingers, Violin Player, 1979, Miniature 15.00
Women's Lib, 1976, Miniature, Pair 10.00

HOUSEHOLD

Many household cleaning products have been packaged in glass bottles since the nineteenth century. Shoe polish, ammonia, stove blacking, bluing, and other nonfood products are listed in this section. Most of these bottles have attractive paper labels that interest the collector.

HOUSEHOLD, ADR Blacking, Albany, Emerald, Embossed, Rolled Lip, Oval 100.00
Ammonia, S. F. Gaslight Co., Aqua, Tooled Lip, 7 7/8 In. .... 30.00 To 40.00
Ammonia, San Francisco Gaslight, Yellow Green, 8 1/4 In., Pt. 40.00
Black Cat Stove Enamel, Cat 15.00
Blacking, Blown, Yellow Amber, OP, 4 3/8 In. 66.00
Bullard's Soap, Vial, Cleaning Coat Collars, Blown, Label 10.00
Carbona Cleaning Fluid, Clear, 12 Panels, Some Contents, 7 In. 7.50
Cleveland's Oil Shoe Polish, Amber 15.00
E-Z Stove Polish, Clear, BIMAL, 5 1/2 In. 4.00
Furniture Cream, Amber, Indian Scene Label 9.00
H. A. Bartlet & Co., Shoe Dressing, Sponge, 7 In. ....Illus   65.00

Household, H.A.Bartlet & Co., Shoe Dressing,
Sponge, 7 In.

Household, Holy Water,
Behold The Heart That Love Men, 6 In.

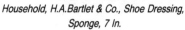

Holy Water, Behold The Heart That Love Men, 6 In. ....*Illus*	45.00
Inman's Household Ammonia, Stoneware, Tan Neck, 10 7/8 In.	58.00
Jar, Borax, Lid, Pottery, Black Transfer All Around, 4 3/4 In.	88.00
Jumbomonia, Plynine Co., Pottery, Blob Top, 11 3/8 In.	200.00
Knowles Insect Destroyer, 8 In.	75.00
Kwik–Lite Lighter Fluid, Boyle–Midway Inc., N. J., 5 3/4 In.	4.00
Larkin Soap Co., Buffalo, N. Y., Emerald, Square, BIM, 3 In.	18.00
Launders Household Ammonia, Olive Green, 12 In.	75.00
Lazell's Sachet Powder, Ground Stopper, Some Contents, Label	20.00
Life Plant, Amber, Embossed Bird	50.00
Milliken's Parlor Pride Stove Paint	8.00
Osborn's Liquid Polish, Yellow Amber, OP, Cylinder, 3 5/8 In.	275.00
Plynine Co. Ltd. A, Ammonia, Stoneware, 10 7/8 In.	46.00
Prices Soap Company, Ltd., Cobalt Blue, Stopper, Label, 7 1/4 In.	150.00
Rolyat Automatic Disinfector Simplex, Gray Pottery, 3 3/4 In.	37.00
Utility Jar, Aqua, Crude Flaring Lip, Pontil, 1830–1860, 9 In.	100.00
Utility Jar, Blown, Medium Yellow, Olive Tone, OP, 4 1/2 In.	357.00
Utility Jar, Blue Green, OP, Cylinder, 3 3/4 In.	19.00
Utility Jar, Deep Olive Amber, Rolled Lip, 1800–1830, 7 In.	468.00
Utility Jar, Deep Olive, Straight Sides, Cylinder, Pontil, 12 In.	155.00
Utility Jar, Free–Blown, Light Green, Uneven Folded Rim, 9 In.	110.00
Utility Jar, Free–Blown, Olive Amber, Cylindrical, Pontil, 9 In.	413.00
Utility Jar, Free–Blown, Olive Green, 1830–1850, 12 In.	176.00
Utility Jar, Howel & Stevens Family, Dye Colors, Aqua, Oval, 4 In.	33.00
Utility Jar, Medium Olive Green, Pontil, 7 1/4 In.	341.00
Utility Jar, Olive Amber, Double Collared Mouth, Pontil, 7 In.	220.00
Utility Jar, Olive Amber, Rectangular, Long Neck, 7 3/4 In.	55.00
Utility Jar, Olive Amber, Straight Sides, 1830–1850, 11 1/2 In.	187.00
Utility Jar, Olive Amber, Tooled Flared Mouth, Pontil, 4 7/8 In.	220.00
Utility Jar, Stoddard Type, Olive Amber, OP, Window, 10 In.	28.00
Warren's Blacking, Jar	18.00

INK

Ink was first used about 2500 B.C. in ancient Egypt and China. It was made of carbon mixed with oils. By the fifteenth century, ink was usually made at home by the housewife who bottled it for later use. In the late eighteenth century, ink was sold by apothecary shops and bookstores. The first patented ink was made in England in 1792. Ink bottles were first used in the United States about 1819. Early ink bottles were of ceramic and were often imported. Small ink bottles were made to be opened and used with a dip pen. Large ink bottles, like the cathedral–shaped Carter's inks, held a quart of ink to be poured into small bottles with dips. Inks can be identified by their shapes. Collectors have nicknamed many and the auctions often refer to *teakettles, cones, igloos,* or *umbrellas.*

Ink bottles were made to be hard to tip over. Some inks, especially English examples, were made with *bust–off* tops. The glass was cracked to open the bottle and the rough edge remained. In general the shape tells the age. Cones and umbrellas were used from the early 1800s to the introduction of the automatic bottle machine in the early 1900s. Hexagonal and octagonal bottles were preferred from about 1835 to 1865. Igloos, or turtles, were introduced in 1865 and were very popular for schools until about 1895. Barrels were made from 1840 to 1900. Square bottles became popular after 1860. Rectangular was the shape chosen in the 1900s. Figural bottles, especially ceramic types, were also made.

For further research, consult the book *Ink Bottles and Inkwells* by William E. Covill Jr. There is a national club, The Society of Inkwell Collectors, 5136 Thomas Avenue South, Minneapolis, MN 55410.

INK, 12–Sided, Dark Olive Green, Pour Spout, IP, 1 Gal.	4400.00
12–Sided, Light Yellow Green, OP, Rolled Lip, 1 2/7 In.	121.00
3 Snail Wells, Clear, Cast Iron Revolving Stand, 3 x 8 In.	231.00
3–Piece Mold, Amber	100.00
3–Piece Mold, Amber, Mt. Vernon Glass Works, Cylindrical, 1 5/8 In.	88.00
3–Piece Mold, Clear, Pontil, 1 3/4 In.	1815.00
3–Piece Mold, Clear, Pontil, 2 In.	1430.00
3–Piece Mold, Coventry, Conn., Amber, Cylindrical, 1 1/2 In.	88.00
3–Piece Mold, Deep Olive Amber, Coventry Glass, Pontil, 1 1/2 In.	77.00
3–Piece Mold, Folded Over Lip, Pontil, Coventry, 1 1/2 In.	132.00
3–Piece Mold, IP, 9 3/4 In., Qt.	90.00
3–Piece Mold, Keene, Marlboro, Yellow Amber, Pontil, 2 In.	230.00
3–Piece Mold, Olive Amber, Folded Over Lip, Pontil, Coventry, 1 3/4 In.	165.00
3–Piece Mold, Olive, Folded Over Lip, Pontil, Coventry, 1 1/2 In.	121.00
3–Piece Mold, Teal Blue, Master, Blob Top	35.00
3–Piece Mold, Yellow Amber, Cylindrical, Pontil, 1820–1840, 1 1/2 In.	99.00
3–Piece Mold, Yellow Olive, Cylindrical, Depressed Disc, 1 1/2 In.	72.00
A & F Pat., Violet, 1872, 1 7/8 In.	50.00
AM Bertinguiot, Black, Embossed, Sheared Lip, Pontil, 2 1/4 In.	88.00
Aqua, Embossed J. C., OP, 1 3/8 In.	55.00
Armchair, Dark Green	98.00
Barrel, Clear, Pat. March 1, 1870	49.00
Barrel, Clear, Pat. Oct. 1865	49.00
Barrel, Light Blue Green, Floral, Small	2200.00
Barrel, Opdyke Bros., Embossed Front, Aqua	90.00
Barrel, S. I. Comp., Milk Glass, Horizontal, Original Stopper, 2 9/16 In.	413.00
Bell, Aqua, 2 1/2 In.	12.00
Benjamin Franklin Head, Fountain, Pale Aqua, 1880–1920, 2 3/4 In.	330.00
Bertinquiot, Medium Olive Green, Sheared Top, OP, 2 In.	303.00
Birdcage, Sheared Lip, Clear	275.00
Birdcage, Square Base, Clear, M Embossed Side, 3 1/4 In.	29.00
Black Amber, Cylindrical, Pontil, 1 7/8 In.	121.00
Black Glass, Octagonal, Pontil, 1790–1800, 2 1/8 In.	500.00
Black Glass, Pontil, Round, 1790–1800, 1 7/8 In.	300.00
Black Glass, Rectangular, Chamfered Corners, 1790–1800, 2 3/8 In.	825.00
Black Glass, Round, Raised Pattern Around, Center Quill Hole, 1820–1840	131.00
Blackwood & Co., Blue Black Inks, Pottery, Rectangular Base, 2 1/2 In.	54.00
Blackwood & Co., London, Igloo, Deep Blue, Whittled, Sheared Lip, 2 In.	127.00

Blackwood & Co., London, Syphon, Bird's Beak Spout, Blue, 5 1/2 In. 155.00
Block House, Fort Pitt .... 100.00 To 400.00
Blown, 3–Piece Mold, Dark Yellow Olive, Cylindrical, Pontil, 1 1/2 In. 88.00
Blown, Cobalt Blue, Squat Dome Form, Pontil, Cover, 1830–1860, 2 In. 253.00
Blown, Master, Yellow Amber, IP, Applied Mouth, Spout, 9 5/8 In. 110.00
Blown, Yellowish Amber, OP, Sheared & Tooled Lip, 3 3/4 In. 72.00
Boat, Emerald Green, 2 1/2 In. 30.00
Boat, Green, Brown Swirls 40.00
Bonney, Barrel, Aqua, Green Striation Front, 2 3/4 In. 75.00
Boy Pushing Cart, Cast Iron Stand, Clear Snail In Cart, 6 x 6 x 4 In. 231.00
Brickett & Thayer, New Ipswich, Olive Amber, OP, Master, 4 1/8 In. 275.00
Bulldog's Head, Milk Glass, Revolving, Black Metal Base, 4 1/2 In. 357.00
Butler's Ink, Cincinnati, 12–Sided, Aqua, Pontil, 2 3/4 In. 176.00
Cabin, Clear, Squared–Off Collar, 2 1/2 In. 550.00
Cabin, Golden Amber, America, c.1850 .... 2530.00
Carter's, Boston, New York & Chicago, Red & Gold Label, BIMAL 29.00
Carter's, Cathedral, Cobalt Blue, Master, 6 1/4 In. 209.00
Carter's, Cathedral, Cobalt Blue, Master, 9 3/4 In. 105.00
Carter's, Cathedral, Cobalt Blue, Qt. 25.00
Carter's, Cone, Bright Sea Green 25.00
Carter's, Cone, Embossed, Amber, 1897 .... 15.00
Carter's, Contents, 2 Oz. 4.00
Carter's, Emerald Green, 1/2 Pt. 25.00
Carter's, Jug, Brown & Cream, Spout, Handle, Master, Gal. 180.00
Carter's, Label, Contents, Master, Box, 16 Oz. 15.00
Carter's, Made In U.S. A., Cone, Amber 8.00
Carter's, Medium To Yellow Amber, Applied Mouth, Spout, 8 In. 85.00
Carter's, Paperweight Block, Clear, 4 x 4 x 4 In. 85.00
Carter's, Stoneware, Display Bottle, Large 1250.00
Caws Ink, N. Y. 20.00
Centennial Exhibition Hall, April 11, 1876, 3 3/8 In. 264.00
Centennial Exhibition Hall, Clear, Metal Cap, 4 1/2 In. 287.00
Chas. Lippincott & Co., Philadelphia, Pa., Keystone, Master, Pt. 15.00
Clark's Superior Record, Boston, Olive Amber, Master, 6 In. 1320.00
Columbian Expo, 1893 .... 35.00
Cone, Aqua, BIMAL, 2 1/2 In. 5.00
Cone, Electric Blue Green, Octagonal, Bubbles, 4 3/8 In. 20.00
Cone, Light Tan Stoneware, 3 5/8 In. 7.50
Cone, Medium Cobalt Blue, Tooled Top, 2 3/8 In. 176.00
Cone, Turquoise, Tooled Top, 2 1/2 In. 121.00
Cottage, Aqua, Crosshatched Roof, Spare Chunk Glass, 2 3/4 In. 139.00
Cottage, Aqua, Master, 5 1/2 In. 495.00
Crock, Circular 10.00
Crock, Cone 10.00
Dark Olive Green, Ringed, Cylindrical, Pontil, 1820–1840, 1 9/16 In. 82.50
Davids & Black, Emerald Green, Cylindrical, Master, 5 1/8 In. 165.00
Davids & Black, New York, Emerald Green, OP, 4 3/4 In. 110.00
Derby, Triangular, Aqua, Contents, Cork, England 18.00
Derby, Triangular, Wax Sealed, Aqua 18.00
Dickson, Spring Pour Spout, ABM, Master, 9 In. 10.00
Domed Beehive Form, Aqua, 1860–1880, Ground Mouth, 1 x 2 1/4 In. 143.00
Double Font, Yellow Aqua, BIMAL, 3 1/2 In. 135.00
E. Waters, Troy, N. Y., Aqua, Cylindrical, Pontil, 2 11/16 In. 176.00
E. Waters, Troy, N. Y., Aqua, Cylindrical, Pontil, 2 3/8 In. 220.00
E. Waters, Troy, N. Y., Aqua, Cylindrical, Pontil, 3 7/16 In. 1045.00
E. Waters, Troy, N. Y., Aqua, Fluted Shoulders, OP, 3 1/2 In. 250.00
E. Waters, Troy, N. Y., Aqua, Pontil, 1/2 Pt. 475.00
E. Waters, Troy, N. Y., Light Green, Cylindrical, Flared Mouth, 2 3/8 In. 495.00
E. Waters, Troy, N. Y., Small 950.00
E. Waters, Troy, N. Y., Yellow Green, IP, Master, 6 1/4 In. 2200.00
Eells' Writing Fluid, Brown Glaze, Cylindrical, 4 3/8 In. 60.00
Embossed R. F., Deep Puce, Flaring Lip, Pontil, 1850 .... 385.00
Embossed R. F., Light Olive Amber, Rolled Lip, Pontil, 2 In. 715.00

Face of Jester, Pottery, Brown Glaze, 1860–1900, 1 5/8 x 3 In. 88.00
Fahnestock's Neutral Ink, 6 Concave Panels, OP, Rolled Lip, 4 1/8 In. 330.00
Farley's, Embossed, Multi–Sided 385.00
Farley's, Octagonal, Olive Amber, Flared Lip, Pontil, 2 1/2 In. 935.00
Farley's, Octagonal, Olive Amber, Pontil, 3 1/2 In. 165.00
Farley's, Octagonal, Yellow Amber, 3 1/2 In. 357.00
Farley's, Olive Amber, Octagonal, Pontil, 1 3/4 In. 187.00
Felt Stationers, Hall Writing, Black Fluid, N. Y., Pottery, 1840s, 7 In. 160.00
Field's, Non–Corrosive, Cream Pottery, Cylindrical, 2 1/2 In. 66.00
Figural, Fort Pitt, Pittsburgh, Pa. 100.00
Figural, Swan, Whimsey, Sea Green, Round Base, England, 4 5/8 In., Pair 1210.00
Floral Design, Hand Painted, China, 3 1/8 In. 66.00
Fountain, Aqua, Pen Rests, 1860–1890, 1 5/8 In. 99.00
Fountain, Automatic Constant Level, Clear, 1890–1920, 3 3/8 In., 2 Pc. 132.00
Fountain, Porcelain, Multicolor Floral, White, England, 5 In. 55.00
Free–Blown, Doorknob Form, Aqua, Stopper, Paperweight, 4 1/4 In. 253.00
Free–Blown, Igloo, Light Yellow Green, Pontil, 2 1/2 In. 1650.00
Geometric, Deep Amber, Disc Mouth, Coventry, Conn., 1 1/2 In. 105.00
Geometric, Olive Yellow, Disc Mouth, 1 5/8 In. 358.00
Gray Martinego & Co., Negroe's Head, Mouth Holds Bowl, Pottery, 5 In. 309.00
Gross & Robinson's American Writing Fluid, Aqua, OP, 3 7/8 In. 385.00
Haley's Ink, Amber, Cylindrical, Tall 27.00
Half–Barrel, 3 Quill Holes, Pottery, Robert Whitfields, 3 1/2 In. 279.00
Hand On Box, Porcelain, Multicolored Glazes, 3 x 4 1/4 In. 121.00
Hard Cider, Tippecanoe Extract, Barrel, Clear, Pontil, 1 7/8 In. 77.00
Harrison's Columbian, Aqua, 12–Sided, IP, Master, 7 1/2 In. 176.00
Harrison's Columbian, Aqua, 12–Sided, Master, 11 1/8 In. 990.00
Harrison's Columbian, Aqua, Embossed, Octagonal, Pontil, 1 1/2 In. 105.00
Harrison's Columbian, Aqua, OP, 4 7/8 In. 160.00
Harrison's Columbian, Blue Black Fluid, Sapphire, Label, 5 1/2 In. 385.00
Harrison's Columbian, Blue Green, Rolled Lip, OP, 1 7/8 In. 121.00
Harrison's Columbian, Bright Green, Cylindrical, Pontil, 2 3/8 In. 1348.00
Harrison's Columbian, Carmine, Smoky Gray Tint, Octagonal, 1 15/16 In. 220.00
Harrison's Columbian, Cobalt Blue, 12–Sided, IP, Master, Gal. 17600.00
Harrison's Columbian, Cobalt Blue, Cylindrical, Pontil, 2 In. 407.00
Harrison's Columbian, Cobalt Blue, OP, 3 7/8 In. 225.00
Harrison's Columbian, Cobalt Blue, Pontil, Master, 5 13/16 In. 1045.00
Harrison's Columbian, Cobalt Blue, Small Master 900.00
Harrison's Columbian, Deep Cobalt Blue, OP, 4 5/8 In. 500.00
Harrison's Columbian, Green, Octagonal, Small 1225.00
Harrison's Columbian, Octagonal, Aqua, 2 3/4 In. 148.00
Harrison's Columbian, Octagonal, Aqua, OP, 1 5/8 In. .... 55.00 To 77.00
Harrison's Columbian, Octagonal, Aqua, Pontil, 2 1/2 In. 93.00
Harrison's Columbian, Pale Green Aqua, Octagonal, 1840–1860, 3 In. 88.00
Harrison's Columbian, Sapphire Blue, Cylindrical, IP, Master, 7 In. 385.00
Harrison's Columbian, Sapphire Blue, Cylindrical, Pontil, 4 In. 523.00
Hexagonal, Cobalt Blue, Pontil, 2 3/4 In. 98.00
Hexagonal, Embossed, Patent, Aqua, OP, Rolled Lip, 2 1/2 In. 357.00
Hill's Pennsylvania Writing Ink, 12–Sided, Aqua, Pontil, 4 1/8 In. 88.00
Hoffman, Label 15.00
Hogan & Thompson, Commercial Red Ink, Cone, Aqua, OP, 1 3/4 In. 303.00
House, Aqua, Applied Lip, 1870–1880, Master, 6 1/2 x 5 x 3 In. 715.00
House, Fort Pitt Block House 100.00
Hover, Philadelphia, Light Green, Cylindrical, Pontil, 5 3/8 In. 148.00
Hover, Philadelphia, Light Green, Rolled Lip, 1850–1860, 2 1/4 In. 190.00
Hover, Philadelphia, Medium Olive Green, OP, 5 7/8 In. 226.00
Hover, Philadelphia, Sapphire Blue, Cylindrical, Pontil, 2 5/8 In. 264.00
Hover, Philadelphia, Umbrella, Aqua, Octagonal, Tooled Mouth, 2 1/4 In. 77.00
Hover, Umbrella, Bright Green, 12–Sided, Pontil, 1840–1860, 1 7/8 In. 55.00
Hover, Yellow Amber, Cylindrical, Pontil, 2 1/2 In. 60.00
Igloo, Blackwood & Co., London, Smoky Green, 2 1/2 In. 33.00
Inverted Funnel, Cobalt Blue, OP, Europe, 2 In. 154.00
Isaacs, Liverpool, Deep Amethyst, Bulbous Cylinder, 5 In. 473.00

Ink, Ma & Pa Carter, Porcelain, Germany, 3 1/2 In.

J. & I. E. M., Turtle, Yellow Amber, 1 5/8 In.	187.00
J. A. Williamson Chemist, Medium Blue Green, Applied Mouth, Spout, 7 In.	110.00
J. B. Fondersmiths, Deep Aqua, Octagonal, OP, Rolled Lip	330.00
J. Field, Aqua, Contents, Square	16.00
J. I. E. M., Igloo, Aqua, BIMAL, 1 7/8 In.	60.00
J. I. E. M., Igloo, Panel	30.00
J. J. Butler, Cincinnati, Oh., Cone, Aqua, OP, Rolled Lip, 2 1/4 In.	204.00
J. Raynald, Globe, Countries Embossed, Aqua, 1870s, 2 1/4 In.	660.00
J. S. Mason, Philadelphia, Green Aqua, Rolled Mouth, Pontil, 4 1/2 In.	143.00
J. S. Mason, Philadelphia, Master, Cylindrical, Aqua, 4 3/8 In.	99.00
J. Underwood, New York, Cream Stoneware, Pouring Lip, 3 1/4 In.	40.00
J. W. Seaton, Louisville, Light Green, 10–Sided, OP, 1830–1850	440.00
Jacobs & Brown, Hamilton, Oh., 12–Sided, Pale Green, OP, 2 1/2 In.	375.00
John Wyeth Bros., Pottery, Blue Gray, No Cap, 7 1/2 In.	7.50
Jones Empire Ink, N. Y., Deep Green, Embossed, Master, Qt.	1400.00
Keens, 3–Piece Mold, Geometric, McK G III–029, Olive Amber	200.00
Keller's, Pottery, Cream Glaze, Spout, Master, Qt.	70.00
Kents Commercial Black Ink, Dark Olive, Label, Cylindrical, 4 3/4 In.	247.00
L. Poincelet, Octagonal, Black Amber, Flared Lip, 2 In.	798.00
L. Poincelet, Octagonal, Chocolate Amber, Europe, Embossed, 1780–1820	1485.00
Laughlin's & Bushfield, Wheeling, W. Va., Octagonal, Aqua, 2 7/8 In.	105.00
Lion's Head, Ceramic, White Glaze, Painted, 2 1/4 In.	341.00
Log Cabin, Clear, 2 1/4 In.	200.00
Lynn Burnishing Ink, Honey Amber, BIM, Master, 7 1/2 In.	18.00
Ma & Pa Carter, Porcelain, Germany, 3 1/2 In. ....*Illus*	230.00
Melon, 28 Ribs, Swirled Left, Olive Amber, Pontil, 2 1/8 In.	2420.00
Milk Glass, Square, Pressed Metal Stand, Cherubs, 4–Footed, 3 1/4 In.	82.00
NE Plus Ultra Fluid, House, Deep Aqua, 2 5/8 In. .... 220.00 To 413.00
Oval, Gold Amber, Neck With Tooled Lip, 2 7/8 In.	53.00
Palmer's, Cleveland, Oh., Gutta Percha, Label, 2 1/2 In.	125.00
Palmer, Madigan, Providence, Pottery, Cobalt Embossed, Large	50.00
Palmers Superior Dark Blue Writing Ink, Green, Label, 4 1/2 In.	154.00
Parker Quink, Contents, Box, 2 Oz.	4.00
Parker Quink, Label, Contents, Master, Box, 32 Oz.	15.00
Parker Super Chrome, Contents, 4 Oz.	4.00
Penn Mfg. Works, P, Garrett, Milk Glass, Octagonal, Stopper, 2 3/4 In.	121.00
Pennsylvania Dutch, Brass Top	100.00
Pentagonal, Half Round, 2 1/2 In.	25.00
Perine Guyot, Cornflower Blue, Embossed, Sheared Lip, 1850, 2 In.	660.00
Perine Guyot, Olive Green, Embossed, Sheared Lip, Pontil, 2 In.	100.00

Perry & Co., London, Salt Glaze, Cream, 1860–1880, 3 5/8 In.	87.00
Perry & Co., London, Waisted Cylinder Shape, Pottery, 2 1/2 In.	18.00
Pitkin Type, 36 Broken Ribs Swirled Left, Olive, 1 5/8 In.	303.00
Pitkin Type, 36 Ribs Swirled Left, Deep Olive, Pontil, 1 5/8 In.	66.00
Pitkin Type, 36 Ribs Swirled Left, Olive Green, Square, 1 5/8 In.	385.00
Pitkin Type, 36 Ribs Swirled Left, Olive Yellow, 1 7/8 In.	253.00
Pitkin Type, 36 Ribs Swirled Left, Olive Yellow, 1832 Note, 1 3/4 In.	303.00
Pitkin Type, 36 Ribs Swirled Left, Yellow Olive, Pontil, 1 3/8 In.	2805.00
Pitkin Type, 36 Ribs Swirled Right, Dark Yellow Olive, 1 5/8 In.	578.00
Pitkin Type, 36 Ribs Swirled Right, Olive Yellow, OP, 1 5/8 In.	495.00
Pitkin Type, Swirled Right, Deep Olive Amber, Pontil, 1 7/8 In.	165.00
Pitkin Type, Tooled Double Mouth	525.00
Pitkin Type, Yellow Olive, Funnel Shaped Mouth, Pontil, 1 7/16 In.	468.00
Polygon, Deep To Cobalt Blue, Square Base, 2 In.	49.00
Porcelain, Hand Painted, Red, Blue, & Gold Design, 2 5/8 x 5 6/8 In.	66.00
Pot, Hall's Patent Simplex Hektograph, Pottery, 5 In.	54.00
Pottery, Blue Gray, Pour Lip, Master, 7 1/2 In.	9.00
R. B. Snow, St. Louis, 12–Sided, Aqua, OP, Rolled Lip, 1 7/8 In.	400.00
Revolving, Cast Iron Anchor & Rope Design, Snail, 4 1/4 x 2 1/2 In.	150.00
Robert Keller Inks & Mucilage, Detoit, Mich., Aqua, Spout, Qt.	45.00
Robert Whitfields, Half Barrel, Pottery, Brown Flecking, 3 1/4 In.	145.00
Round, Dark Salt Glaze, 3 Outer & 1 Center Hole, Derbyshire, 3 3/4 In.	164.00
S. Fine Black Ink, Dark Amber, OP, Rolled Lip, 1830–1850, 3 1/8 In.	880.00
S. Fine Black Ink, Medium Yellow Green, Cylindrical, Pontil, 2 7/8 In.	358.00
S. Fine Black Ink, Yellow Amber, OP, Flared Lip, 3 In.	330.00
S. Fine Black Ink, Yellow Amber, OP, Flared Lip, 3 In.	605.00
S. I. Comp., Cottage, Senate Ink Co., Aqua, Tooled Lip, 2 9/16 In.	226.00
S. M. Co., Light Green, Embossed, 2 3/8 In.	30.00
Sanford's, Boat, Pat. Applied For, Aqua, 2 In.	12.00
Sanford's, Inks & Mucilage, Stoneware, Cream, Brown, Handle, 9 1/2 In.	72.00
Sanford's, SMCO Monogram, Clear, Pt.	55.00
Shaeffer's Skript, Contents, Box, 2 Oz.	4.00
Shaeffer's Skript, Label, Contents, Master, Box, 16 Oz.	15.00
Sheared & Tooled Lip, Olive Amber, OP, 3 3/4 In.	165.00
Shoe, Clear, Embossed N. Antoine, France, 2 1/6 x 4 1/4 In.	77.00
Silliman & Co., Traveling, Chester, Conn., Wood, Black Top, 3 In.	85.00
Silver Plated Cap, Emerald Green, Clear Applied Feet, 2 3/4 In.	143.00
Skull, Bisque, White Enamel Teeth, Black & Maroon, 1870–1890, 2 1/4 In.	110.00
Snail, Ceramic, White Glazed, Gold Designs, 3 1/2 In.	54.00
Snail, Clear, Iron Anchor & Rope Revolving Stand, 4 1/4 In.	150.00
Snail, Iron Stand, Clear, 1870–1880, 3 1/2 x 5 In., Pair	165.00
Snail, Milk Glass, Cast Iron Revolving Stand, 4 1/4 In.	105.00
Snails, Cobalt Blue, Milk Glass, Revolving, Iron Stand, 3 1/2 In.	341.00
Snake, Nest With Eggs, Pottery, Painted, 1920–1950, 2 5/8 In.	22.00
Souter Jonny, Smiling Face, Pottery, Salt Glaze, 1 1/2 In.	419.00
Stafford's, Aqua, Round, Master, 9 3/4 In.	75.00
Stafford's, Cobalt Blue, Spout, Small	55.00
Stafford's, Cone, Amber, BIMAL, Master, Qt.	50.00
Stafford's, Deep Cobalt Blue, BIM, Master, Qt.	40.00
Stafford's, Fountain Pen, Cobalt Blue, Screw, Rubber Spout, Wooden Box	25.00
Stafford's, Green, Master, 7 1/2 x 3 In.	60.00
Stoneware, Spout, Master	12.00
Strong Cobb & Co., Cleveland, Oh., Brilliant Cobalt Blue, 6 1/4 In.	25.00
T & M Ink, Aqua, Dark Green Swirl, Rolled Lip, OP, 2 3/8 In.	94.00
T & M Ink, Dark Blue Green, Rolled Lip, OP, 2 1/2 In.	60.00
Teakettle, 7–Sided, Medium Sapphire Blue, Gold Paint, 2 In.	275.00
Teakettle, Barrel, Cornflower Blue, Ground Mouth, 2 1/8 In.	853.00
Teakettle, Barrel, Light Blue Green, Gilt Design, 1830–1860, 2 3/16 In.	2420.00
Teakettle, Barrel, Medium Sapphire, 2 1/4 In.	605.00
Teakettle, Bell, Blue Clambroth, Brass Closure, 1830–1860, 2 3/4 In.	495.00
Teakettle, Ceramic, Bell Form, Ribbed White Glaze, 1830–1870, 3 In.	413.00
Teakettle, Clambroth, Sheared & Polished Lip, 2 1/4 In.	468.00
Teakettle, Clear, Blue & Gold Painted Design, 1830–1860, 1 1/8 In.	440.00

Ink, Tint Assenzio, Montovani, 1 3/4 In.

Ink, Umbrella, 3 In.

Teakettle, Clear, Cone, Octagonal, 1870–1890, 2 3/8 In.	82.00
Teakettle, Clear, Red & Blue Painted Design, 1830–1860, 2 1/4 In.	412.00
Teakettle, Cobalt Blue, Sheared & Ground Lip, 2 1/4 In., C–1267	1430.00
Teakettle, Cranberry & White Mottled Ceramic, Hexagonal, 2 1/8 In.	176.00
Teakettle, Cut & Polished Side Panels, Diamond–Shaped Top, Canary	1050.00
Teakettle, Cut, Clear, Lime Overlay, Ribbed, England, 1 7/8 In.	633.00
Teakettle, Emerald Green, Brass Collar, 1830–1860, 1 7/8 In.	360.00
Teakettle, Fiery Opalescent, Hand Painted Design, 2 In.	385.00
Teakettle, Fountain, Golden Amber, 8 Panels With Petals, 2 1/8 In.	468.00
Teakettle, Fountain, Raised & Recessed Panels, Aqua, 1 7/8 In.	172.00
Teakettle, H. Morrell, London, Brown Glazed Stoneware, 2 5/8 In.	115.00
Teakettle, Henry Thacker & Co., London, Pottery, Blue Glazed, 3 1/4 In.	254.00
Teakettle, Hexagonal, Orange, White Mottled Ceramic, France, 2 1/8 In.	176.00
Teakettle, Josiah Johnson's Fluid, Pottery, Hexagonal, 2 3/4 In.	121.00
Teakettle, Lime Green Overlay, Clear Ribs, Pat. London, 1870–1880, 2 In.	137.00
Teakettle, Medium Yellow Green, BIMAL, 2 In.	575.00
Teakettle, Milk Glass, Cone, Multifaceted, Spout Cap Missing, 3 1/4 In.	131.00
Teakettle, Octagonal Fluted Panels, Cobalt Blue, 1830–1860, 1 7/8 In.	193.00
Teakettle, Octagonal, Cobalt Blue, 1830–1860, 2 7/16 In.	165.00
Teakettle, Octagonal, Opalescent, Yellow Flashed, Floral, 2 3/8 In.	210.00
Teakettle, Octagonal, Orange Yellow, Small	475.00
Teakettle, Octagonal, Sheared Mouth, Aqua, 2 x 4 In.	110.00
Teakettle, Orange Yellow, BIMAL, 2 In.	578.00
Teakettle, Pottery, Shiny Brown Top, Gold Band Around, 2 1/2 In.	27.00
Teakettle, Pyramid, Black Amethyst, Embossed Depose, 2 1/4 In.	1210.00
Teakettle, Stephens, London, Clear, Swans Neck Opening, 2 In.	55.00
Teakettle, Straker, Stoneware	255.00
Teakettle, Vaseline, Ground Mouth, 1830–1860, 2 In.	758.00
Teakettle, Yellow Amber, Sheared & Ground Lip, 2 1/8 In.	750.00
Tent, Aqua	18.00
Thaddeus Davids & Co., N. Y., Olive Green, Label, 5 In.	413.00
Thaddeus Davids & Co., N. Y., Pen Ink, Blue Green, 6 In.	110.00
Thaddeus Davids & Co., N. Y., Stoneware, Brown, Cream, Handle, 11 1/2 In.	61.00
Tint Assenzio, Montovani, 1 3/4 In. ....*Illus*	400.00
Toper, Staffordshire	54.00
Turtle, Fountain, Clear, Sheared Mouth, 1880–1920, 1 7/8 In.	154.00
Ugly Woman, Pottery, Multi–Cream Body, Hole In Forehead, 2 1/2 In.	136.00
Umbrella, 3 In. ....*Illus*	18.00
Umbrella, America, c.1850–1870	1045.00
Umbrella, Black Brown Glass, Pontil, 2 1/2 In.	150.00

Umbrella, Blue Green, Octagonal, OP	39.00
Umbrella, Bright Yellow Green, 1 3/4 In.	16.00
Umbrella, Cherry Red Puce, OP, America, c.1850, 2 3/8 In.	1265.00
Umbrella, Emerald, Olive Hue, Rolled–In Lip, OP, 2 1/2 In.	550.00
Umbrella, James S. Mason & Co., Octagonal, Aqua, Pontil, 2 1/2 In.	165.00
Umbrella, John Tilton, Newburyport, Mass., Aqua, OP, Label	75.00
Umbrella, Medium Green	50.00
Umbrella, Octagonal, Aqua, Sheared Neck, BIMAL, 3 In.	7.00
Umbrella, Octagonal, Brilliant Deep Cobalt Blue, 2 3/4 In.	330.00
Umbrella, Octagonal, Cobalt Blue, OP, Rolled Lip, 2 3/8 In.	798.00
Umbrella, Octagonal, Cobalt Blue, Rolled Lip, 2 1/2 In.	450.00
Umbrella, Octagonal, Cornflower Blue	59.00
Umbrella, Octagonal, Dark Olive Amber, Pontil, 1840–1860, 2 1/2 In.	132.00
Umbrella, Octagonal, Deep Cobalt Blue, Tooled Lip, 2 5/8 In.	330.00
Umbrella, Octagonal, Deep Olive Green, OP, Sheared Lip, 2 3/8 In.	143.00
Umbrella, Octagonal, Light Green, Rolled Lip, Pontil, 2 1/2 In.	66.00
Umbrella, Octagonal, Olive Green, Yellow Tint, OP, 2 1/2 In.	198.00
Umbrella, Octagonal, Orange Amber, Pontil, 1840–1860, 2 1/2 In.	220.00
Umbrella, Octagonal, Reddish Amber, Sheared Lip, Pontil, 2 1/2 In.	121.00
Umbrella, Octagonal, Teal	55.00
Umbrella, Octagonal, Yellow Olive, Root Beer Amber, OP, 2 1/2 In.	176.00
Umbrella, Octagonal, Yellowish Olive Green, Rolled Lip, 2 1/2 In.	143.00
Umbrella, Overlapping CPC Monogram, 12–Sided, Aqua, 3 In.	24.00
Umbrella, Puce, Rolled–In Lip, OP, 2 5/8 In.	1595.00
Umbrella, Puce, Rolled–In Lip, Smooth Base, 2 1/2 In.	1364.00
Umbrella, Red Amber, Large Dot On 2 Panels, OP, 2 3/8 In.	413.00
Umbrella, Thaddeus Davids, Blue Green, 1845–1860, 2 1/2 In.	100.00
Umbrella, Yellow, Orange Hue, Rolled–In Lip, OP, 2 1/2 In.	715.00
Umbrella, Yellow, Rolled–In Lip, OP, 1850–1860, 2 1/2 In. .... 1350.000 To	1485.00
W. E. Bonney, Barrel, Embossed, Aqua, Green Striation Front, Whittled	95.00
Waterlow & Sons, Limited, Pottery, 7 1/2 In.	25.00
Waterman's, Contents, Box, 2 Oz.	4.00
Waterman's, Ideal, Label, Contents, Master, Box, 16 Oz.	15.00
Waterman's, Patrician, Purple, Contents, Box, 2 Oz.	4.00
Weber Carmine, F. Weber & Co., Philadelphia, BIMAL, Cylinder	25.00
Whitall, Tatem & Co., Cabin, Clear, 2 3/8 In.	77.00
Williams & Carlton, Hartford, Conn., Aqua	35.00
Williams & Carlton, Hartford, Conn., Light Green	35.00
Williston's Superior Indelible, Aqua, Rectangular, OP, 2 3/8 In.	176.00
Winslow's Improved Chemical Indelible Ink, Olive Amber, Label, 5 In.	330.00
Woman, Reclining On Couch, Pottery, Brown Glaze, 3 1/4 In.	193.00
Yellow Amber, IP, Spout, New England, Master, 9 5/8 In.	110.00

--------------------------------- **JAR** ---------------------------------

Jar is the name for a container of a special shape. It has a wide mouth and almost no neck. Today we see jars of cold cream, but in earlier days jars made of glass or ceramic were used for storage of home–canned produce and for many commercial products.

JAR, 3–Piece Mold, Clear, Pontil, 5 7/8 In.	358.00
Barrel Shape, Red Rock Emblem, Stippled, 8 Oz.	12.00
Beech–Nut, Counter, Tin Lid, Imprinted Lettering, 9 1/2 In.	99.00
Begg's Liver Pills, Counter, Pressed Glass, Etched Lettering, 11 In.	578.00
Blown, Wide Mouth, Olive Green, Pontil, 9 In.	150.00
Blueberry, Golden Amber, Paneled Shoulder, Cylindrical, 11 1/4 In.	303.00
Borden's Malted Milk Has No Equal, Amethyst, No Stopper, 7 In.	25.00
Cobalt Blue, ABM, 5 1/4 In.	33.00
Display, Country Store, Clear, Amethyst Tint	110.00
Display, Druggist, Aloe Soco, Coat of Arms, Clear, Painted, 1880s, 24 In.	633.00
Display, Fine Sponges, Clear, Painted, Domed Lid, 14 In.	825.00
F & R Pratt, Mottled, Passing The Pipe, Pottery, 1850s, 3 3/4 In.	173.00
Free–Blown, Clear, Gold Painted Tin Top, Cylindrical, Pontil, 9 In.	55.00
Free–Blown, Yellow Olive, Cylindrical, OP, 1820–1860, 10 3/4 In.	300.00
Gooseberry Jam, Baxter & Co., Edinburgh, Salt Glaze, 6 1/8 In.	118.00

Green Gage Jam, Gunter & Co., London, Speckled Salt Glaze, 7 1/8 In. 73.00
Harrison's Columbian Perfumery Pomade, Octagonal, 1 1/2 In. 242.00
Hockin, Duke St., London, Dark Olive Green, Improved Pontil, 4 In. 110.00
Ice Cream Cone, Metal Top & Cone Holder, 14 In. .... 220.00 To 325.00
Joseph Prime & Sons, Royal Standard Cheese, England, Stoneware, 4 In. 40.00
Nicholls & Campbell Kings Lynn, 3–Piece Mold, Aqua, Narrow Neck 53.00
Ocean Spray Cranberry Juice Cocktail, 50 Years, 1930–1980, Qt. 22.00
Paterson's Extract of Malt, Red Brown Transfer, Pottery, 5 In. 27.00
Pill, Blown, Medium Yellow Amber, 12–Sided, OP, 2 1/2 In. 523.00
Salve, Owl Drug Co., Milk Glass, Screw Top, ABM, 2 1/2 In. 88.00
Saratoga, Counter, Wooden Top, Raised Lettering All Sides, 8 In. 132.00
Schall, Counter, Raised Lettering, Flame Finial Handle, 14 1/2 In. 77.00
Stephen's Rheumatic Remedy, Cleveland, Oh., Aqua, Octagonal, OP, 3 In. 577.00
Storage, Blown, Dark Olive Amber, Pontil, 12 1/4 In. 257.00
Storage, Blown, Yellow, Sheared Lip, Deep Kick–Up Base, 12 3/4 In. 176.00
Storage, Greenish Aqua, Free–Blown, OP, Rolled Lip, 11 7/8 In. 121.00
Tobacco, 6 Panels, Honey Amber, Lid 45.00
Tobacco, Cream Glazed Pottery, Coat of Arms, Lions, Floral, 8 1/4 In. 49.00

─────────────────────── **JIM BEAM** ───────────────────────

JIM BEAM, see Beam

─────────────────────────── **JUG** ───────────────────────────

A jug is a deep container with a narrow mouth and a handle. It is usually made of
pottery. Jugs were often used as containers for liquor. Messages, mottoes, and the name of
the distillery or bar are often printed on the jug.

JUG, Amber, Flattened Chestnut Shape, OP, No Handle 45.00
   Cambridge Springs Mineral Water, Pig Ears, Wire Bail, Miniature 85.00
   Chimney Corner Bourbon, W. P. Squibb, Lawrenceburgh, 10 In. ....*Illus* 400.00
   City Liquor Store, Nicholas Gludt, Prop., Square, Spout, 1/4 Pt. 80.00
   Flattened Chestnut Form, Puce, Handle, Flame Finial, Pontil, 14 1/8 In. 148.00
   Heather Dew, Scotch, Beige Stoneware, Scotsman Transfer, 5 1/4 In. 50.00
   Hendrick's Cafe & Hall, Albany, N. Y., Brown, Cream, Square, Spout, 1/2 Pt. 60.00

Jug, Chimney Corner Bourbon, W.P.Squibb,
Lawrenceburgh, 10 In.

Jug, Red, White, & Blue Pure Apple Cider,
Baldwin, Ga., 10 In.

Jug, Saratoga Table Water, Royal Spring Co.,
Handle, 7 3/4 In.

Jug, Wm.Radam's Microbe Killer, No.2,
Pottery, Cork, Gal., 11 In.

J. F. T. & Co., Philadelphia, Handle, Golden Amber, Bulbous, 7 1/8 In. 330.00
J. W. Orr, Brown & Tan Pottery, California, 1/2 Gal. 605.00
Locke's Kilbeggan, 2 Tone Brown Stoneware, Transfer, 7 1/2 In. 50.00
M. J. Miller's Sons Whiskey, Pottery, Dark Top, Cream Base, Cork, 3 Gal. 200.00
Mancuiso & LoGalbo, Importer, Amphora Shape, 2 Handles, Pottery 40.00
Merry Christmas & Happy New Year, Brown & White Glaze, Small 25.00
Motto, Detrick Distilling Co., Dayton, Eat Drink & Be Merry, 1/4 Pt. 75.00
Newport Bar, A Merry Christmas, Newport, E. O. S. 1910, 1/4 Pt. 75.00
Oakland Wine Co., Richmond, Ind., Miniature 70.00
Old Continental Hand Made Sour Mash Whiskey, B. Bros., Miniature 75.00
Parker Rye, N. M. Uri & Co., Louisville, Ky., 1/4 Pt. 55.00
Radium Water, Sequoyah Hotel, Claremore, Okla., 1/4 Pt. 85.00
Red, White, & Blue Pure Apple Cider, Baldwin, Ga., 10 In. ....*Illus* 85.00
Rock Castle Pure Rye, W. P. Squibb & Co., Lawrenceburgh, Ind., Gal. 75.00
Saratoga Table Water, Royal Spring Co., Handle, 7 3/4 In. ....*Illus* 75.00
Victoria Whiskey, Tan & Brown Pottery, Man & Woman Each Side, 9 In. 38.50
W. I. Johnson Kentucky Whiskey, Handle, Golden Amber, Pear Form, 8 In. 187.00
Wm. Radam's Microbe Killer, No. 2, Pottery, Cork, Gal., 11 In. ....*Illus* 65.00
X. Brazin's Old Holland Cologne, 1/4 Pt. 40.00

―――――――――――――――― **KENTUCKY GENTLEMAN** ――――――――――――――――

Kentucky Gentleman bottles were made in 1969. The six bottles in the set were called
Frontiersman, Kentucky Gentleman, Pink Lady, Revolutionary Soldier, Union Soldier, and
Confederate Soldier.

KENTUCKY GENTLEMAN, Frontiersman, 1969 .... 12.00
  Gentleman, 1969 .... 12.00
  Pink Lady, 1969 .... 35.00
  Revolutionary Soldier, 1969 .... 13.00
  Union Soldier, 1969 .... 13.00

―――――――――――――――― **KONTINENTAL CLASSICS** ――――――――――――――――

Kontinental Spirits Kompanie of Bardstown, Kentucky, made figural bottles from 1976 to
1981 to hold Kontinental Kentucky bourbon. Most of the bottles were full–length figures
of people from earlier times, although a bust of John Lennon was added in 1981.

KONTINENTAL CLASSICS, Editor, 1976, Miniature 12.00
  Gandy Dancer, 1976 .... 14.00
  Gunsmith, 1977, Miniature 12.00
  Homesteader, 1978 .... 24.00

Lennon, Bust, Silver, 1981	38.00
Saddle Maker, 1977, Miniature	12.00
School Marm, 1977	30.00
Statue of Liberty, 1976	19.00

———————————————— LACEY ————————————————

Haas Brothers of San Francisco, California, was established in 1851. They made W. A. Lacey and Cyrus Noble bottles in the 1970s. The firm discontinued its ceramic business about 1981 and destroyed all of the molds. Lacey bottles include the log animal series (1978–1980) and the tavern series (1975).

LACEY, see also Cyrus Noble

LACEY, Bank Exchange, Exterior, 1976, Miniature	20.00
Bank Exchange, Interior, 1976, Miniature	20.00
Continental Navy, 1975, Miniature	8.00
Fargo Bank, 1975, Miniature	16.00
Rabbit, Log, 1978	28.00
Rabbit, Log, 1980, Miniature	14.00
Raccoon, Log, 1978	44.00
Raccoon, Log, 1980, Miniature	14.00
Squirrel, Log, 1979	28.00
Tennis, Men, 1976, Miniature	15.00
Tennis, Women, 1976, Miniature	15.00
Tonapah Saloon, 1975, Miniature	11.00

———————————————— LAST CHANCE ————————————————

Last Chance Whiskey was presented in ceramic figural bottles in 1971 and 1972. One series of 8–ounce bottles called Professionals pictured a doctor, dentist, banker, entertainer, politician, and salesman. Another series was a group of six bottles that joined together to form a long bar scene. Two versions of this bar scene were made, one with and one without a frame.

LAST CHANCE, Bar Scene, 1971, Miniature, 6 Piece	120.00
Dentist, 1971, Miniature	8.00
Doctor, 1971, Miniature	8.00
Entertainer, 1971, Miniature	8.00
Politician, 1971, Miniature	8.00
Salesman, 1971, Miniature	8.00
Wyoming Stockgrowers	75.00

———————————————— LEWIS & CLARK ————————————————

Lewis & Clark bottles were created by Alpha Industries of Helena, Montana. The first bottles, full–length representations of historical figures, were made from 1971 to 1976. The pioneer series of 1977–1978 was released in two–bottle sets. Each bottle was 13 inches high and two placed together created a scene. For example, one was an Indian (bottle) offering to sell some furs to a white man (bottle). A set of six troll bottles was made in 1978–1979.

LEWIS & CLARK, Arizona, 1981, Miniature	8.00
California, 1981, Miniature	8.00
Daughter Troll, 1978	24.00
Idaho, 1981, Miniature	8.00
Indian Peacepipe, 1978	40.00
Iowa, 1981, Miniature	8.00
Maryland, 1981, Miniature	8.00
Minnesota, 1981, Miniature	8.00
New Mexico, 1981, Miniature	8.00
North Dakota, 1981, Miniature	8.00
Oregon, 1981, Miniature	8.00
South Carolina, 1981, Miniature	8.00
South Dakota, 1981, Miniature	8.00
Utah, 1981, Miniature	8.00
Wisconsin, 1981, Miniature	8.00

Wyoming, 1981, Miniature 8.00

---------------------------------- **LIONSTONE** ----------------------------------

Lionstone Distilleries Inc. of Lawrenceburg, Kentucky, started making porcelain figural bottles to hold their whiskey for national sale in 1969. The first bottles were Western figures, each with a black label that told the historical facts about the figure. About 15,000 bottles were made for each of the first six subjects, the cowboy, proud Indian, casual Indian, sheriff, gentleman gambler, and cavalry scout. About half of the bottles were never filled with liquor because they leaked. These *leakers* were used by bars as display items on shelves and were clearly labeled with decals stating that they were for display only. More bottles were made for the series, about 4,000 of each. The set had 16 bottles. Lionstone then made a series of race cars (1970–1984), more Western figures (1970–1976), a Western bar scene (1971), birds (1970–1977), circus figures (1973), dogs (1975–1977), European workers (1974), oriental workers (1974), Bicentennial series (1976), clowns (1978–1979), sports series (1974–1983), and others. They also made many miniature bottles. The whiskey was distilled in Bardstown, Kentucky, but the bottles were made in Chicago. Lionstone was sold to Barton Brands in December 1979. It was sold back to Mark Slepak, the original owner, in December 1983. Collectors can contact the company at 1955 Raymond Drive, Suite 102, Northbrook, IL 60062.

LIONSTONE, American Indian, No. 2, 1980 .... 37.00
AMVET Riverboat, 1983 .... 10.00
Bass, No. 1, 1982 .... 50.00
Bicentennial, Betsy Ross, 1975 .... 20.00
Bicentennial, Blacksmith, 1973 .... 25.00
Bicentennial, George Washington, 1975 .... 15.00
Bicentennial, Mecklenburg, 1975 .... 22.00
Bicentennial, Molly Pitcher, 1975 .... 20.00
Bicentennial, Paul Revere, 1975 .... 22.00
Bicentennial, Sons of Freedom, 1975 .... 24.00
Bicentennial, Valley Forge, 1975 .... 13.00 To 15.00
Bird, Blue Jay, 1971 .... 18.00
Bird, Blue–Crowned Chlorophonia, 1974, Miniature 42.00
Bird, Bluebird, Eastern, 1972 .... 10.00
Bird, Bluebird, Western, 1972 .... 15.00 To 18.00
Bird, Canada, Goose, 1980 ....*Illus* 50.00
Bird, Canary, 1973, Miniature 40.00
Bird, Capistrano Swallow, Gold Bell, 1972 .... 19.00 To 21.00
Bird, Capistrano Swallow, Gold Bell, 1972, Miniature 7.00
Bird, Capistrano Swallow, Silver Bell, 1972 .... 39.00
Bird, Cardinal, 1972 .... 30.00
Bird, Cardinal, 1973, Miniature 15.00
Bird, Doves of Peace, 1977, Miniature 35.00
Bird, Emerald Toucanet, 1974 .... 16.00
Bird, Falcon, 1973 .... 15.00 To 19.00
Bird, Hummingbird, 1973, Miniature 35.00
Bird, Meadowlark, 1969 .... 20.00
Bird, Mourning Dove, 1981 .... 45.00
Bird, Northern Royal Flycatcher, 1974, Miniature 40.00
Bird, Ostriches, 1977, Miniature 15.00
Bird, Owls, 1973 .... 19.00
Bird, Painted Bunting, 1974, Miniature 15.00
Bird, Pheasant, 1977 .... 52.00
Bird, Pheasant, No. 6, 1981 .... 41.00
Bird, Quail, 1969 .... 10.00 To 12.00
Bird, Roadrunner, 1969 .... 17.00 To 25.00
Bird, Roadrunner, 1969, Miniature 8.00
Bird, Robin, 1975 .... 35.00
Bird, Robin, 1975, Miniature 12.00
Bird, Scarlet Macaw, 1974, Miniature 36.00
Bird, Snow, Goose, 1981 .... 68.00
Bird, Wood Duck, 1981 .... 52.00
Bird, Woodhawk, 1969 .... 15.00 To 24.00

Bird, Woodhawk, 1969, Miniature 20.00
Bird, Woodpecker, 1975 .... 24.00
Bird, Woodpecker, 1975, Miniature 11.00
Bird, Yellow Head, 1974, Miniature 42.00
Buccaneer, 1973 .... 29.00
Car, Corvette, 1984 Model, 1984 .... 65.00
Car, Corvette, 1984 Model, Black, 1984 .... 125.00
Car, Duesenberg, 1978, Miniature 15.00
Car, Jaguar, 1936 Model, 1978 .... 18.00
Car, Johnnie Lightning, No. 1, Gold, 1972 .... 80.00
Car, Johnnie Lightning, No. 2, Silver, 1973 .... 50.00 To 58.00
Car, Mercedes, 1978, Miniature 15.00
Car, Olsonite Eagle, No. 6, 1970 .... 69.00 To 94.00
Car, Stutz Bearcat, 1978, Miniature 15.00
Car, Turbo Car STP, Gold, 1972 .... 150.00
Car, Turbo Car STP, Platinum, 1972 .... 150.00
Car, Turbo Car STP, Red, 1972 .... 40.00
Cherry Valley, 1971, Gold .... 17.00 To 19.00
Cherry Valley, 1971, Silver 36.00
Circus Set, 1973, Miniature, 9 Piece 125.00
Circus, Burmese Girl, 1973, Miniature 12.00
Circus, Fire Eater, 1973, Miniature 12.00
Circus, Snake Charmer, 1973, Miniature 12.00
Circus, Strongman, 1973, Miniature 12.00
Circus, Sword Swallower, 1973, Miniature 12.00
Circus, Tattooed Lady, 1973, Miniature 12.00
Clown Set, 1978–1979, 6 Piece 245.00
Clown, No. 1, Monkey Business, 1978 .... 36.00
Clown, No. 1, Monkey Business, 1978, Miniature 21.00
Clown, No. 2, Sad Sam, 1978 .... 35.00
Clown, No. 2, Sad Sam, 1978, Miniature 21.00
Clown, No. 3 Say It With Music, 1978 .... 35.00
Clown, No. 3, Say It With Music, 1978, Miniature 21.00
Clown, No. 4, Salty Tails, 1978 .... 35.00
Clown, No. 4, Salty Tails, 1978, Miniature 19.00

Lionstone, Bird, Canada, Goose, 1980

Lionstone, Old West, Camp Cook, 1969

Lionstone, Old West, Riverboat Captain, 1969

Clown, No. 5, Pie Face, 1979 .... 35.00
Clown, No. 5, Pie Face, 1979, Miniature 19.00
Clown, No. 6, Lampy, 1979 .... 35.00
Clown, No. 6, Lampy, 1979, Miniature 19.00
Dog, Afghan, 1977, Miniature 18.00
Dog, Alaskan Malamute, 1977, Miniature .... 15.00 To 18.00
Dog, Beagle, 1977, Miniature 15.00
Dog, British Pointer, 1975, Miniature .... 15.00 To 16.00
Dog, British Rough Collie, 1975, Miniature 14.00
Dog, Cocker Spaniel, 1975, Miniature 15.00
Dog, Collie 15.00
Dog, Doberman, 1977, Miniature 15.00
Dog, French Poodle, 1975, Miniature .... 15.00 To 18.00
Dog, German Boxer, 1975, Miniature 18.00
Dog, German Dachshund, 1977, Miniature 15.00
Dog, German Shepherd, 1975, Miniature 18.00
Dog, Golden Retriever, 1977, Miniature 15.00
Dog, Great Dane, 1977, Miniature 18.00
Dog, Irish Setter, 1977, Miniature .... 15.00 To 16.00
Dog, Labrador Retriever, 1977, Miniature 15.00
Dog, Schnauzer, 1977, Miniature 16.00
Dog, Scottish Terrier, 1977, Miniature 16.00
Dog, St. Bernard, 1977, Miniature 15.00
Duck, Canvasback, 1981 .... 36.00
Duck, Mallard, 1981 .... 30.00 To 35.00
Duck, Pintail, 1981 .... 49.00
Duck, Wood, 1981 .... 55.00
European Worker, Cobbler, 1974 .... 30.00
European Worker, Horseshoer, 1974 .... 30.00
European Worker, Potter, 1974 .... 30.00
European Worker, Silversmith, 1974 .... 30.00
European Worker, Watchmaker, 1974 .... 30.00
European Worker, Woodworker, 1974 .... 30.00
F. O. E. Eagle, Las Vegas, 1982 .... 20.00
F. O. E. Eagle, Nashville, 1983 .... 28.00
F. O. E. Eagle, White, 1983 .... 18.00
Firefighter, Fire Alarm Box, Red, 1983 .... 110.00
Firefighter, Fire Equipment, 1976, Miniature, 3 Piece .... 42.00 To 65.00
Firefighter, Fire Extinguisher, No. 9, 1983 .... 95.00
Firefighter, Fire Hydrant, No. 6, 1981 .... 95.00
Firefighter, Fireman No. 1, Red Hat, 1972 .... 105.00 To 125.00
Firefighter, Fireman No. 1, Yellow Hat, 1972 .... 145.00
Firefighter, Fireman No. 2, With Child, 1974 .... 125.00
Firefighter, Fireman No. 3, Down Pole, 1975 .... 80.00 To 95.00
Firefighter, Fireman No. 4, Emblem, 1978 .... 30.00
Firefighter, Fireman No. 5, Emblem, 1979 .... 24.00 To 25.00
Firefighter, Fireman No. 7, Hat, 1982 .... 94.00
Firefighter, Fireman No. 8, Fire Alarm Box, 1983 .... 70.00
Fish, Goldfinch, 1972 .... 24.00
God of War, 1978 .... 20.00
Goddess of Love, 1978 .... 20.00
Horse, Cannonade, 1976 .... 50.00
Horse, Secretariat, 1977 .... 75.00
Horse, Secretariat, 1977, Miniature 17.00
Lantern, Brass, 1983 .... 61.00
Mailman, 1974 .... 20.00
Oil Filter, Delco 65.00
Old West, Annie Christmas, 1969 .... 13.00
Old West, Annie Oakley, 1969 .... 13.00
Old West, Bar Scene, 1970, Framed, 4 Piece 600.00
Old West, Barber, 1976 .... 45.00
Old West, Barber, 1976, Miniature 14.00
Old West, Bartender, 1969 .... 20.00

Old West, Bartender, 1969, Miniature 14.00
Old West, Bath, 1976 .... 60.00 To 75.00
Old West, Bath, 1976, Miniature 16.00
Old West, Belly Robber, 1969 .... 12.00
Old West, Buffalo Hunter, 1973 .... 32.00
Old West, Calamity Jane, 1973 .... 25.00
Old West, Camp Cook, 1969 ....*Illus* 15.00
Old West, Camp Follower, 1969 .... 15.00
Old West, Cavalry Scout, 1969 .... 10.00
Old West, Cavalry Scout, 1970, Miniature 13.00
Old West, Chinese Laundry Man, 1969 .... 14.00 To 20.00
Old West, Country Doctor, 1969 .... 12.00
Old West, Cowboy, 1969 .... 10.00
Old West, Cowboy, 1970, Miniature 12.00
Old West, Cowgirl, 1973 .... 25.00 To 28.00
Old West, Custer's Last Stand, 1979 .... 360.00
Old West, Dancehall Girl, 1973 .... 52.00
Old West, Frontiersman, 1969 .... 15.00
Old West, Gambler, 1969 .... 10.00
Old West, Gambler, 1969, Miniature 12.00
Old West, Gold Panner, 1969 .... 35.00 To 48.00
Old West, Highway Robber, 1969 .... 13.00
Old West, Indian, Bust, No. 1, 1980 .... 35.00
Old West, Indian, Bust, No. 2, 1980 .... 35.00
Old West, Indian, Casual, 1969 .... 12.00
Old West, Indian, Casual, 1970, Miniature 15.00
Old West, Indian, Proud, 1969 .... 12.00
Old West, Indian, Proud, 1970, Miniature 15.00
Old West, Indian, Squaw, 1973 .... 18.00
Old West, Indian, Squawman, 1969 .... 28.00
Old West, Indian, Tribal Chief, 1973 .... 22.00
Old West, Jesse James, 1969 .... 14.00
Old West, Judge Roy Bean, 1973 .... 35.00
Old West, Judge, Circuit Riding, 1969 .... 10.00
Old West, Lonely Luke, 1974 .... 26.00
Old West, Lonely Luke, 1975, Miniature 12.00
Old West, Lucky Buck, 1974 .... 30.00
Old West, Lucky Buck, 1975, Miniature 10.00
Old West, Madame, 1969 .... 42.00 To 50.00
Old West, Molly Brown, 1973 .... 27.00
Old West, Mountain Man, 1969 .... 15.00
Old West, Photographer, 1976 .... 45.00
Old West, Photographer, 1976, Miniature 15.00
Old West, Professor, 1973 .... 49.00
Old West, Railroad Engineer, 1969 .... 20.00
Old West, Rainmaker, 1976 .... 30.00
Old West, Rainmaker, 1976, Miniature 14.00
Old West, Renegade Trader, 1969 .... 15.00
Old West, Riverboat Captain, 1969 ....*Illus* 10.00
Old West, Sheepherder, 1969 .... 38.00
Old West, Sheepherder, 1975, Miniature 16.00
Old West, Sheriff, 1969 .... 10.00
Old West, Sheriff, 1970, Miniature 14.00
Old West, Shootout At OK Corral, 1971 .... 395.00
Old West, Shootout At OK Corral, 1971, Miniature 125.00
Old West, Sodbuster, 1969 .... 15.00
Old West, Stage Driver, 1969 .... 13.00
Old West, Telegrapher, 1969 .... 16.00
Old West, Tinker, 1974 .... 26.00
Old West, Trapper, 1976 .... 22.00
Old West, Vigilante, 1969 .... 10.00
Old West, Wells Fargo Man, 1969 .... 10.00
Oriental Worker Set, 1974, 8 Piece 228.00

Oriental Worker, Basket Weaver, 1974	30.00
Oriental Worker, Egg Merchant, 1974	30.00
Oriental Worker, Gardener, 1974	30.00
Oriental Worker, Sculptor, 1974	30.00
Oriental Worker, Tea Vendor, 1974	30.00
Oriental Worker, Timekeeper, 1974	30.00
Police Association Convention, 1980	18.00 To 20.00
Prima Donna Club, 1978, 5 Piece	315.00
Professor, 1975, Miniature	12.00
Rose Parade, 1973	15.00
Safari, Buffalo, 1977, Miniature	15.00
Safari, Elephants, 1977, Miniature	16.00
Safari, Gazelles, 1977, Miniature	15.00
Safari, Giraffes, 1977, Miniature	15.00
Safari, Hippos, 1977, Miniature	15.00
Safari, Kangaroos, 1977, Miniature	15.00
Safari, Koala Bear, 1977, Miniature	15.00
Safari, Leopards, 1977, Miniature	15.00
Safari, Lion & Cub, 1977	27.00
Safari, Lion & Cub, 1977, Miniature	10.00
Safari, Mona Monkeys, 1977, Miniature	15.00
Safari, Rhinos, 1977, Miniature	16.00
Safari, Zebras, 1977, Miniature	15.00
Shamrock, 1983	33.00
Sport, Backpacker, 1980	28.00
Sport, Baseball Players, 1974	85.00
Sport, Basketball Players, 1974	30.00
Sport, Boxers, 1974	49.00
Sport, Brooks Robinson, 1983	71.00
Sport, Fisherman, 1983	30.00 To 39.00
Sport, Football Players, 1974	35.00 To 65.00
Sport, Golfer, 1974	35.00
Sport, Hockey Players, 1974	65.00
Sport, Johnny Unitas, 1983	95.00
Sport, Sahara Invitational, 1976	27.00
Sport, Sahara Invitational, 1977	25.00
Sport, Tennis Player, Female, 1980	28.00
Sport, Tennis Player, Male, 1980	28.00

--------------------------------- **LORD CALVERT** ---------------------------------

Lord Calvert Canadian whiskey has been sold in several types of special decanters. A series of glass flasks with ball stoppers was offered in 1961, and a series of duck decanters was made from 1978 to 1980.

LORD CALVERT, Canada Goose, 1977	50.00
Canvasback Duck, 1979	20.00
Common Eider Duck, 1980	20.00
Wood Duck, 1978	25.00

--------------------------------- **LUXARDO** ---------------------------------

In 1821 Girolamo Luxardo began making a liqueur from the marasca cherry. The company literature calls this famous drink *the original maraschino.* The business has remained in the family through five generations. Decorative Luxardo bottles were first used in the 1930s at Torreglia near Padua, Italy. Most of the Luxardo bottles found today date after 1943. The date listed here is the first year each bottle was made. The bottles are still being made and some are sold at stores in the United States and Canada. Bottles are of glass or ceramic and come in many sizes, including miniatures. Many of the bottles were pictured in the now-out-of-print book *Luxardo Bottles* by Constance Avery and Al Cembura (1968).

LUXARDO, African Head	20.00
Amphora, 1956, Miniature	10.00
Ampulla, 1959	25.00

Luxardo, Decanter, Ships

Apothecary Jar, 1960	25.00
Apothecary Jar, 1960, Miniature	16.00
Autumn Wine Pitcher, 1958	35.00
Babylon, 1960	20.00
Bacchus, 1969	25.00
Bantu, 1962	15.00
Bizantina, 1959	32.00
Black Cat, Miniature	12.00
Blue & Gold Amphora, 1968	25.00
Buddha, Jogan, Gray, 1962	18.00
Burma Ashtray, 1960	22.00
Burma Ashtray, 1960, Miniature	18.00
Burma Pitcher, 1960	13.00 To 15.00
Calypso, 1962	22.00
Candlestick, Alabaster, 1961	33.00
Cannon, Brass Wheels, 1969	25.00
Cellini, 1952	40.00
Cellini, 1968	15.00
Ceramic Barrel, 1968	15.00
Chess, Horse, Quartz, 1969	38.00
Clock, 1960	10.00
Clock, Beam Label	20.00
Clown, Miniature	16.00
Coffeepot, 1962	12.00
Congo, 1960	20.00
Decanter, Ships	*Illus* 25.00
Deruto Cameo, 1959	28.00
Dog, Bulldog, Miniature	20.00
Dog, English Bulldog, Miniature	6.00
Dolphin, 1959	45.00
Duck, Green, 1960	40.00
Eagle, Onyx, 1970	50.00
Faenza, 1972	8.00
Fakir, 1960	30.00
Fish, Alabaster, 1960	35.00
Fish, Green & Gold, 1960	35.00
Fish, Quartz, 1969	36.00
Fish, Ruby, 1961	36.00
Frog, Miniature	7.00
Fruit, 1960, Miniature	27.00

Gambia, 1961	10.00
Gambia, 1961, Miniature	6.00
Gazelle, 1957	35.00
Goose, Alabaster, 1960	30.00
Maraboo, 1957	35.00
Mayan, 1960	20.00
Mazzo, Amphora, 1954	25.00
Medieval Palace, 1952	35.00
Medieval Palace, 1970	9.00
Miss Luxardo, 1970	15.00
Mosaic Ashtray, 1959, Miniature	20.00 To 22.00
Mud Bucket, Miniature	15.00
Nubian, 1959	16.00
Nubian, 1959, Miniature	8.00
Owl, Miniature	12.00
Owl, Onyx, 1970	45.00
Paestum, 1959	20.00
Paestum, 1959, Miniature	5.00
Pagliacci, 1959	18.00
Penguin, 1968	36.00
Pheasant, Black, 1968	170.00
Pheasant, Modern, 1960	50.00
Pheasant, Quartz, 1969	45.00
Pheasant, Red & Gold, 1960	50.00
Pierrot, 1959	50.00
Pre–Historic, Miniature	10.00
Puppy, Cicciola, 1961	28.00
Puppy, Cicciola, On Base, 1960	35.00
Safari Animals, Miniature	10.00
Santa Maria Ship, 1969	20.00
Sphinx, 1961	12.00
Squirrel, 1968	45.00
Tamburello, 1959	25.00
Torra Bianca, 1962	20.00
Torre Tinta, 1962	20.00
Tower of Flowers, 1968	22.00
Tower of Fruit, 1968	20.00
Turkey, 1961	35.00
Turkey, 1961, Miniature	30.00
Twist, Miniature	10.00
Venetian, Gold Rosy, 1952	22.00
Venetian, Merletto, 1957	25.00
Venus, 1969	22.00
Wobble Bottle, 1957	10.00
Zodiac, 1970	30.00

MBC, see Miniature, MBC

─────────── **MCCORMICK** ───────────

It is claimed that the first white men to find the limestone spring near Weston, Missouri, were Lewis and Clark on their famous expedition. Over 20,000 gallons of fresh water gush from the spring each day. An Indian trading post was started near the spring by a man named McPhearson about 1830. His friend Joseph Moore decided to establish a town and paid a barrel of whiskey for the land. Bela Hughes and his cousin Ben Holladay came to the new town in 1837. They soon had a dry goods store, a drugstore, a tavern, and a hotel. They even built a Pony Express station. In 1856, Ben Holladay and his brother David started a distillery to make bourbon using the spring water. David's daughter later married a man named Barton and the distillery was renamed Barton and Holladay. It was sold in 1895 to George Shawhan but closed from 1920 to 1936. The property became a cattle and tobacco farm.

In 1936, after the repeal of Prohibition, Isadore Singer and his two brothers purchased the plant and began making Old Weston and Old Holladay bourbon. About 1939 they bought the name *McCormick* from a nearby distillery founded years before by E. R. McCormick. Legend says that Mrs. McCormick would not allow her husband to reopen the distillery because she had *gotten religion*. The Singer brothers' new distillery used part of the grain for the mash, and their cattle feed lot used the leftover parts.

During World War II, alcohol was needed by the government and Cloud L. Cray bought the distillery to make industrial alcohol at a company he called Midwest Solvents. After the war, Bud and Dick Cray, sons of Cloud Cray, started making bourbon at the old plant by old-fashioned methods, producing about 25 barrels a day. The bourbon was sold in Missouri, Kansas, Iowa, and Oklahoma. The old plant, listed in the National Register of Historic Sites, is open for tours. In about 1980 the company, under the direction of the new president, Marty Adams, started marketing on a national instead of a local scale, and it is now selling in all of the states. They have a full line, including wine, beer, and many alcoholic beverages such as rum, tequila, vodka, dry gin, blended whiskey, and brandy that are now sold under the McCormick name.

McCormick Distilling Company, now a subsidiary of Midwest Grain Products, has created many types of figural bottles for their bourbon, ranging from a bust of Elvis Presley (made in 1979) to a musical apple (1982). The company discontinued making decanters in 1987.

MCCORMICK, Abe Lincoln, 1976	35.00
Air Race Pylon, 1970	10.00
Arizona Sun Devil	46.00
Barrel, With Stand, Gold Hoops, 1968	18.00
Bat Masterson, 1972	30.00
Benjamin Franklin, 1975	16.00
Benjamin Franklin, 1976, Miniature	16.00
Betsy Ross, 1975	25.00
Betsy Ross, 1976, Miniature	35.00
Billy The Kid, 1973	35.00
Buffalo Bill, 1979	55.00
Calamity Jane, 1974	30.00
Captain's Lamp, No. 2, Captain, 1983	17.00
Charles Lindbergh, 1977, Miniature	12.00
Daniel Boone, 1975	18.00
Doc Holiday, 1972	30.00
Dune Buggy, 1976	35.00
Elvis, Aloha, 1981	115.00
Elvis, Bust, 1978	28.00
Elvis, Designer, No. 1, 1981	75.00
Elvis, Gold, 1984	185.00
Elvis, No. 1, White, 1978	75.00
Elvis, No. 1, White, 1978, Miniature	42.00
Elvis, No. 2, Pink, 1980	50.00
Elvis, No. 2, Pink, 1980, Miniature	35.00
Elvis, No. 3, Black, 1980	55.00
Elvis, No. 3, Black, 1980, Miniature	35.00
Elvis, Sergeant, 1983	45.00
FOE Stein, 1986	25.00
George Washington, 1975	25.00
George Washington, 1975, Miniature	37.00
Henry Ford, 1977, Miniature	12.00
Imperial Council, 1984	23.00
Jefferson Davis, 1976	28.00
Jesse James, 1973	30.00
Jester, Mirth King, 1972	34.00
John Hancock, 1975	16.00
John Hancock, 1976, Miniature	16.00
Johnny Rogers, No. 2, 1973	90.00
Jug, Bourbon, White, 1976	10.00

Julia Bullette, 1974	135.00
Kansas City Royals, 1971	12.00
Kit Carson, 1975	16.00
Lamp, Victorian, 1984	17.00
Lobsterman, 1979	28.00
Mark Twain, 1977	20.00
Mark Twain, 1978, Miniature	13.00
Meriwether Lewis, 1978	18.00
Mississippi Rebel, 1974	8.00
Nebraska Corn Huskers, 1974	13.00
New Mexico Lobo, 1973	30.00
Oregon Beavers, 1974	10.00
Ozark Ike, 1979	30.00
Packard, 1937 Model, Cream, 1980	40.00
Packard, Hood Ornament, 1985	25.00
Patrick Henry, 1976, Miniature	16.00
Paul Bunyan, 1979	28.00
Paul Revere, 1975	25.00
Paul Revere, 1976, Miniature	35.00
Pirate, No. 1, 1972, 1/2 Pt.	8.00
Pirate, No. 2, 1972, 1/2 Pt.	8.00
Pirate, No. 5, 1972. 1/2 Pt.	8.00
Pirate, No. 6, 1972, 1/2 Pt.	8.00
Pirate, No. 7, 1972, 1/2 Pt.	8.00
Pirate, No. 9, 1972, 1/2 Pt.	8.00
Queen Guinevere, 1979	20.00
Robert E. Lee, 1976	30.00
Robert Peary, 1977	32.00
Rose Garden, 1980, Miniature	22.00
Sam Houston, 1977	25.00
Sir Lancelot, 1979	16.00
Spirit of 76, 1976	48.00
Spirit of 76, 1977, Miniature	20.00
Telephone, French, 1969	22.00
Texas Longhorns, 1972	27.00
Texas, 150th Anniversary	20.00
Thomas Jefferson, 1976, Miniature	16.00
Train, Locomotive, 1969	18.00
Train, Mail Car, 1969	18.00
Train, Passenger Car, 1970	32.00
Train, Set, 1980, Miniature, 4 Piece	60.00
Train, Wood Tender, 1969	15.00
U.S. Marshall, 1979	30.00
Wild Bill Hickock, 1973	30.00
Will Rogers, 1977	22.00
Will Rogers, 1978, Miniature	13.00
William Clark, 1978	18.00
Wood Duck, 1980	35.00
Wyatt Earp, 1972	30.00

MEDICINE

If you have friends with scrofula or cattarh, they probably can find a medicine from the nineteenth century. The extravagant claims for cures and the strange names for diseases add to the fun of collecting early medicine bottles. Bottles held all of the many types of medications used in past centuries. Most of those collected today date from the 1850–1930 period. Some of the names, like Kickapoo Indian Oil, Lydia Pinkham's Female Compound, or Wahoo Bitters, have become part of the slang of America. Bitters, cures, sarsaparilla, and a few other types of medicine are listed under their own headings in this book. Collectors prefer early bottles with raised lettering. Labeled bottles in original boxes are also sought. For more information, look for *The Bottle Book: A Comprehensive Guide to Historic, Embossed Medicine Bottles* by Richard E. Fike.

MEDICINE, see also Cure; Drug

MEDICINE, A. D. Elemers Pain Killing Balm, Label 20.00
A. McEckron's Ring Bone Liniment, New York, Aqua, OP, 7 1/4 In. 75.00
Allen's Nerve & Bone Liniment, ABM, 3 3/4 In. 14.00
Aqua, Blown, Rectangular, Flat Corner Panels, OP, 6 1/4 In. 22.00
Atlas Worm Killer, Aqua, Label, Contents, BIMAL 15.00
Ayer's Cherry Pectoral, Aqua, BIMAL, 5 1/4 In. 12.00
B. B. B., Philadelphia & St. Louis 25.00
Baby Brand Castor 3.00
Bach's American Compound, N. Y., Aqua, OP, Rectangular, 7 1/2 In. 105.00
Barnes & Park, Balsam of Wild Cherry & Tar, Aqua, 7 5/8 In. 198.00
Barry's Tricopherous For Skin & Hair, Aqua, Rectangular, 6 In. 32.00
Begg's Diarrhea Balsam 12.00
Bermingham Nasal Douch, 1890, Box 18.00
Bon–Opto, For The Eyes 12.00
Boswell & Warner's Colorific, Milk Glass, Indented Panels, 5 In. 668.00
Bradfield's Female Regulator, Aqua, Rectangular, 8 1/2 In. 20.00
Brant's Indian Pulmonary Balsam, M. T. Wallace, Octagonal, OP 85.00
Brant's Purifying Extract, Aqua, OP, D Variant 200.00
Bristol's Extract of Sarsaparilla, Buffalo, Aqua, OP, 5 5/8 In. 90.00
Bromo Celery, Arnold Chemical Co., Chicago, Amber, BIM, 3 In. 16.00
Bromo–Seltzer, Dispenser, Cobalt Blue, 7 1/2 In. 6.00
Bromo–Seltzer, Emerson Drug, Baltimore, Cobalt Blue, 2 1/2 In. 4.00
Buchan's Hungarian Balsam, London, Aqua, OP, 5 3/4 In. .... 45.00 To 72.00
Burnett's Cocaine, Boston, Aqua, Odd Shape 45.00
C. C. Taylor Liniment Or Oil of Life, Label, 16 Oz. 15.00
C. Heimstreet & Co., Troy, N. Y., Medium Blue, 6 3/4 In. 320.00
C. Toppan, Cocoa Nut Oil, Violin Shape, Aqua, Pontil, 5 7/8 In. 132.00
Cantrell's Pectoral Or Cough Syrup, Philadelphia, OP, 6 In. 185.00
Catarrh Remedy, Olive Green, 3–Piece Mold, Pontil, Label 42.00
Cha. Pfiser Co., N. Y., Factory On Label, Aqua, 7 1/2 In. 12.00
Chamberlain's Colic, Cholera & Diarrhoea Remedy, Aqua, ABM, 4 In. 8.00
Chesbro's Liquid Corn Plaster, Cobalt Blue .... 10.00 To 20.00
Ciroux Mfg. Co., Buffalo, Fort Erie, Clear, Parisian Sage, 7 In. 15.00
Citrate–Magnesia, Porcelain Stopper, Pt. 5.00
Clark's Syrup, Medium Emerald Green, 9 3/4 In. 75.00
Clarke's–Lincoln–World Famed Blood Mixture, Blue, 7 1/4 In. 33.00
Cod Liver Oil, Fish, ABM, 9 1/3 In. 18.00
Cole Bros. Perfection Liniment, Binghamton, N. Y. 8.00
Collins' Cough Elixir, Kemp & Elmitt, Aqua, Octagonal, 5 5/8 In. 10.00
Davis Vegetable Pain Killer, Clear, Rectangular, ABM, 6 1/2 In. 8.00
Davis Vegetable Pain Killer, IP, Rectangular, 6 5/8 In. 45.00
Davis Vegetable Pain Killer, Label Dated 1868, 4 5/8 In. 14.00
Dose Measure, Appliance Co., Providence, R. I., Clear, 2 Oz. 20.00
Dr. A. C. Daniels Wonder Worker Lotion, Boston, Rectangular, 6 In. 10.00
Dr. B. J. Kendall's Blackberry Balsam, Clear, BIMAL 7.00
Dr. Blackman's Genuine Healing Balsam, Clear, OP 85.00
Dr. Broughton's Invigorating Syrup, Manhood Restorer, Aqua, 5 In. 38.00
Dr. Browder's Compound Syrup, Indian Turnip, Aqua, 7 In. .... 120.00 To 210.00
Dr. C. F. Basford's Home Guard Medicines, Cincinnati, Oh. 185.00
Dr. C. F. Brown's Young American Liniment, Aqua, OP, Round, 4 In. 220.00
Dr. Clark, N. Y., Brilliant Emerald, Applied Tapered Lip, IP, 9 In. 880.00
Dr. Crook's Wine of Tar, Deep Aqua, 8 3/4 In. 45.00
Dr. D. Jayne's Alterative, Sunken Front Panel, Oval, 7 In. 45.00
Dr. D. Jayne's Tonic Vermifuge, Philadelphia, Pa. 70.00
Dr. D. Kennedy's Favorite Remedy, Kingston, N. Y., BIM, 8 1/2 In. 22.00
Dr. Denig's Cough Balsam, Aqua, IP, 6 1/8 In. 110.00
Dr. Duncan's Expectorant Remedy, Aqua, Tapered Collar, 6 3/8 In. 88.00
Dr. E. G. Gould's Pin Worm Syrup, Aqua, OP 55.00
Dr. Engles' Balsam of Life, Dark Aqua, Rectangular, 7 7/8 In. 275.00
Dr. Fenner's Peoples Remedy, Amber, Pt. 20.00
Dr. G. Kerr & Bertolet, Compound Asiatic Balsam, Aqua, Embossed 65.00
Dr. G. W. Denig's, Oh., Aqua, Rectangular, 1840–1860, Pontil, 6 In. 198.00
Dr. Gordak's Iceland Jelly 175.00

Medicine, Dr.J.H.McLean's Liniment Oil,
Volcanic, Box, 4 In.

Medicine, Elleman's Universal Embrocation,
10 1/2 In.

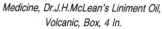

Dr. H. A. Ingham's Nervine Pain Extract, Aqua, BIM, 5 In.	7.00
Dr. H. Swayne's Compound of Wild Cherry, Square, Indented Panels	65.00
Dr. Henley's Celery, Beef & Iron, San Francisco, Amber, 9 1/2 In.	121.00
Dr. Hershey's Worm Syrup, Small Burst Bubble	75.00
Dr. Hoofland Balsamic Cordial, Philadelphia, Aqua, 6 3/4 In.	105.00
Dr. Hostetter's, Honey Amber, Embossed Base	15.00
Dr. Ira Warren's Blood & Bile Purifier, Aqua, 8 3/4 In.	225.00
Dr. J. Blackman's Genuine Healing, Clear, Octagonal, 5 1/2 In.	39.00
Dr. J. Cheever's Life Root Mucilage, Mass., Aqua, 8 3/8 In.	215.00
Dr. J. F. Churchill's Hypophosphites, Lime Soda, Potash, Aqua, 8 In.	330.00
Dr. J. H. McLean's Liniment Oil, Volcanic, Box, 4 In. ....*Illus*	15.00
Dr. J. W. Bull's Vegetable Baby Syrup, English & German, Aqua	35.00
Dr. Jayne's Carminative Balsam, Aqua, Rolled Lip, OP	20.00
Dr. Jayne's Indian Expectorant, Clear, OP	75.00
Dr. Jewett's Celebrated Pulmonary Elixir, Aqua, OP, Dug, 5 1/4 In.	25.00
Dr. John Roake's Iodine Liniment, N. Y., Rectangular, 7 1/4 In.	240.00
Dr. Johnson's Dog Remedies, N. Y. Vet. Hospital, Aqua, 3 1/2 In.	26.00
Dr. Kelinger's Magic Fluid, New York, Aqua, 4 7/8 In.	70.00
Dr. Kennedy's Rheumatic Liniment, Roxbury, Mass.	105.00
Dr. Kilmer's Ocean Weed Heart Remedy, Binghamton, Aqua, 8 In.	121.00
Dr. Kilmer's Swamp Root Kidney, Liver & Bladder Remedy, Aqua	12.00
Dr. King's New Discovery, Chicago, Ill., Aqua, Rectangular, 4 In.	18.00
Dr. King's New Discovery, Coughs & Colds, ABM, 6 5/8 In.	7.50
Dr. L. B. Wright's Liquid Cathartic Or Physic, Aqua, OP, 6 3/4 In.	84.00
Dr. M. F. Marbles Blood Syrup, Cardiner, Me.	16.00
Dr. Mackenzie's Smelling Catarrh Salt, Ball Stopper, Green, 3 In.	40.00
Dr. Mann's Celebrated Ague Balsam, Galion, Oh., Aqua, IP, 6 3/4 In.	198.00
Dr. McBride, World's Relief, San Francisco, Aqua	80.00
Dr. McMunn's Elixir of Opium	14.00
Dr. O. Phelp's Brown, Jersey City, N. J., Deep Aqua, 8 3/4 In.	38.00
Dr. P. Hall's Cough Remedy, Aqua, Rolled Lip, OP, 1850, 4 3/4 In.	132.00
Dr. Pettit's American Eye Water, Aqua, Wooden Cylinder, 8 1/4 In.	523.00
Dr. Pierce's Extract of Smart-Weed	15.00
Dr. Pierce's Favorite, Buffalo, N. Y., Light Blue, 8 In.	15.00
Dr. Pierce's Golden Med. Discovery, Medium Aqua, BIM, 9 In.	38.00

Dr. Pinkham's Emmenagogue, Aqua, OP, Applied Mouth, 6 In.	160.00
Dr. Pinkham's Emmenagogue, Deep Aqua, OP	59.00
Dr. R. Ansom & Co., King of The Blood, Aqua, BIM, 8 1/2 In.	32.00
Dr. R. Goodales American Catarrh Remedy, Aqua, 6 In.	121.00
Dr. Roback Swedish Remedy, Aqua, Embossed, Octagonal	165.00
Dr. Roger's Liverwort, Tar, Canchalagua, Rectangular, IP, 7 1/2 In.	60.00
Dr. S. Feller's Lung Balsam, Aqua, IP, Rectangular, 6 3/4 In.	142.00
Dr. S. Pitcher's Castoria, Aqua	8.00
Dr. S. S. Fitch, 707 Broadway, N. Y., Label, Aqua, 1840, 3 1/4 In.	275.00
Dr. Sanford's Invigorator Or Liver Remedy, N. Y., Aqua, 7 1/2 In.	72.00
Dr. Sawen's Celebrated Oil Liniment, Watertown, N. Y., Aqua, 6 In.	20.00
Dr. Seth Arnold's Balsam, Aqua, OP, Rectangular, 4 Panels, 5 In.	26.00
Dr. Shoop's Family Medicine, German & English Label, BIMAL, 5 In.	9.00
Dr. Steeling's Pulmonary Syrup, N. J., Aqua, OP, Rectangular, 6 In.	105.00
Dr. Stone's Oxford Drops For Coughs & Cold, Aqua, OP, 5 In.	95.00
Dr. Thatcher's Improved Liver Pills, Wooden Vial, 25 Cents	6.00
Dr. Thorne's Arnica & Chloroform Liniment, Oval, c.1860, 6 In.	20.00
Dr. Warren's Expectorant, White & Hill, Aqua, Rectangular, 6 In.	84.00
Dr. Wing's Corn Remedy	12.00
Dr. Wistar's Balsam of Wild Cherry, Phila., Aqua, Octagonal, OP	45.00
Drake's, 6 Logs, Yellow Amber	75.00
Dyer's Healing Embrocation, Providence, R. I., Aqua, OP, 6 1/8 In.	45.00
E. G. Lyons & Co., Jamaica Ginger, San Francisco, Dark Lime, 6 In.	286.00
Electric Brand Laxative, Clear, BIMAL, Square, Contents, 9 1/2 In.	17.50
Elleman's Universal Embrocation, 10 1/2 In. ....*Illus*	2500.00
Eno's Fruit Salt, Aqua, Glass Stopper	8.00
Family Embrocation, All Healing Liniment, Aqua, Whittled	55.00
Father John's Medicine, Lowell, Mass., Dark Amber, 7 1/4 In.	7.00
Fenner's St. Vitus Dance	28.00
Fletcher's Castoria, Blue Aqua, ABM, Cork	6.00
Forhan's Pyorrhea Astringent, N. Y., Label, Stopper, 2 1/4 In.	15.00
G. W. Merchant, Lockport, N. Y., Dark Aqua, OP, 1850, 5 In. ....93.00 To	120.00
Gardiners Liniment, Aqua, Round, Rolled Lip, 4 1/8 In.	25.00
Gauss, Elixir On Opposite Sides, Amber, Rectangular, 8 In.	12.00
Gibb's Bone Liniment, Olive Green, OP, Hexagonal, 6 1/4 In.	688.00
Gladstone's Celery & Pepsin Compound, Amber, Contents, 7 1/4 In.	35.00
Gold Medal Mosquito Lotion, Clear, BIMAL, Label, Contents, Box	16.00
Grant German Magnetic Liniment, Albany, N. Y.	22.00
Gunn's Pioneer Blood Renewer, Macon, Ga., Amber, 10 7/8 In.	125.00
MEDICINE, H.H. WARNER'S, see Medicine, Warner's	
H. Lake's Indian Specific, Aqua, Rectangular, Pontil, 8 1/4 In.	286.00
Hall's Balsam For The Lungs	125.00
Hall's Painless Corn	20.00
Hamptons V. Tincture, Mortimer & Mowbray, Copper, 6 1/4 In.	330.00
Hanford's Balsam of Myrrh, Vet, Aqua, 12–Sided, Box, 2 3/4 In.	20.00
Hartshorn's Sarsaparilla & Iron TC	4.00
Haven's Cough Syrup, Lowell, Mass., Label, Cylinder, 4 3/4 In.	100.00
Haven's Diarrhea & Colera Syrup, Flared Lip, Cylinder, 4 In.	125.00
Hemlock Oil Co., West Derry, N. H., Label, Contents	20.00
Henry Wampole Co. Ltd., Perth, Ontario, Canada, Light Blue, 8 In.	10.00
Herrick's German Horse Liniment, L. W. Warner, Rectangular, 8 In.	25.00
Holman's Nature's Grand Restorative, Aqua, Large	140.00
Homeopathic Tincture, Label	5.00
Hood's Vegetable Pills, Contents, Box	25.00
Hospital Association, Mo., Railway Employees, Amethyst, 4 3/4 In.	12.00
Howard's Vegetable Cancer & Canker Syrup, Amber, 7 1/4 In.	743.00
Humphrey's Homeopathic Leucorrhea, Nude On Lion, Cork, 2 1/2 In.	16.00
Hunnewell's Tolu Anodyne, Aqua, OP, 3 3/4 In.	40.00
Hunnewell's Universal Cough Remedy, Aqua, OP, 4 1/2 In.	45.00
Hunter's Pul. Balsam Or Cough Syrup, Rectangular, 6 In.	85.00
J. F. Davis Crimean Liniment, Stickney's Corner, Me., 4 3/4 In.	17.00
J. G. Royce's Universal Relief, Mass., Aqua, OP, Rectangular, 5 In.	53.00
J. H. Fisher's Wildfire Rheumatic Liniment, Flemington, N. J.	130.00

J. L. Mathieu's Cough Syrup, Marlboro, Mass., Oval, 6 1/2 In. 25.00
J. Paul Liebe, Dresden, Golden Yellow 15.00
J. R. Burdsall's Arnica Liniment, New York, Aqua, OP, 5 1/2 In. 50.00
J. R. Spalding's Rosemary & Castor Oil, Aqua, OP, 5 In. .... 35.00 To 55.00
J. Russell Spalding, Boston, Aqua, Rectangular, Pontil, 7 1/8 In. 33.00
Jadwin's Subduing Liniment, Aqua, Hinged Mold, 8 3/4 In. 35.00
Jenk's Vegetable Extract, Aqua, Rectangular, 4 In. 88.00
Jewett's Stimulating Liniment, Aqua, OP, Rectangular, 2 1/4 In. 58.00
John Hart & Co., Heart Shape, c.1870 .... 412.50
John M. Winslow, Compound Balsam of Horehound 140.00
John Youngson Extract of American Oil, Aqua, OP 150.00
Jones Drops, For Humors Or Anti–Impetigines 110.00
Kennedy's Prairie Weed, Boston, Mass., 1878–1900 .... 25.00
Kennedy's Salt Rheum Ointment, Wide Mouth, Aqua, OP, 2 In. 75.00
Keough's Foul Remedy 50.00
     MEDICINE, KICKAPOO OIL, see Medicine, Healy & Bigelow
Kilmer's Cough Consumption Oil 25.00
Kilmer's Oceanweed Heart Remedy, Embossed Heart 285.00
Kodol Nerve Tonic, Sample 15.00
Kurnitzki Swire Grall Liver & Kidney, Charleston, Aqua, Oval 45.00
Kuro Medicine Co., Boston, For Coughs, Triangular, 8 1/4 In. 35.00
Lindsey's Blood Searcher, Light To Medium Teal, 9 1/4 In. 1050.00
Liquid Opodeldoc, Aqua, Seed Bubbles, Flared Lip, Cylindrical 25.00
Log Cabin Cough & Consumption Remedy, Amber, Large 150.00
Log Cabin Scalpine, Rochester, N. Y., Amber, 9 In. 90.00
Lydia E. Pinkham's Vegetable Compound, Aqua, BIM, 8 1/2 In. 18.00
Lydia E. Pinkham's Vegetable Compound, Clear, 8 In. 15.00
M. B. Roberts Vegetable Embrocation, Lime, OP, 1850, 5 1/4 In. 88.00
Magnesia, S. Tompkins & Bro., New Bedford, OP, Label 25.00
Mathewson's Infallible Remedy, 50 Cents, Aqua 150.00
McClellan's Diphtheria Remedy, Aqua, Tooled Top, 8 1/4 In. 99.00
McDonald's Annihilator For Consumption, Aqua, OP, 7 5/8 In. 495.00
McDonald's Celebrated Soothing Syrup, Label 10.00
McLean's Strengthening Cordial, Aqua, Oval, Civil War 15.00
McLean's Strengthening Cordial, Aqua, Pontil, Oval, 9 3/8 In. 105.00
McMunn's Elixir of Opium, Aqua, Flared Lip, OP 24.00
Medical Department, U.S. Other Side, Clear, 500 Cc, 8 1/2 In. 35.00
Menthocol Expectorant, Milk Glass, Screw Lid, Box, 1921, 3 1/8 In. 15.00
Mexican Mustang Liniment, Lyon Mfg. Co., N. Y., Round, 7 1/2 In. 16.00
Miller Mfg. Co. Anti–Mole, Lincoln, Neb. 25.00
Mingay's Cough Balsam, Aqua, 4 1/8 In. 14.00
Monroe's Compound Arnica Liniment, 5 3/4 In. 150.00
Morse's Celebrated Syrup, Providence, Emerald, OP, Oval 565.00
Morse's Indian Root Pills, W. H. Comstock, Amber, 2 1/2 In. 45.00
Mrs. Dinsmore's Cough & Croup Balsam, Lynn, Mass., Aqua, Embossed 15.00
Mrs. Winslow's Soothing Syrup, Curtis & Perkins, Aqua, BIM, 5 In. 7.00
Mrs. Winslow's Soothing Syrup, Marine Blue .... 49.00 To 69.00
N. Woods, Portland, Me., Aqua, OP, Rectangular, Beveled Edges 45.00
N. Y. College of Medicine Pharmacy, W. Richardson Agent, Oval, Neck 125.00
Nasal Douche, 1890, Orange Box 18.00
Nature's Remedy, Acid, Iron & Earth, Mobile, Ala., Amber, 6 1/7 In. 15.00
O'Neill's Catholicon, Light To Medium Green, OP, Round, 7 5/8 In. 935.00
Opium Habit, Cured By Dr. S. B. Collins, Laporte, Ind., 1890, 8 In. 264.00
Oregon Blood Purifier, Embossed Baby's Face, Amber, Tooled Lip 30.00
Osgood's Indian Cholagogue, N. Y., Crude 35.00
Page's Vegetable Syrup, Females, Aqua, Whittled, 8 1/8 In. 132.00
Paine's Celery Compound 5.00
Pearl's White Glycerine, Cobalt Blue, Tooled Collar, 6 3/8 In. 48.00
Peptenzyme, Cobalt Blue, 3 In. 10.00
Phillips Emulsion Cod Liver Oil, Amber 10.00
Preston's Ve–Purifying Catholican Ports, N. Y., Aqua, 9 1/2 In. 225.00
Prickly Ash Poke Root Potassium, Blood Purifier, Amber, Large 25.00
R. D. Porter's Genuine Oriental Life Liniment, Aqua .... 75.00 To 100.00

Medicine, Scudder's Syrup, Chicago, Ill., Qt., 10 1/4 In.

Medicine, Sevoin's Panacea, Phila., Pa., Yellow Green, 8 1/2 In.

Medicine, Vapo-Cresolene Co., July, 1872, 4 In.

Race's Indian Blood Renovator, Aqua, Embossed, 9 In.	25.00
Radam's Microbe Killer, Amber, Square, 10 1/2 In.	45.00
Reed & Carnrick Peptenzyme, Cobalt Blue, Screw Top, Caster Oil	20.00
Renne's Pain Killing Magic Oil, Aqua, BIMAL	8.00
Rev. N. H. Downs Vegetable Elixir, Aqua, 12–Sided, BIMAL	6.00
Rheumatism Swift Specific Co., Atlanta, Amber, ABM, Label, 7 In.	10.00
Roger's Liverwort Canchalagua, Aqua, IP, Crude	70.00
Roussel–Type Single Collar, Yellow Green, OP, Squat	98.00
Rustin's Oil For Rheumatism, Aqua, OP, Tapered Collar, 5 In.	53.00
S. B. Goff's Magic Oil Liniment, Aqua, Label	12.00 To 15.00
S. B. Packer's Cutaneous, Aqua	6.00
Salve, 12–Sided, Olive Amber, Keene Marlboro, Pontil, 2 1/4 In.	540.00
Schenck's Pulmonic Syrup, Aqua, OP, Octagonal, 1850, 7 1/4 In.	330.00
Schenck's Pulmonic Syrup, OP, Octagonal	65.00
Scott's Emulsion Cod Liver Oil, Lime & Soda, Aqua, BIM, 9 In.	22.00
Scudder's Syrup, Chicago, Ill., Qt., 10 1/4 In. *Illus*	35.00
Seethatdicey & Co., Light Green Aqua, Flared Lip, Embossed, 6 In.	75.00
Sevoin's Panacea, Phila., Pa., Yellow Green, 8 1/2 In. *Illus*	300.00
Shaker Anodyne, N. H., Aqua, Pontil, Rectangular, 3 1/2 In.	77.00
Shepherd's Sarsaparilla, Aqua, OP	300.00
Shield's German Cough Syrup, Label	10.00
Skelton's Pectoral Balsam of Life, Lung Disease, Aqua, 7 3/8 In.	185.00
Skin–A–Fire For Eczema, Square, Box, 4 1/2 In.	17.00
Snow & Mason Cough & Croup, Wittly, Early Snap Case	20.00
Southern Pacific Co. Hospital Dept., Purple	15.00
Starkweather's Hepatic Elixir, Upton, Mass.	240.00
Stephen Sweet's Infallible Liniment, OP, 1850, 5 1/8 In.	28.00
Swaim's Panacea, Philadelphia, Aqua, OP, 7 7/8 In.	330.00
Swaim's Panacea, Philadelphia, Deep Olive, Pontil, 7 7/8 In.	220.00
Swaim's Panacea, Philadelphia, Light To Medium Green	145.00
Swayne's Syrup, Wild Cherry, Aqua, OP	75.00 To 85.00
T. C. Pomeroy, Blood & Liver Purifier	25.00
T. W. Steeling's Rheumatic Liniment, Aqua, OP, 5 1/8 In.	110.00
The Mother's Friend, Atlanta, Ga.	4.00
Thompson's Wild Cherry Hygeia Phosphate, 4 Panels Form Cross	15.00

Troyer's Vegetable Rheumatic Liniment	80.00
True Daffy Elixir, Deep Aqua, Green Tone, 4 1/4 In.	110.00
Turner Brothers, Blue Green, OP, Oval	80.00
U.S. A. Hospital Dept., Cobalt Blue, Striations, Cylinder, Qt.	688.00
U.S. A. Hospital Dept., Forest Green, Square Collar, 1865, 6 In.	242.00
Urine Specimen, Clear, 7 Oz., 6 In.	4.00
Valentine Hassmer's Lung & Cough Syrup, Blob Top	100.00
Vapo–Cresolene Co., July, 1872, 4 In. ....*Illus*	2.00
Vaughn's Vegetable Lithontriptic Mixture, Buffalo, Aqua, 8 In.	121.00
Vegetable Pain Reliever, Pomfret, Conn., Label	10.00
Venetian Liniment, Dr. Tobias, New York, Aqua, Oval, Pontil	35.00
W. F. Lawrence's Genuine Preparations, Epping, Aqua, 5 5/8 In.	69.00
W. W. Huff's Liniment, Emerald, OP, Cylinder, 4 In.	176.00
Ward's Rheumatic Embrocation, New York	160.00
Warner's Compound A Diuretic, Contents, Label	33.00
Warner's Rattler Oil	25.00
Warner's Safe Cure, London, Deep Olive Green, Oval, 11 In.	605.00
Warner's Safe Kidney & Liver Cure, Golden Amber, 9 3/8 In.	66.00
Warner's Safe Kidney & Liver Remedy, Medium Amber, Blob Top, Pt.	35.00
Warner's Safe Kidney & Liver Remedy, Olive Amber, 9 5/8 In.	21.00
Warner's Safe Nervine	65.00
Warner's Safe Nervine, Amber	45.00
Warner's Safe Nervine, Slug Plate Variant, Amber, 7 3/8 In.	45.00
Warner's Safe Remedies Co., Golden Amber, Label, 7 3/8 In.	88.00
Warner's Safe Remedy Co., Rochester, N. Y., Amber, 7 1/8 In.	25.00
Warner's Safe Remedy, Amber, 12 1/2 Oz.	37.00
Warner's Safe Remedy, Yellow Apricot, ABM	20.00
Warner's Tippecanoe, Cough & Consumption Remedy, Log Cabin, Amber	165.00
Warner's, Log Cabin, Rochester, N. Y., Golden Amber, 8 1/8 In.	143.00
Westlake's Ointment Vegetable, Lima, N. Y.	35.00
Whitwell's Original Opodeldoc, Clear, Flint, OP	65.00
Wm. R. Warner & Co., Tono Sumbul Cordial, Label, 8 1/8 In.	20.00
Wyeth & Bro., Cobalt Blue, Dose Cap, Square, BIM, 6 1/2 In.	32.00
Wyeth Collyrium, Eyecup, Cobalt Blue, Label, Embossed	25.00
Wyeth Sage & Sulphur Compound, Wrap–Around Label, Amber, ABM	25.00
Wyeth, Cobalt Blue, Label, Embossed, Dose Cap	22.00
Wyeth, Sodium Phosphate Salts Dose Bottle	35.00
Zoa–Phora, Woman's Friend, Aqua, BIMAL, 7 1/4 In.	7.00
Zoa–Phora, Woman's Friend, Aqua, Rectangular, 7 1/2 In.	16.00

MICHTER'S

Michter's claims to be America's oldest distillery, established in Schaefferstown, Pennsylvania, in 1753, before it was even the state of Pennsylvania. The building has been named a national historic landmark. Special ceramic jugs were first made in 1955 and figural decanters have been made since 1977. One of the most famous series was King Tut (1978–1980). About 3,000 were made of the large size. Miniature bottles were also made.

MICHTER'S, Christmas Ornament, 1984	38.00
Christmas Tree, 1978	51.00
Conestoga Wagon, 1976	124.00
Fireman, Volunteer Statue, 1979	86.00
Football On Tee, Delaware	49.00
Goddess Selket, 1980	30.00
Halloween Witch, 1979	55.00
Hershey Trophy, 1980	45.00
Ice Wagon, 1979	19.00 To 20.00
Jug, 1957, 1/2 Pt.	16.00
Jug, 1957, Qt.	20.00
Jug, 1976, 1/2 Pt.	7.00
Jug, 1976, Pt.	6.00
Jug, 1976, Qt.	8.00
King Tut, 1978, Miniature	10.00
Packard, 1937 Model, Black, 1980	34.00

Packard, Fleetwood, 1979	30.00
Pennsylvania Hex, 1977	8.00
Queen Nefertiti, 1979	35.00

MIKE WAYNE

Mike Wayne Distilled Products Company was founded in Bardstown, Kentucky, in 1978. The company was formed to sell original ceramic decanters. A John Wayne bust, a portrait, and two full–figure bottles are among the many decanters made until about 1982.

MIKE WAYNE, Grandfather Clock, 1981	42.00
John Wayne, Bust, 1980	45.00
John Wayne, Portrait, 1979	40.00
John Wayne, Statue, White, 1981	87.00
Masonic, Past Master, 1981	35.00
Mercedes Benz, 450 SL, 1980	25.00
Nebraska Cornhuskers, 1982	25.00
Norman Rockwell, Plumber, 1978	15.00
Pheasant, 1981	20.00
Pope John Paul II, 1980	20.00
Razorback Hog, 1982	35.00

MILK GLASS

It makes perfect sense to think that white milk–colored glass is known as *milk glass* to collectors. But not all milk glass is white, nor is all white glass milk glass, so the name may cause a little confusion.

The first true milk glass was produced in England in the 1700s. It is a semi–opaque glass, often with slight blue tones. The glass reached the height of its popularity in the United States about 1870. Many dishes and bottles were made. Both new versions of old styles and new styles have been made continuously since that time, many by the Westmoreland and the Kemple glass companies. These pieces, many very recent, often appear at antiques sales.

Figural bottles of milk glass were used by Westmoreland to hold their food products, especially mustard. Today it is considered correct to talk about blue milk glass or black milk glass. This is glass made by the same formula but with a color added. It is not correct to call a glass that is white only on the surface *milk glass.* Bottles made of milk glass may also be found in this book under many other headings.

milk glass, see also Cologne; Cosmetic; Drug; Figural

MILK GLASS, Champlin's Liquid Pearl, BIM, Rectangular, 5 In.	20.00
G. W. Laird Perfumer, N. Y., BIM, Rectangular, 4 3/4 In.	34.00
Jar, Battleship Maine, Pt.	180.00 To 250.00
Klondyke Nugget, & Cap, Opalescent, Ground Lip, 5 7/8 In.	60.00
Mascot, Pat. Nov. 30 '08, July 20, '86	50.00
Owl Drug Co., 4 1/2 In.	50.00
Owl Drug Co., Tooled Lip, Label, 1895–1908, 3 3/8 In.	303.00
Owl, Figural, 6 1/2 In. *Illus*	75.00
Pinch, 3–Piece Mold, Yellow, Triangular, Mushroom Stopper, 9 In.	44.00
Sazerac Aromatic Bitters, 12 1/8 In.	100.00
Snail, Figural, Iron Wheelbarrow Stand, 1870–1880, 3 1/4 In., Pr.	413.00
Tobacco, Amphora, Dutch Windmill On Side, 6 1/4 In.	25.00
Velvetina Skin Beautifier, Goodrich Drug, Omaha	12.50 To 35.00
World's Fair, 1939, 9 In.	20.00

MILK

The first milk bottle we have heard about was an earthenware jar pictured on a Babylonian temple stone panel. Evidently, milk was being dipped from the jar while cream was being churned into butter.

Milk Glass, Owl, Figural, 6 1/2 In.

Milk, Farmer's Dairy, Cream Top, Qt.

Milk came straight from the cow on early farms; but when cities started to grow in America, a new delivery system was needed. The farmer put the milk into large containers. These were taken to the city in horse–drawn carts and delivered to the consumer. The milkman took a slightly dirty dipper and put it into the milk, ladling a quantity into the customer's pitcher.

Flies, dirt, horse hairs, and heat obviously changed the quality of the milk. By the 1860s iceboxes were developed. One type of milk can claimed to keep milk from becoming sour in a thunderstorm. In 1895, pasturization was invented and another source of disease from milk was stopped. The first milk bottle patent was issued in the 1880s to the Warren Glass Works Company. The most famous milk bottle was designed in 1884 by Dr. Harvey D. Thatcher, a physician and druggist from Potsdam, New York. His glass bottle had a *Lightning* closure and a picture on the side of a cow being milked. In 1889 The Thatcher Company brought out the bottle with a cap that is still used.

The characteristic shape and printed or embossed wording identify milk bottles for collectors. The round bottle was the most popular until 1936, when the squat round bottle was invented. In 1940 a square squat bottle became the preferred shape. A slug plate was used in the manufacture of a special type of round milk bottle. The manufacturer would change the name embossed on the bottle by changing a metal plate in the glass mold. In the following list of bottles, the letters *ISP* refer to this sort of slug plate. Amber–colored glass was used for a short time. Makers claimed it resisted spoiling. A green bottle was patented in 1929. *Pyro* is the shortened form of the word *pyroglaze*, an enameled lettering used on milk bottles after the mid–1930s. Before that, the name had been embossed.

Cop the top, babyface, toothache, and *cream top* are some of the terms that refer to the shapes of bottle necks popular in the 1930s. Near the top of the bottle there was an indentation so the cream, which separated from the standing milk, could be poured off with little trouble. Today, with homogenized milk, few children realize that the cream on natural milk will rise to the top. The glass bottle was displaced by cartons by the 1960s. There is a newsletter for collectors, The Milk Route, 4 Ox Bow Road, Westport, CT 06880–2602.

MILK, A. G. Smalley, Clear, Embossed, Side Handle, 1/2 Pt. 440.00
   A. G. Smalley, Clear, Embossed, Side Handle, Qt. ....87.00 To 154.00
   Alta Crest Farms, Green, Paper Cap .... 700.00 To 770.00
   Alta Crest Farms, Spencer, Mass., Cow's Head, Bright Yellow Green, Qt. 798.00
   Anchorage Dairy, Dutch Girl, With Pails, Orange Pyro, Round, Qt. 65.00
   Angus Dairies, Sheep Herder, England, Orange, Tall, Pt. 13.00
   Arden Milk, Western Dairy Products Inc., In Slug Plate, Qt. 5.00

Batchelor's Better Milk, Canon City, Red On Yellow Pyro, 1/2 Pt. 13.00
Baxter's Dairy, Goderich, Ontario, Black Silk Screen, Round, Qt. 200.00
Belle Springs, B In Bell Emblem Over Bell, ISP, Embossed, Round, Qt. 12.00
Belleview Dairy, Pasteurized Homogenized Milk, Amber, Square, Qt. 10.00
Bernard Dairy, Cow, Red, Square, 1/2 Pt. 7.50
Big Elm Dairy Co., Green, Qt. .... 193.00 To 275.00
Binder Dairy, Oshkosh, Wis., Diamond Neck, Slogan Roll, 3/4 Qt. 7.50
Borden's, R In Circle, Amber, Square, Gal. 45.00
Borden's, Ruby Red 850.00
Brighton Farm Creamery, H. Bahrenburg, Clear, Qt. 61.00
Brighton Place Dairy, Green, Qt. 358.00
Buffalo, Embossed Bison, Clear, Qt. 20.00
Burr, Los Angeles, Bear Emblem, Slug Plate, Round, Embossed, Pt. 25.00
Burroughs Brothers, Knightsen, Calif., 2 Kids In Buggy, Red Pyro, Qt. 10.00
Burroughs Brothers, Walnut Grove Farm, Cream Top, 12 Bulb Rib, Qt. 25.00
C. W. Lilja, Falconer, N. Y., Stippled, Crosshatched, ISP, Round, Qt. 17.50
Carnation, Please Return Empty Bottles, Amber, Square, Qt. 15.00
Chestnut Farms, Chevy Chase Dairy, Washington, D. C., 1/4 Pt. 12.00
Chicago Guernsey Farming, Hinsdale, Ill., Clear, 1/2 Pt. 15.00
Climax, Pat. 1898, Tin Top, Square, Pt. 88.00
Clover Brand Dairy Products, 3–Leaf Clover, Round, Pt. 9.00
Cloverleaf Creamery Co., Boulder, Colo., Cream Top, ISP, Qt. 80.00
Cloverleaf Farms, Blue Ribbon Farms, Stockton, Ca., Round, Red, 1/3 Qt. 8.00
Cloverleaf Farms, Blue Ribbon Farms, Stockton, Ca., Round, Red, 3/4 Qt. 8.00
Cloverleaf Farms, Stockton, Calif., Cream Top, Orange, Square, Qt. 15.00
Cloverleaf Harris, Quality Milk Dairy, Emblem, ISP, Cream Top, 1/2 Pt. 30.00
College Dairy, La Sierra College, Yellow Over Blue, Square, 1/2 Pt. 25.00
College View Dairy, Northfield, Vt., Jumping Horse, Maroon, Square, Pt. 10.00
Columbia Dairy, Geo. H. Pippy, San Francisco, Amethyst, ISP, Pt. 15.00
Cranford Farms, Derby, N. Y., 1/3 Qt. 20.00
Cream Top Dairy, Milk Daily, Cream Top, Green, Square, Qt. 20.00
Creamer, All State Dairies, 2 In. ....*Illus* 15.00
Creamer, Anthony's Cream, Red, Round, 1/2 Oz. 20.00
Creamer, Badger Farms Creameries 21.00
Creamer, Bergren's Dairy Farms, Script, Red, 3/4 Oz. 20.00
Creamer, Blue Jay Cafe, Blue, Round, 1/2 Oz. 20.00
Creamer, Borden's, Red, Round, 1/2 Oz. 15.00
Creamer, Borden's, Red, Round, 3/4 Oz. 20.00
Creamer, Bowler's Creamery, Saltglaze, 3 In. 12.00
Creamer, Brookside Creamery, Manville, N. J., Fleur–De–Lis, Red, 3/4 Oz. 20.00

Milk, Creamer, All State Dairies, 2 In.

Milk, Creamer, Heath, 2 Large H's, 2 1/8 In.

Milk, Creamer, Quality Dairy, 1 3/4 In.

Milk, Creamer, Sealtest, 1 3/4 In.

Creamer, Chicago Guernsey Farm, Maroon, Round, 1/2 Oz. 20.00
Creamer, Colvert's Pasteurized Dairy Products, Red, Round, 1/2 Oz. 20.00
Creamer, Creamland, Albuquerque, Green, Round, 3/4 Oz. 20.00
Creamer, Crescent Pasteurized Milk & Cream, Orange, Round, 1/2 Oz. 20.00
Creamer, Crowley's, Clear, Maroon Oval, Round, 1/2 Oz. 20.00
Creamer, Davis Dairy, Creston, Iowa 21.00
Creamer, Deep South Creamery, Star, Udderly Delicious, Orange, 1/2 Oz. 20.00
Creamer, Dressel–Young, Granite City, Ill., Orange, Round, 3/4 Oz. 20.00
Creamer, G. E. Thomas & Sons, In Diamond, Black, Round, 1/2 Oz. 20.00
Creamer, Galloway Preserved Cream, Stoneware, 5 In. 18.00
Creamer, Golden Royal, Red Lettering, Clear, 1 In. 6.00
Creamer, Hailwoods Cream, Cow Picture, Brown Top, Stoneware, 4 1/2 In. 9.00
Creamer, Heath, 2 Large H's, 2 1/8 In. ....*Illus* 10.00
Creamer, Ingram's Milweek, Cap 15.00
Creamer, Jersey Pride Creamery, Red, Round, 1/2 Oz. 20.00
Creamer, Meadow Gold, In Split Circle, Red, Round, 1/2 Oz. 20.00
Creamer, Meadow Gold, R In Shield, Red, Round, 1/2 Oz. 20.00
Creamer, Nadler Bros. Inc. 24.00
Creamer, National Dairy Sealtest Prod. Co., Tru–Li–Pure, Red, 1/2 Oz. 20.00
Creamer, Neidig's Dairy, Pennsylvania 21.00
Creamer, Provincial Dairies Leeds, Oak Acorn, White Stoneware, 3 In. 24.00
Creamer, Pulaski Pure Milk Co., Pulaski, Tennessee 27.00
Creamer, Quality Dairy, 1 3/4 In. ....*Illus* 5.00
Creamer, Quality Dairy, None Better, Red, Round, 1/2 Oz. 12.50
Creamer, Richardson's Thick Cream, Sheffield, White Stoneware, 3 In. 15.00
Creamer, Sealtest, 1 3/4 In. ....*Illus* 3.00
Creamer, Sealtest, In Script, Red, Round, 1/2 Oz. 20.00
Creamer, Sunset Dairy, Tucson's Oldest Since 1921, Maroon, 1/2 Oz. 20.00
Creamer, Valley Gold, Script, Orange, Round, 3/4 Oz. 20.00
Crescent Milk, Reno, Nev., Qt. 35.00
Cronenweth Dairy, Buttermilk, Security, Wide Mouth, Orange, 1/2 Gal. 25.00
Curles Neck Dairy Inc., Baby Top, Cops, Emblem, Square, Qt. 45.00
Curly's Dairy, Quality Checked, Q With Check Mark, Amber, Square, Qt. 18.00
D. F. Smith Quality Dairy, Gloversville, N. Y., Cream Reservoir, 10 In. 16.00
Damascus Creamery, Pasteurized Milk & Cream, In Slug Plate, 1/2 Pt. 15.00
Damascus Fresh Homogenized Nu–Rich Milk, Amber, White, Square, Qt. 7.50
Darigold, Quality Homogenized Milk, Portland, Amber, Square, White, Qt. 12.50
Dellinger Dairy Farm, Jefferson, Ind. 15.00
Deluxe Cream Separator, Clear, Red Pyro, Square, Qt. 385.00
E. F. Mayer, Emblem, Amber, In Slug Plate, Round, Qt. 60.00
E. F. Mayer, Red Amber, Round, Emblem In Slug Plate, Qt. 85.00
Edgemar Farms, Embossed 4 Sides, Flowers, Amber, Square, Qt. 18.00
El Paso Dairy, Multisided, 1/2 Pt. 20.00
Elmhurst Dairy, Qt. 6.00
Eureka Dairy, Keystone Weber, Churn Shape, Amethyst, ISP, Pt. 20.00
F. E. R. G. Co., Amber, Wash & Return On Side, Pre–1920, Qt. 33.00
Fairmont's Better Butter, Omaha, Neb., Red, Yellow, Pyro, Round, 1/2 Pt. 13.00
Farmer's Dairy Association, Portland, Ore, ISP, Round, Qt. 12.50
Farmer's Dairy, Cream Top, Qt. ....*Illus* 7.00
Farmer's Dairy, Howell & Demarest, ISP, Round, Embossed, Qt. 25.00
Fredericktown Ice & Dairy, Wash & Return, Embossed, ISP, Round, Qt. 15.00
Furtado Dairy, Antioch, Ca., In Slug Plate, Round, Qt. 10.00
Gascoyne Dairy, Clear Cream Separator 70.00
Gold Medal Creamery, Long Beach, Cream Top, ISP, Round, Qt. 30.00
Golden Arrow, Finest Quality, Ca., Amber, Yellow, Square, Qt. 10.00
Golden State Brand Dairy Products, Ca., Red Pyro, 1/2 Pt. 13.00
Golden State Company, Ltd., Shield, California, 1/2 Pt. 7.50
Golden State Company, Ltd., Shield, Cream Top, Qt. 18.00
Gulf Hill, Dartmouth, Round, 1/3 Qt. 7.50
Hage's Locally Owned, 6 Emblems, Orange Pyro, Round, 1/2 Pt. 8.00
Hampden Registered Creamery Co., Cow's Head, ISP, Tin Top, 1/2 Pt. 45.00
Hartford Dairy, 1/2 Pt. 30.00
Herrington's Dairy, Picton, Ontario, Blue Silk Screen, Round, Pt. 175.00

*Milk, Kornely, Guernsey Farms Dairy,
Amber, Qt.*

Milk, Midwest Dairy, With Cap, Qt.

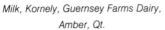

Highland Hill Dairy, Exeter, Ontario, Orange Silk Screen, Round, Qt.	275.00
Hillside Dairy Milk, Peter Gallick, Carbondale, Pa., ISP, Pt.	13.00
Hilo Dairymen's Center, Clarabell The Cow, Black Pyro, 1/2 Pt.	75.00
Hollow Hill Farm, Crown Top, Amethyst, In Slug Plate, Round, Qt.	30.00
Holsgern Farms Dairy, McClellan Bros., Clear, Tin Top & Closure, Qt.	85.00
Hoppy's Favorite, Wm. Boyd, Northland, Mich., Maroon, Square, Qt.	40.00
Hostess Pasteurized Milk, Hewett & Eckel, Orange Pyro, Round, Qt.	35.00
Indian Head Farm, Framingham, Mass., Embossed Indian's Head, Pt.	110.00
Indian Hill Dairy, Greenville, Me., Indian Head, Orange Pyro, Qt.	8.00
J. Boyles, Lead, S. D., ABM	20.00
John Brown, Troy N. Y., Embossed Cow, Qt.	25.00
John W. Boak & Son Grandview Dairy, Jamestown, N. Y., ISP, Pt.	20.00
Jos. Simmons, Brooklyn, Clear, Climax 66, Tin Lid & Wire Closure, Qt.	16.50
Kee & Chapell Dairy Company, Shield, Amethyst, Pt.	12.00
Kornely, Guernsey Farms Dairy, Amber, Qt. ....*Illus*	18.00
Lang's Creamery, Buffalo, N. Y., Green, Qt.	300.00
Laurentia, Crown Top, Unusual Shape, Canada, 1920s, Imperial Qt.	75.00
Liberty Milk Co., Buffalo, 1/2 Pt.	4.00
Liberty Milk Co., Buffalo, Pt. ....4.00 To 10.00	
Liberty Milk Co., Buffalo, Qt.	10.00
Loma Linda Sanitarium Dairy, Loma Linda, Ca., Orange, Square, Qt.	27.00
London City Dairies, Green Silk Screen, Round, 1/2 Pt.	175.00
Long Beach Dairy & Creamery Co., Long Beach, Amber, ISP, Round, Qt.	125.00
Long Sault Dairy, Phone 462–W, Black Silk–Screen, Round, Qt.	155.00
Lucas Valley Dairy, San Rafael, Calif., Amber, White, Square, Qt.	9.00
Lucerne Homogenized Vitamin D Milk, S. A. Safeway, Red, Square, Gal.	40.00
M. B. S., Indianpolis, Ind., Clear, 5 1/2 In., Qt.	6.00
Maple City Dairy, Paw Paw, Mich.	15.00
Meadowland Approved Ayrshire, Portland, Ore., Amber, Square, Qt.	20.00
Meyer Dairy, Bethlehem, Pa., Embossed Cow, Qt.	25.00
Midwest Dairy, With Cap, Qt. ....*Illus*	8.00
Milk Protector, Thatcher Mfg. Co., Man Milking Cow, Clear, Qt.	305.00
Milk, Sunrise Dairy, 1st Line of Health Defense, Red, Squat, Qt.	30.00
Miller Dairy, Ione, Ca., Red Pyro, Round, Qt.	30.00
Milverton Creamery Co., Milverton, Ont., Green Silk–Screen, Round, Qt.	225.00
Minges Dairies, Wellsville, N. Y., Stippled, Screw, Orange, Square, Qt.	10.00
Monterey Bay Milk Distributors Inc., Hobnailed Neck, 1/4 Pt.	20.00
Morningside Farms, Stockton, Ca., Orange Pyro, Round, Qt.	10.00
Moss Farm Dairy, Chesterland, Oh., Farm Scene, 1/2 Pt.	12.00
Mountain Dairies, M. Burgmann Inc., Amethyst, In Slug Plate, Round, Qt.	24.00

Mt. Whitney Pasteurized Dairy Products Co., Embossed, 1/2 Pt. 25.00
New London Dairy, Conn., Clear, 1/2 Pt. 20.00
Newans Diary Co., Des Moines, Ia., Emblem, 1/2 Pt. 10.00
NL Martin, Climax 107, Boston, Tin Top, Square, Qt. 410.00
North Shore Dairy Co., Cow, Orange, Round, Squat, 1/2 Gal. 12.00
Nu–Method Dairy Products Co., Los Angeles, Ca., In Slug Plate, 8 Oz. 30.00
Oak Grove Dairy, Manchester, Conn., Baby–Table, Green Pyro, Round, Pt. 10.00
Ohio Farmers, Script Over Map of Ohio, Round, Pt. 35.00
Oldfield, Farm Parker Bros., Clark's Summit, In Slug Plate, Pt. 12.00
Orchard Park & Jewett Stock Farm Milk Co., Round, 1/2 Pt. 15.00
Otath–He–Waugh–Pe–Qua, Off In A Jiffy, Amber, 1/2 Gal. ....*Illus* 28.00
Pacific Union Angwin College, In Slug Plate, Round, 1/2 Pt. 35.00
Pacific Union Angwin College, In Slug Plate, Round, Pt. 30.00
Paramount For Health, Embossed, Round, Qt. 9.00
People's Milk Co., Emblem, Amber, Round, In Slug Plate, Qt. 60.00
Peter Pan Dairy Farms, Granada Hills, Amber, Yellow, Square, Qt. 10.00
Play Safe, Use Gold Spot Dairy Products, Green, Orange Pyro, 1/2 Gal. 75.00
Polish American Dairy, Health Dept. Permit 67, In Slug Plate, Pt. 30.00
Portland Damascus Milk Co., In Slug Plate, Ribbon Overlay, Pt. 12.00
Portsmouth, England, Emblem, Tall, Pt. 10.00
Powell Valley Creamery, Orange Pyro, Squat, Qt. 18.00
Price's Dairy Co., El Paso, Tex., Ribbed Neck, Embossed, Round, Qt. 25.00
Pure Milk Dairy, Adlam Pat., Tin Screw Lid With Handle, Qt. 935.00
Pure Milk Dairy, Round Embossed, In Slug Plate, Qt. 15.00
Purity Dairy, Lovelock, Nev., Pt. 55.00
Purity Ice & Ice Cream Co., In Slug Plate, Embossed, Round, Qt. 15.00
Quaker Maid Dairy, Quaker Woman, Whittier, Calif., Amber, Square, Qt. 20.00
R. Bedford Dairy Co., Brooklyn, N. Y., Tin Top, Bowling Pin, Qt. 100.00
Red Rock, Plaid Pattern Mid Body, Barrel Shape, 1/2 Pt. 15.00
Red Top, Embossed Top, Qt. 10.00
Reehl's Dairy, Vitamins, Greenbush, N. Y., Amber, White, Square, Qt. 10.00
Reno Model Dairy Inc., In Slug Plate, 14 Neck Ribs, 1/4 Pt. 40.00
Riverview Dairy, Cream Top, In Slug Plate, Round, Qt. 25.00
Riverview Dairy, Wash & Return, Crown Top, In Slug Plate, 1/2 Pt. 12.00
Riverview Damascus, Portland, Ore, Emblem, Cream Top, Round, Qt. 35.00
Robertson Jersey Farm, Molalla, Ore., Wire Handle, Yellow, Round, Gal. 60.00
Rosedale Dairy, Laramie, Wyo., Emblem, In Slug Plate, Cream Top, Qt. 40.00
Safeway Grocery, S In Circle, Rectangular, Red, 1/2 Gal. 6.00
San Bernardino Creamery, Crown Top, Amethyst, In Slug Plate, Pt. 15.00
San Carlos Dairy, Bowling Pin, Slug Plate, Round, 1/2 Pt. 15.00

Milk, Otath–He–Waugh–Pe–Qua,
Off In A Jiffy, Amber, 1/2 Gal.

Milk, Weckerle, Green, Pt.

Sanitary Dairies Co., Eureka, Slug Plate, Round, Embossed, Pt.	15.00
Scheider's, Wash & Return, Crown Top, In Slug Plate, 1/2 Pt.	9.00
Scott's Dairy, Hanford, Ca., Embossed, Qt.	25.00
Service Milk, Buffalo, Monogram, Amber, Round, Qt.	75.00
Shamrock Dairy, Cream Top, In Slug Plate, Round, Qt.	40.00
Shy–Der's, 100 Pure Undiluted Health Juices, Green Pyro, Qt.	15.00
Smith's Model Dairy Inc., Black On Yellow, Pyro, Round, Qt.	12.50
Snider's Dairy, Goderich, Ontario, Red Silk Screen, Round, Qt.	205.00
South Sevier Dairy, Monroe, Utah, Amber, Beige, Square, Qt.	25.00
Spokane Bottle Exchange Inc., Shield, Blue Pyro, Qt.	25.00
St. Louis Dairy Co., St. Louis, Mo., 16 Neck Ribs, Round, Qt.	6.50
Store Bottle, Redeemed For 8 Cents, Walla Walla, Red, Squat, Qt.	8.00
Sun Valley Dairy, Homogenized Milk, Green, Yellow Pyro, 1/2 Gal.	20.00
Sun Valley Dairy, Multi–Vitamin Homo. Milk, Yellow Pyro, 1/2 Gal.	20.00
Sunflower Dairy, Clear, Pt.	8.00
Sunland Dairy, Yuma, Ariz., Amber, White, Square, Qt.	25.00
Sunset Dairy, Tucson, Ariz., In Slug Plate, Emblem, 1/3 Qt.	35.00
Sunshine Dairy, Baby Top, Cops, Orange, Square, Qt.	30.00
Sunshine Dairy, Grade A Milk, Paducah, Ky., Orange Pyro, 1/2 Pt.	10.00
Sunshine Dairy, St. Johns, Newfoundland, Red Pyro, Round, Imperial Qt.	45.00
Superior Milk Products, Carolina Creamery Co., Round, Embossed, Pt.	7.50
Supreme Guaranteed Dairy Farm, Green, Straight Sides, 8 Oz.	25.00
Supreme Milk & Cream Co., Perth Amboy, N. J., Embossed, Round, Qt.	7.50
Taylor's Dairy, Homogenized Milk, Amber, Square, Yellow, 1/2 Pt.	35.00
Thatchers, Absolutely Pure Milk, Potsdam, Man Milking Cow, 1884, Qt.	330.00
Thompson's Dairy, NW Washington, D. C., Emblem, Cream Top, Round, Qt.	20.00
Titusville Dairy Co., Black On Red, Round, Pyro, Qt.	40.00
Troutmere Guernsey Farm, La Honda Canyon, Pear Shape, 1/2 Pt.	18.00
Turner Centre, TCS System, Bowling Pin, Round, Pt.	17.50
Union Milk Co. Ltd., Calgary, 22 Neck Ribs, Red, Square, Imperial Qt.	15.00
Union Milk Co. Ltd., Calgary, 22 Neck Ribs, Round, Imperial Qt.	20.00
Universal Store Bottle, 5 Cents, Embossed, Round, Qt.	15.00
Universal Store Bottle, Ribbed, In Slug Plate, Round, 1/4 Pt.	9.00
Universal, Cap, 5 Cents, Qt.	5.00
Vale Edge Dairy, A Bottle of Health, Brown Pyro, Round, Qt.	35.00
Vale Edge Dairy, Brown Pyro, Buttermilk Cap, Qt.	45.00
Valley Creamery Co., Visalia, Ca., Unlawful–Used By Other, Qt.	25.00
Valley Dairy, Yerington, Nev., Painted Label, Qt.	30.00
Valley Gold Dairies Inc., Orange In Blue Shield, Square, Qt.	12.00
Victoria Guernsey, Over Poppy, San Bernardino, Orange, Square, Qt.	10.00
Voegel's Pasteurized, Minn., Baby Top, Cops, Black, Square, Qt.	45.00
Wagner Bros. Dairy, Best By Test, Anacortes, Wash., ISP, Round, Qt.	17.50
Waihee Dairy, Map of Oahu, Cow's Head, Red, Square, Qt.	25.00
Walker–Gordon Registered Laboratory, Carrier Emblem, Round, ISP, Qt.	20.00
Watcom County Dairymen's Association, Darigold, Metal Cap, ISP, Qt.	25.00
Weckerle, Green, Pt. ....*Illus*	100.00
Weckerle, Green, Qt. .... 165.00 To	170.00
Weiser's Dairy, W. Des Moines, Ia., Orange Pyro, Owl's Head, Square, Pt.	15.00
Western Farm's Dairy Co., Emblem, In Slug Plate, Amber, Round, Qt.	100.00
Wheeler & Taylor Pasteurized Milk, Keene, N. H., Orange, Squat, Qt.	15.00
Whiteman, Dome–Type Tin Cap, Clear, Qt.	330.00
Wildwood Dairy, Santa Rosa, Calif., Emblem, ISP, Cream Top, Qt.	30.00
Winder Dairy, Salt Lake City, Amber, Yellow, Rectangular, 1/2 Gal.	20.00
Windmill Brand Dairy Products, Minden, Nev., Red, Square, 1/2 Pt.	15.00
Windsor Farm Dairy, Script, Emblem, 12 Bulb Ribs, Cream Top, 1/2 Pt.	15.00
Wm. Colteryahn & Sons Co., Orange Pyro, 1/2 Gal.	25.00

MINERAL WATER

Although today it is obvious which is soda water and which is mineral water, the difference was not as clear in the nineteenth and early–twentieth centuries. Mineral water bottles held the fresh natural spring waters favored for health or taste. Even though some had a distinct sulfur or iron taste, the therapeutic values made them seem delicious. Some mineral waters had no carbonation, but many were naturally carbonated. Soda water today is made with artificial carbonation and usually has added flavor.

Mineral water was mentioned by the ancient Greeks, and the Romans wrote about visiting the famous springs of Europe. Mineral springs were often the center of resorts in nineteenth-century America, when it was fashionable to *take the waters*. Often the water from the famous springs was bottled to be sold to visitors. Most of the mineral water bottles collected today date from the 1850-1900 period. Many of these bottles have embossed lettering and blob tops. The standard shape was cylindrical with thick walls to withstand the pressure of carbonation. Most were made in a snap case mold although a few can be found with open or iron pontils. Common colors are clear, pale aqua, and light green. More unusual are dark green, black, and amber bottles, while cobalt blue ones are rare. The bottles were sealed with a cork. A few places, like Poland Springs and Ballston Spa, made figural bottles.

MINERAL WATER, see also Seltzer; Soda

MINERAL WATER, A. Schroth Superior, Medium Cobalt Blue, IP	375.00
A. Schroth Superior, Medium Sapphire Blue, IP, 7 3/8 In.	467.00
Adirondack Spring, Westport, N. Y., Emerald Green, Qt.	253.00
Adirondack Spring, Whitehall, N. Y., Emerald, Pt.	115.00
Archdeacon's, Patterson, N. J., Emerald Green, IP, 7 1/4 In.	330.00
Artesian Spring Co., Ballston Spa, Yellow Olive, Pt.	176.00
Artesion Spring, Sweet Spring Co., Golden Amber, Pt.	121.00
Avon Spring Water, Deep Olive Green, Qt.	500.00
B. R. Lippincott & Co., Cobalt Blue, IP, 7 3/8 In.	467.00
Bango City Mineral Water Co., Aqua, Octagonal, Codd, 9 In.	74.00
Bear Lithia Water, Elkton, Va., Aqua, 1/2 Gal.	95.00
Benoni Mineral Water Works, Skittle Shape, Aqua, Codd, 9 In.	67.00
Black-Artesian Water, Louisville, Ky., 12 Panels, Pontil, Pt.	275.00
Blout Springs Natural Sulphur Water, Cobalt Blue, Pt.	50.00
Blout Springs Natural Sulphur Water, Cobalt Blue, Qt.	178.00
Boyd & Beard, Yellow Green, IP, 6 1/2 In.	232.00
Brand's, Toledo, Oh., Cobalt Blue, IP, 7 In.	303.00
Buffalo Mineral Springs Water, Honey Amber	90.00
Buffum Sarsaparilla & Lemon, Cobalt, 10-Sided, 7 5/8 In.	825.00
Buffum Sarsaparilla & Lemon, Deep Aqua, 10-Sided, 7 3/8 In.	242.00
Buffum Sarsaparilla & Mineral Water, Cobalt Blue, 8 In.	715.00
Burr & Waters Bottlers, Buffalo, N. Y., Sapphire	1400.00
C. A. Reiners Improved, Moon & Stars, Deep Aqua	45.00
C. Cleminshaw, Troy, N. Y., Sapphire Blue, IP, 6 7/8 In.	192.00
C. Garforth Mineral Water, Wheeling, W. Va., IP	250.00
Caladonia Spring, Wheelock, Vt. Honey Amber, 1870-1880, Qt.	605.00
Clarke & Co., Saratoga, N. Y., Green, Pontil, Pt.	125.00
Clarke & Co., Saratoga, N. Y., Olive, IP, Pt.	85.00
Clarke & White, New York With C, Olive, BIM, Qt.	52.00
Clarke & White, New York, Deep Olive Green, 1850-1860, Pt.	60.00
Clarke & White, New York, Deep Yellow Olive, Cylindrical, Pt.	154.00
Clarke & White, New York, Olive Green, Pt.	50.00 To 75.00
Clarke & White, New York, Olive Green, Pt., Variant	88.00
Coffes Potash Water, Birmingham, Cobalt Blue, Cylinder	450.00
Congress & Empire Spring Co., Emerald Green, 1870s, Qt.	72.00
Congress & Empire Spring Co., Golden Amber, Cylindrical, Qt.	99.00
Congress & Empire Spring Co., Green, Cylindrical, Qt.	132.00
Congress & Empire Spring Co., Olive Green, Qt.	77.00
Congress & Empire Spring Co., Teal, BIM, Pt.	38.00
Congress & Empire Spring Co., Teal, Qt.	58.00
Congress & Empire Spring Co., Yellow Olive, Pt.	88.00
Congress Spring Co., Emerald, Burst Bubble, Pt.	15.00
Darien Mineral Springs, Darien Centre, N. Y., Blue Green, Pt.	385.00
Deep Rock Artesian Fresh, Green, White & Red Pyro, 1/2 Gal.	65.00
Deep Rock Spring, Oswego, N. Y., Aqua, Qt.	88.00
Deep Rock Spring, Oswego, N. Y., Blue Green, Pt.	453.00

Edwards, Columbia, Pa., Green Aqua, Pontil	60.00
Enterprise Mineral Water Co., Milford, Dela., Fluted, 8 In.	12.50
Excelsior Spring, Saratoga, N. Y., Green, 1860–1870, Pt.	110.00
Excelsior Spring, Saratoga, N. Y., Yellow Olive, 1870, Pt.	55.00
F. Gleasons, Rochester, N. Y., Cobalt Blue, Tenpin, 8 1/4 In.	1073.00
Florida Water, Murray & Lanman, N. Y., Label, ABM, Corker	16.00
Franklin Spring, Ballston Spa, Emerald, 7 3/4 In.	523.00
G. W. Weston, Green, Qt.	90.00
Gardner & Landon Sharon Sulphur, Olive Green, Qt.	825.00
Gettysburg Katalysine Water, Yellow Green, Qt.	45.00
Geyser Soda Springs, Aqua, Pt.	65.00
Geyser Spring, Saratoga Spouting Spring, Aqua, Pt.	90.00
Ghirardelli's Branch, Oakland, Cobalt Blue, 7 3/8 In.	413.00
Gleason & Cole, Pittsburgh, Cobalt Blue, 10–Sided, 7 1/4 In.	358.00
Gleason's, Rochester, N. Y., Cobalt Blue, Tenpin	525.00
Gleason's, Rochester, N. Y., Sapphire Blue, Tenpin, 1/2 Pt.	1705.00
Guilford Mineral Spring Water, Guilford, Vt., Olive, Qt.	83.00
Hathorn Springs, Amber, Qt.	25.00
Hathorn Springs, Black Amber, Qt.	35.00
Hathorn Springs, Dark Amber, Pt.	40.00
Hennicker Magnetic Springs	430.00
High Rock Congress Springs, Saratoga, N. Y., Olive Yellow, Pt.	231.00
High Rock Congress Springs, Saratoga, Twig Sides, Green, Pt.	358.00
Highland Spring Water, Blue Forest, St. Paul, Mn., 1/2 Gal.	10.00
Honesdale Glassworks, Pa., Medium Emerald Green	50.00
J. & A. Dearborn, N. Y., Sapphire Blue, Octagonal, 7 3/4 In.	242.00
J. B. Edwards, Columbia, Pa., Aqua, IP	30.00
J. Boardman, New York, Cobalt Blue, Octagonal, IP ....*Illus*	314.00
J. Dowdall, Superior Mineral Water, Cobalt Blue, 7 In.	605.00
J. N. Gerdis, Aqua, Octagonal, Blob Top	45.00
J. Simonds, Boston, Aqua, 1850, 7 1/8 In.	120.00
J. Simonds, Boston, Green, IP, 7 1/8 In.	105.00
John Clarke, New York, Olive Green, Saratoga, 1860–1870, Qt.	143.00
Kissing Water, Hanbury Smith, Olive Green, 1/2 Pt.	50.00
Lamoille Spring, Milton, Vt., Honey Amber, 1870–1880, Qt.	935.00
Lynch & Clarke, Deep Yellow Olive, Cylindrical, Pontil, Pt.	88.00
Lynch & Clarke, N. Y., Olive Amber, Cylindrical, Pontil, Qt.	110.00
Lynch & Clarke, N. Y., Olive Amber, Pontil, Pt.	210.00
Lynch & Clarke, N. Y., Yellow Olive, Cylindrical, Pontil, Pt.	176.00
M. Altenbauch's, Pittsburgh, Cobalt, 10–Sided, IP, 7 In.	550.00
M. T. Crawford, Hartford, Ct., Cobalt Blue, IP, 7 1/2 In.	275.00
Massena Spring, Monogram, Light Blue, AP, Qt.	135.00
Massena Spring, Monogram, Light Blue, Applied Lip, Qt.	135.00
Middletown Healing Springs, Middletown, Vt., Amber, Qt.	70.00
Middletown Healing Springs, Middletown, Vt., Emerald, Qt.	550.00
Missisquoi Springs, Squaw, Medium Olive Green, Qt.	400.00
Moses, Figural, Poland Springs, Green, Flared Lip, 10 7/8 In.	192.00
Moses, Figural, Poland Springs, Honey Amber, 11 In.	495.00
Mt. Clemens Mineral Spring Co. Ltd., Golden Yellow, Pt.	550.00
Oak Orchard Acid Springs, Alabama, Blue Green, Qt.	187.00
Oak Orchard Acid Springs, N. Y., Emerald, Qt.	132.00
Oak Orchard Acid Springs, N. Y., Yellow Amber, Qt.	83.00
Oak Orchard Acid Springs, Saratoga, Amber, Qt.	75.00
Oldham Aerated Water Co., Ltd., Aqua, Green Lip, Codd, 7 In.	488.00
Pavilion & U.S. Spring Co., Saratoga, N. Y., Emerald, Pt.	440.00
Pavilion & U.S. Spring Co., Saratoga, N. Y., Yellow Olive, Pt.	880.00
Purities Distilled Water, Amber, Qt.	25.00
Quaker Springs, I. W. Meader & Co., Pt.	650.00
Richfield Springs, N. Y., Sulphur Water, Emerald, Pt.	375.00
Roussel's, Philadelphia, Dark Blue Green, IP, 7 In.	77.00
Rutherford's Premium, Cincinnati, 10–Sided, Cobalt Blue	150.00
S. Moore Superior, Phila., Deep Blue Green, IP .... 120.00 To 135.00
S. Premium, Deep Green, Octagonal, IP, 7 5/8 In.	220.00

Mineral Water, Well Picture, Embossed,
Green, 9 In.

Mineral Water, J.Boardman, New York,
Cobalt Blue, Octagonal, IP

Saratoga Seltzer Water, Teal, 1/2 Pt.	115.00
Saratoga Seltzer Water, Teal, Rolled Lip, Pt.	40.00
Saratoga Spring Co., Large A, Olive Green, 1866–1889, Pt.	154.00
Saratoga Star, Spring, Backward S., Green, Qt.	100.00
Saratoga Vichy Water, Golden Amber, Cylindrical, Qt.	137.00
Saratoga Vichy Water, Reddish Amber, Cylindrical, Qt.	377.00
Saratoga Vichy Water, Saratoga, N. Y., Amber, Qt.	220.00
Saratoga Vichy Water, Yellow Amber, Cylindrical, Pt.	154.00
Seitz & Bro., Easton, Pa., Emerald Green, Octagonal	25.00
Seitz & Bro., Easton, Pa., Premium, Sapphire, Octagonal	190.00
Seltz & Bro., Easton, Pa., Cobalt Blue, IP	50.00
South Omaha Independent Mineral Springs, Aqua, Crown Top	8.00
St. Regis Water Massena Springs, Blue Green, 1870–1880, Qt.	143.00
Stevens & Co., Lancaster Glassworks, Cobalt Blue, 6 3/4 In.	2200.00
Stirling's Magnetic Mineral Spring, Amber, Saratoga, Qt.	100.00
Summit Mineral, Garrison, Maine, Decanter, 1870–1880, 10 In.	50.00
Superior, B & C, San Francisco, Deep Cobalt Blue, 6 1/2 In.	293.00
Superior, Embossed D, Morristown, N. J., Deep Green	325.00
Superior, Octagonal, Cobalt Blue, IP	125.00 To 175.00
Superior, Phila., Green, 10–Sided, Mug Base	395.00
Superior, Twitchell, Emerald Green, IP, 6 7/8 In.	176.00
Superior, Twitchell, Green, Pontil, Lip Ring, 7 1/4 In.	170.00
Superior, Twitchell, Philadelphia, Blue Green, IP	39.00
Superior, Twitchell, Philadelphia, Blue Green, Squatty	19.00
Superior, Union Glass, Philadelphia, Cobalt Blue, IP	150.00
Superior, Utica Bottling, A. L. Edic, Superior, Green, IP	150.00
Superior, V. Mager, Cobalt Blue, IP	575.00
Syracuse Springs Excelsior, A. J. Delatour, Citron, 1/2 Pt.	335.00
Syracuse Springs Excelsior, Amber Shaded, 7 3/4 In.	305.00
Syracuse Springs Excelsior, Yellow Amber, Pt.	314.00
Thompson's, Union Soda Works, Aqua, Tenpin, 7 5/8 In.	154.00
Tifft & Perry, Darien Centre, N. Y., Blue Green, Pt.	450.00
Vermont Saxe & Co., Sheldon, Vt., Olive, BIM, Qt.	58.00
Vermont Spring, Saxe & Co., Sheldon, Vt., Yellow Amber, Qt.	413.00
Virginia Etna Springs Co., Vinton, Va., Tenpin, ABM	6.00
W. Eagle Superior, Cobalt Blue, Pontil	110.00
W. Eagle, N. Y., Sapphire Blue, IP, 7 1/4 In.	242.00
Washington Spring, Washington, Ballston Spa, Emerald, Pt.	425.00
Well Picture, Embossed, Green, 9 In. ....*Illus*	16.00
Witter Springs, Amber, Paper Label	18.00

Wm. A. Carpenter's, Hudson, Yellow Green, Octagonal, 7 In.	495.00
Wm. Betz, Pittsburgh, Aqua, 10–Sided, 1850, 8 In.	357.00
Wm. Betz, Salem, Oh., Light Apple Green, 10–Sided, 7 1/4 In.	220.00
Wm. P. Davis & Co., Brooklyn, Cobalt, Octagonal, 7 1/2 In.	126.00
Wm. W. Lappeus Premium, Cobalt Blue, 10–Sided, 7 3/8 In.	385.00
Ypsilanti Salts, Mich., Aqua, Contents, Round, 6 In.	12.00

MINIATURE

Most of the major modern liquor companies that make full–sized decanters and bottles quickly learned that miniature versions sell well too. Modern miniatures are listed in this book by brand name. There are also many older miniature bottles that were made as give–aways. Most interesting of these are the small motto jugs that name a liquor or bar, and the comic figural bottles. Collectors sometimes specialize in glass animal miniatures, beer bottles, whiskey bottles, or other types. Interested collectors can join the Lilliputian Bottle Club, 5626 Corning Ave., Los Angeles, CA 90056; or subscribe to Miniature Bottle Collector, P.O. Box 2161, Palos Verdes, CA 90274.

MINIATURE, Ballantine, Scotch, Jug, White, Cobalt, 3 In.	15.00
Beer, Acme Beer, San Francisco, Amber, Paper Label, 4 In.	8.00
Beer, Barbarosa Beer, Amber, Paper Label, 4 In.	12.00
Beer, Barbarosa Beer, Brown, 3 In.	10.00
Beer, Berkart, Amber, Paper Label, 4 In.	5.00
Beer, Blatz, Amber, Paper Label, 4 In.	5.00 To 8.00
Beer, Blatz, Brown	5.00
Beer, Carling Black Label, Brown	16.00
Beer, Carling, Amber, Paper Label, 4 In.	16.00
Beer, Coors, Brown, Salt Celler Top, 3 In.	1.00
Beer, Country Cook, Amber, Paper Label, 4 In.	5.00
Beer, East Side, Amber, Paper Label, 4 In.	12.00
Beer, East Side, Brown	12.00
Beer, Esslinger Premium, Amber, Paper Label, 4 In.	13.00
Beer, Esslinger Premium, Brown	13.00
Beer, Falsenbrau, Brown	8.00
Beer, Falsom Brown, Amber, Paper Label, 4 In.	12.00
Beer, Falstaff Super X, Brown, 3 In.	10.00
Beer, Flex Beer, Brown	10.00
Beer, Genuine Porter, Amber, Paper Label, 4 In.	7.00
Beer, Gold Bond, Amber, Paper Label, 4 In.	40.00
Beer, High–Life, Clear, 3 In.	10.00
Beer, Lonestar, Brown	16.00

Miniature, Benton, Myers & Co., Cleveland, Oh., Whiskey, Jug

Miniature, J. Fries, Cleveland, Oh., Whiskey, Jug

Miniature, Wine, Duroy Wine Co., Tokay, Cleveland, Oh., Jug

Miniature, Schlitz, Beer, 4 In.

Miniature, Budweiser, Beer, 4 In.

Beer, Lonestar, San Antonio, Amber, Paper Label, 4 In. 16.00
Beer, Lord Derby Premium, Amber, Paper Label, 4 In. 8.00
Beer, Misner Brand, Pilsner, Amber, Paper Label, 4 In. 12.00
Beer, Old Colony Chief Stout, Boston, Amber, Paper Label, 4 In. 10.00
Beer, Old Dutch, Amber, Paper Label, 4 In. 20.00
Beer, Old Vienna, Amber, Paper Label, 4 In. 6.00
Beer, Pabst Blue Ribbon, Brown, 3 In. 6.00
Beer, Prior, Amber, Paper Label, 4 In. 20.00
Beer, Real German Brand, Conelsburg, Amber, Paper Label, 4 In. 10.00
Beer, Red–Top Ale, Amber, Paper Label, 4 In. 15.00
Beer, Red–Top Ale, Brown 15.00
Beer, Rupert, Brown, 3 In. 10.00
Beer, Schlitz, Amber, Paper Label, 4 In. 12.00
Beer, Silver Label Lager, Amber, Paper Label, 4 In. 8.00
Beer, Steins Canandagua Light Ale, Amber, Paper Label, 4 In. 8.00
Beer, Tip–Top Bohemian, Amber, Label, Salt Shaker Top, 4 In. 40.00
Beer, Trophy, Amber, Paper Label, 4 In. 7.00
Beer, Valley Forge, Amber, Paper Label, 4 In. 20.00
Beer, Valley Forge, Brown 20.00
Beer, Virginia Special Export Beer, Amber, Paper Label, 4 In. 60.00
Bells 8, Blended Scotch Whiskey, Amber, Label 14.00
Benton, Myers & Co., Cleveland, Oh., Whiskey, Jug ....*Illus* 65.00
Bird Set, Fremont Abbey, 6 Piece 60.00
Blown, Olive Amber, Flared Lip, Pontil, 1800–1840, 2 3/4 In. 220.00
Budweiser, Beer, 4 In. ....*Illus* 3.50
Cointreau, White Nun, Whiskey 20.00
Cottage, Mead 5.00
Cream Pure Rye, Amber, Rectangular, Fluted Shoulders 8.00
Dog, Spotted, 3 3/4 In. ....*Illus* 24.00
Dr Pepper, Cap 2.00
Dr. Bouvier's Buchu Gin, Square, BIM, 4 1/4 In. 28.00
Duffy's Malt, Whiskey, Rochester, N. Y., Amber, 3 3/4 In. 15.00
Duffy's Malt, Whiskey, Sample 20.00
Dug's Nevada Brothels, Barbara's My Place, No. 10, 1981 .... 25.00
Dug's Nevada Brothels, Desert Club, No. 16. No. 1982 .... 25.00
Dug's Nevada Brothels, Doll House, No. 13, 1982 .... 25.00
Dug's Nevada Brothels, Julia Bulette, 1991 .... 39.00
Dug's Nevada Brothels, La Belle, No. 7, 1980 .... 29.00
Dug's Nevada Brothels, Lucky Strike, No. 3, 1978 .... 29.00
Dug's Nevada Brothels, Moonlight Ranch, 20th Anniversary, 1991 .... 375.00
Dug's Nevada Brothels, Moonlight Ranch, No. 1, 1977 .... 295.00
Dug's Nevada Brothels, Patricia's Hacienda, No. 8, 1981 .... 35.00
Dug's Nevada Brothels, Raft 15.00
Dug's Nevada Brothels, Sharon, 1991 .... 35.00
Fabb Maraschino, M. Magazzino Azar, Turquoise, Square, 6 In. 66.00
Ferd Westheimer & Sons, Whiskey, Red Top, Amber, 4 1/2 In. 25.00
Food, Yoo–Hoo Chocolate Drink, Clear, Yellow Label, 3 In. 5.00
Four Roses, Amber, Emblem Roses, 1/10 Pt. 20.00
Gin, Herman Vansen Schiedam, Black Glass, Applied Lip, 4 3/8 In. 55.00
Golden Wedding, 1/10 Pt. .... 16.00 To 25.00
Goose, Ryenbende 11.00
Guinness, Brown, Champagne Shaped, Label, Crown Cap, 3 1/3 In. 27.00
Hardy Capt. Junior, Cognac, Crystal 65.00
Henry McKenna, White, Blue Pyro, 1/10 Pt. 20.00
Herman Jansen, Schiedam, Case, Gin, Black, 4 1/2 In. 54.00
Hotel Donnelley, Tacoma, Whiskey, Flask, Matching Lid, 2 Oz. 40.00
House, Canal No. 9, Ryenbende 10.00
Iler's Eagle Gin, Willow Springs Distillery, Omaha, Neb. 40.00
J. Fries, Cleveland, Oh., Whiskey, Jug ....*Illus* 65.00
J. Lewis, London, Key Design, Aqua, Embossed Hamilton, 2 5/8 In. 118.00
J. Reiger & Co., Distributors, Whiskey, Kansas City, Mo. 12.00
Jug, A Cordial Greeting, H. S., Handle, 1 3/4 In. 25.00
Jug, Bronte, Label 18.00

Miniature, Dog, Spotted, 3 3/4 In.

Miniature, Sechsamtertropfen, Figural,
Liqueur, 5 1/2 In.

Jug, Queen's Castle, Scotland, Label, 2 1/2 In.	15.00
Kellerstrauss Distilling Company	18.00
Laughlan Rose & Co., Leith, Golden Amber, Cylinder, 3 7/8 In.	182.00
Liqueur, Kahlua, Black Russian	12.00
Liqueur, Kahlua, Goddess, Green	7.00
Loch Ness Monster, Beneagle	8.00
MBC, 1st National Bank	20.00
MBC, Foxes, Pair	20.00
MBC, Geisha, Set of 6	42.00
MBC, Globe	9.00
MBC, Horseshoe, Las Vegas	9.00
MBC, Horseshoe, Reno	9.00
MBC, Landmark Hotel	8.00
MBC, Peddler	11.00
MBC, Pennsylvania Dutch	20.00
Mitt, What A Catch, Silver State Specialties	12.00
Monarch Old Scotch Whiskey, Scotland, Jug, 3 1/2 In.	10.00
Mount Vernon Pure Rye, Amber, 3 In.	10.00
Muff Warmer, Cream Glazed, Applied Leaves, West Bros., 4 In.	118.00
Olde Curiosity Shop, Aidee	7.00
Orange Crush	2.00
Paul Jones Pure Rye, Louisville, Amber	7.00
Rabbit, Aidee	5.00
Rabbit, Ryenbende	11.00
RC Cola, Cap	2.00
Red Roses, Amber	15.00
Rose & Co., Black, Classic Vines 2 Sides, 5 In.	102.00
Royal Flush, Silver State Specialties, Miniature	12.00
Schlitz, Beer, 4 In. ....*Illus*	3.50
Sechsamtertropfen, Figural, Liqueur, 5 1/2 In. ....*Illus*	75.00
Shoe, Ryenbende	12.00
Soda, Be One Lime–Lemon Soda, Colonial Beverages Esq., 6 Oz.	5.00
Soda, Dr. Nuf, 6 1/2 Oz.	5.50
Soda, Good Drink Chase & Mixer, Green	6.00
Soda, Hires Root Beer, 3 In.	15.00
Soda, Hires Root Beer, Brown, Yellow Label, Pyro	6.00
Soda, Orange Crush, 3 In.	26.00
Soda, Pep–Up, Big Boy Beverage, Cleveland, Green, 6 1/2 Oz.	6.00
Soda, Royal Crown Cola, 3 In.	15.00
Soda, Squirt, Plastic Top, 3 In.	5.00
Soda, White Rock Ginger Ale, 7 Oz.	4.00
Sprite, Cap	2.00
Squirrel, Beneagle	9.00

Squirrel, Forcol	6.00
Squirrel, Mead	5.00
Swan, Ryenbende	11.00
Teacher's, Crystal, Scotch, Cylindrical, Tall	13.00
Teem, Cap	2.00
Urn, Ryenbende, Round	10.00
Violin, Light Aqua, No Music On Back	12.00
Whiskey, Crown Distiller	30.00
Whiskey, Duffy's Malt, Bright Yellow, Sample, 4 1/2 In.	30.00
Whiskey, Irish Mist, Guard	8.00
Whiskey, Jack Daniels, Bell of Lincoln	18.00
Whiskey, Jack Daniels, Gold Medal	25.00
Whiskey, Jack Daniels, Maxwell House	30.00
Whiskey, Jack Daniels, Riverboat Captain	20.00
Whiskey, Jesse Moore	55.00
Whiskey, King Kamehameha, Hawaiian Distillers	12.00
Whiskey, King of Kings, Jug	18.00
Whiskey, Mt. Vernon Pure Rye	13.00
Whiskey, Tribute To Tennessee	25.00
Wilshire Dry Gin, C. F. Heublein & Co., Gin, Clear, ABM, 3 1/8 In.	12.00
Wine, Duroy Wine Co., Tokay, Cleveland, Oh., Jug ....*Illus*	60.00
Wine, Grande Wine, Extravielle, Light Green, 3 7/8 In.	3.25
Yoo-Hoo, Cap	2.00
Zara Seal, Turquoise, Crude Applied Lip, 6 1/4 In.	78.00
Zara Seal, Turquoise, Square Body, 6 1/4 In.	91.00

MR. BOSTON, see Old Mr. Boston

--------------------------------- **NAILSEA TYPE** ---------------------------------

The intricate glass called *Nailsea* was made in the Bristol district of England from 1788 to 1873. The glass included loopings of white or colored glass worked in patterns. The characteristic look of Nailsea was copied and what is called Nailsea today is really Nailsea type made in England or even America. Nailsea gemel bottles are of particular interest to collectors.

NAILSEA TYPE, Bar, White Looping, Large Neck Ring, Pontil, 1860–1880, 12 In.	165.00
Clear, Opaque White Looping, Pontil, Late 19th Century, 8 In.	88.00
Clear, White Looping, Free–Blown, Pontil, Mid–19th C., Pt.	100.00
Dark Olive, White Flecks, Gloppy Applied Handle, 9 In.	1558.00
Flask, Clear, Cobalt Ribs	150.00
Flask, Clear, Pink, Yellow, White, Green Loopings, Pontil, 5 In.	121.00
Flask, Teardrop Form, Cranberry, Pontil, 6 3/8 In.	286.00
Rolling Pin, Dark Olive Amber, White Flecks, 13 1/4 In.	88.00

----------------------------------- **NURSING** -----------------------------------

Pottery nursing bottles were used by 1500 B.C. If a bottle was needed, one was improvised, and stone, metal, wood, and pottery, as well as glass bottles were made through the centuries. A glass bottle was patented by Charles Windship of Roxbury, Massachusetts, in 1841. Its novel design suggested that the bottle be placed over the breast to try to fool the baby into thinking the milk came from the mother. By 1864 the most common nursing bottle was a nipple attached to a glass tube in a cork that was put into a glass bottle. Unfortunately, it was impossible to clean and was very unsanitary. The nursing bottle in use today was made possible by the developement of an early 1900s rubber nipple.

Nursing bottles are easily identified by the unique shape and the measuring units that are often marked on the sides. Some early examples had engraved designs and silver nipples but most are made of clear glass and rubber. There is a collectors club, The American Collectors of Infant Feeders, 5161 West 59th Street, Indianapolis, IN 46254, and a publication called *Keeping Abreast*. A reference book, *A Guide to American Nursing Bottles* by Diane Rouse Ostrander, is also available.

NURSING, 24 Vertical Ribs	150.00
Acme, WT & Co., Star, Turtle, 1880, 8 Oz.	25.00

Avondale Milk, Hygeia Screw Top, Round	15.00
Babee & Brockway, Words For Cross, Hexagonal, 1930s, 8 Oz.	11.00
Baby Bunting, Clear, 4 Oz.	6.00
Baby Dear, Midget	15.00
Baby's Delight, Baby, With Turtle Bottle, McKee, 1890, 8 Oz.	75.00
Baby's First Ayrton's, Double Ended, England, 7 Lines For Oz.	22.50
BB Safety Nursing, Flask, Push Base, Aluminum Collar, 1897	25.00
Blown, 16 Diamonds, Pale Green, Midwestern, 7 In.	210.00
Blown, 16 Ribs, Light Green, 6 5/8 In.	50.00
Blown, 16 Ribs, Presentation Label Dated 1894, 5 7/8 In.	75.00
Boy & Girl, Words Hansel & Gretel, Blue Paint, 8 Oz.	12.50
Burr, Boston, Aqua, Medallion	40.00
Clifton Feeder, AB Monogram, Pale Green, Bubbles, 8 Oz.	30.00
Clifton Feeder, Pear Shape, Glass Stopper, Tablespoons, 9 In.	9.00
Crown Feeding, Crown In Circle, Turtle, Threaded Mouth, 1885, 8 Oz.	30.00
Curity, Kendall Co., Concave Waist, Square, 8 Oz.	7.00
Davol, Anti–Colic, Blue Paint, Square, 1950s, 8 Oz.	8.00
Dimples Hygienic Feeding, Double Ended, England, 7 Lines For Oz.	22.50
Echo Farm Milk, Blue Paint, Round, 8 Oz.	10.00
Echo Farm Milk, Safe For Babies, Blue, Pyro, Round, Pullover Finish	12.00
Embossed Baby, 7 In. ....*Illus*	9.00
Embossed Bottom Baby Care, Round, Flat Side, Green Dome, 8 Oz.	8.00
Embossed Rabbit, 7 In. ....*Illus*	9.00
Empire, WT & Co. Monogram, Clear, Teardrop	12.00
Evenflo, Calib, Hexagon, Double Lined, Red Paint, Cover, 8 Oz.	7.00
Franklin	4.00
Free–Blown, Narrow Teat End, 4 Glass Attachments, 7 1/2 In.	82.00
Garipwell, H. B. M., Double Ended, Oblong, England, 7 Lines For Oz.	22.50
Golden Arrow, Hexagonal, Complete Top, Orange, Oz. & Ml.	30.00
Good Health For Baby, Taxston Dairy, Red, Round, Pullover Finish	15.00
Graduated, Amethyst, 8 Oz.	15.00
Grip–Tite, Box	20.00
Gulf Life Ins. Co., Red Paint, Screw Cap, 8 Oz.	15.00
Happy Baby, Baby Picture, Oval, 1930–1944, 8 Oz.	10.00
Hygeia, Ball, Embossed, Round, 8 Oz.	5.00

Nursing, Embossed Baby, 7 In.   *Nursing, Embossed Rabbit, 7 In.*

Hygeia, Calibrated, Dull Red Paint, Round, Screw Top, 4 Oz.	3.00
Hygeia, Life of Virginia, Torch, Green Paint, Screw Cap, 8 Oz.	15.00
Hygeia, Round, Pat. June 19, 1894 & Dec. 5, 1916, 8 Oz.	30.00 To 40.00
Hygeia, Southern Diaper Service, Red Paint, Round, 8 Oz.	12.50
Ideal, Pean Co., Shield, Double Ended, Bubbles, England	22.50
Independent Life & Accident Ins. Co., Blue Paint, Round, 8 Oz.	15.00
Liberty National Life Ins. Co., Red Pyro, Round, Screw Cap, 8 Oz.	15.00
Life Insurance Co. of Ga., Blue Paint, Round, Screw Cap, 8 Oz.	15.00
Life Insurance Co. of Ga., Green Pyro, Round, Screw Cap, 8 Oz.	15.00
Life Security With Life & Casualty Ins., Tenn., Blue, Screw Top	50.00
Lifeboat, Double Ended, Bubbles, France, Numbers Up To 15	35.00
Michigan State University, Green Paint, Round, Cap, 8 Oz.	20.00
Milverton & Norman & Leamington, Aqua Tint, 1864–1915, 8 Oz.	30.00
Muted Broken Swirl, Pale Green, Molded, 1820–1840, 8 1/8 In.	75.00
Muted Diamond, Pale Green, Molded, 1820–1840, 6 In.	70.00
N. Woods & Sons, Turtle, 1870s, 8 Oz.	25.00
National Baby's Formula Service, Chicago, Orange Pyro, Square	40.00
Nursmatic Insta–Value Nurser, Rounded Hexagon, Red Paint, 8 Oz.	8.00
Nursmatic Words Finest Nurser, Blue Paint, Rounded Hexagon, 8 Oz.	8.00
Nursmatic, Hanks Craft, Thermoglas, Hexagonal, 8 Oz.	5.00
Paulus Dairy, New Brunswick, Blue, Flat Sides, Pullover Finish	15.00
Phoenix Ovale, Oval, 1940, 8 Oz.	8.00
Pyrex, Upright, Round, Clear	10.00
Pyrex, Words Form Cross, Hexagonal, 8 Oz.	5.00 To 7.00
Rigo Improved, Montreal, Quebec, Oblong, Pat. 1922, 8 Oz.	15.00
San Diego State University, Black Paint, Round, 8 Oz.	20.00
San Diego State University, Evenflo Emblem, Hexagonal, Orange	35.00
Sears, Pinched Waist, Baby, Yellow Pyro, 8 Oz.	8.00
Sears, Pinched Waist, Flowers, Yellow Pyro, 8 Oz.	8.00
SMA Wyeth, Nipple Retainer Ring, Frosted Shoulders, Round, 4 Oz.	2.00
Steadifeed, Hexagonal, Embossed, Black Cap	6.00
Stork, Easily Cleaned & Hygienic, Round, Waisted, 8 Oz.	15.00
Stork, Nipple Valve Nurser, Light Blue Paint, Hexagon, 8 Oz.	9.00
Toothsome Tit Bit, In Circle, BS & B, Threaded, 18 Tbsp. & 9 Oz.	30.00
Universal Feeder, Monogrammed, Clear	25.00
Walker Gordon Modified Milk Laboratory, 12 Oz.	35.00

--------------------------------------- **OBR** ---------------------------------------

Old Blue Ribbon, or OBR, bottles were made from 1969 to about 1974.

OBR, Balloon, 1962	10.00
Bus, 5th Avenue, 1971	18.00
Caboose, 1973	28.00
Engine, General, 1974	15.00
Football Player, 1972	18.00
Pierce Arrow, 1969	12.00
Prairie Wagon, 1969	8.00
River Queen, 1967	10.00
Titanic, 1970	38.00
W. C. Fields, Top Hat, 1976	26.00

--------------------------------------- **OIL** ---------------------------------------

Motor oil, battery oil, and sewing machine and lubricating oils were all sold in bottles. Any bottle that has the word *oil* either embossed in the glass or on the paper label falls in this category. A battery jar has straight sides and an open top. It was filled with a chemical solution. The jars were usually made with a zinc plate or a copper plate plus a suspended carbon plate. With the proper connections the chemicals and metals generated an electric current. Many companies made batteries that included glass jars, and the jars are now appearing at bottle shows. In the Edison battery, the solution was covered with a special protective layer of oil which kept it from evaporating. Edison battery oil jars, dating from about 1889, were specially made to hold the protective and can still be found.

OIL, American Oil, Cumberland River, Ky., Aqua, OP, 6 7/8 In.	495.00

Oil, Kalos Mani-Rosa Manicuring Oil, E. Burnham, 3 1/4 In.

Oil, Sewing Machine, Singer, Square, 5 In.

Oil, Three In One, Cleans & Polishes, Paper Label, Box

Bear's Oil, Bear At Stream Label, Aqua, 4 In.	6.00
Edison Battery, ABM	5.00
Edison Battery, Aqua	5.00
Electrical Bicycle Lubricating Oil, Flask, Pumpkin Seed, Contents	180.00
Gargling Oil, Lockport, N. Y., Emerald Green, Rectangular, BIM, 5 1/4 In.	14.00
Gargling Oil, Lockport, N. Y., Olive Amber, 5 3/4 In.	385.00
Gargling Oil, Lockport, N. Y., Yellow Amber, Part Label, 5 1/2 In.	132.00
Hamlin's Wizard Oil, Cincinnati, Ohio, Aqua, OP, Oval, 4 In.	58.00
I. Rokeach & Sons Inc. Oil Refiners, Brooklyn, N. Y., Amethyst, 7 7/8 In.	30.00
Kalos Mani–Rosa Manicuring Oil, E. Burnham, 3 1/4 In. ....*Illus*	7.00
Kickapoo Oil	3.00
Little's White Oil, Scottsville, Va., Aqua, OP, 6 1/16 In.	154.00
McLeans Volcanic Oil Liniment, Aqua, OP, Square, Indented Panels, 4 In.	80.00
Prof. DeGrath's Electric Oil, Clear, Rolled Lip, OP	40.00
Salvation Oil, Meyer Co., Baltimore, Aqua, Oval, Indented Panel, 7 In.	25.00
Sewing Machine, F. S. Pease, Buffalo, N. Y. Cornflower Blue, OP, 5 3/4 In.	300.00
Sewing Machine, Singer, Square, 5 In. ....*Illus*	5.00
Sewing Machine, Small	3.50
Standard Oil Co., Ind., Metal Spout & Screw Cap, Clear, Qt.	10.00
Three In One, Cleans & Polishes, Paper Label, Box ....*Illus*	15.00
Tiolene Motor Oil, Pure Oil Co., Clear, Qt.	20.00
Youatt's Gargling Oil, Comstock & Brother, N. Y., Aqua, OP, 7 5/8 In.	495.00
Youatt's Gargling Oil, Comstock & Brother, N. Y., Aqua, OP, 9 In.	275.00

OLD BARDSTOWN

Old Bardstown was made and bottled by the Willit Distilling Company in Bardstown, Kentucky. Figural bottles were made from about 1977 to 1980. One unusual bottle pictured Foster Brooks, the actor who is best known for his portrayal of drunks.

OLD BARDSTOWN, Bulldog, 1980	110.00
Christmas Card, 1977	16.00
Delta Queen Riverboat, 1980	40.00
Foster Brooks, 1978	17.00
Horse, Citation, 1979	133.00
Iron Worker, 1978	31.00

Keg, With Stand, 1977, 1/2 Gal.	16.00
Keg, With Stand, 1977, Gal.	27.00
Surface Miner, 1978	21.00
Trucker, 1978	20.00
Wildcat, No. 2, 1979	31.00

─────────────── **OLD COMMONWEALTH** ───────────────

Old Commonwealth bottles have been made since 1975 by J. P. Van Winkle and Sons, Louisville, Kentucky. They also put out bottles under the Old Rip Van Winkle label. An apothecary series with university names and other designs has been made from 1978 to the present. As few as 1,600 were made of some of these designs. Other bottles depict firemen, coal miners, fishermen, Indians, dogs, horses, or leprechauns. Some of the decanters were made with music box inserts. The distillery will sell empty bottles to collectors interested in completing a set. Write to 2843 Brownsboro Road, Louisville, KY 40206.

OLD COMMONWEALTH, Alabama Crimson Tide, 1981	18.00
Auburn Tigers, 1979	37.00
Castles of Ireland, 1990	28.00
Chief Illini, No. 1, 1979	120.00
Chief Illini, No. 2, 1981	60.00
Chief Illini, No. 3, 1983	70.00
Clemson Tigers, 1979	44.00
Coal Miner, Coal Shooter, 1983	30.00
Coal Miner, Coal Shooter, 1983, Miniature	20.00
Coal Miner, Lunch Time, 1980 ....*Illus*	35.00
Coal Miner, Lunch Time, 1983, Miniature	16.00
Coal Miner, Pick, 1976	30.00
Coal Miner, Pick, 1982, Miniature	20.00
Coal Miner, Shovel, 1977	90.00
Coal Miner, Shovel, 1981, Miniature	25.00
Coins of Ireland, 1979	25.00
Cottontail Rabbit, 1981	31.00
Dogs of Ireland, 1980	20.00
Fireman, 75th Anniversary, 1976	115.00
Fireman, Modern No. 1, Black Hat, 1982 .... 20.00 To	35.00
Fireman, Modern No. 1, Black Hat, 1982, Miniature	10.00
Fireman, Modern No. 1, Yellow Hat, 1982	50.00
Fireman, Modern No. 1, Yellow Hat, 1982, Miniature	22.00
Fireman, Modern No. 2, Nozzle Man, 1983	38.00
Fireman, Modern No. 2, Nozzle Man, 1983, Miniature	17.00
Fireman, Modern No. 3, On Call, 1983	50.00
Fireman, Modern No. 3, On Call, 1983, Miniature	20.00
Fireman, Modern No. 3, Yellow Helmet, 1983	47.00
Fireman, Modern No. 3, Yellow Helmet, 1983, Miniature	20.00
Fireman, Modern No. 4, Fallen Comrade, 1983	38.00
Fireman, Modern No. 4, Fallen Comrade, 1983, Miniature	24.00
Fireman, Modern No. 5, Harmony, 1984	45.00
Fireman, Modern No. 5, Harmony, 1984, Miniature	22.00
Fireman, No. 2, Volunteer, 1978	56.00
Fireman, No. 3, Valiant Volunteer, 1979	50.00
Fireman, No. 4, Heroic Volunteer, 1981	60.00
Fireman, No. 5, Lifesaver, 1983	45.00
Fireman, No. 5, Lifesaver, 1983, Miniature	24.00
Fireman, No. 6, Breaking Through, 1983	45.00
Fireman, No. 6, Breaking Through, 1983, Miniature	24.00
Fisherman, Keeper, 1980	37.00
Flowers of Ireland, 1983	20.00
Georgia Bulldog, 1982	25.00
Golden Retriever, 1979	35.00
Horses of Ireland, 1981 ....*Illus*	24.00
Houston University, 1977	28.00
Irish At The Sea, 1989	25.00
Irish Idyll, 1981	15.00

Irish Lore, 1988	24.00
Kansas State Wildcats, 1982	35.00
Kentucky Peach Bowl, 1977	30.00
Leprechaun, No. 1, Elusive, 1980	33.00
Leprechaun, No. 2, Irish Minstrel, 1982	32.00
Leprechaun, No. 3, Lucky, 1983	25.00
Leprechaun, No. 3, Lucky, 1983, Miniature	20.00
Louisville Champs, 1980	30.00
LSU Tiger, 1979	50.00
Lumberjack, Old Time, 1979	24.00
Maryland Terps, 1977	25.00
Missouri Tigers, 1979	40.00
North Carolina University, 1979	25.00
North Carolina, Bicentennial, 1975	25.00
Oktoberfest, 1983	40.00
Princeton University, 1976	18.00
Sons of Erin, No. 2, 1978	23.00
Sports of Ireland, 1987	23.00
St. Patrick's Day Parade, 1984	20.00
Symbols of Ireland, 1985	25.00
Tennessee Walking Horse, 1977	34.00
Thoroughbreds, Kentucky, 1977	35.00
USC Trojan Centennial, 1980	50.00
USC Trojan Centennial, 1980, Miniature	11.00
Virginia University, 1979	6.00
Waterfowler, No. 1, Hunter, 1978	45.00
Waterfowler, No. 2, Here They Come, 1980	35.00
Waterfowler, No. 3, Good Boy, 1981	37.00
Western Boot, 1982	20.00 To 22.00
Western Logger, 1980	30.00
Yankee Doodle, 1982	16.00

OLD CROW

Dr. James Crow of Kentucky was a surgeon and chemist from Edinburgh, Scotland. He started practicing medicine but decided to improve the quality of life by distilling corn whiskey instead. In those days, about 1835, whiskey was made by a family recipe with a bit of that and a handful of the other. The results were uneven. Dr. Crow was a scientist and used corn and limestone water to make a whiskey that he put into kegs and jugs. He used charred oak kegs, and the liquid became reddish instead of the clear white of corn liquor. More experiments led to his development of the first bourbon, named after northeastern Kentucky's Bourbon County, which had been named for the French royal family.

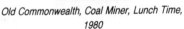

Old Commonwealth, Coal Miner, Lunch Time, 1980   *Old Commonwealth, Horses of Ireland, 1981*

Old Crow became a popular product in all parts of the country and was sold to saloons. Salesmen for competing brands would sometimes try to ruin the liquor by putting a snake or nail into the barrel. In 1870, for the first time, bourbon was bottled and sealed at the distillery. The distillery was closed during Prohibition, and when it reopened in 1933, Old Crow was purchased by National Distilleries. That Old Crow would be packaged in a crow–shaped decanter was inevitable, and in 1954 National Distillers Products Corporation of Frankfort, Kentucky, put Old Crow bourbon into a ceramic crow. Again in 1974 a crow decanter was used; this time 16,800 Royal Doulton bottles were made. The bourbon was sold in the 1970s in a series of bottles shaped like light or dark green chess pieces.

OLD CROW, Chess Set, No Rug, 32 Piece 250.00
Chess Set, With Rug, 32 Piece 300.00
Crow, Red Vest, 1974 .... 12.00 To 14.00
Crow, Royal Doulton 40.00
Knight, Green 20.00
Old Crow, Advertising 25.00
Queen, Light Green .... 10.00 To 20.00
Rook, Light Green 10.00

───────────────── **OLD FITZGERALD** ─────────────────

Stitzel Weller of Louisville, Kentucky, had a letterhead in 1971 that said *established 1849, America's oldest family distillery.* In 1972 the distillery was sold to Somerset Importers, Ltd., a division of Norton Simon Company, Inc. Somerset Importers continued to market the Old Fitzgerald series until 1978, when they sold it to Julian P. Van Winkle. He had started the series while president of the Old Fitzgerald Distillery. He continued making the decanter series under the brand Old Commonwealth. The Van Winkle series of bottles for both brands included only 20 bottles through 1986. In 1968 the Old Fitzgerald decanter carried the words *plase God.* Federal laws ruled this objectionable and the decanters were changed to read *prase be.* Esmark purchased Norton Simon in 1984, then sold the Old Fitzgerald label to Distillers of England in 1985, who sold it to Guinness Stout of Ireland in 1986. Guinness Stout has since become Guinness PLC of London, and its Louisville distillery is called United Distillers Production, Inc.

An out–of–print pamphlet called *Decanter Collector's Guide* pictures Old Fitzgerald decanters offered since 1951. Most are glass in a classic shape. A series of apothecary jars was made from 1969 to 1983. In 1971, when J. P. Van Winkle Jr. was president, the company, of course, made a Rip Van Winkle decanter. The distillery makes Old Fitzgerald bourbon, Cabin Still bourbon, and W. L. Weller bourbon. The Cabin Still decanters are also listed in this book. These include a series of hillbilly bottles made in the 1950s and 1960s, apothecary jars, and classic glass decanters.

OLD FITZGERALD, America's Cup, 1970 .... 15.00 To 17.00
American Sons, 1976 .... 15.00 To 16.00
Around We Go, Export Only, 1983 .... 20.00 To 22.00
Birmingham, 1972 .... 40.00
Blarney, Irish Toast, 1970 .... 15.00 To 16.00
Cabin Still, Anniversary, 1959 .... 10.00
Cabin Still, Copper Still, 1957 .... 6.00
Cabin Still, Deer Browsing, 1967 .... 7.00
Cabin Still, Diamond, 1961 .... 10.00
Cabin Still, Dog, Left, 1968 .... 18.00
Cabin Still, Dog, Right, 1965 .... 10.00
Cabin Still, Double Image, 1967 .... 15.00
Cabin Still, Ducks Unlimited, 1972 .... 20.00
Cabin Still, Early American, 1970 .... 5.00
Cabin Still, Hillbilly, 1954, Pt. ....*Illus* 31.00
Cabin Still, Pheasants Rising, 1964 .... 7.00
Cabin Still, Quail, 1968 .... 5.00
Candlelite, 1955 .... 18.00
Candlelite, 1961 .... 9.00
Classic, 1972 .... 5.00 To 6.00
Colonial, 1969 .... 5.00
Countries, 1973 .... 18.00

Old Fitzgerald, Cabin Still, Hillbilly, 1954, Pt.   *Old Fitzgerald, Rip Van Winkle, 1971*

Crown, 1957	7.00
Davidson, N. C., 1972	30.00
Diamond, 1959	12.00
Diamond, 1961	12.00
Double Candlelite, 1956	8.00
Eagle, 1973	6.00 To 7.00
Early American, 1970	5.00
Executive, 1960	7.00
Flagship, 1967	4.00 To 6.00
Fleur–De–Lis, 1962	7.00 To 10.00
Florentine, 1961	7.00 To 9.00
Four Seasons, 1965	5.00

Old Fitzgerald, Ohio State, 1970   *Old Fitzgerald, Old Monterey, 1970*

Gallon In Cradle	15.00
Geese, 1970	5.00
Gold Coaster, 1954	11.00
Gold Web, 1953 .... 10.00 To	12.00
Golden Bough, 1970 .... 5.00 To	6.00
Hospitality, 1958	7.00
Hostess, 1977	6.00
Huntington, W. V., 1971	26.00
Illinois, 1972	12.00
Irish Charm, 1977 .... 17.00 To	20.00
Irish Counties, 1973	17.00
Jewel, 1951	8.00
Leprechaun, Plase God, 1968 .... 25.00 To	27.00
Leprechaun, Praise Be, 1968	20.00
Lexington, 1968 .... 6.00 To	8.00
LSU, 1970	26.00
Luck, 1972	28.00
Man of War, Horse, 1969 .... 5.00 To	6.00
Memphis, 1969 .... 10.00 To	12.00
Monticello, Left Handle, 1968	23.00
Monticello, Right Handle, 1968	5.00
Nebraska, 1972 .... 20.00 To	30.00
Ohio State, 1970 ....*Illus*	13.00
Old Fitz, 1978	5.00
Old Ironsides	5.00
Old Monterey, 1970 ....*Illus*	15.00
Patriots, 1971	24.00
Pheasant, 1972 .... 6.00 To	8.00
Pilgrim Landing, 1970	17.00
Ram, Bighorn, 1971 .... 4.00 To	5.00
Rip Van Winkle, 1971 ....*Illus*	32.00
Songs of Ireland, 1969	10.00
Sons of Erin, 1969 .... 12.00 To	15.00
South Carolina, 1970	11.00
Texas University, 1971	15.00
Tournament, 1963 .... 6.00 To	8.00
Tree of Life, 1964 .... 4.00 To	6.00
Triangle, 1976	4.00
Venetian, 1966	5.00
Vermont, 1970	18.00
Virginia, 1972	16.00
W. V. Forest Festival, 1973	10.00
Wish, 1975	20.00

—————————————— **OLD MR. BOSTON** ——————————————

It seems strange that a liquor company began as a candy factory, but that is part of the history of Old Mr. Boston. The Ben Burk Candy Company started in 1927 making nonalcoholic cordials during Prohibition. After Repeal, they became the first Massachusetts company to get a license for distilled spirits. They built a still and started making gin. One of the first brand names used was Old Mr. Boston. There was even a live Mr. Boston, an actor who made appearances for the company. In the early 1940s the company was sold to American Distilleries, but four years later Samuel Burk and Hyman Burkowitz, brothers, bought the company back. They expanded the Old Mr. Boston brand to include other beverages, such as flavored cordials and homogenized eggnog. They claim to be the first to introduce the quarter–pint size. In the mid–1960s the company began putting the liquor in decanters that are in demand by today's collectors. No decanters were made after the early 1970s. They also made Rocking Chair Whiskey in a bottle that actually rocked. Traditionally, whiskey barrels were rolled back and forth on ships to improve the taste. Ships' captains liked the improved flavor and when they retired they would tie barrels of whiskey to their rocking chairs. A series of liquors in glass cigar–like tubes called *The Thin Man* were made in the mid–1960s. Glenmore Distilleries acquired Old Mr. Boston in 1969. The brand name was changed to Mr. Boston about 1975.

The Mr. Boston trademark was redesigned in the 1950s and again in the 1970s. Each time he became thinner, younger, and more dapper. The slogan *An innkeepers tradition since 1868* was used in the 1980s. It refers to the year the Old Mr. Boston mark was first registered.

OLD MR. BOSTON, AMVETS, Iowa Convention, 1975 ....9.00 To 10.00
   AMVETS, Scroll, 1976 .... 12.00
   Anthony Wayne, 1970 .... 8.00
   Assyrian Convention, 1975 .... 21.00
   Bart Starr, No. 15 .... 15.00
   Beckley, W. V. 24.00
   Bell, Liberty, 1976 .... 16.00
   Bingo In Illinois, 1974 .... 12.00
   Black Hills Motor Club, 1976 .... 22.00
   Circus Lion, 1974 .... 14.00
   Circus Lion, Signature, 1974 .... 20.00
   Clown Head, 1973 .... 15.00
   Clown Head, Signature, 1974 .... 26.00
   Cog Railway, 1978 .... 29.00
   Concord Coach, 1976 .... 26.00
   Dan Patch, 1970 .... 15.00 To 20.00
   Dan Patch, 1973 .... 15.00 To 20.00
   Daniel Webster Cabin, 1977 .... 19.00
   Deadwood, South Dakota, 1975 .... 15.00
   Eagle Convention, 75th Anniversary, 1973 .... 14.00 To 16.00
   Eagle Convention, 78th Anniversary, 1973 .... 10.00 To 13.00
   Eagle Convention, Atlanta, 1972 .... 12.00
   Eagle Convention, Boston, 1971 .... 11.00
   Elkins, W. V., Stump, 1975 .... 20.00
   Fire Engine, 1974 .... 29.00 To 30.00
   Green Bay, No. 87 .... 23.00 To 45.00
   Greensboro Open, Gold Bag, 1976 .... 30.00
   Greensboro Open, Golf Shoe, 1978 .... 37.00
   Guitar, Music City, 1968 .... 15.00 To 17.00
   Illinois Capitol, 1970 .... 13.00
   Lincoln Horseback, 1972 .... 10.00
   Miss Nebraska 16.00
   Mississippi Bicentennial, 1976 .... 16.00
   Molly Pitcher, 1975 .... 8.00
   Monticello, 1974 .... 11.00
   Mooseheart, 1972 ....9.00 To 12.00
   Nathan Hale, 1975 .... 12.00 To 15.00
   Nebraska No. 1, Gold, 1970 .... 15.00 To 30.00
   New Hampshire, 1976 .... 16.00
   New Hampshire, Frigate, 1975 .... 13.00
   New Hampshire, Independence, 1976 .... 15.00
   Paul Bunyan, 1971 .... 10.00
   Paul Revere, 1975 .... 10.00
   Polish American Legion, 1975 .... 15.00
   Presidential Inauguration, 1953 .... 10.00 To 12.00
   Prestige Bookend, 1970 .... 7.00
   Race Car, No. 9 .... 26.00
   Red Dog Dan, 1974 .... 10.00
   Sherry Pitcher 5.00
   Ship Lantern, 1974 .... 18.00
   Shriner, AAONMA, Camel, 1975 .... 12.00 To 14.00
   Shriner, Bektash Temple, 1976 .... 25.00
   Steelhead Trout, 1976 .... 15.00
   Tennessee Centennial 10.00
   Town Crier, 1976 .... 15.00
   W. V. National Guard, 1973 .... 36.00

OLD RIP VAN WINKLE

Old Rip Van Winkle apothecary jars and figurals shaped like Rip Van Winkle were made from 1968 to 1977. J. P. Van Winkle and Sons, Louisville, Kentucky, made these bottles and others under the Old Commonwealth label.

OLD RIP VAN WINKLE, Bay Colony, 1975	15.00
Cardinal, 1974	15.00
Colonial Virginia, 1974	14.00
Kentucky Sportsman, 1973	25.00
New Jersey Bicentennial, 1975	20.00
New York, 1975	17.00
Rip Van Winkle, No. 1, Sitting, 1975	25.00 To 37.00
Rip Van Winkle, No. 2, Reclining, 1975	25.00 To 35.00
Rip Van Winkle, No. 3, Standing, 1977	20.00 To 25.00
Sanford, N. C., Centennial, 1974	10.00 To 12.00
University of Kentucky, Wildcat, 1974	27.00

PACESETTER

Bottles shaped like cars and trucks were made under the Pacesetter label from 1974 to about 1983.

PACESETTER, Corvette, 1978, Gold, Miniature	18.00
Corvette, 1978, Silver, Miniature	15.00
Corvette, 1978, White, Miniature	15.00
Corvette, 1978, Yellow, Miniature	15.00
Corvette, 1980, White, 1 Ltr.	57.00
Corvette, 1980, Yellow, 1 Ltr.	57.00
Pontiac Firebird, 1980	37.00
Tractor, No. 1, John Deere, 1982	110.00
Tractor, No. 3, International Harvester, 1983	85.00
Tractor, No. 3, International Harvester, 1983, Miniature	42.00
Tractor, No. 4, 4–Wheel–Drive, Big Red, 1983, 200 Ml.	70.00
Tractor, No. 4, 4–Wheel–Drive, Green Machine, 1983, 200 Ml.	70.00
Tractor, No. 4, Ford, Big Blue, 1983	70.00
Tractor, No. 4, Ford, Big Blue, 1983, Miniature	35.00
Tractor, No. 5, Allis Chalmers, Big Orange, 1984, Miniature	45.00

PEPPER SAUCE

There was little refrigeration and only poor storage facilities for fresh meat in the nineteenth century. Slightly spoiled food was often cooked and eaten with the help of strong spices including pepper. Small hot chili peppers were put into a bottle of vinegar. After a few weeks the spicy mixture was called *pepper sauce.* A distinctive bottle, now known as a pepper sauce bottle, was favored for this mixture. It was a small bottle, 6 to 12 inches high, with a long slim neck. The bottle could be square or cylindrical or decorated with arches or rings. Most were made of common bottle glass in shades of aqua or green. A few were made of cobalt or milk glass. Very early examples may have a pontil mark. More information on pepper sauce can be found in *Ketchup, Pickles, Sauces* by Betty Zumwalt.

PEPPER SAUCE, Aqua, 8 Rounded Panels, OP, Applied Mouth	25.00
Aqua, Ribbed, 3 Rings On Neck	20.00
C. L. Stickney, Aqua, OP, 9 In.	88.00
Cathedral, 6 Panels, Aqua, OP, 8 1/2 In.	65.00
Cathedral, Aqua, 6 Panels, 8 5/8 In.	35.00
Cathedral, Aqua, Cylinder, Embossed Design, 9 In.	73.00
Cathedral, Aqua, Pontil	75.00
Cathedral, Aqua, Square, 8 3/8 In.	35.00
Cathedral, Deep Aqua, Green Hint, OP, 9 In.	110.00
Cathedral, Pale Yellow Green, Square, 1860–1880, 8 1/2 In.	100.00
Cathedral, Square, Aqua, Cross & Tassel, 9 3/8 In.	77.00
Cathedral, Square, Aqua, OP, 10 3/8 In.	95.00
Cathedral, W. K. Lewus & Co., Aqua, OP, 10 1/8 In.	577.00
Clear, 21 Rings, Oval	6.00

Pepper Sauce, Milk Glass,   *Pepsi-Cola, Forest City,*   *Pepsi-Cola, Miniature,*
9 In.   *Ark., 10 Oz.*   *3 1/2 In.*

Deeley, Stourbridge, Aqua, Allover Raised Diamond, 13 1/4 In.	115.00
E. R. Durkee & Co., New York, Aqua	20.00
E. R. Durkee & Co., Pat. Feb. 17, 1874, Amber, 7 7/8 In.	578.00
Jumbo Brand, Elephant Head, Clear, 6 1/2 In.	30.00
Lutz Bros. Tomato Catsup & Pepper Sauce, Label	25.00
M. & G. M., N. Y., Aqua, OP, 10 1/8 In.	44.00
Milk Glass, 9 In. ....*Illus*	95.00
SCA, 18 Rings, 6 1/2 In.	8.00
Stickney & Poor, Pat. App. For, Teal, Tooled Lip, 8 In.	55.00
Stickney & Poor, Spiral, Teal, 8 In. .... 20.00 To 22.00
W. & E., Aqua, OP, 8 7/8 In., 8 7/8 In.	176.00
Wells, Miller & Provost, New York, Aqua, 8 1/4 In.	35.00

─────────────────── **PEPSI–COLA** ───────────────────

Caleb Davis Bradham, a New Bern, North Carolina, druggist, invented and named Pepsi–Cola. Although he registered the trademark, the word *Pepsi–Cola* in calligraphy script, in 1903, he claimed that it had been used since 1898. A simpler version was registered in 1906. The bottle is marked with the name. The name in a hexagonal frame with the words *A Sparkling Beverage* was registered in 1937. This logo was printed on the bottle. About 1950, the modern logo in an oval was introduced. The simulated cap logo was used at the same time. The name *Pepsi* was started in 1911, but it was not until 1966 that the block–lettered logo was registered. Both names are still used. A few very early Pepsi bottles were made of amber glass. Many other Pepsi bottles with local bottlers' names were made in the early 1900s. Modern bottles made for special events are also collected. There is a club, Pepsi–Cola Collectors Club, P.O. Box 1275, Covina, CA 91722. The company has archives at One Pepsi Way, Purchase, NY 10589.

PEPSI–COLA, Anderson, S. C., Clemson Football, Undefeated Season, 12 Oz.	9.00
Applied Colored Label, Swirl, 1961, 10 Oz.	8.00
Bethlehem, Pa., Script Around Middle, Pennant On Drum	60.00
Burlington, N. C., ACL Emblem, Red, White, & Blue, 1948, 12 Oz.	12.50
Charlotte, N. C., Flower's Shoulder, Green	12.00
Charlotte, N. C., Light Green, 1918–1926, 6 1/2 Oz.	35.00
Charlotte, N. C., Script At Base, Slug Plate, BIM, Straight Sides	20.00
Colorado Centennial–Feelin' Free, 1976, 16 Oz.	12.00
Diet Pepsi, Blue Dots, 10 Oz.	4.00
Durham, N. C., Pinched In Corset, Script In Rectangle	60.00
Durham, N. C., Script At Shoulder, Base, BIM, Straight Sides	30.00
Durham, N. C., Script Embossed, Clear, BIMAL, 1910, 7 Oz.	60.00
East Tennessee State University, Johnson City, 1975, 16 Oz.	14.00
Forest City, Ark., 10 Oz. ....*Illus*	5.00
Greensboro, N. C., Green, Block Embossed, 1918–1926, 6 1/2 Oz.	44.00
Greensboro, N. C., Star Boys, Light Green, Cathedral Windows	15.00

Greensboro, N. C., White Rose Ginger Ale, Rose 15.00
Greenville, S. C., 75th Anniversary, Swirl, 1973, 12 Oz. 9.00
Hickory, N. C., Superior Beverages, Light Green 15.00
Illinois Brewing Co., Socorro, N. M., Amber, Paper Label 70.00
Iowa Vs. Iowa State University Football, 1977, 16 Oz. 12.00
Jacksonville, Fla., Slug Plate, Script Embossed, 1910, 7 Oz. 85.00
Jessup Bottling, Charlottesville, Va., Aqua, ABM, Slug 15.00
Littleton, N. C., ACL Emblem, Red, White, 1948, 8 Oz. 12.00
Memphis, Tn., Fountain Syrup, ACL Emblem, Red, White, 1943, 12 Oz. 30.00
Miniature, 3 1/2 In. ....*Illus* 50.00
Mr. Energizer, 1980 South Carolina Jaycees, Contents, 10 Oz. 12.00
Myrtle Beach, S. C., 50th Anniversary, Contents 7.00
Newport News, Va., Smoky, Block Letters, Straight Sides 25.00
Ohio Bicentennial, Canal, Railroad, 1976, 16 Oz. 12.00
Raleigh, N. C., Aqua, Script Embossed, 1912, 7 Oz. 85.00
Red, White, & Blue, No. 12025 .... 10.00
Richard Petty, 7 Time Winston Cup Champion, Commemorative 7.00
Rocky Mount, N. C., Green, Orange Crush Bottling Co. 30.00
Script On Middle & Base 20.00
Set, Washington, Eagle, Flag, Drum, & Cannon Emblems, 1976, 5 Pc. 40.00
St. Louis Blues Hockey, Screw Cap, 1974, 16 Oz. 9.00
Suffolk, Va., Aqua, Script At Base, BIM, Straight Sides 25.00
Sunbo Beverages, Ga., Sun Over Mountains Picture, White Paint 5.00
University of Nebraska Cornhuskers, Contents, 1974, 16 Oz. 12.00
Virginia Famous Statesmen, 1976, 16 Oz. 9.00
Wilmington, N. C., Light Green, 1912, 7 Oz. 80.00
Winston–Salem, N. C., Block Letters On Shoulder, Straight Sides 15.00
Winston–Salem, N. C., Vertical Ridges 15.00

PERFUME

Perfume is a liquid mixture of aromatic spirits and alcohol. Cologne is similar but has more alcohol in the mixture so it is not as strong. Perfume bottles are smaller than colognes and usually more decorative. Most perfume bottles today are from the twentieth century. Some were made by famous glass makers such as Lalique or Webb, and some held expensive perfumes such as Schiaparelli, Nina Ricci's Coeur de Joie, or D'Orsay's Le Lys D'Orsay. DeVilbiss is a manufacturer of the spray tops used on perfume bottles and the name sometimes appears in a description. The club Perfume & Scent Bottle Collectors publishes a newspaper (P.O. Box 6965, Rockford, IL 61125–6965). The Tops & Bottoms Club has a matching service for Rene Lalique bottles. If you have a bottle without a stopper, or a stopper and no bottle, contact them at P.O. Box 15555, Plantation, FL 33317.

PERFUME, see also Cologne; Scent
PERFUME, 3 Spiraling Pleated Swirl, Frosted, Clear Base, Lalique, 2 3/4 In. 325.00
Allover White Flowers, Turquoise, Bristol, 5 3/4 In. 75.00
Alternating Diamond & Panel, Light To Medium Amethyst, 7 1/4 In. 495.00
Amber, Beveled, Metal Footed & Stopper 50.00
Ambre D'Orsay, Lalique, Black Glass 1200.00
Amethyst, 12 Panels, Burst Bubble, New England, 1860–1880, 5 In. 110.00
Arabian Cream Perfume, 2 1/2 In. ....*Illus* 4.00
Aurene, Blue Iridescent, DeVilbiss, Dipper Shape, 6 1/2 In. 385.00
Baccarat, Fan Stopper, 4 1/4 In. ....*Illus* 65.00
Ballet Dancer, Blues, Japan, 7 1/2 In. 68.00
Barrel, Miniature, Clear, OP 100.00
Basketweave, Aqua, Oval Label Panel, 1830–1860, 2 7/8 In. 11.00
Beer Shape, Black Glass, Bass & Co. Pale Ale, 3 In. 19.50
Black Crystal, Frosted 2 Tango Dancers Stopper, Dauber, Czech 660.00
Black Crystal, Geometric Diamond Shape Malachite Stopper, Czech 523.00
Black Crystal, Round Columnar, Maidens & Pan, Frosted Stopper 55.00
Blown, Opaque Blue Gray, Tooled Lip, Pontil, 1850, 7 1/2 In. 132.00
Blown, Smoky Gray Blue, Rolled Lip, Pontil, 1850–1860, 7 3/8 In. 83.00
Blue Aurene, Melon Ribbed 1760.00
Boots The Chemist & Perfumers, Green, Pocket Watch Shape 22.00

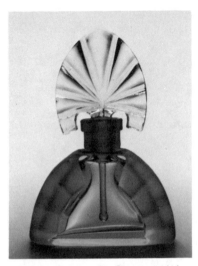

Perfume, Baccarat, Fan Stopper, 4 1/4 In. *Perfume, Cut Glass, Oval Fancy Stopper,*
11 1/2 In.

Boots, Figural, Flask Type, Green	16.00
Boston & Sandwich, 3–Piece Mold, Purple, Stopper, Pontil, 6 In.	220.00
Bourjois, Kobako, Clear & Frosted, Snuff Bottle Shape, Stopper	88.00
Bourjois, Paris, Cobalt Blue, Clear Frosted Stopper	22.00
Boy In Bag, Figural, Pottery, Painted, Metal Crown Top, Germany	198.00
Boy Swami, Figural, Pottery, Balloon Pants, Crown Stopper, Germany	99.00
Bunker Hill, Monument, Clear, 1870–1880, 12 In.	30.00
Burner, Clear, Etched Floral, A. De Caranza, Metal Top, Wick	149.00
C. Depinoix, Clear, Frosted, Green Waves, Kneeling Woman Stopper	825.00
Calliste, Mon Studio, Black Glass, Rectangular, Inner Stopper	231.00
Cameo Glass, D'Argental, Landscape & Sailboats, Signed, 6 3/4 In.	1250.00
Cameo Glass, Daum Nancy, Scenic, 6 In.	2600.00
Cameo, Lay–Down, Carved Water Lilies & Dragonfly, Blue, 3 3/4 In.	3250.00
Cameo, Lay–Down, Flower, Gold, Pointed Base, Faberge Cap, 3 3/4 In.	6500.00
Caron, Chez Moi, Green Enameled Stopper	220.00
Caron, Chez Moi, Rectangular, Stopper, Box	50.00
Caron, With Pleasure, Baccarat, 3 7/8 In.	40.00
Carven, Robe D'Un Soir, Clear, Rectangular, Metallic Label, Stopper	11.00
Caswell & Massey, Verbena, Apothecary Shape, Clear, Stopper	66.00
Charbert, The French Touch, Clear, Feathers Label, Stopper, Box	143.00
Charles Jourdan, Votre, Display, Yellow, Umbrella Stopper, Large	154.00
Charlie McCarthy, Figural, With Hat, Clear	20.00
Circe, Black Glass, Frosted Frieze Woman, Lion & Dog, Stopper	286.00
Ciro, Acclaim, Folds of Drapery Shape, Stopper, Gold Letters	33.00
Ciro, Surrender, Faceted Gemstone Shape, Labels, Baccarat On Base	88.00
Clear, Glass Inner Stopper, Gold Metal Overcap, Hexagonal	33.00
Clear, Silver Overlay, Stylized Lilies, Stopper, Initialed KMB	385.00
Cloisonne, Blue, Red Roses, Purse, 2 In.	75.00
Cobalt Blue, 15 Ribs, Tapered Cylinder, Pontil, 5 1/4 In.	577.00
Cobalt Blue, Label, 1870, 8 1/2 In.	44.00
Colonial Woman, China, Pink, White, Germany, 3 1/2 In.	40.00
Corday, L'Orchidee Bleue, Clear, Flower Shape & Stopper, Baccarat	105.00
Coty, Embossed Floral Design, Signed	125.00
Coty, L'Aimant, Clear, Reddish Brown Leaf Design Stopper	55.00
Coty, L'Origan, Clear, Frosted, Flask Shape, Floral Design, Box	83.00

Coty, Muse, Clear, Frosted, Inner Stopper, Opulent Box	253.00
Cranberry, White Boy & Girl, Mary Gregory Type, 9 1/2 In., Pair	265.99
Crystal, Holder, Allover Grooved Design, Czech, Pair	28.00
Crystal, Leaded, Hand–Cut	35.00
Cut Glass Base, Green, Art Deco Stopper, Czechoslovakia, 7 In.	220.00
Cut Glass, Etched Flower Stopper, Czechoslovakia	165.00
Cut Glass, Fan Stopper, Czecholovakia, 8 1/2 In.	145.00
Cut Glass, Geometric, Double Lay–Down, Silver Repousse Tops	135.00
Cut Glass, Oval Fancy Stopper, 11 1/2 In. ....*Illus*	47.50
Cut Glass, Steeple Stopper, Czechoslovakia, 6 1/4 In.	95.00
D'Orsay, Intoxication, Pleated Star Shape, Stopper, White Box	77.00
D'Orsay, Toujours Fidele, Clear, Pillow Shape, Sitting Dog Stopper	198.00
Dans La Nuit, Lalique	475.00
Deep Red Cut To Create Clear Windows, Atomizer, Bohemian	110.00
Deux Aigles, Gray Stained, 2 Facing Eagles, Paperweight, Lalique	1664.00
DeVilbiss, 24 Ribs, No Bulb Atomizer, 1937	8.00
Double Swan	65.00
Dropper, Yellow Opaque, Black Enameled, Footed, Atomizer, 7 In.	85.00
Duchese Perfume, Colorful Label, 5 In.	20.00
Eau De Cologne, Purple, Fancy, ABM	7.50
Elizabeth Arden, Memoire Cherie, Clear, Stopper, Gold Label	55.00
Emerald Green, Diamond Cut, Oval, Silver Screw, Laydown & Upright	285.00
Etched Scroll Design, Deer & Gardens, Octagonal Stopper, 3 In.	100.00
Flamme De Gloire, Green, 3 3/4 In. ....*Illus*	45.00
Floral, Pink, Stopper, 9 In. ....*Illus*	225.00
Forvil, Les Cinq Fleurs, Flask Shape, Black Rope, Knots, Lalique	665.00
Frosted Dancing Nudes, Stopper, Molinard Creation, Lalique	225.00
Frosted Green, Classical Cylindrical, Enameled Art Deco, Czech	55.00
Fry, Art Glass, Opalescent, Lavender Base, Mushroom Dauber, 7 In.	295.00
G. T. Barney, Aqua, OP, Square, 7 In.	42.00
Gothic Knight, Aqua, Flared Lip, OP, 1830–1860, 4 1/8 In.	47.25
Green Base, Nude Stopper, Czechoslovakia, 5 1/2 In.	165.00
Green, Pedestal, Stopper, 5 In. ....*Illus*	35.00
Green, Sterling Silver Lattice of Daisies & Leaves, Stopper	275.00
Guerlain Mitsouko, Baccarat	125.00

Perfume, Flamme De Gloire, Green, 3 3/4 In.

Perfume, Prince Matchabelli, 7/8 In.
Perfume, Le De Givenchy, Paris, 1 1/2 In.

Perfume, Triple Extract Hyacinth, Vail Bros., Phila., Pa., 4 In.

Perfume, Floral, Pink, Stopper, 9 In.

Perfume, Green, Pedestal, Stopper, 5 In.

Guerlain, Coq D'Or, Baccarat, 3 1/16 In. 400.00
Guerlain, Coq D'Or, Cobalt Blue, Bowtie Shape, Gold Enameled 495.00
Guerlain, Ejedi, Clear, Gold Metal Medallion Stopper, Baccarat 165.00
Guerlain, L'Heure Bleue, 7 1/2 In. 25.00
Guerlain, Ode, Clear, Rosebud Stopper, Baccarat Emblem Base 154.00
Gump, Pikake Lei, Carved Monkeypod Wood, 2 Leaves Shape, Stopper 55.00
Harrison's Columbian Perfumery, Flared Lip, Round, 3 1/4 In. 10.00
Hattie Carnegie, 2 1/2 In. 150.00
Hattie Carnegie, Carnegie Blue, Clear, Woman's Head & Shoulders 358.00
Head, Man & Woman's, Googly–Eye, White Glass, Germany, Pair 83.00
Hijang, Van Tines, Frosted Florals, 2 1/4 x 3 In. 95.00
Honeycomb, Atomizer 15.00
Houbigant, Fan Shape, Triangular Stopper, Lalique, 4 Bottles, Box 5225.00
Houbigant, Premier Mai, Clear, Stopper, Round Label, Box 50.00
Internally Enameled Green, Dancing Nude, Atomizer 55.00
Jade Green, Brass Stopper & Dauber, 1 1/2 In. 37.50
Jaytho, Frosted Tulips, Sienna Stained, Clear, Lalique, 4 In. 1800.00
Je Reviens, Blue Glass 95.00
Jean Patou, 1000, Hexagonal, Clear, Molded JP Logo Stopper, Label 55.00
Jean Patou, Amour Amour, 8 1/2 In. 120.00
Jean Patou, Amour Amour, Flask Shape, JP Logo Cut In Stopper 33.00
Jet Corday, 1 1/4 Oz. 75.00
Jet Corday, 5/8 Oz. 55.00
Jonteel, 3 3/4 In. 35.00
Kewpie Doll, Figural, Pottery, Metal Crown Stopper, Germany 88.00
L. E. Smith, Hobnail, Crystal, Amethyst Dipstick 30.00
Lady, Holding Bouquet, Figural, Pottery, Crown Stopper, Germany 94.00
Lalique, Cat, Sitting, Signed, 9 In. 425.00
Lalique, Elephant, Signed, 6 In. 180.00
Lalique, Lovebirds, Signed, 4 1/2 In. 120.00
Lalique, Nude Maiden & Fawn, Signed, 4 1/2 In. 100.00
Lalique, Nude, Signed, 10 In. 300.00
Lalique, Nudes, Stopper, Signed, 5 In. 400.00
Lalique, Pearl, Blue Wash, Stopper, 6 1/2 In. 950.00
Lalique, Rooster, Fighting, Signed, 8 In. 225.00

Lamp, Dog, Figural, Pottery, Air Holes Top of Head, Germany 88.00
Lancome, Magie, Frosted, Sphere Shape, Metal Screw Cap 220.00
Lancome, Tresor, Lay–Down, Gold Metal Screw Top, Blue Ribbon 77.00
Lander Gardenia, Floral Stopper, 4 1/2 In. ....*Illus* 7.00
Langlois, Duska, Red, Black Glass Stopper, Skyscraper Shape, 2 In. 39.00
Lanvin, A Veil of My Sin, Frosted, 4 In. 10.00
Lanvin, Arpege, Ball Shape, Black Glass, Gilded Raspberry Stopper 220.00
Lapis Lazuli, Molded Nude On Flat Octagonal Form, Bakelite Cap 297.00
Larkin, Green, Crown Top, 5 Oz., 3 In. 16.00
Latticinio, Flower Cluster Stopper, Banjo Shape, 11 In., Pair 450.00
Lazell's, N. Y., Dated 1881, 4 In. 45.00
Lazell's, Sachet Powder, Label, Ground Stopper, 3 In. 20.00
Le De Givenchy, Paris, 1 1/2 In. ....*Illus* 1.50
Light Amethyst, 12 Panels, Rolled Lip Pontil, 7 3/4 In. 357.00
Lovebirds Design, Clear & Frosted, Atomizer, Ovoid, France 187.00
Lucien Lelong, Indiscreet, Frosted, Drapery & Bow Shape, Stopper 110.00
Lucien Lelong, Mon Image, Clear, Intended Rectangular, Stopper 50.00
Lucien Lelong, Sirocco, Clear, Stopper, Swirled, Gold Highlights 61.00
Luster, Greens, Germany, 5 In. 68.00
Man In Moon, Figural, Pottery, Brown Glaze, Crown Top, Germany 143.00
Marquay, L'Elu, Faceted Gemstone Shape Stopper, Clear, Peach Bag 65.00
Marquay, Prince Douka, Swami Stopper, Cream Satin Cape, 3 3/4 In. 116.00
Marquay, Prince Douka, Swami Stopper, Green Satin Cape, 3 In. 66.00
Maurice Modele, Sachet, Jar, Barrel Shape, Cupid With Grapes Top 171.00
Medium Blue Gray, 12 Panels, Rolled Lip, Pontil, 4 1/4 In. 186.00
Melon Ribbed, Green Crystal Teardrop Stopper, Steuben, 5 In. 295.00
Milk Glass, Roped Corners, Rose Spray 3 Sides, Square, 6 1/4 In. 115.00
Milk Glass, Square With 2 Ribs On Each Side, 7 1/4 In. 126.00
Millot, Crepe De Chine, Clear, Octagonal Stopper, Gold Label, Box 39.00
Molinelle, English Roses, M Intaglio Cut Flat Octagonal Stopper 66.00
Monument, Teal, 6 1/2 In. 630.00
Morell Factice, 8 3/8 In. 150.00
Narcissus, Lander, Basketweave Bottle, 3 1/2 In. 15.00
Nina Ricci, Capricci, Quilted, Clear, Faceted Stopper, Lalique 50.00
Nina Ricci, Coeur Joie, Clear, Frosted, Lay–Down, 2 Hearts, Lalique 600.00
Nina Ricci, Fille D'Eve, Lalique 50.00
Nina Ricci, L'Air Du Temps, Clear, Lay–Down, Doves On Sides, Lalique 235.00
Nude, Dancing Among Waves, Figural, Pottery, Crown Stopper, Germany 145.00
Opalescent, Beaded, 1870, 8 In. 85.00
Palmer, Green, 4 In. 15.00
Palmer, Script Front, Emerald Green, Oval, 4 In. 32.00
Phalon Perfumers, N. Y., Medicine Bottle Shape, OP, 5 In. 25.00
Pierre Dune, Sequoia, Round Cushion Shape, Kneeling Nude Stopper 525.00
Pierrot, Figural, White, Yellow Hat, Pottery, Stopper, Germany 66.00
Pig, Silver Overlay, Original Stopper, 4 In. 175.00
Pressed Glass, Dogwood Metal Top, Dauber, England, 6 In., Pair 95.00
Prince Matchabelli, 7/8 In. ....*Illus* 2.50
Prince Matchabelli, Clear, 2 3/4 In. 10.00
Prince Matchabelli, Duchess of York, Crown, Red Bakelite Top 187.00
Prince Matchabelli, Frosted, 2 3/4 In. 10.00
Renaud, Sweet Pea, Green, Gold Medallion Label, Fitted Case 121.00
Renoir, Chi–Chi, Heart Shape, Amber Bakelite Arrow End Screw Cap 75.00
Richard Hudnut, Clear, Frosted, Nymph Standing Stopper, Tall 2970.00
Richard Hudnut, Wooden Base, 3 In. ....*Illus* 5.00
Roger & Gallet, Extrait De Violette De Parme, Stopper, 2 3/4 In. 15.00
Sandwich, Paneled, Medium Amethyst, 6 1/2 In. 550.00
Saville, Mischief, Black Glass, Chrome & Black Screw Top 75.00
Schiaparelli, Embossed S, Pink Cap, 3 1/2 In. 65.00
Schiaparelli, Shocking, 1 3/4 In. 45.00
Schiaparelli, Shocking, Dress Dummy Shape, Metal Cap, 2 1/4 In. 176.00
Schiaparelli, Shocking, Rectangular, Clear, Stopper, Pink Label, Box 44.00
Schiaparelli, Sleeping, 5 1/2 In. 150.00
Schiaparelli, Snuff Pipe Shape 295.00

Schuco Teddy Bear, 1910, 3 In.	350.00
Scrolls, Daisies, Applied Collar, Pontil, 1830–1860, 3 1/4 In.	42.00
Sprays of Bleeding Heart, White On Amethyst, 7 1/2 In.	500.00
Street Lamp, Ashtray, Metal, Green, 3 Bottles In Lamps, 8 In.	32.00
Stuart, Perfume Hi–Lights, 3 Miniature Bottles In Lamp Shade, Box	66.00
Swirled, Orange, Gold & Blue, Metal Crown Stopper, European	61.00
Swirled, Orange, Gold & Blue, Stopper With Dauber, European	99.00
Teissier Prevost A Paris, Bell & Ribbon, Emerald, BIM, 7 1/2 In.	125.00
Teissier Prevost A Paris, Bell & Ribbon, Teal, 7 1/2 In.	95.00
Tigress, Faberge, 3 In.	10.00
Tre–Jur, Woman, Figural, Stopper Torso With Long Dauber, Frosted	385.00
Triple Extract Hyacinth, Vail Bros., Phila., Pa., 4 In. ....*Illus*	12.00
Urn Base, Flower Basket Stopper, Czechoslovakia, 9 In.	195.00
Vigny, Le Golliwogg, Figural, Frosted, Black Sealskin Hair, Label	275.00
Vine Design, Sandwich Glass, Amber, Octagonal, Steepe Stopper	325.00
Vogue, Lily of The Valley, 3 3/4 In.	40.00
Volupte, Frosted Round Bottle, In Brass Standing Nude's Hands	253.00
Watkins, Box, 5 1/2 In.	30.00
Wells Hackmetack Persian Perfum, Leroy, N. Y., Clear, BIM, 4 In.	14.00
White Lilac, Dorothy Gray, Hot Weather, 6 In.	5.00
White Satin Glass, Applied Pink Flowers, Atomizer, 6 In., Pair	145.00
Woman, Figural, 18th Century Type, Pottery, Blue Dress, Germany	105.00
Woman, Figural, Hooped Skirt, Frosted, Head Stopper, 6 In.	350.00
Woman, Figural, Hooped Skirt, Pottery, Stopper, Germany	77.00
Worth, Gardenia, Impressed Flowers, Clear, Stopper, Gold Label	275.00
Worth, Je Reviens, Dark Blue, Turquoise Stopper, Round	44.00
Yellow Crystal, Geometric, Intaglio Nude On Ball Stopper, Czech	220.00
Yellow Flower Stopper, Czechoslovakia, 5 1/2 In.	95.00

PICKLE

Pickles were packed in special jars from about 1880 to 1920. The pickle jar was usually large, from one quart to one gallon size. They were made with four to eight sides. The mouth was wide because you had to reach inside to take out the pickle. The top was usually sealed with a cork or tin cover. Many pickle jars were designed with raised gothic arches as panels. These jars are clear examples of the Victorian gothic revival designs, so

Perfume, Richard Hudnut, Wooden Base, 3 In.
Perfume, Lander Gardenia, Floral Stopper, 4 1/2 In.
Perfume, Arabian Cream Perfume, 2 1/2 In.

Pickle, Cathedral, 8 1/2 In.   *Pickle, R.& F.Atmore, Cathedral, 11 1/2 In.*

they are often included in museum exhibitions of the period. Their large size and attractive green to blue coloring make them good accessories in a room, and designers often use them on a kitchen counter. Bottle collectors realize that pickle jars are examples of good bottle design, that they are rare, and that a collection can be formed showing the works of many glasshouses. Pickle bottles are so popular that they are being reproduced. For more information on pickle jars, see *Ketchup, Pickles, Sauces* by Betty Zumwalt.

PICKLE, Aqua, 4 Scalloped Sides, Concave, 14 5/8 In. 75.00
Aqua, Pontil, Square, 3 1/8 In. 29.00
Atmore's, Cathedral, Light Green, Rolled Lip, 11 1/4 In. 132.00
Barrel, Green, 1/2 Gal. 45.00
Bunker Hill Pickles, Skilton Foote, Light Green, No Stopper, Pt. 14.00
California Home Sweet Gherkins, San Francisco, Purple, Label 25.00
Cathedral Arch Sides, Aqua, Square, 8 1/2 In. 15.00
Cathedral, 8 1/2 In. ....*Illus* 140.00
Cathedral, Aqua Green, Hexagonal, 1860–1880, 13 1/8 In. 176.00
Cathedral, Aqua Green, Rolled Lip, 14 In. 303.00
Cathedral, Aqua, 4 Panels, Floral Sprig Above, Pontil, 13 In. 190.00
Cathedral, Aqua, 6 Panels, 2 Designs In Arch Panel, 13 1/4 In. 200.00
Cathedral, Aqua, Applied Mouth, 8 3/4 In. 38.50
Cathedral, Aqua, IP, 9 1/8 In. 275.00
Cathedral, Aqua, IP, 10 1/2 In. 121.00
Cathedral, Aqua, IP, Rolled Lip, 9 In. 220.00
Cathedral, Aqua, OP, 7 1/2 In. 85.00
Cathedral, Aqua, OP, 9 1/4 In. 95.00
Cathedral, Aqua, Rolled Lip, 13 3/4 In. 358.00
Cathedral, Aqua, Rolled Lip, 1870–1880, 9 1/4 In. 75.00
Cathedral, Aqua, Square, 7 1/2 In. 65.00
Cathedral, Aqua, Tooled Collared Mouth, Square, 13 3/4 In. 170.00
Cathedral, Blue Green, 6 Panels, Leaf Design, 13 1/4 In. 275.00
Cathedral, Crown & Tassels In 4 Panels, 1860–1865, 11 1/2 In. 210.00
Cathedral, Deep Aqua, Green Tone, IP, 8 7/8 In. 523.00
Cathedral, Deep Aqua, IP, 8 7/8 In. 440.00
Cathedral, Deep Aqua, Rolled Lip, 11 3/4 In. 215.00
Cathedral, Deep Emerald Green, Rolled Lip, 9 In. 643.00
Cathedral, Emerald Green, IP, 14 1/2 In. 908.00
Cathedral, Light Green, IP, 11 3/4 In. 495.00
Cathedral, Medium Blue Green, Square Base, Gal. 200.00
Cathedral, Sunken Panels, 1880, Rectangular, 8 3/4 In. 60.00
Cathedral, Yellow Green, 6 Panels, Rolled Lip, 13 1/8 In. 358.00

Cathedral, Yellow, Amber Tones, 6 Panels, 11 3/8 In. 2695.00
Clear, Flute Around Shoulder, Rectangular, Master 12.00
E. H. V. B., Cathedral, Deep Emerald, 6 Panels, IP, 9 In. 660.00
E. H. V. B., N. Y., Cathedral, Deep Aqua, IP, 9 In. 187.00
E. T. Cowdrey & Co., Boston, Amber, 6 1/2 In. 55.00
Embossed C. U., Aqua, Octagonal, Qt. 29.00
Embossed Fruit, Emerald Green 35.00
Espy, Phil., Aqua, OP, 9 1/2 In. 16.50
Figural, Medium Green, Ground Lip, 1880–1900, 4 1/2 In. 143.00
G. P. Sanborn & Son, Boston, Aqua, Rolled Lip, 5 In. 60.50
Gherkins–Boston, Cathedral, Aqua, 13 3/4 In. 77.00
Goofus, 3–Piece Mold, Grapes, Leaves, Vines, Milk Glass, 12 In. 200.00
Goofus, Milk Glass, Ground Lip, 15 1/8 In. 187.00
Gothic Arch, Clear, 13 1/2 In. 205.00
Gothic Arch, Light Green, Applied Lip, 11 3/4 In. 475.00
Heinz Noble & Co., Pittsburgh, Pa., Deep Aqua, 7 7/8 In. 77.00
I. G. Co., Cathedral, 6 Panels, Aqua, Embossed, 13 In. 175.00
J. M. Clark & Co., Louisville, Ky., Yellow Amber, 6 7/8 In. 55.00
J. McCollick & Co., N. Y., Deep Green Aqua, IP, 8 1/2 In. 176.00
J. McCollick & Co., N. Y., Embossed, c.1850 .... 990.00
Light Green, Unembossed, OP, 7 3/8 In. 61.00
Milwaukee Pickle Co., Wauwatosa, Wisc., Orange Amber, 12 5/8 In. 231.00
Mold Blown, Aqua, Applied Lip, IP, 11 1/2 In. 150.00
Octofoil, Rolled Lip, 1860–1870, 8 In. 440.00
P. D. Code & Co., S. F., Deep Olive Amber, 11 3/8 In. 468.00
R. & F. Atmore, Cathedral, 11 1/2 In. ....*Illus* 150.00
R. P. Co., Paterson, N. J., Urn Shape, Bright Green, Laid On Lip 39.00
Shaker Brand, E. D. Pettengill & Co., Yellow, Amber Tone, 5 In. 745.00
SJG, Cathedral, Aqua, Pt. 125.00
Skilton Foote & Co., Bunker Hill Pickles, Amber, 6 3/4 In. 77.00
Skilton Foote & Co., Bunker Hill Pickles, Amber, Square, Pt. 45.00
Skilton Foote & Co., Bunker Hill Pickles, Cork, 5 1/4 In. 8.00
Skilton Foote & Co., Bunker Hill Pickles, Light Yellow, Qt. 50.00
Skilton Foote & Co., Bunker Hill Pickles, Olive Amber, Lighthouse 210.00
Sol Wangenheim & Co., Monogram, San Fran., Aqua, Square, 11 1/4 In. 65.00
T. B. Smith & Co., Cathedral, Medium To Deep Blue Green, 8 7/8 In. 550.00
T. B. Smith & Co., Philadelphia, Aqua, 6 Panels, Round, 11 In. 688.00
T. B. Smith & Co., Philadelphia, Aqua, IP, 11 1/8 In. 165.00
T. B. Smith & Co., Philadelphia, Aqua, OP, Collared Mouth, 10 1/2 In. 35.00
Trade, Embossed Griffin, C. P. Co., Aqua, Rolled Lip, 9 In. 71.50
W. D. Smith, N. Y., Deep Aqua, IP, Rolled Lip, 8 5/8 In. 495.00
W. K. Lewis & Bros., Boston, Label, Light Green, 12 In. 71.50
W. K. Lewis, Cathedral, Boston, Square, Pontil 350.00
W. Numsen & Co., Baltimore, Yellow Green, OP, 9 In. 275.00
W. Numsen & Son, Baltimore, Aqua, Qt., 8 1/2 In. 143.00
W. T. & Co., Cathedral, Golden Amber, 13 3/8 In. 825.00
W. T. & Co., Cathedral, Golden Amber, Hexagonal, 13 1/4 In. 423.00
Wells–Miller & Provost, Aqua, IP, 11 1/2 In. 220.00
Wells–Miller & Provost, Cathedral, Emerald, IP, 11 1/2 In. 1650.00
Whitney Glass Works, Coffin, Aqua, 1860–1880, 14 1/4 In. 132.00
Wm. Underwood & Co., Boston, Aqua, OP, 11 3/8 In. 220.00
Wm. Underwood & Co., Cathedral, Boston, Blue Aqua, IP, 11 1/2 In. 650.00

POISON

Everyone knows you must be careful about how you store poisonous substances. Our ancestors had the same problem. Nineteenth–century poison bottles were usually made with raised designs so the user could feel the danger. The skull and crossbones symbol was sometimes shown, but usually the bottle had ridges or raised embossing. The most interesting poison bottles were made from the 1870s to the 1930s. Cobalt blue and bright green glass were often used. The bottle was designed to look different from any type of food container. One strange British poison bottle made in 1871 was shaped like a coffin and was often decorated with a death's head. Another bottle was shaped like a skull.

Poison collectors search for any bottle that held poison or that is labeled poison. Included are animal and plant poisons as well as dangerous medicines. A helpful reference book is *Poison Bottle Workbook* by Rudy Kuhn.

POISON, 1 Wing Owl, Cobalt Blue, Triangular, 3 1/2 In. 95.00
   4–Pointed Stars, Embossed, Amber, Irregular Hexagon, 2 1/2 In. 50.00
   Acetate Potassa, U.S. A. Hosp. Dept., Aqua, Cylinder, 6 1/2 In. 55.00
   Admiralty, Deep Cobalt Blue, Ribbed, Square, Stopper, 7 1/2 In. 100.00
   Amber, Ground Glass Stopper, Ribbed, ABM, 3 5/8 In. 25.00
   Amber, J. T. M. & Co., Triangular, Sawtooth Ribs, BIMAL, 10 In. 725.00
   Amber, P. D. & Co., Embossed 1890, Amber, Triangular, BIMAL, 2 3/4 In. 22.00
   Amber, Poison On Reverse, 3 5/8 In. 15.00
   Amber, Ribbed, 3 3/4 In. 18.00
   Amber, Ribbed, BIM, 3 3/4 In. 18.00
   Amber, Tinct, Skull & Crossbones, Square, ABM, BIMAL, 2 3/16 In. 20.00
   Amber, Triangular, Rounded Back, 4 3/4 In. 12.00
   Ammonia, Aqua, Rows of Dots, Oval, BIMAL, 9 1/2 In. 30.00
   Ammonia, S. F. Gas Light Co., Blue Aqua, Blob Top, Whittle, 9 In. 75.00
   Ammonia, S. F. Gaslight Co., Aqua, Green Whirled Neck, Bubbles, 9 In. 33.00
   Aqua, Horizontal Not To Be Taken, Burst Lip, 5 3/4 In. 15.00
   Bowker's Pyrox Poison, Jar, Clear, Lid .... 20.00 To 40.00
   Bowker's Pyrox Poison, Jar, White Glaze, Black Marked, Part Label 100.00
   Bowman's Drug Stores, Pat. Applied For, Cobalt Blue, 7 1/2 In. 577.00
   C. L. G. Co., Hexagon, Cobalt Blue, Horizontal Ribs, 2 Oz. 35.00
   C. L. G. Co., Poison–Poison, Cobalt Blue, Irregular Hexagon, 6 1/4 In. 110.00
   Carbolic Acid, Cobalt Blue, Hexagon With Flat Back, 3 Oz. 45.00
   Champion Embalming Fluid, Springfield, Oh., Clear, Square, 7 1/2 In. 22.50
   Chemical Cat, Chases Rats & Mice, St. Louis, Mo., 8 Oz. ....*Illus* 5.00
   Chloroform, Ribbed, Bright Green, Label, Stopper, 1900, 5 3/4 In. 72.00
   Cobalt Blue, Embossed 24 Oz., N–Arrow, Stopper, 7 1/2 In. 115.00
   Cobalt Blue, Ground Lip, Embossed Poisonous, Rectangular, 4 1/4 In. 25.00
   Cobalt Blue, Irregular Hexagon, 3 Front Panels, 4 1/2 In. 45.00
   Cobalt Blue, Square, Vertical Ribs, Beveled, BIMAL, 6 5/8 In. 75.00
   Cobalt Blue, Triangular Front, Not To Be Taken, 1900, 3 1/4 In. 38.00
   Coffin, Amber, Embossed Poison, BIMAL, ABM, 3 5/8 In. 210.00
   Coffin, Light Cobalt Blue, Embossed, 1890, BIMAL, ABM, 3 1/2 In. 99.00
   Coles Patent, Poison Ossidine, England, Cobalt Blue, 7 5/8 In. 105.00
   Cross Stitching, Dots, Poison, Light Cobalt, Triangular, ABM, 3 In. 38.00
   Cyona, Morgan X, 24, Cobalt Blue 380.00
   Dark Green, Rounded Rectangular, Lattice Front, 1900, 6 1/4 In. 38.00

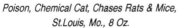

Poison, Chemical Cat, Chases Rats & Mice,
St.Louis, Mo., 8 Oz.

Poison, Fly–Tox, Kills Flys, 6 1/2 In.

Decanter, Skeleton Shape, Ceramic, 4 Skull Cups, 6 3/4 In.	220.00
Diamond Antiseptics, Embossed, ABM, BIMAL, Triangular, 3 5/8 In.	125.00
Diamond Antiseptics, Embossed, Gold Amber, Triangular, 10 3/4 In.	385.00
Dodge, Graduated Scale, Clear, 8 3/4 In.	83.00
Dr. Oreste Sinanide's Medicinal Prep., Coffin, 4 1/2 In.	660.00
Durfee Embalming Fluid Co., Grand Rapids, Mich., Clear, 10 7/8 In.	50.00
Eccles–Chemist, Napier Poison–Take Care, Cobalt, Square, 2 5/8 In.	70.00
Embossed Not To Be Taken, Amber, Hexagonal, ABM, 4 3/8 In.	15.00
Embossed Not To Be Taken, Cobalt Blue, 5 1/8 In.	22.00
Embossed Not To Be Taken, Cobalt Blue, Hexagonal	15.00
Embossed Not To Be Taken, Diamond Point, Hexagonal, Green, 5 In.	12.00
Embossed Not To Be Taken, Hexagonal, 7 In.	30.00
Embossed Not To Be Taken, Ribbed Side, Burst Lip, 4 1/4 In.	12.00
Embossed Not To Be Taken, Ribbed, Aqua, Hexagonal, BIMAL, 5 In.	17.00
Embossed Not To Be Taken, Ribbed, Emerald, Rectangular, 4 1/4 In.	12.00
Embossed Not To Be Taken, Ribbed, Olive, Rectangular, 5 1/2 In.	15.00
Embossed Poison, Amber, Tooled Lip, BIMAL, ABM, 3 1/4 In. .... 44.00 To	72.00
Embossed Poison, Cobalt Blue, Octagonal, Ground, Lip, 2 5/8 In.	61.00
Embossed Poison, Emerald, Vertically Ribbed, Rectangular, 3 1/2 In.	10.00
Embossed Poison, Front Ribbing, Cobalt, BIMAL, Hexagonal, 3 1/2 In.	18.00
Embossed Poison, Front Ribbing, Grass Green, BIMAL, 4 1/8 In.	24.00
Embossed Poison, Lattice & Diamond, Deep Cobalt Blue, 5 1/2 In.	143.00
Embossed Poison, Medium Amber, Tooled Lip, 4 3/4 In.	330.00
Embossed Poison, Teal, Cylindrical, BIMAL, 3 1/4 In.	17.00
Embossed Poisonous Not To Be Taken, Aqua, Ribbed, Oval, 5 5/8 In.	20.00
Embossed Poisonous, Half Ribbed, Amber, Hexagonal, ABM, 2 1/2 In.	4.00
Embossed Rating On Shoulder, Cobalt Blue, BIMAL, Hexagonal, 5 In.	30.00
Embossed Use With Caution, Cobalt Blue, 8 7/8 In.	110.00
Emerald Green, 2 Ribbed Panels, Hexagonal, BIMAL, ABM, 6 In.	10.00
Emerald Green, Embossed Not To Be Taken, BIMAL, 5 1/2 In.	25.00
Figural, Skull, Cobalt Blue, Crossed Bones On Base, 4 1/8 In.	1430.00
Figural, Skull, Pat. June 26th, 1894, Cobalt Blue, BIMAL, 3 1/2 In.	1045.00
Figural, Skull, White Opalescent, 3 In.	65.00
Flask, Clear, Amethyst Tint, Diamond Pattern, OP, 1850, 5 1/4 In.	412.00
Flask, Hobnail, Blown Half–Post Type, Germany, 1820–1850, 6 In.	165.00
Fly–Tox, Kills Flys, 6 1/2 In. ....*Illus*	3.00
Frosted Skull, Clear, Cork, ABM, 2 3/4 In.	15.00
Goffe Potash Water, Birmingham, Cobalt Blue, Round Torpedo	440.00
Green, Ribbed Cylinder, Stopper, 6 3/4 In.	30.00
H. B. Co., Lattice & Diamond Pattern, Cobalt Blue, Round, 3 7/8 In.	35.00
H. B. Co., Lattice & Diamond Pattern, Cobalt Blue, Round, 6 7/8 In.	72.00
Imperial Fluid Company Poison, Syracuse, Embalming, Clear, Gal.	95.00
Imperial Fluid Company, Syracuse, Clear, 11 1/2 In.	50.00
J. T. M. & Co., Embossed Poison, Amber, Tooled Lip, Triangular, 3 In.	99.00
Jacob Hulle, Not To Be Taken, Strychnine, Octagonal, Blue, 3 1/2 In.	15.00
Kilner Bros. Makers, Clear, 6 5/8 In.	17.50
Kilner Bros. Makers, Cobalt Blue, Tapered, Round, 8 1/4 In.	85.00
Lattice & Diamond, Clear, Cylindrical, BIMAL, 3 7/8 In.	50.00
Lattice & Diamond, Cobalt Blue, Flat Shoulder, 7 1/4 In.	121.00
Lattice & Diamond, Cobalt Blue, Round, 4 5/8 In.	44.00
Lysol Ltd., Cylinder, Embossed Not To Be Taken, Amber, 3 1/4 In.	10.00
Lysol, Jug, Deep Olive Green, Cross Banding, 8 In.	60.00
M. C. C. Co., Skull & Crossbones, Tinct Iodine, Cobalt Blue, 3 1/8 In.	94.00
Melvin & Badger, Irregular Hexagon, Cobalt Blue, 5 In.	75.00
Mercurous Iodide Yellow, 500 Tablets, Black, Neck Insignia, 4 In.	22.00
Mercury Bichloride, Amber, Rectangular, ABM, BIMAL, 2 11/16 In.	14.00
Myer & Co., Death Dust, Aqua, 7 In.	3.00
Neuroline, Miniature	162.00
Norwich Coffin 4A, Embossed, Amber, Coffin Shape, 4 15/16	1595.00
Norwich Coffin, Embossed, Amber, Tooled Lip, Contents, 3 3/8 In.	94.00
Norwich Pharmacal Co., Norwich, N. Y., Coffin, Cobalt Blue, 3 1/2 In.	61.00
Owbridge's Embrocation Hull, Deep Cobalt, Hexagonal, BIMAL, 5 In.	30.00
Owl Drug Co., 2 3/4 In.	25.00

Poison, Rat–Nip, Kills Rats,
Wartime Package, 3 In.

Poison, Strychnia, Philadelphia, 2 1/2 In.

Owl Drug Co., Clear, Small	75.00
Owl Drug Co., Cobalt Blue, Triangular, 1880–1900, 7 3/4 In.	577.00
Owl Drug Co., Owl Sitting On Mortar, Cobalt Blue, 3 3/8 In.	66.00
Owl Drug Co., Owl, Cobalt Blue, Tooled Lip, Slug Plate, 5 1/8 In.	220.00
Owl Drug Co., Owl, Cobalt Blue, Tooled Top, Slug Plate, 2 3/4 In.	83.00
Owl Drug Co., Owl, Cobalt Blue, Triangular, 3 3/16 In.	71.50
Owl Drug Co., Owl, Cobalt Blue, Triangular, 4 3/4 In.	215.00
Owl Drug Co., Owl, Cobalt Blue, Triangular, 9 3/8 In.	478.00
Owl Drug Co., Slug Plate 2 2/3 In.	12.00
Owl, Sparkling, 8 In.	300.00
P. D. & Co., Skull & Crossbones, Amber, Rectangular, 2 1/2 In.	55.00
P. D. & Co., Skull Has Smile, Crossbones, Amber, 2 5/8 In.	100.00
Pearlite Mfg. Co., Amber, Diamond Shape, X's Along Edges, ISP, 9 In.	25.00
Photo Chemical, Eastman, Rochester, N. Y., Clear, BIM, 5 In.	9.00
Plumber Drug Co., Lattice & Diamond, Deep Cobalt, 7 1/2 In.	94.00
Poison On 2 Panels, Amber, Oval, BIMAL, 3 In.	20.00
Poison On 2 Panels, Cobalt Blue, Triangular, ABM, 3 1/4 In.	30.00
Poison On 2 Panels, Cobalt, Irregular Hexagon, BIMAL, 4 1/8 In.	55.00
Poison Panel, Amber, Triangular–Rounded Back, 2 5/8 In.	4.00
Poison, Quilted Cobalt Blue, Stopper, Cylinder	115.00
Poison–Poison, Amber, 2 Flat Panels, 8 1/8 In.	85.00
Pot, Stoneware, Poison Embossed Around Shoulder, 1910, 5 1/2 In.	88.00
Powers & Weightman, Strychnine Sulphate Crystals, 2 1/8 In.	14.00
Quilt Pattern, Cobalt Blue, Poison Stopper, Tooled Top, 5 1/2 In.	66.00
Quilted, Cobalt Blue, Cork, Cylindrical, 5 1/2 In.	45.00
Quilted, Cobalt Blue, Cork, Cylindrical, 6 1/4 In.	352.00
Quilted, Cobalt Blue, Round, Quilted Embossed Stopper, 4 3/4 In.	50.00
Quilted, Cobalt Blue, Stopper, 6 In.	90.00
Quilted, Cobalt Blue, Stopper, ABM, 7 1/8 In.	120.00
Rat–Nip, Kills Rats, Wartime Package, 3 In. ....*Illus*	4.00
Sharp & Dohme, Baltimore, Md., Amber, Quilted	35.00
Sharp & Dohme, Skull & Crossbones, Yellow Amber, 4 5/8 In.	908.00
Sharp's Ammonia, Apple Green, 9 1/4 In.	120.00
Skeleton, Pottery, Clock, Brown & White Glazes, Germany, 5 3/4 In.	198.00
Skull & Crossbones, Cobalt Blue, Embossed, 1910–1920, 2 3/4 In.	66.00
Skull & Crossbones, DP Poison, Cobalt Blue, Tooled Lip, 3 In.	2035.00
Skull & Crossbones, Tinct Iodine, Amber, ABM, 3 1/4 In.	30.00
Skull & Crossbones, Tinct Iodine, Amber, Square, 2 5/8 In.	15.00
Skull & Crossbones, Tinct Iodine, Amber, Square, 3 1/4 In.	12.00
Skull & Crossbones, Tinct Iodine, Cobalt Blue, 1900, 2 1/8 In.	52.00

Skull & Crossbones, Tinct Iodine, Cobalt Blue, 3 1/16 In. 125.00
Skull & Crossbones, Yellow Amber, Tooled Lip, 4 5/8 In. 578.00
Skull, Figural, Deep Cobalt Blue, 1880–1890, 4 1/4 In. 1045.00
Slanted Horizontal Ribbing, Light Green, Crescent, 4 1/2 In. 35.00
Star, Emerald Green 126.00
Strychnia, Philadelphia, 2 1/2 In. ....*Illus* 240.00
Submarine, Embossed Poison, Cobalt Blue, Small .... 480.00 To 600.00
Sulpholine, Cobalt Blue, Rectangular, 6 In. 18.00
Sun Drug, Green, 2 3/4 In. 130.00
Sun Drug, Hexagonal, Cobalt Blue, England, 3 3/8 In. 14.00
Tinct Iodine, Cobalt Blue, Embossed, 1900, 2 1/8 In. 130.00
Tinct Iodine, M. C. C. Co., Cobalt Blue, 1900, 3 1/8 In. 120.00
Tinct Iodine, Scull & Crossbones, Amber, Rubber Stopper, 3 In. 38.00
Tinct Iodine, Skull & Crossbones, Light Cobalt 90.00
Tippers Thretipene 3 Tips Disinfectant, Amber, 9 In. 290.00
Triangular, Cobalt Blue, 3 1/4 In. 25.00
U. D. Co., Cobalt Blue, Triangular, 1890–1910, 8 1/8 In. 440.00
U. D. Co., Mercury Bichloride, Triangular, Cobalt, 5 1/4 In. 187.00
Vapo Cresolene Use Kerosene, 6–In. Lamp, Bottle With Contents 105.00
W. T. & Co., Cobalt Blue, 3 3/4 In. 35.00
W. T. & Co., Lattice & Diamond, Poison Stopper, Cobalt Blue, 4 3/4 In. 71.50
Webbers, Indian Oil of Cream, Cobalt Blue, Hexagonal, 6 In. 65.00
Wilberts Javex, Amber, Concave & Ribbed, 9 In. 45.00
Wm. Radam's Microbe Killer, No. 3, Crock, Applied Handle, Gal. 85.00
Wyeth & Bro., Phila., Cobalt, Rectangular, BIMAL, 2 3/4 In. .... 70.00 To 77.00

POTTERY

Many bottles were made of pottery. In this section we have included those that have no brand name and do not fit into another category. Many figural flasks, such as those made at the Bennington, Vermont, potteries or the Anna pottery, are listed. Another section lists stoneware bottles.

POTTERY, Ballantine's Liquor Blended Scotch, Blue Top & Handle, 3 3/8 In. 22.00
Blue & White, Mason's Mallet Shape, Applied Boys, 8 1/4 In. 164.00
Coachman, Figural, 11 In. ....*Illus* 650.00
Coronation Whiskey, Wilkinson & Co., King & Queen, 7 1/2 In. 510.00
Cream of Irish Whiskey, Shamrock, Sepia, Pear Shape, 8 In. 137.00
Crock, St. Regis Everbearing Raspberry, Lid, Pat. 1896, 1/2 Gal. 69.00
Decanter, Gin, Tan Top, Cream Base, Square, Strap Handle, 7 In. 76.00
Dewar's Whisky, Green Top, Scene, Doulton Lambeth, 1 1/2 In. 337.00
Dodson & Braun's Fine Pickles, St. Louis, Barrel, Bail, 14 1/2 In. 160.00
Dr. Cronk, Large Letters 35.00
Flagon, R. J. Fullwood & Bland's Dairy, White, Handle, 3 3/8 In. 73.00

Pottery, Pig, Mottled Brown, Kneeling, 7 In.

Pottery, Coachman, Figural, 11 In. *Pottery, S.O.B. Bourbon, 2 Handles, 11 In.*

Flagon, Whiskey, Darhind & Co. Ltd., London, Handle, 2 3/4 In.	55.00
Galley of Lorne, Transfer of Ship, Bulbous, 6 7/8 In.	482.00
Glenmore Kentucky, Bourbon Whiskey, Buff, Brown, 2 Handles, 7 In.	30.00
Greer's Brig O'Weir Liquor Whiskey, Crossed Flags, 7 In.	155.00
Hot Water Bottle, Adaptable, Fulham Pottery, Stopper, 2 Pt.	49.00
Jug, Buff Top & Handle, Brown Base, No Lip, 8 1/4 In.	15.00
Jug, Compliments of Hirsch, Louisville, Ky., Tan & Brown, 3 In.	89.00
Jug, Cream of Highland Whiskeys, My Queen, Sepia Print, 7 1/2 In.	273.00
Jug, Face, Wm. Greer & Co. Ltd., Glasgow, Sarreguemines, 5 7/8 In.	182.00
Jug, Mohawk, Labels, Qt.	20.00
Jug, O. V. I. Scotch, Henry Simpson & Co., Cobalt Blue Top, 6 3/5 In.	746.00
Jug, Robbie Burns Famed Old Scotch Whiskey, Red Brown, 6 In.	455.00
Jug, Spicy Cologne, Blue Stenciled, 3 In.	29.00
Jug, White Horse Whiskey, Deep Blue Transfer, 5 In.	819.00
Keller's Inks, Mucilage Paste & Sealing Wax, Blue, No Lid, Gal.	60.00
Old Valley Whiskey, Perfection, Blue Transfer, 7 3/8 In.	127.00
Owl Drug Co., 1 Wing, White, Display, 4 5/8 In.	220.00
Pig, Mottled Brown, Kneeling, 7 In. ....*Illus*	550.00
Pig, Railroad Guide, Anna–Type, 1890, 4 x 8 In.	4070.00
Pig, Railroad, Greyish Beige, Anna Pottery, 1882, 7 In.	6325.00
S. O. B. Bourbon, 2 Handles, 11 In. ....*Illus*	75.00
Scotch Malt & Whiskey, Glencoe Distillery, Blue Transfer, 7 In.	218.00
Skeleton, Brown & White Glaze, Poison At Waist, 8 In.	320.00
Tobacco Jar, Martin Bros., Southall, 1890, Salt Glaze, Dated	1000.00
Vulcanizing Solution, Goodyear Tire & Rubber, White, 4 3/4 In.	60.00
Warmer, Buchans Blue Bottle, Blue Top, Stand Up Cylinder, 10 In.	36.00
Wise's Old Irish Whiskey, Foliage Transfer, 7 1/2 In.	86.00
Wm. Kraas Celebrated Root Beer, 12–Sided	45.00

---------------------------------- **PURPLE POWER** ----------------------------------

Purple power is the Kansas State University slogan. A series of bottles was made from 1970 to 1972 picturing the wildcat at a sporting event. They were distributed by Jon–Sol.

PURPLE POWER, Football Player, 1972	11.00
Wildcat On Basketball, Kansas State U.	12.00 To 15.00
Wildcat On Football	15.00
Wildcat Walking, Kansas State U.	17.00 To 22.00

---------------------------------- **ROYAL DOULTON** ----------------------------------

Royal Doulton is the mark used on Doulton and Company pottery from 1902 to the present. Doulton and Company of England was founded in 1853. The company made many advertising pieces. Bottles include a series of brown Kingsware flasks (often marked with a product name) and figural bottles such as the crow for Old Crow or the Don (Zorro) for Sandeman sherry. The Don held either a yellow or red glass, depending on the type of sherry in the bottle. For additional information, check *Doulton Kingsware Whisky Flasks* by Jocelyn Lukins and *Royal Doulton Jugs* by Jean Dale.

ROYAL DOULTON, Bonnie Prince Charlie, Kingsware, Dewars, 7 In. .... 118.00 To 164.00
Dewar's Scotch Whiskey, Beefeater, Pear Shape, Brown, 7 In. 218.00
Flagon, Advertising, Miniature 273.00
Flagon, Bulmers Cider, Green Glaze, Metal Handle, 16 1/2 In. 41.00
Flagon, Handle, Lambeth, For Brewers & Distillers, 2 3/4 In. 182.00
Flask, Ben Jonson, Kingsware, Dewar's Whisky, 1909, 7 1/4 In. 111.00
Flask, Gillie & Fisherman, Dark Brown, 8 1/4 In. 277.00
Flask, Hip, Punch & Judy, Lambeth, 8 1/2 In. 382.00
Flask, Pipe Major, Kingsware, Dewar's Whisky, 1916, 8 1/2 In. 49.00
Flask, Spirit, Green Top, Lion & Crown, Miniature 33.00
Footwarmer, Brown Print .... 25.00 To 63.00
Ginger Beer, Allover Brown Salt Glaze, Blob Top, 2 1/4 In. 27.00
Ginger Beer, John Dewar, Cork, 7 In. 98.00
Ginger Beer, Salt Glaze, Dark Top 27.00
Grant Mackay & Cos. Scotch, Plated Stopper, Blues, 9 In. 155.00
Grouse 250.00
Ink, Baby, Hinged Back, Brown Salt Glaze, L. Harradine 369.00
Ink, Hoof Shape, Triumph Patent, Blue & Green Glaze, 3 In. 356.00
Ink, Isobath, Figural, Artware, Blue, Brown, Cream, 6 1/8 In. 131.00
Ink, Woman, Votes For Women, Brown Salt Glaze, 3 3/8 In. 410.00
Inkwell, Ushers Scotch Whiskey Around, Blue, 3 1/2 In. 200.00
Jovial Monk, Flask, Kingsware, Dewars Whisky, 7 1/4 In. 210.00
Jug, 5 Portraits Charles Dickens Memories, Brown, 9 In. 328.00
Jug, Alchemist, Yellow, Kingsware, 1913, 9 In. 1580.00
Jug, Bellarmine, Face Mask Top, Salt Glaze, Miniature 139.00
Jug, Connoisseur, Kingsware, Flattened Pear Shape, 8 1/2 In. 453.00
Jug, Fine Old Scotch Whiskey, Salt Glaze, Leaves, 8 In. 182.00
Jug, Heart's Content, Kingsware, 3 In. 82.00
Jug, Huntingware, Salt Glaze, Applied Sprigs, 1 3/4 In. 38.00
Jug, John Dewar & Sons, Blue Top, Squat, Lambeth, 5 7/8 In. 437.00
Jug, John Dewar & Sons, Hunting Scenes, Green Top, 6 1/2 In. 155.00
Jug, John Dewar & Sons, Whisky, Perth, Stoneware, Qt. 135.00
Jug, Motto, Black Green Top, Salt Glaze, Waisted, 8 7/8 In. 100.00
Jug, Mr. Micawber, Yellow Glaze, 8 In. 1183.00
Jug, Special Highland Whisky, Tan, Brown Handle, Ship 125.00
Jug, Watchman, Kingsware, Cylindrical, 10 1/2 In. 181.00
Jug, Watchman, Kingsware, Flattened Globular, 7 1/4 In. 167.00
Jug, Whiskey, Handle, Dark Top, 1 7/8 In. 22.00
King George IV, Deep Blue, Spherical, Border, 7 1/2 In. 137.00
McNab, Kingsware, Dewar's Whisky, Stopper, 9 1/2 In. 230.00
Mr. Pickwick, Kingsware, Cylindrical, 8 1/4 In. 349.00
Spirit Barrel, Scenes On Side, Pottery Stand, 6 3/4 In. 546.00
Watchman, Kingsware, 4 1/8 In. 1230.00
Watchman, Kingsware, Dewar's Whisky, Cylindrical, 11 In. 131.00
Watchman, Kingsware, Dewer's Whisky, Cylindrical, 8 In. 82.00
Zorro, Sandeman 25.00
    SANDWICH GLASS, see Cologne; Scent

---------------------------------- **SARSAPARILLA** ----------------------------------

The most widely distributed syphillis *cure* used in the nineteenth century was sarsaparilla. The roots of the smilax vine were harvested, cleaned, dried, and sold to apothecaries and drug manufacturers. They added alcohol and other flavorings, such as the roots of yellow dock, dandelion, or burdock or the bark from prickly ash, sassafras, or birch trees. A few

Sarsaparilla, Brown's For The Kidneys, Liver & Blood, 9 1/4 In.

Sarsaparilla, Sand's, New York, 10 In.

Seal, Bols, Ring Handle, 7 In.

makers also added fruit or vegetable juice and clover blossoms. All of this was mixed to make the medicine called *sarsaparilla*. It was claimed to cure many diseases, including skin diseases, boils, pimples, piles, tumors, scrofulous conditions including king's evil (a swelling of the neck), and rheumatism. It could cleanse and purify the blood, a process doctors thought should take place regularly for good health.

The first labeled sarsaparilla was made in the early 1800s. Some bottled products called sarsaparilla are still made today. The bottles were usually rectangular with embossed letters, or soda-bottle shaped. Most were light green or aqua but some amber and cobalt bottles were made. Later bottles had paper labels.

SARSAPARILLA, Ayer's Compound, Aqua, BIM, 8 1/2 In. 32.00
  Ayers Concentrated Sarsaparilla, Rectangular, 7 3/4 In. 65.00
  Brown's For The Kidneys, Liver & Blood, 9 1/4 In. ....*Illus* 15.00
  Buffum Sarsaparilla & Lemon Mineral Water, Aqua, IP 100.00
  Buffum Sarsaparilla Mineral Water, Aqua, 10–Sided, Pontil 200.00
  Bush's Smilax, Aqua, OP, 10 In., DeG–33 .... 275.00
  C. M. Townsend & Co., Lima, Ohio, Clear, 9 1/4 In. 225.00
  Carl's Sarsaparilla & Celery Compound, Aqua, 7 3/8 In. 63.00
  Concentrated Compound Extract, Ayers, Mass., Aqua, OP 69.00
  Dana's, Belfast, Maine, Aqua, BIM, 8 3/4 In. 28.00
  Dodge City 10.00
  Dr. Belding's Wild Cherry, Minneapolis, Minn., Aqua, 9 1/4 In. 65.00
  Dr. Cronk's Compound Beer, Deep Aqua, IP, 8 1/4 In. 523.00
  Dr. Denison's, Medium Green, Oval, OP, 7 1/5 In. 495.00
  Dr. Guysott's Extract of Yellow Dock, Emerald, 9 In. 1870.00
  Dr. Guysott's Yellow Dock & Sarsaparilla, Aqua, 10 1/4 In. 110.00
  Dr. James, Pittsburgh, Pa., Pale Aqua, 9 1/8 In. 150.00
  Dr. Marshalls' Extract, Sarsaparilla, Dandelion, Aqua, 8 In. 30.00
  Dr. Reinhauser's Hydriodated, Rochester, Deep Aqua, 8 5/8 In. 1018.00
  Dr. Townsend's Sarsaparilla, Albany, N. Y., Green, IP 235.00
  Dr. Townsend's Sarsaparilla, Albany, N. Y., Pontil, Olive 155.00
  Dr. Townsend's, Albany, N. Y., Olive Amber, 9 1/2 In. 264.00
  Dr. Townsend's, Albany, N. Y., Pale Apple Green, 4 1/2 In. 150.00
  Dr. Townsend's, Deep Yellow Olive, Square, Pontil, 9 3/4 In. 132.00
  Dr. Townsend's, Emerald 50.00
  Dr. Townsend's, Light Olive, Large OP 195.00
  Dr. Townsend's, N. Y., Blue Green, Square, IP, 9 1/2 In. 193.00
  Edward Wilders, Sarsaparilla & Potash, Louisville, 8 1/2 In. 175.00
  Edwin Joy, San Fran., Aqua, Rectangular, 8 1/2 In. .... 18.00 To 25.00

F. Gleason's Sarsaparilla & Lemon Mineral Water, Sapphire	375.00
Foley's Sarsaparilla, Chicago, Light Amber	35.00
Graefenberg Co., New York, Aqua, OP, Label, 7 1/8 In.	225.00
Grants, Fremont, Neb. Aqua	30.00
Hood's, Lowell, Mass., Aqua, 9 In.	32.00
John Bull Extract of Sarsaparilla, Aqua, BIMAL, 9 1/2 In.	35.00
John Bull Extract of Sarsaparilla, Emerald, IP, 8 3/4 In.	743.00
John Bull Extract of Sarsaparilla, Louisville, Aqua, 9 In.	175.00
Jone's & Co., Williamsport, Pa., Aqua, 8 3/4 In.	195.00
Joy's, San Francisco, Aqua, Rectangular, 8 1/2 In.	18.00
Kennedy's Sarsaparilla & Celery Compound, 1890, 9 3/4 In.	38.00
King's Celery & Sarsaparilla Compound, Amber, 9 3/4 In.	38.00
King's Celery & Sarsaparilla Compound, Amber, 10 In.	195.00
Langley's Compound, San Francisco, Aqua, 10 3/4 In.	320.00
Log Cabin, Deep Golden Amber, 1880s, 8 7/8 In.	88.00
Log Cabin, Rochester, Golden Amber, Round Blob Lip, 9 In.	55.00
Masury's Sarsaparilla Compound, Aqua, Embossed, OP, Qt.	275.00
Old Dr. Townsend's, New York, Light Green Aqua, 9 1/2 In.	60.00
Radway's Sarsaparilla Resolvent	20.00
Rush's Sarsaparilla & Iron, Flanders, M. D., N. Y., 8 1/2 In.	12.50
Rush's, Aqua	25.00
Sand's, New York, 10 In. ......Illus	65.00
Shepherd's Genuine Preparation, Baltimore, Aqua, 5 3/4 In.	660.00
Sir Astley Coopers U.S. & Jamaica, London Lab., Aqua, 8 In.	40.00

SCENT

Perfume and cologne are not the same as scent. Scent is smelling salts, a perfume with ammonia salts added for a sharp vapor that could revive a person who was feeling faint. Because our female ancestors wore tightly laced corsets and high starched collars, the problem of feeling faint was common. Scent bottles were sometimes small mold–blown bottles in the full spectrum of glass colors. Sometimes the bottles were free blown and made in elaborate shapes to resemble, perhaps, a seahorse. By the mid–nineteenth century molded scents were made, usually of dark green, cobalt, or yellow glass. These were rather squat bottles, often with unusual stoppers. There is much confusion about the difference between cologne and scent bottles because manufacturers usually made both kinds.

SCENT, see also Cologne; Perfume

SCENT, Amber, Pewter Cap, 2 1/2 In.	75.00
Amethyst, 16 Ribs, Swirled Right, 2–Piece Mold, Pontil, 2 7/8 In.	175.00
Amethyst, Pewter Cap, 2 1/2 In.	120.00
Baroque Pattern, Opalescent, 2–Piece Mold, Hinged Lid, 2 1/2 In.	75.00
Beaded Flute, Opalescent, Label, 5 5/8 In.	165.00
Blue & White Swirl, Lozenge Shape, Mid–Victorian, 3 1/8 In.	55.00
Clear, Applied Rigaree, 3 1/8 In.	45.00
Clear, Sitting Oriental Frosted Stopper	775.00
Cobalt Blue, 12–Sided, Ring Lip, 5 3/4 In.	30.00
Cut Glass, Clear, Threaded Mouth, 2 3/4 In.	50.00
Deep Puce, Blown, Flared Lip, 3 1/8 In.	45.00
Diamond Daisy, Clear, Nickel Plated Cap, Castor, 3 5/8 In.	10.00
Diamond Panels, Fiery Opalescent, Threaded Pewter Cap, 3 1/8 In.	35.00
Faceted Diamond, Clear, Screw Cap, 2 1/8 In.	10.00
Geometric Pattern, Citron, 3 1/4 In.	60.00
High Top Shoe, Figural, Aqua, Saratoga Dressing, 4 3/4 In.	22.50
Horizontal & Vertical Ribs, Opalescent, 3 1/4 In.	25.00
Horizontal & Vertical Ribs, Sapphire Shaded To Cobalt, 3 3/8 In.	265.00
Molded, Shell Design, Blue, Sheared Lip, 2 3/8 In.	265.00
Octagonal, Opaque White, Cap, 3 1/4 In.	55.00
Oval, Molded Design, Blue, 2 5/8 In.	170.00
Paneled, Amethyst, Flared Lip, 4 7/8 In.	85.00
Peacock Green, Teardrop Shape, Ribbed, 3 1/8 In.	95.00
Powder Blue, Gold Bands & Stars, Silver Stopper, 2 1/8 In.	247.00
Ribbed, Deep Violet Blue, Fire Polished Lip, 3 In.	75.00
Ribbed, Swirled To Right, Amethyst, OP	129.00

Scroll, Clear, Threaded Neck, Nickel Plated Copper Cap, 2 7/8 In.	305.00
Scroll, Clear, White Looping, Applied Rigaree, 2 3/8 In.	65.00
Scroll, Deep Amethyst, Pewter Cap, 2 5/8 In.	45.00
Scroll, Opaque White Opalescent, Pewter Cap, 2 1/2 In.	15.00
Scroll, Peacock Blue Pewter Cap, 2 5/8 In.	110.00
Scroll, Yellow Green, Pewter Cap, 2 1/2 In.	130.00
Seahorse, Clear, Applied Rigaree, 2 5/8 In. .... 45.00 To 90.00	
Seahorse, Clear, White Looping, Applied Cobalt Rigaree, 2 3/8 In.	85.00
Smooth Sides, Emerald Green, Pewter Cap, 2 3/8 In.	22.50
Spiral Ribs, Clear, Screw Cap, 1 1/4 In.	10.00
Sunburst, Clear, Sheared & Polished Lip, Pontil, 2 7/8 In.	66.00
Waisted Hexagonal, Cobalt Blue, Cap, 2 1/2 In.	75.00
Waisted Octagonal, Opaque White, Threaded Mouth, 2 1/4 In.	50.00

-------------------------------- SEAL --------------------------------

Seal or sealed bottles are named for the glass seal that was applied to the body of the bottle. While still hot, this small pad of glass was impressed with an identification mark. Seal bottles are known from the second century but the earliest examples collectors can find today date from the eighteenth century. Because the seal bottle was the most popular container for wine and other liquids shipped to North America, broken bottles, seals alone, or whole bottles are often found in old dumps and excavations. Dutch gin, French wine, and English liquors were all shipped in large seal bottles. Seal bottles also held rum, olive oil, mineral water, and even vinegar. It is possible to date the bottle from the insignia on the seal and from the shape of the bottle.

SEAL, Bols, Ring Handle, 7 In. ....*Illus*	600.00
Coat of Arms, Held By 2 Lions, Olive Amber, 9 7/8 In.	275.00
Joseph Peabody, Olive Amber, 10 1/2 In.	160.00
R. Gafkell, Olive Amber, Pontil, 1761	750.00
Royal Crown Above Letter C, Olive Amber, 10 3/4 In.	160.00
T. C. Pearsall, Olive Amber, Pontil	240.00
T. Herbert Chester, Olive Amber, Pontil, 1808	425.00

-------------------------------- SELTZER --------------------------------

The word *seltzer* was first used for mineral water with medicinal properties at Selters, Germany. Seltzer was thought to be good for intestinal disorders. The word soon was used for any of the artificially carbonated waters that became popular in the nineteenth century. Seltzer bottles were advertised in Philadelphia by 1816. *Soda* and *seltzer* mean the same thing. Collectors want the bottles that say *seltzer* and the special pump bottles that dispensed it. These pump bottles were usually covered with a metal mesh to keep glass from flying in case of an explosion. The top of the bottle was a spigot and carbonation was added to the water when the spigot was pressed.

SELTZER, see also Coca–Cola; Mineral Water; Pepsi–Cola; Soda

SELTZER, Club Seltzer, Pittsburgh Seltzer Co., Green, Embossed, Round	27.50
G. A. Signitz, Dayton, Oh., Blue, Metal Spout, 12 In.	30.00
Leverenz Sparkling Water, Blue, Round, 28 Oz.	12.50
Leverenz Sparkling Water, Green, 10 Panels, 28 Oz.	12.50
Ribbed, Clear, Metal Spout, England, 6 1/8 In.	22.00
South Devon Mineral Water Co., Deep Green, Blob Lip, 5 1/2 In.	31.00
Wm. Thompson, Aberdeen, Dark Green, Blob Lip,, 6 1/8 In.	27.00

-------------------------------- SKI COUNTRY --------------------------------

Ski Country bottles are issued by The Foss Company of Golden, Colorado. The first bottles were made in 1973. By 1975 the company wrote us that they were making about 24 different decanter designs in each size each year, plus one decanter in the gallon size. The firm has marketed many series of decanters. The National Ski Country Bottle Club, at 1224 Washington Avenue, Golden, CO 80401, will send lists and information.

SKI COUNTRY, Ahrens–Fox Fire Engine, Customer Speciality, 1981 .... 126.00 To 250.00	
Animal, Antelope, Pronghorn, 1979 .... 42.00 To 75.00	
Animal, Badger, 1981 .... 29.00 To 64.00	
Animal, Badger, 1981, Miniature .... 17.00 To 31.00	

Animal, Bear, Brown, 1974 .... 24.00 To 45.00
Animal, Bear, Polar, 1984 .... 39.00 To 75.00
Animal, Bear, Polar, 1984, Miniature .... 24.00 To 45.00
Animal, Bobcat, 1981 .... 45.00 To 80.00
Animal, Bobcat, 1981, Miniature .... 18.00 To 31.00
Animal, Buffalo, Stampede, 1982 .... 45.00 To 75.00
Animal, Buffalo, Stampede, 1982, Miniature .... 20.00 To 35.00
Animal, Bull, Charolais, 1974 .... 33.00 To 55.00
Animal, Cow, Holstein, 1973 .... 73.00 To 99.00
Animal, Coyote, Family, 1978 .... 39.00 To 65.00
Animal, Coyote, Family, 1978, Miniature .... 18.00 To 38.00
Animal, Deer, White Tail, 1982 .... 81.00 To 150.00
Animal, Deer, White Tail, 1982, Miniature .... 29.00 To 49.00
Animal, Dog, Basset Hound, 1978 .... 39.00 To 67.00
Animal, Dog, Basset Hound, 1978, Miniature .... 28.00 To 47.00
Animal, Dog, Labrador With Mallard, 1978 .... 81.00 To 135.00
Animal, Dog, Labrador With Mallard, 1978, Miniature .... 23.00 To 39.00
Animal, Dog, Labrador With Pheasant, 1978 .... 54.00 To 90.00
Animal, Dog, Labrador With Pheasant, 1978, Miniature .... 24.00 To 40.00
Animal, Elk, American, 1980 .... 135.00 To 225.00
Animal, Elk, American, 1980, Miniature .... 48.00 To 90.00
Animal, Ferret, Blackfooted, 1976, Miniature .... 36.00 To 69.00
Animal, Fox, and Butterfly, 1983 .... 42.00 To 75.00
Animal, Fox, and Butterfly, 1983, Miniature .... 24.00 To 41.00
Animal, Fox, Family, 1979 .... *Illus* 82.00
Animal, Fox, Family, 1979, Miniature .... 21.00 To 35.00
Animal, Fox, On A Log, 1974 .... 81.00 To 135.00
Animal, Fox, On A Log, 1974, Miniature .... 141.00 To 235.00
Animal, Fox, On A Log, 1981, 1. 75 L. .... 165.00 To 275.00
Animal, Goat, Mountain, Family, Miniature .... 35.00 To 65.00
Animal, Goat, Mountain, Single, 1975 .... 81.00 To 135.00
Animal, Goat, Mountain, Single, 1975, Gal. .... 750.00 To 900.00
Animal, Goat, Mountain, Single, 1975, Miniature .... 36.00 To 60.00
Animal, Jaguar, 1983 .... 87.00 To 160.00
Animal, Jaguar, 1983, Miniature .... 35.00 To 59.00
Animal, Kangaroo, 1974 .... 24.00 To 42.00
Animal, Kangaroo, 1974, Miniature .... 15.00 To 32.00
Animal, Koala, 1973 .... 24.00 To 42.00
Animal, Leopard, Snow, 1979 .... 39.00 To 65.00
Animal, Leopard, Snow, 1979, Miniature .... 20.00 To 35.00

Ski Country, Animal, Fox, Family, 1979   *Ski Country, Christmas, Bob Cratchit, 1977*

Animal, Lion, Mountain Cat, Family .... 54.00 To 62.00
Animal, Lion, Mountain Cat, Family, Miniature .... 18.00 To 27.00
Animal, Lion, Mountain, 1973 .... 34.00 To 75.00
Animal, Lion, Mountain, 1975, Miniature .... 18.00 To 37.00
Animal, Lions, African, Safari .... 35.00 To 60.00
Animal, Lions, African, Safari, Miniature .... 15.00 To 30.00
Animal, Moose, Bull, 1982 .... 57.00 To 115.00
Animal, Moose, Bull, 1982, Miniature .... 27.00 To 50.00
Animal, Mountain Goat, Gal. .... 510.00 To 800.00
Animal, Otter, River, 1979 .... 47.00 To 79.00
Animal, Otter, River, 1979, Miniature .... 20.00 To 36.00
Animal, Raccoon, 1975 .... 29.00 To 65.00
Animal, Raccoon, 1975, Miniature .... 15.00 To 45.00
Animal, Raccoons, 1982, Club Decanter .... 42.00 To 108.00
Animal, Raccoons, 1982, Club Decanter, Miniature .... 26.00 To 49.00
Animal, Ram, Big Horn, 1973 .... 56.00 To 95.00
Animal, Ram, Big Horn, 1973, Miniature .... 24.00 To 45.00
Animal, Sheep, Dall, Grand Slam, 1980 .... 90.00 To 195.00
Animal, Sheep, Dall, Grand Slam, 1980, Miniature .... 27.00 To 55.00
Animal, Sheep, Desert, Grand Slam, 1980 .... 75.00 To 125.00
Animal, Sheep, Desert, Grand Slam, 1980, Miniature .... 24.00 To 50.00
Animal, Sheep, Rocky Mt., Grand Slam, 1981 .... 42.00 To 75.00
Animal, Sheep, Rocky Mt., Grand Slam, 1981, Miniature .... 23.00 To 50.00
Animal, Sheep, Stone, Grand Slam, 1981 .... 48.00 To 80.00
Animal, Sheep, Stone, Grand Slam, 1981, Miniature .... 27.00 To 45.00
Animal, Skunk, Family, 1978 .... 36.00 To 60.00
Animal, Skunk, Family, 1978, Miniature .... 21.00 To 35.00
Animal, Squirrels, 1983, Club Decanter .... 75.00 To 135.00
Animal, Squirrels, 1983, Club Decanter, Miniature .... 81.00 To 105.00
Animal, Walrus, Alaskan .... 30.00 To 60.00
Animal, Walrus, Alaskan, Miniature .... 12.00 To 25.00
Bird, Blackbird, Redwing, 1977 .... 29.00 To 50.00
Bird, Blackbird, Redwing, 1978, Miniature .... 15.00 To 30.00
Bird, Blue Jay, 1978 .... 54.00 To 90.00
Bird, Blue Jay, 1978, Miniature .... 41.00 To 69.00
Bird, Cardinal, 1977 .... 59.00 To 99.00
Bird, Cardinal, 1979, Miniature .... 36.00 To 62.00
Bird, Condor, 1973 .... 44.00 To 74.00
Bird, Condor, 1973, Miniature .... 24.00 To 40.00
Bird, Dove, Peace, 1973 .... 51.00 To 85.00
Bird, Dove, Peace, 1973, Miniature .... 22.00 To 35.00
Bird, Duck, Blue Wing Teal, 1976 .... 174.00 To 300.00
Bird, Duck, Blue Wing Teal, 1976, Miniature .... 59.00 To 102.00
Bird, Duck, Blue Wing Teal, Banded, 1985 .... 41.00 To 800.00
Bird, Duck, Blue Wing Teal, Banded, 1985, Miniature .... 63.00 To 200.00
Bird, Duck, Bufflehead, 1984 .... 45.00 To 85.00
Bird, Duck, Bufflehead, 1984, Miniature .... 21.00 To 40.00
Bird, Duck, Canvasback, 1981 .... 45.00 To 75.00
Bird, Duck, Canvasback, 1981, Miniature .... 18.00 To 43.00
Bird, Duck, Green Wing Teal, 1983 .... 119.00 To 210.00
Bird, Duck, Green Wing Teal, 1983, Miniature .... 27.00 To 55.00
Bird, Duck, King Eider, 1977 .... 39.00 To 75.00
Bird, Duck, King Eider, 1977, Miniature .... 27.00 To 45.00
Bird, Duck, Merganser, Female Hooded, 1981 .... 48.00 To 80.00
Bird, Duck, Merganser, Female Hooded, 1981, Miniature .... 24.00 To 40.00
Bird, Duck, Merganser, Male Hooded, 1983 .... 49.00 To 82.00
Bird, Duck, Merganser, Male Hooded, 1983, Miniature .... 18.00 To 35.00
Bird, Duck, Pintail, 1978 .... 78.00 To 145.00
Bird, Duck, Pintail, 1978, Miniature .... 21.00 To 46.00
Bird, Duck, Pintail, 1979, 1/2 Gal. .... 150.00 To 250.00
Bird, Duck, Red Head, 1974 .... 53.00 To 111.00
Bird, Duck, Red Head, 1974, Miniature .... 40.00 To 67.00
Bird, Duck, Widgeon, 1979 .... 27.00 To 70.00

Ski Country, Bird, Eagle, Birth of Freedom, 1976

Ski Country, Bird, Eagle, Harpy, 1973

Ski Country, Bird, Swallows, Barn, 1977

Bird, Duck, Widgeon, 1979, 1. 75 L. .... 159.00 To 325.00
Bird, Duck, Widgeon, 1979, Miniature .... 15.00 To 39.00
Bird, Duck, Wood, 1974 .... 150.00 To 250.00
Bird, Duck, Wood, 1974, Miniature ....93.00 To 155.00
Bird, Duck, Wood, Banded, 1982 ....75.00 To 125.00
Bird, Duck, Wood, Banded, 1982, Miniature .... 36.00 To 60.00
Bird, Ducks, Wood, 1980, Club Decanter ....225.00 To 375.00
Bird, Ducks, Wood, 1980, Club Decanter, Miniature .... 33.00 To 70.00
Bird, Eagle, Birth of Freedom, 1976 ....*Illus*   139.00
Bird, Eagle, Birth of Freedom, 1976, Miniature ....65.00 To 109.00
Bird, Eagle, Birth of Freedom, 1977, Gal. .... 1500.00 To 2500.00
Bird, Eagle, Easter Seals, 1980 .... 34.00 To 82.00
Bird, Eagle, Easter Seals, 1980, Miniature .... 19.00 To 35.00
Bird, Eagle, Harpy, 1973 ....*Illus*   165.00
Bird, Eagle, Harpy, 1973, Miniature ....76.00 To 127.00
Bird, Eagle, Hawk, 1974 .... 105.00 To 175.00
Bird, Eagle, Hawk, 1977, Miniature .... 59.00 To 99.00
Bird, Eagle, Majestic, 1971 .... 285.00 To 500.00
Bird, Eagle, Majestic, 1971, Miniature ....99.00 To 199.00
Bird, Eagle, Majestic, 1973, Gal. .... 1380.00 To 2300.00
Bird, Eagle, Mountain, 1973 .... 117.00 To 195.00
Bird, Eagle, Mountain, 1973, Miniature ....93.00 To 155.00
Bird, Eagle, On A Drum, 1976 ....99.00 To 180.00
Bird, Eagle, On A Drum, 1977, Miniature .... 46.00 To 85.00
Bird, Eagle, On The Water, 1981 .... 100.00 To 175.00
Bird, Eagle, On The Water, 1981, Miniature .... 36.00 To 65.00
Bird, Falcon, Gyrfalcon, 1983 .... 61.00 To 85.00
Bird, Falcon, Gyrfalcon, 1983, Miniature .... 32.00 To 39.00
Bird, Falcon, Peregrine, 1979 .... 57.00 To 95.00
Bird, Falcon, Peregrine, 1979, Gal. .... 330.00 To 550.00
Bird, Falcon, Peregrine, 1979, Miniature .... 15.00 To 35.00
Bird, Falcon, Prairie, 1981 ....49.00 To 120.00
Bird, Falcon, Prairie, 1981, Miniature ....36.00 To 65.00
Bird, Falcon, White, 1977 ....63.00 To 105.00
Bird, Falcon, White, 1977, Miniature .... 29.00 To 55.00
Bird, Flycatcher, 1979 ....59.00 To 165.00
Bird, Flycatcher, 1979, Miniature .... 33.00 To 65.00
Bird, Gamecock, Survivor .... 54.00 To 90.00
Bird, Gamecock, Survivor, Miniature .... 24.00 To 40.00
Bird, Gamecocks, Fighting, 1980 ....99.00 To 179.00

Bird, Gamecocks, Fighting, 1982, Miniature .... 36.00 To 60.00
Bird, Goose, Canada, Banded, 1986 ....92.00 To 125.00
Bird, Goose, Canada, Banded, 1986, Miniature .... 18.00 To 49.00
Bird, Goose, Canada, Family, 1980 .... 39.00 To 65.00
Bird, Goose, Canada, Family, 1980, Miniature .... 18.00 To 40.00
Bird, Goose, Canada, Single, 1973 ....81.00 To 135.00
Bird, Goose, Canada, Single, 1973, Miniature .... 59.00 To 99.00
Bird, Goose, Snow, 1988 .... 34.00 To 76.00
Bird, Goose, Snow, 1988, Miniature .... 19.00 To 33.00
Bird, Grouse, Ruffled, 1981 .... 39.00 To 65.00
Bird, Grouse, Ruffled, 1981, Miniature .... 17.00 To 33.00
Bird, Grouse, Sage, 1974 .... 45.00 To 95.00
Bird, Grouse, Sage, 1974, Miniature .... 27.00 To 47.00
Bird, Hawk, Red Shoulder, 1973 ....63.00 To 105.00
Bird, Hawk, Red Shoulder, 1973, Miniature .... 27.00 To 45.00
Bird, Hawk, Red–Tailed, 1977 ....55.00 To 115.00
Bird, Hawk, Red–Tailed, 1977, Miniature .... 36.00 To 60.00
Bird, Kestrel, Club Decanter .... 34.00 To 80.00
Bird, Kestrel, Club Decanter, Miniature .... 12.00 To 40.00
Bird, Mallard, Banded, 1980 .... 57.00 To 75.00
Bird, Mallard, Banded, 1980, Miniature .... 30.00 To 43.00
Bird, Mallard, Drake, 1973 .... 45.00 To 85.00
Bird, Mallard, Drake, 1973, Miniature .... 30.00 To 50.00
Bird, Mallard, Family, 1977 .... 51.00 To 85.00
Bird, Mallard, Family, 1977, Miniature .... 35.00 To 59.00
Bird, Meadowlark, 1980 .... 39.00 To 70.00
Bird, Meadowlark, 1980, Miniature .... 15.00 To 35.00
Bird, Oriole, Baltimore, 1977 .... 34.00 To 76.00
Bird, Oriole, Baltimore, 1977, Miniature .... 15.00 To 40.00
Bird, Osprey, 1974, Miniature .... 108.00 To 200.00
Bird, Osprey, 1976 .... 120.00 To 200.00
Bird, Osprey, Family, 1984, 2 Piece ....75.00 To 125.00
Bird, Osprey, Family, Miniature, 1984, 2 Piece .... 33.00 To 65.00
Bird, Owl, Baby Snow, 1976, Miniature .... 39.00 To 75.00
Bird, Owl, Barn, 1979 .... 48.00 To 89.00
Bird, Owl, Barn, 1979, Miniature .... 18.00 To 36.00
Bird, Owl, Great Gray, 1985 .... 38.00 To 85.00
Bird, Owl, Great Gray, Miniature, 1985 .... 20.00 To 35.00
Bird, Owl, Great Horned, 1974 ....60.00 To 100.00
Bird, Owl, Great Horned, 1974, Gal. ....720.00 To 1600.00
Bird, Owl, Great Horned, 1974, Miniature .... 66.00 To 110.00
Bird, Owl, Northern Snowy, 1972 ....90.00 To 150.00
Bird, Owl, Northern Snowy, 1972, Miniature ....60.00 To 100.00
Bird, Owl, Saw Whet, 1977 .... 40.00 To 70.00
Bird, Owl, Saw Whet, 1977, Miniature .... 18.00 To 37.00
Bird, Owl, Screech, Family, 1977 ....81.00 To 145.00
Bird, Owl, Screech, Family, 1977, Miniature .... 66.00 To 110.00
Bird, Owl, Screech, Family, 1979, Gal. .... 295.00 To 550.00
Bird, Owl, Spectacled, 1975 ....66.00 To 110.00
Bird, Owl, Spectacled, 1975, Miniature ....57.00 To 105.00
Bird, Owls, Barred, 1981, Club Decanter ....45.00 To 100.00
Bird, Owls, Barred, 1981, Club Decanter, Miniature .... 24.00 To 49.00
Bird, Owls, Burrowing .... 42.00 To 60.00
Bird, Owls, Burrowing, Miniature .... 12.00 To 30.00
Bird, Partridge, Chukar, 1979 .... 34.00 To 69.00
Bird, Partridge, Chukar, 1979, Miniature .... 15.00 To 29.00
Bird, Peacock, 1973 ....81.00 To 135.00
Bird, Peacock, 1973, Miniature .... 45.00 To 75.00
Bird, Pelican, Brown, 1976 .... 40.00 To 67.00
Bird, Pelican, Brown, 1976, Miniature .... 18.00 To 35.00
Bird, Penguin, Family, 1978 .... 45.00 To 75.00
Bird, Penguin, Family, 1978, Miniature .... 18.00 To 40.00
Bird, Pheasant, Golden .... 39.00 To 65.00

Bird, Pheasant, Golden, Miniature .... 23.00 To 39.00
Bird, Pheasant, In Corn, 1982 .... 51.00 To 95.00
Bird, Pheasant, In Corn, 1982, Miniature .... 30.00 To 59.00
Bird, Pheasant, Standing, 1977, Miniature .... 47.00 To 78.00
Bird, Pheasants, Fighting, 1977 .... 50.00 To 115.00
Bird, Pheasants, Fighting, 1977, Miniature .... 39.00 To 65.00
Bird, Pheasants, Fighting, 1979, 1/2 Gal. .... 135.00 To 225.00
Bird, Pigeons, Passenger, 1983 .... 66.00 To 135.00
Bird, Pigeons, Passenger, 1983, Miniature .... 29.00 To 69.00
Bird, Prairie Chicken, 1976 .... 45.00 To 75.00
Bird, Prairie Chicken, 1977, Miniature .... 32.00 To 54.00
Bird, Robin, 1975, Miniature .... 45.00 To 80.00
Bird, Seagull, Club Decanter .... 24.00 To 60.00
Bird, Seagull, Club Decanter, Miniature .... 12.00 To 35.00
Bird, Swallows, Barn, 1977 .... *Illus*   60.00
Bird, Swallows, Barn, 1977, Miniature .... 33.00 To 61.00
Bird, Swan, Black, 1974 .... 33.00 To 65.00
Bird, Swan, Black, 1974, Miniature .... 19.00 To 39.00
Bird, Turkey, 1975 .... 75.00 To 135.00
Bird, Turkey, Miniature, 1976 .... 98.00 To 164.00
Bird, Whooping Crane, 1983 .... 30.00 To 55.00
Bird, Whooping Crane, Miniature .... 30.00 To 50.00
Bird, Woodpecker, Gila, 1972 .... 54.00 To 90.00
Bird, Woodpecker, Gila, Miniature, 1973 .... 24.00 To 40.00
Bird, Woodpecker, Ivorybill, 1976 .... 34.00 To 64.00
Bird, Woodpecker, Ivorybill, 1976, Miniature .... 15.00 To 34.00
Bluebirds, 1984, Club Decanter .... 25.00 To 75.00
Bluebirds, 1984, Club Decanter, Miniature .... 17.00 To 40.00
Bonnie, Customer Speciality, 1974 .... 20.00 To 33.00
Bonnie, Customer Speciality, 1974, Miniature .... 12.00 To 20.00
C. S. M. Burro, Customer Speciality, 1973 .... 45.00 To 85.00
C. S. M. Burro, Customer Speciality, 1974, Miniature .... 42.00 To 70.00
Caveman, Customer Speciality, 1974 .... 18.00 To 30.00
Caveman, Customer Speciality, 1974, Miniature .... 12.00 To 20.00
Christmas, Bob Cratchit, 1977 .... *Illus*   65.00
Christmas, Bob Cratchit, 1977, Miniature .... 20.00 To 35.00
Christmas, Cardinals, 1990 .... 36.00 To 69.00
Christmas, Cardinals, 1990, Miniature 35.00
Christmas, Cardinals, Special Edition, 750 Ml. 95.00
Christmas, Cardinals, Whiteware 100.00
Christmas, Cedar Waxwings .... 36.00 To 75.00
Christmas, Cedar Waxwings, Miniature .... 18.00 To 32.00
Christmas, Chickadees, 1981 .... 45.00 To 79.00
Christmas, Chickadees, 1981, Miniature .... 24.00 To 45.00
Christmas, Mrs. Cratchit, 1978 .... 37.00 To 81.00
Christmas, Mrs. Cratchit, 1978, Miniature .... 21.00 To 35.00
Christmas, Scrooge, 1979 .... 55.00 To 79.00
Christmas, Scrooge, 1979, Miniature .... 12.00 To 24.00
Christmas, Woodland Trio, 1980 .... 42.00 To 85.00
Circus, Clown, 1974 .... 42.00 To 73.00
Circus, Clown, 1974, Miniature .... 31.00 To 45.00
Circus, Elephant, 1974 .... 27.00 To 50.00
Circus, Elephant, 1974, Miniature .... 26.00 To 44.00
Circus, Horse, Lipizzaner, 1976 .... 33.00 To 65.00
Circus, Horse, Lipizzaner, 1976, Miniature .... 27.00 To 55.00
Circus, Horse, Palomino, 1976 .... 36.00 To 65.00
Circus, Horse, Palomino, 1976, Miniature .... 27.00 To 45.00
Circus, Jenny Lind, Blue, 1976 .... 54.00 To 92.00
Circus, Jenny Lind, Blue, 1976, Miniature .... 45.00 To 75.00
Circus, Jenny Lind, Yellow, 1976 .... 117.00 To 195.00
Circus, Jenny Lind, Yellow, 1976, Miniature .... 111.00 To 185.00
Circus, Lion, 1975, Miniature .... 20.00 To 33.00
Circus, Lion, 1976 .... 22.00 To 49.00

Circus, P. T. Barnum, 1976 .... 27.00 To 45.00
Circus, P. T. Barnum, 1976, Miniature .... 18.00 To 37.00
Circus, Ringmaster, 1974 .... 18.00 To 35.00
Circus, Ringmaster, 1974, Miniature .... 14.00 To 29.00
Circus, Tiger, 1975 .... 27.00 To 45.00
Circus, Tiger, 1975, Miniature .... 22.00 To 37.00
Circus, Tom Thumb, 1974 .... 18.00 To 32.00
Circus, Tom Thumb, 1974, Miniature .... 14.00 To 23.00
Circus, Wagon, 1977 .... 27.00 To 55.00
Clyde, Customer Speciality, 1974 .... 22.00 To 37.00
Clyde, Customer Speciality, 1974, Miniature .... 18.00 To 30.00
Cowboy Joe, Customer Speciality, 1980 .... 45.00 To 75.00
Fish, Muskellunge, 1977 .... 27.00 To 42.00
Fish, Muskellunge, 1977, Miniature .... 14.00 To 29.00
Fish, Salmon, 1977 .... 27.00 To 45.00
Fish, Salmon, 1977, Miniature .... 18.00 To 30.00
Fish, Trout, Brown, 1976, Miniature .... 24.00 To 40.00
Fish, Trout, Rainbow, 1976 .... 36.00 To 60.00
Fish, Trout, Rainbow, 1976, Miniature .... 24.00 To 40.00
Indian, Ceremonial Antelope Dancer, 1982 .... 50.00 To 90.00
Indian, Ceremonial Antelope Dancer, 1982, Miniature .... 36.00 To 60.00
Indian, Ceremonial Basket Dancer .... 72.00 To 95.00
Indian, Ceremonial Basket Dancer, Miniature .... 19.00 To 39.00
Indian, Ceremonial Buffalo Dancer, 1979 .... 150.00 To 250.00
Indian, Ceremonial Buffalo Dancer, 1980, Miniature .... 38.00 To 55.00
Indian, Ceremonial Butterfly Dancer .... 62.00 To 88.00
Indian, Ceremonial Butterfly Dancer, Miniature .... 32.00 To 40.00
Indian, Ceremonial Deer Dancer, 1980 .... 90.00 To 150.00
Indian, Ceremonial Deer Dancer, 1982, Miniature .... 65.00 To 79.00
Indian, Ceremonial Eagle Dancer, 1979 .... 177.00 To 295.00
Indian, Ceremonial Eagle Dancer, 1979, Miniature .... 34.00 To 50.00
Indian, Ceremonial Falcon Dancer, 1983 .... 87.00 To 145.00
Indian, Ceremonial Falcon Dancer, 1983, Miniature .... 39.00 To 75.00
Indian, Ceremonial Olla Maiden .... 77.00 To 89.00
Indian, Ceremonial Olla Maiden, Miniature .... 24.00 To 41.00
Indian, Ceremonial Rainbow Dancer .... 47.00 To 95.00
Indian, Ceremonial Rainbow Dancer, Miniature .... 55.00 To 80.00
Indian, Ceremonial Wolf Dancer, 1981 .... 77.00 To 90.00
Indian, Ceremonial Wolf Dancer, 1981, Miniature .... 33.00 To 55.00
Indian, Cigar Store, 1974 .... 30.00 To 50.00
Indian, Cigar Store, 1975, Miniature .... 21.00 To 35.00
Indian, Dancers of Southwest, 1975, 6 Piece .... 212.00 To 395.00
Indian, Dancers of Southwest, 1975, Miniature, 6 Pc. .... 135.00 To 280.00
Indian, End of The Trail, 1976 .... 153.00 To 272.00
Indian, End of The Trail, 1977, Miniature .... 75.00 To 150.00
Indian, Great Spirit, 1976 .... 90.00 To 150.00
Indian, Great Spirit, 1979, Miniature .... 15.00 To 30.00
Indian, Lookout Indian, 1977 .... 54.00 To 92.00
Indian, Lookout Indian, 1978, Miniature .... 15.00 To 39.00
Indian, North American Tribes, 1977, 6 Piece .... 150.00 To 250.00
Indian, North American Tribes, 1977, Miniature, 6 Pc. .... 81.00 To 160.00
Indian, Warrior, Hatchet, Chief No. 1, 1975 .... 105.00 To 175.00
Indian, Warrior, Hatchet, Chief No. 1, 1979, Miniature .... 15.00 To 28.00
Indian, Warrior, Lance, Chief No. 2, 1975 .... 105.00 To 175.00
Indian, Warrior, Lance, Chief No. 2, 1979, Miniature .... 16.00 To 27.00
Lady of Leadville, Blue, Customer Speciality, 1973 .... 16.00 To 27.00
Lady of Leadville, Blue, Customer Speciality, 1973, Miniature 15.00
Lady of Leadville, Brown, Customer Speciality, 1973 .... 24.00 To 27.00
Lady of Leadville, Brown, Customer Speciality, 1973, Miniature 15.00
Mill River Country Club, Customer Speciality, 1974 .... 27.00 To 45.00
Phoenix Bird, Customer Speciality, 1981 .... 51.00 To 85.00
Phoenix Bird, Customer Speciality, 1981, Miniature .... 27.00 To 45.00
Political Donkey, Customer Speciality, 1976 .... 24.00 To 55.00

Political Donkey, Customer Speciality, 1976, Miniature	20.00
Political Elephant, Customer Speciality, 1976	20.00 To 50.00
Political Elephant, Customer Speciality, 1976, Miniature	20.00
Rodeo, Barrel Rider, 1982 ....50.00 To 105.00
Rodeo, Barrel Rider, 1982, Miniature .... 22.00 To 38.00
Rodeo, Bull Rider, 1980 .... 45.00 To 75.00
Rodeo, Bull Rider, 1980, Miniature .... 25.00 To 45.00
Rodeo, Snake River Stampede, 1980 .... 51.00 To 85.00
Rodeo, Wyoming Bronco, 1978 .... 54.00 To 91.00
Rodeo, Wyoming Bronco, 1979, Miniature .... 26.00 To 44.00
Skier, Blue, Customer Speciality, 1972 .... 22.00 To 42.00
Skier, Blue, Customer Speciality, 1975, Miniature .... 52.00 To 69.00
Skier, Gold, Customer Speciality, 1972 ....75.00 To 170.00
Skier, Olympic, Customer Speciality, 1980 .... 36.00 To 62.00
Skier, Olympic, Customer Speciality, 1980, Miniature .... 17.00 To 30.00
Skier, Red, Customer Speciality, 1972 .... 22.00 To 39.00
Skier, Red, Customer Speciality, 1975, Miniature .... 27.00 To 54.00
Submarine, Customer Speciality, 1976, Miniature .... 18.00 To 30.00

SNUFF

Snuff has been used in European countries since the fifteenth century, when the first tobacco was brought back from America by Christopher Columbus. The powdered tobacco was inhaled through long tubes. The French ambassador to Portugal, Jean Nicot, unknowingly made his name a household word when he sent some of the powdered tobacco to his queen, Catherine de Medici. The stuff became known as *nicotine.*

Tobacco was at first considered a remedy and was used in many types of medicines. In the sixteenth and seventeenth centuries, royalty enjoyed snuff and kept it in elaborate gold and silver snuffboxes. Snuff was enjoyed by both royalty and laboring classes by the eighteenth century. The nineteenth–century gentleman no longer used snuff by the 1850s, although poor Southern women used snuff by dipping, not sniffing, and putting it in the mouth, not the nose.

Snuff bottles have been made since the eighteenth century. Glass, metal, ceramic, ivory, and precious stones were all used to make plain or fancy snuff holders. Commercial bottles for snuff are made of dark glass, usually shaped more like a box than a bottle. Snuff was also packaged in stoneware crocks. Most oriental snuff bottles have a small stick with a spoon end as part of the closure. The International Chinese Snuff Bottle Society, 2601 North Charles Street, Baltimore, MD 21218, has a colorful, informative publication.

SNUFF JAR, Olive Amber, 9 1/4 In.	325.00
SNUFF, 1000 Figure Design, Reverse Painted, Flat Body, Chinese, 3 1/4 In.	1210.00
Agate, Carved Carnelian Dragon, Agate, 2 7/8 In.	150.00
Agate, Cat's-Eye, Carved, 1 1/2 In.	127.00
Agate, Mottled, Oriental, 2 In.	66.00
Amber Dragon Design, Overlay, Flat Body, Peking, 19th Century, 3 In.	275.00
Amber, Blown, Deep Root Beer Color, Square, OP, 4 5/8 In.	578.00
Amber, Chinese, Square, 2 1/4 In.	385.00
Amber, Flat Body, Jade Stopper, Chinese, 2 1/4 In.	165.00
Amber, Horseshoe Shape, Metal Screw Cap, 5 Oz.	4.00
Amber, Levi Garrett, Square, 4 1/4 In.	3.00
Aventurine, Carved Monkey, Brown, 2 1/2 In.	80.00
Aventurine, Carved Monkey, With Peach, Green, 3 In.	90.00
Banded Agate, Carved Eagle, 2 3/8 In.	85.00
Banded Agate, Carved Fish, With Seaweed, 2 1/8 In.	85.00
Birds 1 Side, Flowers Other, Enameled, 2 3/4 In.	125.00
Black Glass, Pontil	124.00
Black Glass, Rectangular, 1840	164.00
Black, Speckled, Plant Design, Overlay, Flat Body, Peking, 2 3/4 In.	275.00
Bloodstone Agate, Carved Turtle, Lily Leaves, 2 1/2 In.	125.00
Blown, Globular, Small	950.00
Blown, Medium Olive Green, Rectangular, OP, 4 1/4 In.	55.00

Snuff, Lorillard's MacCoboy Snuff, Rose Scented, 7 In.

Snuff, Cinnabar, Running Horse, 2 1/2 In.

Blown, Medium Yellow Olive, Flared & Tooled Lip, OP, 4 1/4 In.	121.00
Blown, Olive Amber, Cylindrical, Keene Marlboro, 1820–1850, 3 1/2 In.	230.00
Blown, Olive Amber, Tooled Mouth, Pontil, Square, 4 In.	198.00
Blown, Rectangular, Cork	625.00
Blown, Yellow Olive, Rectangular, Chamfered, Pontil, 6 5/8 In.	935.00
Blue Glass, Carved Foo Dog, Flat Body, Chinese, 2 1/2 In.	303.00
Bright Olive Green, Flared Mouth, Rectangular, 4 7/8 In.	688.00
Brown Amber, Flared Lip, 1840, OP, 4 x 2 3/8 In.	132.00
Caramel Jade, Carved Man On Base, Flat Body, Chinese, 2 1/4 In.	247.00
Carved Bird & Mum Spray, Turquoise, Chinese, 19th Century, 2 In.	330.00
Carved Rose Quartz, Stand, Flat Body, Chinese, 19th C., 2 1/2 In.	715.00
Chinese Hornbill, Carved Figural Scenes, Stand, 8 In.	990.00
Cinnabar, Figural & Mountain Scenes, Oriental, 2 In.	94.00
Cinnabar, Running Horse, 2 1/2 In. ....*Illus*	100.00
Cloisonne, Multicolored Flowers & Birds, Black, 3 1/2 In.	25.00
Copper, Deer Each Side, 3 In.	35.00
Dark Cherry, Jade Stopper, Flat Body, Peking Glass, 2 1/2 In.	143.00
Dark Cherry, Peking Glass, 3 In.	275.00
Deep Green, Bubbly, Chamfered Corners, Rectangular, 4 5/8 In.	275.00
Dr. Marshall's Catarrh Snuff, Aqua	12.00
Dr. Marshall's Catarrh Snuff, Deep Blue Aqua, BIMAL, Cork	20.00
Dr. Marshall's Snuff, Aqua, Pontil, 3 1/2 In.	36.00
E. Roome, Troy, New York, Black Green, Rectangular, 4 3/8 In.	180.00
Fish In Water Design, Reverse Painted, Flat Body, Chinese, 3 In.	495.00
Green Porcelain, Raised Wildflower, Flat Body, Chinese, 3 1/4 In.	440.00
Howlite, Carved Cat, With Rat, 2 1/2 In.	85.00
Jade, Carved Foo Dog & Urn Form, Oriental, 19th Century, 2 1/4 In.	385.00
Jar, Medium Olive Green, Sheared Top, OP, 4 1/8 In.	50.00
Lapis Lazuli, Carved Buddha, With Bag, Blue, 2 3/4 In.	150.00
Lapis Lazuli, Wooden Stand, Chinese, 2 1/2 In.	165.00
Leopard Skin Agate, Carved Cat, 2 5/8 In.	85.00
Lorillard's MacCoboy Snuff, Rose Scented, 7 In. ....*Illus*	45.00
Malachite, Carved Eagle, 2 7/8 In.	150.00
Olive Amber, Beveled Corners, Rectangular, Pontil, 6 In.	357.00
Olive Amber, Blown, Flared & Tooled Lip, OP, 4 3/4 In.	550.00
Olive Amber, Chamfered Corners, Rectangular, Pontil, 5 1/4 In.	105.00
Olive Amber, Outwardly Flaring Lip, OP, Square, 1820–1850, 4 3/4 In.	132.00
Olive Green, Octagonal, Outwardly Flaring Lip, 1820–1850, 4 1/8 In.	770.00
Olive Green, Rectangular, Chamfered Corners, 1790–1830, 6 1/4 In.	33.00
Olive Green, Rectangular, New England, 6 3/4 In.	193.00
Peking Glass, Blue & White Enameled, Porcelain, 2 1/2 In.	110.00
Peking Glass, Carved Vine & Lotus Design, Flat Body, 2 1/2 In.	275.00
Peking Glass, Yellow, Flat Body, Coral Stopper, 2 3/4 In.	605.00

| Soda, A & W Root Beer, Sugar Free, 11 1/2 In. | Soda, Big Red, 1980 National Champions, Louisville, 16 Oz. | Soda, Chocolate Soldier, 7-Up Bottling, Memphis, Tenn., 7 Oz. |

Porcelain, Blue Dragon Design, White Ground, Chinese, 2 3/4 In. 193.00
Porcelain, Eagle Shape, Spoon Stopper, Floral, China, 2 1/4 In. 35.00
Porcelain, Elephant Shape, Spoon Stopper, Design, China, 2 1/4 In. 35.00
Porcelain, Man In Landscape, Blue, Chinese, 2 3/4 In. 110.00
Porcelain, Man On Horse, Hand Painted, Flat Body, Chinese, 2 3/4 In 385.00
Purple Flourite, Carved Dragon, 2 1/2 In. 90.00
Red To Speckled Plant Design, Overlay, Flat Body, Peking, 3 In. 330.00
Reverse–Painted Landscape & House, Peking, 2 1/2 In. 83.00
Rhodonite, Carved Fish, In Basket, Rose, Black Accents, 2 1/2 In. 125.00
Rock Crystal, Interior Landscape Scene, Zhou Leyuan, 2 1/4 In. 1210.00
Rose Quartz, Carved Eagle, 2 1/2 In. 90.00
Serpentine, Carved Oriental Characters, 2 1/2 In. 94.00
Sodalite, Carved Elephants, 3 In. 85.00
Stoddard Glass, Dark Olive Green, Improved Pontil, Snap Case 35.00
Tiger's–Eye, Carved Elephants, 3 In. 150.00
Weymans Snuff, Pottery, Cream, 5 1/2 In. ....7.50 To 10.00
White Jade, Carved Oxen, Ovoid, Oriental, 19th Century, 2 1/4 In. 110.00
White Jade, Flat Body, Chinese, 19th Century, 2 1/4 In. 330.00
Whitwells, 2 Sides Embossed, Crude 55.00
Yellow Amber, Blown, Flared & Tooled Lip, OP, 4 In. 143.00

──────────────────────────── **SODA** ────────────────────────────

All forms of carbonated drink—naturally carbonated mineral water, artificially carbonated and flavored pops, and seltzer—are forms of soda. The words are often interchanged. Soda bottles held some form of soda pop or carbonated drink. The soda bottle had a characteristic thick blob top and heavy glass sides to avoid breakage from the pressure of the carbonation. Tops were cleverly secured; the Hutchinson stopper and Coddball stopper were used on many early bottles. The crown cap was not developed and used until 1891.

The first soda was artificially carbonated in the 1830s by John Matthews. He used marble chips and acid for carbonation. It is said he took all the scrap marble from St. Patrick's Cathedral in New York City to use at his plant, which made, so they say, 25 million gallons of soda water. In 1839 a Philadelphia perfume dealer, Eugene Roussel, had the clever idea of adding flavor to the soda. Soon colors were added and the soft drink industry had begun. The late 1800s saw the beginning of Coca–Cola (1886), Pepsi–Cola (1898), Moxie (1876), Dr Pepper (1885), and others. The English brand Schweppes was already established, but they added artificially carbonated sodas as well.

Collectors search for the heavy blob top bottles and the newer crown top sodas with embossed lettering or silk–screened labels. Recent commemorative bottles are also in demand. In this book, the soda bottle listing includes modern carbonated beverage bottles as well as the older blob tops, Hutchinsons, and other collectible soda bottles. Coca–Cola and Pepsi–Cola bottles are listed in their own sections. Collectors can contact the Saratoga–type Bottle Collectors Society, 238 South St., Mechanicville, NY 12118. For modern soda bottles, contact the Dr Pepper Collectors Club, 1614 Ashbury Drive, Austin, TX 78723, or the clubs listed in this book in the Coca–Cola and Pepsi–Cola sections.

SODA, see also Coca–Cola; Mineral Water; Pepsi–Cola; Seltzer

SODA, A & W Root Beer, Sugar Free, 11 1/2 In. ....*Illus*	1.00
A. L. Rapp & Co., Mineral Waters, Medium Cobalt Blue, 10–Sided, IP	325.00
A. M. McFarland, Philadelphia, Green, IP, 1850, 7 1/2 In.	55.00
A. R. Cox, Norristown, Pa., Cobalt Blue, Union Glass, IP	1750.00
Abel & Voellger, Pittsburgh, Pa., Deep Amber	110.00
ACC Soda, Clear, Jumbo, 10 Oz.	6.00
ACC Soda, Kickapoo Joy Juice, Green, 10 Oz.	7.00
Ace Ginger Beer, City Bottling Works, Indianapolis, Amber, 7 In.	5.00
Acme Soda Water Co., Pittsburgh	20.00
Acme Soda Works, Pittsburgh	7.00
Albert Von Harten, Savannah, Ga., Hutchinson, Green, Blob Top, 7 1/4 In.	21.50
Aman, Cheyenne, Wyo., Hutchinson	40.00
Arabia Dry Ginger Ale, Green, Sheik On Horse Label	17.00
Arizona Bottling Works, Phoenix, Aqua, 4 Mold, Hutchinson, 6 3/4 In.	80.00
Arny & Shinn, Georgetown, D. C., Bottle Is Never Sold, Deep Blue Green	89.00
Aunt Ida, Favorite Drink, Green ....*Illus*	10.00
B. W. & Co., New York, Brilliant Cobalt Blue, IP, Blob Top	165.00
Big Red, 1980 National Champions, Louisville, 16 Oz. ....*Illus*	10.00
Billman & Hain, Reading, Pa., Cobalt Blue, IP	900.00
Black Cow, Picture of Cow's Face Label, Amber	7.00
Bolen & Byrne, Clear, Torpedo	30.00
Boyd & Beard, Mineral Water, Yellow Green, 1850, 6 3/4 In.	143.00
Boyd, Baltimore, Tenpin Shape, Deep Olive Green, 8 1/2 In.	605.00
Bromber–Aginsim, Newark, N. J., Aqua, Reverse Eagle, Blob Top, 7 1/2 In.	35.00
Buffum & Co., Pittsburgh, Deep Aqua, IP, Embossed Around	40.00
Buffum, Pittsburgh, Cobalt Blue, IP	350.00
C. A. Cole, C. F. Brown, Baltimore, Medium Sapphire, Tenpin Shape	450.00
C. A. Dubois & Bro., Philadelphia, Aqua, Blob Top, Embossed, Large	39.00
C. Abel & Co., St. Louis, Mo., 7 3/4 In. ....*Illus*	35.00
C. C. Habenicht, Columbia, S. C., Hutchinson, Aqua, 6 1/2 In.	17.50
C. Cleminshaw Soda & Mineral Water, Sapphire Blue, Applied Mouth	75.00
C. D. Egert & Co., Albany, N. Y., Reddish Puce, Blob Lip, 1860–1875, 7 In.	320.00
C. Schaal, Philadelphia, Aqua, Squatty	15.00
C. Whittemore, N. Y., Emerald Green, IP, Blob Top	15.00
Calumet, Ill., Bottling Works, Hutchinson, Clear, 7 In.	10.00
Canada Dry Ginger Ale, Carnival Glass	15.00
Canada Dry, Crown Top	2.50
Carl Schultz, Pat. May, 1868, N. Y., Green, Squat	75.00
Carpenter & Cobb, Knickerbocker, Light Green, 10–Sided, 7 1/4 In.	121.00
Carpenter & Cobb, Knickerbocker, Sapphire Blue, 10–Sided, 7 5/8 In.	1100.00
Cedar Rapids Bottling Works, Aqua, Hutchinson, 6 1/2 In.	26.00
Chapman's, Aqua, Rolled Lip, Pontil, Round Base, 8 In.	357.00
Chief Artesian Bottling Works, Waterford, N. Y., Aqua, BIM, 9 3/4 In.	28.00
Chocolate Soldier, 7–Up Bottling, Memphis, Tenn., 7 Oz. ....*Illus*	7.50
Clark & White, Saratoga	40.00
Comal Bottling Works, New Braunfels, Tx., Clear, Pt.	12.00
Compton Bottling Co., Wyo., Cloverleaf, Hutchinson	700.00
Concord Bottling, Concord, N. H., Hutchinson	18.50
Corvallis Soda Works, Corvallis, Or., Hutchinson	100.00
Crown Bottling Works, Buffalo, N. Y., Hutchinson	7.00
Crystal Palace, W. Eagle, N. Y., Emerald Green, IP, 7 1/4 In.	467.00
Cub Beverage, Shreveport, La. ....*Illus*	15.00
D. Heenan, Philadelphia, Olive, Embossed, Double Collar, Squat, IP	169.00

Soda, Frostie Old Fashion Root Beer, Baltimore, Md. *Soda, Tom Collins Jr., Tasty Lemon*
Soda, Cub Beverage, Shreveport, La. *Drink, With Display*
Soda, Fox Beverages, Cherry Cola, Fremont, Oh.

D. L. Ormsby, N. Y., Cobalt Blue, Embossed, IP, 1860, 7 In. 55.00
D. O'Kane, Dyottville Glassworks, Phila., Double Collar, Green, IP 98.00
Dark Amethyst, Aqua Marble, Codd, 8 3/4 In. 619.00
Dawson, Norwich, London, Dark Green To Black, Codd, 7 7/8 In. 113.00
De Snelle, Sprong, Tegelen, Deep Green, Girl Pouring Water, Codd, 7 In. 382.00
Deer Park, L. I., Medium Cobalt Blue, Octagonal, IP, 7 In. 633.00
DeMott's Celebrated Soda Or Mineral Waters, Cobalt Blue, IP 150.00
Diamond Trade Mark Soda Works Co., San Francisco 12.50
Distilled Soda Water Co. of Alaska, Aqua, Mug Hutchinson, 7 1/4 In. 358.00
Dr Pepper, King of Beverage, Waco, Tex. 75.00
Dr. Brown, Green, Pontil, B On Reverse, 7 In. 240.00
Dyottville Glassworks, Philadelphia, Aqua, Squatty 12.00

Soda, C.Abel & Co., St.Louis, Mo., 7 3/4 In. *Soda, J.Pablo & Co. Seltzer & Mineral Water,*
8 1/2 In.

Dyottville Glassworks, Philadelphia, Green, Pontil, 7 In. 220.00
E. Duffy & Son, 44 Filbert St., Philadelphia, Deep Green, IP 135.00
E. Duffy & Son, 44 Filbert St., Philadelphia, Teal, IP 39.00
E. L. Billing's Sac City, Geyser Soda, Sapphire Blue, 7 1/4 In. 176.00
E. Roussel, Dyottville Glassworks, Philadelphia, Blue, IP 300.00
E. Roussel, Philadelphia, Dark Green, Embossed, IP, 1850, 7 1/2 In. 60.00
E. S. & H. Hart, Superior, Emerald Green, IP, 7 1/2 In. 110.00
E. Young, Pittsburgh, Ice Blue Embossed Vertically, IP 49.00
East Tex Bottling Works, Beaumont, Tex., Hutchinson, Aqua, 6 1/2 In. 25.00
Edward Patent, London, Aqua, Wired On Metal Cap, Codd, 8 1/4 In. 634.00
Excelsior Soda Works, Savannah, Ga., Cobalt Blue, 1870, 7 1/4 In. 99.00
F. Aure, Lebanon, Ill., Hutchinson 10.00
F. Gleason, Rochester, N. Y., Tenpin Shape, Aqua 250.00
F. McKinney, Large F On Rear, Cloudy Aqua 15.00
F. Schrader, Dunmore, Pa., Cobalt Blue, IP 625.00
Felix Ginger Ale, Qt. 18.00
Fox Beverages, Cherry Cola, Fremont, Oh. ....*Illus* 7.50
Frank Mateijka, Chicago, Embossed Star, Hutchinson 10.00
Frostie Old Fashion Root Beer, Baltimore, Md. ....*Illus* 7.50
G, Cornett, Liverpool, Codd, Narrow Neck, Angular Base, 7 1/8 In. 49.00
G. Burkhardt, Philadelphia, Blue Green 15.00
G. S., Salem, Or., Hutchinson 25.00
G. W. Mallison, Barnsley, Aqua, Amber Marbled, Codd, 10 Oz. 36.00
Gardner & Brown, Bright Yellow Green, Round Base 475.00
Geo. Eagle, Medium Green, Embossed Ribs, IP, 6 7/8 In. 660.00
Geo. Gemenoen, Savannah, American Eagle, Flags, Green, 7 1/4 In. 231.00
Geo. Munson, So. Bethlehem, Pa., Aqua, Fluted Base, Hutchinson, 6 1/2 In. 9.50
Geo. Upp, Jr., York, Pa., Aqua, Tenpin Shape, 8 1/2 In. 412.00
George Hiscox, Guildford, Dark Copper Blue, Codd, 9 1/8 In. 468.00
George Russel Aromatic Ginger Ale, Brooklyn 10.00
Glazer Beverages, Siphon, Vaseline, Etched Bear, Czech., 13 In. 55.00
Goff & Jackson, Stanford, Ct., Blob Top, 9 1/2 In. 7.00
Green Valley Beverages, Colored Flavor & Fruit Acid Added, 7 Oz. 10.00
Green Valley Beverages, Poulson Creamery Co., 7 Oz. 10.00
Groves & Whitnall Ltd., Salford, Bright Golden Amber, Codd, 10 Oz. 66.00
H. A. Loveland, Herkimer, N. Y., Almost Yellow, Blob, Lightning Stopper 20.00
H. Amon, Cheyenne, Wyo., Hutchinson 65.00
H. Denhalter Bottle Co., Salt Lake, Utah, Hutchinson, 6 1/2 In. 22.00
H. M. Martin, Minneapolis, Minn., Hutchinson, Aqua, Slug Plate, Qt. 38.00
H. Maillard, Lead City, S. D., Hutchinson 17.00
Hagerty's Glass Works, N. Y., Green Aqua, Sparkling 35.00
Hamilton Glass Works, Aqua, Graphite Pontil, Blob Top 40.00
Hanford Soda Works, J. S. 17.50
Harvey Bottling Works, Calumet, Mich., Hutchinson, Aqua, 6 1/2 In. 9.50
Hayward's Pure Juice of The Grape, Aqua, Dean Foster, Boston 25.00
Hazen Brown Co., Pluto, Boston, Amber, Blob Top, 4 1/2 In. 15.00
Heiss Superior, Cobalt Blue, IP, 10–Sided 300.00
Hennessy & Nolan, Albany, N. Y., Empire State Back & Base, Aqua 30.00
Henry C. Hall, Manchester, N. H., Dark Green, 1870, 7 1/2 In. 247.00
Henry Kuck, Savannah, Ga., 1878, Green, Blob Top 45.00
Hewlett Bros., Salt Lake City, Utah, Hutchinson, Aqua, 6 1/2 In. 17.50
Hires Improved Root Beer, Philadelphia, USA, 10 In. ....*Illus* 35.00
Hobbelskirt, Kalamazoo, Mich., 1915 .... 15.00
Hoffman Bros., W. T., Hutchinson 300.00
Hund & Eger, St. Joseph, Mo., Pale Green, Pt. 6.00
Isaac A. Moran & Bro., N. Y., Glass Stopper 10.00
J. & A. Dearborn & Co., New York, Deep Cobalt Blue, Inverted Pontil 300.00
J. & D. Miller, Hutchinson, Applied Mouth, Cobalt Blue 250.00
J. & J. W. Harvey, Norwich, Conn., Emerald Green, 1850, 7 3/4 In. 285.00
J. A. Lomax, Chicago, Hutchinson, Cobalt Blue, 6 1/2 In. 21.50
J. A. Wallis, Bangor, Me., Hutchinson 35.00
J. Andrews, Philadelphia, Double Collar, Green, Squatty 19.00
J. B. Bacon, Wellington, Aqua, Green Lip, Codd, 7 1/2 In. 897.00

J. E. Edisbury & Co., Shield, Crossed Seals, Torpedo, Aqua, 6 Oz. 20.00
J. F. Deegan, Pottsville, Pa., Yellow, Hutchinson 675.00
J. J. Mettham, Mansfield, Aqua, Codd, Octagonal, 7 1/2 In. 100.00
J. J. Sprenger, Holidaysburgh, Pa., Cobalt Blue, IP 850.00
J. L. Pampell, Kerrville, Tex., Painted 6.00
J. Lake, Schenectady, N. Y., Sapphire Blue, Tenpin Shape, 7 5/8 In. 231.00
J. McLaughlin, Philadelphia, Blue Green, Squatty, IP 19.00
J. Monteith, F. Road, Philadelphia, Emerald, IP, Squat 69.00
J. Naylor & Sons, Philadelphia, Horseshoe Emblem, Hutchinson 10.00
J. O. Kane, Philadelphia, Peacock Blue, Double Collar 49.00
J. Pablo & Co. Seltzer & Mineral Water, 8 1/2 In. ....*Illus* 25.00
J. T. Brown Chemist, Boston, Medium Green, Torpedo, 9 In. 385.00
J. T. Brown, Chemist, Boston, Deep Aqua, Torpedo, 8 7/8 In. 88.00
J. W. Harris, New Haven, Conn., Sapphire Blue, Octagonal, 7 1/4 In. 303.00
J. Waeckerlin, Rawlins, Wyo., Hutchinson 250.00
J. Wise, Allentown, Cobalt Blue 75.00
J. Wismann, Dayton, Oh., 12 Panels, Aqua, Graphite Pontil, Squat 200.00
J. Zerbe, Duncansville, Cobalt Blue, IP 625.00
James H. Gorman, Logansport, Ind., Hutchinson, Aqua, 6 1/2 In. 12.50
Jas. McDonough, Geneva, N. Y., Cobalt Blue, Applied Mouth, IP 240.00
Jas. Watson, Philadelphia, Embossed Flower, Double Collar, Porter Type 149.00
Jerh. Deegan, Pottsville, Pa., Emerald Green, Smooth Base 400.00
John Fehr, Reading, Pa., Blue Green, IP 48.00
John M. Wagner & Sons, Yonkers, N. Y., Aqua, Blob Top, BIM, 9 1/4 In. 16.00
John O'Brien, St. Louis, Mo., Aqua, Round Base, Collared Mouth 45.00
John Yost Jr., Lebanon, Pa., Deep Emerald Green, IP 425.00
Katton & Maag, CMN, Boston, Mass., Pale Aqua, Lightning Stopper 16.00
Keach, Baltimore, Medium Yellow Green, Round Base 375.00
Kinsella & Hennessy, Albany, N. Y., Emerald Green, 6 3/4 In. 42.00
Knicker–Bocker Soda Water, Deep Teal, Octagonal, IP 375.00
Knicker–Bocker Soda Water, N. Y., Cobalt Blue, 10–Sided, 1848, 7 In. 575.00
Knicker–Bocker, C. C., Cobalt Blue, 10–Sided, IP, 7 In. 578.00
Knicker–Bocker, Medium Cobalt Blue, 10–Sided, IP, 7 1/4 In. 413.00
L. L. Beland, Newark, N. J., Blue Green, Squatty 59.00
Lakeview, Green, 7 Oz. 7.00
Lancaster Glassworks, N. Y., Teal, Blob Lip, IP, 7 In. 165.00
Lander Bottling Works, 1894, Wyo., Hutchinson 750.00
Leigh & Co., Salford, Codd, Small 22.00
Lexington, Kentucky, Crown Top 3.00
Lieberman's, Allentown, Pa., Hutchinson, Clear, Blob Top, 8 In. 22.50

Soda, Hires Improved Root
Beer, Philadelphia, USA,
10 In.

Soda, Moxie, Since 1884,
Needham Hts., Mass., 11 In.

Soda, Mr. Cola Jr., Grapette
Bottling Co., New Albany,
10 In.

Little Tom, 6 Oz.	7.00
M. Cronar, Sacramento, Hutchinson	45.00
M. Gressle, Pottsville, Pa., Star, Medium Emerald Green, Qt.	275.00
Mammy Beverage Co., Embossed Mammy, Clear, 30 Oz.	27.00
Mammy Beverage Co., Embossed Mammy, Clear, 60 Oz.	27.00
Manhattan, Clear, 7 Oz.	7.00
Mansfield Bottling Works, Mansfield, Ark., Hutchinson, Aqua, 6 1/2 In.	17.50
Masabe Bottling Works, Virginia, Minn., Slug Plate, Aqua, Qt.	38.00
Mason's Root Beer, Chicago, Ill., Amber, Painted	8.00
Maumee Valley, Label, Clear	10.00
Maverick, T. Shone Bishop, Hutchinson, Aqua	55.00
Mellor & Sons, Manchester, Pineapple & Leaves, Codd, Aqua, 6 Oz.	20.00
Mission Beverages, Hillsboro, Oregon, Crown Top	2.50
Mission Dry Sparkling, Black, Crown Top	3.50
Mission Orange Dry, Black, Crown Top	3.50
Morrison & Townsend, Castleford, S. Yorks, Aqua, Codd, 9 In.	12.00
Mosher Heam Bottling Works, Lock Haven, Pa., Multi–Sided, Clear	10.00
Moxie, Since 1884, Needham Hts., Mass., 11 In. ....*Illus*	10.00
Mr. Cola Jr., Grapette Bottling Co., New Albany, 10 In. ....*Illus*	2.00
Mug Old Fashioned Root Beer, Amber, Label, Crown Top, 28 Oz.	2.50
Mynderse & Fink, Schenectady, N. Y., Mug Base, Embossed Eagle	15.00
N. R. Pearson, Pittsfield, Mass., Cobalt Blue, Embossed, 1850, 7 3/8 In.	165.00
Napa Lemonade, Green, Label	25.00
National Dope Co., Hutchinson, Brass Wire Stopper, 1890s	180.00
Nesbitts, Los Angeles, Calif., Crown Top	2.50
Newton Bottler, New York, Cobalt Blue, IP, 7 1/8 In.	797.00
Northwestern Bottling Co., Butte, Mont., Hutchinson, Aqua, 6 1/2 In.	21.50
Nu–Icy Flavors, Can't Forget, Charleston, Aqua, Hobbleskirt, 8 Oz.	8.00
O. C. M. Caines, Columbia, Pa., Emerald Green, IP	400.00
Oakland Pioneer Soda Water Co., Hutch Bottle Picture	35.00
Ogden & Gibson, Pittsburgh, Medium Green, IP, 7 1/8 In.	393.00
Omaha Bottling Co., Omaha, Nebr., Hutchinson, Aqua, 7 In.	15.00
Owl, Emerald	45.00
Owl, Teal	45.00
P. Bable Bolt, Green, Blob Top, Graphite Pontil	55.00
P. Divine Bottler, Philadelphia, Teal, Double Collar, Squatty, IP	79.00
P. H. Murat & Co., Manchester, Aqua, Dumpy, Codd, 7 1/4 In.	25.00
P. Hall, Philadelphia, Blue Green, Double Collar, Porter Type, Squatty	109.00
P. Murat & Co., Manchester, Deep Aqua, Codd, 5 7/8 In.	519.00
P. Paul, Honesdale, Pa., Medium Green, Octagonal, IP	1250.00
Pacific Bottling Works, Tacoma, Wash., Hutchinson ....17.00 To 35.00	
Ph. J. Tholey, Philadelphia, Blue Green, Squatty	29.00
Philadelphia Glassworks, Burgin & Sons, Blue Green, IP	49.00
Philadelphia Glassworks, Burgin & Sons, Emerald Green, IP, 7 1/4 In.	60.00
Point Richmond Soda Works, F. S. W., Point Richmond	18.00
Pokagon, Indian Picture, Clear	5.00
Popular Soda Water Co., San Francisco, Hutchinson	24.00
R. C. & T., New York, Strawberry Puce, Cylindrical, IP, 1/2 Pt.	2420.00
R. Hodgson's Improved Soda Water, Olive, Round, Pontil	1850.00
R. M. Becker, Waterford, Miss., Hutchinson, Stained	60.00
R. T. Smith, Troy, N. Y., Aqua, BIM, 7 In.	18.00
R. White, Camberwell, Dark Aqua, Deep Red Amber Lip, Codd, 10 Oz.	85.00
Redfearn Bros., Barnsley, Aqua With Black Marble, Codd, 9 In.	49.00
Reifs Special, Embossed, Amber, Crown Top	5.00
Rev. F. W. H., Headman, Philadelphia, Green, Blob Top, Graphite Pontil	70.00
Revett & Co., Sheffield, Aqua, Codd, Faceted Base, 9 In.	5.50
Riley Mfg. Co., Ltd., London S. W., Bright Green, Codd, 10 Oz.	69.00
Rocky Mountain Co. Springs, Hutchinson	30.00
Roussel, Philadelphia, Dyottville, Cobalt Blue, Tenpin Shape, IP	2500.00
Royal Crown, Painted Label, Cap, Contents, 3 1/2 In.	12.00
Royal German Spa, Seltzer, Amber, Blob Lip, 1860, Codd, 5 3/4 In.	49.00
Royal Soda, Hillsboro, Ore., Embossed, Crown Top	2.50
S. H. Boughton Root Porter, Rochester, Cobalt Blue, IP	325.00

Soda, Turk Bros., Newark, N.J., Hutchinson,
7 1/2 In.

Soda, Uncle Joe, Amber
Soda, Aunt Ida, Favorite
Drink, Green

S. S. Knicker–Bocker, Cobalt Blue, 10–Sided, IP, 7 1/2 In. 198.00
S. Smith, Auburn, N. Y., Cobalt Blue, 10–Sided, IP, 1857 .... 425.00
S. Smith, Auburn, N. Y., Cobalt Blue, Tenpin Shape, 8 3/8 In. 687.00
Safford Bottling Works, Safford, Ariz., Dark Amethyst, 1885–1895, 7 In. 1100.00
Samuel Fogg & Co., San Francisco, Dog's Head, Codd, Aqua, 6 Oz. 20.00
San Francisco Soda Works, Hutchinson 140.00
Scarboro & Whitby Breweries Ltd., Knottingley, Green, Codd, 7 3/4 In. 344.00
Seitz & Bro., Easton, Pa., Deep Cobalt Blue, IP, 1850, 7 7/8 In. 93.00
Seltzer, Gate City Bottling Works, Rapid City, S. D. 50.00
Seltzer, Richardson's, Lead, S. D. 40.00
Seven–Up, Cleveland Browns .... .50
Seven–Up, Green, Crown Top, 7 Oz. 2.50
Seven–Up, Liberty Bell, 1st Rung, July, 8, 1776 .... .50
Seven–Up, Ohio Model 1.00
Seven–Up, Ohio University, 175 Years .... .50
Seven–Up, United States Bicentennial .... .50
Sheffield Chemists Aerated Water, Amber, Embossed, Codd, 8 1/8 In. 364.00
Silver State, Reno, Embossed Mole & Miner, Hutchinson, ABC Crown Top 25.00
Smedley & Brandt, Blue Green, IP 42.00
Smith & Grove, Columbia, Pa., Brilliant Yellow Green, IP 1150.00
Snowdrop, J. Lyon & Co., Manchester, Aqua, Codd, 8 7/8 In. 350.00
South Bend, Wash., Soda & Bottling Works, BIMAL, 6 3/4 In. 13.00
Southwick & Tupper, N. Y., Blue Green, IP 35.00
Southwick & Tupper, N. Y., Green, Blob Top, Graphite Pontil 60.00
Standard Bottling Works, Cripple Creek, Co., Aqua, Hutchinson, 6 In. 62.00
Star, Clear, Blue Marble, Codd, 10 Oz. 22.00
Stubbs Mugs Root Beer, Amber, Label, Crown Top, Small 2.50
Sun Crest, Atlanta, Ga., Crown Top 2.50
Superior, American Eagle, Cobalt Blue, IP, 7 3/8 In. 495.00
Sutton, Aqua, IP 75.00
Swansea United Breweries, Green, Horse In Shield, Codd, 8 1/2 In. 566.00
Syrup, Peacock 5 Cents, Bird of A Drink, Enameled Letters, 11 1/4 In. 145.00
T. Burkhardt, Braddock, Pa., D. C. Co., Hutchinson, Yellow Olive 180.00
T. Cecil, Dyottville, Green, Double Collar, Porter Type, IP 139.00
T. W. Gillett, New Haven, Medium Cobalt Blue, Octagonal, IP, 7 5/8 In. 385.00

Tarr & Smith, Worcester St., Boston, Teal 79.00
Taylor & Co., San Francisco, Eureka, Cobalt Blue, 6 3/4 In. 253.00
Teem, ACL, Green, 1972, 12 Oz. 10.00
Tergen & Thieme, Lafayette, Ind., Hutchinson, Aqua, 6 1/2 In. 12.50
Theo Clements, Philadelphia, Hutchinson 10.00
Thomas Leonard Sonora Soda Works, Sonora, Calif., Hutchinson, Green 25.00
Tom Collins Jr., Tasty Lemon Drink, With Display ....*Illus* 30.00
Torpedo, Hong Kong Soda Water, Green Aqua 60.00
Turk Bros., Newark, N. J., Hutchinson, 7 1/2 In. ....*Illus* 100.00
Twitchell T., Philadelphia, Medium Green 15.00
Uncle Joe, Amber ....*Illus* 10.00
Union Glass Works, Philadelphia, Tea, Double Collar, Squatty, IP 49.00
Vess, Family Size, 24 Oz. ....*Illus* 5.00
Vincent Hathaway & Co., Boston, Medium Green, Round Base 140.00
Vonharten & Grogan, Savannah, Ga., Medium Blue Green 65.00
W. & G. Roseveare, Barnsley, Aqua, Codd, 9 In. 25.00
W. Dubois, Philadelphia, Deep Green, Double Collar, Letters All Around 69.00
W. Eagle's Superior, W. E., Dark Cobalt Blue, IP, 6 7/8 In. 132.00
W. H. H., Chicago, Cobalt Blue, Applied Blob Collar, IP, 7 1/2 In. 90.00
W. J. Hopps, Long Eaton, Aqua, Cobalt Blue Lip, Codd, 6 Oz. 180.00
W. M. & D. T. Cox, Port Jervis, N. Y., Light Teal, Squat, Round 32.00
W. P. Knickerbocker, Sapphire Blue, 10–Sided, 7 1/2 In. 220.00
W. Riddle, Philadelphia, Blue Green, Squatty, IP 39.00
W. Ryer, Deep, Sapphire Blue, Cylindrical, IP, 1/2 Pt. 100.00
W. S. Wright, Pacific Glass Works, Blue Green, Applied Top, 7 1/4 In. 1000.00
W. S. Wright, Virginia City, Nev., Dark Blue Green, Blob, 7 1/4 In. 1100.00
W. T. Gray, South Norwalk, Conn., Hutchinson 10.00
Wallis Bottling Works, Wallis, Tex., Hutchinson, Clear, 6 1/2 In. 17.50
Walter & Brother, Reading, Pa., Brilliant Cobalt Blue 725.00
Wanseahurns High Class Mineral Water, Suitcase, Torpedo, 6 Oz. 22.50
Welchade, Carbonated Water, Louisville, Ky., 6 Oz. ....*Illus* 5.00
William B. Scaife & Sons Co., Pittsburgh, Pa., Citrate Type, Sample 18.00
William Young, Redcar, Deep Green, Central Star, 9 In. 410.00
Williams & Severance, Cobalt Blue, Round, IP, 7 1/2 In. 154.00
Williams & Severance, San Francisco, Deep Cobalt Blue, IP, Blob Top 200.00

Soda, Vess, Family Size, 24 Oz.   Soda, Welchade, Carbonated Water,
Louisville, Ky., 6 Oz.

Williams & Son, Leicester, Golden Amber, Codd, 9 In. 780.00
Wilmer & Sons, Newport Pagnall, Ice Blue, Codd, 8 5/8 In. 25.00
Wm. Dulley & Sons, Ltd., Wellingborg, Bright Brown, Codd, 10 Oz. 53.00
Wm. Eagle, New York, Cobalt Blue, Octagonal, IP, 7 1/4 In. 176.00
Wm. Petrie, Leith, Green Marble, Vertically Embossed, Codd, 9 In. 49.00
Wm. Russell, Baltimore, Bright Yellow, Round Base 700.00
Wunder Bottling Works, Stockton, Calif., Amber, Blob Top, 9 1/2 In. 10.00
Youngblood, Philadelphia, Twitchell Type Top, Green 49.00
  SPIRIT, see Flask; Gin; Seal

————————————————— STIEGEL TYPE —————————————————

Henry William Stiegel, an immigrant to the colonies, started his first factory in
Pennsylvania in 1763. He remained in business until 1774. Glassware was made in a style
popular in Europe at that time and was similar to the glass of many other makers. It was
made of clear or colored glass that was decorated with enamel colors, mold blown designs,
or etchings. He produced window glass, bottles, and useful wares. It is almost impossible
to be sure a piece is a genuine Stiegel, so the knowing collector now refers to this glass as
Stiegel type. Almost all of the enamel–decorated bottles of this type that are found today
were made in Europe.

STIEGEL TYPE, Amethyst, 12 Diamond, Pocket, 5 In. 3800.00
Amethyst, 28 Ogival Over 28 Flutes, Pocket, 5 1/4 In. 4300.00
Amethyst, Daisy In Hexagon, Pocket, 5 1/2 In. 1500.00
Amethyst, Flask, Diamond Over Flute, Pocket, 1770–1773, 5 In. 4840.00
Bright Amethyst, Daisy In Diamond Over Flutes, 4 1/16 In. 8855.00
Bright Amethyst, Daisy In Diamond Over Flutes, 4 7/8 In. 2310.00
Deep Amber, 14 Ribs, Swirled, Pocket, 4 3/4 In. 800.00
Medium Amethyst, Daisy Over Flutes, 5 1/8 In. 2255.00
Medium Pink Amethyst, 12 Diamond, 5 In. 1760.00
Sapphire Blue, 16 Melon Ribs, Half–Post 950.00
Sapphire Blue, 16 Ribs, 1/2 Post, Pocket, 4 1/2 In. 950.00
Sapphire Blue, Salt, 12 Honeycomb Over Diamonds, 3 In. 165.00

————————————————— STONEWARE —————————————————

Stoneware is a type of pottery, not as soft as earthenware and not translucent like
porcelain. It is fired at such a high temperature it is impervious to liquid and so makes an
excellent bottle. Although glazes are not needed, they were often added to stoneware to
enhance its appearance. Most stoneware bottles also have the name of a store or brand
name as part of their decoration.

STONEWARE, Cream Pot, Buttercup Cream, Blue Top, 4 1/8 In. 40.00
Cream Pot, Buttercup Cream, Blue Top, 4 3/4 In. 67.00
Cream Pot, C. W. S. Limited, Somerset, Churn Shape, Brown Top, 4 In. 36.00
Cream Pot, Eland's Pure Devonshire Clotted Cream, Print, 4 In. 91.00
Cream Pot, J. A. Ferguson, Glasgow, All White, 4 1/2 In. 18.00
Cream Pot, J. E. Bannister, Huddersfield Dairies, Spout, 5 In. 82.00
Cream Pot, Rose Bower Dairy Co., White, Milkmaid, 3 3/4 In. 118.00
Crock, Parama Pottery, Sacramento, Cal., Cream Glaze, 3 Gal. 75.00
Crock, Peoria Pottery, Multi–Brown Glazed, Wax Sealer, 1/2 Gal. 50.00
Crock, Port Edward Stoneware Co., Applied Handle, Tan, Gal. 125.00
Dr. Cronk's Sarsaparilla Beer, 12–Sided, 9 3/4 In. .... 38.50 To 75.00
Finest Riviera Olive Oil Brillat Brand, Tan, 1/4 Gal. 49.00
Ink Pot, White, Blue Lettering, Cover, Gal. 55.00
Invalid Feeder, Pitcher Type, 2–In. Neck 7.50
Jar, Blacking, Orange Salt Glaze, 6 1/2 In. 36.00
Jar, Los Angeles Olive Growers, Qt. 150.00
Jar, Mason's Patent, 2 Tone, Debossed Around Opening 65.00
Jar, Warren's Liquid Blacking, Salt Glaze, 1805–1815, 7 In. 860.00
Jar, Weir, Pat. Mar. 1st, 1892, 2 Tone, Cover, Wire Bail, Qt. 25.00
Jug, Bulbous, Salt Glaze, 8 In. 455.00
Jug, Cudahy Packing Co., Tan, Brown, Blue Stencil, Handle 29.00
Jug, Gray & Co., Spokane, Wash., Label, 1 Gal. 100.00
Jug, Hagner, Crock Type, Gal. 50.00

Jug, O'Keefe's Pure Malt Whiskey, Oswego, N. Y., White, Qt. 45.00
Jug, Walkers Dairy, J. Stiff & Sons, Salt Glaze, Dogs, 3 In. 40.00
Jug, Wildeman, Dutch Farmer, Windmill, Gray Blue, Handle, 6 1/4 In. 65.00
Lemon Beer, Burr & Waters, Salt Glaze, 12–Sided, 8 1/4 In. 132.00
Pen–Yan, Handle, Cobalt Blue Flower, Gal. 130.00
Porter, Harman & Sons, Norwich, Red Brown Glaze, 9 1/2 In. 76.00
Porter, R. Rowson Warrington, Blob Lip, Brown Salt Glaze, 8 In. 36.00
Porter, Thos. Griffiths Bowling Green Inn, Salt Glaze, 9 1/8 In. 100.00
Salzman & Signalman Whiskey, Brooklyn, N. Y., Brown, Cream, 7 In. 35.00
Union Stoneware Co., Red Wing, Minn., Blue, 2 Gal. 125.00
Vulcanizing Solution, 5 In. 15.00
William Radam's Microbe Killer, N. Y. C., Cream, Gal. 50.00
Wm. Bros. & Charbonneau, Quebeck Maple Syrup, Detroit, Gal. 30.00

--------------------------------- TARGET BALL ---------------------------------

Target balls were first used in England in the early 1830s. Trapshooting was a popular sport. Live birds were released from a trap and then shot as they tried to fly away. The target balls, thrown into the air, replaced the live birds. The first American use was by Charles Portlock of Boston, Massachusetts, about 1850. A mechanical thrower was invented by Captain Adam Bogardus and with this improvement, trap shooting spread to all parts of the country. Early balls were round globes but by the 1860s they were made with ornamental patterns in the glass. Light green, aqua, dark green, cobalt blue, amber, amethyst, and other colors were used. Target balls went out of fashion by 1880 when the *clay pigeon* was invented.

TARGET BALL, Bogardus, Apr. 10, 1877, Cobalt Blue, Diamond, 2 3/4 In. 798.00
Bogardus, Apr. 10, 1877, Olive Amber, Cross Hatched All Over 98.00
Bogardus, Apr. 10, 1877, Olive Amber, Diamond, 2 3/4 In. 440.00
Bogardus, Apr. 10, 1877, Olive Green, Diamond, 2 3/4 In. 440.00
Bogardus, Apr. 10, 1877, Olive Yellow, Diamond, 2 3/4 In. 418.00
C. Newman, Yellow Amber, Diamond, 2 3/4 In. 880.00
Cobalt Blue, Squares, 1870–1880, 2 1/2 In. 99.00
Cobalt Blue, Squares, Center Band, 2 3/4 In. 127.00
E. Jones, Blackburn Lancashire, Light Blue, Cross Hatching 49.00
Hockey's Patent Trap, Light Green, Diamond, 2 5/8 In. 770.00
Ira Paine's, Oct. 23, 1877, Yellow Amber, 2 3/4 In. 209.00
L. Jones Gunmaker, Blackburn, Aqua, Diamond, 2 3/4 In. 303.00
L. Jones Gunmaker, Blackburn, Cobalt Blue, Diamond, 2 3/4 In. 242.00
Man, Gun, In Circle, Amethyst, Diamond, Striations, 2 3/4 In. 187.00
Man, Gun, In Circle, Blue Gray, Diamond, 2 3/4 In. 385.00
Man, Gun, In Circle, Clear, Diamond, 2 3/4 In. 231.00
Man, Gun, In Circle, Cobalt Blue, Diamond, 2 3/4 In. 385.00
Man, Gun, In Circle, Green, Diamond, 2 3/4 In. 231.00
Medium Amber, 2 3/4 In. 61.00
N. B. Glassworks, Perth, Aqua, Diamond, 2 7/8 In. 88.00
N. B. Glassworks, Perth, Cobalt Blue, Cross–Hatched, 2 1/2 In. 54.00
N. B. Glassworks, Perth, Cobalt Blue, Diamond, 2 3/4 In. 100.00
W. W. Greener, London, Amethyst, Diamond, 2 3/4 In. 165.00
W. W. Greener, London, Cobalt Blue, Diamond, 2 3/4 In. 88.00
Yellow Amber, Embossed Square On Base, 2 3/4 In. 66.00
    TOILET WATER, see Cologne

------------------------------------ TONIC ------------------------------------

Tonic is a word with several meanings. Listed here are medicine bottles that have the word *tonic* either on a paper label or embossed on the glass. In this book *hair tonic* is listed with cosmetics or medicine.

    TONIC, see also Cure; Medicine
TONIC, Chief Tonic, San Francisco, Clear, Tooled Mouth, 2 Labels, 9 3/4 In. 193.00
Dr. Harrison's Chalybeate Tonic, 4 1/2 In. 20.00
Dr. Harter's Iron Tonic, Amber, BIMAL, 9 1/4 In. 8.00
Dr. Miles, Label, Contents, ABM, Box 28.00
Fenner's Blood & Liver Remedy & Nerve Tonic, Label 23.00

Tonic, Plank's Chill Tonic
Co., Chattanooga, Tenn.,
6 1/2 In.

Vinegar, Buy Leo Vinegar,
O.J. Gregory, Rogers,
Pottery, 4 1/2 In.

Vinegar, Cabiria Apple
Cider, Stute & Co., St. Louis,
9 3/4 In.

Happy Home & Blood Purifer & Health Tonic, Aqua, Label, 10 1/2 In.	242.00
Hood's Blood & Nerve	15.00
Hop–Cel Co., Nerve, Blood & Brain Tonic, San Francisco, Amber, 9 In.	27.50
J. T. Higby Tonic Bitters, Yellow Amber	80.00
Kodol's Nerve Tonic, Label, Sample	35.00
O–Joy Vegetable Compound, T–Lax Products, 12 Oz., 3 3/4 x 7 1/2 In.	8.00
Parvin's Tonic Mixture, Cincinnati, Aqua, OP, 6 In.	121.00
Plank's Chill Tonic Co., Chattanooga, Tenn., 6 1/2 In. ....*Illus*	65.00
Primley's Iron & Wahoo Tonic, Elkhart, Ind., Amber, Square, 8 1/2 In.	28.00
Rohrer's Expectorial Wild Cherry Tonic, Lancaster, Pa., Amber, IP	225.00
Schenck's Seaweed Tonic .... 20.00 To 25.00
Sims Tonic Elixir, Pyrophosphate, Iron, Antwerp, Amber, 7 1/2 In.	15.00
V. T. T–Lax Products, Birmingham, Ala., 8 Oz., 8 1/2 In.	8.00
Warner's Safe Tonic, Rochester, Slug Plate, Amber, 9 1/2 In.	189.00
Web's No Cathartic Tonic	25.00

─────────────────── **VINEGAR** ───────────────────

Vinegar was and is sold in glass bottles. Most vinegar packers prefer a large glass jug–shaped bottle with a small handle, the shape used today even for modern plastic vinegar bottles. The collector wants any bottle with the name *vinegar* on a paper label or embossed on the glass. The most famous vinegar bottles were made by National Fruit Product Company for their White House Brand vinegar. Bottles with the embossed brand name and a picture of a house, the trademark, were made in the early 1900s. Jugs in three or four sizes, apple–shaped jars, canning jars, fancy decanters, cruets, a New York World's Fair bottle, rolling pins, vases, a refrigerator water jar, and other fanciful reusable shapes were used until the 1940s. The company is still in business.

VINEGAR, Buy Leo Vinegar, O. J. Gregory, Rogers, Pottery, 4 1/2 In. ....*Illus*	75.00
Cabiria Apple Cider, Stute & Co., St. Louis, 9 3/4 In. ....*Illus*	14.00
Maple Sap Boiled Cider–Vinegar, Cobalt Blue, Cylinder, 1870–1885	525.00
Pure Radish White, J. Bruning, N. J., Aqua, Square, 6 1/4 In.	25.00
Skilton Foote & Co., Bunker Hill, Yellow Green, 11 1/4 In.	550.00
White House, 8 In.	8.00
White House, Jug, Handle, 10 In.	16.00
White House, Lighthouse Shape, 10 In.	45.00
W.A. LACEY, see Lacey	
WATER, MINERAL, see Mineral Water	

WHISKEY

Whiskey bottles came in assorted sizes and shapes through the years. Any container for whiskey is included in this category. Although purists spell the word *whisky* for Scotch and Canadian and *whiskey* for bourbon and other types, we have found it simpler in this book to use only the spelling *whiskey*. There is also blended whiskey, which includes blended bourbon, Scotch, Irish, or Canadian. Although blends were made in Scotland and Ireland for many years, it was not a process popular in the United States until 1933. One way to spot very new whiskey bottles is by the size. The 1 3/4–liter bottle is slightly less than a half gallon, the 1–liter bottle slightly more than a quart, and the 3/4–liter bottle almost the same size as a fifth. These bottles were introduced in 1976.

Several years ago there was a contest to find the oldest bourbon bottle made in America. It was thought to be one dated 1882. The contest turned up an even older bottle, a Bininger made in 1848. Bourbon was first made in 1789 in Kentucky. Rum was made in America by the mid–seventeenth century; whiskey made of corn, rye, or barley, by the early 1700s. It was the tax on this whiskey that caused the so–called Whiskey Rebellion of 1794.

A museum of interest to collectors is the Seagram Museum, 57 Erb St., Waterloo, Ontario, Canada.

WHISKEY, see also modern manufacturers by brand name

WHISKEY, A. B. Co., Wright & Taylor Distillers, Louisville, Amber, BIM, Qt.	4.00
Adler Co., Cleveland, Oh., Deep Red Amber, Unusual Shape, 7 1/2 In.	42.00
Allman Irish Whiskey, Handle, Stencil	60.00
Altschul Distilling Co., Springfield, Oh., Square, Qt.	20.00
Always Pure Old Elk Whiskey, Elk, Emerald, Stopper, 11 1/4 In.	688.00
B. M. & E. A. Whitlock & Co., Aqua, Unusual Shape, 8 5/8 In.	176.00
B. M. & F. A. W. & Co., Ambrosial, Chestnut Shape, Amber, 8 3/4 In.	132.00
Barclay 76, Amber, BIMAL, Partial Label, Cylinder, 12 In.	35.00
Barrel, Figural, Cobalt Blue, 9 7/8 In.	908.00
Belle of Anderson, Old Fashion–Sour Mash, Milk Glass, 8 In.	137.00
Belle of Anderson, Sour Mash, Star, Milk Glass, 8 1/8 In.	55.00
Benedictine, Olive Green, Crude, Pt.	19.00
Benedictine, Qt.	14.00
Bennett & Carrol, Pittsburgh, Barrel, Figural, Amber, 9 3/8 In.	633.00
Berry's Diamond Wedding, Clear	12.00
WHISKEY, BININGER, see Bininger	
Blackberry, Clear, Woman On Label, Backbar, 11 1/4 In.	303.00
Blackberry, Cut Fancy Leaves, Clear, Amethyst Tint, Backbar	39.00
Blake's Rye & Bourbon, Embossed Barrels	20.00
Bloch Bros. Scotch Whiskey, Glascow, Dark Amber, Triangular, Qt.	16.00
Bohemian Cocktail & Supply Co., San Francisco, Calif., 40 Oz.	12.00
Bonnie Brown, Louisville, Ky., 1/2 Pt.	5.00
Bourbon, Black Amethyst, Silver Overlay Letters, Stopper, Backbar	95.00
Bourbon, Gothic Letters, Amethyst, 3 Mold, Pinched, Stopper, Backbar	85.00
Buchanan's Absolutely Pure Malt Whiskey, Amber, 9 In.	1265.00
Buchanan's, Cannon, Golden Amber	250.00
Bulkey Fiske Brandy, Chestnut, Yellow, Aqua Handle, 8 3/8 In.	6600.00
Bull Durham, Golden Amber, Cylindrical, Side Base, Qt.	1040.00
Burger Spital, Wurzburg, Bird, Flattened Chestnut, Amber, 7 5/8 In.	248.00
Burlingame Cream of Whiskeys, Nipper, White China, Germany, 1915	50.00
C. W. Middleton, 1825 Wheat Whiskey, Phila., Red Amber, 9 1/2 In.	48.00
Caldwell's Rum, Amber, Emblem Ship & Kegs, Pt.	10.00
Carhart & Brother, N. Y., Copper, Chestnut Shape, IP, 8 3/4 In.	770.00
Caspers Whiskey, Cobalt Blue	425.00
Chapin & Gore Sour Mash, Chicago, Amber, Screw Cap, 8 1/2 In.	121.00
Chestnut Grove, C. W., Reddish Amber, Flattened Chestnut, 9 In.	154.00
Chivas Regal, Jug, Wade	18.00
Clear, Marble Stopper, Backbar, Octagonal, 10 1/4 In.	132.00
Cognac Brandy, Amber, Wicker, Woman's Bust, 11 1/2 In.	303.00
Cognac W. & Co., Amber, Handle, Embossed Seal, OP	275.00
Colburn Co., Clear	35.00

WHISKEY, CORDIAL, see Cordial

Cortwright Rye, Clear, Gold Letters, Backbar	35.00
Creme DeMenthe, Claw On Globe Emblem, Red Amber, 11 In.	20.00
Crown Distilleries Co., Crown & Shield, Cylinder, Fifth	15.00
Cunningham & Bailey, Harzardville, Conn., 1/2 Pt.	35.00
Daniel, Bail Handle, Gal.	325.00
Daniel, Cylindrical, Qt.	95.00
Daniel, Square, Qt.	40.00
Davy Crockett Pure Old Bourbon	50.00
Deep Olive Green, Case, Applied Lip, 12 1/2 In.	187.00
Dewar's, Perth Whisky, Onion Shape, Free–Blown, Black Glass, 8 In.	91.00
Dr. Abernathy Green Ginger Brandy, San Fran., Amber, 10 3/4 In.	25.00
Dr. Girard's London Ginger Brandy, Inverted Cone, Amber, 9 1/4 In.	330.00
Duffy Malt Whiskey, Baltimore, Label, BIMAL	40.00
Duffy Malt Whiskey, Rochester, Label, BIMAL	25.00
Duffy's Malt Whiskey, Sample	20.00
Dyottville Glassworks, Philadelphia, Olive Amber	19.00
Dyottville Glassworks, Philadelphia, Olive Citron, Cylinder	29.00
Dyottville, 3–Piece Mold, Deep Green, 11 1/8 In.	22.00
E. G. Booz's Old Cabin Whiskey, Cabin, Amber, Whitney, Qt.	880.00
E. G. Booz's Old Cabin Whiskey, Cabin, Golden Amber, Whitney, Qt.	1210.00
E. G. Booz's Old Cabin Whiskey, Green, Clevenger, Reproduction	75.00
E. G. Booz's Old Cabin, Cabin, Amber, 7 1/2 In.	440.00
E. G. Booz's Old Cabin, Cabin, Amber, Whitney, 7 3/4 In.	1045.00
E. G. Booz's Old Cabin, Philadelphia, Cabin, Amber, 7 5/8 In.	898.00
E. G. Booz's, Amber, Wheaton, Reproduction	40.00
E. G. Booz's, Dark Lavender, Nuline, Dark Lavender, Reproduction	45.00
E. G. Booz's, Deep Royal Blue, Reproduction	125.00
E. G. Booz's, Deep Sea Green Base, Jersey Green, Reproduction	85.00
E. G. Booz's, Old Cabin, Amber, Paper Label, Clevenger, Reproduction	40.00
E. H. Taylor Jr. Co. Distillers, Frankfort, Ky.	20.00
Ellenville Glass Works, Embossed, Olive, 3–Piece Mold, 11 1/8 In.	50.00
Eye Opener, Clear, Painted Eye & Letters, Ovoid, Cap, 5 1/2 In.	72.00
Famous Maple Leaf Pure Rye, Backbar, Clear, Swirled Rib, 11 In.	1155.00
Ferd. Westheimer & Sons, Flask, Amber, Red Top, 1/2 Pt.	30.00
Figural, Scallop, Silver Painted	70.00
Fine Old Brandy, Young Woman, Clear, Bar, Cylindrical, 11 1/2 In.	1980.00
Fine Old Rum, Backbar, Woman In Blue Dress Label, 1880–1910	605.00
Fine Old Wheat Whiskey, Chestnut, 24 Ribs, Amber, Handle, 9 1/8 In.	242.00
Fine Old, Clear, Wicker, Anna Held's Bust, 1880–1910, 11 1/2 In.	1348.00
WHISKEY, FLASK, see Flask	
Flora Temple Harness Trot, Red Amber, Embossed Horse, 8 5/8 In.	468.00
Fluted Base, Clear, Ornate Etched Sherry, Petaled Shoulders	35.00
Forest Lawn, J. V. H., Olive Green, Seed Bubbles, IP, 7 3/8 In.	110.00
G. H. Moore's Old Bourbon & Rye, J. Moore, Louisville, Orange Amber	25.00
G. O. Blake's Bourbon Co., 2 Barrels, Dark Amber, 11 1/2 In.	231.00
WHISKEY, GIN, see Gin	
Glen Garry Old Highland Whiskey, Pottery, Brown, Corkscrew, Qt.	39.00
Glencoe Distillery Scotch Malt Whiskey, Cream, Transfer, 7 In.	30.00
Glendisco B. Rum Blend, Boston, Mass., Backbar, Clear, 10 1/2 In.	743.00
Golden Wedding, Clear, Embossed Bells, Screw Cap, Pt.	8.00
Grandpa's Whiskey, Clear, Fluted Shoulder & Neck, 11 7/8 In.	72.00
Greeley's Bourbon, Barrel, Pink Puce, 9 1/4 In.	200.00
H. A. Graef's Son, N. Y., Canteen, Olive Green, 6 5/8 In.	413.00
H. C. Myers Co., New York, N. Y., Flask, Ribbed, Oval, BIM, 7 3/4 In.	18.00
H. Feurerstein, New York, Octagonal, Amber, 12 3/8 In.	66.00
H. Heye Bremen, Olive Green, 3–Piece Mold, Embossed	25.00
Hanover Rye, Clear, Horse's Head, Cylindrical, Backbar, Pontil, Qt.	495.00
Hanover Rye, Gold Words Cut Into Bottle, Backbar, 11 1/8 In.	303.00
Harvard Rye, Qt. ....4.00 To 6.00	
Hayner Whiskey, Troy, Oh.	5.00
Hayner, Clear, Round, Paper Labels, 11 1/2 In.	15.00
Herald Rye, Man Blowing Horn, Cut Fluted Neck, Backbar, 10 In.	660.00

Highspire Straight Rye, Barrel Label, June 30, 1906, Amber, 1/2 Pt. 29.00
Homer's Bleached Jamaica Ginger Brandy, Amber, Cylinder 16.00
Homer's California Ginger Brandy, Amber, Cylinder 16.00
Horse's Head, Porcelain, Liquor Spout 16.00
I. W. Harper, Wicker Encased, Handle, Amber, Qt. 45.00
Imperial Levee J. Noyes, Hollywood, Miss., Golden Amber, 9 1/2 In. 2090.00
Indian Chief, Embossed, Clear 45.00
Indian, Figural, H. Pharazyn, Philadelphia, Yellow Amber, 12 1/8 In. 935.00
Irish W., Bar, Woman's Bust, Cylindrical, 1880–1910, 10 5/8 In. 1320.00
J. A. Millers, Nelson County, Houston, Tex., Clear, Qt. 175.00
J. H. Cutter Crown, A. P. Hotaling, 4–Piece Mold, Amber, Blob Top 60.00
J. H. Cutter, Bird, Blob Top, Amber, 5th 150.00
J. H. Cutter, Old Bourbon, Star, Medium Olive Green, 11 7/8 In. 600.00
J. Reiger & Co., Kansas City, Qt. 11.00
J. T. Gayen, Cannon, Altoona, Amber, 1860–1880, 13 1/2 In. 605.00
Jack Daniels, Jug, 1/2 Gal. 10.00
Jesse Moore & Co., Louisville, Ky., Amber, 11 3/4 In. 20.00
Jesse Moore Hunt Co., San Francisco, Calif., Amber 15.00
John Winn, Jr., Seal Spirits, 3–Piece Mold, Olive Green, 8 1/2 In. 303.00
Jug, Bronte, Yorkshire Liquor, Label, 3/4 Qt. 14.00
Jug, Chestnut Grove, Chestnut Form, Handle, Amber, Qt. 467.00
Jug, Cream of Old Scot Whiskey Bonnie Castle, Castle Picture 89.00
Jug, Glen Garry Old Highland, Stoneware, Ball Shape, Pour Lip, Qt. 59.00
Jug, Mohawk Liquor, Demitasse Coffee Drip, 25/32 Qt. 25.00
Jug, Pure Old Liquor, J. H. Kearns, Lebanon, Ky., Cream, Brown, 1/2 Pt. 99.00
Kellerstrauss Distilling Co., Kansas City, Mo., Qt. 25.00
King William IV Scotch Whisky, Olive, Paper Label, Round, Qt. 18.00
Liqueurs De Fruits, Cabin, Roped Corners, France, 1860–1890, 9 In. 66.25
Louis Taussic & Co., San Francisco, Clear 18.00
M. Gruenberg Old Judge Bourbon, San Francisco, Blob Top 350.00
M. Salzman Purity Above All, Deep Amber, ABM, 11 1/2 In. 28.00
McCallums, Jug, Handle 127.00
Meadowview Whiskey, Clear, Pinch, Gold Letters, Glass Stopper 20.00
Melrose Drove Ltd., Apricot Brandy, Aqua, Lady's Leg, Label 39.00
   WHISKEY, MINIATURE, see Miniature, Whiskey
Mitchell's Old Irish Whiskey, Belfast, Pottery, Near Qt. 29.00
Mohawk Peach Liquor, Stoneware, White & Red Mottled, Label, Sealed 20.00
Mohawk Whiskey Pure Rye, Indian Shape, Golden Amber, 12 5/8 In. 752.00
Mohawk, Figural, Pure Rye, Pat. Feb. 11, 1868, Amber, 12 1/2 In. 176.00
Monticello Club Pure Rye, Strauss Bros., Chicago, Qt. 20.00
Moore Trimble & Co., Jug, Amber, Applied Handle & Mouth, 8 3/4 In. 209.00
Mount Vernon Pure Rye, Lady's Leg Neck, Black, 3 1/4 In. 29.00
Munron Dalwinnie Scotland, Amber, Square, Qt. 19.00
N. D. Co., Bear, Walking, Amber 15.00
Neal's Ambrosia, Philadelphia, Cobalt Blue, Striations, 9 1/2 In. 2035.00
Norhouse Kornschnapps, Cream, Transfer, Jug, 7 1/2 In. 30.00
Old Belle of Anderson, Sour Mash, Milk Glass, Tooled Lip, 8 In. 50.00
Old Continental Soldier, Deep Yellow Amber, Square, 9 1/4 In. 715.00
Old Judge Hand Made Pot Still, 3–Piece Mold, Clear, Round, Qt. 50.00
Old Rye, For Pikes Peak, Pittsburgh, Pa., Deep Aqua, Qt. 145.00
Old Velvet Brandy, S. M. & Co., Inverted Cone, Amber, 9 3/4 In. 523.00
Palmer & Madigan Importers, Providence, Flask, Strap Sides, Clear 25.00
Paul Jones, Clear, Multicolored Enamel, Ground Stopper, 8 5/8 In. 187.00
Paul Jones, Louisville, Ky., Amber, Wicker, Handle, 11 1/2 In. 15.00
Pennsylvania Club Rye Whiskey, Polished Pontil, Backbar, 11 In. 110.00
Picnic Jellison Wines & Liquors, San Francisco 55.00
Poland Rye, As Pure As The Spring, Heublein, Hartford, Conn., Amber 25.00
Pretty Girl Litho, Whiskey, Pat. Nov. 1902, Rectangular, 10 3/4 In. 2833.00
Pride of Kentucky Old Bourbon, Amber, Applied Top, 12 In. 1705.00
Pride of Kentucky Old Bourbon, Livingston & Co., Amber, 12 In. 1550.00
Pusser's Rum, Jug, Liter 20.00
Quaker Maid Whiskey, Clear, Pt. 9.00
R. Cummins Old Process Sour Mash Whiskey, Slug Plate, 10 In. 10.00

Red Top Rye, Cylinder, Pt.	10.00
Red Top, Amber, 1/2 Pt.	5.00
Red Top, Clear, Pt.	7.00
Remy Martin, Baccarat Crystal, Case	65.00
Rose Valley, Louisville, Ky., Label, 17 In.	660.00
Roth & Co., Lawton Rye, San Francisco, Amber, Rectangular, 10 In.	15.00
Rye, Amber, Wicker, Woman Bust, Cylindrical, 11 1/2 In.	440.00
Rye, Aqua, Wicker, Woman Bust, Ovoid Kidney Form, Cork, 8 1/2 In.	660.00
Rye, Label, Horse & Bird–Dog, Painted, 1900	69.00
S. Tobias & Son, Philadelphia, Black, Unusual Shape, 9 1/2 In.	143.00
Schiedam Aromatic, Udolpho Wolfe's Schnapps, Teal, Square, 8 In.	85.00
Scotch, Label, Man & Dog, Backbar, Painted, 1900	69.00
Seal Spirits, Embossed E. Greene 1805, Olive Green, 1805, 10 In.	468.00
Seal Spirits, P. W. A. 1799, Deep Olive, Cylindrical, 10 1/2 In.	258.00
Seal Spirits, Sir W. Strickland, Boynton, Amber, Backbar, 10 In.	198.00
Shea Bocqueraz Co., San Francisco, Amber	22.00
Southern Comfort, Gen. Robert E. Lee	200.00
Star Whiskey, N. Y., Inverted Cone	400.00
Star Whiskey, N. Y., W. B. Crowell, Amber, Handle, 8 In.	523.00
Star Whiskey, W. B. Crowell, Jr., Inverted Cone, Yellow, 8 1/8 In.	660.00
Taylor & Williams Distillers, Louisville, Ky., BIMAL, 3 1/2 In.	10.00
Turner Brothers, Barrel, Golden Amber, 9 7/8 In.	83.00
Turner Brothers, Barrel, Light Olive Green, 1860–1880, 9 7/8 In.	396.00
Udolpho Wolfe's Aromatic Schnapps, Light Apricot	65.00
Udolpho Wolfe's Schiedam Aromatic Schnapps, Black, IP, 9 3/4 In.	85.00
Udolpho Wolfe's Schiedam Aromatic Schnapps, Olive, IP, 9 3/4 In.	66.00
Udolpho Wolfe's Schnapps, Light Green, Pt.	25.00
Van Beil, Philadelphia, Jug, Amber, Applied Mouth, Handle, 8 3/4 In.	688.00
Vidvard & Sheehan, Jug, Bright Yellow Green, Flattened, 9 3/4 In.	1430.00
Voldner's Aromatic Schnapps, Schiedam, Olive, 1860, 9 7/8 In.	55.00
W. I. Johnson, Kentucky, Amber, Applied Handle & Mouth, OP, 8 1/2 In.	66.00
W. J. Van Schuyver, Portland, Ore.	20.00
Wadsworth Whiskey, Clear, Pinch, Gold Letters, Glass Stopper	20.00
Waldorf Cafes, Becker Bros., Flask, Amethyst, Rectangular, 1915, Pt.	55.00
Warton's Whiskey, Medium Amber, Spout, Handle, 10 In.	95.00
Wharton's, Chestnut Grove, Flask, Medium Blue, 5 1/2 In.	242.00
Wharton's, Chestnut Grove, Jug, Amber, Spout, Handle, 10 In.	330.00
Whichman, Lutgen & Co., Amber, Inside Treads, Cylinder, 11 1/2 In.	20.00
White Horse Whisky, Dark Green	12.00
Wie's Old Irish Whiskey, Cream, Transfer, 7 1/2 In.	45.00
Willington Glass Works, 3–Piece Mold, Amber, 11 1/4 In.	44.00
Wilson Fairbanks, For Medical Purpose Only, Aqua, Square	100.00
Wilson, Fairbank & Co., Old Bourbon Whiskey, Square	55.00
Woman & Word Whiskey Label, Backbar, 1880–1910	358.00
Words Scotch, Cobalt Blue, Clear Stopper, Backbar, 9 In.	198.00
Wright & Taylor Distillers, Louisville, Ky., Amber, Cork, Qt.	8.00
Zeiger, El Paso, Tex., BIMAL, Diamond Label, 1930, Fifth	17.00

---------------------------- **WILD TURKEY** ----------------------------

Wild Turkey is a brand of bourbon made by Austin Nichols Distillery. The company says the bourbon was originally made as a gift for some hunting companions and so was named for their favorite gamebird. A crystal bottle with an etched flying turkey design was made in 1951. The company made turkey–shaped ceramic bottles from 1971 to 1989. The first bottle, filled with bourbon, sold for $20. In 1981 the company added miniature bottles. For a short time during the 1980s, the company marketed a line of *go–withs* such as plates and plaques. Today, Wild Turkey sells two imported limited–edition bottles, a Rare Breed Whiskey bottle in a teardrop shape and a Kentucky Legend decanter shaped like a violin. The Kentucky Legend bottle is available only in duty–free shops.

WILD TURKEY, Charleston Centennial, 1974	65.00 To 70.00
Decanter, Baccarat, Crystal, 1979	200.00
Decanter, Crystal Anniversary, 1955	1540.00 To 2250.00
Decanter, Wedgwood, 1 Ltr.	200.00 To 225.00

Fliers Club, Pitcher, 1987 .... 75.00
King of American Forest Birds, 1st Edition, 1987 .... 299.00
Liggett & Meyers, 1971 .... 310.00 To 350.00
Mack Truck, 1975 .... 20.00 To 25.00
Series 1, No. 1, Male, 1971 .... 165.00 To 265.00
Series 1, No. 1, Male, 1981, Miniature .... 6.00 To 7.00
Series 1, No. 2, Female, 1972 .... 150.00 To 250.00
Series 1, No. 2, Female, 1981, Miniature .... 6.00 To 7.00
Series 1, No. 3, On The Wing, 1973 .... 40.00 To 70.00
Series 1, No. 3, On The Wing, 1982, Miniature .... 10.00 To 15.00
Series 1, No. 4, With Poult, 1974 .... 70.00 To 100.00
Series 1, No. 4, With Poult, 1982, Miniature .... 10.00 To 15.00
Series 1, No. 5, With Flags, 1975 .... 20.00 To 45.00
Series 1, No. 5, With Flags, 1983, Miniature .... 15.00 To 17.00
Series 1, No. 6 Striding, 1976 .... 25.00 To 30.00
Series 1, No. 6, Striding, 1983, Miniature .... 15.00 To 17.00
Series 1, No. 7, Taking Off, 1977 ....*Illus*   35.00
Series 1, No. 7, Taking Off, 1983, Miniature .... 15.00 To 17.00
Series 1, No. 8, Strutting, 1978 .... 25.00 To 35.00
Series 1, No. 8, Strutting, 1983, Miniature .... 15.00 To 17.00
Series 2, No. 1, 1979 .... 20.00 To 25.00
Series 2, No. 2, Winter Forest, 1980 .... 22.00 To 25.00
Series 2, No. 3, Keenness of Sight, 1981 .... 30.00 To 35.00
Series 2, No. 4, Ready To Fight, 1982 .... 35.00 To 38.00
Series 3, No. 1, In Flight, 1983 .... 75.00 To 95.00
Series 3, No. 1, In Flight, 1984, Miniature .... 33.00 To 35.00
Series 3, No. 2, Turkey & Bobcat, 1983 .... 95.00 To 108.00
Series 3, No. 2, Turkey & Bobcat, 1985, Miniature .... 29.00 To 35.00
Series 3, No. 3, Turkeys Fighting, 1983 .... 89.00 To 125.00
Series 3, No. 3, Turkeys Fighting, 1983, Miniature 35.00
Series 3, No. 4, Turkey & Eagle, 1984 .... 60.00 To 70.00
Series 3, No. 4, Turkey & Eagle, 1984, Miniature .... 38.00 To 45.00
Series 3, No. 5, Turkey & Raccoon, 1984 .... 49.00 To 75.00
Series 3, No. 5, Turkey & Raccoon, 1984, Miniature .... 19.00 To 35.00
Series 3, No. 6, Turkey & Poults, 1984 .... 45.00 To 65.00
Series 3, No. 6, Turkey & Poults, 1984, Miniature .... 19.00 To 35.00
Series 3, No. 7, Turkey & Fox, 1985 .... 49.00 To 72.00
Series 3, No. 7, Turkey & Fox, 1985, Miniature .... 25.00 To 35.00
Series 3, No. 8, Turkey & Owl, 1985 .... 39.00 To 75.00
Series 3, No. 8, Turkey & Owl, 1985, Miniature 35.00
Series 3, No. 9, Turkey & Bear Cubs, 1985 .... 65.00 To 70.00
Series 3, No. 9, Turkey & Bear Cubs, 1985, Miniature 35.00
Series 3, No. 10, Turkey & Coyote, 1986 .... 65.00 To 70.00
Series 3, No. 10, Turkey & Coyote, 1986, Miniature .... 19.00 To 35.00
Series 3, No. 11, Turkey & Falcon, 1986 ....   80.00
Series 3, No. 11, Turkey & Falcon, 1986, Miniature .... 25.00 To 35.00
Series 3, No. 12, Turkey & Skunk, 1986 .... 80.00 To 81.00
Series 3, No. 12, Turkey & Skunk, 1986, Miniature .... 29.00 To 35.00
Series 3, No. 12, Turkey & Skunk, 1987, 1. 75 Ltr. 340.00
Series 4, No. 1, Habitat, Female, 1988 .... 95.00 To 104.00
Series 4, No. 1, Habitat, Female, 1988, Miniature .... 45.00 To 52.00
Series 4, No. 2, Habitat, 1989 .... 95.00 To 105.00
Series 4, No. 2, Habitat, 1989, Miniature .... 45.00 To 52.00

---------------------------------- **WINE** ----------------------------------

Wine has been bottled since the days of the ancient Greeks. Wine bottles have been made in a variety of sizes and shapes. Seal bottles were used from the second century and are listed in their own section in this book. Most wines found today are in the standard shapes that have been used for the past 125 years. The Bordeaux shape has square shoulders and straight sides while the Burgundy shape is broader with sloping shoulders. The German or Rhine wine flute bottle is tall and thin. Other wines, such as Champagne, are bottled in slightly different bottles.

WINE, MINIATURE, see Miniature, Wine

WINE, Black Glass, European, 11 1/4 In.	33.00
Black Glass, European, Swirling Line of Bubbles, 10 3/4 In.	16.40
Black Green, European, Very Narrow Neck, Bubbles, 10 In.	16.40
Blown, Olive Amber, Applied Mouth, Pontil, 9 3/8 In.	61.00
Blue Green, Ribs Around Base & Shoulder, Pontil, 15 3/4 In.	160.00
C. Carpy, San Francisco, Aqua, Blob Seal Shoulder, Small	55.00 To 65.00
Catawba Wine, Gold & White Label, Black Letters, Backbar, 11 1/2 In.	204.00
Febrifuge Wine, N. Y., Deep Aqua, IP, 13 In.	577.00
Fredonia Wine Co., Amber, Blob	14.00
Free–Blown, Black Glass, Champagne Shape, Pontil Top Kick Up, 11 In.	22.00
Free–Blown, Crude, Green, 1850s	5.00
G & C & E Nuthall & Sons Ltd., Wine Merchants, Pottery, 7 In.	55.00
Garrett & Co., American Wines, Eagle, Amethyst, Embossed	10.00
Garrett & Co., American Wines, Norfolk Va., BIM, 5 1/2 In.	24.00
Geo. Zantziner, Philadelphia, Olive Amber, Pontil, 11 5/8 In.	165.00
Hock, Blown, Red Amber, 14 In.	5.00
Honeymoon Arkansas Natural Grape Wine, Tontitown, 9 In. ....*Illus*	7.50
James Durkin Wines & Liquors, Spokane, Wash., Amber, Cylinder, Qt.	50.00
Jug, Langert Wine Co., Spokane, Wash., Beehive Shape, Stenciled, 3 Gal.	125.00
Kingdon's, Devonshire Cider, Champagne Form, Green, 10 3/4 In.	100.00
Lake Keuka Vintage Co. Winery, Bath, N. Y., Fancy	25.00
Olive Green, Label, France, 1964	7.00
Onion, Pierpont Family Crest, Black Glass, 1700, 4 3/4 In.	656.00
Pure Blackberry, Label, Qt. ....*Illus*	40.00
Ricketts Glassworks, Bristol, 3–Piece Mold, Black, Cylinder, 12 In.	361.00
Schlesinger & Bender Inc. Pure Calif. Wines & Brandies, Amber	29.00
Sherry, Amber, Wicker, Backbar, Woman's Bust, Cylindrical, 11 3/8 In.	358.00
Stoneware, Black & White, Label, Germany, 1972	7.50
Vieux Cognac 1811, 3–Piece Mold, Dark Green, 13 In.	163.00
Vin Portens, Clear, Ground Stopper, OP, 12 In.	25.00 To 40.00
Wedding Veil Picture, Amber, 1966	12.00
Wine Company, Bordeaux, Black, Turn Mold, Large Kick Up, 9 5/8 In.	33.00

Wild Turkey, Series 1, No. 7, Wine, Honeymoon Arkansas Wine, Pure Blackberry,
Taking Off, 1977   Natural Grape Wine,   Label, Qt.
*   Tontitown, 9 In.*

ZANESVILLE

The Zanesville Manufacturing Company started making glass in Zanesville, Ohio, in 1815. This glassworks closed in 1838 but reopened from 1842 to 1851. The company made many types of blown and mold blown pieces. At least one other glassworks operated in Zanesville from 1816 to the 1840s. The products of all the Zanesville factories are sometimes identified as *Midwestern* glass and are grouped with pieces made in Mantua, Kent, Ravenna, and other Ohio towns. The blown glass pieces include diamond patterned and ribbed pieces in clear, blue, amethyst, aquamarine, and amber colored glass. Collectors prize the Zanesville swirl pieces and identify them as *right* or *left* swirl.

ZANESVILLE, 24 Vertical Ribs, Honey Amber, 8 1/2 In. 2100.00
  Amber, 4 In. 3630.00
  Blown, 24 Swirled Ribs, Aqua, 7 3/4 In. 250.00
  Blown, 24 Swirled Ribs, Globular, Aqua, 8 In. 250.00
  Club, 24 Ribs, Broken Swirl, Aqua, 8 In. 250.00
  Club, Aqua, Midwestern, 7 3/4 In. 40.00
  Flask, 24 Ribs, Golden Amber, Globular, 1815–1840, 7 3/4 In. 490.00
  Flask, Chestnut, 10 Diamond, Citron, Pontil, 5 1/8 In. 4400.00
  Flask, Chestnut, 10 Diamond, Deep Amber, 5 3/8 In. 2200.00
  Flask, Chestnut, 24 Ribs, Aqua, Pontil, 7 In. 225.00
  Flask, Chestnut, 24 Swirled Ribs, Aqua, 6 1/8 In. 150.00
  Flask, Chestnut, 24 Swirled Ribs, Golden Amber, 5 In. 220.00

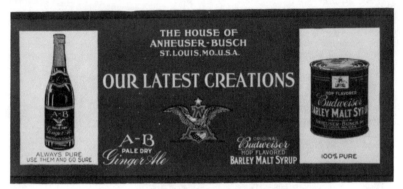

Blotter, House of Anheuser-Busch, Bottle, Can, 4 × 9 In.

--- **GO–WITHS** ---

There are many items that interest the bottle collector even though they are not bottles: all types of advertising that picture bottles or endorse bottled products like whiskey or beer, many small items like bottle openers or bottle caps, and related products by well-known companies like trays and plaques. Collectors call all of these *go-withs*. A variety of the items are listed here. Many others can be found under company names in other price lists such as *Kovels' Antiques & Collectibles Price List.* Clubs and publications that will help collectors are listed in the bibliography and club list.

AD, Pond's Bitters, Dollar Bill Form	10.00
ADVERTISING CARD, Hires Root Beer, Little Boy, 1898	50.00
ALMANAC, Moffatt's Phoenix Bitters, 1849	12.00
ASHTRAY, Rainier Pale Beer, Roseville Pottery Co.	35.00
Sierra Beer, Reno, Spur On Copper	35.00
Taittinger Champagne, France	75.00
BANK, Coca–Cola, Owl, Red Plastic, Drink Coca–Cola, 4 1/4 In.	4.00
Coca–Cola, Thirst Knows No Season, Atlanta, 3/12 x 4 In.	2.00
Pepsi–Cola, Vending Machine, Plastic	95.00
BAR FIGURE, Bust, Elizabethan Man, Flowers, Plaster	82.00
Landlord, In Pub Door, Bullard's Bitter Beer, 14 In.	82.00
Soldier, Irish Mist, Ireland's Liqueur, 9 3/8 In.	39.00
BEACH BAG, Pepsi–Cola, Blue Nylon Mesh, Wild One Logo, 16 x 18 In.	14.00
BEANIE, Coca–Cola, Felt, 1950s	5.00
BILLHEAD, C. Berry & Co., Diamond Wedding Whiskey, Colorful	10.00
BLACKBOARD, Nehi, Tin	75.00
BLENDER, Barroom, Southern Comfort Liquor, Electric	225.00
BLOTTER, Coca–Cola, 1913	35.00
House of Anheuser–Busch, Bottle, Can, 4 x 9 In. *Illus*	9.50
Pepsi–Cola, Pepsi & Pete	60.00
BOOK, Ball Blue Canning, 1943	1.50
Bitters Bottle Book, James H. Thompson, 1947	35.00
Calendar, Woman's, Burnett's Cocaine, 1876	8.00
Kerr Canning, 1945	1.50
BOOKCOVER, Coca–Cola, Basketball, Cheerleader & Referee Signals, 1960	3.00
Coca–Cola, Football Design, 1957	10.00
BOOKLET, Hood's Sarsaparilla, My Mother–In–Law, 16 Pages, 4 In.	8.00
Hood's Sarsaparilla, Palette Shape, 1894	45.00
Orange Crush, Fable	18.00
Warner's Safe Cure, Little Girl Cover, 6 x 8 1/2 In.	36.00
BOOKMARK, Coca–Cola, Celluloid, Lithograph, Lettering, 2 1/4 In.	132.00
Coca–Cola, Hilda Clark, 1903	250.00
BOTTLE CAP, Brownie Chocolate	.50
Cliquot Club Strawberry Cream Soda, Crown Type	.50

Fruit Bowl, Crown Type	.50
Grapefruit Crush	.50
Grapette, Crown Type	.50
Howdy Cola	.50
Mission Royal Punch	.50
Mr. Cola, Crown Type	.50
Nehi Red, Crown Type	.50
Nesbits Ginger Ale	.50
Orange Blossom, Crown Type	.50
Pepsi–Cola, 1950s & 1960s, 5 Piece	2.00
Red Arrow, Crown Type	.50
Spur, Crown Type	.50
Triple AAA Root Beer	.50
Zimba Cola, Crown Type	.50
BOTTLE OPENER, Alligator, Green, Rhinestone Eyes, 3 In.	35.00
Bar Bum, Comes Apart, Bar Tools Inside, Opener In Hat	85.00
Beer Drinker, Cast Iron	38.00
Bulldog, White, Green Collar, Cast Iron, 4 1/8 In.	25.00
Coca–Cola, 6 In.	5.50
Cocker Spaniel, Black, Cast Iron, 3 3/4 In.	65.00
Cowboy, At Signpost, Iron, Painted, John Wright Co., 4 1/2 In.	125.00
Donkey, Polychrome Paint, Cast Iron, 3 1/8 In.	35.00
Glersberg Select Wine, Corkscrew In Handle	25.00
Mother Goose, Painted Aluminum	45.00
Pabst Blue Ribbon Beer, 4 In.	10.00
Pepsi–Cola, 5 Cents	40.00
Pepsi–Cola, Bottle Shape, Tin Lithograph, 1930a	35.00
Rooster, Polychrome Paint, Cast Iron, 3 1/4 In.	75.00
Solano Bottling Works, J. Manuel, Prop., Flat Metal	15.00
BOTTLE, Squeeze, Pepsi–Cola, Allstars	1.50
BOX, Blood Wine, Louis Daudelin, Worcester, Mass., Wooden, 11 In.	83.00
Blue Mountain Bitters, S. E. Hubbel Proprietor, Wooden	65.00
Brown's Sarsaparilla, Bangor, Me., Wooden, 10 x 12 x 10 In.	60.00
Cotton Patch Bitters, Terrell, Tx., Wooden, 12 x 9 x 10 In.	143.00
Dr. Greene's Nervura Nerve Tonic, Wooden, 10 x 11 x 8 In.	55.00
Duffy's Malt Whiskey, 1860, Rochester, N. Y., Wooden, 11 x 8 In.	110.00
Electric Bitters, World's Great Cure, Wooden, Lid, 10 In.	55.00
Gall Complete Fruit Jars, Wooden, 1 Doz., 1/2 Gal. On Both Ends	94.00
Griesedieck Beer, Wooden, Hinged Lid	60.00
Hood's Sarsaparilla, Lowell, Mass., Wooden, 14 x 15 x 10 In.	60.00
Lockport Mason Fruit Jars, Porcelain, Wooden	160.00
Zoagriane, Asthma Conqueror & Catarrh Cure, No Bottle	15.00
BROOM HOLDER, Nichols Creamery, Ahlbrecht, Minn., Metal, Wall Mount	10.00
BUTTON, Let's Talk Avon	1.00
Thanks America For Making Avon No. 1	1.00
CALENDAR, Coca–Cola, 1947, Paper	97.50
Coca–Cola, Color Lithograph, 1950–1951, 22 In.	11.00
Hood's Sarsaparilla, Children, Sewing Circle, 1892	10.00
Nehi, Color Lithograph, 20 In.	11.00
Owl Drug Co., Dr. Miles Weather, 1937	61.00
CANNING SET, Gunnard, 24–Page Booklet, Box, 3 Piece	18.00
CAP, Coca–Cola, Baseball, Felt, 1940s	8.00
Mountain Dew, Green, Mesh Back	6.00
Pure Milk Dairy Co., Pasteboard, 4–In. Diam.	1.50
CARD, Dewar's Whiskey, Gold Letters, Border, 27 1/2 x 22 1/2 In.	137.00
Playing, Coca–Cola, 1943	65.00 To 70.00
Playing, Owl Drug Co., 1 Wing, 1900–1908, 54 Piece	231.00
CARRIER, Coca–Cola, Cardboard, 6 Pack, 1929	75.00
Coca–Cola, Cardboard, 6 Pack, 1933	40.00
Dr Pepper, Stenciled Wood, Red Lettering, 14 3/4 In.	22.00
Milk, Maine Dairy, 4 Slots	10.00
Pepsi–Cola, 12 Bottles, Carton, 1940s	45.00
Seven–Up, Aluminum, 12 Bottles	50.00

CASE, Blatz Beer, Wooden, Hinged Lid	35.00
Good Old Hoosier Beer, S. Bend Brewing, Wooden, Bottles	55.00
CASSEROLE, Moxie, China	75.00
CASSETTE PLAYER, Coca–Cola, AM/FM, Molded Plastic, Box, 10 In.	60.00
CATALOG, California Perfume Company, 1927, Color Pictures	100.00
Dominion Glass Co., Canada Druggist, No. 12, 1910, 72 Pages	60.00
CHANGE RECEIVER, Old Rippy Whiskey, Copper	35.00
CHARM, Orange Crush, Good Luck, 1930s	35.00
CLAMPOVER LID, Foremost Milk, Orange Plastic	10.00
Gustafson's Milk, Burlington, Ia., Aluminum	.10
Littleton's Milk, San Bernardino	.25
CLOCK, Coca–Cola, Electric, Reverse Stenciled, Box, 18 In.	523.00
Coca–Cola, Light–Up, Reverse Stenciled Glass, 19 1/2 In.	242.00
Dr Pepper, Bottle Shape, Tin	140.00
Fehr's Beer, Plastic, It's Always Fehr Weather	22.50
Nu–Grape, Light–Up, Bottle Shape, 1940s	150.00
Pabst Blue Ribbon, Electric	20.00 To 30.00
Pepsi–Cola, Can Shape, Electric, Box, 12 1/2 x 24 In.	120.00
Pepsi–Cola, Schoolhouse, Oak, Pendulum, Quartz, Battery Operated	200.00
Pepsi–Cola, Wall, 1940s	275.00 To 350.00
Royal Crown Cola, Glass Front, Square, 15 In.	30.00
Ward's Orange Crush, Regulator, 1908	1600.00
COASTER SET, Pepsi–Cola, Sports Trivia, Cardboard, 1970s, 4 Piece	12.50
COASTER, Coca–Cola, 8 Piece	3.00
Ruppert Beer, Tin, Set	22.00
COOKBOOK, Ball Blue Book, 1932	10.00
Ball Blue Book, 1938	8.00
Ball Blue Book, 1944	9.00
Ball Blue Book, 1956	2.00
Ball Blue Book, 1972	3.00
Carnation, 1935, 97 Pages	5.00
Fisher's Blend Sour Milk Recipes, 1930s, 48 Pages	1.00
Goodness By Arden, 1937, 21 Pages	2.00
Kerr, 1943	1.00
Kerr, 1947	4.00
Kerr, 1958	2.00
Kerr, 1969	3.00
Knudsen Recipes, 1950s, 48 Pages	4.00
Warner's Safe Cure, 9th Edition	45.00
When The Cows Come Home, From Ca. Dairy Council, 1930	3.00
COOKIE JAR, Coca–Cola, Coke Can, U.S. A.	25.00
COOLER, Curtis & Moore's Orangeade	65.00
Gordon's Gin, Bottle, Derby Hat	20.00
Schlitz, 1950s	25.00
CORKSCREW, Anheuser–Busch, Eagle Facing Leaf, Looks At Label	53.00
New Life Rye Whiskey, Edward Appel, Wooden Handle	20.00
Wm. J. Lemp Brewing Co., St. Louis, 6 In.	28.00
CRATE, Blatz Beer, Wooden, 12 x 18 x 11 In.	30.00
CREAMER, F. B. B. Co., Dairy, Embossed, 2 Oz., 2 1/2 In.	10.00
CUTOUT, Nehi, Circus, 1929	100.00
DECAL, Window, Orange Crush, 1943, Large, Set of 3	150.00
DICE, Seven–Up, Always Roll 7, Pair	16.00
DISPENSER, Buckeye Root Beer Syrup	695.00
Cherry Smash, 5 Cent, Glass, Original Pump	2500.00
Hires Syrup, Hourglass, Pump	800.00 To 850.00
Howell's Orange Julep, 5 Cent, 15 In.	990.00
Orange Crush, Painted Crushie, Glass, Chrome, 30 In.	1150.00
Ward's Lime Crush	975.00 To 1278.00
DISPLAY, Bottle, Carter's Inks, Stoneware, Gray, 1880–1900, 27 In.	522.00
Dr Pepper, Santa Claus, Vinyl Face, 30 In.	64.00
DOOR PULL, Coca–Cola, Plastic, Steel, 8 In.	88.00
DOOR PUSH, Canada Dry, Bottle	45.00
Hires Root Beer	60.00

Jar Cap, HFJ Co., Pat.Dec.6, 1964, 2 1/2 In.   *Jar Cap, HFJ Co., Pat.Feb.27, '97, 3 1/4 In.*

Orange Crush	75.00
DOSE CUP, W. R. Warner & Co., Phila., Pa., Cobalt Blue, 1 1/2 In.	22.00
DOSE GLASS, A Little Cuban Bitters Please, Etched, 2 1/2 In.	94.00
Adlerika Natural Bowel Cleanser	17.50
C. C. Burnet G. Apothecary, San Francisco	25.00
Cobalt Blue, Holds Heaping Dessert Spoon	15.00
Dr. Petzold's German Bitters, Clear, Etched, 2 In.	83.00
Henry J. Martin, Prescriptions, Los Angeles	25.00
Indian Herb Co., Washington, D. C., Amethyst	18.00
John Wyeth & Brother, Cobalt Blue	13.00
Owl Drug Co., Clear, 2 5/8 In.	38.50
Thos. McGuire–Druggist, Petaluma, Calif.	45.00
Try Greenhut's Bitters, Clear, Etched, 2 1/4 In.	143.00
W. W. Gavitt's Topeka, Kans., Clear, Embossed, 2 In.	12.00
DOSE SPOON, Duffy's Pure Malt Whiskey, A Medicine, Clear, Glass	20.00
ENVELOPE, Hotel Riverside–Grey Mineral Spring, Cambridge, 1888	30.00
EYECUP, Wyeth, Cobalt Blue	18.00
FAN, Dr Pepper, 1931	60.00
Moxie, Boy On Moxiemobile, Cardboard, 1922, 7 x 8 In.	85.00
Moxie, Muriel Ostriche Portrait, Cardboard, 1918	75.00
Seven–Up, Art Deco Bathing Beauty, Cardboard, 1931	12.50
FIGURE, Beefeater Gin, Composition, Wood Base, 17 In.	49.00
Bottle, Display, Carter's Ink, Stoneware	1200.00
Butler, Moxie, Carved Wood, Painted, 35 In.	220.00
Duquesne Beer	40.00
Hamm's Bear, By Campfire, Fish In Pan	49.00
Healing Vital Oil, Man Form, With Bottle, Painted, 22 In.	377.00
Old Dutch Beer, Plaster, 14 In.	120.00
Pabst Blue Ribbon, White Metal, Painted, 15 In.	72.00
FLAG, Extra Order, For Milkman, Driftwood Dairy	3.50
FLASHLIGHT, Seven–Up, Bottle Shape	35.00
HARMONICA, Coca–Cola, Enjoy Coca–Cola, Hohner	20.00
HOT WATER BOTTLE, Owl Drug Co., Nickle Plated Brass, 9 x 8 In.	154.00
JACKET, Pepsi–Cola, Employee Driver's, Blue, Quilted Liner, Zipper	25.00
Wild Cherry Pepsi, White Nylon Pullover, Extra Large	30.00
JAR & CAP REMOVER, C. B. Co., Pat. 2–28–22	2.00
JAR CAP, HFJ Co., Pat. Dec. 6, 1964, 2 1/2 In. ......*Illus*	2.00
HFJ Co., Pat. Feb. 27, '97, 3 1/4 In. ......*Illus*	4.00
JAR WRENCH, Boye, Metal	2.00
Easy Twist, Foley	1.50

Gunnard	2.00
Sure Grip, Rubber	1.50
KEYCHAIN, Bottle Shape	3.50
Coca–Cola Classic, Medal Shape, Round	3.50
Coca–Cola, Rectangular	3.50
Coca–Cola, Says Coke, Can Shape	3.50
KNIFE, Pocket, Pepsi–Cola, White, 1 Blade, Bookend Logo	4.00
LABEL, Old Black Joe Gin, Black Man, Jug, 1930s, 3 1/2 x 4 In.	3.00
Smith, Hamway Druggist, Baltimore, Small	3.00
LAMP, Schmidt Beer, Canvas Tepee	150.00
LICENSE PLATE, Pepsi–Cola, Aluminum, Regular Size	3.50
LID, Plug Type, MSC, Michigan State, Half & Half	.50
LIGHTER, Cigarette, Squirt, 1957	28.00
Hamm's Beer, Bear On Log	25.00
Pepsi–Cola, Bottle Shape	27.00
Pepsi–Cola, Musical, Box	125.00
Regal Beer, Bottle Shape	35.00
Royal Crown Cola, Bottle Shape	19.50
LIQUOR CASE, Traveling, Oak, 6 Case Bottles, Engraved, Shot Glass	220.00
MAP, Warner's Safe Cure Prize Map, Folded	350.00
MATCH HOLDER, Dr Pepper	55.00 To 60.00
Moxie, Die Cut Metal, Bottle Shape, Wall	300.00
MATCH SAFE, Anheuser–Busch, Eagle Logo Both Sides, Brass	120.00
Schlitz Beer	55.00
Val Blatz Brewing Co., Trademark On Reverse	35.00
MENU BOARD, Coca–Cola, Embossed Tin Lithograph, Art Deco, 27 In.	176.00
Pepsi–Cola, Art Deco, 1940s	250.00
Seven–Up, Tin, 1940s	65.00
MILK BOTTLE TOP, Borden's Hi–Protein Milk, 1 1/2 In. ....*Illus*	1.00
Borden's Pasteurized Milk, 1 In. ....*Illus*	1.00
Grade D Raw Milk, 1 1/2 In. ....*Illus*	1.00
Shady Grove Ice Cream, 1 1/2 In. ....*Illus*	1.00
MILK CARRIER, Maine Dairy, 4 Slots	10.00
MIRROR, Crane Whiskey, Pocket	60.00
Duffy's Malt Whiskey, Pocket, 2 3/4 In.	15.00
Old Crane Whiskey, Round, Small	35.00
MUG, A & W Root Beer, Arrow Logo, Glass, 3 1/2 In.	10.00
A & W Root Beer, Embossed, 3 1/4 In.	2.00
Augsburger Beer, Logo, Commemorative, 4 3/16 In.	20.00
Ball Mason, 47 Years' Service, Bill Wade, 1937–1984, Clear	18.00

Milk Bottle Top, Shady Grove Ice Cream, 1 1/2 In.

Milk Bottle Top, Borden's Pasteurized Milk, 1 In.

Milk Bottle Top, Borden's Hi-Protein Milk, 1 1/2 In.

Milk Bottle Top, Grade D Raw Milk, 1 1/2 In.

Ballantine Beer, Sing Along, 5 1/4 In.	15.00
Beer, J. Ruppert's Centennial Prize Medal Lager Beer, 10 In.	715.00
Budweiser Beer, 1980	175.00
Carnation Hot Cocoa Mix, Just Add Hot Water	5.00
Clipper, The Light Dark Beer, Blue Logo, 5 1/16 In.	5.50
Coors Herman, Joseph Black, Irish Creme	15.00
Coors, State Fair, 1939	25.00
Crystal Bottling Mfg. Co., Pine Bluff, Hutchinson, Amethyst	12.00
Culmbacher Beer, East St. Louis	135.00
Dad's, Have A Dad's Black Cow, Red & Yellow, 5 In.	6.00
Dove Ginger Ale, Dove Picture, Ornate Handle, Green, Brown	145.00
Edelweiss Beer, Ceramic, 4 1/2 In.	16.00
Falstaff Beer, Glass, Embossed Trademark, 7 In.	25.00
Falstaff, Logo, Pressed Glass, Gold Rim, 7 In., 4 Piece	28.00
Frostie Root Beer, Beer Type, Plastic	3.00
Graf's Beer, Since 1873, 4 3/4 In.	6.00
Hamm's Beer, Red, Logo, 5 5/8 In.	25.00
Hires Root Beer, Since 1876, Red & White, 3 1/4 In.	7.00
Hires Root Beer, Stoneware, Hourglass Shape	22.00
Moxie, Handle, 5 In.	45.00
Pioneer Dairy, Great Falls, Mont., Milk Glass, Red Pyro	10.00
Richardson's Root Beer, Rochester, N. Y., 6 5/8 In.	37.00
Schlitz Beer, Blue & Gray, Impressed Design, 4 1/2 In.	60.00
NAPKIN HOLDER, Rolling Rock Beer, Mountain Stream Picture	20.00
PATCH, Meadow Gold Products, Shield	.75
Steere's Milk	.75
PEN, Pepsi–Cola, Bottle Shaped Clip, Logo On Top & Bottom, 1937	200.00
PENCIL CASE, Coca–Cola, Complete 1940s	65.00
PENCIL, Pepsi–Cola	.50
Regal Pale Beer, With 1951 Yearly Calendar	15.00
PENNANT, Pepsi–Cola, Dark Blue Felt, White Script Logo, 27 1/2 In.	4.50
PIN, Cherry Coke, Can Shape	3.50
Coca–Cola, Bottle Shape	3.50
Coca–Cola, Can Shape	3.50
Coca–Cola, Round, 50th Anniversary	3.50
Coca–Cola, Tip of Arrow Shape	3.50
Coca–Cola, U.S. Country Shape	3.50
Miller High Life, Celluloid, Die Cut, Pin Back, 1905	75.00
Pepsi–Cola, Choice of A New Generation	1.25
Pepsi–Cola, Ted Turner Goodwill Games, Moscow, 1986	15.00
Slice, 100th Rose Bowl Parade, 1984	6.00
PITCHER SET, Pepsi–Cola, White Plastic, Blue Logo, 5 Piece	7.00
PITCHER, A & W Root Beer, Orange, White & Brown Bear, 8 1/8 In.	22.00
Champale Beer, Red On White, 10 1/2 In.	15.00
Dr. Harter's Little Liver Pills, Silver Plate, 13 In.	297.00
Dr. Harter's Wild Cherry Bitters, 13 In.	325.00
Elsie The Cow, Elsie's Head Shape	75.00
Heilman's Special Export Beer, Red, 9 1/8 In.	9.50
Miller Beer, Nasty Habit Pub, Logo On Side, 6 7/8 In.	12.00
Pabst Blue Ribbon Beer, Blue, 9 1/8 In.	70.00
PLACE MAT, Pepsi–Cola, Cartoon Character, Plastic, 1976	4.00
PLATE, Avon, Worldwide Avon Club Plate, 1973	5.00
California Perfume Company, 10th Anniversary	8.00
PLATTER, Central Creamery, Pottery, Blue Border, 1920–1945	20.00
PORCH BOX, Mayflower Milk Products, Masonite, 12 x 15 x 10 In.	20.00
Szep's Dairy, Aluminum, 11 x 11 x 9 In.	20.00
POSTCARD, Budweiser Lager Beer, Folding, 11 x 3 1/2 In.	15.00
Chamberlin Medicine, Des Moines, Iowa	6.00
Dr. Shoop Family Medicines, Racine, Wisc., 1900s	12.00
POSTER, Bring Nintendo–Pepsi Home For The Holidays, 18 x 27 In.	9.00
POT LID, J. B. Thorn Chemist, London, N. Y., Transfer, 2 3/4 In.	110.00
Jules Hauel Perfumer, World's Fair, Transfer, 3 1/2 In.	66.00
RADIO, Coca–Cola, Cooler Shape	575.00

Pepsi–Cola, Bottle Shape, 1930s, 23 In. 450.00
RECIPE CARD, 3 Famous Desserts, From Bottle of Milk, 1930s 1.00
REFRIGERATOR JUICE BOTTLE, Lebanon Cty., Goodness Wengert's Milk 11.00
RING, Home Canning, American, Rubber, 1 Doz., Box 2.00
SALT & PEPPER, Pepsi–Cola .... 10.00 To 15.00
SHADE, Lamp, Coca–Cola, Frosted Glass, Red Lettering, 12 1/2 In. 385.00
SHEET MUSIC, Emerson Drug Co., Bromo–Seltzer Advertising, Cures 12.00
SHOEHORN, Kirn Beer, 19 In. 15.00
SHOT GLASS, Brown & Wilson Pharmacists, Longmont, Colo., BIM, 2 In. 38.00
   Drink Burlingame Whiskey 37.00
   Helpalax Helpavit Hepa Inc., Cleveland, Oh., ABM, 2 In. 24.00
   J. F. Cutter Whiskey, Star In Shield, E. Martin & Co. 30.00
   J. H. Cutter, Slanted Script 20.00
   Old Fitzgerald Straight Bourbon, 2 3/8 In. 4.00
   Smith's Green Mountain Renovator, BIM, 1 3/4 In. 38.00
SIGN, Anheuser–Busch, Custer's Last Stand, 32 x 36 In. 275.00
   Baccarat, Clear, Asymmetrical Chunk of Ice, 3 x 7 In. 176.00
   Brown's Iron Bitters, Girl, Paper, 14 7/8 In. 400.00
   Budweiser, Attach On Overland Stage, Cardboard, 30 In. 33.00
   Canada Dry, Flange, Steel, Stenciled, 2 Sides, 15 In. 60.00
   Cherry Cola, Perry's Quality Beverages, Tin, 14 x 20 In. 40.00
   Cleveland & Sandusky Brewing, Man, Tin Lithograph, Oval, 28 In. 578.00
   Cliquot Club, 2 Sides, Cardboard, 1930s, 2 1/4 In. x 7 In. 3.00
   Coburgen Beer, Maiden, Painted In, 20 x 16 In. 110.00
   Coca–Cola, 1950s, Tin, 20 x 28 In. 125.00
   Coca–Cola, Barrel, Stenciled Tin, 14 1/2 In. 28.00
   Coca–Cola, Bathing Beauty, Reach For Coke, 1952, 18 x 36 In. 150.00
   Coca–Cola, Santa Claus, Fiberboard, Color Lithograph, 42 In. 44.00
   Coca–Cola, Woman, Hand Up, Fiberboard, Color Lithograph, 49 In. 88.00
   Commonwealth Distiller, Mother–of–Pearl Windows 8250.00
   Dr Pepper, Embossed Tin Lithograph, Nail Hole, 23 1/2 In. 165.00
   Dr. B. J. Kendall's Tonic & Blood Purifier, Paper, 6 x 24 In. 39.00
   Dr. Hoofland's German Bitters, Paper, 7 1/4 x 8 3/4 In. 72.00
   Dr. Seigert's Angostura Bitters, Framed, 30 In. 525.00
   Dr. Swett's Root Beer, 5 Cents, 2 Sides, Die Cut Tin, 6 In. 245.00
   Drink Braems Bitters, Metal On Cardboard, 7 x 13 In. .... 80.00 To 94.00
   Ebblinger Beer, Light–Up, Reverse Stenciled, Metal, 15 In. 132.00
   For Kidney Ills Nyal's Kidney Pills, Cardboard, 11 x 7 In. 19.00
   G & W Stands For Great Whiskey, Electric 110.00
   Grapette Soda, Embossed Tin, Oval, 27 In. 50.00
   Great Western Champagne, Tin Lithograph, Framed, 20 3/4 In. 77.00
   Green River Whiskey, Tin Lithograph, Black Mule, 24 In. 800.00
   Hires, Drink Hires In Bottles, Metal, 1920s, 5 x 14 In. 160.00
   I. W. Harper Whiskey, Dog, Indoor Scene, Frame, 17 x 23 In. 495.00
   Lakeside Bouquet Whiskey, Glass, 15 1/2 x 19 1/2 In. 3850.00
   Loreley Whiskey, Reverse Painting, 19 1/2 x 22 1/2 In. 5500.00
   Mad. Manchester, Botanic Doctress, 1853, 9 x 12 In. 125.00
   Mil–Kay Vitamin Drink, Orange Phosphate, Tin Lithograph, 40 In. 176.00
   Moxie, Tin Lithograph, Oval, 28 x 19 1/2 In. 110.00
   National Brewery Co., White Seal, Crystaloid, 14 In. 660.00
   Nu–Grape, Bottle Shape, Tin, 14 In. 85.00
   Paul Jones & Co., Temptation, Tin, 19 1/2 x 13 1/4 In. ....*Illus* 1,000
   Pepsi–Cola, 5 Cent Refreshing & Healthful, Tin 275.00
   Pepsi–Cola, Electric, Block Logo, Metal, Plastic, 36 x 48 In. 400.00
   Pepsi–Cola, Embossed Red Border, Green, Tin, 1910s, 3 x 8 In. 275.00
   Pepsi–Cola, Enjoy Pepsi–Cola, Porcelain, 2 Sides, 56 In. 357.00
   Pepsi–Cola, Round, Celluloid & Tin, 1940s, 9 In. 90.00
   R. C. Cola, Coed Drinks Cola, Cardboard, 1940s, 11 x 28 In. 20.00
   Seven–Up, Embossed Tin Lithograph, 18 In. 44.00
   T. O. D. Co., Owl Drug, Cardboard, Fold, 1908–1920, 12 x 7 In. 38.50
   Try A Milkshake, 3 Milkshakes Pictured, Cardboard, 24 x 8 In. 3.00
SILVER COIN, Houchk's Panacea, Liberty 50 Cent, c.1832, 1 1/4 In. 248.00
SPOON, Baby's, Owl Drug Co., Silver Plated, 1900–1905, 5 In. 33.00

STEIN, Budman, Budweiser, Mid–1970s 290.00
   German Olympia, 1975 .... 240.00
   Schlitz, 125th Anniversary 151.00
STREET SIGN, Pepsi–Cola Ave., Blue, Red Letters, 6 x 29 1/2 In. 20.00
STRING HOLDER, Pepsi–Cola, Tin, 1930s 375.00
SWEATSHIRT, Pepsi–Cola, White, Eagle Head, Medium 23.00
T–SHIRT, Diet Pepsi Logo, 2 Bicyclists, White, Blue Trim, Large 8.25
TELEPHONE, Seven–Up Can 25.00
THERMOMETER, Coca–Cola, 1900s, Wooden, 21 x 5 In. 450.00
   Coca–Cola, Art Deco, Embossed Tin Lithograph, 16 In. 154.00
   Coca–Cola, Bottle Picture, Embossed Tin Lithograph, 16 In. 50.00
   Coca–Cola, Woman, With Bottle, Tin Lithograph, 16 In. 94.00
   Dr Pepper, 1930s 250.00
   Grapette, Embossed Tin Lithograph, 16 1/2 In. 44.00
   Hires Root Beer, Die Cut Bottle .... 55.00 To 85.00
   Jim Beam, Tin, 25 1/2 x 10 In. 45.00
   Orange Crush, Fiberboard, Stenciled, 16 In. 28.00
   Paul Jones Whiskey, Tin, Red, Black, White Dial, 13 In. 50.00
   Pepsi–Cola, Say Pepsi Please, Tin, 1960s 50.00
   Pepsi–Cola, Tin, 1950s, 27 x 7 In. 100.00
   Scott Bros. Dairy, Pomona, Calif., Key Shape, Hanging 2.00
   Triple XXX Root Beer 65.00
TIN, Borden's Improved Malted Milk, Square, 5 Lb. 25.00
TIP TRAY, Coca–Cola, 1909, Coca–Cola Girl 220.00
   Coca–Cola, 1912, Girl With Red Rose In Hat 350.00
   Coca–Cola, 1914, Betty .... 93.50 To 195.00
   Coca–Cola, 1917, Elaine .... 135.00 To 165.00
   Mapeline Syrup, 4 1/8 In. 20.00
   Miller High Life, 1952 .... 10.00
   Moxie, Purple Flower 250.00
   National Brewing Co., Cowboy Holding Beer Bottle 715.00
   Old Angus Scotch 10.00
   Schlitz, 1955 .... 10.00
   Seagrams 7 Crown 10.00
   Sterling Beer, 1930s 18.00
TOKEN, Angeles Co–Op Creamery, 5 Cents Upon Return of Bottle 6.00
   Fuller Rancho Corona, 1 Qt. Milk, Aluminum, Square, Hole 1.00
   It's Lucky To Drink Green River Whiskey, Brass, 1 1/2 In. 24.00
   Keystone Dairy, Pa., 3 Cents Return Bottle, Aluminum, Round 4.00
   Shively's, 2 Gal. Dairy, Rounded 4 Sides, Aluminum 3.00
TONGS, Sunny Maid Farms, The Better Milk, Santa Ana, Calif. 6.00
TRADE CARD, Hood's Sarsaparilla, Grover Cleveland 5.00
TRAY, Christian Fiegenspan Beer, Color Lithograph, Round, 13 1/2 In. 28.00
   Coca–Cola, 1914, Betty, Oval 935.00
   Coca–Cola, 1914, Betty, Rectangular 495.00
   Coca–Cola, 1917, Elaine 400.00
   Coca–Cola, 1924, Smiling Girl .... 135.00 To 225.00
   Coca–Cola, 1930, Girl With Telephone 220.00
   Coca–Cola, 1936, Hostess .... 150.00 To 400.00
   Coca–Cola, 1937, Girl, Running .... 55.00 To 99.00
   Coca–Cola, 1938, Girl In Afternoon .... 50.00 To 75.00
   Coca–Cola, 1941, Ice Skater 100.00
   Coca–Cola, 1942, Two Girls At Car .... 110.00 To 300.00
   Coca–Cola, 1943, Girl With Wind In Her Hair 50.00
   Deer Park Brewing Co., Lithograph, 11 1/2 In. 165.00
   Dr Pepper, 2 Cats, Drinking Milk, Tin Lithograph, 2 1/2 In. 220.00
   Edelweiss Beer, Red–Headed Woman, 1913 .... 120.00
   Enterprise Beer, Woman, 1905 .... 200.00
   Falstaff Lemp Brewery, 1910, 24 In. 275.00
   Frank's Pale Dry Ginger Ale, Soda Bottle, 1930s 65.00
   Ginsing Beverages, Lithograph of Woman On Rickshaw 110.00
   Green River Whiskey, Black Man, Mule In Front of Inn .... *Illus* 275.00
   Hires Root Beer, Haskell Coffin Girl, 13 x 10 In. 210.00

Liberty Beer, Rochester, N. Y., Indian Maiden, 12 In. 82.50
Miller Beer, Girl On Moon, 13 1/4 In. .... 30.00 To 45.00
Nu–Grape, Girl With Bottle 95.00
Orange Julep Drink, Tin Lithograph, 13 In. 59.00
Pepsi–Cola, 1940s 75.00
Pepsi–Cola, Lithograph, Red, White, & Blue, 13 3/4 In. 39.00
Pepsi–Cola, Woman At Bar, c.1909 .... 2500.00
Velvet Beer, Color Lithograph, Oval, 15 1/2 In. 198.00
Virginia Brewing Co., Pilsener Export, 10 In. Diam. 1250.00
TRUCK, Milk Tank, 4 In. 7.50
TUMBLER, A & W Cream Soda, Frosted Glass, Metal Holder, 5 In. 7.00
Beer, Fresno Brewing Company, Etched Glass, 1900s 91.00
Coca–Cola, Terry Bradshaw 40.00
Coors, Centennial, 1959 .... 15.00
Dense Olive Bottle Type, OP, Cylindrical, 2 1/4 x 3 In. 175.00
Dr Pepper, Happy Days, Fonz, 6 1/8 In. 3.00
Dr Pepper, I'm A Pepper, Richard Gittus, Red, 5 In. 3.00
Dr Pepper, U.S. S. Enterprise 83.00
Hamm's, Burgie 151.00
Measuring, Borden's, Elsie, Brown Over Yellow, Lid, 8 Oz. 12.00
Measuring, Enjoy Sealtest Milk, Red & White, 8 Oz. 6.00
Measuring, Harrisburg Dairies, Building, Red, 8 Oz. 6.00
National Bohemian Beer, One–Eyed Man, 5 13/16 In. 9.00
Old Milwaukee Beer, Logo In Circle, 3 1/4 In. 3.00
Pepsi–Cola, Boris & Natasha 32.00
Pepsi–Cola, Mighty Mouse 307.00
Tyndall' Creamery Co., Tyndall, S. D., Red 8.00
UMBRELLA, Beach, Coca–Cola, Stenciled Cloth, Metal, 65 In. 143.00
UNIFORM PATCH, Pepsi–Cola Logo, 8 x 6 In. 3.00
VISOR, Pepsi–Cola, Paper, Unused 20.00
WATCH, Pepsi–Cola, Man's, Gold Tone Curvex Style, Pigskin Strap 65.00
Pepsi–Cola, Pocket, Employee Award, Gold Tone, Chain 65.00
WRISTWATCH, Seven–Up, Leather Band 35.00
YO–YO, Pepsi–Cola, Blue Plastic 1.00

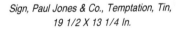

Sign, Paul Jones & Co., Temptation, Tin,
19 1/2 X 13 1/4 In.

Tray, Green River Whiskey, Black Man,
Mule In Front of Inn

K O V E L S

SEND ORDERS & INQUIRIES TO: **Crown Publishers, Inc.**
201 East 50th Street, New York, NY 10022
ATT: SALES DEPT.

SALES & TITLE INFORMATION
1-800-733-3000

NAME _____

ADDRESS _____

CITY & STATE _____   ZIP _____

PLEASE SEND ME THE FOLLOWING BOOKS:

ITEM NO.	QTY.	TITLE		PRICE	TOTAL
584727	_____	Kovels' Antiques & Collectibles Price List 24th Edition	PAPER	$13.00	_____
54668X	_____	American Country Furniture 1780–1875	PAPER	$14.95	_____
001411	_____	Dictionary of Marks-Pottery and Porcelain	HARDCOVER	$12.95	_____
559145	_____	Kovels' New Dictionary of Marks	HARDCOVER	$17.95	_____
568829	_____	Kovels' American Silver Marks	HARDCOVER	$40.00	_____
589443	_____	Kovels' Bottles Price List 9th Edition	PAPER	$13.00	_____
584441	_____	Kovels' Depression Glass & American Dinnerware Price List 4th Edition	PAPER	$13.00	_____
578069	_____	Kovels' Know Your Antiques Revised and Updated	PAPER	$14.95	_____
588404	_____	Kovels' Know Your Collectibles Updated	PAPER	$15.00	_____
58008X	_____	Kovels' Guide to Selling Your Antiques & Collectibles Updated Edition	PAPER	$ 9.95	_____
573334	_____	Kovels' Antiques & Collectibles Fix-It Source Book	PAPER	$ 9.95	_____

_____ TOTAL ITEMS

TOTAL RETAIL VALUE _____

CHECK OR MONEY ORDER ENCLOSED MADE PAYABLE TO
CROWN PUBLISHERS, INC., 201 East 50th Street.
New York, N.Y. 10022
or telephone 1-800-733-3000
(No cash or stamps, please)

Shipping & Handling
Charge $2.00 for one book;
50¢ for each additional book.
Please add applicable
sales tax.   _____

Charge: ☐ MasterCard ☐ Visa ☐ American Express
Account Number (include all digits)   Expires MO. YR.

TOTAL AMOUNT DUE _____

_____

Signature _____
Thank you for your order.

PRICES SUBJECT TO CHANGE
WITHOUT NOTICE. If a more
recent edition of a price list has
been published at the same price, it
will be sent instead of the old edition.